# CAMP THE U.S. FOR $5.00 OR LESS
## Western States

## MARY HELEN & SHUFORD SMITH

The Globe Pequot Press

P.O. Box 833, Old Saybrook, CT 06475

**Library of Congress Cataloging-in-Publication Data**

Smith, Mary Helen
  Camp the U.S. for $5 or less. Western states / Mary Helen and Shuford Smith. — 1st ed.
    p.  cm.
  "A voyager book."
  Includes index.
  ISBN 1-56440-173-1
  1. Camp sites, facilities, etc. —West (U.S.)—Directories.
I. Smith, Shuford. II. Title. III. Title: Camp the U.S. for five dollars or less. Western states.
GV191.42.W47S65   1993
647.947809—dc20                               92-42401
                                                              CIP

Manufactured in the United States of America
First Edition / First Printing

# Contents

# Authors

At ages 39 and 43, Mary Helen and Shuford Smith embarked on an odyssey to see North America and, ultimately, the world. For four years they journeyed with their van, tent, cameras, and computers. With hundreds of nights under the stars and hundred of miles of trails under their boots, they've received insights into the splendors of our natural world.

They've written newspaper and magazine articles on travel, food, and computers. Soon they hope to publish their first novel as well as the cookbook they've created for any stove top.

With this book, the Smiths invite you to experience the real West. With a forthcoming version on the Eastern United States, explore all that's natural in America.

# Introduction

When we were asked to write this book, we did a lot of soul-searching. We realized here was an opportunity to write the guide we had wanted to own during our four years of full-time camping on the North American continent. To write it, however, meant we would have to make a few changes in our nomadic lifestyle–including giving up travel for a year. Obviously, we decided compiling America's best camping values for thousands of other campers was worth our time and effort.

This book is dedicated to **all** campers looking for **positive** experiences in the **natural** environment–whether they're adventurous RVers or tenters. That includes fishermen, hikers, backpackers, bicyclists, boaters, mountain climbers, skiers–an endless number of people with as many styles of camping.

We share tips we've learned and observed in our years of camping. These ideas are rooted in common sense and deep concern for our land and our world.

We've gathered the information on camping America's public lands from numerous sources. We've made an honest attempt to be as up-to-date and as accurate as possible. Campgrounds located within national and state parks/recreation areas are listed under the park's name. All appear alphabetically within each state.

To be included in this book, a campground must meet these criteria: cost of $5 or less, access by vehicle or short walk, and provision of at least one facility such as water spigot, pit toilet, or picnic table. (Backcountry sites, of course, have no provisions.) For space reasons, we've eliminated most group camps, horse camps, boat-ins, and long hike-ins except for popular Grand Canyon and Na Pali Coast. All the listed campgrounds are actual places to camp–not just wide spots beside the road.

Use the index at the back of this guide to help you locate places to camp by administrator, body of water, or nearest town. Here bonus alternatives appear in bold as well as in listings of nearby campgrounds.

Look at this book as a way to get in touch with the real America. Pack it along with your adventurous spirit and go camping. Hopefully, you'll discover our information rings true to your personal experiences. We welcome your comments. Write us through our mail service:

Mary Helen & Shuford Smith
1508 West Jefferson Avenue
Dade City, FL 33525

▲ ▲ ▲ ▲ ▲ ▲ ▲ ▲ ▲ ▲ ▲ ▲ ▲ ▲ ▲ ▲ ▲ ▲ ▲ ▲ ▲ ▲ ▲ ▲

# HOW TO READ LISTINGS

Each state begins with State Map and Overview of $5-or-less camping.

Every alphabetical Listing follows this form:

## CAMPGROUND NAME

*Administrator*
*Information Phone Number*
*State Map Coordinates*
*Directions*
*Fee and Season*
*Sites and Facilities*
*Natural Description and*
*Recreational Opportunities*
*Concerns*
*Altitude*

Alongside the handy Locator Map, find the *Administrator* and *Information Phone Number* as well as the official *State Map Coordinates*. In the *Directions*, NEAREST TOWNS appear in all capital letters and metric distances in parentheses. Whenever road conditions create hazards for vehicles, they're indicated here. (If you're driving a RV or pulling a trailer, be sure to check for restrictions on type of sites as well as concerns). Also in directions, find **unlisted alternatives** in bold as well as cross-referenced options in parentheses.

*Fee* is in bold type whether it's **FREE** or up to **$5**. These days free camping options are becoming fewer and fewer because of maintenance costs. There are ways, however, we campers can contain costs and add to our enjoyment of natural environments. When the listing includes the slogan "choose a chore," take the initiative to pick up litter, clean fire rings.... See more ideas on page vii.

*Season* varies with location. If off-season camping is allowed, that's indicated. If it's dry camping (no drinking water), that's stated too. Opening and closing dates are as specific as possible. Call the information phone number to verify.

*In Sites*, find out how many sites and what types. They may be undesignated, a combination of tent and RV, or only tent sites due to topography. Rangers tell if sites are scattered or close as well as open or screened.

Under *Facilities*, basics are listed first: water, then toilets. Whenever possible, specifics are given (such as hand water pumps or flush toilets) to aid your decision-making. Sometimes you'll find improvements such as boat ramps, playgrounds, and pay phones. Generally trash cans are available. If not, that's indicated in concerns.

The *Natural Description* gives you an idea of what to expect when you get there–a creek, a spring, or a lake; pine trees or no trees; tall mountain or flat desert landscapes.

*Recreational Opportunities* vary with location. This information helps you decide whether you want to spend one night, a weekend, or two weeks. Fishing and hiking are readily available at most campgrounds. When other opportunities such as swimming, boating, mountain climbing, cross-country skiing, or, even, gold panning are available, they're indicated too.

*Concerns* list other awareness areas. If there's no drinking water, that's marked with a capital NO so you can adequately provision yourself. Rangers have indicated restrictions on length of stay or length of vehicle as well as problems with insects, noise, etc.

Last, but not least, *Altitude* is noted wherever that information has been provided. This knowledge helps you know where the nights turn cool and the air becomes rare.

Happy camping!

▲ ▲ ▲ ▲ ▲ ▲ ▲ ▲ ▲ ▲ ▲ ▲ ▲ ▲ ▲ ▲ ▲ ▲ ▲ ▲ ▲ ▲ ▲ ▲ ▲ ▲ ▲ ▲ ▲

## ABBREVIATIONS

Besides accepted abbreviations for directions (such as N), geography (Mt), measurement (ft), months (Aug), roads (Hwy), states (WA), we use these from various governmental agencies:

| | |
|---|---|
| ATV | All Terrain Vehicle |
| BLM | Bureau of Land Management |
| BOR | Bureau of Reclamation |
| COE | Corps of Engineers |
| CR | County Road |
| DNR | Department of Natural Resources (WA) |
| FAS | Fishing Access Site (MT) |
| FH | Forest Highway |
| FR | Forest Road |
| FWP | Fish, Wildlife & Parks (MT) |
| I- | Interstate |
| LTVA | Long-Term Visitor Area |
| NF | National Forest |
| NHP | National Historical Park |
| NPS | National Park Service |
| NS | National Seashore |
| NRA | National Recreation Area |
| NWR | National Wildlife Refuge |
| RA | Recreation Area |
| RS | Recreation Site |
| SF | State Forest |
| SHP | State Historical Park |
| SMA | Special Management Area (AK) |
| SP | State Park |
| SF | State Forest |
| SHP | State Historical Park |
| SP | State Park |
| SRA | State Recreation Area |
| SRS | State Recreation Site |
| SWA | State Wildlife Area (CO) |

▲ ▲ ▲ ▲ ▲ ▲ ▲ ▲ ▲ ▲ ▲ ▲ ▲ ▲ ▲ ▲ ▲ ▲ ▲ ▲ ▲ ▲ ▲ ▲ ▲ ▲ ▲ ▲ ▲

## CHOOSE A CHORE

Here are some ideas on how to keep free campgrounds free:

▲ Pick up litter ▲
▲ Clean fire rings ▲
▲ Untie ropes from trees ▲
▲ Remove wax from tables ▲
▲ Tighten loose screws ▲
▲ Tidy toilets ▲
▲ Leave a roll of toilet paper ▲
▲ Ask if ranger needs any assistance ▲

viii

▲ ▲ ▲ ▲ ▲ ▲ ▲ ▲ ▲ ▲ ▲ ▲ ▲ ▲ ▲ ▲ ▲ ▲ ▲ ▲ ▲ ▲ ▲ ▲ ▲ ▲ ▲

## ACKNOWLEDGMENTS

Although we count by thousands the hours to compile this book, it would have been impossible without equal hours spent to provide the data. Originally, we wanted to thank by name each person who completed a questionnaire. The book size, however, has prevented that courtesy. We hope all agree what's important is to list the campground information.

We thank each person who helped make this book as accurate and as detailed as possible plus all administrators who cooperated in the data collection. In alphabetical order on the federal level, we thank personnel of the Bureau of Land Management, Bureau of Reclamation, Corps of Engineers, Fish and Wildlife Service, Forest Service, National Park Service, and, of course, Postal Service. In each of the thirteen western states, we thank various departments of tourism, state parks, forests, and wildlife. We thank many counties and cities. Too, we want to thank all the research librarians who helped us locate materials to refine the concept of this guide then the addresses to contact the various administrators.

Also, we thank numerous friends and fellow travelers who took time to share their experiences, ideas, and selves with us. For encouragement and inspiration, we thank our families and:

Karen & Henry Alexander
Dorothy & Bruce Baynes
Brenda & Terry Berezan
Betty Bertrand
Phyllis & Bruce Bierle
Virginia & David Bint
Carol & John Blackmore
Shirley Bragg
Marge & Lenny Bruss
Karen Carter
Sandy McAvoy & Alan Christensen
Cecil & Allen Compton
Deena & Bill Culp
Meg Danby
Connie & Steve Dieleman
Veronica & Howard Diesel
Barbara Erol
Helen & Dan Faris
Charles Fertig
Dominique & Jean Fuseau
Jim & Jan Gambill
Linde & Russell Gee
Diana & Bill Gleasner
Triona Gogarty
Joyce & Nelson Graves
Marilynn Friley & Pat Grediagin
MJ & Chuck Halstead
Charlotte & Robert Hope
Gwen Hoppe
Allison & Ches Hortenstine
Deborah & Victoria Joy
Karen Lindsay

Evelyn & Frank Lloyd
Retta & Donald Lyons
Phylliss & Larry Mabry
Heike Mayer
Marsha & Charles Milford
Hope & Bill Moffett
Nathalie & Charles Neal
Charles Neifeld
Kris Nye
Nancy Parks
Suzanne & Dustan Rine
Sylvia & Dick Rortvedt
Gloria & Hub Schleicher
Vicky & Jay Semple
Deborah & Robert Sesco
Marilyn Shadford
Barbara & Jim Shanks
Chris Sheehy
Jean Shula
Pat Soares
Mary Jackson & Bill Staton
Deborah & Jack Streich
Danny Hoyt & Ron Stuttle
Jane Tappan
Connie Toops
Duryea & Dan Wills
Debi & Bill Winski
Carolyn Ellis & Earll Wolcott
Sandy & Herb Wright
Lyle Yazzie
Bill Zack
Peter Zmyj

# ABC's of Camping

**911:** This emergency telephone number works across most of United States.

**Animals:** Bears, rodents, and other furry creatures are attracted to campsites by food. Keep food stored in tamper-proof containers out of sight (car trunk) or out of reach (two balanced bags hanging from tree limb).

**Attitude:** Keep an "Are we having fun yet?" frame-of-mind. Whatever the situation, try not to panic.

**Backpacking:** Get away from it all. Learn how little you really need to survive and how much rates as "nice." High on the essentials list are: water, waterproof matches, food, map and compass.

**Bathing:** If showers are unavailable, hang waterbag in sunny place to absorb rays and heat water. Rinse off with plain water or, for spot cleanup, use baby wipes. You'll sleep better; your sleeping bag/linens will stay fresher.

**Birds:** Observe birds and other animals. Never feed them as you may become their executioner. Research has proved feeding birds and other animals interferes not only with their instinct but their ability to survive. Animals accustomed to eating human junk foods are less likely to live through winter. They absorb their insulating layer of body fat before winter is over and natural foods become available.

**Blanket, Space:** This lightweight, coated-on-one-side piece of Mylar is an example of beneficial spinoffs from space technology. Take along space blanket when hiking. In case of sudden hypothermia, wrap individual in blanket (reflective side in) to conserve body heat. If day gets too hot, rig space blanket as reflective tarp. Keep it in your tent nightsack. If weather turns cold during night, spread it (reflective side down) over sleeping bag to trap body heat.

**Books:** Guidebooks add to your understanding and enjoyment of the world around you. Select one or two well-recommended books so you're not overburdened with information or weight. Well-paced novels can also add to your "great escape."

**Budget:** Whether trip is weekend jaunt or extended tour, it pays to plan your finances. Allocate money for necessities such as food and any camp fees before niceties such as that raft trip or hot air balloon ride.

**Choose a chore:** see page vii.

**Clothing:** Learn art of layering clothes. It allows garments to perform more than one duty to keep you comfortable. Dressing in layers has other benefits: you buy less and you pack less. Always prepare for the worst-case weather scenario.

**COE Projects:** Federal law requires one free campground per project. Ask, if you don't see it on project map.

**Compass:** Carry one (and use it) when you're hiking.

**Cooking Pots & Pans:** Pots that nest inside one another take up less space, that valuable commodity when camping or traveling. If you're concerned about weights and oxides, purchase lightweight stainless steel. A pressure cooker makes sense while camping (as long as you're not backpacking). It can turn out an entire meal in a half-hour whether bean pot or three-course chicken dinner.

**Dishes:** Carry reusable cups, dishes, and flatware. Think twice about buying paper plates, plastic forks and spoons.

▲ ▲ ▲ ▲ ▲ ▲ ▲ ▲ ▲ ▲ ▲ ▲ ▲ ▲ ▲ ▲ ▲ ▲ ▲ ▲ ▲ ▲ ▲ ▲ ▲ ▲ ▲ ▲ ▲

These items really aren't "disposable." They're extravagant wastes of world's resources. When washing dishes outdoors, use that indispensable waterbag to rinse dishes. After drying, place utensils out of animals' reach.

**Documents:** While traveling in US, Americans need only their driver's licenses. Travelers from other countries also need visas or passports.

**Ethics:** Here is where golden rule applies. If you take care of plants, animals, objects, and structures as you wish you or your property were treated, there would be no need for any other rules or regulations.

**Exercise:** Make exercise a natural part of your day. Take a walk, bike ride, paddle, or swim. If it's raining, perform isometrics in your tent or RV.

**Fires:** If you must have a campfire (so you can smell smoke in your hair and clothes all night and, maybe, all day), build a small one. Make certain it's totally out before you leave it.

**First-Aid (Basic Kit):** In alphabetical order, pack aloe cream for sun or wind burn; antibiotic (such as penicillin or erythromycin) to treat infections; antihistamine (such as *Benadryl*) for respiratory problems; aspirin to lower fever; band-aids/bandages; DEET (diethylmetatoluamide) to prevent mosquito bites; hydrocortisone cream (such as *Cortaid*) to relieve skin irritations; rubbing alcohol to clean cuts; and *Sting-eze* (if ice unavailable) to treat insect bites.

**Fishing:** What a rewarding way to let your mind wander. While you solve world's problems or simply get lost in wonder of nature, you might catch dinner!

**Flashlight:** To prevent accidental draining of batteries, rubber band flashlight switch "off."

**Focus:** Choose interest area if you're planning extended trip–bird sightings, battlefields, emigration trails, Native American petroglyphs....

**Foods:** Buy fresh, locally-grown foods whenever possible. Not only do they taste better and have more food value,

generally they're less expensive. Store all food items carefully against pests as well as spoilage.

**Footwear & Footcare:** Sandals, shoes, and boots that fit can make or break you. It's important to choose comfortable as well as appropriate footwear. For example, in camp change from hiking boots to moccasins or sandals to avoid unnecessary trampling of vegetation. If you're sweating or blistering, take off your socks and shoes, then bathe your feet in rubbing alcohol. Another way to avoid blisters is to wear two pair of socks: a thin pair next to your feet with a thicker pair on top.

**Guns:** Statistics indicate–carry no guns.

**Hiking:** Your feet set the best pace for your mind to absorb the wonders of nature.

**Hunting:** Over America's two-hundred year history, hunting has evolved from necessity for survival to sport. Now as population centers encroach on country's last wild places, hunting must be carefully regulated.

**Insects:** In alphabetical order ants, bees, chiggers, flies, hornets, mosquitoes, no-see-ems, scorpions, ticks, and wasps can make you miserable no matter where you are. Practice avoidance: shun scented soaps and lotions; camp in breezy locations; wash dishes and pack away food after eating; check shoes, clothes, and linens before using; dress appropriately (for example, to avoid mosquitoes or ticks, wear light-colored long sleeves and pants); use DEET sparingly. If bitten, remove insect. Wash area with soap and water then cool with ice, if available. In case of swelling or itching, take antihistamine (such as *Benadryl*). If bitten by tiny yellow or yellow-green scorpion in Southwest (Centuroides scultuatus), seek immediate medical attention.

**Itineraries:** Let someone (friend, family member, or ranger) know your plans, including arrival place and time.

**Kids:** #1 rule is keep your sense of humor. #2 rule is pack plenty of

▲ ▲ ▲ ▲ ▲ ▲ ▲ ▲ ▲ ▲ ▲ ▲ ▲ ▲ ▲ ▲ ▲ ▲ ▲ ▲ ▲ ▲ ▲ ▲ ▲ ▲

snacks that can become pleasurable distractions as well as energizers. #3 rule is dress children in bright colors so they're easy to spot outdoors. Child carriers allow babies who can hold up their heads to accompany you on walks and hikes. Carry baby gently. Plan on stops for diaper changes, feedings, and stret:hes. Check baby's body temperature and adjust clothing frequently. If child is toddling, expect any foot travel to take about one hour per half-mile. Plan accordingly and carry as little as possible, in case you have to pick up child. Older children love to bring along friends on day trips or overnight excursions. For overnights, pack separate tent for them. They'll love "responsibility;" you'll love relative peace.

**Knots:** Take time to learn basic knots. They'll save you much frustration in rainstorms or windstorms.

**Lantern, Makeshift:** Place candle in empty tuna can to catch melting wax.

**Litter:** Carry litter bag to pick up trash marring natural beauty of landscape.

**Mail:** When you're out for extended time, arrange for post office, family member, or friend to number (for example, 1 of 10) then forward your mail "General Delivery" to appointed place. Specify when to forward. Allow one week for all items to arrive.

**Maps:** These necessary items help take frustration out of travel. You can figure out where you want to go and how to get there. Carry official state maps in your vehicle and US Geological Survey (USGS) topographical maps in your backpack.

**Medical Information:** Wear any medical identification bracelets/tags and know yourself (for example, when you last had tetanus shot).

**Messages:** At least one no-fee *Gold MasterCard* offers free message service.

**Money:** This commodity is relatively easy to obtain this day and time. Automatic teller machine networks crisscross the country; advances on charge cards are available at most banks; many auto club members can purchase free travelers checks.

**Nature:** Take only pictures; leave only footprints. Show consideration to all living things you see. Picking wildflowers and feeding or capturing wild creatures for pets is forbidden—it's hard to improve on Mother Nature's schemes. (Too, never buy souvenirs made from endangered animals.)

**Moon & Stars:** In our electric world, we've lost familiarity with these stellar objects. Buy star chart to get reacquainted. Learn phases of moon.

**Nightsack:** Pack books, flashlight and batteries, tissues, baby wipes and powder, space blanket—all those little necessities—into one carryall.

**Nocturnal Animals:** Meet wide range of animals that come out at night.

**Observation:** Try to use all your senses to identify all that surrounds you.

**Options:** Keep your eyes open to more efficient ways of doing anything and everything. Remember that goal of camping is to enjoy it—not work at it.

**Organization:** Develop systems for loading your backpack, your automobile, your RV.... For example, carry heavy items in backpack near your pelvis and back for balance. Many campers have adapted almost-indestructible milk crates to their needs. Each crate serves a different purpose such as pantry, his or her clothes.... Designate specific places for water bottles, maps, first-aid kit, raingear.... Always put any item back in place so you can find it when you need it.

**Passes:** Purchasable Golden Eagle Pass allows you into unlimited number of national park service locations. Golden Age Pass qualifies anyone over age 62 to camping and entrance discounts. Golden Access Pass guarantees disabled individuals to free entrance to national park sites. Check out state and local passes too.

**Pets:** Pets can create problems when traveling. If you must bring one, be prepared to make allowances for needs of other people and animals as well as your pet.

▲ ▲ ▲ ▲ ▲ ▲ ▲ ▲ ▲ ▲ ▲ ▲ ▲ ▲ ▲ ▲ ▲ ▲ ▲ ▲ ▲ ▲ ▲ ▲ ▲ ▲ ▲

**Photography:** Here is another focus that allows you to enjoy trip again and again.

**Poisonous Plants:** Know how poison ivy, oak, and sumac look to avoid them. Pack cortisone cream in case you have a close encounter.

**Quiet:** Now recognized as a resource in need of protection in many parks, rules have been made to restrain generators and other noise during specific hours. If fellow camper is noisy, approach immediately and courteously request quiet.

**Recreational Equipment:** Keep it simple. How about a frisbee?

**Rules & Regulations:** Take responsibility to determine if there are any specifics beyond golden rule.

**RV Ethics:** Use generator sparingly. Dump gray/black water at appropriate locations–never at campsite.

**Safety:** Always consider safety of others as well as self.

**Sanitation:** If toilets unavailable, walk as far away from camp or trail as feasible. Dig small hole at least four inches deep. Afterward, fill hole with soil and tamp down. Cover with large rock or branch to keep animals from digging. Carry plastic bags for toilet paper, sanitary napkins, and tampons.

**Shelters (Tents, Screenhouses, RVs):** Select best option according to your needs–not salesman's.

**Site Selection:** Choose inside curve along roads to avoid headlights. Look around. Avoid low places for water drainage and never trench area. Look overhead to avoid dead tree limbs. To hold your place, leave large but inexpensive item–for example, a lawn chair.

**Sleeping Gear (Pads, Bags, Liners, Pillows):** Make yourself comfortable. A washable liner acts as a sheet and protects your sleeping bag.

**Smoking:** If you must, dispose of matches, ashes, and cigarette butts in responsible manner–they're litter as well as fire hazards.

**Snakes:** Remember that snakes tend to shy away from humans.

**Stoves:** To lessen site impact, use campstove instead of fire. Select reliable model and take care of it for dependable service.

**Styrofoam:** Avoid purchasing Styrofoam containers whenever possible. These containers cannot be recycled, creating hazards to our environment. In addition, they're manufactured at great expense to important habitats such as rainforests.

**Sun Protection:** As world's ozone layer depletes and allows ultraviolet rays to harm skin, you must take steps to protect yourself and, especially, your children. When sun is bright, wear hats or sunscreen or both. Pay special attention to noses.

**Telephone Cards:** These pieces of plastic come in handy at pay phones. Make sure you have long-distance carrier's customer service number for any assistance.

**Time:** Take your time, but know when to go. Be aware of time zones and daylight savings time changes.

**Tools & Spare Parts:** Keep it simple–for example, a hubcap works as a shovel.

**Trails:** Stay on trails. Avoid trampling fragile undergrowth or causing erosion by taking switchbacks.

**Transportation:** Choose your wheels–bicycle, motorcycle, car, RV–then maintain for reliable service. Consider options of boat, plane....

**Trash:** Make sure your garbage doesn't end up in ocean, lake, creek, gully, or side of road. Pack it in; pack it out.

**Volunteer:** Get involved in special places and projects. Often, you receive as much as you give.

**Water:** Importance of water cannot be underestimated. Carry and drink plenty. A multi-gallon container allows freedom to camp where water is unavailable–often saving you a camp fee. If backpacking and collecting water from streams and lakes, carry water filter or purifying tablets.

**Weather:** Watch the weather so you can decide when to pack up, tie down, or bring extra gear inside tent or RV.

# Alaska

Grid conforms to official state map. For your copy, write:
Division of Tourism, PO Box 110801, Juneau, AK 99811-0801.

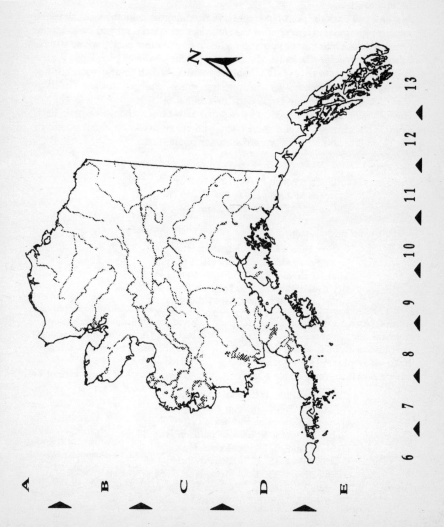

Most Alaska campgrounds open when the tourists begin to arrive–around May 15. Summer seems to happen overnight. It's a delight to watch leaves grow, salmon swim upstream, moose cows teach their calves to graze on willow bushes. The summer solstice, the longest day in June and the year, has real meaning here. Then the days grow shorter. The plants and animals complete their growth cycles preparing for the long winter. Most tourists are on their way home by first frost, so most campgrounds begin to close–around Sep 15.

Find camping in Alaska along the ferry routes and along the highways whose names you'll soon know intimately: Elliott, Glenn, Parks, Richardson, Seward, Steese, Sterling, Taylor. In addition to federal agencies such as the **Bureau of Land Management** (BLM), **National Park Service** (NPS), **US Fish and Wildlife**, and **US Forest Service** offering camping in Alaska, a great number of towns welcome each summer's tourists.

**Alaska State Park** (SP) camping fees have risen dramatically the last few years. These campgrounds no longer meet the $5-or-less criterion until you consider the $75 annual pass. Once you've spent 15 nights in any of these parks, you're paying less than $5 per night. Alaska has done a magnificent job developing lands for the public to appreciate this state's beauty, history, wildlife, and recreational opportunities. Each park has its own offering, from clamming in Clam Gulch to viewing hanging glaciers on Lynn Canal in Chilkat SP.

The following list is alphabetical by region, nearest town, then state park. Each park includes milemarker and fee to help you make decisions about where to spend those few hours each northern summer night.

## CHUGACH

| Anchorage | **Chugach SP-Bird Creek**, 101.5 Seward Hwy, $8 |
| | **Chugach SP-Eagle River**, 12.6 Glenn Hwy, $12 |
| Eagle River | **Chugach SP-Eklutna**, 26.5 Glenn Hwy, $10 |

## COPPER RIVER BASIN/VALDEZ

| Chitina | **Liberty Falls SRS**, 23.5 Edgerton Hwy, $6 |
| Copper Center | **Little Tonsina SRS**, 65 Richardson Hwy, $6 |
| | **Squirrel Creek SRS**, 79.5 Richardson Hwy, $6 |
| Glenallen | **Dry Creek SRS**, 117.5 Richardson Hwy, $6 |
| | **Lake Louise SRA**, 160 Glenn Hwy, $6 |
| | **Little Nelchina SRS**, 137.4 Glenn Hwy, $6 |
| Tok | **Porcupine Creek SRS**, 64 Tok Cutoff, $6 |
| Valdez | **Blueberry Lake**, 23 Richardson Hwy, $6 |

## NORTH

| Delta Junction | **Birch Lake SRS**, 305.5 Richardson Hwy, $6 |
| | **Clearwater SRS**, 1415 Alaska Hwy, $6 |
| | **Delta SRS**, 267 Richardson Hwy, $8 |
| | **Donnelly Creek**, 238 Richardson Hwy, $6 |
| | **Fielding Lake SRS**, 200.5 Richardson Hwy, $6 |
| | **Harding Lake**, 321.4 Richardson Hwy, $6 |
| | **Quartz Lake SRS**, 277.8 Richardson Hwy, $6 |
| | **Salcha River SRS**, 323.3 Richardson Hwy, $6/vehicle |
| Fairbanks | **Chena SRA-Rosehip**, 27 Chena Hot Springs Rd, $6 |
| | **Chena SRA-Tors Trail**, 39 Chena Hot Springs Rd, $6 |

▲ ▲ ▲ ▲ ▲ ▲ ▲ ▲ ▲ ▲ ▲ ▲ ▲ ▲ ▲ ▲ ▲ ▲ ▲ ▲ ▲ ▲ ▲ ▲ ▲ ▲ ▲ ▲

|  |  |
|---|---|
|  | **Chena River SRS**, University Ave, $12 |
|  | **Lower Chatanika River SRA-Olnes Pond**, 10.5 Elliott Hwy, $6 |
|  | **Lower Chatanika River SRA-Whitefish**, 11 Elliott Hwy, $6 |
|  | **Upper Chatanika River SRS**, 39 Steese Hwy, $6 |
| Tok | **Eagle Trail SRS**, 109.5 Tok Cutoff, $8 |
|  | **Moon Lake SRS**, 1332 Alaska Hwy, $8 |
|  | **Tok River SRS**, 1309 Alaska Hwy, $8 |

## KENAI PENINSULA

|  |  |
|---|---|
| Homer | **Anchor River SRA**, 157 Sterling Hwy, $6 |
|  | **Anchor River SRS**, 162 Sterling Hwy, $6 |
|  | **Deep Creek SRA**, 138 Sterling Hwy, $6/vehicle |
|  | **Kachemak Bay SP**, by boat or plane, $6 |
|  | **Ninilchik SRA**, 135 Sterling Hwy, $8 |
|  | **Stariski SRS**, 151 Sterling Hwy, $8 |
| Kenai | **Bernice Lake SRS**, 23 Kenai Spur Rd, $6 |
|  | **Capt Cook SRA-Discovery**, 39 Kenai Spur Rd, $8 |
| Nikiski | **Capt Cook SRA-Bishop Creek**, 36 Kenai Spur Rd, $6 |
| Seward | **Caines Head SRA**, by boat, $6 |
| Soldotna | **Clam Gulch SRA**, 117 Sterling Hwy, $6 |
|  | **Crooked Creek SRS**, Coho Loop Rd, $6 |
|  | **Johnson Lake SRA**, 110 Sterling Rd, $8 |
|  | **Kasilof River SRS**, 109.5 Sterling Hwy, $6 |
|  | **Kenai River SMA-Bings Landing**, 79 Sterling Hwy, $6 |
|  | **Kenai River SMA-Izaak Walton**, 81 Sterling Hwy, $8 |
|  | **Kenai River SMA-Morgans Landing**, 85 Sterling Hwy, $6/vehicle |
|  | **Kenai River SMA- Scout Lake**, 85 Sterling Hwy, $6 |
|  | **Kenai River SMA-Funny River**, 10 Funny River Rd, $6/vehicle |

## KODIAK

|  |  |
|---|---|
| Kodiak | **Fort Abercrombie SHP**, 4.0 E Rezanof Dr, $6 |
|  | **Buskin River SRS**, 4.5 W Rezanof Dr, $6/vehicle |
|  | **Pasagshak SRS**, 40 Pasagshak River Rd, $6 |

## MATANUSKA-SUSITNA

|  |  |
|---|---|
| Big Lake | **Big Lake N SRS**, 5 N Big Lake Rd, $6/vehicle |
|  | **Big Lake S SRS**, 5.2 S Big Lake Rd, $6/vehicle |
|  | **Rocky Lake SRS**, 3.5 Big Lake Rd, $6 |
| Palmer | **Bonnie Lake SRS**, 83.3 Glenn Hwy, $6 |
|  | **Finger Lake SRS**, Bogard Rd, $6/vehicle |
|  | **King Mountain SRS**, 76 Glenn Hwy, $6 |
|  | **Long Lake SRS**, 85.3 Glenn Hwy, $6 |
|  | **Matanuska Glacier SRS**, 101 Glenn Hwy, $6 |
|  | **Moose Creek SRS**, 54.4 Glenn Hwy, $6 |
|  | **Wolf Lake SRS**, 2.5 Engstrom Dr, $6 |
| Talkeetna | **Montana Creek SRS**, 97.6 Parks Hwy, $6/vehicle |
| Trapper Creek | **Denali SP-Byers Lake**, 147 Parks Hwy, $8 |
|  | **Denali SP-Lower Troublesome Creek**, 137.2 Parks Hwy, $6/vehicle |
| Willow | **Nancy Lake SRA-S Rolly Lake**, 6.5 Nancy Lake Pkwy, $6 |
|  | **Nancy Lake SRS**, 66.5 Parks Hwy, $6 |
|  | **Willow Creek SRA-Deception Creek**, 48 Hatcher Pass Rd, $6/vehicle |

▲ ▲ ▲ ▲ ▲ ▲ ▲ ▲ ▲ ▲ ▲ ▲ ▲ ▲ ▲ ▲ ▲ ▲ ▲ ▲ ▲ ▲ ▲ ▲ ▲

**SOUTHEAST**

| Haines | **Chilkat SP**, 7 Mud Bay Rd, $6/vehicle |
| | **Chilkoot Lake SRS**, 10 Lutak Rd, $8/vehicle |
| | **Mosquito Lake SRS**, 27.2 Haines Hwy, $6/vehicle |
| | **Portage Cove SRS**, 1 Beach Rd, $6/tent |
| Ketchikan | **Settler's Cove SRS**, 18 N Tongass Hwy, $6/vehicle |

**SOUTHWEST**

| Dillingham | **Wood-Tikchik SP**, by boat or plane, $6 |

If you've put your rig on a "Big Blue Canoe" as an Alaska Marine Highway ferry is called, if you've driven across British Columbia and the Yukon Territory, or if you've flown from the "Lower 48," you've already made an investment in money. While you're here, you might want to charter a boat to one of the national parks offering backcountry opportunities or a float plane to an Inuit village.

Spend more than a couple of weeks here. Slow down and smell the Alaska roses, see how many lynx you can count, savor the smoked salmon, hear the rushing wind and water, feel the greatness.

▲ ▲ ▲ ▲ ▲ ▲ ▲ ▲ ▲ ▲ ▲ ▲ ▲ ▲ ▲ ▲ ▲ ▲ ▲ ▲ ▲ ▲ ▲ ▲ ▲

## ALAGANIK SLOUGH

Chugach NF
(907) 271-2500
State map: C10
From CORDOVA at milepost 17 on Copper River Hwy (AK 10), take 3-mile (4.8 k) gravel road.
FREE but choose a chore.
Open May 15–Sep 15, weather decides.
Undesignated sites.
Pit toilets, tables, boat launch.
On Copper River Delta flowing into Prince William Sound.
Boat and fish. Observe and photograph wildlife–trumpeter swan and moose.
Store food carefully–bears frequent area.

## ANIAKCHAK NM-Backcountry

(907) 246-3305
State map: D8
For information on scheduling a backcountry trip (and making plane arrangements) to Aniakchak NM, call Katmai NP (above number) or write PO Box 7, King Salmon, AK 99613.
FREE. Open All Year.
Fly over volcanically active Aleutian Mountains where 30-square-mile caldera (one of world's largest) erupted in 1931.
Raft Aniakchak National Wild and

Scenic River formed by Surprise Lake's breach of crater wall. Observe wildlife and fish.
Lots of preparations to travel here.

## AUKE VILLAGE

Tongass NF (907) 747-6671
State map: D13
Drive 2 miles (3.2 k) N of ferry terminal–3 miles (4.8 k) W of AUKE BAY and 15 miles (24 k) N of JUNEAU–on Glacier Hwy.
$5. Open May 15–Sep 15.
12 sites. Water, flush/pit toilets, tables, grills, shelters.
Beside SE Passage gravel beach.
Fish. Walk beach and nature trail.
Observe marine wildlife.
14-day/25-ft limits.

## BRUSHKANA CREEK

BLM (907) 822-3217
State map: C10
Drive 31 miles (49.6 k) E of CANTWELL to mile 104.3 of Denali Hwy (AK 8), a rutted gravel road at this point.
FREE but choose a chore.
Open Jun–Oct, snow decides; dry camping off-season.
17 scattered sites in open or screened

settings. Hand water pump, pit toilets, tables, fire rings.
On creek near scenic Alaska Range. Enjoy hiking, wildlife viewing, photography, and fishing.
7-day limit. Store food carefully–grizzly bears frequent area. Avoid trampling fragile tundra. Crowded hunting season (mid Aug–mid Sep).
2600 ft (780 m)

### CCC

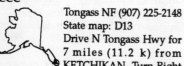

Tongass NF (907) 225-2148
State map: D13
Drive N Tongass Hwy for 7 miles (11.2 k) from KETCHIKAN. Turn Right (NE) on gravel FR 39 (Ward Creek Rd) and go 1 mile (1.6 k). (After Signal Creek but before Last Chance campgrounds.)
$5. Open approximately Apr 15–Oct 15.
4 close, screened sites. Hand water pump, pit toilets, tables, grills, fire rings.
Near Ward Lake and 2-mile Perseverance Trail.
Hike, view wildlife, take photographs, fish, or canoe. Enjoy an under-cover picnic in massive-beamed, CCC-built shelter on other side of Ward Lake.
14-day limit. Lots of rain and insects.
0 ft (0 m)

### CHENA LAKE RA

BLM (907) 356-5385
State map: C10
S of FAIRBANKS at milepost 347 on Richardson Hwy (AK 2), drive N on Laurence Rd.
$5. Open All Year.
82 sites. Hand water pumps, pit toilets, dump station, tables, grills, fire rings, shelters, pay phone, store (ice and equipment rentals), playground, volleyball court, horseshoe pits, dock, boat ramp.
Alaska-resort camping among wildlife next to flood-control lake.
Boat, swim, and fish in river or lake. Cycle and hike trails. Play volleyball and horseshoes on site. Cross-country ski and snowmobile in winter.
600 ft (180 m)

### CIRCLE PUBLIC CAMPGROUND

Circle City Park
State map: B11
Find at milepost 162 on Steese Hwy (AK 6).
FREE but choose a chore.
Open May 15–Sep 15, weather decides.
Undesignated sites. Pit toilets, tables.
In grassy area along Yukon River.
Walk around town once thought to be on Arctic Circle. Soak at nearby hot spring. Fish.
NO water.
600 ft (180 m)

### COEUR D'ALENE

Chugach NF
(907) 271-2500
State map: C10
Before you enter HOPE (at milepost 16 of Hope Hwy), turn Left (S) on Resurrection Creek Rd. Bear Left (SE) on steep, narrow Palmer Creek Fork (FR 901) for 7.5 miles (12 k)–not recommended for trailers or RVs.
FREE but choose a chore.
Open Jun 1–Oct 15.
6 scattered sites in open and screened setting. Pit toilet, tables, fire rings.
On hillside around stream footbridge.
Fish. Hike to admire alpine scenery and pick berries, in season.
14-day limit. Hunting/mining nearby.
1400 ft (420 m)

### CRIPPLE CREEK

BLM (907) 356-5385
State map: C10
Drive NE of FAIRBANKS to milepost 60.5 on Steese Hwy (AK 6).
FREE. Open All Year.
21 (6 tent-only) sites. Hand water pump, pit toilets, tables, fire rings.
On pretty creek.
Fish. Paddle Chatanika River Canoe Trail to Chatanika River SP. Walk nature trail. Photograph wildlife and scenery.
7-day/20-ft limits. No pets. Hunting in season.
700 ft (210 m)

ALASKA 6

▲ ▲ ▲ ▲ ▲ ▲ ▲ ▲ ▲ ▲ ▲ ▲ ▲ ▲ ▲ ▲ ▲ ▲ ▲ ▲ ▲ ▲ ▲ ▲ ▲

**DENALI NP-Morino Walk-In**

(907) 683-2294
State map: C9
Drive 238 miles (386 k) N
from ANCHORAGE or
126 miles (193 k) S from
FAIRBANKS on George Parks Hwy
(AK 3). From Depot, follow signed
walkway .25 mile (400 m) to self-
registration station.
$3/person plus park entrance fee of
$3/individual or $5/family. Other NPS
campgrounds cost $12. Also, free
backcountry permits are available in
person at Visitor Access Center by area
quota system.
Open May 23–Sep 14.
60 walk-in tent sites (for visitors without
vehicles), scattered in open setting.
Central water faucet, chemical toilets,
food storage containers, tables.
In Alaska Range near North America's
tallest mountain, Denali, at 20320 ft.
Take shuttle bus to view scenery of this
subarctic wilderness–its mountain slopes
and its wild river valleys. View flora
(virgin spruce and alpine flowers) and
fauna (caribou, Dall sheep, grizzly bear,
wolf). Bring your camera! Hike. Attend
scheduled ranger programs.
Obey all NPS guidelines for preserve,
park, and wilderness areas.
2000 ft (600 m)

**DENEKE PARK**

Palmer City Park
State map: C10
Find in PALMER at 435 S
Denali Street–near Visitor
Center and Old Glenn
Hwy and Alaska Railway.
$4.50. Open May 15–Sep 15.
Undesignated sites. Water, flush toilets,
dump station, hot showers, tables.
On grassy area in birch grove.
Fish in nearby Matanuska River. Tour
Visitor Center agricultural exhibits.
Purchase Matanuska Valley vegetables at
roadside stands. Attend Alaska State Fair
(late Aug–Labor Day).
240 ft (72 m)

**EAGLE**

BLM (907) 356-5385
State map: C11
From Mile 160.3 of Taylor
Hwy (AK 5) heading
toward EAGLE, drive
1 mile (1.6 k) W.
FREE but choose a chore.
Open Jun 1–Sep 30.
16 scattered, screened sites. Spring water,
pit toilets, picnic tables, fire rings.
On bluff overlooking spring that
provided water to fort (follow pipes).
Tour historic US Army Fort Egbert and
town of Eagle on Yukon River. Walk
trails. Fish.
Be careful crossing fort parade
ground–it's town airstrip. 10-day limit.
820 ft (246 m)

**EAGLES NEST**

Tongass NF (907) 828-3304
State map: D13
On Prince of Wales Island
from town of THORNE
BAY, take gravel AK 30
W for 18 miles (28.8 k)–check current
road and weather conditions.
$5. Open May 15–Sep 30; dry camping
off-season.
10 (2 walk-in, tent-only) sites in close but
screened setting. ๔
Hand water pump, chemical toilets,
tables, grills, fire rings.
Along mountain creek among Sitka
spruce, yellow cedar, and hemlock. On
Balls Lake with canoe launch and board-
walk trail around part of lake.
Canoeing, fishing (cutthroat trout and
salmon), hiking, photography, and wildlife viewing (duck, geese, swan, crane,
otter, beaver, deer, bear).
14-day/30-ft limits. ATV/pet leash rules.
1500 ft (450 m)

**FOREST ACRES &**
**WATERFRONT PARK**

Seward City Parks
(907) 224-3331
State map: C10
In SEWARD, find Forest
Acres 2.5 miles (4 k) S on

▲ ▲ ▲ ▲ ▲ ▲ ▲ ▲ ▲ ▲ ▲ ▲ ▲ ▲ ▲ ▲ ▲ ▲ ▲ ▲ ▲ ▲ ▲ ▲ ▲ ▲ ▲ ▲ ▲

Seward Hwy (AK 9). Waterfront Park lies between Ballaine Blvd and 3rd Ave. $5. Open May 15–Sept 30.

Close, open parking for RVs.

Harbormaster Building contains public restrooms, pay showers, pay phones, mailbox. Dump station and water at small boat harbor at 4th Ave. More public restrooms along Ballaine Blvd at waterfront.

In rebuilt town on eastern Kenai Peninsula between rugged mountains and Resurrection Bay.

Try saltwater fishing, boating, swimming, sightseeing (including 1964 Earthquake library slide show).

No tables (picnic shelters on waterfront).
10 ft (3 m)

## GLACIER BAY NP-Bartlett Cove

(907) 697-2230
State map: D12
Arrive in GUSTAVUS by boat or commercial flight out of Juneau. Glacier Bay NP lies 9 miles (14.4 k) from town and offers bus service from airstrip to park headquarters. This whole trip gets expensive, but the longer you stay, the lower the daily cost.

FREE. Also, free backcountry permits available. Open mid May–mid Sep.

35 walk-in tent sites .25 mile (400 m) from park lodge. Food storage facilities, warming hut with woodstove, beach.

In deep spruce-hemlock woods just off bay shore surrounded by fjords and glacier-clad mountains.

Hike, watch and photograph wildlife (particularly seabirds and marine mammals as well as wolf and bear). Fish and kayak. Attend ranger programs too. NO water/trash facilities. 14-day limit. Black bears and insects.
10 ft (3 m)

## HILLSIDE

Homer City Parks
(907) 235-7740
State map: D9
In HOMER at milepost 174 of Sterling Hwy

(AK 1), turn N on Bartlett St and follow signs.

$3 for tents, $7 for RVs.
Open May 15–Sep 15.

26 sites. Water, pit toilets, tables, fire rings.

On wooded overlook above town and Kachemak Bay.

Photograph view. Catch a summer ballgame or two. Enjoy Homer–the Key West of the North.

14-day limit.
200 ft (60 m)

## HOMER SPIT

Homer City Parks
(907) 235-7740
State map: D9
Drive 4 miles (6.4 k) S of HOMER on Spit Rd.

$3 for tents, $7 for RVs (pay at Spit Visitor Center). Open May 15–Sep 15, weather decides.

Undesignated, close, open sites.

Water, flush/chemical/pit toilets, tables, boat ramp.

On narrow gravel bar formed by Kachemak Bay currents.

Absorb view of bay and nearby mountains. Boat and fish. Observe marine wildlife. Explore town.

14-day limit.
5 ft (1 m)

## KATMAI NP & PRESERVE
### Brooks Camp

(907) 246-3305
State map: D8
Locate park 250 air miles (400 k) SW of ANCHORAGE. Access campground by float plane from KING SALMON, 20–30 minutes away.

FREE (may add fee in '93); reservations required. Also, free backcountry permits available at Brooks Contact Center.

Open Jun 1–Sep 17; dry camping off-season.

20 grassy tent sites near beautiful Naknek Lake and woods.

Central water faucet, elevated food caches, garbage can .25 mile (400 m) from campground, pit toilets, tables, fire rings, non-motor boat rentals.

Visit Valley of Ten Thousand Smokes created by 1912 eruption of Novarupta Volcano in wilderness setting of rugged mountains and shorelines. Hike, take photographs, attend ranger programs. Fish, boat, and view wildlife (especially, bald eagle and brown bear).

7-day limit. Crowded July. Frequent rain, wind, mosquitos, and bears.

40 ft (12 m)

## KENAI CITY PARK

(907) 283-1991
State map: C9
In KENAI, take Kenai Spur through town to milepost 12, turn Left (S) on Forest Dr. Campground behind National Guard Armory.

FREE but choose a chore.

Open May 15–Sep 15, weather decides.

30 sites. Water, pit toilets, tables, shelters, playground.

On wooded overlook onto Cook Inlet and snowcapped volcanos, Mt Redoubt and Mt Iliamna.

Fish. Watch for whales at Beluga Lookout. Explore Russian influence in 1791 fur trading settlement.

3-day limit.

40 ft (12 m)

## KENAI NWR

(907) 262-7021
State map: C9
On western slopes of Kenai Mountains of Kenai Peninsula with many forests, lakes, and rivers providing habitation for large and small mammals, birds, as well as spawning areas for fish.

FREE, except Upper Skilak Lake.

14-day limit, except Jim's Landing.

400 ft (120 m)

**▲ Dolly Varden Lake**

11 miles (17.6 k) from SOLDOTNA at milepost 83 on Sterling Hwy (AK 1), drive 15 miles (24 k) N on Swanson River Rd–not for large RVs.

FREE but choose a chore.

Open May 1–Oct 1.

12 sites. Water, pit toilets, tables, fire rings, boat ramp.

On lake named for its trout.

Boat (10-ft limit), swim, fish. Pick berries when ripe.

16-ft limit.

**▲ Engineer Lake**

Find at mile 9.5 of Skilak Lake Rd.

FREE but choose a chore.

Open All Year.

8 sites. Water, pit toilets, tables, fire rings, boat ramp.

Fish for silver salmon. Hike Seven Lakes Trail. Enjoy winter sports here.

**▲ Jean Lake**

Travel about 11–12 miles from COOPER LANDING to mileposts 59–60 on Sterling Hwy (AK 1).

FREE but choose a chore.

3 sites. Pit toilets, tables, boat ramp.

Fishing!

NO water.

**▲ Jim's Landing**

From STERLING, drive 9 miles (14.4 k) E to milepost 72 on Sterling Hwy (AK 1) then less than a mile on Skilak Lake Rd.

FREE but choose a chore.

5 sites. Water, pit toilets, boat ramp.

On Kenai River.

Canoeing and fishing.

7-day/16-ft limits. Crowded.

**▲ Kelly Lake**

Take 1-mile access road at mile 68.5 Sterling Hwy (AK 1), between towns of COOPER LANDING and STERLING.

FREE but choose a chore.

Open May 1–Oct 20.

3 sites. Water, pit toilets, tables, fire rings, boat ramp.

Boat and fish lake. Hike Seven Lakes Trail. Watch for wildlife, especially moose. Pick berries in season.

**▲ Lower Ohmer Lake**

18 miles (28.8 k) E of STERLING, take Skilak Lake Rd SE for 8 miles (12.8 k).

FREE but choose a chore.

Open May 1–Oct 20; camping allowed off-season.

3 sites. Pit toilets, fire rings, boat ramp.

On lake in wooded hills with backdrop of Kenai Mountains.

Boat (be careful of gusty winds). Fish for rainbow trout. Pick berries when ripe. NO water. 20-ft limit.

▲ **Lower Skilak Lake**
10 miles (16 k) from COOPER LANDING at milepost 58 of Sterling Hwy (AK 1), take Skilak Lake Rd. Go 15 miles (24 k) SW.
FREE but choose a chore.
Open All Year.
14 sites. Water, pit toilets, tables, fire rings, boat ramp.
In summer, fish for salmon, trout, and whitefish or hike along lake. In winter, ice fish, snowshoe, or cross-country ski.
14-day limit. Gusty winds. Bears.
400 ft (120 m)

▲ **Petersen Lake**
Find access road S at mile 68.5 of Sterling Hwy (AK 1).
FREE but choose a chore.
Open May 1–Oct 20.
3 sites. Water, pit toilets, tables, fire rings, boat ramp.
Boat. Fish for trout. Hike Seven Lakes Trail. Watch for moose. Pick berries when ripe.

▲ **Rainbow Lake**
West of STERLING at milepost 83 on Sterling Hwy (AK 1), take Swanson River Rd N 16 miles (25.6 k).
FREE but choose a chore.
Open May 1–Oct 20; dry camping off-season.
4 sites. Water, pit toilets, fire rings, boat ramp.
Fish for rainbows here. Pick berries when ripe. In winter, ice fish, ice skate, snowshoe, and cross-country ski.
20-ft limit.

▲ **Swanson River**
W of STERLING at milepost 83 on Sterling Hwy (AK 1), take Swanson River Rd for 18 miles (28.8 k).
FREE but choose a chore.
Open May 1–Oct 20; dry camping off-season.
8 sites. Water, pit toilets, tables, fire rings, and boat ramp.
Canoe Swanson River to access point at Captain Cook SRA. Fish. Enjoy winter

sports in off-season.
20-ft limit.

▲ **Tustamena Lake**
18 miles (28.8 k) SW of SOLDOTNA at milepost 110 on Sterling Hwy (AK 1), drive 6 miles (9.6 k) SE on gravel Tustamena Lake Rd.
FREE but choose a chore.
10 sites. Water, pit toilets, tables, fire rings, boat ramp on river.
On Kasilof River with Tustamena Lake 1 mile (1.6 k) upstream.
Fish. Boat (be careful of river currents and lake winds). Observe and photograph wildlife. Pick berries. Enjoy winter activities in season.
20-ft limit. Often crowded.

▲ **Upper Skilak Lake**
10 miles (16 k) W of COOPER LANDING at milepost 58 on Sterling Hwy (AK 1), turn SW on Skilak Lake Rd. Go 8.5 miles (13.6 k) to lake access road then 1.3 miles (2.1 k) S on gravel road not maintained in winter.
$5. Snow determines season; dry camping off-season.
25 sites (10 tent-only in open setting; 15 tent/RV scattered in screened setting).
Hand water pump, chemical and pit toilets, tables, fire rings, and boat ramp.
In forest on glacially-fed lake.
Boating and fishing are primary activities. There's also hiking, viewing and photographing scenery and wildlife, and attending ranger programs. In winter, cross-country ski.
Quiet 11pm–6am. Crowded Jun–Jul. Pet leash rules. Extremely cold lake water, but only thin ice in winter.
400 ft (120 m)

▲ **Watson Lake**
Find lake 10 miles (16 k) E of STERLING at mile 70.8 on Sterling Hwy (AK 1).
FREE but choose a chore.
Open May 1–Oct 20
3 sites.
Pit toilets, tables, fire rings, boat ramp.
Boat and fish for red salmon. Hike Seven Lakes Trail. Pick berries when ripe. Enjoy outdoor winter activities in season.
NO water. Moose hunting in season.

▲▲▲▲▲▲▲▲▲▲▲▲▲▲▲▲▲▲▲▲▲▲▲▲▲▲▲▲▲

## KLONDIKE GOLD RUSH NHP-Dyea

(907) 983-2921
State map: D12
Follow narrow, winding one-lane road with turn-outs from SKAGWAY to historic town site of Dyea–road unsuitable for large RVs or trailers.
FREE. Also, free backcountry permits available at Skagway Visitor Center to backpack Chilkoot Trail. Open All Year.
27 (22 RV, 5 tent-only) scattered, screened sites.
Pit toilets, tables, fire rings.
In shade along Taiya River, approximately .25 mile (400 m) from present-day trailhead of historic 35-mile (56-k) Chilkoot Trail used by 1898 gold miners through mountain passes and alpine ecologies to Yukon Territory.
Hike along Chilkoot Trail. View historic artifacts. Take photographs. Fish and birdwatch. Attend ranger programs and tour NPS exhibits on gold rush at Visitor Center while in Skagway.
NO potable water.
0 ft (0 m)

## LAKE #3

Tongass NF (907) 828-3304
State map: D13
Locate on FR 2030-790, a 20-minute drive from Prince of Wales Island's THORNE BAY and 5.5 miles (8.8 k) S of junction of AK 929 and FR 2030. (Other free campgrounds on island include Staney Bridge and Staney Creek in 1980 clear-cut area.)
FREE but choose a chore.
Open All Year.
2 sites. Pit toilets, tables, fire rings.
On gently sloping, brushy hill overlooking lake.
Fish, canoe, hike, view wildlife, take photographs, and explore historic Tlingit culture and modern logging operations.
NO water/trash arrangements. Hunting in season. Check road and weather conditions.
200 ft (60 m)

## LAST CHANCE

Tongass NF (907) 225-2148
State map: D13
Drive N Tongass Hwy for 7 miles (11.2 k) from KETCHIKAN. Turn on gravel FR 39 (Ward Creek Rd) and go 3 more miles (4.8 k). (Pass Signal Creek and CCC campgrounds.)
$5. Open generally Jun 1–Aug 31.
22 close, screened sites. Central water faucet, pit toilets, tables, grills, fire rings. Among towering trees and running creeks.
Find opportunities for wildlife viewing, photography, and solitude on Conneu Lake Trail. Enjoy non-motorized boating as well as fishing.
14-day/22-ft limits. Rain. Insects.
0 ft (0 m)

## MENDENHALL

Tongass NF (907) 747-6671
State map: D13
From JUNEAU and milepost 9 of Egan Expressway, turn onto Mendenhall Loop Rd and drive almost 4 miles (6.4 k). Turn on Montana Creek Rd and continue .5 mile (800 m).
$5. Open May 15–Sep 15.
61 scattered, screened sites. Water, pit toilets, dump station, tables, fire rings.
On lake with spectacular views of Mendenhall Glacier, ice floes, and mountains.
Boat (no motors) on lake. Hike to glacier and ice pinnacles. Take lots of photos. Tour Visitor Center across lake.
14-day/25-ft limits.

## ODIAK PARK

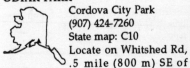

Cordova City Park
(907) 424-7260
State map: C10
Locate on Whitshed Rd, .5 mile (800 m) SE of downtown.
$5. Open May 15–Sep 15, weather decides.
Gravel lot for RVs (tents on "Ski Hill").
Water, flush toilets, showers.

On compacted and landscaped old town dump in fishing community situated on Orca Inlet of Prince William Sound with views of Mt Eccles.
Explore impact of fishing, mining copper, transporting oil on this beautiful town. Hike up Mt Eyak ("Ski Hill") and to Crater Lake for panoramas.
Primarily for summer cannery workers.
50 ft (15 m)

## OHMER CREEK

Tongass NF (907) 772-3871
State map: D13
Take Mitkof Hwy from PETERSBURG for 22 miles (35.2 k). 1900-ft (580-m) access road meanders through two tidally influenced, grassy meadows.
FREE but choose a chore.
Open May 15–Sep 15.
15 sites. Central hand water pump, pit toilets, tables, grills, fire rings.
Undesignated, open sites nestled in coniferous vegetation. (Scheduled for improvement in '94).
On creek with seasonal returns of steelhead, coho, and king salmon. Hiking, wildlife viewing, photo taking as well as exploring town with strong native American and Norwegian influences.
14-day/32-ft limits–more suitable to trailers than RVs because of dense forest canopy. No ATVs. Insects.
0 ft (0 m)

## SAWMILL CREEK

Tongass NF (907) 747-6671
State map: D12
On Baranof Island from SITKA, drive 6 miles (9.6 k) SE on FR 11–not recommended for trailers or large RVs.
($5 Starrigavan Campground is .7 mile (1.1 k) from ferry terminal.)
FREE but choose a chore. Open May 15–Sep 15, weather decides.
6 sites. Pit toilets, fire rings.
In mountainous setting.
Swim and fish in creek. Hike trail to Blue Lake. Observe wildlife. Explore beautiful, historic Sitka's native

American, Russian, and modern-day American influences.
Boil creek water before drinking.

## SHOEMAKER BAY

Wrangell City Parks
(907) 874-3770
State map: D13
On Wrangell Island, drive almost 5 miles (8 k) S of WRANGELL on Zimovia Hwy. (An overnight option is Wrangell City Park.)
FREE but choose a chore. Open May 15–Sep 15, weather decides.
Undesignated sites.
Water, flush toilets, dump station, tables, playground, tennis court, boat launch.
In woods on creek near small boat harbor and forest trailhead.
Boat and fish on bay. Walk to Rainbow Falls. Explore industrious Wrangell.
10-day limit.

## SIGNAL CREEK

Tongass NF (907) 225-2148
State map: D13
Travel N Tongass Hwy for 7 miles (11.2 k) out of KETCHIKAN. Turn on gravel FR 39 (Ward Creek Rd) and continue .75 mile (1.2 k). (CCC and Last Chance campgrounds are also on FR 39.)
$5. Open Memorial Day–Labor Day
24 close, screened sites. Hand water pump, pit toilets, tables, grills, fire rings.
In old-growth hemlock-spruce forest with meandering stream.
Hike, view wildlife, and take photos.
Boat (no motors) and fish Ward Lake.
See totem pole collection at nearby Totem Bight State Park.
14-day/22-ft limits. Rain. Insects.
0 ft (0 m)

## SOURDOUGH CREEK

BLM (907) 822-3217
State map: C10
Find near village of SOURDOUGH, about 20 miles (32 k) N of GULKANA at mile 147.5 on Richardson Hwy (AK 4), a paved road with frost

▲ ▲ ▲ ▲ ▲ ▲ ▲ ▲ ▲ ▲ ▲ ▲  ▲ ▲ ▲ ▲ ▲ ▲ ▲ ▲ ▲ ▲ ▲ ▲

FREE but choose a chore.
Open May 15–Oct 1, snow decides; camping allowed off-season.
43 scattered sites in open or screened settings. (Under reconstruction in '93.)
Pit toilets, tables, fire rings, boat ramp.
With views of Alaska Range, Wrangell and Chugach Mountains.
Year around, view and photograph scenery and wildlife. In summer, fish and boat (access to Gulkana River) or walk trail along Sourdough Creek. In winter, cross-country ski. Learn why sourdough breads became popular here. (Try sourdough pancakes at Alaska's oldest existing roadhouse).
NO water. 7-day limit. Crowded July 4th. Hunting in season.
2000 ft (600 m)

## STANEY BRIDGE

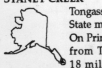

Tongass NF (907) 828-3304
State map: D13
On Prince of Wales Island from THORNE BAY, drive 18 miles (28.8 k) W on Thorne Bay Rd. Turn Right (N) on FR 20 (North Island Rd). Drive 4.8 miles (7.7 k) and turn Left on FR 2050–.5 mile (800 m) S of Staney Creek Bridge approximately an hour-and-a-half drive from THORNE BAY. (Other free campgrounds on island include Lake #3 and Staney Creek.)
FREE but choose a chore.
Open All Year.
2 close sites. Pit toilets, tables, fire rings.
In stand of second-growth Sitka spruce, hemlock, and yellow cedar near creek.
Fish for steelhead, salmon, and trout.
Enjoy photographing flora and fauna.
NO water/trash arrangements (pack it out). Hunting in season. Check road and weather conditions.
200 ft (60 m)

## STANEY CREEK

Tongass NF (907) 828-3304
State map: D13
On Prince of Wales Island from THORNE BAY, go 18 miles (28.8 k) W on Thorne Bay Rd. Turn Right (N) on FR 20 (North Island Rd). Go 10.9 miles (17.4 k) and turn Left on FR 2054, approximately an hour-and-a-half drive from THORNE BAY. (Also see Lake #3 and Staney Bridge.)
FREE but choose a chore.
Open All Year.
2 close sites. Pit toilets, tables, fire rings.
In 1980 clear-cut area but close to popular fishing hole known as Horseshoe Hole.
Fishing. Watching and photographing wildlife. Comparing modern methods to Tlingit traditions.
NO water/trash facilities. Check weather and road conditions. Hunting in season.
100 ft (30 m)

## STARRIGAVAN CREEK

Tongass NF (907) 747-6671
State map: D12
On Baranof Island, drive 7 miles (11.2 k) N of SITKA on paved Halibut Point Rd–only .7 mile (1.1 k) from Alaska Marine Hwy terminal. (Free campground on other side of town is Sawmill Creek.)
$5. Open Apr 15–Nov 1; dry camping off-season.
27 (3 walk-in tent) sites on two loops.
Hand water pump, pit toilets, tables, grills, fire rings.
In old-growth rainforest on ocean bay and estuary with magnificent mountain views. In summer, wildflowers bloom early and salmon spawn late.
Beachcomb and fish. Hike to view and photograph nature. Tour town of Sitka.
14-day/30-ft limits. Quiet 10pm–6am.
Crowded Jun 15–Jul 31.
0 ft (0 m)

## TANGLE LAKES

BLM (907) 822-3217
State map: C10
Travel 22 miles (35.2 k) W of PAXSON to mile 21.5 of Denali Hwy (AK 8), a paved road with frost heaves.
FREE but choose a chore.

▲ ▲ ▲ ▲ ▲ ▲ ▲ ▲ ▲ ▲ ▲ ▲ ▲ ▲ ▲ ▲ ▲ ▲ ▲ ▲ ▲ ▲ ▲ ▲ ▲ ▲ ▲ ▲

Open Jun–Oct, snow decides; dry camping off-season.

23 scattered, open sites.

Hand water pumps, pit toilets, tables, fire rings, boat ramp.

In Tangle Lakes Archeological District with view of Alaska Range as well as access to Delta National Wild, Scenic, and Recreational River.

Lots of recreational opportunities: hiking, fishing, rafting, canoeing, boating, photography, and, in season, berrying.

7-day limit. Crowded July 4 and hunting season (mid Aug–mid Sep). Fragile tundra. Grizzly bears.

3000 ft (900 m)

## TANGLE RIVER

BLM (907) 822-3217
State map: C10
Drive W of PAXSON to mile 21.7 of Denali Hwy (AK 8)–paved road with frost heaves.

FREE but choose a chore.

Open Jun–Oct, snow decides; dry camping off-season.

7 close, open sites. Hand water pump, pit toilets, tables, fire rings, boat ramp.

On banks of Tangle River with access to canoe trail on Upper Tangle Lakes and, with portages, to Middle Fork of Gulkana River.

Watch and photograph wildlife year-round. Enjoy summer hikes and boating excursions as well as fishing. In winter, cross-country ski.

7-day limit. Crowded July 4. Hunting in season (mid Aug–mid Sep). Fragile tundra. Grizzly bears.

3000 ft (900 m)

## TENT CITY

Petersburg City Park
(907) 772-3646
State map: D13
Locate on Haugen Drive in SE Passage town of PETERSBURG.

$3 plus $25 deposit.

Open May 15–Sep 15, weather decides.

Wooden platforms for 3–5 tents. Water,

toilets, tables, cooking area platform. On muskeg.

Explore Petersburg–historic influences of native Americans and Norwegians as well as contemporary fishing industry. Primarily for summer cannery workers.

## TETLIN NWR

(907) 883-5312
State map: C11
Find between YUKON border and TETLIN JUNCTION.

In wooded areas around small lakes in Tetlin NWR, part of North American migratory bird flyway.

FREE but choose a chore.

Open May–Sep.

NO potable water. No generator use within refuge. Mosquitos.

1750 ft (525 m)

▲ **Deadman Lake**

Drive Alaska Hwy (AK 2) to milepost 1249. Take sandy road 1 mile (1.6 k).

18 (10 tent or pickup camper, 8 RV) sites in scattered, screened settings.

Pit toilets, tables, fire rings.

Walk nature trail, swim, boat, fish, watch and photograph wildlife. (Be careful not to harass animals by venturing too close.) Attend ranger-scheduled programs in season.

▲ **Lakeview**

At Alaska Hwy (AK 2) milepost 1256.7, drive .25 mile (400 m) on packed sand road. Due to no turnaround space here, trailers, 5th wheels, and RVs need to use Deadman Lake Campground (see above.)

8 (tent and pickup camper) sites in scattered, screened settings.

Pit toilets, tables, fire rings.

By small but pretty Yarger Lake.

Fishing, boating, swimming, bird-watching, and photography. (Do not harass animals by venturing close.)

## VALDEZ GLACIER

Valdez City Parks
(907) 835-2531
State map: C10
From VALDEZ at mile 3.4 of Richardson Hwy (AK

4), drive 2 miles (3.2 k) N on Airport Rd.
$5. Open May 1–Oct 1.
101 sites. Hand water pumps, pit toilets, tables, grills, fire rings.
Within scenic views of glacier.
Boat and fish (fresh and saltwater). See glacier and farthest-north ice-free port in Americas. Examine impact of industries (oil, fishing, and tourism) on town set between beautiful Prince William Sound and rugged Chugach Mountains. Outside of town, view Keystone Canyon and its waterfalls, Horsetail and Bridal Veil.
15-day limit. Bears.

## WALKER FORK

BLM (907) 356-5385
State map: C11
Drive 14 miles (22.4 k) N of CHICKEN to milepost 82 on Taylor Hwy (AK 5).
FREE but choose a chore.
Open May 15–Sep 30.
20 sites. Water, pit toilets, tables, fire rings.
At confluence of Jack Wade Creek and Walker Fork of Fortymile National Wild and Scenic River.
From bluff above creek, watch beaver at work. Fish. Hike. Pan for gold in river.
10-day limit.

## WEST FORK

BLM (907) 356-5385
State map: C11
Travel 19 miles (30.4 k) S of CHICKEN to milepost 49 on Taylor Hwy (AK 5).
FREE but choose a chore.
Open May 15–Sep 30.
25 close, open sites.
Pit toilets, tables, fire rings.
On Fortymile National Wild and Scenic River. Canoe. Observe wildlife. Fish.
NO water. 10-day limit.

## WRANGELL CITY PARK

(907) 874-3770
State map: D13
On Wrangell Island, drive through town of WRANGELL then 2 miles (3.2 k) S on Zimovia Hwy. (Find more modern and longer-term facilities at Shoemaker Bay, 3 miles–4.8 k–farther.)
FREE but choose a chore.
Open May 15–Sep 15, weather decides.
8 sites. Water, flush toilets, tables, picnic shelter, ball field.
On shore of Inland Passage.
Enjoy the view: channel, wooded islands, snowcapped mountains, bald eagles. Catch a summer ballgame. See petroglyphs, totem poles, Chief Shakes' Community House.
Overnight only.
0 ft (0 m)

## WRANGELL-ST ELIAS NP-Backcountry

(907) 822-5234
State map: C11
Access park perimeter via old McCarthy or Nebesna mining roads. Fly into interior and its glacier fields on chartered aircraft. Call, or write PO Box 29, Glenallen, AK 99588, for details on permits and recommendations.
FREE. Open All Year.
Encompasses Wrangell and St Elias mountains (including 9 of 16 highest peaks in US). Park/preserve conjoins Canada's Kluane National Park to create refuge from human encroachment for black and grizzly bear, caribou, moose, Dall sheep, wolverine. This vast, remote area full of ice fields has great impact on the continent's weather.
Mountain bike, hike, backpack, mountain climb, cross-country ski, fish, raft, and take lots of photos.
Lots of preparations to travel here.

# Arizona

Grid conforms to official state map. For your copy, write:
Arizona Office of Tourism, 1100 West Washington, Phoenix, AZ 85007.

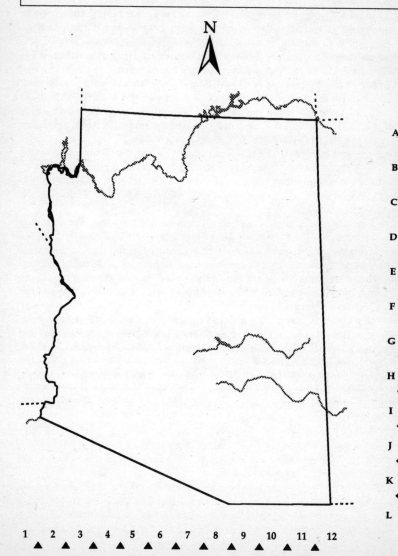

Study the Arizona map for camping opportunities and become impressed with the impact of natural forces. Campsites cluster around water sources, where the living is easy. Starting in the northern part of the state, the Colorado River winds its way through the Grand Canyon, across the state, and down into the Mohave Desert, where many snowbirds boondock their rigs each winter. Looking east, most preferred summer camping lies above the Mogollon Rim, stretching above and past Prescott, Phoenix, and Safford. Below Safford there are popular "islands in the sky," mountains rising above the desert floor and enjoying cooler ecologies.

Find $5-or-less camping offered by US Department of the Interior's agencies. The **National Park Service** (NPS) lists Canyon de Chelly National Monument (NM), Grand Canyon NP, Navajo NM, Organ Pipe Cactus NM, Petrified Forest NP (backcountry), and Saguaro NM (backcountry). **US Fish and Wildlife Service** allows primitive camping in the Kofa National Wildlife Refuge (NWR). The **Bureau of Land Management** (BLM) provides many opportunities, but most are provide by the US Department of Agriculture's Forest Service.

In the **Apache-Sitgreaves National Forest** (NF), the Mogollon Rim rises vertically in places as high as 1000 feet. Experience the Mount Baldy, Bear Wallow, and Escubilla wilderness areas plus the Blue Range Primitive Area. Watch for bald eagle and, perhaps, fish for Apache trout. Retrace Coronado's search for the fabled Seven Cities of Cibola, now US 666.

Deep canyons (such as Oak Creek), tall peaks ("sacred" San Francisco), remote wilderness areas (scenic Sycamore Canyon) as well as intriguing ruins of prehistoric native American villages (Sinagua) are found in the **Coconino NF**. Wildlife observations list the threatened bald eagle and peregrine falcon, black bear, and mountain lion.

The **Coronado NF** stretches from the Tucson area to the Mexico border, then across the bottom of the state to the New Mexico border. Consequently, there's a lot of diversity here: exotic Mexican flora and fauna can be seen in Sycamore Canyon; distinct ecological zones can be examined by road up Mount Lemmon. Eight wilderness areas, including the Chiricahua, provide habitation for jaguar, jaguarundi, ocelot, coatimundi, Chiricahua fox squirrel, trogon, and Gila chub as well as the desert bighorn sheep.

On the plateaus surrounding the Grand Canyon, the **Kaibab NF** contains three wilderness areas. Look for the Kaibab squirrel (dark body with light tail and tufted ears) as well as bald eagle and peregrine falcon. The forest's southern portion reveals volcanic activity.

In central Arizona, the **Prescott NF** encompasses two long mountain ranges, varying in elevation from 3000 to 8000 feet. In the high elevations, watch for bald eagles and peregrine falcons. There are eight wilderness areas in the Prescott NF; Pine Mountain is particularly scenic.

Northeast of Phoenix is the **Tonto NF**. Drive the exciting Apache Trail. Hike into one of seven wilderness areas with such evocative names as Hellgate and Superstition. Admire ancient cliff dwellings. Look for lost gold mines and quartz crystals. Slow down for gopher tortoise.

While Arizona State Parks (SPs) are too expensive ($7 per vehicle) to qualify, check out two county park options: Dirty Shirt Campground in Maricopa County's Lake Pleasant Regional Park and Cataract Lake in Coconino County.

Tour Arizona's highways, camp its public lands, experience its grandeur.

## AIRPLANE FLAT

Tonto NF (602) 462-3311
State map: F9
From PAYSON, head E on
AZ 260 for 33 miles
(52.8 k)–8 miles (12.8 k) W of FOREST
LAKES. Turn Right (S) on gravel FR 512
(Young Rd). In 3 miles (4.8 k) at Colcord
Ridge, turn Left (E) on FR 33. Go
4.5 miles (7.2 k).
FREE but choose a chore.
Open Apr–Nov.
Scattered open sites. Pit toilets, tables.
In ponderosa pine near Canyon Creek.
Fishing is main lure. Good wildlife
observations include bear, elk, and
mountain lion.
NO water. 14-day/16-ft limits. No ATVs.
6600 ft (1980 m)

## ALDERWOOD

Tonto NF (602) 462-3311
State map: F9
Travel E from PAYSON for
24 miles (38.4 k) to gravel
FR 291. Turn Right (SE). Travel 4 miles
(6.4 k) to FR 200. Turn Right again and
go another 7 miles (11.2 k) to FR 249.
Turn Right (W) and continue 1 more
mile (1.6 k). (Also see Haigler Creek.)
FREE but choose a chore.
Open Apr–Nov.
Undesignated, scattered, open sites.
Pit toilets, tables.
On banks of Haigler Creek.
Splash in creek's swimming holes or pull
out fishing rods. Many just relax in
peaceful setting.
NO water/trash arrangements (pack it
out). 14-day limit. No ATVs.
5200 ft (1560 m)

## ALPINE DIVIDE

Apache-Sitgreaves NF
(602) 339-4385
State map: G12
Take US 666 N from ALPINE
for 3 miles (4.8 k).
$5. Open May 15–Oct 15; dry camping
off-season.
13 scattered, open sites.
Water, pit toilets, tables, grills, fire rings.

Adjacent to AZ 666 in thick stand of
ponderosa pine and Douglas fir.
Fishing possibilities.
14-day/32-ft limits. Crowded around
July 4. Hunting in season. Closed by
snow in winter.
8500 ft (2550 m)

## APACHE LAKE

Tonto NF (602) 225-5200
State map: H8
From APACHE JUNCTION,
take AZ 88 (Apache Trail) NE
for 31.5 miles (50.4 k). Turn Left on
FR 79 and go 1 mile (1.6 k).
$2 (when renovated, fees changed).
Open All Year.
12 close, open sites. Water, pit toilets,
tables, grills, boat ramp.
On shores of lake.
Enjoy water-based activities such as
skiing, swimming, boating, and fishing.
14-day/22-ft limits.
1900 ft (570 m)

## ARCADIA

Coronado NF (602) 428-4150
State map: I11
From SAFFORD, head S on
US 666 for 7.5 miles (12 k).
Turn Right (SW) on AZ 366. Ascend for
11 miles (17.6 k) on paved but steep and
winding road. (See Hospital Flat for
high-elevation alternative.)
$5. Open Mar 1–Nov 30.
17 scattered, open sites.
Water, pit toilets, tables, grills, fire rings.
Halfway up Mt Graham along old Swift
Trail among pine and oak.
Pleasant hiking and birdwatching.
14-day limit.
6700 ft (2010 m)

## BACHELORS COVE

Tonto NF (602) 467-2236
State map: G8
From ROOSEVELT, go 2 miles
(3.2 k) NW on AZ 88 then
4 more miles (6.4 k) on AZ 188.
FREE but choose a chore.
Open All Year.
Undesignated, open sites.

▲ ▲ ▲ ▲ ▲ ▲ ▲ ▲ ▲ ▲ ▲ ▲ ▲ ▲ ▲ ▲ ▲ ▲ ▲ ▲ ▲ ▲ ▲ ▲

Pit toilets, tables.
By lake among desert scrub: mesquite,
catclaw, cholla, and burro weed.
Relish water sports on Roosevelt Lake.
NO water. Clean up area—use trash cans.
14-day/16-ft limits. No ATVs.
2100 ft (630 m)

## BATHTUB

Coronado NF (602) 364-3468
State map: K12
Take US 666 N from ELFRIDA
for 3 miles (4.8 k). Turn Right
(E) on unpaved CR 74. Go 23 miles
(36.8 k) then turn Left (NE) on FR 75E.
Go 5 more miles (8 k). (Also see Camp
Rucker, Cypress Park, and Rucker.)
$3. Open All Year.
11 close, open sites.
Water, pit toilets, tables, fire rings.
In stand of ponderosa pine near small
fishing lake.
Hike, birdwatch, and fish.
No trash facilities. 14-day limit. No
trailers. Generator rules.
6300 ft (1890 m)

## BEAR CANYON LAKE

Apache-Sitgreaves NF
(602) 289-2471
State map: F9
From HEBER, drive SW on
AZ 260 approximately 22 miles (35.2 k)
to FR 300. Turn Right (W) and follow
signs about 13 miles (20.8 k).
FREE but choose a chore.
Open Spring—Fall (closed by weather).
50 scattered, open sites.
Chemical/pit toilets.
Along sides of lake. Walk .25 mile
(400 m) to water.
Boat (if you can carry your craft) and
fish. Explore and enjoy area scenery.
NO water/trash arrangements (come
prepared and pack it out). 14-day limit.
Crowded weekends.
8000 ft (2400 m)

## BEAVER CREEK

Coconino NF (602) 567-4510
State map: E7
From MCGUIREVILLE, go NE
on I-17 for 5 miles (8 k). Take
Exit 298 (AZ 179) and turn E on
unpaved FR 618 for 3 miles (4.8 k).
$5. Open All Year.
13 close, open sites.
Water, pit toilets, tables, grills, fire rings.
On banks of Wet Beaver Creek in
riparian environment contrasting with
surrounding Sonoran Desert. Sheltered
by cottonwood and sycamore with
natural gardens of prickly pear and
banana yucca.
Swim, wade, or fish in creek. Take
hiking excursion into adjacent Beaver
Creek Wilderness.
14-day/22-ft limits.
3800 ft (1140 m)

## BERMUDA FLAT

Tonto NF (602) 467-2236
State map: G8
From ROOSEVELT, go 2 miles
(3.2 k) NW on AZ 88 then
7 more miles (11.2 k) on AZ 188.
FREE but choose a chore.
Open All Year.
Undesignated, open sites.
Pit toilets, tables, dirt boat launch.
In open, fairly level area by lake among
mesquite.
Indulge in water-play in Roosevelt Lake.
NO water. Clean up area—use trash cans.
14-day/16-ft limits. No ATVs.
2100 ft (630 m)

## BLACK CANYON RIM

Apache-Sitgreaves NF
(602) 535-4481
State map: F9
From FOREST LAKES, take
AZ 260 for 2.5 miles (4 k) SE to FR 300.
Turn Left (S) and continue another
2.5 miles (4 k).
$4. Open Apr—Oct; dry camping
off-season.
20 scattered, screened sites.
Water, chemical toilets, tables, fire rings.
Among ponderosa pine, only 3 miles

(4.8 k) from Black Canyon Lake.
Hiking and birdwatching. Nearby
boating and fishing.
14-day/16-ft limits.
7600 ft (2280 m)

## BLACKJACK

Apache-Sitgreaves NF
(602) 865-4129
State map: H12
From CLIFTON, go S on
US 666 for 15 miles (24 k) to AZ 78.
Turn Left (E) on AZ 78 and drive
19 miles (30.4 k). (Also see Coal Creek.)
FREE but choose a chore.
Open May 15–Oct 15; camping allowed
off-season.
5 scattered, open sites.
Pit toilets, tables, grills.
Under trees near New Mexico border.
Hiking, birding, and taking photos.
NO water/trash arrangements (pack it
out). 14-day limit. No generators.
Hunting in season.
6200 ft (1860 m)

## BLUE CROSSING

Apache-Sitgreaves NF
(602) 339-4385
State map: G12
Find near BLUE at intersection
of FR 281 and 567. Road can flood.
FREE but choose a chore.
Open All Year.
4 scattered, open sites.
Pit toilets, tables, grills, fire rings.
Underneath cottonwood, on banks of
Blue River.
Great spot to hike with access to more
remote areas.
Water needs treating. No trash facilities
(pack it out). 14-day/18-ft limits.
Hunting in season.
5800 ft (1740 m)

## BLUE RIDGE

Coconino NF (602) 477-2255
State map: F8
From STRAWBERRY or
FLAGSTAFF, proceed to
CLINTS WELL (intersection of FH 3 and
AZ 87). From crossroads, go NE on

AZ 87 for 7.5 miles (12 k). Turn Right on
unpaved FR 138 and continue SE for
1 mile (1.6 k). (Also see Rock Crossing.)
$5. Open Memorial Day–Sep 15.
10 close, open sites. Water, pit toilets,
tables, grills, fire rings, boat ramp.
In shady secluded spot along Blue Ridge
Reservoir.
Fish for three types of trout. Mountain
bike, hike, observe wildlife, or just relax.
14-day/22-ft limits. Forest roads close in
winter.
7500 ft (2250 m)

## BOG SPRINGS

Coronado NF (602) 281-2296
State map: K9
Head S from GREEN VALLEY
on US 89 for 3 miles (4.8 k).
Turn Left (SE) on FR 62 and continue
7 miles (11.2 k) to FR 70. Go S another
6 miles (10.2 k).
$5. Open All Year.
13 close, open sites.
Water, pit toilets, tables, grills, fire rings.
Among deciduous trees in Madera
Canyon's riparian setting.
Birdwatching, taking photographs, and
hiking.
14-day limit. Crowded fall and spring.
5600 ft (1680 m)

## BUFFALO CROSSING

Apache-Sitgreaves NF
(602) 339-4385
State map: G12
Located at junction of FR 25
and 24–about 35 miles (56 k) SW of
ALPINE.
FREE but choose a chore.
Open May 15–Oct 15; camping allowed
off-season.
19 scattered, open sites.
Pit toilets tables, grills, fire rings.
Along banks of East Fork of Black River.
Fish, take photographs, and enjoy ranger
programs.
Water must be treated. 14-day limit.
Crowded July 4 weekend.
7600 ft (2280 m)

▲ ▲ ▲ ▲ ▲ ▲ ▲ ▲ ▲ ▲ ▲ ▲ ▲ ▲ ▲ ▲ ▲ ▲ ▲ ▲ ▲ ▲ ▲

## BURNT CORRAL

Tonto NF (602) 467-2236
State map: G8
From ROOSEVELT, take AZ 88
(narrow, steep, dirt Apache
Trail) W for 6 miles (9.6 k). At mile
marker 236, turn Right on FR 183.
FREE but choose a chore.
Open All Year.
79 close, open sites.
Pit toilets, tables, boat ramp.
On shore of Apache Lake.
Play in water–swimming to waterskiing.
Attend summer campfire programs.
NO water. Clean up area–use trash cans.
14-day/22-ft limits. No ATVs.
1900 ft (570 m)

## BURRO CREEK

BLM (602) 757-3161
State map: E4
From WICKIEUP, go 14 miles
(22.4 k) SE on US 93. About
1 mile (1.6 k) S of bridge, turn Right (W)
on Burro Creek Rd. Continue another
1.25 miles (2 k).
$4. Open All Year.
21 scattered, open sites.
Water, flush/pit toilets, tables, grills, fire
rings, sun ramadas, dump station.
On year-round creek with pools and
waterfalls supporting lush vegetation
and incredible diversity of wildlife.
Excellent opportunity to study and
photograph desert ecologies, complete
with desert garden and nature trail.
Swim in creek too.
14-day limit. Crowded in winter.
Rattlesnakes.
1960 ft (588 m)

## CAMP RUCKER

Coronado NF (602) 364-3468
State map: K12
Take US 666 N from ELFRIDA
for 3 miles (4.8 k). Turn Right
(E) on unpaved CR 74. Go 23 miles
(36.8 k) then turn Left (NE) on FR 75E
for 200 yards (185 m). (Also see Bathtub,
Cypress Park, and Rucker.)
$3. Open All Year.
14 scattered, open sites.

Water, pit toilets, tables, grills, fire rings.
In pine-oak forest near stream.
Hiking and fishing.
14-day/16-ft limits. Generator rules.
6100 ft (1830 m)

## CANYON CREEK

Tonto NF (602) 462-3311
State map: F9
From PAYSON, head E on
AZ 260 for 33 miles
(52.8 k)–8 miles W of FOREST LAKES.
Turn Right (S) on gravel FR 512 (Young
Rd). In 3 miles (4.8 k) at Colcord Ridge,
turn Left (E) on FR 33. Go 5 miles (8 k).
FREE but choose a chore.
Open Apr–Nov.
Scattered open sites. Pit toilets, tables.
Across road from Canyon Creek Fish
Hatchery (self-guided tours).
Fishing is IT (artificial flies and lures).
NO water. 14-day/16-ft limits. No ATVs.
6700 ft (2010 m)

## CANYON DE CHELLY NM
### Cottonwood

(602) 674-5436
State map: B12
From CHINLE, drive E on
access road (Navajo 7/64) for
3 miles (4.8 k) to Visitor Center.
FREE plus $3 entrance fee (or pass).
Open All Year.
106 (38 tent-only, 26 RV-only) close sites.
Water (foul-tasting), flush toilets, tables,
grills, pay phone, dump station.
In grove of cottonwood.
Take Rim Dr for impressive overviews.
Hike down White House Ruins Trail.
More extensive exploration of ancient
area possible, if you (and up to 9 others)
hire authorized Navajo guides at Visitor
Center for $10/hour. Be protective of
fragile ruins and artwork.
5-day/35-ft limits. Crowded Apr–Sep.
Generator rules. Water turned off
Nov–Mar. No ATVs. Peddlers.
5500 ft (1650 m)

▲ ▲ ▲ ▲ ▲ ▲ ▲ ▲ ▲ ▲ ▲ ▲ ▲ ▲ ▲ ▲ ▽ ▲ ▲ ▲ ▲ ▲ ▲ ▲ ▲ ▲ ▲ ▲

## CATARACT LAKE

Coconino County Parks
(602) 774-5139
State map: D6
From WILLIAMS, take I-40 W
to Exit 161 (Country Club). Go 1 mile
(1.6 k) N.
$4. Open May 1–Sep 30.
56 (28 tent-only) close, open sites.
Pit toilets, tables, grills, fire rings.
On lakeshore among ponderosa pine.
Enjoy water activities.
NO water. 14-day limit. 8 hp boat motor
limit.
6500 ft (1950 m)

## CCC

Tonto NF (602) 488-3441
State map: G7
From CAREFREE, take FR 24
(Cave Creek Rd) N for 20 miles
(32 k) to Seven Springs (keep bearing
Left). Go another .5 mile (800 m). Last
9 miles (14.4 k) are gravel with blind
curves–not recommended for trailers
over 16 ft. (Also see Seven Springs.)
FREE but choose a chore.
Open All Year.
8 close, open sites.
Pit toilets, tables, grills.
At former site of Civilian Conservation
Corps camp, next to small creek under
large sycamore trees.
Good birding plus access to Cave Creek
trail system for hiking and exploring.
NO water/trash arrangements (pack it
out). 14-day limit. No ATVs.
3500 ft (1050 m)

## CHEVELON CROSSING

Apache-Sitgreaves NF
(602) 289-2471
State map: E9
From WINSLOW, take AZ 99 S
for 28 miles (44.8 k) to FR 504. Turn Left
(E) and follow signs.
FREE but choose a chore.
Open All Year.
7 close, open sites.
Chemical toilets, tables, fire rings.
Next to Chevelon Creek.
Fish or simply enjoy remote location.

NO water/trash facilities. 14-day limit.
Crowded holiday weekends.
6000 ft (1800 m)

## CHEVELON LAKE

Apache-Sitgreaves NF
(602) 289-2471
State map: F9
From HEBER, drive SW on
AZ 260 approximately 22 miles (35.2 k)
to FR 300. Turn Right (W) and drive
about 11 miles (17.6 k) to junction of
FR 169. Follow signs on 169 about
20 miles (32 k).
FREE but choose a chore.
Open All Year.
20 scattered, open sites. Pit toilets.
Close to Chevelon Lake (within .75 mile).
Fish and boat (small motors only) in lake
or hike surrounding area.
NO water/trash arrangements (pack it
out–keep location clean). 14-day limit.
6500 ft (1950 m)

## CHOLLA BAY

Tonto NF (602) 467-2236
State map: G8
From ROOSEVELT, go 2 miles
(3.2 k) NW on AZ 88 then
8 more miles (12.8 k) on AZ 188.
FREE but choose a chore.
Open Sep–Jun.
Undesignated, open sites. Pit toilets.
Along Roosevelt Lake next to developed
Cholla RS, popular with snowbirds.
Enjoy water-based activities.
NO water/trash arrangements (pack it
out). 14-day/16-ft limits.
2200 ft (660 m)

## CLEAR CREEK

Coconino NF (602) 567-4510
State map: F7
From CAMP VERDE, take
FH 9 (General Crook Hwy) E
for 5 miles (8 k). Turn Left (N) on
unpaved FR 626.
$5. Open All Year.
18 close, open sites.
Water, pit toilets, tables, grills, fire rings.
In grassy setting under stand of
cottonwood beside West Clear Creek,

▲ ▲ ▲ ▲ ▲ ▲ ▲ ▲ ▲ ▲ ▲ ▲ ▲ ▲ ▲ ▲ ▲ ▲ ▲ ▲ ▲ ▲ ▲ ▲ ▲

creating mini-oasis in desert canyon country.

Enjoy swimming, wading, or fishing for bass and sunfish. Birdwatching for both raptors and songbirds.

14-day/32-ft limits. Sometimes crowded (especially group site).

3200 ft (960 m)

## CLINTS WELL

Coconino NF (602) 354-2216
State map: F8
Find at intersection of FH 3 and AZ 87—about 22 miles (35.2 k) NE of STRAWBERRY or 50 miles (80 k) SE of FLAGSTAFF.

FREE but choose a chore.

Open Apr–Nov; dry camping off-season.

12 close, open sites.

Water, pit toilets, tables, grills.

In stand of old ponderosa near several fishing lakes as well as Mogollon Rim. Hiking, wildlife observing, and fishing.

14-day/22-ft limits. Winter storms occasionally close area.

7000 ft (2100 m)

## COAL CREEK

Apache-Sitgreaves NF
(602) 865-4129
State map: H12
From CLIFTON, travel S on US 666 for 15 miles (24 k). Turn Left (E) on AZ 78 and drive 15 miles (24 k). (Also see Blackjack.)

FREE but choose a chore.

Open May 15–Oct 15; camping allowed off-season.

5 close, open sites.

Pit toilets, tables, fire rings.

Under shade trees.

Wander peaceful surroundings.

NO water/trash facilities. 14-day limit. No generators. Hunting in season.

5680 ft (1704 m)

## COCHISE STRONGHOLD

Coronado NF (602) 364-3468
State map: K10
16 miles (25.6 k) S of I-10 on US 666 (just N of SUNSITES), take CR 84 W for 7.5 miles (12 k). Turn

W on unpaved FR 84 and go 2 miles (3.2 k), crossing stream several times.

$5. Open All Year.

23 close, screened sites.

Water, pit toilets, tables, grills, fire rings.

At site of old Apache stronghold among great rock formations and erratic creek. Hiking and birdwatching rate high.

14-day limit. Generator rules.

5000 ft (1500 m)

## COLCORD RIDGE

Tonto NF (602) 462-3311
State map: F9
From PAYSON, head E on AZ 260 for 33 miles (52.8 k)–8 miles W of FOREST LAKES. Turn Right (S) on gravel FR 512 (Young Rd) and travel 3 miles (4.8 k).

FREE but choose a chore.

Open Apr–Nov.

Undesignated, scattered sites.

Pit toilets, tables.

On fairly level spot among pine and fir. Fishing in nearby Canyon Creek and wildlife observing (bear, elk, mountain lion, javelina, and deer).

NO water/trash arrangements (pack it out). 14-day/32-ft limits. No ATVs.

7600 ft (2280 m)

## CROOK

Apache-Sitgreaves NF
(602) 289-2471
State map: F9
From HEBER, go SW on AZ 260 approximately 22 miles (35.2 k) to FR 300. Turn Right (W) and drive about 3.5 miles (5.6 k) to FR 105. Sites are .25 mile (400 m) up FR 105–tricky when muddy. (Also see Mogollon.)

$5. Open May 1–Oct 31.

26 close, open sites. Water, pit toilets, tables, fire rings, dump station, boat ramp, nearby store with ice and rentals. On lakeshore in ponderosa pine.

Enjoy ranger programs during summer plus boating, fishing, hiking, wildlife viewing, and taking photographs.

14-day limit. Crowded holiday weekends.

7000 ft (2100 m)

## CROSSROADS

BLM (602) 855-8017
State map: F2
From PARKER, cross to
California side of river and go
N for 8 miles (12.8 k) on Parker Dam Rd.
(Also see Empire Landing in CA.)
FREE but choose a chore.
Open All Year.
8 scattered, open sites.
Pit toilets, tables, grills.
Under trees beside Colorado River in highly-developed area. Temperature rarely below 60°F.
Swimming, boating, and jet-skiing.
14-day limit. Generator rules. Often noisy between power boats, nearby ATV areas, and crowds of people.
395 ft (117 m)

## CYPRESS PARK

Coronado NF (602) 364-3468
State map: K12
Take US 666 N from ELFRIDA
for 3 miles (4.8 k). Turn Right
(E) on unpaved CR 74. Go 24 miles
(38.4 k). (Also see Bathtub, Camp Rucker, and Rucker.)
$3. Open Mar–Oct; dry camping off-season.
7 scattered, open sites.
Water, pit toilets, tables, grills, fire rings.
In pine-oak forest.
Hiking and fishing.
14-day/16-ft limits. Generator rules.
6000 ft (1800 m)

## DIAMOND ROCK

Apache-Sitgreaves NF
(602) 339-4385
State map: G12
From ALPINE, go 2 miles
(3.2 k) NW on US 666. Turn Left (W) on gravel FR 1249 and travel 9 miles (14.4 k). Turn Left (SW) on FR 276 and go 5.9 miles (9.4 k).
FREE but choose a chore.
Open May 1–Oct 30; dry camping off-season.
13 close, screened sites.
Water, pit toilets, tables, fire rings.
Along banks of Black River's East Fork.

Trout fishing outside your door. Hiking and wildlife observation in forest.
14-day/18-ft limits. Crowded July 4 and Labor Day.
7900 ft (2370 m)

## EAST FORK-BLACK RIVER

Apache-Sitgreaves NF
(602) 339-4385
State map: G12
Drive about 15 miles (24 k) SW
of ALPINE on unpaved FR 276. (Also see West Fork.)
FREE but choose a chore.
Open May 1–Oct 31; dry camping off-season.
60 scattered, screened sites.
Water, few pit toilets.
On 6 mile (9.6 k) stretch of trout stream. Fishing and wildlife viewing. Attending ranger programs too.
Pack out your trash. Crowded July 4 and Labor Day. 14-day limit.
7600 ft (2280 m)

## EAST RIM VIEWPOINT

Kaibab NF (602) 643-7395
State map: B6
From JACOB LAKE at North
Kaibab Visitor Center, take
AZ 67 S for 26.5 miles (42.4 k)–.7 mile (1.1 k) beyond **DeMotte** Campground. Turn Left (E) on FR 611 and travel another 4.4 miles (7 k).
FREE but choose a chore.
Open late spring–late fall.
Undesignated sites. Pit toilets.
In small grassy openings of oak-aspen forest with rim views, including House Rock Valley, Vermillion Cliffs, Marble Canyon, and North Canyon.
Enjoy excellent photography and sightseeing opportunities. Wildlife observation ranges from wild turkey and grouse to deer and fox. For solitude, access East Rim Trail #7 into Saddle Mountain Wilderness.
NO water/trash arrangements (come prepared and pack it out). Cool even in summer.
8800 ft (2640 m)

▲ ▲ ▲ ▲ ▲ ▲ ▲ ▲ ▲ ▲ ▲ ▲ ▲ ▲ ▲ ▲ ▲ ▲ ▲ ▲ ▲ ▲ ▲ ▲ ▲ ▲ ▲

## FLOWING SPRINGS

Tonto NF (602) 474-7900
State map: G8
From PAYSON, go 4 miles
(6.4 k) N on AZ 87. Near mile
marker 257, turn Right (E) on gravel
FR 272. Site is within .5 mile (800 m).
FREE but choose a chore.
Open May–Sep.
Undesignated, open sites. Pit toilet.
On East Verde River with waterfalls and
unusual rock formations.
Trout fishing is another draw.
NO water/trash arrangements (pack it
out–keep it clean). 14-day/16-ft limits.
4600 ft (1380 m)

## FOUR MILE CANYON

BLM (602) 428-4040
State map: I10
From PIMA, go 5 miles (8 k) W
on US 70. Turn Left (SW) on
Aravaipa–Klondyke Rd, driving about
40 miles (64 k) on unpaved road to
Klondyke. Turn Left and travel .5 mile
(800 m)–impassable when wet.
FREE but choose a chore.
Open All Year.
10 close, open sites.
Water, flush toilets, tables, fire rings.
Among desert scrub and mesquite in
colorful canyon with views of
surrounding mountains. Near Aravaipa
Canyon Wilderness (permits required).
Hike. Swim in Aravaipa Creek. Find
solace in canyons. Photograph some of
200 species of birds.
14-day limit. Crowded in Sep–Oct with
hunters and in Jan with snowbirds.
3000 ft (900 m)

## GENERAL HITCHCOCK

Coronado NF (602) 749-8700
State map: J9
From TUCSON, take Hitchcock
Hwy (Left off Tanque Verde)
toward Mt Lemmon. Campground is
at milepost 12. (Also see Molino Basin.)
FREE but choose a chore.
Open Apr 15–Oct 15.
13 close-together sites with some
screening. Water, pit toilets, tables, grills.

Midway up Mt Lemmon from Tucson
among pines in small canyon.
Explore and hike surrounding area.
14-day limit. Generator rules.
6000 ft (1800 m)

## GENTRY

Apache-Sitgreaves NF
(602) 535-4481
State map: F9
Take AZ 260 17 miles (27.2 k)
SW from HEBER. Turn Left (S) on
FR 300 and go 3 miles (4.8 k).
FREE but choose a chore.
Open May–Oct; camping allowed
off-season.
6 scattered, open sites.
Pit toilets, tables, fire rings.
In secluded setting among tall ponderosa
pine near Gentry fire tower.
Hike, watch birds, or just enjoy solitude.
14-day/16-ft limits.
7700 ft (2310 m)

## GRAND CANYON NP

(602) 638-7805
State map: B4–B6
$10 entrance fee (or pass). All
rim camps (except Toroweap
Point) cost $8-10. Also, free backcountry
permits and trail maps available from
Backcountry Office–reservations
accepted at (602) 638-7888.
At one of seven natural wonders of
world, enjoy incredible rim views.
Explore into canyon to absorb grandeur.
▲ Bright Angel Walk-In
Walk down about 9 miles (14.4 k) from
South Rim with 5000-ft (1524-m) drop.
Open All Year.
33 close, screened tent sites. Water,
flush/pit toilets, tables, pay phone.
At bottom of quintessential canyon in
low-altitude desert environment with
shade next to stream flowing into
Colorado River.
Hike to relish and photograph desert
environments.
Permit required. Pack out all trash. Hike
down and up strenuous anytime.
Extremely hot summers.
2300 ft (690 m)

▲ ▲ ▲ ▲ ▲ ▲ ▲ ▲ ▲ ▲ ▲ ▲ ▲ ▲ ▲ ▲ ▲ ▲ ▲ ▲ ▲ ▲ ▲ ▲ ▲ ▲ ▲

**▲ Cottonwood Walk-In**
Walk down about 7 miles (11.2 k) from North Rim with 4500-ft (1372-m) drop.
Open May 15−Oct 31; dry camping off-season.
12 close, screened tent sites.
Water, pit toilets, tables.
Near stream about two-thirds down spectacular canyon with few shade trees.
Rewarding hiking. Good birdwatching and photography.
Permit required. Pack out all trash. Hike down and up strenuous anytime.
Extremely hot summers.
3900 ft (1170 m)

**▲ Indian Garden Walk-In**
Walk down about 4.5 miles (7.2 k) from South Rim with 3000-ft (914-m) drop.
Open All Year.
16 close, screened tent sites.
Water, pit toilets, tables.
Midway into canyon, with desert feeling despite cottonwood trees.
Additional hiking opportunities on exceptional Tonto Trail. Excellent birdwatching and photography too.
Permit required. Pack out all trash. Hike down and up strenuous anytime.
Extremely hot summers. Mules use trail.
3000 ft (900 m)

**▲ Toroweap Point**
From FREDONIA, head SW on AZ 389 for 9 miles (14.4 k). Turn Left (S) on dirt Mt Trumbill Rd. Continue 60 miles (96 k) on very rough, unimproved, long, dirt road to point on North Rim−not recommended for RVs.
Open All Year.
5 sites. Chemical toilets, tables.
In rock-covered area on edge of Grand Canyon.
Hiking, sightseeing, and taking photos.
NO water/trash facilities (pack it out).
4600 ft (1380 m)

**GRANITE BASIN**
Prescott NF (602) 445-7263
State map: E5
Leaving PRESCOTT, go NW on Iron Springs Rd (on West Gurley to Grove. North on Grove to 4th traffic light. Turn Left.) Drive Iron Springs Rd for 3.2 miles (5.1 k) to Granite Basin turnoff. Turn N (FR 374) and go 4 miles (6.4 k).
FREE but choose a chore.
Open All Year.
18 close, screened sites.
Pit toilets, tables, grills, fire rings.
Beneath ponderosa pine and rugged, boulder-strewn cliffs.
Take short walk to Granite Basin Lake.
Hike to view nature. Fish (lake not stocked) or boat (electric motors permitted).
NO water. 14-day limit. No swimming.
5600 ft (1680 m)

**GRANVILLE**
Apache-Sitgreaves NF
(602) 865-4129
State map: H12
Travel N on US 666 from CLIFTON and MORENCI for 15 miles (24 k).
FREE but choose a chore.
Open May 15−Oct 15; dry camping off-season.
12 scattered, screened sites.
Water, pit toilets, tables, grills.
In relaxing setting plus lots of shade.
Birdwatching and photo opportunities in camp. Hike for more.
14-day limit. Crowded weekends and holidays. Generators discouraged.
Hunting in season.
6800 ft (2040 m)

**HAIGLER CREEK**
Tonto NF (602) 462-3311
State map: F9
Drive E from PAYSON for 24 miles (38.4 k) to gravel FR 291. Turn Right (SE). Travel 4 miles (6.4 k) to FR 200. Turn Right again. Go 7 miles (11.2 k). (Also see Alderwood.)
FREE but choose a chore.
Open Apr−Nov.
Scattered open sites. Pit toilets, tables.
On banks of creek in riparian setting with canyons and wide variety of plant and animal life.
Splash in creek's swimming holes or pull out fishing rods (regular trout stocking).

Many just relax in peaceful setting.
NO water/trash arrangements (pack it
out). 14-day/16-ft limits. No ATVs.
5300 ft (1590 m)

## HANNAGAN

Apache-Sitgreaves NF
(602) 339-4385
State map: G12
Take US 666 for 22 miles
(35.2 k) SW from ALPINE.
FREE, donations accepted.
Open May 15–Oct 15; camping allowed
off-season.
8 close, screened sites.
Pit toilets, tables, grills, fire rings.
Among tall spruce, fir, and aspen
adjacent to Coronado Scenic Byway.
Hike and relish high-country beauty. Ski
in winter.
NO water/trash facilities. 14-day/28-ft
limits. Crowded July 4 and Labor Day.
9100 ft (2730 m)

## HONEYMOON

Apache-Sitgreaves NF
(602) 865-4129
State map: H12
From CLIFTON and
MORENCI, go N on US 666 for 24 miles
(38.4 k). Turn Left (W) on FR 217 and
follow to end–20 miles (32 k). Dirt road
crosses water 3 times–difficult to
impossible in wet conditions.
FREE but choose a chore.
Open May 15–Oct 15; camping allowed
off-season.
4 scattered, screened sites.
Pit toilets, tables, fire rings.
In shady location along Eagle Creek.
Getaway with fishing and hiking
opportunities. Also, wildlife identification or relaxation.
NO water/trash arrangements (come
prepared and pack it out). 14-day limit.
5400 ft (1620 m)

## HORSESHOE

Tonto NF (602) 488-3441
State map: G7
From CAREFREE, take FR 24
(Cave Creek Rd) N for 6 miles
(9.6 k) to FR 205. Continue Right on
FR 205 for 6 miles (9.6 k) to intersection
with FR 19 (pavement ends). Continue
Left on FR 205 for another 10 miles
(16 k) to FR 205A. Site is less than
.5 mile (800 m) down FR 205A. Narrow
access roads not recommended for
trailers. (Also see Mesquite.)
FREE but choose a chore.
Open All Year.
8 close, open sites.
Pit toilets, tables, grills.
Under large mesquite trees with good
shade near Verde River and Horseshoe
Reservoir.
Enjoy water activities.
NO water/trash arrangements (pack it
out). 14-day/16-ft limits. No ATVs. No
motors on Verde River or reservoir.
1900 ft (570 m)

## HOSPITAL FLAT

Coronado NF (602) 428-4150
State map: I11
From SAFFORD, head S on
US 666 for 7.5 miles (12 k).
Turn Right (SW) on AZ 366. Ascend for
23 miles (36.8 k) on steep, winding,
paved access road. (Also see Shannon
and Soldier Creek.)
$5. Open May 1–Nov 14.
10 scattered, open sites. Water, flush and
chemical toilets, tables, grills, fire rings.
In dense pine-fir forest high in Pinaleno
Mountains.
Pleasant for hiking and birdwatching.
Though high, hot and crowded during
summer. Heavy snowfall during
transition periods.
9000 ft (2700 m)

## INDIAN CREEK

Prescott NF (602) 445-7263
State map: F5
Leaving PRESCOTT, go S on
US 89 for 5.7 miles (9.1 k).
Turn Left (E) on FR 97 and drive about
1 mile (1.6 k).
FREE but choose a chore.
Open May 15–Sep 30.
27 close, screened sites.
Pit toilets, tables, grills.

▲ ▲ ▲ ▲ ▲ ▲ ▲ ▲ ▲ ▲ ▲ ▲ ▲ ▲ ▲ ▲ ▲ ▲ ▲ ▲ ▲ ▲ ▲ ▲ ▲ ▲ ▲ ▲

Near town among rolling hills covered with ponderosa pine and live oak. Create base for exploring area. Good birdwatching too.
NO water. 14-day/32-ft limits.
5800 ft (1740 m)

## INDIAN HOLLOW

Kaibab NF (602) 643-7395
State map: B6
From FREDONIA, take unpaved FR 422 SE for 27 miles (43.2 k) to BIG SPRINGS. Continue 5 more miles (8 k) then turn Left (SW) on FR 425. In 8 miles (12.8 k), turn Left on FR 232—last 4.5 miles (7.2 k) of access impassable when wet or icy.
FREE but choose a chore.
Open May 1–Nov (depends on snowfall).
3 close, open sites.
Pit toilets, tables, grills.
Near access to Kanab Creek Wilderness and Grand Canyon's Thunder River Trail (permit from park needed to hike into Grand Canyon).
Good hiking and wildlife viewing.
NO water/trash arrangements.
6300 ft (1890 m)

## JONES WATER

Tonto NF (602) 425-7189
State map: G9
Take US 60 NE from GLOBE for 17 miles (27.2 k).
FREE but choose a chore.
Open All Year.
12 close, open sites.
Pit toilets, tables, grills.
In riparian area, surrounded by chaparral.
Excellent spot for birdwatching.
NO water. 14-day/16-ft limits. No ATVs.
4500 ft (1350 m)

## K P CIENEGA

Apache-Sitgreaves NF
(602) 339-4385
State map: G12
Go SW on US 666 from ALPINE for 25 miles (40 k). Turn Left (E) to campground—about 2 miles (3.2 k).

FREE, donations accepted.
Open May 15–Oct 15; dry camping off-season.
5 close, screened sites.
Water, pit toilets, tables, grills, fire rings. Amidst corkbark fir and Engelmann spruce next to beautiful meadow.
Excellent area for hiking and photography. Birdwatching and fishing opportunities too.
No trash arrangements (pack it out).
14-day/18-ft limits. Crowded July 4 and Labor Day. Hunting in season.
9200 ft (2760 m)

## KEHL SPRINGS

Coconino NF (602) 354-2216
State map: F8
From STRAWBERRY, go about 14 miles (22.4 k) N on AZ 87 to unpaved FR 300 (General Crook Trail). Turn Right (E) and drive 6 miles (9.6 k).
FREE but choose a chore.
Open Memorial Day–Sep 30.
8 close, open sites.
Pit toilets, tables, grills.
In shade near fabulous Mogollon Rim.
Good hiking and mountain biking on General Crook Historic Trail and Rim Country Scenic Dr.
NO water. 14-day/22-ft limits.
7500 ft (2250 m)

## KENTUCK SPRINGS

Prescott NF (602) 445-7263
State map: F6
From CROWN KING, take FR 259A S for .5 mile (800 m) to FR 52. Bear Left (SE) and continue 6 miles (9.6 k)—beyond Horsethief Basin.
FREE but choose a chore.
Open May 1–Nov 30.
15 close, screened sites.
Pit toilets, tables, grills.
In pines at southern end of Bradshaw Mountains in Horsethief Basin with flowing stream (after rains).
Hike to observe nature. Fishing nearby.
NO water/trash arrangements (pack it out). 14-day limit.
6000 ft (1800 m)

## KINNIKINICK

Coconino NF (602) 774-1147
State map: E8
From FLAGSTAFF, head S for
30 miles (48 k) on paved FH 3
(past Lake Mary). Turn Left (E) on
unpaved FR 125 for 4 miles (6.4 k). Turn
Right on FR 82 and go 5.5 miles (8.8 k)–
road usually closed by snow and mud in
winter.
FREE but choose a chore.
Open Memorial Day–Sep 30; dry
camping off-season.
18 close, open sites.
Pit toilets, tables, fire rings, grills.
Under weathered trees surrounding
Kinnikinick Lake with prairies and San
Francisco Peaks in background.
Elk, antelope, plus bald eagles in winter,
make lake good wildlife viewing location
as well as fishing hole.
NO water. 14-day/22-ft limits. No boat
motors over 8 hp.
7000 ft (2100 m)

## KNOLL LAKE

Coconino NF (602) 477-2255
State map: F8
From STRAWBERRY, go about
14 miles (22.4 k) N on AZ 87 to
unpaved FR 300 (General Crook Trail).
Turn Right and go 30 miles (48 k). Turn
Left (N) on FR 295E. Go 4 miles (6.4 k).
$5. Open Memorial Day–Sep 15.
33 close, open sites. Water, pit toilets,
tables, grills, fire rings, boat ramp.
In secluded setting on picturesque lake
near fantastic views of Mogollon Rim.
Hike and mountain bike for views. Fish
for trout.
14-day/22-ft limits.
7400 ft (2220 m)

## KOFA NWR-Backcountry

(602) 783-7861
State map: H2
Find 5 entrances to refuge
along E side of US 95 between
QUARTZSITE and YUMA.
FREE but choose a chore.
Open All Year.
Undesignated, open camping except
within .25 mile (400 m) of waterholes.
Refuge is for wildlife; peoples' needs are
secondary.
Rising above desert, two small, rugged
mountain ranges, Kofa and Castle Dome,
dominate setting for desert bighorn
sheep refuge.
Hike in Palm Canyon. Take lots of time
to watch wildlife and observe myriad
varieties of plant life.
NO water, toilet, or trash arrangements
(come prepared). 14-day limit. Many
high-clearance roads–4-WD only.
3000 ft (900 m)

## LA POSA LTVA

BLM (602) 726-6300
State map: G2
Take US 95 for 1 mile (1.6 k) S
from QUARTZSITE. Find sites
on both sides of road.
$50 annual pass or $10/week.
Open Sep 15–Apr 15; dry camping
off-season.
10000 scattered, open sites. Water, pit
toilets, pay phone, dump station.
In wide-open Sonoran Desert
topography with gravelly soil and
numerous small washes.
Attend Quartzsite's many gem-related
festivals, popular with rockhounds and
winter snowbirds who flock to area.
Generator rules. Coyotes and snakes.
927 ft (276 m)

## LAKE PLEASANT-Dirty Shirt

Maricopa County Parks
(602) 506-2930
State map: G6
From PHOENIX, take I-17 N to
AZ 74 Exit. Head W about 13 miles
(20.8 k) to Lake Pleasant entrance.
$4. Open All Year.
28 scattered, open sites.
Chemical toilets, boat ramp.
Around lake's shoreline.
Boating, fishing, hiking, birdwatching,
and taking photos.
NO water. 14-day limit. Quiet hours.
1600 ft (480 m)

▲ ▲ ▲ ▲ ▲ ▲ ▲ ▲ ▲ ▲ ▲ ▲ ▲ ▲ ▲ ▲ ▲ ▲ ▲ ▲ ▲ ▲ ▲ ▲ ▲

## LOS BURROS

Apache-Sitgreaves NF
(602) 368-5111
State map: F11
From MCNARY, take FR 224
(Road to Vernon) N for 7.5 miles (12 k).
Turn Right (E) on FR 20 to camp.
FREE but choose a chore.
Open May 1–Oct 30.
5 scattered, open sites.
Pit toilets, tables, fire rings.
Beside 1910 Los Burros Ranger Station.
Enjoy natural setting and wildlife
viewing.
NO water/trash arrangements (pack it
out). No ATVs. Hunting during season.
9000 ft (2700 m)

## LOWER & UPPER JUAN MILLER

Apache-Sitgreaves NF
(602) 865-4129
State map: H12
From CLIFTON and
MORENCI, take US 666 N for 25 miles
(40 k). Turn Right (E) on unpaved
FR 475 and drive 1 mile (1.6 k). Two
small camps within .5 mile (800 m).
FREE but choose a chore.
Open May 15–Oct 15; camping allowed
off-season.
7 scattered, screened sites.
Pit toilets, tables, grills.
With lots of shade and space.
Nice place to relax and do a little
walking (as Colin Fletcher calls hiking).
NO water of trash arrangements (pack it
out). 14-day limit. Hunting in season.
5750 ft (1725 m)

## LOWER WOLF CREEK

Prescott NF (602) 445-7263
State map: F6
Leaving PRESCOTT, go S on
Senator Rd for 6 miles (9.6 k)
to pavement end. 500 ft (152 m) later,
turn Right (W) on FR 97 and go
1.25 miles (2 k).
FREE but choose a chore.
Open May 15–Nov 15.
20 close, screened sites.
Pit toilets, tables, grills.
In boulder-strewn area shaded by pine,

interspersed with walnut and live oak.
Create base for exploring area. Nice
birdwatching and relaxing too.
NO water. 14-day limit.
6000 ft (1800 m)

## MARBLE VIEWPOINT

Kaibab NF (602) 643-7395
State map: B6
From JACOB LAKE at North
Kaibab Visitor Center, take
AZ 67 S for 26.5 miles (42.4 k)–.7 mile
(1.1 k) beyond DeMotte Campground.
Turn Left (E) on FR 611 and travel
another 1.4 miles (2.2 k) to FR 610. Turn
Right and head S for 6 miles (9.6 k) to
FR 219. Turn Left (N) and go about
4 miles (6.4 k) to end of road.
FREE but choose a chore.
Open late spring–late fall.
Undesignated, scattered sites. Pit toilets.
In small grassy openings in oak-aspen
forest with views of House Rock Valley,
Vermillion Cliffs, Marble Canyon, North
Canyon, and Saddle Mountain
Wilderness.
Excellent photography and sightseeing.
Wildlife viewing includes wild turkey,
grouse, deer, fox, hawks, and eagles.
NO water/trash arrangements (come
prepared). Cool even in summer.
8900 ft (2670 m)

## MESQUITE

Tonto NF (602) 488-3441
State map: G7
From CAREFREE, take FR 24
(Cave Creek Rd) N for 6 miles
(9.6 k) to FR 205. Continue Right on
FR 205 for 6 miles (9.6 k) to intersection
with FR 19 (pavement ends). Continue
Left on FR 205 for another 9 miles
(14.4 k) to sign. (Also see Horseshoe.)
FREE but choose a chore.
Open All Year.
Undesignated, close, open sites.
Pit toilets.
Under large mesquite trees on banks of
Verde River.
Enjoy water activities.
Be careful: river proves treacherous to
poor swimmers. NO water/trash

facilities (pack it out). 14-day limit. Not recommended for trailers. No motors on Verde River.
1900 ft (570 m)

## MINGUS MOUNTAIN

Prescott NF (602) 567-4121
State map: E6
From PRESCOTT, go E on US 89A for 19 miles (30.4 k). Turn Right (SW) on dirt FR 104 and drive 4 miles (6.4 k).
FREE but choose a chore.
Open Apr 1–Nov 30; camping allowed off-season.
25 close, screened sites.
Pit toilets, tables, grills, fire rings.
In shady pine grove on mountaintop with spectacular vistas of Verde Valley. Hike and relish natural beauty. Savor animal and birdwatching chances.
NO water/trash arrangements (pack it out). 14-day/22-ft limits.
7500 ft (2250 m)

## MOGOLLON

Apache-Sitgreaves NF
(602) 289-2471
State map: F9
From HEBER, go SW on AZ 260 about 22 miles (35.2 k) to FR 300. Turn Right (W) and drive about 4.5 miles (7.2 k)–dirt road can challenge when wet. (Also see Crook.)
$5. Open May 15–Oct 15.
26 close, open sites.
Water, pit toilets, tables, fire rings, dump station, boat ramp.
In ponderosa pine forest.
Water activities include boating and fishing. Land opportunities involve walking nature or longer trails and attending seasonal ranger programs.
14-day limit.
7000 ft (2100 m)

## MOLINO BASIN

Coronado NF (602) 749-8700
State map: J9
From TUCSON, take Hitchcock Hwy (Left off Tanque Verde) toward Mt Lemmon. Locate camp at milepost 6. (Also see General Hitchcock.)
FREE but choose a chore.
Open Oct 15–Apr 15.
49 close, open sites. ♿
Pit toilets, tables, grills.
In oak canyon at road bend (first camp from Tucson). As winter-only camp, open sunny sites usually more desirable than those in shade.
Explore and hike surrounding area.
NO water. 14-day limit. Generator rules. Closed summers.
4500 ft (1350 m)

## NAVAJO NM-Main

(602) 672-2366
State map: A9
From KAYENTA, go 19 miles (30.4 k) W on US 160. Turn Right (N) on AZ 564 and continue 10 miles (16 k) to monument.
FREE. Open mid Apr–mid Oct; dry camping off-season. Also, free backcountry permits to Keet Seel ruin available at Visitor Center (offered summers to 20 people per trip; reservations required two months in advance).
30 close, screened sites. ♿
Water, flush toilets, tables, grills, pay phone.
In pinyon-juniper growth on top of red mesa with interesting rock outcroppings and spectacular sunsets.
Take ranger-led hike to one of best ruins on continent, Betatakin. Sign up early. Hike is 5 miles (8 k) round-trip including 700-ft (200-m) elevation change. Walk easy Sandal Trail. View exhibits on Anasazi at Visitor Center. Enjoy Tsegi Canyon panoramas and evening ranger programs.
7-day/25-ft limits. Crowded weekends and holidays. Quiet hours and generator rules. Be careful around fragile ruins and unstable rocks.
7300 ft (2190 m)

## NEEDLE ROCK

Tonto NF (602) 488-3441
State map: G7
In SCOTTSDALE, take Pima
Rd to Dynamite Rd. Turn Right
(E), go 5 miles (8 k), and merge with Rio
Verde. Continue another 9.5 miles
(15.2 k) to unpaved FR 20. Turn Left (N)
and go 3 miles (4.8 k) to Needle Rock.
FREE but choose a chore.
Open All Year.
Undesignated, scattered sites. Pit toilets.
Along Verde River with rocky beach,
unusual rock formations, and riparian
habitats for interest.
Boat, fish, or just splash about in river.
NO water/trash arrangements (pack it
out–leave it cleaner than you found it).
14-day limit. No trailers or ATVs.
1600 ft (480 m)

## OAK FLAT

Tonto NF (602) 425-7189
State map: H8
From SUPERIOR, go E on
US 60 for 4 miles (6.4 k). Turn
Right (S) on FR 469 and go 1 mile (1.6 k).
FREE but choose a chore.
Open All Year.
16 close, open sites.
Pit toilets, tables, grills.
On Gila Pinal Scenic Route among shady
oak with rolling hills and nearby Devils
Canyon.
Observe wildlife, explore, and do a little
rock climbing.
NO water. 14-day/16-ft limits. No ATVs.
4200 ft (1260 m)

## ORANGE PEEL

Tonto NF (602) 467-2236
State map: G8
From ROOSEVELT, go 2 miles
(3.2 k) NW on AZ 88 then
9 more miles (14.4 k) on AZ 188. Turn
Right (E) into site.
FREE but choose a chore.
Open All Year.
Undesignated, open sites.
Pit toilets, tables.
By Roosevelt Lake in walking distance of
Tonto Creek's riparian habitat.

Enjoy water-based activities on Roosevelt
Lake and wildlife viewing.
NO water. Clean up area–use trash cans.
14-day/32-ft limits. No ATVs.
2100 ft (630 m)

## ORGAN PIPE CACTUS NM
### Alamo Canyon

(602) 387-6849
State map: J5
From LUKEVILLE, go 2 miles
(3.2 k) N on AZ 85 to Visitor
Center. Obtain required permit and
directions–approximately 12 miles
(19.2 k) N on AZ 85 then 4 miles (6.4 k)
E on unmarked, gravel road.
FREE but $3 entrance fee or pass.
(Developed campground near Visitor
Center costs $8.) Also, free backcountry
permits are available.
Open All Year.
4 scattered, open sites. Pit toilets.
In Sonoran desert at canyon mouth
among large saguaro and organ pipe
cacti.
Savor fantastic hiking and viewing of
plants and animals found nowhere else
in United States.
NO water/trash arrangements (pack it
out). 14-day limit.
1800 ft (540 m)

## PACKSADDLE

BLM (602) 757-3161
State map: D2
From KINGMAN, go 18 miles
(28.8 k) NW on US 93. Turn
Right (E) on BLM's Chloride/Big Wash
Rd. Travel another 9 miles (14.4 k) on
steep, gravel road.
FREE but choose a chore.
Open May–Oct (depends on snow).
7 scattered, screened tent sites.
Pit toilets, grills, fire rings.
In pinyon-juniper woodland with vistas
of lower valleys and distant mountains–
a high desert experience with yucca,
creosotebush, deer, and coyote.
Hike Cerbat Mountains, rockhound,
view wildlife, or explore hundreds of old
mines in area.
NO water. 14-day limit. Night temper-

▲ ▲ ▲ ▲ ▲ ▲ ▲ ▲ ▲ ▲ ▲ ▲ ▲ ▲ ▲ ▲ ▲ ▲ ▲ ▲ ▲ ▲ ▲ ▲

atures can fall to 30's in summer.
5700 ft (1710 m)

## PAINTED ROCK-Petroglyph Unit

BLM (602) 863-4464
State map: H4
From GILA BEND, travel
20 miles (32 k) W on I-8. Take
Painted Rocks Rd N for 11 miles (17.6 k).
FREE but choose a chore.
Open All Year.
30 close, open sites.
Pit toilets, tables, grills, sun shelters.
In volcanic region near Gila River with
views from top of Painted Rock.
Study numerous petroglyphs and canals
left by early Americans (do not deface).
Wide variety of rocks, birds, and animals
provide additional interest.
NO water. 14-day limit.
600 ft (180 m)

## PEPPERSAUCE

Coronado NF (602) 749-8700
State map: J9
From ORACLE, go 15 miles
(24 k) SE on unpaved FR 38.
FREE but choose a chore.
Open All Year.
21 close, open sites.
Water, pit toilets, tables, fire rings.
In riparian canyon with deciduous
vegetation. Near popular caving areas.
Spelunking and gold panning.
No trash arrangements (pack it out).
14-day limit. Crowded weekends during
spring and fall.
4700 ft (1410 m)

## PETRIFIED FOREST NP-Backcountry

(602) 524-6228
State map: D11
From HOLBROOK, go 25 miles
(40 k) E on I-40 to Exit 311.
Obtain permit and directions at Visitor
Center.
FREE but $5 entrance fee (or pass).
Open All Year.
Backpack into Painted Desert or among
petrified wood (permits assigned by
area). Among 50000 acres of wilderness,
find colorful and remote opportunities.

Enjoy hiking and taking photographs.
Carry adequate water-extreme heat.
Protect fragile ruins and petroglyphs.
5500 ft (1650 m)

## PINAL & UPPER PINAL

Tonto NF (602) 425-7189
State map: H9
In GLOBE, take Jess Hayes Rd
SE until junction of FR 112
(Icehouse Canyon) and FR 222
(Sixshooter Canyon). Take gravel FR 112
for 2.4 miles (3.8 k) to FR 55. Bear Right
on FR 55 and proceed 3 miles (4.8 k) to
FR 651. Turn Left and follow narrow,
winding FR 651 for 12.5 miles (20 k).
FREE but choose a chore.
Open May – Nov; dry camping
off-season.
28 (22 in Pinal, 6 in Upper Pinal) sites.
Water, pit toilets, tables, grills, shelters.
In shady locale beneath tall pines and
white fir with views of distant valleys.
Wonderful place to hike and become
attuned to wildlife observation as trails
comb ridges (no fewer than 10 within
1 mile of Pinal and Upper Pinal).
No trash arrangements (pack it out). NO
water during winter. 14-day/16-ft limits.
No ATVs.
7500 ft (2250 m)

## PINERY CANYON

Coronado NF (602) 629-6483
State map: K12
From PORTAL, take CR 42 W
about 18 miles (28.8 k).
(Creates alternative to nearby Rustler
Park and accessible from Willcox side).
FREE but choose a chore.
Open Apr–Nov.
5 close, open sites.
Pit toilets, tables, fire rings.
In pretty Cave Creek area not far from
Chiricahua NM.
Relax or hike.
NO water/trash arrangements (pack it
out). 14-day/16-ft limits.
7000 ft (2100 m)

▲ ▲ ▲ ▲ ▲ ▲ ▲ ▲ ▲ ▲ ▲ ▲ ▲ ▲ ▲ ▲ ▲ ▲ ▲ ▲ ▲ ▲ ▲ ▲ ▲

## PIONEER PASS

Tonto NF (602) 425-7189
State map: H9
▲ In GLOBE, take Jess Hayes Rd
SE until junction of FR 112
(Icehouse Canyon) and FR 222
(Sixshooter Canyon). Take gravel FR 112
for 2.4 miles (3.8 k) to FR 55. Bear Left
on FR 112 for another 6 miles (9.6 k).
FREE but choose a chore.
Open May-Nov; dry camping
off-season.
27 close, open sites.
Water, pit toilets, tables, grills.
In Pinal Mountains with relief from
intense summer heat.
Hike nearby Squaw Springs and East
Mountain trails.
No trash arrangements (pack it out). NO
water in winter. 14-day limit. No ATVs.
6000 ft (1800 m)

## PORTER SPRING

Tonto NF (602) 467-2236
State map: G8
▲ From ROOSEVELT, go 6 miles
(9.6 k) SE on AZ 188. Turn Left
(E) on gravel FR 82. Go 3 miles (4.8 k).
(Also see Windy Hill.)
FREE but choose a chore.
Open All Year.
Undesignated, open sites.
Pit toilets, tables.
By Roosevelt Lake along southern shore
of Salt River arm.
Enjoy water-based activities.
NO water. Clean up area–use trash cans.
14-day/22-ft limits. No ATVs.
2100 ft (630 m)

## POTATO PATCH

Prescott NF (602) 567-4121
State map: E6
▲ From PRESCOTT, go E on
US 89A about 19 miles (30.4 k)
to dirt FR 106. Turn Right (SW) and
drive 1 mile (1.6 k).
FREE but choose a chore.
Open Apr 1-Nov 30.
15 close, screened sites.
Pit toilets, tables, grills, fire rings.
Among pine–cool in summer.

Make base for exploring area or just
taking a break.
NO water/trash facilities. 14-day/22-ft
limits. Hunting in season.
7000 ft (2100 m)

## POWELL SPRINGS

Prescott NF (602) 567-4121
State map: E6
▲ From DEWEY, take AZ 169 E
for 6 miles (9.6 k) to dirt
FR 372. Turn Left (N) and drive 5 miles
(8 k).
FREE but choose a chore.
Open All Year.
10 close, open sites.
Water, pit toilets, tables, grills, fire rings.
In pine trees near town of Cherry.
Try relaxed pace of birdwatching and
animal observation.
No trash arrangements (pack it out).
14-day/22-ft limits. Hunting in season.
5300 ft (1590 m)

## RATTLESNAKE

Tonto NF (602) 488-3441
State map: G7
▲ From CAREFREE, take FR 24
(Cave Creek Rd) N for 6 miles
(9.6 k). Continue Right on FR 205 for
6 miles (9.6 k). Turn Right on FR 19 and
drive about 7 miles (11.2 k). Turn Left on
FR 459 and in .5 mile (800 m), you're at
cove on Bartlett Reservoir. Also on lake
are three similar camping areas–Bartlett
Flat, South Cove, and South Bend Cove.
(Also see Riverside.)
FREE but choose a chore.
Open All Year.
Undesignated, scattered, open sites.
Pit toilets.
On reservoir with beach and nice vistas
of surrounding mountains.
Swimming, boating, and fishing.
NO water/trash arrangements (pack it
out–keep it clean). 14-day limit. Not
recommended for trailers. No ATVs.
1800 ft (540 m)

## REEF TOWNSITE

Coronado NF (602) 378-0311
State map: L10
From SIERRA VISTA, drive S
on AZ 92 for 7 miles (11.2 k).
Turn Right (W) on FR 368. Ascend for
5 miles (8 k) on difficult, narrow, steep,
winding dirt access–not recommended
for trailers or long vehicles.
$5. Open All Year.
16 scattered, open sites.
Water, pit toilets, tables, grills, fire rings.
In historic mining townsite high above
Sierra Vista.
Good hiking and birdwatching.
Can be hot at night.
7200 ft (2160 m)

## RIM

Apache-Sitgreaves NF
(602) 535-4481
State map: F9
From FOREST LAKES, take
AZ 260 SW for 7 miles (11.2 k). Turn
Right (N) on FR 300. Travel 1 mile
(1.6 k). (Also see Sink Hole.)
$5. Open May–Sep; dry camping
off-season.
26 scattered, screened sites.
Water, pit toilets, grills, fire rings.
Around large cul-de-sac in ponderosa
pine grove.
Boating and fishing nearby. Hiking and
birdwatching at hand.
14-day limit.
7600 ft (2280 m)

## RIVERSIDE

Tonto NF (602) 488-3441
State map: G7
From CAREFREE, take FR 24
(Cave Creek Rd) N for 6 miles
(9.6 k) to FR 205. Continue Right on
FR 205 for 6 miles (9.6 k) to intersection
with FR 19. Right on FR 19 about 7 miles
(11.2 k) to Jojoba Boating Site (road
becomes gravel). Continue another
3 miles (4.8 k) to site near Bartlett
Reservoir Dam. (Also see Rattlesnake.)
FREE but choose a chore.
Open All Year.
8 close, open sites.

Pit toilets, tables, grills.
In Verde River riparian area excellent for
birdwatching (occasional bald eagles).
Enjoy nearby swimming, boating, and
fishing plus wildlife observation.
NO water/trash arrangements (pack it
out–keep it clean). 14-day limit. Not
recommended for trailers. No ATVs.
1600 ft (480 m)

## ROCK CROSSING

Coconino NF (602) 477-2255
State map: F8
From STRAWBERRY or
FLAGSTAFF, proceed to
CLINTS WELL (intersection of FH 3 and
AZ 87). From crossroads, go NE 4 miles
(6.4 k) to unpaved FR 751. Turn Right
and continue SE for 3 miles (4.8 k). (Also
see Blue Ridge.)
$5. Open Memorial Day–Sep 15.
10 close, open sites. Water, pit toilets,
tables, grills, fire rings, boat ramp.
In shady seclusion at Blue Ridge
Reservoir.
Fish for three types of trout. Mountain
bike, hike, observe wildlife, or just relax.
14-day/22-ft limits. Forest roads close in
winter.
7500 ft (2250 m)

## ROOSEVELT MARINA

Tonto NF (602) 225-5200
State map: G8
Find near ROOSEVELT.
FREE but choose a chore.
(When reconstructed, fees added.)
Open All Year.
50 open sites.
Pit toilets, tables, boat ramp.
Enjoy water activities–skiing to fishing.
NO water. Clean up area–use trash cans.
14-day limit. No ATVs.
2100 ft (630 m)

## ROSE CREEK

Tonto NF (602) 462-3311
State map: G9
From YOUNG, go 22 miles
(35.2 k) S on AZ 288. Enter just
N of mile marker 281.
FREE but choose a chore.

Open Apr–Nov.
5 close, open sites.
Water, pit toilets, tables, grills.
Near two wilderness areas: Salome and Sierra Ancha.
Hike and explore for wide variety of wildlife and prehistoric ruins (quite fragile–be protective of America's heritage).
No trash arrangements (pack it out).
14-day/16-ft limits. No ATVs.
5400 ft (1620 m)

## RUCKER

Coronado NF (602) 364-3468
State map: K12
Take US 666 N from ELFRIDA for 3 miles (4.8 k). Turn Right (E) on unpaved CR 74. Go 23 miles (36.8 k) then turn Left (NE) on FR 75E. Go 5.75 miles (9.2 k). (Also see Bathtub, Cypress Park, and Camp Rucker.)
$3. Open All Year.
14 close, open sites.
Water, pit toilets, tables, fire rings.
In stand of ponderosa pine near small fishing lake.
Fishing, hiking, and birdwatching.
14-day/16-ft limits. Generator rules.
6500 ft (1950 m)

## SAGUARO NM-East Unit Backcountry

(602) 296-8576
State map: J9
From TUCSON, go 3 miles (4.8 k) E from city limits on Old Spanish Trail Rd. Obtain permit and directions at Visitor Center.
FREE but $3 entrance fee (or pass).
Open All Year.
In giant Saguaro cacti forests (unique to Sonoran Desert) and Rincon Mountains–all rate spectacular.
Walk or ride horseback into one of seven remote-feeling, backcountry sites.
Carry more than adequate water.

## SCHOOLHOUSE POINT

Tonto NF (602) 467-2236
State map: G8
From ROOSEVELT, go 11 miles (17.6 k) SE on AZ 188. Turn

Left (E) on gravel FR 447. Go 13 miles (20.8 k).
FREE but choose a chore.
Open All Year.
Undesignated, open sites.
Pit toilets, tables, dirt boat launch.
By Roosevelt Lake along southern shore of Salt River arm within walking distance of riparian area.
Enjoy good canoeing between AZ 288 and Schoolhouse as well as water-based sports on lake.
NO water. Clean up area–use trash cans.
14-day/32-ft limits. No ATVs.
2100 ft (630 m)

## SCOTT RESERVOIR

Apache-Sitgreaves NF
(602) 368-5111
State map: F11
From PINETOP–LAKESIDE, go E on AZ 260 only .1 mile (160 m) and turn Left (E) on FR 45 (Porter Mountain Rd). Continue 1.5 miles (2.4 k) and watch for sign on Right to Reservoir.
FREE but choose a chore.
Open Apr 1–Nov 30.
Undesignated, scattered sites. Pit toilets.
Under ponderosa pine with surrounding pinyon-juniper growth.
Boat (electric motors only), fish, and watch many varieties of birds.
NO water. 14-day limit. Muddy during rainy/snowy seasons.
6900 ft (2070 m)

## SECOND CROSSING

Tonto NF (602) 474-7900
State map: F8
At N end of PAYSON, turn Right (E) on FR 199 (Houston Mesa Rd). Go 8.5 miles (13.6 k) on mainly gravel road. (Also see Third Crossing, Verde Glen, and Water Wheel.)
FREE but choose a chore.
Open May–Sep.
Undesignated, open sites. Pit toilet.
On East Verde River for access to trout fishing.
NO water/trash arrangements (pack it out). 14-day/16-ft limits.
5100 ft (1530 m)

▲ ▲ ▲ ▲ ▲ ▲ ▲ ▲ ▲ ▲ ▲ ▲ ▲ ▲ ▲ ▲ ▲ ▲ ▲ ▲ ▲ ▲ ▲ ▲ ▲

## SEVEN SPRINGS

Tonto NF (602) 488-3441
State map: G7
From CAREFREE, take FR 24
(Cave Creek Rd) N for 20 miles
(32 k)–always bearing Left. Last 9 miles
(14.4 k) are gravel with blind curves–not
recommended for trailers over 16 ft.
(Also see CCC.)
FREE but choose a chore.
Open All Year.
23 close, open sites.
Pit toilets, tables, grills.
CCC-built, next to creek under large
sycamores.
Make base to hike (access Cave Creek
trail system), explore, observe wildlife,
or just play in water.
NO water/trash arrangements (pack it
out). 14-day limit. No ATVs.
3400 ft (1020 m)

## SHANNON

Coronado NF (602) 428-4150
State map: I11
From SAFFORD, head S on
US 666 for 7.5 miles (12 k).
Turn Right (SW) on AZ 366 and ascend
for 21 miles (33.6 k) on steep, winding
paved road. Continue .5 mile (.8 k) N up
unpaved FR 137. (Also see Hospital Flat
and Soldier Creek.)
$5. Open May 20–Nov 14.
10 close, open sites.
Water, pit toilets, tables, grills.
In thick pine-fir forest high in Pinaleno
Mountains.
Pleasant hiking and birdwatching.
Though high, hot during summer.
Heavy snowfall during transition
periods.
9300 ft (2790 m)

## SINK HOLE

Apache-Sitgreaves NF
(602) 535-4481
State map: F9
From FOREST LAKES, take
AZ 260 SW for 6 miles (9.6 k). Turn
Right (N) on FR 149 toward Willow
Springs Lake. Locate entrance within
.25 mile (400 m). (Also see Rim.)

$5. Open May–Sep; dry camping
off-season.
26 scattered, screened sites.
Water, pit toilets, tables, grills, fire rings.
On large loop in ponderosa pine grove.
Boating and fishing nearby; hiking and
birdwatching at hand.
14-day limit.
7600 ft (2280 m)

## SOLDIER CREEK

Coronado NF (602) 428-4150
State map: I11
From SAFFORD, head S on
US 666 for 7.5 miles (12 k).
Turn Right (SW) on AZ 366. Ascend for
28 miles (44.8 k) on steep, winding road.
Continue .5 mile (800 m) N on unpaved
FR 803 then .25 mile (400 m) E on
FR 656. (Also see Hospital Flat and
Shannon.)
$5. Open May 20–Nov 14.
12 close, open sites. Water, flush toilets,
tables, grills, fire rings.
In dense pine and fir.
Nice hiking and birdwatching.
Though high, hot during summer.
Heavy snowfall during transition
periods.
9300 ft (2790 m)

## SOUTH FORK

Coronado NF (602) 629-6483
State map: K12
From PORTAL, take CR 42 W
about 6 miles (9.6 k).
FREE but choose a chore.
Open All Year.
4 close, open tent sites.
Pit toilets, tables, fire rings.
Near stream in pretty Cave Creek area of
Chiricahua Mountains.
Hiking and relaxing.
NO water/trash arrangements (pack it
out). 14-day limit. No trailers.
5300 ft (1590 m)

## SOUTH FORK CAMP

Apache-Sitgreaves NF
(602) 333-4372
State map: F12
Locate about 8 miles (12.8 k) W

▲ ▲ ▲ ▲ ▲ ▲ ▲ ▲ ▲ ▲ ▲ ▲ ▲ ▲ ▲ ▲ ▲ ▲ ▲ ▲ ▲ ▲

of EAGAR off AZ 260 on gravel FR 560.
**FREE** but choose a chore.
Open May–Sep.
8 scattered, open sites.
Pit toilets, tables, grills.
In shade on South Fork of Little Colorado.
Fishing and hiking dominate scene.
NO water.
7600 ft (2280 m)

**STOCKTON PASS**
Coronado NF (602) 428-4150
State map: I11
From SAFFORD, head S on US 666 for 15 miles (24 k).
Turn Right (W) on AZ 266 and continue 11 miles (17.6 k).
**FREE** but choose a chore.
Open All Year.
11 close, open sites.
Pit toilets, tables, fire rings.
In high desert with rolling hills dotted with juniper.
Explore surrounding area.
Intermittent water. No trash arrangements (pack it out). 14-day limit.
5600 ft (1680 m)

**STRAYHORSE**
Apache-Sitgreaves NF
(602) 865-4129
State map: H12
Go 56 miles (89.6 k) NW from CLIFTON and MORENCI on US 666.
**FREE** but choose a chore.
Open May 15–Oct 15; dry camping off-season.
6 close, open sites.
Water, pit toilets, tables, grills.
Nice shady spot.
Good hiking.
14-day limit. Hunting in season.
7600 ft (2280 m)

**SULPHIDE DEL RAY**
Tonto NF (602) 425-7189
State map: H9
In GLOBE, take Jess Hayes Rd SE to junction of FR 112 (Icehouse Canyon) and FR 222 (Sixshooter Canyon). Take gravel FR 112

for 2.4 miles (3.8 k) to FR 55. Bear Right on FR 55. Go 3 miles (4.8 k) to FR 651.
Turn Left and follow narrow, winding FR 651 5.5 miles (8.8 k).
**FREE** but choose a chore.
Open All Year.
10 close, open sites.
Pit toilets, tables, grills.
At former mining community set high so workers could escape heat below. A few stones remain beneath pines.
Relax as miners did many years ago.
NO water/trash arrangements (come prepared and pack it out). 14-day/16-ft limits. No ATVS.
4500 ft (1350 m)

**SYCAMORE**
Coronado NF (602) 364-3468
State map: K12
From WILLCOX, take AZ 186 SE for 23 miles (36.8 k). Head S on AZ 181 another 10 miles (16 k). Turn Left (E) on dirt FR 41. Continue 9 miles (14.4 k).
**FREE** but choose a chore.
Open All Year.
3 scattered, open sites.
Pit toilets, tables, fire rings.
Along dirt road in pine forest.
Hike or relax.
Intermittent water. 18-ft limit.
6200 ft (1860 m)

**THIRD CROSSING**
Tonto NF (602) 474-7900
State map: F8
At N end of PAYSON, turn Right (E) on FR 199 (Houston Mesa Rd). Go 9.5 miles (15.2 k) on mainly gravel road. (Also see Second Crossing, Verde Glen, and Water Wheel.)
**FREE** but choose a chore.
Open May–Sep.
Undesignated, open sites. Pit toilet.
On East Verde River.
Fishing is big lure.
NO water/trash arrangements (pack it out–keep site clean). 14-day/16-ft limits.
5160 ft (1548 m)

▲ ▲ ▲ ▲ ▲ ▲ ▲ ▲ ▲ ▲ ▲ ▲ ▲ ▲ ▲ ▲ ▲ ▲ ▲ ▲ ▲ ▲ ▲

## TONTO CREEK

Tonto NF (602) 474-7900
State map: F8
From PAYSON, take AZ 260 E
for 16 miles (25.6 k). Turn Left
(N) on FR 289 just beyond Kolh's Ranch
at mile marker 269. Locate site within
.5 mile (800 m).
$5. Open All Year.
17 close, open sites.
Water, pit toilets, tables, grills.
Near Tonto Creek with year-round trout
fishing.
Try hiking (Derrick Spur Trail at FR 289
and AZ 260 links up with Highline
National Recreation Trail).
7-day/16-ft limits. NO water/trash
arrangements between Labor Day and
Memorial Day. No ATVs.
5600 ft (1680 m)

## UPPER BLUE

Apache-Sitgreaves NF
(602) 339-4385
State map: G12
From ALPINE, go E on AZ 180
for 4 miles (6.4 k). Turn Right (S) on
unpaved FR 281. Go 12 miles
(19.2 k)–road not for trailers.
FREE but choose a chore.
Open All Year.
3 tent sites.
Water, pit toilets, tables, grills, fire rings.
In secluded spot nestled among red cliffs
with pinyon pine and alligator juniper.
Remove yourself from crowds;
reestablish contact with nature.
No trash pickup. 14-day limit.
7000 ft (2100 m)

## UPPER TONTO CREEK

Tonto NF (602) 474-7900
State map: F8
From PAYSON, take AZ 260 E
for 16 miles (25.6 k). Turn Left
(N) on FR 289 just beyond Kolh's Ranch
at mile marker 269. Go .75 mile (1.2 k)
and turn Right into camp.
$5. Open May–Sep.
9 close, open sites.
Water, pit toilets, tables, grills.
At confluence of Tonto and Horton

creeks with trailheads for Horton Creek
and Derrick trails–both access Highline
National Recreation Trail.
Trout fishing as well as hiking.
7-day/16-ft limits. No ATVs.
5600 ft (1680 m)

## VALENTINE RIDGE

Tonto NF (602) 462-3311
State map: G9
From PAYSON, head E on
AZ 260 for 33 miles
(52.8 k)–8 miles W of FOREST LAKES.
Turn Right (S) on gravel FR 512 (Young
Rd). Travel 5.5 miles (8.8 k) to FR 188.
Turn Left (E). Go another 2 miles (3.2 k).
FREE but choose a chore.
Open Apr–Nov.
10 close, open sites.
Pit toilets, tables, grills.
Near Canyon Creek with rainbow trout.
At base of 9-mile mountain-bike trail.
Fishing, mountain biking, hiking, and
wildlife viewing (from javelina to bear).
NO water/trash arrangements (pack it
out). 14-day/16-ft limits. No ATVs.
6700 ft (2010 m)

## VERDE GLEN

Tonto NF (602) 474-7900
State map: F8
At N end of PAYSON, turn
Right (E) on FR 199 (Houston
Mesa Rd). Go 10 miles (16 k) on mainly
gravel road and turn Right (E) on FR 64.
Find site within .5 mile (800 m). (Also
see Second Crossing, Third Crossing,
and Water Wheel.)
FREE but choose a chore.
Open May–Sep.
Undesignated, open sites. Pit toilet.
On East Verde River for access to trout
fishing.
NO water/trash arrangements (pack it
out). 14-day/16-ft limits.
5600 ft (1680 m)

## VIRGIN RIVER

BLM (801) 673-3545
State map: A3
From LITTLEFIELD, travel
16 miles (25.6 k) N on I-15. Exit

▲ ▲ ▲ ▲ ▲ ▲ ▲ ▲ ▲ ▲ ▲ ▲ ▲ ▲ ▲ ▲ ▲ ▲ ▲ ▲ ▲ ▲ ▲ ▲ ▲

at Cedar Pockets.

**$4.** Open All Year.

115 sites. Water, flush toilets, tables.

In impressive Virgin River Gorge with abundance of willow, cottonwood, and rushes below and occasional desert bighorn sheep above.

Good hiking, including access to Paiute and Beaver Dam wilderness areas.

14-day limit.

2500 ft (750 m)

## WATER WHEEL

Tonto NF (602) 474-7900
State map: F8
At N end of PAYSON, turn Right (E) on FR 199 (Houston Mesa Rd). Go 8 miles (12.8 k) on mainly gravel road. (Also see Second Crossing, Third Crossing, and Verde Glen.)

**FREE** but choose a chore.

Open May–Sep.

Undesignated, open sites. Pit toilet.

On East Verde River with easy access to trout fishing and waterfalls.

NO water/trash arrangements (pack it out). 14-day/16-ft limits.

5000 ft (1500 m)

## WEST FORK-BLACK RIVER

Apache-Sitgreaves NF
(602) 339-4385
State map: G12
From ALPINE, go S on US 666 for 13 miles (20.8 k). Turn Right (W) on unpaved FR 26 and continue another 12 miles (19.2 k). Turn Right (N) on FR 24 for 4 more miles (6.4 k). Left on FR 25 for 3 miles (4.8 k). (See East Fork.)

**FREE** but choose a chore.

Open May 1–Oct 30; dry camping off-season.

40 scattered, open sites. Water, pit toilets. Along trout stream.

Fishing and hiking dominate. Also, ranger programs and wildlife studies.

Pack out trash. 14-day limit. Crowded after July 4.

7500 ft (2250 m)

## WEST TURKEY CREEK

Coronado NF (602) 364-3468
State map: K12
From WILLCOX, take AZ 186 SE for 23 miles (36.8 k). Head S on AZ 181 another 10 miles (16 k). Turn Left (E) on dirt FR 41 and continue 8 miles (12.8 k).

**FREE** but choose a chore.

Open All Year.

7 close, open sites.

Pit toilets, tables, fire rings.

In pine forest along dirt road.

Relax and do a little birdwatching.

Intermittent water source.

5900 ft (1770 m)

## WHITE ROCK

Coronado NF (602) 281-2296
State map: L8
7 miles (11.2 k) N from NOGALES on I-7, take AZ 289 W. Continue 9 miles (14.4 k).

**$5.** Open All Year.

15 close, open sites.

Water, pit toilets, tables, fire rings.

Near small reservoir.

Fishing and boating (small motors) opportunities close-by. Good bird-watching in camp.

14-day limit. Crowded, especially holiday weekends.

4000 ft (1200 m)

## WILD COW SPRINGS

BLM (602) 757-3161
State map: D3
From KINGMAN, go 14 miles (22.4 k) S on Hualapai Mountain Rd. Turn Right at Pine Lake firehouse and proceed 5 miles (8 k) on steep, dirt access road–high clearance, under 20-ft vehicles only.

**FREE** but choose a chore.

Open May–Oct (depends on snow).

24 scattered, screened sites.

Pit toilets, tables, grills, fire rings.

Among ponderosa pine and walnut. In canyon home of over 80 species of birds and numerous animals including elk and bobcat.

Watch wildlife and take photographs.

▲ ▲ ▲ ▲ ▲ ▲ ▲ ▲ ▲ ▲ ▲ ▲ ▲ ▲ ▲ ▲ ▲ ▲ ▲ ▲ ▲ ▲ ▲ ▲ ▲ ▲ ▲ ▲

NO water. 14-day limit. Bring your own firewood. Summer night temperatures fall into 30's.
6200 ft (1860 m)

## WINDY HILL

Tonto NF (602) 467-2236
State map: G8
From ROOSEVELT, go 6 miles (9.6 k) SE on AZ 188. Turn Left (E) on gravel FR 82. Go 3 miles (4.8 k). (Also see Porter Spring.)
**FREE** but choose a chore.
Open All Year.
Undesignated, open sites.
Pit toilets, tables, paved boat launch.
By Roosevelt Lake along southern shore of Salt River arm.
Relish water-based activities on lake.
NO water. Clean up area—use trash cans. 14-day/32-ft limits. No ATVs.
2100 ft (630 m)

## WINDY POINT

BLM (602) 757-3161
State map: D2
From KINGMAN, go 18 miles (28.8 k) NW on US 93. Turn Right (E) on BLM's Chloride–Big Wash Rd. Travel another 11 miles (17.6 k) on steep, gravel access road—2 miles (3.2 k) beyond Packsaddle.
**FREE** but choose a chore.
Open May–Oct (depends on snow).
10 scattered, screened sites.
Pit toilets, tables, grills, fire rings.
In high pinyon-juniper setting with spectacular sunsets plus grand views of lower valleys and distant mountains. Hike and rockhound early mining area.
NO water. 14-day limit.
5700 ft (1710 m)

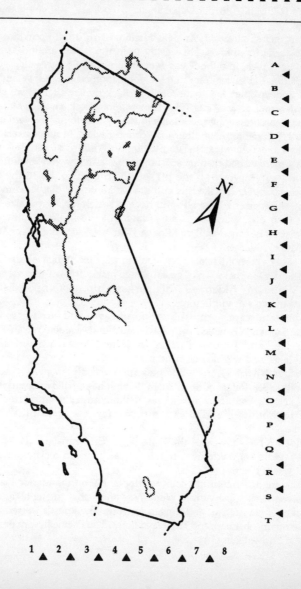

# California

Grid conforms to official state map. For your copy, call (800) 862-2543
or write Office of Tourism, 1121 L Street, Suite 103, Sacramento, CA 95814.

▲ ▲ ▲ ▲ ▲ ▲ ▲ ▲ ▲ ▲ ▲ ▲ ▲ ▲ ▲ ▲ ▲ ▲ ▲ ▲ ▲ ▲ ▲ ▲ ▲ ▲ ▲ ▲ ▲ ▲ ▲

The California challenge: discover fantastic scenery (easy), without hordes of people (hard), for little money (even harder). Northern California claims rugged coasts, redwoods, volcanic wonders, and many off-the-track possibilities. From its coast to its mountain lakes, Central California possesses great natural beauty but far more residents and tourists. Southern California has subtropical weather, desert ecologies, abrupt mountain ranges, and even more folk.

Looking at inexpensive camping choices, you find the US Forest Service is the best bet. The Bureau of Land Management (BLM) has substantial resources. Even the National Park Service (NPS) has a few options. The US Army Corps of Engineers (COE), California Department of Forestry, and some counties also contribute.

In Los Angeles' backyard, **Angeles National Forest** (NF) provides retreats in the San Gabriel mountains. Hike away from the roads–around Mount Baldy, along Soldier Creek, into the Sheep Mountain or San Gabriel wilderness areas.

Perhaps due to its proximity to huge population centers, **Cleveland NF** offers you little in developed, low-price camping. Backcountry alternatives are possible in four wilderness areas: Agua Tibia, Hauser, Pine Creek, and San Mateo Canyon.

Blue lakes and towering mountains in the Crystal Range are two offerings of **Eldorado NF**. Explore the mother lode country with old mining remains (west) as well as Lake Tahoe (east). The Desolation Wilderness rates as marvelous, though it's more visited than most. The forest is also known for winter activities.

The oldest living tree on the planet, the highest point in the Lower 48, mysterious lakes, earthquake rifts you can walk into–all these and more exist in the Sierra Nevadas and **Inyo NF**. You have to search for inexpensive camps, but the do-it-yourself experience is rewarding. Hike to Mount Whitney (2 days), admire bristlecone pines, explore Minaret Wilderness, or photograph wildflowers in John Muir Wilderness.

In the eastern part of **Klamath NF**, you can walk through lava tubes or examine ice caves and glass rocks. The Coastal Range marks the western section and the Marble Mountain Wilderness is its perfect expression: rugged slopes with thousands of acres of virgin forest.

Volcanic landscapes with subterranean caves and surface spatter cones punctuate **Lassen NF**, which completely surrounds Lassen Volcanic NP. In the Caribou, Ishi, and Thousand Lakes wilderness areas, a hiker can also find beautiful lakes and wildflower meadows.

**Los Padres NF** has several wilderness areas to compliment its varied camping opportunities. San Rafael north of Santa Barbara has terrific rock curiosities; Santa Lucia is scenic; Ventana holds some of the country's rarest trees. Also see Machesna Mountain and Dick Smith wilderness areas plus two condor sanctuaries.

**Mendocino NF** showcases the Yolla Bolly (this translates as "snowcovered peaks")–Middle Eel Wilderness. In other areas, you can rockhound, hang glide, or identify rare plants.

For escaping the multitude, look to **Modoc NF** on the Modoc Plateau in the northeastern corner. The Warner Wilderness offers challenging hikes and climbs, alpine lakes, clear streams, and rugged canyons. The forest's western section has Glass Mountain, obsidian, and large lava flows. The Pacific flyway provides some of the best birdwatching possible.

▲ ▲ ▲ ▲ ▲ ▲ ▲ ▲ ▲ ▲ ▲ ▲ ▲ ▲ ▲ ▲ ▲ ▲ ▲ ▲ ▲ ▲ ▲ ▲ ▲ ▲ ▲ ▲ ▲ ▲

Water gives the **Plumas NF** special places. Feather Falls Scenic Area, indeed the whole Middle Fork of the Feather River, offers beauty and grandeur. If you prefer lakes, there's Antelope Lake, Bucks Lake, and Frenchman Reservoir. For marsh-bog aficionados, find the rare cobra plant in the Butterfly Valley Botanical Area.

Rim-of-the-World Highway provides an idea of the possibilities in **San Bernardino NF**. The highest mountains of Southern California plus four wilderness areas (Cucamonga, San Gorgonio, San Jacinto, and Santa Rosa) offer backcountry challenges and rewards.

Magnificent trees are the focal point of **Sequoia NP**, some thirty groves of the giants. Don't miss the rest of the forest, including the wild and scenic Kern and Kings rivers or the Dome Wilderness (plus four more wilderness areas).

More sequoias can be worshipped in **Sierra NF** at the Nelder and McKinley groves. When a forest is between Yosemite NP and Kings Canyon NP, and it administers all or part of six wilderness areas (including the Ansel Adams, John Muir, and Minarets), there's much to experience. The best camping is away from the more popular and concessionaire-run locales.

While Mount Shasta and Lake Shasta with the Whiskeytown NRA dominate the attention of most visitors to the **Shasta–Trinity NF**, two fantastic wilderness areas, the Yolla Bolly–Middle Eel (shared with Mendocino NF) and the Salmon-Trinity Alps, offer secluded, natural experiences.

The 135-mile-long region of northern California administered by **Six Rivers NF** has only two camps whose price allow entry into these listings. Fortunately, there are many make-your-own camp spots along the six rivers and hundreds of streams running through the forest. Explore the possibilities.

Forming the northwest border of Yellowstone NP, the **Stanislaus NF** possesses two excellent wild areas: Emigrant and Mokelumne (shared with Eldorado NF). Unusual rock formations near Dardanelles, rugged canyons cut into the western slope of the Sierra Nevadas, and five major rivers provide a wealth of beauty to discover.

**Tahoe NF** has been blessed and cursed with popularity from last century's gold rush to today's proximity of an interstate highway. Move away from the congestion and find the northernmost group of sequoias, high-elevation conifers, canyon ecologies, gold-flecked streams, and 90 miles of the Pacific Crest Trail.

The **NPS** offers a variety of experiences. Try island camping at Channel Islands NP; walk-in sites at Golden Gate National Recreation Area (NRA), Point Reyes National Seashore (NS), and Redwoods NP; drive-to camps at Death Valley National Monument (NM), Joshua Tree NM, Lassen Volcanic NP, Sequoia-Kings Canyon NP, Whiskeytown NRA, and Yosemite NP; and backcountry (only) opportunities at Devils Postpile NM and Lava Beds NM.

For lake recreation enthusiasts, the **COE** maintains free sites at seven projects in the state (other listings have been transferred to NF control). The **BLM** offers opportunities in the northwest but more profusely in the arid eastern-central and southeastern parts of the state. A couple of Long-Term Visitor Areas (LTVAs) are included where you can boondock for months.

Only two **California State Parks** (SPs), Andrew Molera and Anza Borrego, have any selections at $5 or less (most parks cost $7–$20). Three State Forests (SFs) maintain free sites. Imperial, Inyo, and Mono counties also offer alternatives.

Search and you can find the rare, the sublime, and the perfect retreat in California's wealth of opportunities.

▲ ▲ ▲ ▲ ▲ ▲ ▲ ▲ ▲ ▲ ▲ ▲ ▲ ▲ ▲ ▲ ▲ ▲ ▲ ▲ ▲ ▲ ▲ ▲ ▲ ▲

## A H HOGUE

Modoc NF (916) 667-2246
State map: C5
Take CA 139 S from TULELAKE
for 20 miles (32 k). Turn Right
(W) on CR 97 and drive 25 miles
(40 k). Watch signs. (Also see Headquarters, Hemlock, and Medicine.)
$5, $5/extra vehicle.
Open May 15–Oct 30; dry camping
off-season.
23 scattered, open sites. Water, pit toilets,
tables, grills, fire rings, boat ramp, beach.
Beside fascinating lake in old volcanic
cone ringed by conifers.
Windsurf, swim, fish, and boat. Just lie
on beach or explore caldera.
14-day/22-ft limits. Region cooler than
you anticipate.
6700 ft (2010 m)

## AFTON CANYON

BLM (619) 256-8313
State map: P7
From BARSTOW, take I-15 E for
37 miles (59.2 k) to Afton Rd Exit.
Go S on gravel road for 4 miles
(6.4 k).
$4. Open All Year.
22 close, open sites. Water, pit toilets,
tables, grills, sun shelters.
In special geological area with surface
water from Mojave River attracting
desert wildlife including bighorn sheep.
Create base to explore desert ecology.
Good rockhounding and birdwatching.
No litter or excessive noise (none after
10pm). Crowded winter holidays. Hot
summers. Flash floods anytime.
2500 ft (750 m)

## AH-DI-NA

Shasta-Trinity NF (916) 964-2184
State map: C4
From MCCLOUD, take FR 16
about 16 miles (25.6 k) S to
McCloud Lake. At South edge,
turn Left (S) on unpaved surface and go
4 miles (6.4 k).
$5. Open May 15–Nov 15.
16 sites.
Water, flush toilets, tables, fire rings.

Along beautiful stretch of river.
Fishing, swimming, and walking.
14-day limit.
2300 ft (690 m)

## ALDER CREEK

Lassen NF (916) 258-2141
State map: E4
From CHESTER, go W on CA 36
for 13 miles (20.8 k) to CA 32.
Turn Left (S) and continue
8 miles (12.8 k).
FREE but choose a chore.
Open All Year.
5 scattered, open sites. Water (must
treat), pit toilets, tables, grills, fire rings.
In scenic Deer Creek Canyon about 50 ft
from water.
Fish, hike, and view wildlife.
14-day limit. Not recommended for large
vehicles. Crowded. Hunting in season.
3900 ft (1170 m)

## ALDER CREEK

Los Padres NF (805) 683-6711
State map: K1
From SAN SIMEON, go N on
US 1 for 25 miles (40 k)–just S of
Cape San Martin. Turn Right (E)
on unpaved FR 23S01 and go about
6 miles (9.6 k). For closer (to US 1), but
no-water alternative, shortly after turn-
ing off 1, bear Left on FR 5E08 to check
out **Sycamore Flat**.
FREE but choose a chore.
Open All Year.
5 close, open sites. Water needs treating,
pit toilets, tables, grills, fire rings.
On remote creek.
Take a hike. Relax and picnic.
No trash arrangements. 14-day limit.
2200 ft (660 m)

## ALDER CREEK

Sequoia NF (805) 871-2223
State map: M4
From GLENNVILLE, go E on
CA 155 for 8 miles (14.4 k). Turn
Right (S) on FR 25S04 and go
3 miles (4.8 k). (Also see Cedar Creek.)
FREE but choose a chore.
Open May 1–Oct 31.

12 close, open tent sites.
Pit toilets, tables, grills, fire rings.
Fish, relax, or walk creekbank trails.
NO water/trash facilities. 14-day limit.
3900 ft (1170 m)

## ALGOMA

Shasta-Trinity NF (916) 964-2184
State map: C4
From MCCLOUD, go 13 miles
(20.8 k) E on CA 89 to FR 39N06
(watch for sign). Turn Right, go
.5 mile (800 m). (Also see Cattle Camp.)
**FREE** but choose a chore.
Open May 1–Nov 1; camping allowed
off-season.
8 close, open sites.
Pit toilets, tables, fire rings.
Next to river–close to highway.
Fish, swim, or hike.
NO water. 14-day limit.
3800 ft (1140 m)

## ALISO PARK

Los Padres NF (805) 683-6711
State map: N2
From NEW CUYAMA, go NW
on CA 166 for 3 miles (4.8 k).
Turn Left (W) on Aliso Canyon
Rd. Go 4 miles (6.4 k) staying Right. Bear
Right on FR 11N02 for 1 mile (1.6 k).
**FREE** but choose a chore.
Open All Year.
11 close, open sites.
Pit toilets, tables, grills, fire rings.
In foothills.
Picnic and relax or hike trails (such as
McPherson Peak).
NO water/trash arrangements (pack it
out). 14-day/22-ft limits.
3200 ft (960 m)

## ALPINE MEADOWS-MARTIS CREEK LAKE

COE (916) 639-2342
State map: G5
From TRUCKEE, go S on CA 267
for 4 miles (6.4 k).
**FREE** but choose a chore.
Open Apr 15–Oct 31.
25 close, open sites. &
Water, chemical toilets, tables, grills, fire

rings, pay phone.
On lake in picturesque, high, mountain
valley with snowcapped granite peaks,
pine-covered slopes, grassy meadows,
sagebrush-blanketed alluvial terraces.
Enjoy hiking, catch-and-release fishing,
and occasional ranger programs.
14-day limit. Crowded May–Sep. No
soap in lake.
5800 ft (1740 m)

## AMERICAN CANYON

Los Padres NF (805) 683-6711
State map: M1
From SANTA MARGARITA, go
E on CA 58 for 1 mile (1.6 k).
Turn Right (S) on CR 21 (Poza
Rd) and drive 17.5 miles (28 k). Just after
Salinas River, in Poza, turn Right on
FR 30S02. Go 7 miles (11.2 k). Turn Left
(NE) on FR 30S04. Drive 2 miles (3.2 k).
**FREE** but choose a chore.
Open All Year.
14 close, open sites.
Water, pit toilets, tables, grills, fire rings.
Nestled at edge of Machesna Mountain
Wilderness.
Picnic and relax or hike into wilderness.
No trash facilities. 14-day/16-ft limits.
1700 ft (510 m)

## ANDREW MOLERA SP WALK-IN

(408) 667-2315
State map: K1
From CARMEL, take CA 1 S for
21 miles (33.6 k). Walk in about
.25 mile (400 m).
$3/person, $1/dog.
Open All Year.
Undesignated sites.
Water, chemical toilets, few tables and
fire rings, pay phone, beach.
In gorgeous meadow with trail to beach.
One of two state listings on CA coast to
make book cost-wise–if you're by
yourself (or with a dog).
Watch sea otters and other resident
coastal creatures. Hike.
3-day limit. Crowded weekends and
holidays. Strict quiet hours. Obnoxious
raccoons.
50 ft (15 m)

▲ ▲ ▲ ▲ ▲ ▲ ▲ ▲ ▲ ▲ ▲ ▲ ▲ ▲    ▲ ▲ ▲ ▲ ▲ ▲ ▲ ▲ ▲

## ANNIE MC CLOUD

Tahoe NF (916) 994-3401
State map: G5
From TRUCKEE, take CA 89 N
past I-80 for .5 mile (800 m) to
Prosser Dam Rd. Turn Right (E)
and go 4.5 miles (7.2 k) to camp--beyond
dam. (Also see Lakeside.)
FREE but choose a chore.
Open May 25–Sep 5; camping allowed
off-season.
10 close, open sites.
Reservoir water must be purified, chemical/pit toilets across street, tables.
On northeast shore of Prosser Reservoir
near Emigrants Trail.
Canoe lake or fish. Hike nearby.
14-day/16-ft limits.
5700 ft (1710 m)

## ANZA BORREGO SP

(619) 767-5311
State map: S5
FREE but choose a chore.
Open All Year.
Incredible desert park.

▲ **Blair Valley Walk-In**
From JULIAN, go E on CA 78 for
12 miles (19.2 k) to park road S-2. Turn
Right (S) and drive 5 miles (8 k) to
entrance. Sites are only 100 ft or so from
parking area.
Undesignated sites, pullouts, and
clearings with tables.
In high desert with good hiking nearby.
NO water, toilet, or trash arrangements
(come prepared).
2000 ft (600 m)

▲ **Fish Creek Primitive Camp**
From OCOTILLO WELLS, go S on dirt
and rocky Split Mountain Rd for
12 miles (19.2 k). Access road is difficult
(only rugged vehicles recommended.)
7 close, open sites. Tables, fire rings.
On bare mesa above Fish Creek Wash.
Enjoy views and hiking opportunities.
NO water, toilet, or trash facilities (come
prepared). No generators after 8pm.
700 ft (210 m)

▲ **Mountain Palm Springs**
From OCOTILLO, go N on park road S-2
for 13 miles (20.8 k).

Undesignated, scattered, open sites.
Chemical toilets, trash cans.
Explore nearby trails. Enjoy birding too.
NO water. Crowded winter/ spring
holidays.
1000 ft (300 m)

▲ **Yaqui Well Primitive Camp**
About 1 mile (1.6 k) W of developed
**Tamarisk Grove**--just W of intersection
of S-3 and CA 78.
30 (15 tent-only) scattered, open sites.
Pit toilets.
In mesquite and cacti on San Felipe
Creek at base of Pinyon Ridge.
Great bird and bighorn sheep watching.
Good nature walks and longer hikes.
Ranger programs too.
NO water/trash facilities. Crowded
holidays and winter/spring weekends.
No generators after 8pm. Gnats,
mosquitos, rattlers.
200 ft (60 m)

## ASH CREEK

Modoc NF (916) 299-3215
State map: D5
From ADIN, take unpaved Ash
Valley Rd E for 7 miles (14.4 k).
FREE but choose a chore.
Open All Year.
7 close, open sites.
Pit toilets, tables, fire rings.
Next to scenic creek with good fishing
and fair hiking possibilities.
NO water/trash arrangements (keep
remote spot clean). Hunting in season.
4000 ft (1200 m)

## ASPEN GROVE

Mono County Parks
(619) 934-7504
State map: J5
From LEE VINING, go W for
5 miles (8 k) on CA 120 (Tioga
Rd) toward Yosemite. (Also see Cattle-
guard, Lower & Upper Lee Vining
Creek, and Lundy.)
$5. Open Apr–Nov.
57 close, open sites. Stream water only
(must purify), chemical toilets, tables.
Among aspen near stream.
Hike or fish.

NO water.
7000 ft (2100 m)

## ATMORE MEADOWS
Angeles NF (818) 574-1613
State map: O3
From LAKE HUGHES, go W on
CR 8N03 (Elizabeth Lake Rd)
about 5.5 miles (8.8 k). Continue
on FR 7N23 for 6 miles (9.6 k). Turn Left
(S) on FR 7N19 for 2.5 miles (3.8 k).
(Also see Sawmill Meadows as well as
Lower & Upper Shake.)
FREE but choose a chore.
Open May 1–Nov 30.
6 close, open sites.
Pit toilets, tables, fire rings.
Along creek, picnic and relax. Hike
trails, including Pacific Crest.
NO water/trash arrangements (pack it
out). 14-day/22-ft limits.
4300 ft (1290 m)

## BAKER CREEK
Inyo County Parks
(619) 878-2411
State map: K5
From BIG PINE, go N on US 395
for .5 mile (800 m). Turn Left (W)
on Baker Creek Rd. Drive 1 mile (1.6 k).
If this one's not for you, check out **Big
Pine Triangle** at intersection of 395 and
168 (same fee and amenities).
$5. Open All Year.
65 scattered, open sites.
Water, pit toilets, tables, grills.
In woods along stream.
Explore along nature trails, streams, and
small ponds.
14-day limit. Crowded holidays.
4100 ft (1230 m)

## BARREL SPRINGS
Los Padres NF (805) 683-6711
State map: N1
From SANTA MARIA, head N
on US 101 for 3 miles (4.8 k).
Take CA 166 E for 15 miles
(24 k). Turn Right (S) on Buckhorn
Canyon Rd and drive 8.5 miles (13.6 k).
Turn Left (E) on steep, dirt Colson
Canyon Rd (FR 11N04). Go 8 miles

(12.8 k), bearing Right at fork (impassible
when wet). (Also see Colson Canyon and
Wagon Flat.)
FREE but choose a chore.
Open All Year.
6 close, open tent sites.
Water, pit toilets, tables, grills, fire rings.
Near creek in secluded spot.
Take extended hikes and bike trips. Also,
picnic and relax.
14-day/16-ft limits. Hot summers.
1000 ft (300 m)

## BASIN GULCH
Shasta-Trinity NF (916) 352-4211
State map: D2
From PLATINA, take CA 36 NW
for 5 miles (8 k). Turn Left (SW)
on unpaved Stuart Gap Rd
(FR 29N13) and go 1.25 miles (2 k).
$4, no fee when water turned off.
Open May 20–Oct 31; dry camping
off-season.
16 close, open sites.
Water, pit toilets, tables, fire rings.
At edge of remote part of forest with
many forest roads and trails to
take–check with Yolla Bolly Ranger
Station. Fish too.
14-day/20-ft limits.
2700 ft (810 m)

## BATES CANYON
Los Padres NF (805) 683-6711
State map: N2
From NEW CUYAMA, go NW
on CA 166 for 11 miles (17.6 k).
Turn Left (W) on Cottonwood
Canyon Rd. Go 7.5 miles (12 k).
FREE but choose a chore.
Open All Year.
6 close, open sites.
Pit toilets, tables, grills, fire rings.
In foothills.
Head to various lookouts or hike into
San Rafael Wilderness.
NO water/trash facilities. 14-day limit.
2900 ft (870 m)

▲ ▲ ▲ ▲ ▲ ▲ ▲ ▲ ▲ ▲ ▲ ▲ ▲ ▲ ▲ ▲ ▲ ▲ ▲ ▲ ▲ ▲ ▲ ▲ ▲ ▲ ▲ ▲ ▲

## BAYVIEW

Lake Tahoe Basin Management
(916) 573-2600
State map: H5
From CAMP RICHARDSON, go
5.3 miles (8.5 k) NW on CA 89.
FREE but choose a chore.
Open Memorial Day–Labor Day.
13 close, open sites.
Chemical toilets, tables, grills, fire rings.
Use as base for short backcountry treks
or for overnight stop near Lake Tahoe.
NO water/trash arrangements (pack it
out). 2-night/22-ft limits.
6400 ft (1920 m)

## BEAR CREEK

Mendocino NF (707) 275-2361
State map: E2
From UPPER LAKE, go N on
CR 1N02 for 17 miles (27.2 k).
Turn Right (E) on FR 18N01 and
drive 6 miles (9.6 k). Continue E on
FR 17N33 for 1.5 miles (2.4 k). (Also see
Deer Valley and Lower Nye.)
FREE but choose a chore.
Open May 1–Oct 15; camping allowed
off-season.
16 (5 tent-only) close, open sites.
Pit toilets, tables, fire rings.
On creek with fishing, hiking, mountain
biking, and relaxing possibilities.
NO water/trash arrangements (pack it
out). 21-day/16-ft limits.
2000 ft (600 m)

## BEAR VALLEY

Tahoe NF (916) 994-3401
State map: G5
Just as you leave SIERRAVILLE
on CA 49 heading E, look for
rough Lemon Canyon Rd on
your Right. Go about 7.5 miles (12 k).
FREE but choose a chore.
Open May 15–Oct 15; dry camping
off-season.
10 close, open sites.
Water, pit toilets, tables.
At headwaters of Bear Creek.
Fishing and relaxing here.
14-day/16-ft limits.
6700 ft (2010 m)

## BEAVER

Los Padres NF (805) 683-6711
State map: O2
From OJAI, go N on CA 33 for
15.75 miles (25.2 k). Turn Right
on FR 22W04. Go .5 mile (800 m).
FREE but choose a chore.
Open All Year.
13 close, open sites.
Pit toilets, tables, fire rings.
Along Sespe Creek.
Picnic and relax; splash in water; hike.
NO water/trash arrangements (pack it
out). 14-day/16-ft limits.
3000 ft (900 m)

## BEAVER CREEK

Klamath NF (916) 465-2241
State map: B4
From KLAMATH RIVER, go
.5 mile (800 m) W on CA 96 to
Beaver Creek Rd (FR 48N01).
Turn Right (N) and drive 5 miles (8 k).
FREE but choose a chore.
Open All Year.
8 scattered, open sites.
Water, pit toilets, tables, grills, fire rings.
At pretty spot on banks of creek for
trout fishing.
No trash arrangements. 14-day/24-ft
limits. Hunting in season.
2400 ft (720 m)

## BEEGUM GORGE

Shasta-Trinity NF (916) 352-4211
State map: D2
Just outside PLATINA (SE side),
take rough Beegum Gorge Rd
(FR 29N06) and go 6.5 miles
(10.4 k)–not recommended for RVs.
FREE but choose a chore.
Open May 1–Oct 31; camping
off-season.
3 close, open sites.
Pit toilets, tables, fire rings.
On Beegum Creek.
Make base for hiking and exploring. Too,
fishing at your doorstep.
NO water. 14-day/20-ft limits.
2200 ft (660 m)

▲ ▲ ▲ ▲ ▲ ▲ ▲ ▲ ▲ ▲ ▲ ▲ ▲ ▲ ▲ ▲ ▲ ▲ ▲ ▲ ▲ ▲ ▲

## BEEHIVE POINT

Shasta-Trinity NF (916) 275-1587
State map: C3
Go S from LAKESIDE for 4 miles
(6.4 k) on Lakeside Dr.
FREE but choose a chore.
Open All Year.
Undesignated primitive sites. Pit toilet.
On secluded shore of Lake Shasta.
Swimming, boating, and fishing.
NO water. 30-day limit.
1067 ft (318 m)

## BENNER CREEK

Lassen NF (916) 258-2141
State map: E4
From CHESTER, go 10 miles
(16 k) N on Juniper Lake Rd.
FREE but choose a chore.
Open May 1 – Nov 1; dry camping
off-season.
9 (4 tent-only) scattered, open sites.
Water needs treating, pit toilets, tables,
grills, fire rings.
On creek in high-altitude forest.
Fishing popular. Good birdwatching too.
Road conditions suggest tent camping.
Hunting in season.
5600 ft (1680 m)

## BERGER

Tahoe NF (916) 288-3231
State map: F4
Take CA 49 NE from SIERRA
CITY for 5 miles (8 k) to Gold
Lake Rd at Bassetts. Turn Left N
and drive 1.3 miles (2.1 k) to CR 20N16
(Packer Lake Rd). Turn Left (W) and
drive 2 miles (3.2 k). (Also see Diablo
and Packsaddle.)
FREE but choose a chore.
Open Jun 15 – Oct 15; camping allowed
off-season.
10 close, open sites. Stream water only
(must be purified), pit toilets, tables,
limited space for very small trailers.
On creek in scenic area with good access
to several lakes and streams.
Fish, hike, and snap photos.
14-day limit.
5900 ft (1770 m)

## BIG BAR

Shasta-Trinity NF (916) 623-6106
State map: C2
Only 1 mile (1.6 k) E of BIG BAR
on CA 299.
FREE but choose a chore.
Open Jun 1 – Nov 1; dry camping
off-season.
3 tent sites.
Water, pit toilets, tables, grills.
At tiny, quiet spot on stream.
Fish, splash, hike, and relax.
14-day limit.
1200 ft (360 m)

## BIG FLAT

Six Rivers NF (707) 457-3131
State map: A2
From GASQUET, head W on
US 199 about 8 miles (12.8 k).
Turn Left (S) on CR 427 (South
Fork) and drive 12 miles (19.2 k).
FREE but choose a chore. (Fees have
been charged in past when water on.)
Open All Year.
30 close, open sites.
Pit toilets, tables, grills.
Along Hurdygurdy Creek.
Fish and swim. Head up road to hike
South Kelsey and Summit Valley Trails.
NO water/trash facilities. 14-day limit.

## BIG FLAT

Shasta-Trinity NF (916) 623-2121
State map: C2
Go 3.5 miles (5.6 k) E of BIG BAR
on CA 299.
$5. Open Jun 1 – Nov 1; dry
camping off-season.
10 close, open sites.
Water, pit toilets, tables, grills.
Among trees by Trinity River.
Fish, splash, hike, and relax.
14-day limit.
1300 ft (390 m)

## BIG FLAT

Klamath NF (916) 467-5757
State map: C3
Go 8 miles (14.4 k) N of TRINITY
CENTER on CA 3. Turn Left (W)
on unpaved Coffee Creek Rd and

▲ ▲ ▲ ▲ ▲ ▲ ▲ ▲ ▲ ▲ ▲ ▲ ▲ ▲ ▲ ▲ ▲ ▲ ▲ ▲ ▲ ▲ ▲ ▲ ▲ ▲

drive about 20 miles (32 k). (Also see Goldfield.)

**FREE** but choose a chore.

Open Jul 1–Sep 30; camping allowed off-season.

9 scattered, open sites. &

Pit toilets, tables, fire rings.

In magnificent "Big Tree" area near Shasta-Trinity Alps Wilderness on Coffee Creek. Fish creek or one of nearby lakes (such as pristine Caribou). Hike into wilderness (take map).

NO water/trash arrangements. 14-day limit. No large vehicles. Bears.

5760 ft (1728 m)

## BIG MEADOW

Sequoia NF (209) 338-2251

State map: L4

From GRANT GROVE, take CA 180 S for 1.5 miles (2.4 k). Turn Left (SE) on Generals Hwy (FH 78) and drive 6.5 miles (10.4 k). Turn Left on Big Meadows (FR 14S11) and go 5 miles (8 k). (Also see Buck Rock.)

**FREE** but choose a chore.

Open May–Sep.

25 sites.

Pit toilets, tables, grills, fire rings.

On creek near Kings Canyon NP.

Good hiking with short nature trail and extended treks into nearby wilderness.

NO water. 14-day/22-ft limits.

7600 ft (2280 m)

## BIG PINE

Lassen NF (916) 336-5521

State map: D4

Go .5 mile (800 m) N from intersection of CA 44 and 89.

**$5.** Open May 15–Oct 1.

19 sites.

Water, pit toilets, tables, grills, fire rings.

On stream in mixed conifer forest.

Fish for trout or hike (several trails nearby).

14-day limit. Generator rules.

4500 ft (1350 m)

## BIG ROCK

Angeles NF (805) 944-2187

State map: P4

From LITTLEROCK, go SW on CA 138 to Longview Rd. Go S on Longview to Valyermo Rd. Left on Valyermo to Big Rock Rd. Right on Big Rock to camp. Only .25 mile (400 m) South of **Camp Fenner.**

**FREE** but choose a chore.

Open All Year.

8 scattered, open sites.

Pit toilets, tables, fire rings.

In shade of oaks and fir on creek.

Good hiking when low 4X4 traffic.

NO water. 14-day limit. Crowded summer holidays.

4500 ft (1350 m)

## BIG SAGE

Modoc NF (916) 233-4611

State map: C6

From ALTURAS, head W on CA 299 for 1 mile (1.6 k) to Crowder Flat Rd. Turn Right (N) on dirt road and drive about 10 miles (16 k). (Also see Reservoir C.)

**FREE** but choose a chore.

Open All Year.

Undesignated area.

Pit toilets, tables, fire rings, boat ramp.

Among juniper, sagebrush, cheatgrass, and rock next to reservoir.

Fish and relax at out-of-the-way spot.

NO water/trash facilities.

4900 ft (1470 m)

## BIG SANDY

Sierra NF (209) 467-5155

State map: J4

From FISH CAMP, take CA 41 S for .5 mile (800 m). Turn Left (E) on Jackson Rd (FR 6S07) and go 6 miles (9.6 k). (Also see Little Sandy.)

**FREE** but choose a chore.

Open May–Oct.

14 close, open sites.

Pit toilets, tables, fire rings.

Along Big Creek near Yosemite NP.

Explore region.

NO water. 14-day/16-ft limits.

5800 ft (1740 m)

▲▲▲▲▲▲▲▲▲▲▲▲▲▲▲▲▲▲▲▲▲▲▲▲

## BIG SLIDE

Shasta-Trinity NF (916) 628-5227
State map: C2
From HYAMPOM, go 5 miles
(8 k) NW on CR 311 (Lower
South Fork Rd).
FREE but choose a chore.
Open Apr 20–Oct 15; dry camping
off-season.
8 close, open sites.
Water, pit toilets, tables, grills.
On Trinity River bank.
Swim or fish in river. Hike area.
14-day/16-ft limits.
1200 ft (360 m)

## BIG SPRINGS

Inyo NF (619) 647-6525
State map: J5
From JUNE LAKE, head N on
CA 158 for 2.5 miles (4 k). Turn
Right (SE) on US 395. Drive
7.5 miles (12 k). Turn Left (E) on
CR 2S07 (Owens River). Go 1.5 miles
(2.4 k). (Also see Deadman and Glass
Creek.)
FREE but choose a chore.
Open May 25–Nov 1.
24 close, open sites.
Pit toilets, tables, fire rings.
On creek for restful getaway.
NO water. 14-day limit.
7300 ft (2190 m)

## BLACK ROCK

Lassen NF (916) 258-2141
State map: E3
From PAYNES CREEK, head SE
on rough, gravel Ponderosa Way
for 15 miles (24 k). (Also see
South Antelope.)
FREE but choose a chore.
Open All Year.
4 scattered, open tent sites. Water (must
treat), pit toilets, tables, grills, fire rings.
On scenic Mill Creek in oak woodland.
Hike major trail into Ishi Wilderness.
Fishing and casual nature viewing too.
Crowded. Snakes and poison oak.
2100 ft (630 m)

## BLOOMFIELD

Stanislaus NF (209) 795-1381
State map: H3
From HATHAWAY PINES, head
E on CA 4 for 43 miles (68.8).
Turn Right (S) at Ebbetts Pass on
Highland Lakes Rd (FR 8N01) and drive
2 miles (3.2 k). (Also see Highland Lakes
and Hermit Valley.)
FREE but choose a chore.
Open Jun–Oct; dry camping off-season.
Undesignated scattered, open sites.
Water, chemical toilet, 5 tables, fire rings.
Hike, fish, or use as base to explore area.
No trash arrangements (pack it out).
14-day limit. Not recommended for
trailers.
7800 ft (2340 m)

## BLUE RIDGE

Angeles NF (805) 944-2187
State map: P4
From WRIGHTWOOD, take CA 2
W about 4.5 miles (7.2 k) to
Inspiration Point. Turn E on Blue
Ridge Rd and drive 3 miles (4.8 k). (Also
see Guffy, Cabin Flats, and Lupine.)
FREE but choose a chore.
Open Jun 1–Oct 31.
8 scattered, open sites.
Pit toilets, tables, fire rings.
Among firs and adjacent to Pacific Crest
and Blue Ridge trails.
Hike! Also relax, birdwatch, and tour
Visitor Center.
NO water/trash arrangements. 14-day
limit. Crowded summers.
8000 ft (2400 m)

## BOARDS CROSSING

Stanislaus NF (209) 795-1381
State map: H3
From ALTAVILLE, head E on
CA 4 to DORRINGTON. Turn
Right (S) on Boards Crossing Rd
(FR 5N02) and go 4 miles (6.4 k). (Also
see Sourgrass.)
FREE but choose a chore.
Open Apr–Oct; dry camping off-season.
Undesignated scattered-open sites.
Water, pit toilets, tables (5), fire rings.
In timbered tract on North Fork of

▲ ▲ ▲ ▲ ▲ ▲ ▲ ▲ ▲ ▲ ▲ ▲ ▲ ▲ ▲ ▲ ▲ ▲ ▲ ▲ ▲ ▲ ▲ ▲ ▲ ▲

Stanislaus River.
Fishing, swimming, hiking, and relaxing.
No trash facilities. 14-day limit.
Crowded. Small trailers only. Hunting in
season.
3800 ft (1140 m)

## BOCA

Tahoe NF (916) 587-3558
State map: G5
From TRUCKEE, go 7 miles
(11.2 k) E on I-80 then 2.2 miles
(3.5 k) N on Boca Rd (turn Left
before dam). (Also see Boca Rest and
Boyington Mill.)
FREE but choose a chore.
Open Jun–Oct; camping allowed
off-season.
20 close, open sites.
Lake water must be purified, pit toilets,
tables, boat ramp nearby.
On southwest side of reservoir.
Boat, waterski, swim, and fish.
14-day/16-ft limits.
5600 ft (1680 m)

## BOCA REST

Tahoe NF (916) 587-3558
State map: G5
From TRUCKEE, go 7 miles
(11.2 k) E on I-80 then 2.5 miles
(4 k) N on CR 19N03. (Also see
Boca and Boyington Mill.)
FREE but choose a chore.
Open Jun–Oct; dry camping off-season.
25 close, open sites.
Water, pit toilets, tables.
On northeast side of reservoir, a couple
of miles north of dam.
Boat, waterski, swim, and fish.
14-day limit.
5700 ft (1710 m)

## BOLSILLO

Sierra NF (209) 877-3138
State map: K4
From LAKESHORE (above
Huntington Lake), take FR 80
(Kaiser Pass Rd) E for 15 miles
(24 k). (See Florence Lake, Portal Fore-
boy, Sample Meadow, and Ward Lake.)
FREE but choose a chore.

Open Jun 17–Sep 15; dry camping
off-season.
3 scattered, open tent sites.
Water, pit toilets, tables, fire rings.
At tiny spot near creek and ranger
station.
Hike to lakes or Mono Hot Springs.
No trash arrangements (pack it out).
14-day limit. Crowded holidays. Hunting
in season. Bears.
7400 ft (2220 m)

## BOUQUET

Angeles NF (818) 574-1613
State map: O3
From SAUGUS, head NE on
CR 6N05 (Bouquet Canyon) for
15 miles (24 k). (Nearby are
Spunky and Streamside. Zuni may also
be open.)
FREE but choose a chore.
Open All Year.
4 close, open tent sites.
Pit toilets, tables, fire rings.
Fish in creek (when water level up).
NO water (creek water dangerous).
14-day limit.

## BOWMAN LAKE

Tahoe NF (916) 265-4538
State map: G4
From NEVADA CITY, go E on
CA 20 for 24.5 miles (39.2 k) to
FR 18N18 (Bowman Rd)–that's
3.5 miles (5.6 k) W of CA 20 Exit off I-80.
Go N on gravel Bowman for 13.25 miles
(21.2 k) to CR 843 (Tyler Foote Crossing
Rd). Turn Right (E) and drive 2 miles
(3.2 k). (Also see Canyon Creek and
Jackson Creek.)
FREE but choose a chore.
Open Jun 15–Sep 30; camping allowed
off-season.
7 close, open sites. Lake water only
(must be purified), pit toilets.
At remote spot on popular lake.
Fish and boat lake. Hike to viewpoints.
No trash arrangements. 14-day limit.
5565 ft (1668 m)

▲ ▲ ▲ ▲ ▲ ▲ ▲ ▲ ▲ ▲ ▲ ▲ ▲ ▲ ▲ ▲ ▲ ▲ ▲ ▲ ▲ ▲ ▲ ▲ ▲ ▲

## BOYINGTON MILL

Tahoe NF (916) 587-3558
State map: G5
From TRUCKEE, go 7 miles
(11.2 k) E on I-80 then 5 miles
(8 k) N on CR 19N03. (Also see
Boca and Boca Rest.)
FREE but choose a chore.
Open Jun–Oct; camping off-season.
10 close, open sites. River water must be
purified, pit toilets, tables.
On Little Truckee River just north of
Boca Reservoir.
Fish or splash in river. Take advantage
of nearby lake.
14-day limit.
5700 ft (1710 m)

## BRADY'S CAMP

Plumas NF (916) 283-0555
State map: F4
From QUINCY, head S and E on
US 70 for 6.5 miles (10.4 k). Turn
Left (E) on dirt Squirrel Creek Rd
and drive 8 miles (12.8 k) toward
Argentine Lookout.
FREE but choose a chore.
Open May 15–Oct 31; dry camping
off-season.
4 scattered, open tent sites. Water (must
treat), pit toilets, tables, grills, fire rings.
In large meadow with trout stream.
Fish. Enjoy wildflowers and trails.
No trash arrangements (pack it out).
30-day limit. Bears.
7200 ft (2160 m)

## BRECKENRIDGE

Sequoia NF (805) 871-2223
State map: N3
From BODFISH, go S on road to
Caliente for 9 miles (14.4 k). Turn
Right (W) on FR 28S06. Drive
about 9 miles (14.4 k), bearing Left after
7 miles (11.2 k).
FREE but choose a chore.
Open May–Oct.
8 tent sites.
Pit toilets, tables, grills, fire rings.
At remote, quiet mountain getaway.
NO water/trash facilities. 14-day limit.
7100 ft (2130 m)

## BRETZ

Sierra NF (209) 467-5155
State map: K4
From TRIMMER, take Trimmer
Springs Rd E for 9 miles (14.4 k).
Go N on FR 7 (Big Creek Rd)
about 15 miles (24 k).
FREE but choose a chore.
Open All Year.
10 close, open sites.
Pit toilets, tables, fire rings.
Along Big Creek near Blue Canyon
Work Center.
Enjoy quiet spot to fish, wade, and relax.
NO water. 14-day/22-ft limits.
3300 ft (990 m)

## BRIDGE CAMP

Shasta-Trinity NF (916) 623-2121
State map: C3
Out of WEAVERVILLE, take
CA 3 NE for 17 miles (27.2 k).
Turn Left (W) on Trinity Alps Rd
(CR 112) and drive 2.5 miles (4 k).
$4. Open All Year.
10 close, open sites.
Water, pit toilets, tables, fire rings.
In excellent location for hikes into
wilderness via Stuarts Fork Trail.
For those not into hiking, fish, swim, or
ride horse back.
14-day limit. Small trailers only. Saddle
and pack animals can be odoriferous.
2700 ft (810 m)

## BRIDGE FLAT

Klamath NF (916) 468-5351
State map: B3
From FORT JONES, go 18 miles
(28.8 k) W on Scott River Rd.
(Also see Indian Scotty.)
$4. Open Memorial Day–Oct 1; dry
camping off-season.
8 close, open sites.
Water, pit toilets, tables, grills, fire rings,
pay phone, beach.
Near Scott River and Kelsey Trail.
Swim, raft, or fish. Take day walks or
trek into Marble Mountain Wilderness.
14-day limit. Rattlesnakes.
2500 ft (750 m)

▲ ▲ ▲ ▲ ▲ ▲ ▲ ▲ ▲ ▲ ▲ ▲ ▲ ▲ ▲ ▲ ▲ ▲ ▲ ▲ ▲ ▲ ▲ ▲

## BRIGHTMAN FLAT

Stanislaus NF (209) 965-3434
State map: I3
From SONORA, go 52 miles
(83.2 k) E on CA 108.
FREE but choose a chore.
Open Apr–Nov; camping off-season.
28 close, open sites.
Pit toilets, tables, fire rings.
In pine-fir shade above Stanislaus River.
Fishing, hiking, and relaxing.
NO water. 14-day/22-ft limits. Crowded.
Bears.
6000 ft (1800 m)

## BROOKSHIRE SPRINGS

Los Padres NF (805) 683-6711
State map: N1
From SANTA MARIA, head N
on US 101 for 3 miles (4.8 k).
Take CA 166 E for 15.5 miles
(24.8 k)–just beyond turn for Buckhorn
Canyon Rd. Turn Right (S) on narrow,
rough FR 11N04 (road impassible when
wet). Go 6 miles (9.6 k) bearing Left on
FR 11N04A to three "spring" camps.
Instead of bearing Left on 11N04A,
continue short distance for Horseshoe
Springs or keep driving, bearing Left
onto 11N03 for Miranda Pine Spring.
FREE but choose a chore.
Open All Year.
2 close, open sites.
Pit toilets, tables, fire rings.
At great getaway spot (great hiking too).
NO water/trash facilities. 14-day/16-ft
limits. Hot summers.
1500 ft (450 m)

## BUCK MEADOW

Sierra NF (209) 467-5155
State map: K4
From SHAVER LAKE, take
Dinkey Creek Rd E for 12 miles
(19.2 k). Turn Right (SE) on FR 40
(McKinley Grove Rd). Go 8 miles
(12.8 k). (See Gigantea and Sawmill Flat.)
FREE but choose a chore.
Open May–Oct.
10 close, open sites.
Pit toilets, tables, fire rings.
Along Deer Creek.

Enjoy quiet spot for relaxing and
walking trails. Fishing possibilities too.
NO water. 14-day/16-ft limits.
6800 ft (2040 m)

## BUCK ROCK

Sequoia NF (209) 338-2251
State map: L4
From GRANT GROVE, take
CA 180 S for 1.5 miles (2.4 k).
Turn Left (SE) on Generals Hwy
(FH 78) and drive 6.5 miles (10.4 k). Turn
Left on Big Meadows (FR 14S11) and go
4 miles (6.4 k). (Also see Big Meadow.)
FREE but choose a chore.
Open Jun–Sep.
5 sites. Pit toilets, tables, grills, fire rings.
Close to Kings Canyon NP with good
hiking possibilities.
NO water. 14-day/16-ft limits.
7600 ft (2280 m)

## BURNT RANCH

Shasta-Trinity NF (916) 623-6106
State map: C2
Go .5 mile (800 m) NW of
BURNT RANCH on CA 299.
FREE but choose a chore.
Open Jun 1–Nov 1; dry camping
off-season.
16 close, open sites.
Water, pit toilets, tables, grills.
On Trinity River with waterfalls and
hiking trails nearby.
Hike, fish, splash, and relax.
14-day/25-ft limits.
1000 ft (300 m)

## BUTTE CREEK

Lassen NF (916) 257-2151
State map: D4
From SUSANVILLE, go W for
38 miles (60.8 k) on CA 44. Turn
Left (S) on dirt FR 18 and drive
2 miles (3.2 k).
FREE but choose a chore.
Open May 15–Oct 15; camping allowed
off-season.
20 close, open sites. Pit toilets, tables.
In pine woods on northern boundary of
Lassen Volcanic NP.
Fish nearby lakes or visit park.

▲ ▲ ▲ ▲ ▲ ▲ ▲ ▲ ▲ ▲ ▲ ▲ ▲ ▲ ▲ ▲ ▲ ▲ ▲ ▲ ▲ ▲ ▲ ▲ ▲ ▲ ▲ ▲

NO water. 14-day/30-ft limits.
5000 ft (1500 m)

## CABALLO

Los Padres NF (805) 683-6711
State map: N2
From MARICOPA, go S on
CA 166 for 9 miles (14.4 k). Turn
Left (SE) on FH 95 and drive
15 miles (24 k). Camp is on Left up
FR 9N27. For more privacy continue to
rustic **Marian Camp**. (Also see Campo
Alto, Toad Spring, and Valle Vista.)
**FREE** but choose a chore.
Open May 15–Nov 15.
6 close, open sites.
Pit toilets, tables, fire rings.
Near creek off road to Mt Abel.
At quiet, relaxing spot with hiking.
NO water/trash arrangements (pack it
out). 14-day/16-ft limits.
5800 ft (1740 m)

## CABIN FLATS

Angeles NF (805) 944-2187
State map: P4
From WRIGHTWOOD, take CA 2
W about 4.5 miles (7.2 k) to
Inspiration Point. Turn E on dirt
Blue Ridge Rd. Drive 10 miles
(16 k)–last 7 miles (11.2 k) are tough.
(See Blue Ridge, Guffy, and Lupine.)
**FREE** but choose a chore.
Open Jun 1–Oct 31.
12 scattered, open tent sites.
Pit toilets, tables, fire rings.
In Prairie Fork Canyon adjacent to Sheep
Mountain Wilderness.
Hike trail to East Fork of San Gabriel
River. Fish and watch birds.
NO water/trash arrangements. 14-day
limit. Crowded summers. Little shade.
5300 ft (1590 m)

## CACHUMA

Los Padres NF (805) 683-6711
State map: O2
From SANTA YNEZ, head E on
Armor Ranch Rd. Crossing
CA 154 continue 1.5 miles
(2.4 k)–road will turn sharply. Turn
Right on Happy Canyon Rd and drive

for 9.5 miles (15.2 k). (Also see Nira.)
**FREE** but choose a chore.
Open All Year.
6 close, open tent sites.
Pit toilets, tables, fire rings.
On creek to splash or fish. Mountain
bike, walk, or relax.
NO water/trash facilities. 14-day limit.
2100 ft (630 m)

## CAMP 4, CAMP 4½, & MILL FLAT

Sequoia NF (209) 338-2251
State map: K4
From TRIMMER, go E on
FR 11S12 (Trimmer Springs) for
16.5 miles (26.4 k). Cross over
Kings River bridge and drive 1 mile on
FR 12S01 (Davis Rd). Continue straight
past next bridge for .75–2.2 miles
(1.2–3.5 k).
**FREE** but choose a chore.
Open All Year.
15 close, open sites (5 at each camp).
Pit toilets, tables, fire rings.
In three areas along Kings River.
Splash in water or fish a bunch. Hike a
bit. Picnic and relax.
NO water/trash facilities. 14-day/16-ft
limits. Hot.
1000 ft (300 m)

## CAMP ONE AREA

Jackson SF (707) 964-5674
State map: E1
About 1 mile (1.6 k) S of FORT
BRAGG, take CA 20 E for
5.9 miles (9.4 k). Watch for small
sign pointing to dirt road on Left. Turn
N and go about 3 miles (4.8 k). Also see
Dunlap, Jackson SF-Scattered, as well as
Red Tail.)
**FREE** but choose a chore.
Open All Year.
25 scattered, open sites with some
screening. River water (must treat), pit
toilets, tables, fire rings, pay phone.
On banks of Noyo River among second-
growth redwoods and firs (cut in 1800s).
With shade and usually free of fog since
3 miles (4.8 k) from ocean.
Splash in shallow river (no fishing–
spawning area) or hike.

▲ ▲ ▲ ▲ ▲ ▲ ▲ ▲ ▲ ▲ ▲ ▲ ▲ ▲ ▲ ▲ ▲ ▲ ▲ ▲ ▲ ▲ ▲ ▲

14-day limit. Crowded holidays and summer weekends.
400 ft (120 m)

## CAMPO ALTO

Los Padres NF (805) 683-6711
State map: N3
From MARICOPA, go S on CA 166 for 9 miles (14.4 k). Turn Left (SE) on FH 95. Go 27 miles (43.2 k). (See Caballo and Toad Spring.)
FREE but choose a chore.
Open May 15–Nov 15.
12 close, open sites.
Pit toilets, tables, fire rings.
On Cerro Noreste (Mt Abel).
In fair hiking territory.
NO water/trash facilities. 14-day limit.
8200 ft (2460 m)

## CANYON CREEK

Tahoe NF (916) 265-4538
State map: G4
From NEVADA CITY, go E on CA 20 for 24.5 miles (39.2 k). Go N on gravel FR 18N18 (Bowman Rd) for 13.25 miles (21.2 k). Turn Right (E) on CR 843 (Tyler Foote Crossing Rd) and drive 4 miles (6.4 k). Turn Right (SE) at Jackson Creek and FR 122-80 and go 3 miles (4.8 k). (Also see Bowman Lake and Jackson Creek.)
FREE but choose a chore.
Open Jun 15–Sep 30; camping allowed off-season.
20 (9 tent-only) close, open sites.
Stream water only (must be purified), pit toilets, tables.
In remote location on nice creek.
Fish and boat nearby Faucherie Reservoir. Hike to other lakes.
No trash arrangements (pack it out).
14-day limit. Limited parking.
5565 ft (1668 m)

## CARLON

Stanislaus NF (209) 962-7825
State map: I4
From GROVELAND, drive E on CA 120 about 20 miles (32 k). Turn Left (N) on Evergreen Rd and go about .8 mile (1.3 k). (Also see

Middle Fork.)
FREE but choose a chore.
Open Apr 15–Nov 1; dry camping off-season.
20 (10 tent-only) close, open sites.
Water, pit toilets, tables, grills.
Among fir and pine on banks of South Fork of Tuolumne River.
At good spot for fishing or hiking.
14-day limit. Crowded holidays.
4600 ft (1380 m)

## CASCADE CREEK

Stanislaus NF (209) 965-3434
State map: I3
From SONORA, go 41 miles (65.6 k) E on CA 108. Take dirt road into campground.
FREE but choose a chore.
Open Apr–Nov; camping allowed off-season.
14 scattered, open sites (2 tent-only and 100-ft walk). Pit toilets, tables, fire rings.
Between road and seasonal creek with some shade. Relax.
NO water/trash facilities. 14-day/22-ft limits. ATV routes nearby.
6000 ft (1800 m)

## CASTLE LAKE

Shasta-Trinity NF (916) 926-4511
State map: C4
From MT SHASTA, take county Barr Rd SW for 11.5 miles (18.4 k). Turn on Castle Lake Rd.
FREE but choose a chore.
Open Jun 1–Oct 15; camping allowed off-season.
6 close, open sites. Pit toilets, tables.
In scenic, mountainous area with excellent hiking and photo taking opportunities.
NO water. 14-day limit.
6450 ft (1935 m)

## CATTLE CAMP

Shasta-Trinity NF (916) 964-2184
State map: C4
From MCCLOUD, go 11 miles (17.6 k) E on CA 89 to FR 40N44 (watch for sign). Turn Right and drive about .5 mile (800 m) to site on

your Left. (Also see Algoma.)
**FREE** but choose a chore.
Open May 1–Nov 1; camping allowed
off-season.
30 close, open sites.
Pit toilets, tables, fire rings.
On river with waterfalls nearby.
Close to fishing and swimming. Hike
along riverbanks.
NO water. 14-day limit.
3600 ft (1080 m)

## CATTLEGUARD

Mono County Parks
(619) 934-7504
State map: J5
From LEE VINING, go W for
5 miles (8 k) on CA 120 (Tioga
Rd) toward Yosemite. (Also see Aspen
Grove, Lower & Upper Lee Vining
Creek, and Lundy.)
$5. Open Apr–Oct.
14 close, open sites.
Stream water only (must be purified),
chemical toilets, tables.
Among aspen and pine.
Hiking and fishing possibilities here.
NO water.
7000 ft (2100 m)

## CAVE LAKE

Modoc NF (916) 279-6116
State map: C7
From NEW PINE CREEK, take
unpaved Forest Rd E off US 395.
Climb steeply about 6 miles
(9.6 k). (Also see Lily Lake.)
**FREE** but choose a chore.
Open Memorial Day–Labor Day; dry
camping off-season.
6 scattered, open sites.
Water, pit toilets, tables, fire rings.
In steep, rocky, piney area next to lake.
Boat (no motors) and fish. Find
photographic studies. Relax.
No trash arrangements. 14-day limit.
6600 ft (1980 m)

## CEDAR CAMP

Mendocino NF (916) 963-3128
State map: F2
From STONYFORD, go W on
CR 18N01 (Fouts Spring) for
6 miles (9.6 k). Turn Left (S) on
narrow FR 18N07 (John Smith Rd) and
drive about 13 miles (20.8 k). Turn SW
on FR 17N02–poor access for trailers.
(Also see Old Mill.)
**FREE** but choose a chore.
Open May 15–Oct 15; camping allowed
off-season.
10 close, open sites.
Pit toilets, tables, grills (5), fire rings.
In remote, wooded (pine and fir) spot for
quiet getaway.
NO water/trash arrangements (pack it
out). 14-day/16-ft limits.
4300 ft (1290 m)

## CEDAR CREEK

Sequoia NF (805) 871-2223
State map: M4
From GLENNVILLE, go E on
CA 155 for 10 miles (16 k). (Also
see Alder Creek.)
**FREE** but choose a chore.
Open All Year.
21 (11 tent-only) close, open sites.
Pit toilets, tables, grills, fire rings.
On creek.
Fish, picnic, and relax.
NO water/trash facilities. 14-day limit.
4800 ft (1440 m)

## CEDAR PASS

Modoc NF (916) 279-6116
State map: D6
From CEDAR PASS, head W on
CA 299 for 8 miles (12.8 k). (Also
see Stough Reservoir.)
**FREE** but choose a chore.
Open Memorial Day–Labor Day;
camping allowed off-season.
17 scattered, open sites.
Pit toilets, tables, grills, fire rings.
In pines with small meadow and creek.
Relax or explore surrounding area.
NO water/trash arrangements.
5600 ft (1680 m)

## CHANNEL ISLANDS NP

(805) 658-5730
State map: O2
Find mainland Visitor Center at
1901 Spinnaker Dr in VENTURA.
**FREE**; reservations required.
Open All Year.
0–936 ft (0–234 m)
▲ **Anacapa Walk-In**
Climb 154 steps; walk .25 mile (400 m).
6 close, open tent sites.
Pit toilets, tables.
In fragile ecology on windswept spine of
East Anacapa Island.
After day-users leave, explore by trail
your almost-private enclave with its
varied beauty and marine life.
NO water/trash arrangements (pack it
out). 14-day limit. No shade and fierce
rains–come prepared. Commercial ferry
costs $48 or more.
▲ **San Miguel**
10 close, open tent sites.
Pit toilets, tables, windbreaks, beach.
Among caliche forest, undisturbed
archeological sites, and incredible natural
beauty.
Gear up for 15-mile (24-k) round-trip
hike to Point Bennett for fantastic
wildlife exhibition of sea lion, elephant
seal, harbor seal, and fur seal.
NO water/trash arrangements. 2-day
limit. Stay on trails–protect fragile
ecology. Wind, rain, and fog create
challenges. Commercial ferry costs $90
or more.
▲ **Santa Barbara**
10 close, open tent sites.
Pit toilets, tables.
In island vegetation returning to
preformed state. Marine shore life and
birds abound.
Several trails beckon to fully explore this
small island.
NO water/trash arrangements (pack it
out). Stay on trails to protect fragile
ecology. Be prepared for wind and rain.
Commercial ferry costs $75 or more.
▲ **Santa Rosa**
9 close, open tent sites.
Pit toilets, tables, wind breaks, beach.
On second largest of islands, with high

mountains and deep-cut canyons.
Explore incredible wealth of archeo-
logical sites, birds (over 195 species),
plant life, and marine specimens.
NO water/trash arrangements.
Commercial ferry costs $80 or more.

## CHILKOOT

Sierra NF (209) 467-5155
State map: J4
From BASS LAKE, take CR 434
(Beasore) N for 4.5 tough miles
(7.2 k).
**FREE** but choose a chore.
Open May 15–Oct 1; camping
off-season.
14 (8 tent-only) sites.
Pit toilets, tables, fire rings.
On creek near Bass Lake.
Fish creek, explore area, or relax.
NO water/trash facilities. 14-day limit.
4800 ft (1440 m)

## CHIMNEY CREEK

BLM (805) 861-4191
State map: M5
From INYOKERN, take US 395 N
for 15 miles (24 k). Turn Left
(Γ .V) on CR 152 (Nine Mile
Canyon). Go 13 miles (20.8 k), bearing
Left at ranger station. (See Long Valley.)
**FREE** but choose a chore.
Open All Year.
36 close, open sites.
Water, pit toilets, tables, fire rings.
At quiet spot on Pacific Crest Trail.
Create wonderful base for day hikes.
No trash arrangements. 14-day limit.
5920 ft (1776 m)

## CHUCHUPATE
Los Padres NF (805) 683-6711
State map: O3
From FRAZIER PARK, go W on
FH 95 (Frazier Mountain Park
Rd) for 3.5 miles (5.6 k). Bear Left
(SW) in Lake of the Woods on CR 9N03
(Lockwood Valley Rd) and drive 1 mile
(1.6 k). Turn Left (S) on FR 8N04 and go
2.5 miles (4 k).
**FREE** but choose a chore.
Open May 15–Nov 15.

▲ ▲ ▲ ▲ ▲ ▲ ▲ ▲ ▲ ▲ ▲ ▲ ▲ ▲ ▲ ▲ ▲ ▲ ▲ ▲ ▲ ▲ ▲

20 close, open sites.
Pit toilets, tables, fire rings.
Next to Frazier Mountain Rd.
Biking and hiking possibilities.
NO water. 14-day/22-ft limits.

## CIENEGA

Angeles NF (818) 574-1613
State map: O3
From CASTAIC, head N on I-5
about 8 miles (12.8 k). Take
Templin Rd E about 3 miles
(4.8 k) Turn Right on FR6N32.
**FREE** but choose a chore.
Open Apr 1–Nov 30.
15 (8 tent-only) close, open sites.
Pit toilets, tables, fire rings.
At fairly isolated spot with trails.
Hike!
NO water. 14-day/22-ft limits.

## CLARK SPRINGS

Shasta-Trinity NF (916) 623-2121
State map: C3
Go 18 miles (28.8 k) N of
WEAVERVILLE on CA 3 to Mule
Creek Station.
**$5.** Open All Year.
34 close, open sites. Water, flush toilets,
tables, grills, boat ramp, beach.
On river.
Swimming, boating, and fishing here.
14-day limit.
2400 ft (720 m)

## CLEAR CREEK

Shasta-Trinity NF (916) 623-2121
State map: C3
From FRENCH GULCH, go N on
unpaved Trinity Mountain Rd
about 16 miles (25.6 k) to Hell
Creek and Dog Creek Rd. Turn Right (E)
and go about 1 mile (1.6 k).
**FREE** but choose a chore.
Open All Year.
8 close, open sites.
Pit toilets, tables, fire rings.
In remote, dense forest beside creek.
Hike or fish.
NO water/trash facilities. 14-day/22-ft
limits. Hunting in season.
3400 ft (1020 m)

## COLSON CANYON

Los Padres NF (805) 683-6711
State map: N1
From SANTA MARIA, head N
on US 101 for 3 miles (4.8 k).
Take CA 166 E for 15 miles
(24 k). Turn Right (S) on Buckhorn
Canyon Rd and drive 8.5 miles (13.6 k).
Turn Left (E) on narrow, steep FR 11N04
(Colson Canyon Rd) and go 4 miles
(6.4 k)–road impassible when wet. (Also
see Barrel Springs and Wagon Flat.)
**FREE** but choose a chore.
Open All Year.
10 close, open tent sites.
Water, pit toilets, tables, grills, fire rings.
At secluded spot for extended hikes or
bike trips. Also, picnic and relax.
14-day/16-ft limits. Hot summers.
2000 ft (600 m)

## CONKLIN PARK

Plumas NF (916) 253-2223
State map: F5
From US 395 in MILFORD, head
S then turn Right (SW), going up
Milford Grade to summit. Turn
on gravel FR 26N70 and drive 4 miles
(6.4 k). Turn Left on paved FR 26N70
and go 2.5 miles (4 k).
**FREE** but choose a chore.
Open All Year.
8 close, open sites. Water (needs
treating), pit toilets, tables, grills.
In mixed conifer and brush on intermit-
tent Willow Creek near large burn area.
Observe renewal after fire.
No trash arrangements (pack it out).
14-day limit. Small vehicles.
5900 ft (1770 m)

## COOPER GULCH

Shasta-Trinity NF (916) 623-2121
State map: C3
From LEWISTON, go 4 miles
(6.4 k) N on CR 105.
**FREE** but choose a chore.
Open Apr 1–Oct 31; dry camping
off-season.
9 close, open sites.
Pit toilets, tables, fire rings.
On lake in quiet, scenic area.

▲ ▲ ▲ ▲ ▲ ▲ ▲ ▲ ▲ ▲ ▲ ▲ ▲ ▲ ▲ ▲ ▲ ▲ ▲ ▲ ▲ ▲ ▲ ▲ ▲

Swim, fish, and walk.
NO water. 14-day/16-ft limits.
2000 ft (600 m)

## CORRAL CANYON ORV AREA

Cleveland NF (619) 445-6235
State map: S4
About 8 miles (14.4 k) S of PINE
VALLEY. Head SE on I-8 to
Buckman Springs Rd. Go S to
Corral Canyon turnoff. Drive about
2 miles (3.2 k) on dirt road.
FREE but choose a chore.
Open All Year.
Undesignated scattered, open sites.
Pit toilets, tables, grills, fire rings.
Two camping areas (Bobcat Meadows
and Corral) for price of none.
Good hiking, mountain biking, and
birdwatching opportunities.
NO water. 14-day limit. Noisy with
ATVs. Crowded weekends and holidays.
3500 ft (1050 m)

## COTTONWOOD

Modoc NF (916) 233-4611
State map: C5
From CANBY, take CA 299 SW
for 3 miles (4.8 k) to CR 84-at
North end of Pit River Bridge.
Turn Right (W) and drive gravel road
about 8 miles (12.8 k).
FREE but choose a chore.
Open May-Oct; dry camping off-season.
5 close sites with some screening.
Water, pit toilets, tables, grills.
Among pines overlooking small
meadow. Just relax.
14-day limit. Hunting in deer season.
4700 ft (1410 m)

## CROCKER

Plumas NF (916) 283-2050
State map: F5
From PORTOLA, take CA 70 E
for 2.5 miles (4 k). Turn Left
(NW) on CR 112 (Grizzly) and go
5 miles (8 k). Turn Right (E) on dirt
FR 24N06 and go 3 miles (4.8 k). (Also
see Lightning Tree.)
FREE but choose a chore.
Open May 1-Oct 31; camping

off-season.
5 close, screened sites. Water, pit toilets,
tables, grills.
In scenic mountain meadow near several
streams and lakes.
Explore and hike. Fish or enjoy quiet.
14-day limit. Hunting in season.
6000 ft (1800 m)

## DAVIES CREEK

Tahoe NF (916) 265-4531
State map: G5
From TRUCKEE, head E on I-80
for 7 miles (11.2 k) Take
CR 21N03 (Stampede Reservoir)
N for 9 miles (14.4 k). Turn Left (W) on
CR 19N03 (Henness). Go 2 miles (3.2 k).
FREE but choose a chore.
Open May 1-Oct 31.
10 close, open sites.
Pit toilets, tables, grills.
On creek close to other streams and
lakes for water sports. Good hiking too.
NO water. 14-day/22-ft limits.
6000 ft (1800 m)

## DEAD MULE

Mendocino NF (916) 824-5196
State map: E2
From PASKENTA, go S on
FR 23N02 to FR 23N50. Turn
Right and drive to FR 23N54.
Turn Left to camp-a total of 28 miles
(44.8 k). (Also see Del Harleson.)
FREE but choose a chore.
Open Jun 1-Oct 31; dry camping
off-season.
2 close, open sites.
Water, pit toilets, tables, fire rings.
At quiet getaway.
Picnic and relax.
No trash arrangements. 14-day limit.
Hunting in season.
5100 ft (1530 m)

## DEADLUN

Shasta-Trinity NF (916) 275-1587
State map: C4
From BIG BEND, go NW for
7 miles (11.2 k) on FR 48N11 to
Iron Canyon Reservoir.
FREE but choose a chore.

▲ ▲ ▲ ▲ ▲ ▲ ▲ ▲ ▲ ▲ ▲ ▲ ▲ ▲ ▲ ▲ ▲ ▲ ▲ ▲ ▲ ▲ ▲ ▲ ▲ ▲ ▲

Open All Year.
30 (15 tent-only) close, open sites.
Pit toilets, tables, fire rings, boat ramp.
On less-popular reservoir.
Enjoy lake for fishing, boating, and
swimming. Hiking afoot.
NO water. 14-day/24-ft limits.
1085 ft (324 m)

## DEADMAN

Inyo NF (619) 647-6525
State map: J5
From JUNE LAKE, head N on
CA 158 for 2.5 miles (4 k). Turn
Right (SE) on US 395 and drive
6.5 miles (10.4 k). Turn Right (W) on
FR 2S05 and go 3 miles (4.8 k). (Also see
Big Springs and Glass Creek.)
FREE but choose a chore.
Open Jun 1–Oct 15.
30 close, open sites.
Pit toilets, tables, fire rings.
On peaceful creek.
NO water. 14-day limit.
7800 ft (2340 m)

## DEANES VALLEY

Plumas NF (916) 283-0555
State map: F4
From QUINCY, head W on Bucks
Lake Rd–about 3.5 miles (5.6 k).
Turn Left (S) on Deanes Valley
Rd and drive 6 miles (9.6 k).
FREE but choose a chore.
Open Apr 15–Oct 31; camping allowed
off-season.
7 close, open sites.
Water (needs treating), pit toilets, tables,
grills, fire rings.
In trees on large meadow with stream.
Besides fishing, walk nature trail.
No trash arrangements (pack it out).
30-day limit. Bears.
4400 ft (1320 m)

## DEATH VALLEY NM

(619) 786-2331
State map: L6–M7
From lowest spot in US to snowcovered peaks, from blistering
heat to winter storms, explore
fascinating monument.

$5 entrance fee (or pass). Also, **free**
backcountry permits available at visitor
centers and ranger stations.

▲ **Emigrant**
From STOVETOP WELLS, go 9 miles
(14.4 k) W on CA 190.
FREE. Open May–Oct.
10 close, open sites.
Water, flush toilets, tables, pay phone.
With good views of sand dunes and
Stovetop Wells.
Hike and take photographs.
30-day limit. Summer heat extreme
without shade. No fires. Generator rules.
2100 ft (630 m)

▲ **Mahogany Flat**
From Visitor Center at FURNACE
CREEK, go N and W on CA 190 for
31 miles (49.6 k). Turn Left (S) on paved
road and drive 25 miles (40 k) to
Wildrose Campground. Turn on rough,
dirt Wildrose Canyon Rd and go 9 miles
(14.4 k) to end. (Also see Thorndike.)
FREE. Open Mar–Nov; camping allowed
off-season.
19 close, screened tent sites.
Pit toilets, tables, fire rings.
In heavily treed area. Look down on
lowest point in US or walk 7.6 miles
(12.2 k) up Telescope Peak, 11049 ft
(3368 m), for incredible views.
NO water/trash facilities. 30-day limit.
Crowded summer holidays. No RVs or
trailers (need high clearance or 4WD).
8000 ft (2400 m)

▲ **Mesquite Spring**
Go 4 miles (6.4 k) S from SCOTTY'S
CASTLE on paved road. Take dirt access
road for 1 mile (1.6 k).
**$5.** Open All Year.
30 close, open sites.
Water, flush toilets, tables, grills, fire
rings, pay phone, dump station.
In few shaded areas near Scotty's Castle-
usually 11 degrees cooler than Furnace
Creek. (Mesquite trees at entrance up to
1000 years old–no wood gathering.)
Create base to explore northern area of
monument. Attend occasional ranger
programs in winter.
30-day limit. Crowded holiday weekends. Generator rules. Sporadic floods.

1800 ft (540 m)

▲ **Stovepipe Wells**
At STOVETOP WELLS Village on CA 190.
**$4. Open Oct–May.**
215 (15 tent-only) close, open sites.
Water, flush toilets, pay phone, dump station, nearby village with pool, showers, ice.
In flat, unshaded spot near sand dunes.
Hiking and photo taking opportunities.
Attending occasional ranger programs.
30-day limit. Hot in spring and fall.
Crowded early Nov. Generator rules.
0 ft (0 m)

▲ **Sunset**
Go .5 mile (800 m) S of FURNACE CREEK Visitor Center.
**$4. Open Oct–May.**
1000 close, open sites. Water, flush/pit toilets, pay phone, dump station.
In flat, unshaded, mainly RV, winter camp across from resort.
Explore southern end of monument.
Attend ranger programs during season.
30-day limit. Crowded early Nov. Hot spring and fall. No fires (portable stoves only). Generator rules.
-190 ft (-57 m)

▲ **Texas Spring**
Go 1.5 miles (2.4 k) S of FURNACE CREEK Visitor Center.
**$5. Open Oct–Apr.**
97 close, open sites.
Water, flush/pit toilets, tables, grills, fire rings, pay phone, dump station.
In badlands-type canyon within walking distance of Visitor Center.
Make base for exploring southern end of monument and attending seasonal ranger programs.
No generators. Hot spring and fall. Crowded around holidays. 30-day limit.
0 ft (0 m)

▲ **Thorndike**
From Visitor Center at FURNACE CREEK, go N then W on CA 190 for 31 miles (49.6 k)–past Stovepipe Wells.
Turn Left (S) on paved road. Drive 25 miles (40 k) to Wildrose Campground.
Turn E on rough, dirt Wildrose Canyon Rd. Go 8 miles (12.8 k). (Also see

Mahogany Flat.)
**FREE. Open Mar–Nov; camping allowed off-season.**
8 close, open tent sites.
Pit toilets, tables, grills, fire rings.
Near pinyons and junipers–with little shade. Wildrose Peak trailhead nearby for hiking.
NO water/trash facilities. 30-day limit.
No RVs or trailers (rough, high-clearance road). Summer holidays crowded. Snow possible in spring and fall.
7500 ft (2250 m)

▲ **Wildrose**
From Visitor Center at FURNACE CREEK, go N then W on CA 190 for 31 miles (49.6 k)–past Stovepipe Wells.
Turn Left (S) on narrow, paved road and drive 25 miles (40 k).
**FREE. Open All Year.**
30 close, open sites.
Water (when above freezing), pit toilets, tables, grills, fire rings, pay phone.
At base of Panamint Mountains with trails to peaks.
Create base camp for exploring monument's high country and old charcoal kilns.
30-day/25-ft combined-vehicle-length limits. Generator rules. Crowded holidays. Snow possible.
4100 ft (1230 m)

## DEER VALLEY

Mendocino NF (707) 275-2361
State map: E2
From UPPER LAKE, go N on CR 1N02 for 12 miles (19.2 k).
Turn Right (E) on dirt FR 16N01 and drive 4.2 miles (6.7 k). (Also see Bear Creek and Lower Nye.)
**FREE but choose a chore.**
Open Apr 1–Nov 1; camping allowed off-season.
13 close, open sites.
Pit toilets, tables, fire rings.
At remote spot with hiking, mountain biking, and relaxing opportunities.
NO water/trash facilities. 14-day/16-ft limits. Hunting in season.
3700 ft (1110 m)

▲ ▲ ▲ ▲ ▲ ▲ ▲ ▲ ▲ ▲ ▲ ▲ ▲ ▲ ▲ ▲ ▲ ▲ ▲ ▲ ▲ ▲ ▲ ▲ ▲ ▲ ▲ ▲ ▲ ▲ ▲ ▲

## DEERLICK SPRINGS

Shasta-Trinity NF (916) 352-4211
State map: D2
From PLATINA, go NW on
CA 36 for 5 miles (8 k). Turn
Right (N) on CR B005 and drive
5.25 miles (8.4 k) to FR 30N44. Turn and
go .25 mile (400 m) to FR 31N01. Turn
and travel N for 5.25 miles (8.4 k).
$4. Open May 20–Oct 31; dry camping
off-season.
15 close, open sites.
Water, pit toilets, tables, fire rings.
On restful Browns Creek.
Enjoy walks and water activities.
14-day/20-ft limits.
3100 ft (930 m)

## DEL HARLESON

Mendocino NF (916) 824-5196
State map: E2
From PASKENTA, go S on
FR 23N02 to FR 23N69. Turn Left
and drive to FR 23N03. Turn Left
and go to FR 23N74. Turn Left to camp-
a total of 21 miles (33.6 k). (Also see
Dead Mule.)
FREE but choose a chore.
Open Apr 15–Nov 15; dry camping
off-season.
2 close, open sites.
Water, pit toilets, tables, fire rings.
At tiny, quiet getaway spot for
picnicking and relaxing.
No trash arrangements (pack it out).
14-day limit. Hunting in season.
4500 ft (1350 m)

## DENNY

Shasta-Trinity NF (916) 623-6106
State map: C2
Go 7 miles (11.2 k) NW of
BURNT RANCH on CA 299 to
Denny Rd. Cross river and drive
about 17 winding miles (27.2 k)–difficult
for large vehicles. Site is 1.5 miles (2.4 k)
beyond Denny.
FREE but choose a chore.
Open Jun 1–Nov 1; dry camping
off-season.
16 sites (10 tent-only), close-open
Water, pit toilets, tables, grills.

On wild and scenic New River.
Wonderful hiking in wilderness. Also,
fishing, splashing, and relaxing.
14-day/25-ft limits.
1400 ft (420 m)

## DEVILS POSTPILE NM-Backcountry

(619) 934-2289
State map: J5
Locate on CA 203 near
MAMMOTH LAKES off US 395.
FREE wilderness permits
available at Mammoth and Devils
Postpile ranger stations. (Developed
campground costs $7.)
Open All Year.
View group of basalt columns
resembling giant pipe organ. Enjoy
delightful waterfalls and hot springs as
well as forests via John Muir and Kings
Creek trails.
Bears–store food carefully and pack out
all trash. Treat water. No hunting.
7560 ft (2268 m)

## DIABLO

Tahoe NF (916) 288-3231
State map: F4
Take CA 49 NE from SIERRA
CITY for 5 miles (8 k) to Gold
Lake Rd at Bassetts. Turn Left (N)
and drive 1.3 miles (2.1 k) to CR 20N16
(Packer Lake Rd). Turn Left (W) and go
1.5 miles (2.4 k). (Also see Berger and
Packsaddle.)
FREE but choose a chore.
Open Jun 15–Oct 15; camping allowed
off-season.
Undesignated sites. Stream water only
(purify), pit toilets, tables.
On creek with good fishing and hiking.
14-day limit.
5800 ft (1740 m)

## DIGGER PINE FLAT

Mendocino NF (916) 963-3128
State map: F2
From STONYFORD, go S on
Lodoga-Stonyford Rd for 6 miles
(9.6 k). Turn Right (W) on
narrow, rough Goat Mountain Rd and
drive 3.9 miles (6.2 k).

▲ ▲ ▲ ▲ ▲ ▲ ▲ ▲ ▲ ▲ ▲ ▲ ▲ ▲ ▲ ▲ ▲ ▲ ▲ ▲ ▲ ▲ ▲ ▲

FREE but choose a chore.
Open All Year.
7 close, open sites.
Pit toilets, tables, grills, fire rings.
Along Little Stony Creek.
Good spot for picnicking.
NO water/trash facilities. 14-day/16-ft
limits. Motorcycles.
1500 ft (450 m)

## DILLON

Klamath NF (916) 627-3291
State map: B3
Take CA 96 NE from ORLEANS
for 24 miles (38.4 k).
$4. Open May–Oct; dry camping
off-season.
21 (10 tent-only) scattered, open sites.
Water, pit toilets, tables, grills.
At popular, streamside location.
Excellent swimming, canoeing/kayaking,
plus good fishing. Hiking and nature
trails available too.
14-day/22-ft limits.
775 ft (231 m)

## DODGE RESERVOIR

BLM (916) 257-0456
State map: E6
From SUSANVILLE, take US 395
N for 50 miles (80 k) to Buckhorn
Rd. Turn Right (E) and drive
9 miles (14.4 k). Turn Left (N) and
continue 3 miles (4.8 k) to Marr Rd. Turn
Right and go 3.5 miles (5.6 k) to Stage
Rd. Turn Left and proceed 2 miles (3.2 k)
to Tuledad Rd. Turn Right and go
7 miles (11.2 k).
FREE but choose a chore.
Open All Year.
11 scattered, open sites.
Pit toilets, tables, grills, fire rings.
In juniper on shore of reservoir.
When there's water, boat and fish. Any-
time, birdwatch or just do nothing.
NO water/trash facilities. 14-day limit.
Road impassable during winter.
5600 ft (1680 m)

## DUNLAP

Jackson SF (707) 964-5674
State map: E1
About 1 mile (1.6 k) S of FORT
BRAGG, take CA 20 E for
17 miles (27.2 k). Take signed dirt
entrance road on Right (S). (See Camp
One, Jackson SF-Scattered, and Red Tail.)
FREE but choose a chore.
Open All Year.
17 scattered, screened sites. Water must
be treated, pit toilets, tables, fire rings.
Among oak, madrone, redwood, and fir
on banks of North Fork of Big River.
Choose Chamberlain Creek Demonstra-
tion Trail among others.
14-day limit. Crowded holidays and
summer weekends.
400 ft (120 m)

## DUSTY

Lassen NF (916) 336-5521
State map: D4
From BURNEY, go 5 miles (8 k) E
on CA 299 then about 10 miles
(16 k) N on CA 89.
FREE but choose a chore.
Open All Year.
5 close, open tent sites.
Pit toilets, tables, fire rings.
On lake beneath oak-conifer canopy.
Swim, boat, or fish lake.
NO water. 14-day limit. Crowded and
noisy.
3200 ft (960 m)

## EAGLE CREEK

Shasta-Trinity NF (916) 623-2121
State map: C3
From TRINITY CENTER, go N
on CA 3 for 16 miles (25.6 k).
$5. Open All Year.
17 close, open sites.
Water, pit toilets, tables, grills.
At juncture of Trinity River and Eagle
Creek.
Fish or hike. When hot, splash in water.
14-day limit.
2800 ft (840 m)

▲ ▲ ▲ ▲ ▲ ▲ ▲ ▲ ▲ ▲ ▲ ▲ ▲ ▲ ▲ ▲ ▲ ▲ ▲ ▲ ▲ ▲ ▲ ▲ ▲

## EAST FORK

Klamath NF (916) 467-5757
State map: C3
From CALLAHAN, take FH 93
SW toward CECILVILLE for
27 miles (43.2 k). (Also see
Matthews Creek and Shadow Creek.)
$4. Open May 25–Sep 15; dry camping
off-season.
9 scattered sites with some screening.
Water, pit toilets, tables, grills, fire rings.
At sunny spot near confluence of East
Fork and Main South Fork of Salmon
River. Walk up South Fork and find
several bedrock holes perfect for
swimming. Hike nearby trail (wilderness
permits at Petersburg Work Station). Fish
for steelhead or just relax.
14-day/24-ft limits.
2600 ft (780 m)

## EAST WEAVER

Shasta-Trinity NF (916) 623-2121
State map: C3
From WEAVERVILLE, go NE on
CA 3 for 2 miles (3.2 k). Turn
Left (NW) on East Weaver Rd
(CR 228) and go 1.5 miles (2.4 k).
$5. Open All Year.
15 (8 tent-only) close, open sites.
Water, pit toilets, tables.
On banks of East Weaver Creek.
Fish creek or walk trails.
14-day/16-ft limits.
2800 ft (840 m)

## EEL RIVER

Mendocino NF (707) 983-6118
State map: E2
From COVELLO, go NE on
CA 162 for 2.5 miles (4 k). Turn
Right (E) on CR 338 and drive
11 miles (17.6 k). Turn Right (S) on
FR 1N02 and go .25 mile (400 m). (See
Little Doe.)
FREE but choose a chore.
Open May 15–Oct 31.
16 close, open sites.
Water, pit toilets, tables, grills, fire rings.
Under oaks at confluence of Middle Fork
of Eel and Black Butte Rivers.
Fish or swim. Picnic and relax.

No trash facilities. 14-day/22-ft limits.
1500 ft (450 m)

## EMERSON

Modoc NF (916) 279-6116
State map: D6
From EAGLEVILLE, go S on
CR 1 for 1 mile (1.6 k). Turn
Right (SW) on Emerson access
road and climb steep grade for 3 miles
(4.8 k)–tough when wet (not for large
vehicles or trailers).
FREE but choose a chore.
Open Memorial Day–Labor Day;
camping allowed off-season.
4 scattered, open sites.
Pit toilets, tables, fire rings.
Among pines and cliffs near natural
stone bridge.
Access Warner Wilderness.
NO water/trash arrangements.
6000 ft (1800 m)

## EMPIRE LANDING

BLM (602) 855-8017
State map: R8
From PARKER, AZ, cross to CA
side of river. Go N 9 miles
(14.4 k) on Parker Dam
Rd–1 mile (1.6 k) beyond Crossroads
Camp (in AZ listing).
$5. Open All Year.
75 close, open sites.
Water, flush toilets, cold showers, tables,
beach, dump station.
Near Colorado River among flowering
plants in highly developed
area–surrounded by saguaro, ocatillo,
and creosote bush.
Swim, boat, fish, hike, rockhound, and
birdwatch.
14-day/35-ft limits. Generator rules.
Crowded and noisy.
384 ft (114 m)

## EVANS FLAT

Sequoia NF (805) 871-2223
State map: N5
From WOFFORD HEIGHTS, take
CA 155 SW for 8 miles (12.8 k).
Turn Left (S) on CR 25S15
(Rancheria). Go 8 miles (12.8 k).

▲ ▲ ▲ ▲ ▲ ▲ ▲ ▲ ▲ ▲ ▲ ▲ ▲ ▲ ▲   ▲ ▲ ▲ ▲ ▲ ▲ ▲ ▲ ▲ ▲ ▲ ▲

**FREE** but choose a chore.
Open May 1–Oct 23.
16 close, open sites.
Pit toilets, tables, fire rings.
Enjoy solitude as you relax or hike.
NO water/trash arrangements (pack it out). 14-day/16-ft limits.
6200 ft (1860 m)

## FENCE CREEK

Stanislaus NF (209) 965-3434
State map: I3
From SONORA, go 50 miles (80 k) E on CA 108. Turn Left (N) on Clark Fork Rd and go 1.5 miles (2.4 k). Turn on FR 6N06 and go .25 mile (400 m).
**FREE** but choose a chore.
Open Apr–Nov; camping off-season.
40 scattered, open sites. Pit toilets, tables (for some sites), fire rings.
Beside creek.
Fishing, hiking, and relaxing.
NO water/trash arrangements (pack it out). 14-day/22-ft limits.
6000 ft (1800 m)

## FIDDLE CREEK

Tahoe NF (916) 288-3231
State map: F4
From CAMPTONVILLE, go NE on CA 49 about 9 miles (14.4 k).
**FREE** but choose a chore.
Open All Year.
13 close, open tent sites. River water only (must purify), pit toilets, tables.
On North Yuba River.
Gold panning, fishing, swimming, and hiking here.
14-day limit.
2200 ft (660 m)

## FISH CREEK

Sierra NF (209) 467-5155
State map: J4
From NORTH FORK, go SE on CR 225 for 4.5 miles (7.2 k). Turn Left (NE) on FR 81 (Minarets) and drive 18 miles (28.8 k).
**FREE** but choose a chore.
Open Apr–Nov.
7 close, open sites.

Pit toilets, tables, fire rings.
Beside creek on road to Mammoth Pools Reservoir.
Hike and fish at this free alternative to nearby **Rock Creek** (fee charged).
NO water. 14-day/16-ft limits.
4600 ft (1380 m)

## FISH CREEK

Sequoia NF (619) 376-3781
State map: M5
From INYOKERN, take US 395 N for 15 miles (24 k). Turn Left (NW) on CR 152 (Nine Mile Canyon) and go 23.5 miles (37.6 k). Take FR 21S02 NW for 8.25 miles (13.2 k). (Also see Kennedy and Troy Meadow.)
**FREE** but choose a chore.
Open Jun 1–Nov 15.
40 close, open sites.
Water, pit toilets, tables, fire rings.
On scenic creek.
Walk and hike. Take photos. Fish and picnic.
No trash facilities. 14-day/16-ft limits.
7400 ft (2220 m)

## FLORENCE LAKE

Sierra NF (209) 467-5155
State map: K5
From LAKESHORE, (above Huntington Lake) take FR 80 (Kaiser Pass Rd) E for 10.5 miles (14.4 k). Take dirt Florence turnoff (FR 7S01) for 5 miles (8 k). (Also see Bolsillo, Portal Foreboy, Sample Meadow, and Ward Lake.)
**FREE** but choose a chore.
Open May 15–Oct 15; camping allowed off-season.
14 close, open tent sites.
Pit toilets, tables, fire rings.
On beautiful, high-country lake.
Fish, canoe, raft, or swim. Hike to Ansel Adams or John Muir Wilderness areas.
NO water/trash facilities. 14-day/25-ft limits. Crowded holidays. Hunting in season. Bears.
7400 ft (2220 m)

▲ ▲ ▲ ▲ ▲ ▲ ▲ ▲ ▲ ▲ ▲ ▲ ▲ ▲ ▲ ▲ ▲ ▲ ▲ ▲ ▲ ▲ ▲ ▲ ▲

## FOREST GLEN

Shasta-Trinity NF (916) 628-5227
State map: D2
At West end of FOREST GLEN
on CA 36. (Also see Hell Gate
and Scotts Flat.)
$4. Open May 20–Oct 15; dry camping
off-season.
15 close, open sites. &
Water, pit toilets, tables, grills.
Next to South Fork of Trinity River.
Swim or fish river. Plan ambitious
hiking excursion.
14-day/15-ft limits.
2300 ft (690 m)

## FORT GOFF

Klamath NF (916) 465-2241
State map: A3
From SEIAD VALLEY, go W on
CA 96 for 4.7 miles (7.5 k).
FREE but choose a chore.
Open All Year.
5 scattered, screened tent sites. Pit toilets,
tables, grills, fire rings, pay phone.
On banks of Klamath River.
Canoe, raft, swim, and fish.
NO water/trash arrangements.
14-day/24-ft limits.
1300 ft (390 m)

## FOUTS

Mendocino NF (916) 963-3128
State map: F2
From STONYFORD, go W on
CR 18N01 (Fouts Spring) for
8.8 miles (14.1 k). Turn Right (N)
on FR 18N03 and drive .75 mile (1.2 k).
(Also see Mill Creek and North Fork.)
FREE but choose a chore.
Open All Year.
10 close, open sites.
Water, pit toilets, tables, fire rings.
On creek beneath digger pines.
Picnic and relax.
No trash facilities. 14-day/16-ft limits.
Motorcycles.
1600 ft (480 m)

## FRASIER MILL

Mountain Home SF
(209) 539-2855
State map: M4
From SPRINGVILLE, go W for
25 miles (40 k) on steep, winding
Bear Creek Rd. (Also see Hedrick Pond,
Hidden Falls, Moses Gulch, Shake Camp,
and Sunset Point.)
FREE but choose a chore.
Open May–Nov; dry camping
off-season.
46 close, open sites with some screening.
Water, pit toilets, tables, fire rings.
Under canopy of young redwoods.
Explore magnificent region. Spot
wildlife. Fish nearby.
14-day limit. Generator rules. Crowded
and noisy.
6500 ft (1950 m)

## FRESNO DOME

Sierra NF (209) 467-5155
State map: J4
From OAKHURST, take CA 41 N
about 5 miles (8 k) to FR 10 (Sky
Ranch Rd). Turn Right (NE) and
go 12 miles (19.2 k). Camp is off
FR 6S07. (Also see Kelty Meadow and
Little Sandy.)
FREE but choose a chore.
Open May–Oct.
12 close, open sites.
Pit toilets, tables, fire rings.
Along Big Creek.
Wade, fish, and explore.
NO water. 14-day/16-ft limits.
6400 ft (1920 m)

## FROG MEADOW

Sequoia NF (209) 548-6503
State map: M4
From CALIFORNIA HOT
SPRINGS, take CR 56 E for
4 miles (6.4 k). Turn Right (S) on
FR 23S05 and go about 9 miles (14.4 k)
to FR 23S16. Turn SE on 23S16 and drive
6.25 miles (10 k). Turn Left (N) on
FR 24S50 and go 5 miles (8 k). (Also see
Panorama.)
FREE but choose a chore.
Open Jun 16–Oct 15.

▲ ▲ ▲ ▲ ▲ ▲ ▲ ▲ ▲ ▲ ▲ ▲ ▲ ▲ ▲ ▲ ▲ ▲ ▲ ▲ ▲ ▲ ▲ ▲

10 close, screened sites.
Water, pit toilets, tables, grills, fire rings.
Relax at isolated, quiet spot. Mountain
bike or walk nearby trails.
14-day/16-ft limits. Hunting in season.
7500 ft (2250 m)

## FULLER LAKE

Tahoe NF (916) 265-4538
State map: G4
From NEVADA CITY, go E on
CA 20 for 24.5 miles (39.2 k) to
Bowman Rd (FR 18N18)–that's
3.5 miles (5.6 k) W of CA 20 Exit off I-80.
Go N on Bowman for 4 miles (6.4 k).
(Also see Grouse Ridge.)
FREE but choose a chore.
Open May 23–Sep 30; camping allowed
off-season.
9 tent sites. Lake water only (purify
before using), pit toilets, tables.
On lakeshore.
Fish here. Enjoy hiking possibilities.
No trash arrangements (pack it out).
14-day limit. Limited parking.
5600 ft (1680 m)

## GAGGS CAMP

Sierra NF (209) 467-5155
State map: J4
Just E of NORTH FORK, take
CR 274 (Mallum Ridge) N for
4.5 miles (7.2 k). Turn Right on
tough FR 6S42 (Central Camp). Go about
11 miles (17.6 k). (Also see Whiskers.)
FREE but choose a chore.
Open May–Oct.
9 close, open sites.
Pit toilets, tables, fire rings.
Along Sand Creek in isolated, quiet spot
to wade, fish, and relax.
NO water. 14-day/16-ft limits.
5700 ft (1710 m)

## GIGANTEA

Sierra NF (209) 467-5155
State map: K4
From SHAVER LAKE, take
CA 168 S to Dinkey Creek Rd.
Drive E for 12 miles (19.2 k).
Turn Right (SE) on FR 40 (McKinley
Grove Rd) and go 6 miles (9.6 k). (Also

see Buck Meadow and Sawmill Flat.)
FREE but choose a chore.
Open May–Oct.
11 close, open sites.
Pit toilets, tables, fire rings.
On Dinkey Creek.
Walk interpretive trail through ancient
McKinley Grove of sequoias. Fish creek.
NO water. 14-day/16-ft limits.
6500 ft (1950 m)

## GLASS CREEK

Inyo NF (619) 647-6525
State map: J5
From JUNE LAKE, head N on
CA 158 for 2.5 miles (4 k). Turn
Right (SE) on US 395 and drive
6 miles (9.6 k). Turn Right (W) on FR 2S4
and go .25 mile (400 m). (Also see Big
Springs, Deadman, and Hartley Springs.)
FREE but choose a chore.
Open May 15–Nov 1.
50 close, open sites.
Pit toilets, tables, fire rings.
On creek for peaceful getaway.
NO water. 14-day limit.
7600 ft (2280 m)

## GOLDEN GATE NRA-Walk-In Camps

(415) 331-1540
State map: H1
From SAN FRANCISCO, drive
US 101 N across Golden Gate
Bridge. Take first Exit (Alexander
Ave). Turn Left at bottom and take first
route up bluff to Marin Headlands.
FREE; reservations required.
Open All Year.
12 tent sites at Bicentennial: 150 ft (45
m); Hawk Camp: 3 miles (4.8 k); and
Haypress: .75 mile (1.2 k).
Water at parking lot, chemical toilets,
tables, grills.
With special natural appeals unusual so
close to urban area.
Hike, mountain bike, surf, attend ranger
program, observe nature, and relax.
3-day limit.

▲ ▲ ▲ ▲ ▲ ▲ ▲ ▲ ▲ ▲ ▲ ▲ ▲ ▲ ▲ ▲ ▲ ▲ ▲ ▲ ▲ ▲ ▲ ▲ ▲ ▲ ▲ ▲ ▲ ▲ ▲ ▲ ▲

## GOLDFIELD

Shasta-Trinity NF (916) 623-2121
State map: C3
From TRINITY CENTER, go N
for 8 miles (12.8 k) on CA 3 to
unpaved Coffee Creek Rd. Turn
Left (W) and go 6.5 miles (10.4 k). (Also
see Big Flat.)
**FREE** but choose a chore.
Open May 15–Sep 15; camping allowed
off-season.
6 close, open sites. Pit toilets, tables.
At Boulder Creek Trailhead.
Hike and explore wilderness.
NO water/trash facilities. 14-day limit.
3000 ft (900 m)

## GOODALE CREEK

BLM (805) 861-4191
State map: L5
About 16 miles (25.6 k) S of BIG
PINE on US 395 in village of
Aberdeen, take Aberdeen Rd W
for 2 miles (3.2 k).
**FREE** but choose a chore.
Open May 1–Nov 1.
62 close, open sites.
Pit toilets, tables, fire rings.
On creek with fishing opportunities.
NO water/trash facilities. 14-day limit.
4100 ft (1230 m)

## GRANDVIEW

Inyo NF (619) 873-2500
State map: K6
From BIG PINE, head N on
US 395 for .5 mile (800 m). Turn
Right (NE) on CA 168. Drive
13 miles (20.8 k). Turn Left (N) on
CR 4S01 (White Mountain). Go 5.5 miles
(8.8 k).
**FREE** but choose a chore.
Open May 1–Dec 15.
26 (6 tent-only) close, open sites.
Pit toilets, tables, fire rings.
At suitably named, high-altitude camp.
Great hikes include peaks, old mining
operations, and Bristlecone Pine Forest.
NO water. 14-day limit.
8600 ft (2580 m)

## GRANITE CREEK

Sierra NF (209) 467-5155
State map: J4
From NORTH FORK, go SE on
CR 225 for 4.5 miles (7.2 k). Turn
Left (NE) on FR 81 (Minarets)
and drive about 50 miles (80 k). Turn
Right on FR 5S30 leading to Clover
Meadow Ranger Station and drive
3.5 miles (5.6 k). **Clover Meadow** camp
is fee-charged option.
**FREE** but choose a chore.
Open Jun–Oct.
20 close, open sites.
Pit toilets, tables, fire rings.
Next to Ansel Adams Wilderness.
Make base for exploring with short
walks or more ambitious hikes.
NO water. 14-day/16-ft limits. No
trailers.
6900 ft (2070 m)

## GREGORY BEACH

Shasta-Trinity NF (916) 275-1587
State map: C3
3 miles (4.8 k) S of LAKESIDE on
I-5, take Salt Creek Exit. Head
back N on Gregory Creek Rd for
4 miles (6.4 k). Gregory Beach is before
$6 **Gregory Creek**. (Also see Oak Grove.)
**FREE** but choose a chore.
Open All Year.
Undesignated primitive sites. Pit toilet.
On shore of Lake Shasta.
Swim, boat, fish, or seek solitude.
NO water or other facilities. 30-day limit.
1067 ft (318 m)

## GREYS MOUNTAIN

Sierra NF (209) 467-5155
State map: J4
From OAKHURST, take CA 41 N
about 5 miles (8 k) to FR 10 (Sky
Ranch Rd). Turn Right (NE). Go
7.75 miles (12.4 k). Turn Right (SE) on
FR 6S40 and go 2.3 miles (3.7 k). (Also
see Kelty Meadow and Soquel.)
**FREE** but choose a chore.
Open May–Oct.
12 close, open sites.
Pit toilets, tables, fire rings.
Along Willow Creek.

▲ ▲ ▲ ▲ ▲ ▲ ▲ ▲ ▲ ▲ ▲ ▲ ▲ ▲ ▲ ▲ ▲ ▲ ▲ ▲ ▲ ▲ ▲ ▲ ▲

Find usually quiet, secluded spot to wade, fish, and explore.
NO water. 14-day/16-ft limits.
5200 ft (1560 m)

## GRIDER CREEK

Klamath NF (916) 465-2241
State map: A3
From SEIAD VALLEY, go E on CA 96 for 1.5 miles (2.4 k) to Walker Creek turnoff. Turn Right (SW). Follow signs about 5 miles (8 k).
FREE but choose a chore.
Open All Year.
10 scattered, screened sites.
Pit toilets, tables, grills, fire rings, corral.
On banks of Grider Creek near trailhead for Pacific Crest Trail. Enjoy superb hiking into Marble Mountain Wilderness plus swimming and fishing.
NO water (stream water). No trash arrangements (pack it out). 14-day limit.
1700 ft (510 m)

## GRIZZLY CREEK

Plumas NF (916) 283-2050
State map: F4
Take Oroville-Quincy Rd W from BUCKS LAKE for 3 miles (4.8 k).
(Also see Silver Lake.)
FREE but choose a chore.
Open Jun 1 – Oct 31.
8 close, open sites.
Pit toilets, tables, fire rings.
On creek.
Make base camp for hiking or fishing streams and lakes.
NO water. 14-day/22-ft limits.
5500 ft (1650 m)

## GROUSE RIDGE

Tahoe NF (916) 265-4538
State map: G4
From NEVADA CITY, go E on CA 20 for 24.5 miles (39.2 k) to Bowman Rd (FR 18N18) – that's 3.5 miles (5.6 k) W of CA 20 Exit off I-80.
Go N on Bowman for 5 miles (8 k) to Grouse Ridge Rd. Turn Right (E) and continue additional 6 miles (9.6 k). (Also see Fuller Lake.)
FREE but choose a chore.

Open May 23 – Sep 30; dry camping off-season.
9 tent sites.
Water, pit toilets, tables, grills.
Near Grouse Ridge Lookout.
Fish here or hike to Grouse Lakes.
No trash arrangements. 14-day limit.
7400 ft (2220 m)

## GUFFY

Angeles NF (805) 944-2187
State map: P4
From WRIGHTWOOD, take CA 2 W about 4.5 miles (7.2 k) to Inspiration Point. Turn E on rough, dirt Blue Ridge Rd and drive 6 miles (9.6 k) – last 3 are tough. (Also see Blue Ridge, Cabin Flats, and Lupine.)
FREE but choose a chore.
Open Jun 1 – Oct 31.
6 scattered, open sites.
Pit toilets, tables, fire rings.
In shade of white firs and pines next to Pacific Crest Trail.
Good hiking here.
NO water/trash arrangements. 14-day limit. Crowded summers and holidays.
8300 ft (2490 m)

## GUMBOOT

Shasta-Trinity NF (916) 926-4511
State map: C4
From MT SHASTA, take county Barr Rd SW for 15 miles (24 k).
FREE but choose a chore.
Open Jun 1 – Oct 15; camping off-season.
4 close, open sites. Pit toilets, tables.
On small lake in scenic, mountainous area for excellent hiking and photo taking opportunities. For the brave, swimming in refreshing lake waters.
NO water. 14-day limit.
6000 ft (1800 m)

## HALF MOON

Los Padres NF (805) 683-6711
State map: O3
From FRAZIER PARK, go W on FH 95 (Frazier Mountain Park Rd) for 3.5 miles (5.6 k). Bear Left (SW) in Lake of the Woods on CR 9N03 (Lockwood Valley Rd) and drive

10.5 miles (16.8 k). Turn Left (S) on
FR 7N03 and go 8.5 miles (13.4 k). (Also
see Pine Spring and Thorne Meadows.)
**FREE** but choose a chore.
Open May 15–Nov 15.
10 close, open sites.
Pit toilets, tables, fire rings.
Along creek.
In secluded getaway with hiking.
NO water/trash arrangements (pack it
out). 14-day/22-ft limits.
4700 ft (1410 m)

## HAMMERHORN LAKE
Mendocino NF (707) 983-6118
State map: D2
From COVELLO, go NE on
CA 162 for 2.5 miles (4 k). Turn
Right (E) on CR 338 and drive
11 miles (17.6 k). Turn Left (N) on dirt
FR 1N02 (Indian Dick) and go 17.5 miles
(28 k). (Also see Little Doe.)
**FREE** but choose a chore.
Open May 15–Oct 31.
10 close, open sites.
Water, pit toilets, tables, grills, fire rings.
In woods on stocked, 5-acre lake.
Fish a bunch or hike into Yolla Bolly-
Middle Eel Wilderness.
No trash facilities. 14-day/16-ft limits.
3500 ft (1050 m)

## HARDLUCK
Los Padres NF (805) 683-6711
State map: O3
From GORMAN, take Hungry
Valley Rd (CR 1048) S about
9 miles (14.4 k). At fork, bear Left
and continue another 4 miles (6.4 k).
When road turns to Left, continue
straight (S) on FR for 3 miles (4.8 k).
**FREE** but choose a chore.
Open All Year.
20 close, open sites.
Pit toilets, tables, fire rings.
On quiet creek.
Splash, swim, fish, and relax.
NO water/trash facilities. 14-day limit.
7600 ft (2280 m)

## HARRIS SPRINGS
Shasta-Trinity NF (916) 964-2184
State map: C4
From MCCLOUD, go 16 miles
(25.6 k) E on CA 89 to FR 43N15
(at Bartle). Turn Left (N) on
unpaved road. Drive 17 miles (27.2 k).
**FREE** but choose a chore.
Open Jun 1–Nov 15; dry camping
off-season.
15 close, open sites.
Water, pit toilets, tables, fire rings.
At usually reliable escape just E of Mt
Shasta with good hiking possibilities.
14-day/32-ft limits.
4800 ft (1440 m)

## HARTLEY SPRINGS
Inyo NF (619) 647-6525
State map: J5
From JUNE LAKE, head N on
CA 158 for 2.5 miles (4 k). Turn
Right (SE) on US 395 and drive
2 miles (3.2 k). Turn South on FR 2S78.
Go 1.5 miles (2.4 k). (See Glass Creek.)
**FREE** but choose a chore.
Open Jun 1–Oct 15.
21 close, open sites.
Pit toilets, tables, fire rings.
On creek near Obsidian Dome.
Good hiking and relaxing.
NO water. 14-day limit.
8400 ft (2520 m)

## HAYDEN FLAT
Shasta-Trinity NF (916) 623-6106
State map: C2
Go 6.25 miles (10 k) NW of BIG
BAR on CA 299.
**$5.** Open Jun 1–Nov 1; dry
camping off-season.
35 (11 RV-only) close, open sites.
Water, pit toilets, tables, grills, beach.
Near river or across road in woods.
Swim and boat. Hike and relax.
14-day/22-ft limits.
1000 ft (300 m)

## HEADQUARTERS

Modoc NF (916) 667-2246
State map: C5
Take CA 139 S from TULELAKE
for 20 miles (32 k). Turn Right
(W) on CR 97. Go 25 miles (40 k).
Watch signs to smallest of 4 camps
Located 1 mile (1.6 k) from others and
with more wind protection. (Also see
A H Hogue, Hemlock, and Medicine.)
$5, $5/extra vehicle.
Open May 15–Oct 30; dry camping
off-season.
9 scattered, open sites. Water, pit toilets,
tables, grills, fire rings, boat ramp, beach.
Near fascinating lake in old volcanic
cone ringed by conifers.
Windsurf, swim, fish, boat. Just lie on
beach or explore caldera.
14-day/22-ft limits. Leash pets. Region
colder than you anticipate.
6700 ft (2010 m)

## HEBER DUNES

Imperial County Parks
(619) 339-4384
State map: T6
From HOLTVILLE, take Orchard
Rd S to Heber Rd. Turn Right
(W) and go about 1 mile (1.6 k).
FREE but choose a chore.
Open All Year.
100 scattered, open sites.
Flush toilets, tables, grills, fire rings.
In agricultural area on mainly flat terrain
with gentle, sandy hills and salt cedars.
Picnic, birdwatch, or relax.
NO water. 3-day limit. Hot summers.

## HEDRICK POND

Mountain Home SF
(209) 539-2855
State map: M4
From SPRINGVILLE, go W for
20 miles (32 k) on steep, winding
Bear Creek Rd. (Also see Frasier Mill,
Hidden Falls, Moses Gulch, Shake Camp,
and Sunset Point.)
FREE but choose a chore.
Open Jun–Nov; dry camping off-season.
13 close, open sites.
Water, pit toilets, tables, fire rings.

In trees next to small pond.
Explore scenic region. View wildlife.
14-day limit. Crowded and noisy.
6500 ft (1950 m)

## HELL GATE

Shasta-Trinity NF (916) 628-5227
State map: D2
From FOREST GLEN, go 1 mile
(1.6 k) W on CA 36. If crowded,
check out sites at Scotts Flat not
far up dirt road. (Also see Forest Glen.)
$4. Open May 20–Oct 15; dry camping
off-season.
15 (9 tent-only) close, open sites. &
Water, pit toilets, tables, fire rings, beach.
On South Fork of Trinity River.
Besides river activities, wander river
bank or engage in serious hiking.
14-day/15-ft limits.
2300 ft (690 m)

## HEMLOCK

Modoc NF (916) 667-2246
State map: C5
Take CA 139 S from TULELAKE
for 20 miles (32 k). Turn Right
(W) on CR 97. Go 25 miles (40 k)
on narrow road. Watch signs. (See A H
Hogue, Headquarters, and Medicine.)
$5, $5/extra vehicle.
Open May 15–Oct 30; dry camping
off-season.
18 small, scattered, open sites.
Water, pit toilets, tables, grills, fire rings,
boat ramp, beach.
In conifers beside lake in volcanic cone.
Explore wonderful area. Just lie on beach
or windsurf, swim, fish, and boat.
14-day/20-ft limits. Leash pets. Region
colder than you anticipate.
6700 ft (2010 m)

## HERMIT VALLEY

Stanislaus NF (209) 795-1381
State map: H3
From HATHAWAY PINES, head
E on CA 4 about 44 miles
(70.4 k)–about 5 miles (8 k) from
Ebbetts Pass Summit. (Also see
Bloomfield.)
FREE but choose a chore.

▲ ▲ ▲ ▲ ▲ ▲ ▲ ▲ ▲ ▲ ▲ ▲ ▲ ▲ ▲ ▲ ▲ ▲ ▲ ▲ ▲ ▲ ▲ ▲ ▲ ▲ ▲

Open Jun–Oct; camping off-season.
Undesignated scattered, open sites.
Chemical toilets, tables (3), fire rings.
Near headwaters of Mokelumne River.
Take long treks into wilderness or fish.
NO water/trash arrangements. 14-day
limit. Crowded. Hunting in season.
7100 ft (2130 m)

## HERRING CREEK

Stanislaus NF (209) 965-3434
State map: I3
From SONORA, go 32 miles
(51.2 k) E on CA 108. Turn Right
on Herring Creek Rd and drive
7 miles (11.2 k).
FREE but choose a chore.
Open Apr–Nov; camping off-season.
8 (2 tent-only) close, open sites.
Pit toilets, tables, fire rings.
Next to creek near lake.
Boating and fishing. Hiking and biking
opportunities too.
NO water/trash facilities (pack it out).
14-day/22-ft limits. Crowded. Bears.
7400 ft (2220 m)

## HI MOUNTAIN

Los Padres NF (805) 683-6711
State map: M1
From SANTA MARGARITA, go
E on CA 58 for 1 mile (1.6 k).
Turn Right (S) on CR 21 (Poza
Rd) and drive about 16 miles (25.6 k).
Turn Right (SW) on FR 30S05 and go
3.5 miles (5.6 k).
$5. Open All Year.
11 close, open sites.
Water, pit toilets, tables, grills, fire rings.
Nestled at top of Saint Lucia Wilderness.
Picnic and relax or take rewarding hike
into wilderness.
No trash arrangements (pack it out).
14-day/16-ft limits. Hunting in season.
2800 ft (840 m)

## HIDDEN FALLS

Mountain Home SF
(209) 539-2855
State map: M4
From SPRINGVILLE, go W for
30 miles (48 k) on Bear Creek

Rd–steep and winding with last 5 miles
(8 k) unpaved. (Also see Frasier Mill,
Hedrick Pond, Moses Gulch, Shake
Camp, and Sunset Point.)
FREE but choose a chore.
Open May–Nov.
8 close, open sites with some screening.
Water, pit toilets, tables, fire rings.
Under Sierra redwoods next to Wishon
Fork of Tule River.
Explore magnificent region. View
wildlife. Fish.
14-day limit. Crowded and noisy.
Hunting in season.
6000 ft (1800 m)

## HIGHLAND LAKES

Stanislaus NF (209) 795-1381
State map: H3
From HATHAWAY PINES, head
E on CA 4 for 43 miles (68.8 k).
Turn Right (S) at Ebbetts Pass on
FR 8N01 (Highland Lakes Rd). Go
4.5 miles (7.2 k). (Also see Bloomfield.)
$5. Open Jun–Sep.
35 close, open sites.
Water, chemical toilets, tables, fire rings.
Between two small lakes.
Swim and fish. Hike and view wildlife.
No trash facilities (pack it out). 14-day
limit. Not recommended for trailers.
8600 ft (2580 m)

## HOBO

Sequoia NF (805) 871-2223
State map: N4
From LAKE ISABELLA, take
CA 178 W for 4 miles (6.4 k).
Turn Left (S) on CR 214 and go
2.5 miles (4 k).
FREE but choose a chore.
Open May 1–Sep 30.
35 (25 tent-only) close, open sites.
Pit toilets, tables, grills, fire rings.
On Kern River.
Relax and picnic. Walk nature trail. Fish.
NO water. 14-day/16-ft limits.
2300 ft (690 m)

▲ ▲ ▲ ▲ ▲ ▲ ▲ ▲ ▲ ▲ ▲ ▲ ▲ ▲ ▲ ▲ ▲ ▲ ▲ ▲ ▲ ▲ ▲ ▲

## HOBO GULCH

Shasta-Trinity NF (916) 623-6106
State map: C3
Go 20 miles (32 k) N of HELENA
on rough, dirt Hobo Gulch
Rd—no large vehicles.
FREE but choose a chore.
Open Jul 1–Oct 1; camping off-season.
10 close, open sites.
Pit toilets, tables, grills.
On North Fork of Trinity, at boundary of
Salmon-Trinity Alps Wilderness.
Create base for serious exploration of
wild area–come prepared.
NO water. 14-day limit.
3000 ft (900 m)

## HOLCOMB VALLEY

San Bernardino NF
(714) 866-3437
State map: Q5
From FAWNSKIN, take CA 38 E
for 1.8 miles (2.9 k). Turn Left (N)
on dirt FR 2N09 (Van Duzen) and go
4 miles (6.4 k). Turn Right (E) on
FR 3N16 and go .9 mile (1.4 k).
FREE but choose a chore.
Open All Year.
19 close, open tent sites.
Pit toilets, tables, fire rings.
In open stand of conifers. Hike.
NO water/trash facilities. 14-day limit.
7400 ft (2220 m)

## HOLE-IN-THE-WALL

BLM (619) 326-3896
State map: P7
From NEEDLES, head W on I-40
for 41 miles (65.6 k) to ESSEX
Exit. Go Right (N) for 10 miles
(16 k) to Black Canyon Rd. Continue N
for 10 miles (16 k)–last 9 are dirt and
subject to flash floods. (See Mid Hills.)
$4. Open All Year.
23 close, open sites. Water, pit toilets,
tables, grills, fire rings, dump station.
Near fantastic, sculpted rock formations
in desert.
For special hike, take trail to Banshee
Canyon. View Wild Horse Mesa.
14-day limit.
4200 ft (1260 m)

## HONN

Lassen NF (916) 336-5521
State map: D4
Go 2 miles (3.2 k) S of HAT
CREEK on CA 89.
FREE but choose a chore.
Open All Year.
6 close, open tent sites.
Water needs treating, pit toilets, tables,
grills, fire rings.
In conifer-oak shade next to creek with
lava bed edge.
Hiking trails as well as fishing spots.
14-day limit. Hunting in season.
3400 ft (1020 m)

## HORSE FLAT

Shasta-Trinity NF (916) 623-2121
State map: C3
Go N on CA 3 from TRINITY
CENTER for 16.5 miles (26.4 k).
Turn Left at Eagle Creek and go
2 miles (3.2 k).
FREE but choose a chore.
Open All Year.
16 close, open sites.
Pit toilets, tables, fire rings, corrals.
At Eagle Creek Trailhead.
Make base for equestrian ventures and
backpack trips.
NO water. 14-day limit.
3200 ft (960 m)

## HORSE SPRINGS

San Bernardino NF
(714) 866-3437
State map: Q5
From FAWNSKIN, take CR 3N14
(Rim of the World) NW for
9.6 miles (15.4 k). Turn E on FR 4N17 for
.5 mile (800 m).
FREE but choose a chore.
Open All Year.
17 close, open tent sites.
Pit toilets, tables, fire rings.
In arid setting with pinyon trees.
Take day hikes from this base.
NO water/trash arrangements (pack it
out). 14-day limit. ATVs.
5800 ft (1740 m)

▲ ▲ ▲ ▲ ▲ ▲ ▲ ▲ ▲ ▲ ▲ ▲ ▲ ▲ ▲ ▲ ▲ ▲ ▲ ▲ ▲ ▲ ▲

## HORTON CREEK

BLM (805) 861-4191
State map: K5
From BISHOP, take US 395 N for
5 miles (8 k). Turn Left (W) on
Round Valley Rd and drive
4 miles (6.4 k).
FREE but choose a chore.
Open May 1–Nov 1.
53 close, open sites.
Pit toilets, tables, fire rings.
On western edge of rugged area.
Extended hiking possible here.
NO water/trash arrangements (pack it
out). 14-day limit. Hunting in season.
4975 ft (1491 m)

## HOTELLING

Klamath NF (916) 467-5757
State map: B3
About 43 miles (68.8 k) SW of
ETNA off FH 93; 3 miles (4.8 k)
from Forks of Salmon
village–watch for logging trucks.
FREE but choose a chore.
Open May–Oct; camping off-season.
4 scattered, open sites.
Pit toilets, tables, fire rings.
Beside South Fork of Salmon.
Good river access for swimming, fishing,
canoeing. Hiking nearby.
NO water. 14-day limit.
1760 ft (528 m)

## HOWARD'S GULCH

Modoc NF (916) 233-4611
State map: C5
Take CA 139 N from CANBY for
5.5 miles (8.8 k)–on Left (W).
FREE but choose a chore.
Open May 1–Oct 15.
10 close sites with some screening. &
Water, pit toilets, tables, grills.
In shady woods with stream and nearby
meadow. Hike and observe wildlife.
Fishing fairly close.
14-day limit.
4600 ft (1380 m)

## HULL CREEK

Stanislaus NF (209) 586-3234
State map: I3
From LONG BARN, drive SE on
paved FR 3N01 for 11 miles
(17.6 k).
FREE but choose a chore.
Open Apr–Nov.
20 close, screened sites. Water, chemical/
pit toilets, tables, fire rings.
In trees near seasonal creek.
Nice, quiet getaway (except weekends)
for hiking, biking, and fishing.
No trash arrangements (pack it out).
14-day limit. Hunting in season.
5000 ft (1500 m)

## IDLEWILD

Klamath NF (916) 467-5757
State map: B3
From ETNA, take FR 2E01 (Etna-
Somes Bar Rd) W for 20 miles
(32 k). (Also see Little North Fork
and Mulebridge.)
$4. Open May–Oct; dry camping
off-season.
17 scattered, open sites. Water, pit toilets,
tables, fire rings, grills, pay phone.
In conifer-oak woods near confluence of
Russian Creek and North Fork of
Salmon River.
Good swimming holes plus fishing
opportunities. Near trails into Marble
Mountain and Russian wilderness areas.
14-day limit. Watch for logging trucks.
2600 ft (780 m)

## IMPERIAL DAM LTVA

BLM (602) 726-6300
State map: T7
Take US 95 N from YUMA, AZ,
about 20 miles (32 k) to Imperial
Dam Rd. Turn Left (W) and
continue to Senator Wash Rd.
$50 annual pass or $10/week.
Open Sep 15–Apr 15; dry camping
off-season.
6000 undesignated sites.
Water, flush toilets, cold showers, pay
phone, dump station.
In open Colorado Desert–no trees. Near
Imperial NWR and Squaw Lake.

▲ ▲ ▲ ▲ ▲ ▲ ▲ ▲ ▲ ▲ ▲ ▲ ▲ ▲ ▲ ▲ ▲ ▲ ▲ ▲ ▲ ▲ ▲ ▲

Ample chances for wildlife watching, hiking, swimming, boating, and fishing. Generator rules. Learn to coexist with desert inhabitants including coyotes and snakes.
300 ft (90 m)

## INDIAN CREEK RS

BLM (702) 882-1631
State map: H5
From WOODFORDS, go 3 miles (4.8 k) S on US 89 to Airport Rd. Turn Left and drive around lake to west side and campground.
$4 tent, $6 RV site. Open May 1–Sep 30.
29 (10 tent-only) sites. Water, flush toilets, showers, tables, grills.
Under mixed conifers by pretty lake (when full).
Take nature trail or longer hikes to Summit or Curtz Lakes.
14-day limit.
6000 ft (1800 m)

## INDIAN SCOTTY

Klamath NF (916) 468-5351
State map: D3
From FORT JONES, go 15 miles (24 k) W on Scott River Rd. (Also see Bridge Flat.)
$4. Open Memorial Day–Oct 1; dry camping off-season.
36 close, screened sites.
Water, pit toilets, tables, grills, fire rings, pay phone, beach.
Among trees on flat next to Scott River. Frolic in water or walk into nearby wilderness.
14-day limit. Crowded weekends and holidays. Bears.
2600 ft (780 m)

## JACKASS SPRINGS

Shasta-Trinity NF (916) 623-2121
State map: C3
From TRINITY CENTER, go 5.75 miles (9.2 k) N on CA 3. Turn Right (SE) on CR 106 (Trinity Mountain Rd). Drive about 15 miles (24 k) to CR 119 at Nelson Creek Gap. Turn Right (W) and go 4.5 miles (7.2 k).

FREE but choose a chore.
Open All Year.
21 (1 tent-only) close, open sites.
Water, pit toilets, tables, fire rings.
In only choice on east side of Clair Engle Lake–secluded and priced right.
Swim, fish, explore, or relax.
14-day/32-ft limits.
2600 ft (780 m)

## JACKSON CREEK

Tahoe NF (916) 265-4538
State map: G4
From NEVADA CITY, go E on CA 20 for 24.5 miles (39.2 k) to FR 18N18 (Bowman Rd)–that's 3.5 miles (5.6 k) W of CA 20 Exit off I-80. Go N on gravel Bowman for 13.25 miles (21.2 k) to CR 843 (Tyler Foote Crossing Rd). Turn Right (E) and drive 4 miles (6.4 k). (Also see Bowman Lake and Canyon Creek.)
FREE but choose a chore.
Open Jun 15–Sep 30; camping off-season.
14 close, open sites.
Stream water only (must be purified), pit toilets, tables, grills.
Along creek with nice overlooks.
Hiking. Fishing in creek or nearby lake. No trash arrangements. 14-day limit.
5565 ft (1668 m)

## JACKSON SF-Scattered

(707) 964-5674
State map: E1
About 1 mile (1.6 k) S of FORT BRAGG, take CA 20 E for 5.9 miles (9.4 k). Watch for signed dirt road on Left. Turn N and in about 3 miles (4.8 k) approach Camp One. Find Camp Host and ask for map; sites are spread mainly along Rds 350, 360, and 361. (Also see Camp One, Dunlap, and Red Tail.)
FREE but choose a chore.
Open All Year.
Several scattered areas. Stream water must be treated, pit toilets, tables, fire rings, pay phone (at Camp One).
Find solitude along streams or trails. Splash in shallow streams (no fishing in

▲ ▲ ▲ ▲ ▲ ▲ ▲ ▲ ▲ ▲ ▲ ▲ ▲ ▲ ▲ ▲ ▲    ▲ ▲ ▲ ▲ ▲ ▲ ▲ ▲ ▲ ▲ ▲ ▲ ▲ ▲

these spawning grounds).
14-day limit. Crowded holidays and
summer weekends.
400 ft (120 m)

## JERSEYDALE

Sierra NF (209) 467-5155
State map: J4
From MARIPOSA, go E on
CA 140 for 4.75 miles (7.6 k).
Turn Right (E) on Triangle Rd
and drive 6.5 miles (10.4 k). Turn Left
(NE) on Jerseydale Rd (leads to Jersey-
dale Ranger Station). Go 3 miles (4.8 k).
FREE but choose a chore.
Open May–Oct.
10 close, open sites.
Pit toilets, tables, fire rings.
At base of Chowchilla Mountains.
Explore scenic area by foot or vehicle.
NO water. 14-day/22-ft limits.
3600 ft (1080 m)

## JONES INLET

Shasta-Trinity NF (916) 275-1587
State map: D3
From BELLA VISTA, take Dry
Creek Rd N for 9 miles (14.4 k).
FREE but choose a chore.
Open All Year.
Undesignated primitive sites. Pit toilets.
On shores of Lake Shasta.
Try fishing, swimming, boating, and
skiing (be wary of snags).
NO water/trash facilities (pack it out).
1067 ft (318 m)

## JOSHUA TREE NM

(619) 367-7511
State map: Q6
$5 entrance fee (or pass). Also,
free backcountry permits
available at Visitor Center.
View incredible rocks plus cactus that
gives monument its name. Two deserts,
Mojave and Colorado, meet here and
provide out-of-the-ordinary mix of plant
and animal life.

### ▲ Belle

From TWENTY-NINE PALMS, drive S
on Utah Trail about 8 miles (12.8 k) to
Cottonwood. Bear Left and continue

3 miles (4.8 k).
FREE. Open All Year.
17 scattered, open sites.
Pit toilets, tables, grills.
Near large rock formations.
Explore Mojave Desert's fragile environ-
ment–be especially careful around old
mining operations. Do not collect.
NO water. 14-day/26-ft limits. Crowded
spring and fall plus winter weekends.
Quiet hours.
3800 ft (1140 m)

### ▲ Hidden Valley

At JOSHUA TREE, turn S off CA 62 onto
Park Blvd. Drive 14 miles (22.4 k).
FREE. Open All Year.
39 close, screened sites.
Pit toilets, tables, grills.
Among huge granite rock piles. Popular
with rock climbers from Oct–Apr.
Good introduction to area on nearby
nature trail and at ranger programs.
NO water. 14-day/26-ft limits. Crowded
most of year.
4200 ft (1260 m)

### ▲ Indian Cove

From JOSHUA TREE, take CA 62 E for
15 miles (24 k). Turn Right (S) on Indian
Cove Rd and drive 3 miles (4.8 k).
FREE. Open All Year.
107 scattered, screened sites.
Pit toilets, tables, grills.
At ancient native American camp site on
north side of wonderland of rocks.
Rock climbing and hiking. Birdwatching
and taking photographs. Learning about
desert through ranger programs.
NO water. 14-day/28-ft limits. Quiet
hours. Crowded weekends.
3200 ft (960 m)

### ▲ Jumbo Rocks

From TWENTY-NINE PALMS, go S on
park road (Utah Trail) for 8 miles
(12.8 k) to fork. Bear Right and drive
about 3 miles (4.8 k).
FREE. Open All Year.
130 scattered, open sites.
Pit toilets, tables, grills.
Among gigantic boulders.
Good location for exploring monument
with its varied plant and animal communities (do not gather). Watch for open

▲ ▲ ▲ ▲ ▲ ▲ ▲ ▲ ▲ ▲ ▲ ▲ ▲ ▲ ▲ ▲ ▲ ▲ ▲ ▲ ▲ ▲ ▲ ▲

shafts around old mines.
NO water. 14-day/26-ft limits. Crowded
fall and spring. Extreme temperatures in
summer and winter.
4400 ft (1320 m)

▲ **Ryan**
At JOSHUA TREE, turn S off CA 62 onto
Park Blvd. Drive 16 miles (25.6 k).
FREE. Open All Year.
31 close, open sites.
Pit toilets, tables, grills.
Among large rock piles near remains of
early ranching and mining operation.
Explore historic remnants and hike Ryan
Mountain Trail.
NO water. 14-day/28-ft limits. Crowded
fall, winter, and spring. Watch for old
mine shafts around mines.
4300 ft (1290 m)

▲ **White Tank**
From TWENTY-NINE PALMS, drive S
on Utah Trail about 8 miles (12.8 k) to
Cottonwood. Bear Left and continue
4 miles (6.4 k).
FREE. Open All Year.
15 scattered, open sites.
Pit toilets, tables, grills.
Among rock piles near old ranch's
manmade water-basin.
Walk Arch Rock geologic trail. Photograph desert communities. Attend ranger
programs.
NO water. 14-day/25-ft limits. Quiet
hours. Crowded fall and spring. Extreme
temperature summer and winter.
3800 ft (1140 m)

## JUANITA LAKE
Klamath NF (916) 398-4391
State map: B4
From MACDOEL, go S on CA 97
for 3.75 miles (6 k) to Ball
Mountain Rd. Turn Right (W)
and go 3 miles (4.8 k). Turn Right (N) on
gravel road and go 4 miles (6.4 k).
$5. Open May – Oct; dry camping
off-season.
23 scattered, screened sites. &
Water, pit toilets, tables, grills, boat ramp
(no motors), beach.
In scenic forest setting near 40-acre lake.
Canoe, swim, and fish. Walk easy trail

around lake.
14-day limit. Hunting in season.
5100 ft (1530 m)

## JUNCAL
Los Padres NF (805) 683-6711
State map: O2
From SANTA BARBARA, go N
on CA 154 for 8 miles (12.8 k).
Turn Right (E) on FR 5N12 (East
Camino Cielo). Go 22 miles (35.2 k)
always bearing Left – no trailers. (Also
see Middle Santa Ynez, Mono, or P-Bar
Flat.)
FREE but choose a chore.
Open All Year.
6 close, open sites.
Pit toilets, tables, fire rings.
On Santa Ynez River.
Picnic, relax, and, maybe, fish a little.
NO water/trash facilities. 14-day limit.
1800 ft (540 m)

## JUNCTION
Inyo NF (619) 647-6525
State map: J5
From LEE VINING, head W on
CA 120 for 10 miles (16 k). Turn
Right (N) on FR 1N04 (Saddlebag
Lake). (Also see Sawmill Walk-In.)
FREE but choose a chore.
Open Jun 1 – Oct 15.
10 close, open sites.
Chemical toilets, tables, fire rings.
In gorgeous high country 1 mile (1.6 k)
from Yosemite NP.
Take trail from site #1 into Hall Natural
Area or walk 1 mile (1.6 k) to old
Bennettville mining site.
NO water. 14-day limit.
9600 ft (2880 m)

## KELTY MEADOW
Sierra NF (209) 467-5155
State map: J4
From OAKHURST, take CA 41 N
about 5 miles (8 k) to FR 10 (Sky
Ranch Rd). Turn Right (NE). Go
10.5 miles (16.8 k). (See Fresno Dome,
Nelder Grove, and Soquel.)
FREE but choose a chore.
Open May – Oct.

12 close, open sites.
Pit toilets, tables, fire rings.
Along Willow Creek.
Wade, fish, or explore.
NO water. 14-day/16-ft limits. Share
camp with horses.
5800 ft (1740 m)

## KENNEDY

Sequoia NF (619) 376-3781
State map: M5
From INYOKERN, take US 395 N
for 15 miles (24 k). Turn Left
(NW) on CR 152 (Nine Mile
Canyon) and go 25.75 miles (41.2 k).
Take FR 22S11 N for .25 mile (400 m).
(Also see Fish Creek and Troy Meadow.)
FREE but choose a chore.
Open All Year.
39 close, open sites.
Water, pit toilets, tables, fire rings.
On South Fork of Kern River.
Walk nature trail and hike countryside.
Swim, fish, and picnic.
No trash facilities. 14-day/22-ft limits.
6100 ft (1830 m)

## KINGS CANYON NP-Backcountry

(209) 565-3306
State map: L5
From WILSONIA, take CA 180 E
to end. (Also see Landslide and
Upper Tenmile.)
FREE but $5 entrance fee (or pass).
Reserve permit at least 14 days in
advance. (Developed campgrounds are
$8 and up.)
Hike into spectacular canyon where
walls rise over 1 mile (1.6 k) above river
or into "High Sierras." See giant sequoia,
pine, and fir among lakes, waterfalls,
and meadows.
Bears–store food carefully and pack out
all trash.

## KINGSLEY GLADE

Mendocino NF (916) 824-5196
State map: E2
From PASKENTA, take FR 23N01
(Toomes Camp) W to
FR 24N01–total of 22 miles
(35.2 k). (Also see Three Prong.)

FREE but choose a chore.
Open Jun 1 – Oct 31; dry camping
off-season.
6 close, open sites.
Water, pit toilets, tables, fire rings.
In woods at edge of meadow.
Enjoy getaway for picnicking and relaxing. Find Thomes Creek 5 miles (8 k)
away for swimming and fishing.
No trash arrangements (pack it out).
14-day limit. Hunting in season.
4500 ft (1350 m)

## KIRCH FLAT

Sierra NF (209) 467-5155
State map: K4
From TRIMMER, go E on
FR 11S12 (Trimmer Springs) for
18 miles (28.8 k).
FREE but choose a chore.
Open All Year.
19 close, open sites.
Pit toilets, tables, fire rings.
On King River.
Splash in water, kayak and canoe, or
fish. Mountain bike, hike, and explore.
NO water. 14-day/22-ft limits. Hot.
1100 ft (330 m)

## LA PANZA

Los Padres NF (805) 683-6711
State map: M1
From SANTA MARGARITA, go
E on CA 58 for 1 mile (1.6 k).
Turn Right (S) on CR 21 (Poza
Rd) and drive about 16 miles (25.6 k).
Continue on FR 29S01 (CR M3093) about
10 miles (16 k). Check out **Queen Bee**
camp another mile away, bearing Right
on FR 29S18.
FREE, $5 in hunting season.
Open All Year.
16 close, open sites.
Water, pit toilets, tables, grills, fire rings.
In woodlands of La Panza hills.
Picnic and relax. Take hike into nearby
Machesna Mountain Wilderness.
No trash facilities. 14-day/16-ft limits.
2800 ft (840 m)

▲ ▲ ▲ ▲ ▲ ▲ ▲ ▲ ▲ ▲ ▲ ▲ ▲ ▲ ▲ ▲ ▲ ▲ ▲ ▲ ▲ ▲

## LAKE ALPINE BACKPACKERS CAMP

Stanislaus NF (209) 795-1381
State map: H3
From HATHAWAY PINES, head
E on CA 4 for 34 miles (54.4 k).
Park across road at Chickaree
Picnic Area or at Silver Valley Trailhead.
**FREE** but choose a chore.
Open Jun–Oct; dry camping off-season.
6 close, open tent sites.
Water, flush toilets, tables, grills, fire rings, pay phone, boat ramp, store.
At layover/packup/cleanup spot for backpackers.
No trash arrangements. 1-night limit.

## LAKE ISABELLA-Auxiliary Dam

Sequoia NF (619) 376-3781
State map: N4
From LAKE ISABELLA, go 1 mile
(1.6 k) E on CA 178.
**FREE** but choose a chore.
Open All Year.
Undesignated open sites.
Water, flush toilets, showers, tables, grills, fire rings, dump station.
Along shore in informal setting–often used as overflow.
Swim, boat, waterski, and fish.
14-day limit.
2800 ft (840 m)

## LAKE ISABELLA-Camp 9 (Eastside)

Sequoia NF (619) 376-3781
State map: N4
From KERNVILLE, go S on Sierra
Way for 5 miles (8 k).
**FREE** but choose a chore.
Open All Year.
109 close, open sites. Water, flush toilets, tables, grills, fire rings, dump station.
On north shore of North Fork of Kern River near lake.
Swimming, boating, waterskiing, and fishing. Biking too.
14-day limit.
2800 ft (840 m)

## LAKE KAWEAH-Lime Kiln

COE (209) 597-2301
State map: L4
From VISALIA, go 25 miles (40 k)
E on CA 198. Full-service **Horse
Creek** on South side of lake is
$10/night.
**FREE** but choose a chore.
Open All Year.
10 close, open sites. Chemical toilets.
On west end of lake in Sierra Nevada foothills.
Enjoy water activities May–Jun before irrigation drains water. Find boat ramps and rentals at private operations around shore. Visit Sequoia NP, only 40 miles (64 k) away.
Trash problem from many lake visitors–keep it clean.
700 ft (210 m)

## LAKE STERLING

Tahoe NF (916) 265-4538
State map: G4
Exit off I-80 at CISCO GROVE.
Go W on North frontage road.
Turn Right (N) on Rattlesnake
Rd. Drive 6.5 miles (10.4 k) on steep road–no trailers. (Also see Woodchuck.)
**FREE** but choose a chore.
Open Jun 15–Sep 30; camping allowed off-season.
6 close, open sites. Lake water only (must purify), pit toilets, tables.
Hiking and fishing possibilities.
No trash arrangements. 14-day limit.
7000 ft (2100 m)

## LAKESIDE

Tahoe NF (916) 994-3401
State map: G5
From TRUCKEE, go 4.5 miles
(7.2 k) N on CA 49. Turn Right
(E) on FR 18N47 and drive
.5 mile (800 m). (Also see Annie
McCloud.)
**FREE** but choose a chore.
Open Apr 1–Oct 31; camping off-season.
30 sites.
Water from reservoir (must purify), pit toilets, concrete boat ramp nearby.
On northwest shore of Prosser Reservoir.

▲ ▲ ▲ ▲ ▲ ▲ ▲ ▲ ▲ ▲ ▲ ▲ ▲ ▲ ▲ ▲ ▲ ▲ ▲ ▲ ▲ ▲ ▲ ▲ ▲ ▲

Swimming, boating, and fishing.
14-day limit.
5700 ft (1710 m)

## LAKEVIEW

Mendocino NF (707) 275-2361
State map: E2
From LUCERNE, go 2 miles
(3.2 k) N on CA 20. Turn Right
(E) on FH 8 and drive 5 miles
(8 k). Turn Right (S) on FR 15N09 and go
3 miles (4.8 k).
FREE but choose a chore.
Open May 1–Oct 15.
9 close, open sites. Water, pit toilets,
tables, grills (3), fire rings.
At scenic spot overlooking Clear Lake
and offering varied area to explore.
14-day/16-ft limits.
3400 ft (1020 m)

## LANDSLIDE

Sequoia NF (209) 338-2251
State map: L4
From GRANT GROVE, take
CA 180 N for 6 miles (9.6 k).
Turn Right (SE) on Hume Lake
Rd (FR 13S01) and go 7 miles (11.2 k).
Can also access Hume Lake-Tenmile
Creek Rd from Generals Hwy SE of
Grant Grove. (Also see Upper Tenmile.)
FREE but choose a chore.
Open May 15–Oct 15.
9 (6 tent-only) sites.
Pit toilets, tables, fire rings.
On Tenmile Creek near Hume Lake and
Kings Canyon NP.
Create base for exploring and hiking.
NO water. 14-day/16-ft limits.
5800 ft (1740 m)

## LASSEN CREEK

Modoc NF (916) 279-6116
State map: C7
Halfway between NEW PINE
CREEK and DAVIS CREEK on
US 395, find FR heading E at
Willow Creek Ranch Dump (that's right).
Go E on road through gravel intersection
and follow signs.
FREE but choose a chore.
Open Memorial Day–Labor Day; camp-
ing allowed off-season.
Undesignated, scattered, open sites.
Pit toilets, tables, fire rings.
Amidst rolling hills, in open meadow
with stream and few shade trees.
Rockhound, birdwatch, take photo-
graphs, and fish.
NO water/trash facilities. 14-day limit.

## LASSEN VOLCANIC NP-Juniper Lake

(916) 595-4444
State map: E4
From CHESTER, take rough dirt
road N for 13 miles (20.8 k)–not
recommended for trailers. (Also
see Warner Creek.)
FREE but $5 entrance fee (or pass). Also,
**free** backcountry permits available at
ranger stations.
Open May–Sep; off-season allowed.
18 close, open sites.
Pit toilets, tables, fire rings.
On east side of Juniper Lake far away
from main part of park.
Swim in lake (for hardy). Paddle a
canoe. Hike on trails to explore primal
volcanic landscape.
Treat lake water. 14-day limit.
6792 ft (2037 m)

## LATOUR SF

(916) 225-2418
State map: D4
From WHITMORE, take Bateman
Rd E about 13 miles (20.8 k).
FREE but choose a chore.
Open Jun 1–Oct 15.
5 sites, scattered. Water (may need
treating), pit toilets, tables, fire rings.
At three mini-camps with such names as
**Old Station, Old Cow,** and **Cow Creek.**
Mountain bike and hike this little-used
region. Picnic and relax.
14-day limit. Hunting in season.
5700 ft (1710 m)

## LAUFMAN

Plumas NF (916) 253-2223
State map: F5
From US 395 in MILFORD, head
S then turn Left (SW) going up
Milford Grade for 3 miles

▲ ▲ ▲ ▲ ▲ ▲ ▲ ▲ ▲ ▲ ▲ ▲ ▲ ▲ ▲ ▲ ▲ ▲ ▲ ▲ ▲ ▲ ▲ ▲ ▲ ▲ ▲

(4.8 k)−not recommended for trailers or RVs. Camp .5 mile (800 m) beyond ranger station.
**FREE** but choose a chore.
Open All Year.
8 close, open sites.
Pit toilets, tables, grills.
In high-desert, mixed-conifer forest along intermittent stream.
Picnic and do nothing.
NO water/trash facilities. 14-day limit.
5100 ft (1530 m)

## LAVA BEDS NM-Backcountry
(916) 667-2292
State map: C5
Take CA 139 S from TULELAKE about 20 miles (32 k). Turn Right (W) at signs. Go 15 miles (24 k).
(Also see A H Hogue and Medicine.)
**FREE** but $3 entrance fee (or pass).
**(Indian Well Campground costs $6.)**
Inquire about **free** backcountry permit at Visitor Center. Open All Year.
In surreal landscape with immense subterranean lava tubes and ice caves. On surface, find volcanic beds, forests, even historical sites (Modoc Indian War). Nearby Tule Lake NWR provides excellent birdwatching.
4500 ft (1350 m)

## LAVA CAMP
Modoc NF (916) 299-3215
State map: C5
From LOOKOUT, go 15 miles (24 k) N on CR 91. Turn Left (NW) on unpaved FR 42N03 and continue about 9 miles (14.4 k).
**FREE** but choose a chore.
Open All Year.
12 scattered, screened sites.
Pit toilets, tables, fire rings.
In remote, wild landscape for those who enjoy natural settings.
Relax, kick-back, read, and meditate.
NO water.
4000 ft (1200 m)

## LIGHTNING TREE
Plumas NF (916) 283-2050
State map: F5
From PORTOLA, take CA 70 E for 2.5 miles (4 k). Turn Left (NW) on CR 112 (Grizzly) and go 10 miles (16 k). (Also see Crocker.)
**FREE** but choose a chore.
Open May 1−Nov 15.
56 close, open RV sites.
Tables, fire rings.
In forest on NE shore of Lake Davis.
Fish, swim, or boat.
NO water, trash, or toilet facilities. 7-day limit. No ATVs.
5800 ft (1740 m)

## LILY LAKE
Modoc NF (916) 279-6116
State map: C7
From NEW PINE CREEK, take unpaved FR E off US 395. Climb steeply for 5.5 miles (8.8 k). (Also see Cave Lake.)
**FREE** but choose a chore.
Open Memorial Day−Labor Day; camping allowed off-season.
6 scattered, open sites.
Pit toilets, tables, fire rings.
On remote, small lake with steep terrain and limited shade.
Boat (no motors) and fish. Relax or find photographic studies.
NO water (at Cave Lake). No trash arrangements. 14-day limit.
6600 ft (1980 m)

## LIMESTONE
Sequoia NF (619) 376-3781
State map: M4
From KERNVILLE, take Sierra Way (CR PM99) N along Kern River for 19.5 miles (31.2 k).
**FREE** but choose a chore.
Open Apr 10−Nov 30.
22 close, open sites.
Pit toilets, tables, fire rings.
On river.
Besides fishing, try walking nature trail or mountain biking.
NO water. 14-day/22-ft limits.
3800 ft (1140 m)

▲ ▲ ▲ ▲ ▲ ▲ ▲ ▲ ▲ ▲ ▲ ▲ ▲ ▲ ▲ ▲ ▲ ▲ ▲ ▲ ▲ ▲ ▲ ▲ ▲ ▲ ▲ ▲ ▲ ▲ ▲ ▲

## LITTLE DOE

Mendocino NF (707) 983-6118
State map: D2
From COVELLO, go NE on
CA 162 for 2.5 miles (4 k). Turn
Right (E) on CR 338 and drive
11 miles (17.6 k). Turn Left (N) on
FR 1N02 (Indian Dick) and go 11.5 miles
(18.4 k). (Also see Hammerhorn Lake.)
FREE but choose a chore.
Open May 15–Oct 31.
22 close, open sites.
Pit toilets, tables, fire rings.
Near mountain lake in mixed conifers.
Fish, picnic, and relax. Explore and hike
into scenic surroundings. Take photos.
NO water/trash arrangements (pack it
out). 14-day/16-ft limits.
3600 ft (1080 m)

## LITTLE JACKASS

Sierra NF (209) 467-5155
State map: J4
From NORTH FORK, go SE on
CR 225 for 4.5 miles (7.2 k). Turn
Left (NE) on FR 81 (Minarets)
and drive about 34.5 miles (54.2 k) Turn
Right on FR 6S22 and go 1 mile (1.6 k).
(See Soda Springs and Sweet Water.)
FREE but choose a chore.
Open Apr–Oct.
5 close, open sites.
Pit toilets, tables, fire rings.
On creek perfect to wade and fish.
NO water. 14-day/16-ft limits.
4800 ft (1440 m)

## LITTLE NORTH FORK

Klamath NF (916) 467-5757
State map: B3
From ETNA, take FR 2E01 (Etna-
Somes Bar Rd) W for 25 miles
(40 k)–watch for logging trucks.
(Also see Idlewild.)
FREE but choose a chore.
Open All Year.
4 close, open sites.
Pit toilets, tables, fire rings.
In cool shade along Little North
Fork–near confluence with North Fork
of Salmon River.
Hike Little North Fork and Garden

Gulch trails to Chimney Rock and
English Peak areas with their lakes and
ridges. Swimming and fishing too.
NO water. 14-day limit.
2000 ft (600 m)

## LITTLE NORTH FORK

Plumas NF (916) 534-6500
State map: F4
From BERRY CREEK, take
Oroville-Quincy Rd (CR 27562)
NE for 13.8 miles (22.1 k). Go NE
on unpaved FR 23N60 for 5.5 miles
(8.8 k)–pickups and autos only. (Also
see Milsap Bar and Rogers Cow Camp.)
FREE but choose a chore.
Open All Year.
8 close, open tent sites.
Pit toilets, tables, fire rings.
On North Fork of Feather River.
Relax and observe nature in hard-to-find
getaway.
NO water/trash facilities. 14-day limit.
4000 ft (1200 m)

## LITTLE SANDY

Sierra NF (209) 467-5155
State map: J4
From FISH CAMP, take CA 41 S
for .5 mile (800 m). Turn Left (E)
on Jackson Rd (FR 6S07) and
drive about 8 miles (12.8 k). (Also see
Big Sandy and Fresno Dome.)
FREE but choose a chore.
Open May–Oct.
10 close, open sites.
Pit toilets, tables, fire rings.
Create base along Big Creek not far from
entrance to Yosemite NP. Explore!
NO water. 14-day/16-ft limits.
6000 ft (1800 m)

## LIVE OAK

Angeles NF (818) 899-1900
State map: P3
In SANTA CLARITA, turn off
CA 14 Freeway E at Sand
Canyon. Go S for 4 miles
(6.4 k)–just outside city limits.
$5. Open All Year.
Undesignated sites.
Water, pit toilets, tables, fire rings.

In stand of California live oaks.
When creek runs in winter and spring,
observe wildlife. Hike too.
14-day limit.
2100 ft (630 m)

## LONE PINE

COE (707) 462-7581
State map: E1
Take Lake Mendocino Exit off
US 101 N of UKIAH and go
1.25 miles (2.25 k) E.
FREE but choose a chore.
Open All Year.
6 close, open sites. Water, chemical
toilets, tables, grills, fire rings.
At one land-accessible, free area on Lake
Mendocino.
Enjoy full range of water-based activities:
swim (watch those biting fish), boat, and
fish. Trails to hike too.
14-day limit. Quiet hours. No firewood
cutting. Leash pets.
710 ft (213 m)

## LONG MEADOW

Sequoia NF (209) 548-6503
State map: M4
From CALIFORNIA HOT
SPRINGS, take CR 56 E for
2.5 miles (4 k). Turn Left (N) on
CR M50. Go 12 miles (19.2 k). Turn on
FR FH90. Go NW for 3.5 miles (5.6 k).
FREE but choose a chore.
Open May 15–Oct 15.
6 close, open sites.
Pit toilets, tables, fire rings.
On stream near giant sequoias.
Journey to Redwoods Meadow and walk
Trail of the Hundred Giants. Reflect.
NO water. 14-day/16-ft limits.
6500 ft (1950 m)

## LONG VALLEY

BLM (619) 256-8313
State map: M5
From INYOKERN, take US 395 N
for 15 miles (24 k). Turn Left
(NW) on CR 152 (Nine Mile
Canyon). Go 26 miles (41.6 k), bearing
Left at ranger station. (Also see Chimney
Creek, Fish Creek, Kennedy, and Troy

Meadow.)
FREE but choose a chore.
Open All Year.
13 close, open sites.
Water, pit toilets, tables, fire rings.
Near South Fork of Kern River and
Dome Wilderness.
Explore some wild territory.
No trash arrangements. 14-day limit.
5200 ft (1560 m)

## LOVERS CAMP

Klamath NF (916) 468-5351
State map: B3
From FORT JONES, take Scott
River Rd W for 15 miles (24 k).
Turn Left (S) on one-lane, steep,
gravel FR and go 8 miles (12.8 k).
FREE but choose a chore.
Open Memorial Day–Oct 15; camping
allowed off-season.
13 close, open sites.
Pit toilets, tables, fire rings, corral.
With great name but mixed ratings.
Visually rewarding plus trails to Marble
Mountain Wilderness. (Horses lessen
sensory appeal).
NO water (piped water for livestock
only). No trash facilities. 14-day limit.
Holiday crowds. Hunting in season.
4500 ft (1350 m)

## LOVERS LEAP

Eldorado NF (916) 644-6048
State map: H4
From Twin Bridges (near VADE),
take US 50 W 2.75 miles (4.4 k).
FREE but choose a chore.
Open May 15–Oct 31.
12 tent sites.
Water, pit toilets, tables, fire rings.
On river plus rock climbing and hiking.
14-day limit. No trailers.
5800 ft (1740 m)

## LOWER & UPPER
## LEE VINING CREEK

Mono County Parks
(619) 934-7504
State map: J5
From LEE VINING, go W for
5 miles (8 k) on CA 120 (Tioga

▲ ▲ ▲ ▲ ▲ ▲ ▲ ▲ ▲ ▲ ▲ ▲ ▲ ▲ ▲ ▲ ▲ ▲ ▲ ▲ ▲ ▲ ▲ ▲ ▲ ▲ ▲

Rd) toward Yosemite. (See Aspen Grove, Cattleguard, and Lundy.)
$5. Open Apr–Nov.
116 close, open sites. Stream water only (must purify), chemical toilets, tables.
In aspen grove.
Hiking and fishing opportunities.
NO water.
7000 ft (2100 m)

## LOWER & UPPER SHAKE

Angeles NF (818) 574-1613
State map: O3
From LAKE HUGHES, go NW on Elizabeth Lake-Pine Canyon Rd for 5 miles (8 k). Find two camps, with Lower Shake being tent-only. Upper Shake is .5 mile (800 m) up road. (Also see Atmore Meadows and Sawmill Meadows.)
FREE but choose a chore.
Open May 1–Nov 30.
18 (5 tent-only) close, open sites.
Pit toilets, tables, fire rings.
Picnic and relax or hike trails, including Pacific Crest.
NO water/trash arrangements (pack it out). 14-day/22-ft limits.
4150 ft (1245 m)

## LOWER CARLTON FLAT

Tahoe NF (916) 288-3231
State map: F4
From CAMPTONVILLE, go NE on CA 49 about 9.5 miles (15.2 k)–about 1 mile (1.6 k) beyond bridge.
FREE but choose a chore.
Open All Year.
Undesignated, undeveloped sites. River water only (must purify), pit toilets.
On North Yuba River.
Pan for gold, fish, swim, and hike here.
14-day limit.
2200 ft (660 m)

## LOWER CHIQUITO

Sierra NF (209) 467-5155
State map: J4
From NORTH FORK, go SE on CR 225 for 4.5 miles (7.2 k). Turn Left (NE) on FR 4S81 (Minarets)

and drive about 36 miles (57.6 k). Turn Left (N) on FR 6S71. Go 3.5 miles (5.6 k).
FREE but choose a chore.
Open May–Oct.
17 close, open sites.
Pit toilets, tables, fire rings.
On stream.
Fish and relax. Wander over to Mammoth Pool Reservoir.
NO water. 14-day/16-ft limits.
4900 ft (1470 m)

## LOWER NYE

Mendocino NF (707) 275-2361
State map: E2
From UPPER LAKE, go N on CR 1N02 for 17 miles (27.2 k). Turn Right (E) on FR 18N01 and drive 6 miles (9.6 k). Turn Left (N) on FR 18N04 for 14 miles (22.4 k). (Also see Bear Creek and Deer Valley.)
FREE but choose a chore.
Open May 1–Sep 15; camping off-season.
6 close, open sites.
Pit toilets, tables, grills, fire rings.
On quiet, remote creek.
Take advantage of seclusion. Enjoy good trails in vicinity.
NO water/trash arrangements (pack it out). 14-day/16-ft limits.
3300 ft (990 m)

## LOWER RUSH CREEK

Modoc NF (916) 299-3215
State map: D5
From ADIN, go 7.5 miles (12 k) NE on CA 299 to FR 40N39. Turn Right (E) and go .5 mile (800 m).
(Tenters, see Upper Rush Creek.)
$5. Open May–Oct.
10 close, open sites.
Water, pit toilets, tables, grills, fire rings.
Next to pleasing creek.
Nice fishing and relaxing.
14-day/22-ft limits.
4500 ft (1350 m)

▲ ▲ ▲ ▲ ▲ ▲ ▲ ▲ ▲ ▲ ▲ ▲ ▲ ▲ ▲ ▲ ▲ ▲ ▲ ▲ ▲ ▲ ▲ ▲

## LUMBERYARD

Eldorado NF (209) 295-4421
State map: H4
From PIONEER, take CA 88 E for
20 miles (32 k). Turn Right (S) on
Ellis Rd.
FREE but choose a chore.
Open May 1–Nov 15.
5 close, open sites.
Pit toilets, tables, fire rings.
Close to streams and lakes with fishing.
NO water. 14-day/16-ft limits.
6200 ft (1860 m)

## LUMSDEN & LUMSDEN BRIDGE

Stanislaus NF (209) 962-7825
State map: I4
From GROVELAND, drive E on
CA 120 for 7.5 miles (12 k). Turn
Left (N) on Ferretti Rd. Go about
1 mile (1.6 k) to unpaved Lumsden Rd.
Turn Right (E) and go 5 rough miles
(8 k)–Lumsden Bridge is another 2 miles
(3.2 k). (Also see South Fork.)
FREE but choose a chore.
Open All Year.
23 (10 at Lumsden Bridge) close,
open sites. Pit toilets, tables, fire rings.
In oak and pine on Tuolumne River.
Popular for kayaking (white-water),
fishing, and hiking.
NO water/trash arrangements.
14-day/16-ft limits. Crowded holidays
and fishing-season opening.
1500 ft (450 m)

## LUNDY

Mono County Parks
(619) 934-7504
State map: J5
From LEE VINING, go N for
5 miles (8 k) on US 395. (Also see
Aspen Grove, Cattleguard, as well as
Lower & Upper Lee Vining Creek.)
$5. Open Apr–Oct.
51 close, open sites.
Stream water only (must be purified),
chemical toilets, tables
In pines with interesting scenery nearby.
Hiking, some fishing possibilities.
NO water.
7000 ft (2100 m)

## LUPINE

Angeles NF (805) 944-2187
State map: P4
From WRIGHTWOOD, take CA 2
W about 4.5 miles (7.2 k) to
Inspiration Point. Turn E on
rough, dirt Blue Ridge Rd and drive
8 miles (12.8 k)–last 5 are tough. (Also
see Blue Ridge, Cabin Flats, and Guffy.)
FREE but choose a chore.
Open Jun 1–Oct 31.
8 scattered, open tent sites.
Pit toilets, tables, fire rings.
Along Prairie Fork Creek near bottom of
Blue Ridge Rd.
Hike, watch birds, or do nothing.
NO water/trash arrangements. 14-day
limit. Crowded summers and holidays.
6500 ft (1950 m)

## MADRONE

Shasta-Trinity NF (916) 275-1587
State map: C4
From MONTGOMERY CREEK
(off CA 299), take unpaved
Fenders Ferry Rd N for 21.5 miles
(34.4 k).
FREE but choose a chore.
Open All Year.
13 close, open sites.
Pit toilets, tables, fire rings.
On Squaw Creek.
Take short walks or adventurous back-
pack trips. Go fishing.
NO water/trash arrangements (pack it
out). 14-day/16-ft limits.
1500 ft (450 m)

## MARTIN'S DAIRY

Klamath NF (916) 398-4391
State map: B4
From MACDOEL, go S on CA 97
for 12 miles (19.2 k) to FR 46N10.
Turn Right (W) and go 11 miles
(17.6 k) to FR 46N12. Go 2 miles (3.2 k).
Camp is .2 mile (320 m) to Right.
FREE but choose a chore.
Open May–Oct; dry camping off-season.
7 scattered, open sites.
Water, pit toilets, tables, grills.
In aspen grove at headwaters of Little
Shasta with distant view of Mt Shasta

and wildflower meadow.
Enjoy natural beauty, stocked trout
fishing, plus fantastic mountain biking.
No trash arrangements. 14-day limit.
Crowded hunting season.
6000 ft (1800 m)

## MATTHEWS CREEK

Klamath NF (916) 467-5757
State map: C3
From CALLAHAN, take FH 93
SW toward CECILVILLE for
37 miles (59.2 k). (See East Fork.)
$4. Open May 25–Sep 15; dry camping
off-season.
13 scattered, open sites with some
screening.
Water, pit toilets, tables, grills, fire rings.
Near South Fork of Salmon River.
River swimming fun in deep pools.
Fishing and canoeing/kayaking popular.
14-day/26-ft limits.
1760 ft (528 m)

## MATTOLE

BLM (707) 462-3873
State map: C1
From just S of PETROLIA, take
Lighthouse Rd W to end–about
5.5 miles (8.8 k) of steep, winding
access–no large vehicles.
FREE but choose a chore.
Open All Year.
6 close, open sites.
Water, pit toilets, tables, grills, fire rings.
On Pacific Ocean at river's mouth.
Explore scenic area.
14-day limit.
100 ft (30 m)

## MAYACMUS

BLM (707) 462-3873
State map: E1
From UKIAH, go 1.5 miles (2.4 k)
E on Talmadge Rd. Turn Right
(S) on Eastside Rd and drive
.3 mile (480 m). Turn Left (E) on Mill
Creek Rd and go 2.5 miles (4 k). Turn
Left (N) on Mendo Rock Rd, go 7 miles
(11.2 k). (Also see Sheldon Creek.)
FREE but choose a chore.
Open All Year.

10 tent sites.
Water, pit toilets, tables, fire rings.
On creek in mountains near Russian
River–part of Cow Mountain RA.
Explore, fish, or just get away.
14-day limit. Closed during inclement
weather. Hunting in season.
2500 ft (750 m)

## MEADOWVIEW

Plumas NF (916) 253-2223
State map: F5
From US 395 in DOYLE, go W up
Doyle Grade 7 miles
(11.2 k)–best for small vehicles.
FREE but choose a chore.
Open All Year.
6 close, open sites.
Pit toilets, tables, grills.
In pine forest surrounded by
meadow–close to state game refuge.
Observe and reflect.
NO water/trash facilities. 14-day limit.
6100 ft (1830 m)

## MEDICINE

Modoc NF (916) 667-2246
State map: C5
Take CA 139 S from TULELAKE
for 20 miles (32 k). Turn Right
(W) on CR 97. Drive 25 miles
(40 k). (Also see A H Hogue.)
$5, $5/extra vehicle.
Open May 15–Oct 30; dry camping
off-season.
21 scattered, open sites.
Water, pit toilets, tables, grills, fire rings,
boat ramp, beach.
Near fascinating lake in old volcanic
cone ringed by conifers.
Explore area. Windsurf, swim, fish, boat,
or just lie on beach.
14-day/22-ft limits. Region colder than
you anticipate.
6700 ft (2010 m)

## MESSENGER FLATS WALK-IN

Angeles NF (818) 899-1900
State map: P4
Go E of ACTON on CA 14 to
Angles Forest Hwy heading S.
Drive to Mill Creek Summit and

▲ ▲ ▲ ▲ ▲ ▲ ▲ ▲ ▲ ▲ ▲ ▲ ▲ ▲ ▲ ▲ ▲ ▲ ▲ ▲ ▲ ▲ ▲ ▲ ▲ ▲ ▲

turn Right on Santa Clara Divide. Drive 7 miles (11.2 k). Walk-in about 20–400 ft (6–120 m). Pass FR 4N24 with its primitive **Big Buck Walk-In** (5 sites). **$5.** Open All Year.
10 close, open tent sites.
Water, pit toilets, tables, fire rings.
Along forest ridge.
Hiking and observing nature.
14-day limit. Hunting in season.
5900 ft (1770 m)

## MID HILLS

BLM (619) 326-3896
State map: P7
From NEEDLES, head W on I-40 for 41 miles (65.6 k) to ESSEX Exit. Go N (Right) for 10 miles (16 k) to Black Canyon Rd. Again go N for 17 miles (27.2 k)–only 1 mile (1.6 k) is paved. Turn Left (W) on Wild Horse Canyon Rd and go 2 rough miles (3.2 k)–subject to flash flooding. (Also see Hole-in-the-Wall.)
**$4.** Open All Year.
26 scattered, screened sites.
Water, pit toilets, tables, grills, fire rings.
In pinyon-juniper woodland.
Enjoy excellent hiking options to explore East Mojave ecosystem.
14-day limit. No large vehicles.
5600 ft (1680 m)

## MIDDLE FORK

Stanislaus NF (209) 962-7825
State map: I4
From GROVELAND, drive E on CA 120 about 20 miles (32 k). Turn Left (N) on rough Evergreen Rd and go about 5 miles (8 k). (Also see Carlon.)
**FREE** but choose a chore.
Open Apr 15–Nov 1.
23 close, open sites.
Pit toilets, tables, grills.
Among oak and pine trees on banks of Middle Fork of Tuolumne River.
Good fishing and hiking.
NO water. 14-day/16-ft limits. Crowded holidays.
4700 ft (1410 m)

## MIDDLE LION

Los Padres NF (805) 683-6711
State map: O2
From OJAI, go N on CA 33 for 15 miles (24 k). Turn Right (E) on Sespe River Rd (FR 7N03). Drive 5.5 miles (8.8 k). Turn Right (S) on FR 22W06. Go 1 mile (1.6 k).
**FREE** but choose a chore.
Open All Year.
11 close, open sites.
Pit toilets, tables, fire rings.
At creekside alternative to more developed and expensive **Lion's Canyon** and **Rose Creek** camps.
Splash in creek. Explore Rose Creek Falls and Willette Hot Springs.
NO water/trash arrangements (pack it out). 14-day/16-ft limits.
3300 ft (990 m)

## MIDDLE SANTA YNEZ

Los Padres NF (805) 683-6711
State map: O2
From SANTA BARBARA, go N on CA 154 for 8 miles (12.8 k). Turn Right (E) on FR 5N12 (East Camino Cielo) and go 22 miles (35.2 k) always bearing Left. Turn Left on FR 5N15 and go 8 miles (12.8 k). (Also see Juncal, Mono, and P-Bar Flat.)
**FREE** but choose a chore.
Open All Year.
9 close, open sites.
Pit toilets, tables, fire rings.
On banks of Santa Ynez River.
Picnic and relax. Fish or mountain bike.
NO water/trash facilities. 14-day limit.
Trailers not advised on treacherous road.
1800 ft (540 m)

## MILL CREEK

Mendocino NF (916) 963-3128
State map: F2
From STONYFORD, go W on CR 18N01 (Fouts Spring) for 8.8 miles (14.1 k). Turn Right (N) on FR 18N03. (See Fouts and North Fork.)
**FREE** but choose a chore.
Open All Year.
6 close, open sites.

Pit toilets, tables, fire rings.
On stream running full in spring.
Hike extensive trail system.
NO water/trash facilities. 14-day/22-ft
limits. Motorcycles.
1700 ft (510 m)

## MILL CREEK

Stanislaus NF (209) 965-3434
State map: I3
From SONORA, drive 43 miles
(68.8 k) E on CA 108. Turn on
FR 5N21. Go 1.5 miles (2.4 k).
FREE but choose a chore.
Open Apr–Nov; off-season allowed.
17 close, open sites.
Pit toilets, tables, grills, fire rings.
In pines on seasonal Mill Creek.
Fishing, hiking, and relaxing here.
NO water. 14-day/22-ft limits. Crowded.
6200 ft (1860 m)

## MILL CREEK FALLS

Modoc NF (916) 279-6116
State map: D6
From LIKELY, go E on CR 64
(Jess Valley Rd). When road forks
in 9 miles (14.4 k), bear Left and
continue to end of pavement.
$5. Open Memorial Day–Labor Day; dry
camping off-season.
19 scattered, open sites.
Water, pit toilets, tables, fire rings.
At shady location in steep, rocky, terrain.
Play on rock formations. Hike to falls, to
Clear Lake, or into Warner Wilderness.
Fish too.
14-day limit.
5700 ft (1710 m)

## MILLARD WALK-IN

Angeles NF (818) 578-1079
State map: P4
From I-10, take Lake Avenue N
to Loma Alta Drive. Turn Left
(W) and go to Chaney Trail. Take
Chaney until it deadends in parking
area. Walk 100 yards to sites near
stream. For more remote feeling, hike
3 miles (4.8 k) to Mt Lowe camp–located
at abandoned resort.
FREE but choose a chore.

Open All Year.
6 close, open tent sites.
Water, pit toilets, tables, grills.
In scattered oaks near seasonal waterfall.
Hike several good trails nearby.
14-day limit. Crowded.
1900 ft (570 m)

## MILSAP BAR

Plumas NF (916) 534-6500
State map: F4
From BRUSH CREEK, follow
signs leading S from town, then
SE on rough, unpaved Milsap Bar
Rd for 8 miles (12.8 k). (Also see Little
North Fork and Rogers Cow Camp.)
FREE but choose a chore.
Open All Year.
20 close, screened sites.
Pit toilets, tables, grills, fire rings.
In shade along beautiful Middle Fork of
Feather River.
Kayak wild and scenic river or fish. Hike
South Branch to falls. Just relax.
NO water/trash facilities. 14-day limit.
1600 ft (480 m)

## MOKELUMNE, MOORE CREEK, & WHITE AZALEA

Eldorado NF (209) 295-4251
State map: H4
From PIONEER, take CA 88 E for
20 miles (32 k). Turn Right (S) on
steep, narrow FR 8N25 (Ellis) and
go about 10 miles (16 k)–numbers will
change to FR 8N05 and 8N50.
FREE but choose a chore.
Open May 1–Nov 15.
22 sites (8 tent-only at Mokelumne; 8 at
Moore Creek; 6 tent-only at White
Azalea). Pit toilets, tables, fire rings.
Along shore of Mokelumne River.
Find scenic spots to swim and fish.
NO water. 14-day limit.
3200 ft (960 m)

## MONO

Los Padres NF (805) 683-6711
State map: O2
From SANTA BARBARA, go N
on CA 154 for 8 miles (12.8 k).
Turn Right (E) on FR 5N12 (East

Camino Cielo). Go 22 miles (35.2 k) bearing Left. Turn Left on FR 5N15. Drive 13 miles (20.8 k). (Also see Juncal, Middle Santa Ynez, and P-Bar Flat.)
FREE but choose a chore.
Open All Year.
9 close, open sites.
Pit toilets, tables, fire rings.
On stream above Gibraltar Reservoir.
Picnic, relax, fish, or mountain bike.
NO water/trash facilities. 14-day limit.
No trailers on treacherous road.
1800 ft (540 m)

## MONTE CRISTO
Angeles NF (818) 899-1900
State map: P3
SE of SAN FERNANDO on Foothills Blvd near Sunland Park, head E on Oro Vista which becomes Big Tujunga Rd. At intersection with Angeles Forest Hwy, turn Left (N) and go 5 miles (8 k). If too crowded, there's Fall Creek Walk-In near Hidden Springs Picnic Area.
$5. Open All Year.
19 close, open sites.
Water, pit toilets, tables, grills.
In woods on stream.
Swimming and bicycling popular.
14-day limit.
3100 ft (930 m)

## MOSES GULCH
Mountain Home SF
(209) 539-2855
State map: M4
From SPRINGVILLE, go W for 30 miles (48 k) on Bear Creek Rd—steep and winding with last 5 miles (8 k) unpaved. (Also see Frasier Mill, Hedrick Pond, Hidden Falls, Shake Camp, and Sunset Point.)
FREE but choose a chore.
Open May–Nov.
10 close, open sites with some screening.
Water, pit toilets, tables, fire rings.
In mixed conifers next to Wishon Fork of Tule River.
Explore magnificent region. Spot wildlife especially waterfowl. Fish.
14-day limit. No trailers. Crowded and

noisy weekends and holidays.
5500 ft (1650 m)

## MOSQUITO LAKES
Stanislaus NF (209) 795-1381
State map: H3
From HATHAWAY PINES, head E on CA 4 for 40 miles (64 k). (Also see Pacific Valley.)
FREE but choose a chore.
Open Jun–Sep; camping off-season.
8 close, open tent sites.
Chemical toilets, tables, fire rings.
Across road from two small lakes.
Good lake fishing plus hiking in vicinity.
NO water/trash arrangements. 14-day limit. Not recommended for trailers.
8600 ft (2580 m)

## MT PACIFICO
Angeles NF (818) 578-1079
State map: P4
From I-10, take CA 2 (Angeles Crest Hwy) N about 27 miles (43.2 k)–2 miles (3.2 k) past Newcomb's Ranch. Turn Left (N) on Santa Clara Divide Rd and go 3 miles (4.8 k) to Mt Pacifico Rd (FR 3N17). Drive 3 more miles (4.8 k) on road for high clearance vehicles.
FREE but choose a chore.
Open May 15–Nov 15; camping allowed off-season.
7 scattered, open tent sites.
Pit toilets, tables, fire rings.
Atop Mt Pacifico amidst pines and large boulders with night view of city lights.
Wonderful hiking along Pacific Crest Trail. Good winter skiing too.
NO water/trash arrangements. 14-day limit. Crowded.
7100 ft (2130 m)

## MULE MOUNTAIN LTVA
BLM (619) 256-8313
State map: S7
From BLYTHE, go W on I-10 for 14 miles (22.4 k) to Wiley's Well Rd Exit. Head S on gravel road for 9 miles (14.4 k).
FREE for 14 days. After that, purchase $25 annual permit.

▲ ▲ ▲ ▲ ▲ ▲ ▲ ▲ ▲ ▲ ▲ ▲ ▲ ▲ ▲ ▲ ▲ ▲ ▲ ▲ ▲ ▲ ▲ ▲ ▲ ▲ ▲ ▲ ▲

Open All Year.
450 scattered, open sites in three areas:
**Coon Hollow** (25), **Mule Mountain**
(undesignated), and **Wiley's Well** (21).
Water (at Wiley's Well Rest Area),
flush/pit toilets, tables.
In desert mountain topography.
Excellent rockhounding (geodes) and
hiking opportunities.
Be prepared for self-sufficiency.

## MULEBRIDGE

Klamath NF (916) 467-5757
State map: B3
From ETNA, take Etna-Somes Bar
Rd (FR 2E01) W for 20 miles
(32 k) to Idlewild Camp. Follow
North Fork upstream for 2 miles
(3.2 k)—watch for logging trucks.
FREE but choose a chore.
Open May–Oct; camping off-season.
2 scattered, open sites.
Pit toilet, table, corral.
At trailhead for North Fork Trail.
Explore Marble Mountain Wilderness.
NO water. 14-day limit.
2800 ft (840 m)

## NACIMIENTO

Los Padres NF (805) 683-6711
State map: K1
From JOLON, head W on
US MIL (CR 4004-Nacimiento)
through military area for 12 miles
(19.2 k). Continue NW on FR 22S01 for
5 miles (8 k). (Also see Ponderosa.)
$5. Open All Year.
17 (9 tent-only) close, open sites.
Water, pit toilets, tables, grills, fire rings.
Close to Ventana Wilderness.
Hike in wilderness. Bike or do nothing.
14-day/22-ft limits.
1700 ft (510 m)

## NAVAJO

Los Padres NF (805) 683-6711
State map: M1
From SANTA MARGARITA, go
E on CA 58 for 1 mile (1.6 k).
Turn Right (S) on CR 21 (Poza
Rd) and drive about 18 miles (28.8 k).
Turn Left (NE) on FR 29S02 and drive

about 6 miles (9.6 k). If this isn't isolated
enough, look for primitive **Friis Camp**
about 1 mile (1.6 k) N.
FREE but choose a chore.
Open All Year.
3 close, open sites.
Water (may need to be treated), pit
toilets, tables, fire rings.
In woodlands of La Panza hills.
Picnic and relax. Hike on several trails.
No trash arrangements (pack it out).
14-day/16-ft limits. Hunting in season.
2200 ft (660 m)

## NELDER GROVE

Sierra NF (209) 467-5155
State map: J4
From OAKHURST, take CA 41 N
about 5 miles (8 k) to FR 10 (Sky
Ranch Rd). Turn Right (NE) and
go about 8 miles (12.8 k). Watch for turn
onto narrow, steep entrance road
(FR 6S47 or FR 6S90) toward grove.
(Also see Kelty Meadow and Soquel.)
FREE but choose a chore.
Open May–Oct.
8 close, open sites.
Pit toilets, tables, fire rings.
Next to Nelder Grove of Giant Sequoias.
Wonderful spot for reflection.
NO water. 14-day/16-ft limits.
5300 ft (1590 m)

## NETTLE SPRING

Los Padres NF (805) 683-6711
State map: N2
From MARICOPA, go S on
CA 33/166 for 27 miles (43.2 k),
staying Left on 33 when 166 cuts
off. Turn Left (E) on FR 8N06 (Apache
Canyon Rd) and drive 9 miles (14.4 k).
FREE but choose a chore.
Open All Year.
9 close, open sites.
Pit toilets, tables, grills, fire rings.
In remote area for 4WD adventurers.
Picnicking and hiking too.
NO water/trash facilities. 14-day limit.
4400 ft (1320 m)

▲ ▲ ▲ ▲ ▲ ▲ ▲ ▲ ▲ ▲ ▲ ▲ ▲ ▲ ▲ ▲ ▲ ▲ ▲ ▲ ▲ ▲

## NIAGARA CREEK

Stanislaus NF (209) 965-3434
State map: I3
From SONORA, go 46 miles
(73.6 k) E on CA 108. Turn on
Eagle Meadow Rd (FR 5N01) and
follow signs about 1 mile (1.6 k).
FREE but choose a chore.
Open Apr–Nov; camping off-season.
6 close, open sites.
Pit toilets, tables, grills, fire rings.
On creek under fir trees.
Good hiking on several trails. Fishing on
Donnells Lake.
NO water/trash arrangements.
14-day/22-ft limits. Crowded.
6600 ft (1980 m)

## NIRA

Los Padres NF (805) 683-6711
State map: O2
From SANTA YNEZ, head E on
Armor Ranch Rd. Crossing
CA 154 continue 1.5 miles
(2.4 k)–road turns sharply. Turn Right
on Happy Canyon Rd. Drive 17 miles
(27.2 k) to end. (Also see Cachuma.)
FREE but choose a chore.
Open All Year.
12 close, open tent sites.
Pit toilets, tables, fire rings.
On creek by trailhead into San Rafael
Wilderness.
Make short hikes or extended treks.
NO water/trash arrangements.
14-day/16-ft limits. Crowded.
2000 ft (600 m)

## NORTH FORK

Mendocino NF (916) 963-3128
State map: F2
From STONYFORD, go W on
CR 18N01 (Fouts Spring) for
8.8 miles (14.1 k). Turn Right (N)
on FR 18N03 and drive 2.2 miles (3.5 k).
(Also see Fouts and Mill Creek.)
FREE but choose a chore.
Open All Year.
6 close, open sites.
Pit toilets, tables, grills, fire rings.
On creek beneath oaks.
Hike trails. Try rockhounding.

NO water/trash arrangements (pack it
out). 14-day/16-ft limits.
1700 ft (510 m)

## NORTH SHORE

Eldorado NF (916) 644-2349
State map: H4
From POLLACK PINES, take
US 50 E for 8.5 miles (13.6 k).
Turn Left (N) on CR 17N12 (Soda
Springs-Riverton) and drive 24 miles
(38.4 k). Turn NE on CR 14N01 for
4.5 miles (7.2 k), then turn back N on
CR 13N18 for another 4 miles (6.4 k).
(Also see South Fork.)
FREE but choose a chore.
Open Jun 15–Oct 15.
15 close, open sites.
Pit toilets, tables, fire rings, boat ramp.
On shores of Loon Lake.
Swim, boat, or fish. Hike Desolation
Wilderness Trail.
NO water. 14-day limit.
6500 ft (1950 m)

## NORTHWIND

Eldorado NF (916) 644-2349
State map: H4
From POLLACK PINES, take
US 50 E for 8.5 miles (13.6 k).
Turn Left (N) on CR 17N12 (Soda
Springs-Riverton) and drive 10.5 miles
(16.8 k). Turn Right (E) on FR 11N37 for
1 mile (1.6 k). (Also see Silver Creek and
Strawberry Point.)
FREE but choose a chore.
Open Jun 1–Oct 15.
10 close, open sites.
Pit toilets, tables, fire rings, boat ramp.
On north shore of Ice House Reservoir
offering swimming, boating, and fishing.
NO water. 14-day limit.
5500 ft (1650 m)

## O'NEIL CREEK

Klamath NF (916) 465-2241
State map: B3
From SEIAD VALLEY, go E on
CA 96 for 4.7 miles (7.5 k).
FREE but choose a chore.
Open Jun 1–Nov 15; camping allowed
off-season.

▲ ▲ ▲ ▲ ▲ ▲ ▲ ▲ ▲ ▲ ▲ ▲ ▲ ▲ ▲ ▲ ▲ ▲ ▲ ▲ ▲ ▲ ▲ ▲ ▲ ▲ ▲ ▲ ▲ ▲

18 scattered, screened sites.
Pit toilets, tables, grills, fire rings.
On banks of creek.
Plan hiking or fishing expedition.
NO water (stream water) or trash
arrangements (pack it out). 14-day/22-ft
limits. Hunting in season.
1500 ft (450 m)

## OAK BOTTOM

Klamath NF (916) 627-3291
State map: B3
Take CA 96 E from SOMES BAR
for .5 mile (800 m). Turn Right on
FR 93 and go 3 miles (4.8 k).
**$4**. Open All Year.
26 scattered, open sites.
Water, pit toilets, tables, grills.
On stream.
Good swimming, canoeing/kayaking,
and fishing in Salmon River.
14-day limit.
775 ft (231 m)

## OAK FLAT

Mendocino NF (707) 275-2361
State map: E2
From POTTER VALLEY, drive
18 miles (28.8 k) NE on CA 240.
Continue NE for 3 miles (4.8 k)
on FR 20N01.
**FREE** but choose a chore.
Open May 15–Sep 30.
12 close, open sites.
Pit toilet, tables, fire rings, boat ramp.
Near Lake Pillsbury.
Wonderful area to hike or bike.
Waterski, boat, and swim too.
NO water/trash facilities. 14-day/22-ft
limits. Crowded weekends.
1810 ft (543 m)

## OAK GROVE

Shasta-Trinity NF (916) 275-1587
State map: C3
3 miles (4.8 k) S of LAKESIDE on
I-5, take Salt Creek Exit. Head W
for 2 miles (3.2 k). (Also see
Gregory Beach.)
**$3**. Open May 20–Sep 5.
43 close, open sites.
Water, flush toilets, tables, grills.

On shores of Lake Shasta.
Take time to boat, ski, swim, and fish.
14-day/16-ft limits.
1100 ft (330 m)

## OAK KNOLL

COE (209) 772-1843
State map: H3
From VALLEY SPRINGS, follow
signs to New Hogan Lake by
taking Hogan Dam Rd S about
3 miles (4.8 k). Head toward $10 Acorn
campgrounds.
**FREE** at 10 sites; **$5** at other 40.
Open Mar 1–Sep 30; dry camping
off-season.
50 close, open sites with some screening.
Water, pit toilets, tables, grills, fire rings,
boat ramp, nearby store.
In oak-covered foothills of Sierra
Nevadas, fabled mining area.
4400-acre New Hogan Lake offers
boating, skiing, swimming, and fishing.
Too, there are opportunities for hiking
(How about "River of Skulls" trail?) and
wildlife viewing (bald eagles in winter).
14-day limit. Quiet hours.
725 ft (216 m)

## OBSIDIAN

Toiyabe NF (619) 932-7070
State map: I5
From BRIDGEPORT, go N on
US 395 for 12 miles (19.2 k). Turn
Left (W) on FR 10066 and drive
3.5 miles (5.6 k).
**FREE** but choose a chore.
Open May 25–Oct 15.
14 close, open sites.
Pit toilets, tables, fire rings (scheduled to
add drinking water and fees in future).
On quiet, relaxing creek.
Enjoy fair hiking/backpacking territory.
NO water. 14-day/22-ft limits.
7800 ft (2340 m)

## OLD MILL

Mendocino NF (916) 963-3128
State map: F2
From STONYFORD, go W on
CR 18N01 (Fouts Spring) for
6 miles (9.6 k). Turn Left (S) on

▲ ▲ ▲ ▲ ▲ ▲ ▲ ▲ ▲ ▲ ▲ ▲ ▲ ▲ ▲ ▲ ▲ ▲ ▲ ▲ ▲ ▲ ▲ ▲ ▲ ▲ ▲

narrow FR 18N07 (John Smith Rd) and drive about 7 miles (11.2 k). (Also see Cedar Camp.)
**FREE** but choose a chore.
Open May 1–Nov 1; dry camping off-season.
10 (7 tent-only) close, open sites.
Water, pit toilet, tables, grills, fire rings.
Among mature pine and fir.
Savor solitude.
No trash facilities. 14-day/16-ft limits.
3700 ft (1110 m)

## OWL CANYON

BLM (619) 256-8313
State map: O5
From BARSTOW, take Fort Irwin Rd N for 8 miles (12.8 k) to Fossil Bed Rd. Turn Left (W) Follow signs next 3 miles (4.8 k).
**$4.** Open All Year.
31 scattered, open sites.
Water, pit toilets, tables, grills, fire rings, some sun shelters.
In desert with wonderful panoramas.
Excellent hiking and rockhounding plus good photo taking possibilities.
Keep place clean and quiet. Hot summers. Crowded winter holidays.
3000 ft (900 m)

## OZENA

Los Padres NF (805) 683-6711
State map: N2
From OJAI, go N on CA 33 for 36 miles (57.6 k)–just past ranger station. Turn Right on CR 9N03 (Lockwood Valley) for 1.5 miles (2.4 k). (Also see Reyes Creek.)
**FREE** but choose a chore.
Open All Year.
12 close, open sites.
Pit toilets, tables, grills, fire rings.
In valley with trails.
Find adobe ruins.
NO water/trash facilities. 14-day limit.
3600 ft (1080 m)

## P-BAR FLAT

Los Padres NF (805) 683-6711
State map: O2
From SANTA BARBARA, go N on CA 154 for 8 miles (12.8 k). Turn Right (E) on FR 5N12 (East Camino Cielo) and go 22 miles (35.2 k) always bearing Left. Turn Left on FR 5N15. Go 9.8 miles (15.7 k). (Also see Juncal, Middle Santa Ynez, and Mono.)
**FREE** but choose a chore.
Open All Year.
4 close, open sites.
Pit toilets, tables, fire rings.
On banks of Santa Ynez River.
Picnic, go fishing or mountain biking.
NO water/trash arrangements (pack it out). 14-day limit. Trailers not advised on treacherous road.
1800 ft (540 m)

## PACIFIC VALLEY

Stanislaus NF (209) 795-1381
State map: H3
From HATHAWAY PINES, head E on CA 4 for 42 miles (67.2 k). Turn Right (S) at Pacific Valley and go .25 mile (400 m). (Also see Mosquito Lakes.)
**FREE** but choose a chore.
Open Jun–Sep; camping off-season.
Undesignated scattered tent sites.
Chemical toilets, tables (9), fire rings.
At overlook onto Pacific Creek.
Fish stream or Mokelumne River.
Explore or relax. Ski in winter.
NO water/trash arrangements. 14-day limit. Not recommended for trailers.
7600 ft (2280 m)

## PACKSADDLE

Tahoe NF (916) 288-3231
State map: F4
Take CA 49 NE from SIERRA CITY for 5 miles (8 k) to Bassetts. Turn Left (N) on Gold Lake Rd and drive 1.3 miles (2.1 k). Turn Left (W) on CR 20N16 (Packer Lake Rd). Drive 2.5 miles (4 k). (Also see Berger and Diablo.)
**FREE** but choose a chore.
Open Jun 15–Oct 15; camping allowed

▲ ▲ ▲ ▲ ▲ ▲ ▲ ▲ ▲ ▲ ▲ ▲ ▲ ▲ ▲ ▲ ▲ ▲ ▲ ▲ ▲ ▲ ▲ ▲ ▲ ▲ ▲ ▲ ▲ ▲ ▲ ▲ ▲

off-season.
Undesignated sites. Pit toilets, tables at
picnic area .5 mile (800 m) away.
In rare place in Tahoe NF permitting
pack and saddle animals.
Explore area or fish creeks and lakes.
14-day limit.
5800 ft (1740 m)

## PALO VERDE

Imperial County Parks
(619) 339-4384
State map: S7
From PALO VERDE, take CA 78
S for 3 miles (4.8 k). Also check
out BLM's **Oxbow Camp** just E by
unpaved road on Colorado River.
FREE but choose a chore.
Open All Year.
25 scattered, open sites.
Flush toilets, boat ramp.
In midst of flat agricultural lands, peace-
ful 10-acre area parallel to highway and
Oxbow Lagoon. Beneath salt cedar,
cottonwood, and willow trees.
Picnic, birdwatch, boat, and fish.
NO water. 3-day limit. Holidays
crowded. Mosquitos and flies.
20 ft (6 m)

## PANORAMA

Sequoia NF (209) 548-6503
State map: M4
From CALIFORNIA HOT
SPRINGS, take CR 56 E for
4 miles (6.4 k). Turn Right (S) on
FR 23S05 and go 9 miles (14.4 k). Turn
SE on FR 23S16. Drive 6.25 miles (10 k).
(Also see Frog Meadow.)
FREE but choose a chore.
Open Jun 15–Oct 15.
10 close, open sites.
Pit toilets, tables, fire rings.
In isolated spot–picnic and relax.
Explore scenic area. Take photographs.
14-day/16-ft limits. Hunting in season.
6800 ft (2040 m)

## PANTHER MEADOWS WALK-IN

Shasta-Trinity NF (916) 926-4511
State map: C4
From MT SHASTA, take Everitt
Memorial Hwy NE for 13.5 miles
(21.6 k).
FREE but choose a chore.
Open Jun 15–Sep 30; camping
off-season.
4 tent sites. Pit toilets, tables.
In beautiful area often used as base to
ascend Mt Shasta (at least 2 days).
NO water.
7400 ft (2220 m)

## PATTERSON

Modoc NF (916) 279-6116
State map: D6
From LIKELY, go E on Jess
Valley Rd. When road forks in
about 9 miles (14.4 k), bear Right
and continue 16 miles (25.6 k).
FREE but choose a chore.
Open Memorial Day–Labor Day; dry
camping off-season.
5 scattered, open sites.
Water, pit toilets, tables, grills.
In pines at site of historic Patterson
Guard Station. Excellent access to South
Warner Wilderness for serious exploring
in pristine environment.
No trash arrangements (pack it out).
7200 ft (2160 m)

## PEPPERDINE

Modoc NF (916) 279-6116
State map: D6
In ALTURAS, find CR 56 heading
E. Go 13 miles (20.8 k) to Modoc
NF boundary. Turn on FR 42N31
(Parker Creek Rd). After 6 miles (9.6 k),
take Pepperdine access.
FREE but choose a chore.
Open Memorial Day–Labor Day; dry
camping off-season.
5 scattered, open sites. Water, pit toilets,
tables, grills, fire rings, corrals.
In pines near Warner Wilderness Trail.
No trash arrangements (pack it out).
14-day limit. Hunting in season.
6680 ft (2004 m)

▲ ▲ ▲ ▲ ▲ ▲ ▲ ▲ ▲ ▲ ▲ ▲ ▲ ▲ ▲ ▲ ▲ ▲ ▲ ▲ ▲ ▲ ▲ ▲

## PEPPERMINT

Sequoia NF (209) 539-2607
State map: L4
From SPRINGVILLE, take
CA 190 E for 26.5 miles (42.4 k).
Turn Right (S) on CR FH90 and
drive 3 miles (4.8 k). Turn Left (E) on
CR 21S07 and go .5 mile (800 m).
FREE but choose a chore.
Open May 15–Nov 15.
19 close, open sites.
Pit toilets, tables, fire rings.
Along Peppermint Creek.
Swim and fish creek. Hike nearby trails.
NO water. 14-day/22-ft limits.
7100 ft (2130 m)

## PHILPOT

Shasta-Trinity NF (916) 628-5227
State map: D2
Go 1 mile W of PEANUT on
CA 36 (watch for FR).
FREE but choose a chore.
Open May 20–Oct 15; dry camping
off-season.
6 sites.
Water, pit toilets, tables, fire rings.
Next to stream.
Fish creek and explore surrounding area.
14-day limit. No large vehicles.
2600 ft (780 m)

## PIGEON FLAT WALK-IN

Stanislaus NF (209) 965-3434
State map: I3
From SONORA, go 54 miles
(86.4 k) E on CA 108. Sites are
200 ft (60 m) from parking lot.
FREE but choose a chore.
Open Apr–Nov; camping off-season.
6 close, open tent sites.
Pit toilets, tables, fire rings.
In bit of shade along Stanislaus River.
Take trail to Column of the Giants. Try
more adventurous hiking or mountain
biking. Go fishing.
NO water (or treat stream water). 14-day
limit. Crowded.
6000 ft (1800 m)

## PIGEON POINT

Shasta-Trinity NF (916) 623-6106
State map: C2
From HELENA, go about 2 miles
(3.2 k) W on CA 299.
$2. Open May 20–Oct 30; dry
camping off-season.
10 scattered, open sites. &
Water, pit toilets, tables, grills.
With swimming beach on Trinity River.
Good hiking and fishing too.
14-day/25-ft limits.
1100 ft (330 m)

## PINE MOUNTAIN

Los Padres NF (805) 683-6711
State map: O2
From OJAI, go N on CA 33 for
33 miles (52.8 k). Turn Right on
FR 6N06 (Reyes Peak). Drive
3.5 miles (5.4 k). (Also see Reyes Peak.)
FREE but choose a chore.
Open Apr 1–Dec 31.
6 close, open sites.
Pit toilets, tables, fire rings.
In scenic setting near several springs.
Grab forest map and hike.
NO water (springs are close). No trash
arrangements. 14-day/16-ft limits.
6800 ft (2040 m)

## PINE SPRING

Los Padres NF (805) 683-6711
State map: O3
From FRAZIER PARK, go W on
FH 95 (Frazier Mountain Park
Rd) for 3.5 miles (5.6 k). Bear Left
(SW) in Lake of the Woods on CR 9N03
(Lockwood Valley Rd). Drive 10.5 miles
(16.8 k). Turn Left (S) on FR 7N03 and
go 2.75 miles (4.4 k). Turn Right (W) on
FR 7N03A. Go 1 mile (1.6 k). (Also see
Half Moon and Thorne Meadows.)
FREE but choose a chore.
Open May 15–Nov 15.
10 close, open sites.
Pit toilets, tables, fire rings.
At quiet, remote getaway with biking
and hiking possibilities.
NO water/trash arrangements (pack it
out). 14-day/16-ft limits.
5800 ft (1740 m)

## PINYON FLAT

San Bernardino NF
(714) 659-2117
State map: R5
Take CA 74 E from MOUNTAIN
CENTER for 21 miles (33.6 k).
$5. Open All Year.
19 close, screened sites. &
Water, pit toilets, tables, grills.
In high-desert pinyon-juniper vegetation.
Hike trails. Picnic and relax.
14-day/15-ft limits.
4200 ft (1260 m)

## PLUM VALLEY

Modoc NF (916) 279-6116
State map: C6
From DAVIS CREEK, go just N
of town on US 395 and take
paved road to Right (E). Signed
gravel access road will quickly become
rough. Bounce along for 3 miles (4.8 k).
FREE but choose a chore.
Open Memorial Day – Labor Day;
camping allowed off-season.
15 scattered, open sites.
Pit toilets, tables, fire rings.
In pine grove with nearby stream.
Fishing and relaxing.
NO water/trash facilities. 14-day limit.
5600 ft (1680 m)

## POINT REYES NS-Walk-In Camps

(415) 663-1092
State map: G1
Pick up permit and map at Point
Reyes Station, .5 mile (800 m) S
of OLEMA.
FREE; reservations required (up to 2
months in advance). Open All Year.
45 (3 group) close, open tent sites.
Pit toilets, tables, grills (for charcoal),
food lockers.
Explore awe-inspiring shoreline of
imposing bluffs, sandy beaches, grassy
meadows, wooded valleys, and frequent
fog. View impressive array of marine
life. Attend weekend ranger programs.
NO water/trash arrangements (pack it
out). Ticks, poison oak, mooching skunks
and raccoons.

▲ **Coast** (14 sites) is easy 2-mile (3.2-k)
walk to exposed, windy bluff with
nearby beach.
▲ **Glen** (12 sites) is relatively flat,
4.6-mile (7.4-k) walk to protected,
wooded valley on Bear Valley Trail.
▲ **Sky** (12 sites) is easy 1.7-mile (2.7-k)
walk from Sky Trailhead to highest point
with nice view of Drakes Bay.
▲ **Wildcat** (7 sites) is 6.5-mile (10.4-k)
undulating walk from Bear Valley to
grassy meadow. (From Fivebrooks, it's
shorter, but steeper). Follow stream to
beach.
100 ft (30 m)

## PONDEROSA

Los Padres NF (805) 683-6711
State map: K1
From JOLON, head W on
US MIL (CR 4004-Nacimiento)
through military area for 12 miles
(19.2 k). Continue NW on FR 22S01 for
2 miles (3.2 k). (Also see Nacimiento.)
$5. Open All Year.
23 close, open sites.
Water, pit toilets, tables, grills, fire rings.
Near Ventana Wilderness.
Take hikes and bike trips or do nothing.
14-day/22-ft limits.
1500 ft (450 m)

## POPPY WALK/BOAT-IN

Tahoe NF (916) 367-2224
State map: G4
From FORESTHILL, go E on
FR 96 (Mosquito Ridge Rd) for
41.5 miles (66.4 k). Park at
McGuire Picnic Area (north shore) and
walk (or boat) 1 mile (1.6 k) to site.
FREE but choose a chore.
Open May 25 – Nov 30; camping allowed
off-season.
12 close, open sites. Reservoir water
must be purified (or carry water from
McGuire Picnic Area), pit toilets, tables.
On French Meadows Reservoir.
Swim, boat, and fish. Also, hike and
view wildlife in designated game refuge.
No trash arrangements. 14-day limit.
5300 ft (1590 m)

▲ ▲ ▲ ▲ ▲ ▲ ▲ ▲ ▲ ▲ ▲ ▲ ▲ ▲ ▲ ▲ ▲ ▲ ▲ ▲ ▲ ▲ ▲ ▲ ▲

## PORTAL FOREBOY

Sierra NF (209) 893-2111
State map: K4
From LAKESHORE (above
Huntington Lake), take FR 80
(Kaiser Pass Rd) E for 13 miles
(12.8 k). (Also see Bolsillo, Florence Lake,
Sample Meadow, and Ward Lake.)
FREE but choose a chore.
Open May 15–Oct 15; camping allowed
off-season.
11 scattered, open tent sites.
Pit toilets, tables, fire rings.
In sandy area within walking distance of
Foreboy Lake.
Hike to other lakes. Canoe, raft, fish. Or
just relax.
NO water/trash facilities. 14-day/20-ft
limits. Crowded holidays. Hunting in
season. Bears.
7200 ft (2160 m)

## PREACHER MEADOW

Shasta-Trinity NF (916) 623-2121
State map: C3
From TRINITY CENTER, go
1.5 miles (2.4 k) SW on CA 3 to
FR 36N98. Camp is .25 mile
(400 m) down access road.
$5. Open May 15–Oct 31.
45 close, open sites.
Water, pit toilets, tables, fire rings.
Close to Trinity Lake.
Hike to enjoy nearby streams.
14-day/32-ft limits.
2900 ft (870 m)

## RAMHORN SPRINGS

BLM (916) 257-0456
State map: E6
From SUSANVILLE, take US 395
N for 41 miles (65.6 k) to Patch
Rd. Turn Right (E) and drive
3 miles (4.8 k) to camp.
FREE but choose a chore.
Open All Year.
12 close, open sites. Water, pit toilets,
tables, fire rings, corrals.
In juniper-sage-covered mountains with
wild horses.
Explore and watch wildlife (deer, ante-
lope, rabbit, grouse).

14-day limit. Crowded hunting season.
5500 ft (1650 m)

## RED BANK

Klamath NF (916) 467-5757
State map: B3
From ETNA, take FR 2E01 (Etna-
Somes Bar Rd) W for 33 miles
(52.8 k)–watch for logging trucks.
(See Little North Fork.)
FREE but choose a chore.
Open May–Oct; camping off-season.
4 scattered, open sites.
Pit toilets, tables, fire rings.
Near North Fork of Salmon River.
Enjoy times to swim, fish, and hike.
NO water. 14-day limit.
1760 ft (528 m)

## RED TAIL

Jackson SF (707) 964-5674
State map: E1
About 1 mile (1.6 k) S of FORT
BRAGG, take CA 20 E for
5.9 miles (9.4 k). Watch for
signed dirt road on Left. Turn N. In
.3 mile (500 m), take Left fork on
Road 300 heading W (350 goes to Right).
In 2.3 miles (3.7 k), approach sites. (See
Camp One, Dunlap, and Jackson SF-
Scattered.)
FREE but choose a chore.
Open All Year.
10 close, screened sites. River water must
be treated, pit toilets, tables, fire rings.
Among second-growth redwood and fir
(cut in 1800s) on banks of Noyo River.
Splash in shallow river (no fishing in
these spawning grounds). Seek solitude
among trees and along trails.
14-day limit. Crowded holidays.
300 ft (90 m)

## REDWOOD NP

(707) 464-6101
State map: A2–B2
In NW corner of state, find prime
examples of world's tallest trees
in foggy coastal valleys.
FREE permits available at trailheads or
visitor centers.
Open All Year.

▲ ▲ ▲ ▲ ▲ ▲ ▲ ▲ ▲ ▲ ▲ ▲ ▲ ▲ ▲ ▲ ▲ ▲ ▲ ▲ ▲ ▲ ▲ ▲ ▲ ▲

▲ **DeMartin Walk-In**
Take trailhead at milepost 14.4 of US 101 near Wilson Creek Bridge. Walk 2 miles (3.2 k).
10 scattered, screened tent sites.
Water, chemical toilet, tables.
On hillside with meadows and forest. Explore and photograph magnificent area of coast.
No trash arrangements (pack it out).
Bears, ticks, and poison oak.
750 ft (225 m)

▲ **Flint Ridge Walk-In**
From KLAMATH, take US 101 S across Klamath River Bridge. Turn Right (W) on Klamath Beach Rd and drive 'til oceanview ridge of river mouth. Walk-in .25 mile (400 m).
10 scattered, screened tent sites.
Water, chemical toilet, tables, fire rings.
On high, grassy slope offering views of distant ocean and spruce-redwood forest. On Coastal Trail, explore and photograph this special ecology.
No trash arrangements. Bears, ticks, and poison oak.
500 ft (150 m)

▲ **Nickel Creek Walk-In**
Take US 101 S from CRESCENT CITY for 3 miles (4.8 k). Turn Right (W) on Enderts Beach Rd (signed "Redwood National Park-Crescent Beach"). Trail at end of road. Walk .5 mile (800 m).
5 close, screened tent sites. Chemical toilet, tables, fire rings, food storage.
In valley with scrub vegetation (redwoods up trail), stream, rocky beach, and tidal pools.
Observe and photograph life-filled coastal environment along northern end of Coastal Trail.
No trash arrangements. Bears, ticks, and poison oak.
40 ft (12 m)

▲ **Redwood Creek Walk-In**
Form ORICK, go 2 miles (3.2 k) N to Bald Hills Rd. Follow signs to Redwood Creek Trailhead. Walk as short as .5 mile (800 m). Permit required (obtain at Orick Information Center).
Accessible Jun–Sep; camping off-season.
Undesignated scattered, screened tent sites. Water (needs treating).
Along rocky creekbanks beneath redwoods.
Enjoy fishing, hiking, and photo taking.
No trash or toilet facilities (be prepared; keep area clean). Bears, ticks, poison oak.
25 ft (6 m)

**RESERVOIR C**
Modoc NF (916) 233-4611
State map: C6
From ALTURAS, head W on CA 299 for 1 mile (1.6 k) to dirt Crowder Flat Rd. Turn Right (N) and drive about 13 total miles (20.8 k)–follow signs. (Also see Big Sage.)
FREE but choose a chore.
Open All Year.
Undesignated sites.
Pit toilets, tables, fire rings, boat ramp.
Among sagebrush, cheatgrass, and rock next to fluctuating reservoir.
Fishing and relaxing at out-of-way spot.
NO water/trash arrangements
4800 ft (1440 m)

**REYES CREEK**
Los Padres NF (805) 683-6711
State map: O2
From OJAI, go N on CA 33 for 36 miles (57.6 k)–just past ranger station. Turn Right on CR 9N03 (Lockwood Valley) for 3 miles (4.8 k). Turn Right (S) on FR 7N11 and go 2 miles (3.2 k). (Also see Ozena.)
$5. Open All Year.
19 close, open sites.
Water, pit toilets, tables, grills, fire rings.
On creek with fishing and hiking trails.
Find old adobe ruins.
14-day/22-ft limits.
4000 ft (1200 m)

**REYES PEAK**
Los Padres NF (805) 683-6711
State map: O2
From OJAI, go N on CA 33 for 33 miles (52.8 k). Turn Right on FR 6N06 (Reyes Peak). Drive 4 miles (6.4 k). (Also see Pine Mountain.)
FREE but choose a chore.

▲ ▲ ▲ ▲ ▲ ▲ ▲ ▲ ▲ ▲ ▲ ▲ ▲ ▲ ▲ ▲ ▲ ▲ ▲ ▲ ▲ ▲ ▲ ▲ ▲ ▲

Open Apr 1–Dec 31.
7 close, open sites.
Pit toilets, tables, fire rings.
Near several springs.
Good hiking territory–grab forest map.
NO water (springs are close) or trash
arrangements. 14-day/16-ft limits.
6800 ft (2040 m)

## RIPSTEIN

Shasta-Trinity NF (916) 623-6106
State map: C3
From JUNCTION CITY, go N on
unpaved Canyon Creek Rd
(CR P401) for 14.75 miles (23.6 k).
FREE but choose a chore.
Open Jul 1–Oct 1; camping off-season.
10 (6 tent-only) close, open sites.
Pit toilets, tables, grills.
Enjoy Canyon Creek area. Hike up creek
toward Shasta-Trinity Alps Wilderness.
NO water. 14-day/16-ft limits.
Abandoned mines.
2600 ft (780 m)

## ROAD'S END

Inyo NF (619) 876-5442
State map: L5
From LONE PINE, take CR 15S02
(Whitney Portal Rd) W for
3.5 miles (5.6 k). Go SW on
CR 15S01 (Horseshoe Meadow) to
end–18.5 miles (29.6 k). (Also see Tuttle
Creek.)
FREE but choose a chore.
Open May 15–Nov 15.
15 close, open sites. Pit toilets.
Next to John Muir Wilderness near Mt
Whitney.
Make forays into wilderness.
NO water. 14-day/16-ft limits.
9400 ft (2820 m)

## ROBINSON FLAT

Tahoe NF (916) 367-2224
State map: G4
From FORESTHILL, take narrow,
winding Foresthill Divide Rd NW
for 27 miles (43.2 k). (Also see
Secret House.)
FREE but choose a chore.
Open Jun 15–Sep 30; camping allowed

off-season.
5 close, open sites. Creek water must be
purified, pit toilets, tables.
On remote creek.
Hiking and exploring here.
No trash facilities. 14-day/16-ft limits.
6800 ft (2040 m)

## ROCKY

Lassen NF (916) 336-5521
State map: D4
Drive 4.5 miles (7.2 k) N on
CA 89 from intersection of CA 44
and 89.
FREE but choose a chore.
Open Apr 30–Oct 15.
8 close, open tent sites.
Pit toilets, tables, grills, fire rings.
Next to creek under conifers and oaks.
Fish in Hat Creek or hike on trails.
NO water. 14-day limit. Generator rules.
Crowded.
4000 ft (1200 m)

## ROCKY CABIN

Mendocino NF (916) 824-5196
State map: E2
From PASKENTA, take FR 23N01
(Toomes Camp) NW to
FR 24N04. Turn Right and go to
FR 24N41. Turn Left and drive to
FR 24N38. Turn Right to camp–total of
24 miles (38.4 k). (Also see Whitlock.)
FREE but choose a chore.
Open May 1–Oct 31; dry camping
off-season.
4 close, open sites.
Water, pit toilets, tables, grills, fire rings.
At quiet getaway for relaxing.
No trash arrangements (pack it out).
14-day limit. Hunting in season.
6250 ft (1875 m)

## ROCKY POINT-BUCKS BAY

BLM (916) 257-0456
State map: E5
From SUSANVILLE, take CA 139
N for 31 miles (49.6 k) to CR A2.
Turn Left (W) and follow signs 6
rough, unpaved miles (9.6 k) to Bucks
Bay.
FREE but choose a chore.

Open All Year.
Undesignated sites. Chemical/pit toilets, undeveloped boat ramp.
On pine-juniper-covered peninsula jutting into Eagle Lake.
Swim, waterski, boat, and fish.
NO water/trash facilities. 14-day limit.
5100 ft (1530 m)

## ROCKY REST

Tahoe NF (916) 288-3231
State map: F4
From CAMPTONVILLE, go NE on CA 49 for 10 miles (16 k).
FREE but choose a chore.
Open All Year.
Undeveloped area. River water only (must purify), pit toilets.
On North Yuba River.
Pan for gold, fish, swim, and hike.
14-day limit.
2200 ft (660 m)

## ROGERS COW CAMP

Plumas NF (916) 534-6500
State map: F4
From BRUSH CREEK, continue NE on Oroville-Quincy Rd for 8 miles (12.8 k)–half is unpaved.
(See Milsap Bar and Little North Fork.)
FREE but choose a chore.
Open All Year.
5 close, open tent sites.
Pit toilets, tables, fire rings.
Along stream.
Find solitude. Pick berries when ripe.
NO water/trash arrangements. 14-day limit. Hunting in season.
4000 ft (1200 m)

## SAGEHEN

Tahoe NF (916) 994-3401
State map: G5
From TRUCKEE, go 9 miles (14.4 k) on CA 89 to Sagehen Summit turnoff. Turn Left (W) and go 2 miles (3.2 k).
FREE but choose a chore.
Open Jun 1–Oct 15; camping off-season.
10 close, open sites. Creek water must be purified, pit toilets, tables.
On banks of Sagehen Creek.

Fish creek or just relax.
No trash arrangements. 14-day limit.
6500 ft (1950 m)

## SAMPLE MEADOW

Sierra NF (209) 877-3138
State map: K4
From LAKESHORE (above Huntington Lake), take FR 80 (Kaiser Pass Rd) E for 9 miles (14.4 k). Turn Left on dirt FR 5 (Sample turnoff) for 7 miles (11.2 k). (Also see Bolsillo, Florence Lake, Portal Foreboy, and Ward Lake.)
FREE but choose a chore.
Open May 15–Oct 15; camping allowed off-season.
16 close, open tent sites.
Pit toilets, tables, fire rings.
Within walking distance of Kaiser Creek.
Take wonderful hikes to surrounding lakes. Observe wildlife too.
NO water/trash facilities. 14-day/25-ft limits. Crowded holidays. Hunting in season. Bears.
7800 ft (2340 m)

## SAND FLAT

Stanislaus NF (209) 965-3434
State map: I3
From SONORA, go 50 miles (80 k) E on CA 108. Turn Left (N) on Clark Fork Rd and drive 5 miles (8 k).
$5. Open Apr–Nov.
61 (7 tent-only) close, open sites within 100 ft of parking.
Water, pit toilets, tables, fire rings.
Near Clark Fork River on open flat.
Swim and fish. Hike to Iceberg Meadow.
14-day limit. Crowded. Bears.
7400 ft (2220 m)

## SARAH TOTTEN

Klamath NF (916) 465-2241
State map: B3
Just outside HAMBURG, drive .25 mile (400 m) E on CA 96.
$4. Open May 15–Nov 15; dry camping off-season.
17 scattered, screened sites, 1 group site for $10. Water, pit toilets, tables, grills,

fire rings, pay phone.
On banks of Klamath River.
Canoe, raft, swim, and fish.
14-day limit. Crowded.
2400 ft (720 m)

## SAWMILL FLAT

Sierra NF (209) 467-5155
State map: K4
From SHAVER LAKE, take
CA 168 S to Dinkey Creek Rd.
Drive E for 12 miles (19.2 k).
Turn Right (SE) on FR 40 (McKinley
Grove Rd) and go 13 miles (20.8 k). Turn
S on FR 11S12. Go 3 miles (4.8 k). (Also
see Buck Meadow and Gigantea.)
FREE but choose a chore.
Open May–Oct.
10 close, open sites.
Pit toilets, tables, fire rings.
In Teakettle Experimental Area.
Hike to explore area. Swim, boat, and
fish at nearby lake.
NO water. 14-day/22-ft limits.
6700 ft (2010 m)

## SAWMILL MEADOWS

Angeles NF (818) 574-1613
State map: O3
From LAKE HUGHES, go W on
CR 8N03 (Elizabeth Lake Rd)
about 5.5 miles (8.8 k). Continue
on FR 7N23 for 4.5 miles (7.2 k). (Also
see Atmore Meadows as well as Lower
& Upper Shake.)
FREE but choose a chore.
Open May 1–Nov 30.
9 close, open sites.
Pit toilets, tables, fire rings.
Hike area trails, including Pacific Crest.
NO water/trash arrangements (pack it
out). 14-day/22-ft limits.
5200 ft (1560 m)

## SAWMILL WALK-IN

Inyo NF (619) 647-6525
State map: J5
From LEE VINING, head W on
CA 120 for 10 miles (16 k). Turn
Right (N) on FR 1N04 (Saddlebag
Lake) and drive 1.5 miles (2.4 k). (Also
see Junction.)

FREE but choose a chore.
Open Jun 1–Oct 15.
9 close, open tent sites.
Chemical toilets, tables, fire rings.
Near Yosemite NP in gorgeous high
country. Enjoy fantastic hiking
throughout Tioga region–Hoover
Wilderness and Hall Natural Area (trail
from camp).
NO water. 14-day limit.
9800 ft (2940 m)

## SCOTT MOUNTAIN

Shasta-Trinity NF (916) 623-2121
State map: C3
From TRINITY CENTER, go
24 miles (38.4 k) N on CA 3.
FREE but choose a chore.
Open All Year.
7 close, open tent sites. Pit toilets, tables.
Along Pacific Crest Trail and near
Shasta-Trinity Alps Wilderness.
Hike here.
NO water. 14-day limit.
5400 ft (1620 m)

## SCOTTS FLAT

Shasta-Trinity NF (916) 628-5227
State map: D2
From FOREST GLEN, go 1 mile
(1.6 k) W on CA 36 to Hell's Gate
Campground. Follow dirt road
.5 mile (800 m) out of camp. (Also see
Forest Glen.)
FREE but choose a chore.
Open May 20–Oct 15; dry camping
off-season.
10 close, open sites.
Water, pit toilets, tables, fire rings, beach.
On South Fork of Trinity.
Enjoy river activities plus serious hiking.
14-day/20-ft limits.
2300 ft (690 m)

## SECRET HOUSE

Tahoe NF (916) 367-2224
State map: G4
From FORESTHILL, take narrow,
winding Foresthill Divide Rd NW
for 19 miles (30.4 k). (Also see
Robinson Flat.)
FREE but choose a chore.

Open Jun 15–Sep 30; camping allowed off-season.
2 close, open sites. Pit toilets, tables.
Next to road in heavily forested area.
Picnicking, relaxing, and walking.
NO water/trash arrangements (pack it out). 14-day/16-ft limits.
5400 ft (1620 m)

## SEQUOIA NP

(209) 565-3134
State map: L4
Among giant trees surrounded by high Sierras, feel humble.
$5 entrance fee (or pass). Also, free backcountry permits available by mail at least 7 days in advance.

▲ **Atwell Mill**
Just N of THREE RIVERS on CA 198, turn Right (E) on Mineral King Rd and drive 20 miles (32 k).
$4. Open Spring–mid Nov.
23 close, open tent sites.
Water, pit toilets, tables, grills, fire rings.
On Atwell Creek.
Explore park. Enjoy beautiful, natural surroundings.
14-day limit. Quiet hours. No large vehicles.
6650 ft (1995 m)

▲ **Cold Springs.**
Just N of THREE RIVERS on CA 198, turn Right (E) on Mineral King Rd and drive 25 miles (40 k).
$4. Open Spring–mid Nov.
37 close, open tent sites.
Water, pit toilets, tables, grills, fire rings.
Along Kaweah River.
Walk to one of high-country lakes.
Watch for wildlife.
14-day limit. No large vehicles. Quiet hours.
7500 ft (2250 m)

▲ **South Fork**
Just S of THREE RIVERS on CA 198, turn E on South Fork Dr and go about 23 miles (36.8 k) to end of road.
$4. Open mid May–Oct; dry camping off-season.
13 close, open tent sites.
Water, pit toilets, tables, grills, fire rings.
On Kaweah River.

Create base for day hikes or longer back-country treks into park.
14-day limit. Quiet hours. RVs and trailers not recommended.
3600 ft (1080 m)

## SHADOW CREEK

Klamath NF (916) 467-5757
State map: C3
From CALLAHAN, take FH 93 SW toward CECILVILLE for 23 miles (36.8 k). (Also see East Fork or Trail Creek.)
$4. Open Jun 1–Oct 15; dry camping off-season.
10 scattered, open sites.
Water, pit toilets, tables, grills, fire rings.
In mixed-conifer forest with creek.
Take Deacon Lee Trail to Russian Wilderness and Carter Meadow. Backpack into Trinity Alps Wilderness. Swim, relax, and enjoy tranquil setting.
14-day limit.
2900 ft (870 m)

## SHAFTER

Klamath NF (916) 398-4391
State map: B5
From MACDOEL, go S on CA 97 for 3.75 miles (6 k) to Ball Mountain Rd. Turn Left (E) and go 2.25 miles (3.6 k) to CR 8Q01 (Tennant). Turn Right (S) and drive 5.3 miles (8.5 k).
FREE but choose a chore.
Open All Year.
10 scattered, open sites.
Water, pit toilets, tables, grills, fire rings.
In ponderosa pine next to Butte Creek and lush spring wildflower meadow.
Go fishing. View and photograph wildflowers.
14-day limit. Crowded hunting season.
4300 ft (1290 m)

## SHAKE CAMP

Mountain Home SF
(209) 539-2855
State map: M4
From SPRINGVILLE, go W for 27 miles (43.2 k) on Bear Creek Rd–steep and winding. (Also see Frasier

Mill, Hedrick Pond, Hidden Falls, Moses
Gulch, and Sunset Point.)
**FREE** but choose a chore.
Open May–Nov.
11 close, open sites.
Water, pit toilets, tables, fire rings.
On flat area near pack station.
Take off and explore region.
14-day limit. Crowded and noisy.
6500 ft (1950 m)

## SHELDON CREEK
BLM (707) 462-3873
State map: F1
From HOPLAND, go 3 miles
(4.8 k) E on CA 175. Turn Right
(S) on Toll Rd and go 8 miles
(12.8 k). (Also see Mayacmus.)
**FREE** but choose a chore.
Open All Year.
10 tent sites.
Water, pit toilets, tables, fire rings.
By creek in hilly, wooded area, part of
Cow Mountain RA.
Find nice spot for picnic.
14-day limit. Hunting in season.
2500 ft (750 m)

## SIERRA
Tahoe NF (916) 288-3231
State map: F4
Go 7 miles (11.2 k) NE on CA 49
from SIERRA CITY.
**FREE** but choose a chore.
Open Jun 15–Oct 15; camping allowed
off-season.
16 (9 tent-only) close, open sites.
River water (must be purified), pit
toilets, tables, grills.
On North Yuba River.
Gold pan or fish river. Visit nearby
historic mining operations.
14-day limit.
5600 ft (1680 m)

## SILVER CREEK
Eldorado NF (916) 644-2349
State map: H4
From POLLACK PINES, take
US 50 E for 8.5 miles (13.6 k).
Turn Left (N) on CR 17N12 (Soda
Springs-Riverton) and drive about

9 miles (14.4 k). (Also see Northwind
and Strawberry Point.)
**FREE** but choose a chore.
Open Jun 1–Oct 15.
11 tent sites. Pit toilets, tables, fire rings.
Beside beautiful creek.
Swimming, boating, and fishing at
nearby Ice House Reservoir.
NO water. 14-day limit. No trailers.
5200 ft (1560 m)

## SILVER LAKE
Plumas NF (916) 283-0555
State map: F4
From QUINCY, head W on Bucks
Lake Rd for 7 miles (11.2 k). Turn
Right (N) on Silver Lake Rd. Go
7 miles (11.2 k). (Also see Grizzly Creek.)
**FREE** but choose a chore.
Open May 1 – Oct 31; camping
off-season.
8 scattered, screened sites. Water (must
treat), pit toilets, tables, grills, fire rings.
On scenic lake.
Within two miles, access Bucks Lake
Wilderness and other trails. Canoe lake
(no swimming). Relax.
No trash facilities. 14-day/20-ft limits.
Crowded weekends. Bears.
5800 ft (1740 m)

## SKILLMAN
Tahoe NF (916) 265-4538
State map: G4
From NEVADA CITY, go E on
CA 20 for 15 miles (24 k).
**$5.** Open May 23–Sep 30; dry
camping off-season.
16 close, open sites.
Water, pit toilets, tables, grills.
Near South Yuba River.
Pan for gold or view scenery.
14-day/22-ft limits.
4400 ft (1320 m)

## SNAG LAKE
Tahoe NF (916) 288-3231
State map: F4
Take CA 49 NE from SIERRA
CITY for 5 miles (8 k) to Gold
Lake Rd at Bassetts. Turn Left (N)
and drive 5 miles (8 k)–no trailers.

▲ ▲ ▲ ▲ ▲ ▲ ▲ ▲ ▲ ▲ ▲ ▲ ▲ ▲ ▲ ▲ ▲ ▲ ▲ ▲ ▲ ▲ ▲ ▲ ▲ ▲ ▲

**FREE** but choose a chore.
Open Jun 1–Oct 1; camping off-season.
16 close, open sites. Lake water only
(must be purified), pit toilets, tables.
On banks of good fishing lake.
Just down road, find Gold Lake with
more fishing, boating (no motors), and
swimming (brrr).
14-day limit.
6600 ft (1980 m)

## SNAKE LAKE

Plumas NF (916) 283-0555
State map: F4
From QUINCY, head W on Bucks
Lake Rd for 5 miles (8 k). Turn
Right (N) on dirt road and drive
another 5 miles (8 k).
**FREE** but choose a chore.
Open Apr 1–Oct 31; camping off-season.
7 close, open sites. Water (must treat), pit
toilets, tables, grills, fire rings.
Along small lake covered with water
shield plants (resembles bayou).
Fish, mountain bike, or hike.
No trash arrangements. 14-day limit.
4200 ft (1260 m)

## SODA SPRINGS

Sierra NF (209) 467-5155
State map: J4
From NORTH FORK, go SE on
CR 225 for 4.5 miles (7.2 k). Turn
Left (NE) on FR 81 (Minarets)
and drive 30 miles (48 k). (Also see Little
Jackass and Sweet Water.)
**FREE** but choose a chore.
Open Apr–Oct.
16 close, open sites.
Pit toilets, tables, fire rings.
On creek not far from Mammoth Pool
Reservoir.
Wade, fish, and relax.
NO water. 14-day/22-ft limits.
4400 ft (1320 m)

## SOQUEL

Sierra NF (209) 467-5155
State map: J4
From OAKHURST, take CA 41 N
about 5 miles (8 k) to FR 10 (Sky
Ranch Rd). Turn Right (NE) and

go 7.75 miles (12.4 k). Turn Right (SE) on
FR 6S40 and go 1.25 miles (2 k). (Also
see Greys Mountain, Kelty Meadow, and
Nelder Grove.)
**FREE** but choose a chore.
Open May–Oct.
14 close, open sites.
Pit toilets, tables, fire rings.
Along Willow Creek.
Wade and fish in quiet, secluded spot.
NO water. 14-day/16-ft limits.
5400 ft (1620 m)

## SOUP SPRINGS

Modoc NF (916) 279-6116
State map: D6
From LIKELY, go E on Jess
Valley Rd (CR 64) for 9 miles
(14.4 k). Turn Left (N) on West
Warner Rd and drive 5 miles (8 k). Turn
Right (E) on Soup Loop Rd and go
another 6 miles (9.6 k).
**FREE** but choose a chore.
Open Memorial Day–Labor Day; dry
camping off-season.
14 scattered, open sites.
Water, pit toilets, tables, fire rings.
In pine trees surrounded by open
meadow and sagebrush.
Access South Warner Wilderness.
No trash arrangements (pack it out).
14-day limit. Hunting in season.
6800 ft (2040 m)

## SOURGRASS

Stanislaus NF (209) 795-1381
State map: H3
From ALTAVILLE, head E on
CA 4 to DORRINGTON. Turn
Right (S) on Boards Crossing Rd
(FR 5N02) and go 4 miles (6.4 k). (Also
see Boards Crossing.)
**FREE** but choose a chore.
Open Apr–Oct; dry camping off-season.
15 close, open sites.
Water, chemical toilets, tables, fire rings.
In timbered tract on North Fork of
Stanislaus River.
Swim or fish when warm; ski in winter.
No trash arrangements. 14-day limit.
Crowded summers. Hunting in season.
3900 ft (1170 m)

▲ ▲ ▲ ▲ ▲ ▲ ▲ ▲ ▲ ▲ ▲ ▲ ▲ ▲ ▲ ▲ ▲ ▲ ▲ ▲ ▲ ▲ ▲ ▲

## SOUTH ANTELOPE

Lassen NF (916) 258-2141
State map: E3
From PAYNES CREEK, go
10 miles (16 k) S on rough, gravel
Ponderosa Way. (See Black Rock.)
FREE but choose a chore.
Open All Year.
4 scattered, open tent sites. Water (must treat), pit toilets, tables, grills, fire rings.
On Antelope Creek.
Fish and enjoy natural surroundings.
ATVs. Hunting in season. Snakes and poison oak.
2700 ft (810 m)

## SOUTH FORK

Eldorado NF (916) 644-2349
State map: G4
From POLLACK PINES, take
US 50 E for 8.5 miles (13.6 k).
Turn Left (N) on CR 17N12 (Soda Springs-Riverton) and drive about 22.75 miles (36.4 k). Turn Left (NW) on FR 13N29 and go .5 mile (800 m). (Also see North Shore.)
FREE but choose a chore.
Open Jun 1–Oct 15.
17 (5 tent-only) close, open sites.
Pit toilets, tables, fire rings.
Along Rubicon River.
Relax and fish.
NO water (must treat). 14-day/22-ft limits.
5200 ft (1560 m)

## SOUTH FORK

Stanislaus NF (209) 962-7825
State map: I4
From GROVELAND, drive E on
CA 120 for 7.5 miles (12 k). Turn
Left (N) on Ferretti Rd and go
about 1 mile (1.6 k) to unpaved Lumsden Rd. Turn Right (E) and go 6 tough miles (9.6 k). (Also see Lumsden & Lumsden Bridge.)
FREE but choose a chore.
Open Apr 15–Nov 1.
8 close, open sites.
Pit toilets, tables, fire rings.
In oak-pine setting on Tuolumne River.
Good kayaking (white-water), fishing, and hiking.
NO water/trash arrangements (pack it out). 14-day/16-ft limits. Crowded holidays and opening of fishing season.
1500 ft (450 m)

## SPUNKY

Angeles NF (818) 574-1613
State map: O3
From SAUGUS, head NE on
CR 6N05 (Bouquet Canyon) for
18.5 miles (29.6 k). Turn Left on CR 6N11 (Spunky Canyon). Go 3.7 miles (6 k). (Also see Bouquet and Streamside.)
FREE but choose a chore.
Open May–Nov.
10 close, open sites.
Pit toilets, tables, fire rings.
In canyon with hiking. (Pacific Crest Trail is nearby.)
NO water. 14-day limit.
3200 ft (960 m)

## SQUAW LAKE

BLM (602) 726-6300
State map: T7
From WINTERHAVEN, exit I-8
on CR S-24. Go 20 miles (32 k) N.
Take paved road marked Senator
Wash and Squaw Lake.
$5. Open All Year.
115 close, open sites.
Water, flush toilets, cold showers, tables, grills, beach, boat ramp.
With paved parking areas near Colorado River beaches–no trees though some cattail-marsh areas.
Boat, swim, jet-ski, and fish. In arid landscape, hike and birdwatch.
14-day limit. Crowded and noisy weekends and holidays. Temperatures break 100°F mark 110 days/year.
200 ft (60 m)

## SQUAW LEAP

BLM (805) 861-4191
State map: K4
From AUBERRY, head N toward
river on Powerhouse Rd for
2 miles (3.2 k). Turn Left at sign
to Squaw Leap and go 4 miles (6.4 k).
FREE. Open All Year.

▲ ▲ ▲ ▲ ▲ ▲ ▲ ▲ ▲ ▲ ▲ ▲ ▲ ▲ ▲ ▲ ▲ ▲ ▲ ▲ ▲ ▲ ▲ ▲ ▲ ▲ ▲ ▲ ▲ ▲

5 scattered, open sites.
Pit toilets, tables, fire rings.
On San Joaquin River.
Observe fascinating ecology. Relax too.
NO water/trash facilities. 14-day limit.

## STANISLAUS RIVER

Stanislaus NF (209) 795-1381
State map: H3
From LAKE ALPINE, go W on
CA 4 for 7 miles (11.2 k). At
Tamarack, turn Left (S) on Spicer
Reservoir Meadow Rd and drive
4.5 miles (7.2 k).
**$5**. Open Jun–Oct; dry camping
off-season.
25 close, open sites. Water, chemical/pit
toilets, tables, fire rings.
On North Fork of Stanislaus River.
Swim, hike, or fish during summer. In
winter, ski.
14-day/22-ft limits.
6200 ft (1860 m)

## STEELBRIDGE

BLM (707) 462-3873
State map: C3
From DOUGLAS CITY, head N
on CA 299 for 2.5 miles (4 k).
Turn W on Steelbridge Rd and
drive to camp.
**FREE** but choose a chore.
Open All Year.
8 close, open sites.
Pit toilets, tables, fire rings.
In shade on Trinity River.
Canoe and fish. Explore.
NO water. 14-day limit.
2000 ft (600 m)

## STONEY POINT

Shasta-Trinity NF (916) 623-2121
State map: C3
From WEAVERVILLE, go
14 miles (22.4 k) N on CA 3.
**$5**. Open Nov–Apr (check with
ranger station).
22 close, open tent sites. Water, pit
toilets, tables, fire rings, boat ramp.
Fish, boat, and swim on Trinity Lake.
14-day limit.
2400 ft (720 m)

## STONY CREEK

Los Padres NF (805) 683-6711
State map: M1
From ARROYO GRANDE, take
Husana Rd (CR 32 which changes
to M2023 in Husana) E for
20 miles (32 k). Turn Left on FR 30S02
and go 2 miles (3.2 k). Bear Left on
FR 31S09 for 1.5 miles (2.4 k).
**FREE** but choose a chore.
Open All Year.
8 close, open sites.
Pit toilets, tables, fire rings.
On remote creek.
Savor solitude.
NO water. 14-day limit. Hunting in
season.
2000 ft (600 m)

## STOUGH RESERVOIR

Modoc NF (916) 279-6116
State map: D6
Head W on CA 299 from
CEDARVILLE for 6 miles (9.6 k).
Turn Right (N) on Stough Access
Rd and drive 1 mile (1.6 k). (Also see
Cedar Pass.)
**FREE** but choose a chore.
Open Memorial Day–Labor Day; dry
camping off-season.
8 scattered, open sites.
Water, pit toilets, tables, grills, fire rings.
In pines near small pond and Bear Rock
formation.
Relax and, maybe, take photos.
No trash arrangements. 14-day limit.
Hunting in season.
6200 ft (1860 m)

## STRAWBERRY POINT

Eldorado NF (916) 644-2349
State map: H4
From POLLACK PINES, take
US 50 E for 8.5 miles (13.6 k).
Turn Left (N) on CR 17N12 (Soda
Springs-Riverton). Go 10.5 miles (16.8 k).
Turn Right (E) on FR 11N57. Go 3 miles
(4.8 k). (See Northwind or Silver Creek.)
**FREE** but choose a chore.
Open Jun 1–Oct 15.
10 tent sites.
Pit toilets, tables, fire rings, boat ramp.

▲ ▲ ▲ ▲ ▲ ▲ ▲ ▲ ▲ ▲ ▲ ▲ ▲ ▲ ▲ ▲ ▲ ▲ ▲ ▲ ▲ ▲ ▲ ▲ ▲ ▲ ▲ ▲

On shores of Ice House Reservoir.
Swim, boat, waterski, and fish.
NO water. 14-day limit.
5500 ft (1650 m)

## STREAMSIDE

Angeles NF (818) 574-1613
State map: O3
From SAUGUS, head NE on
CR 6N05 (Bouquet Canyon) for
17.5 miles (28 k). (Also see
Bouquet and Spunky.)
FREE but choose a chore.
Open All Year.
9 close, open tent sites.
Pit toilets, tables, fire rings.
On creek.
Fish (when water level is up) or relax.
NO water (creek water dangerous).
14-day limit.

## SUGAR SPRINGS

Mendocino NF (916) 824-5196
State map: E2
From PASKENTA, go S on
FR 23N02. Turn Right on
FR 23N69. Go to FR 23N41. Turn
Right to camp-total of 35 miles (56 k).
FREE but choose a chore.
Open Jun 1 - Oct 31; dry camping
off-season.
2 close, open sites.
Water, pit toilets, tables, fire rings.
At getaway for picnicking and relaxing.
No trash arrangements (pack it out).
14-day limit. Hunting in season.
5400 ft (1620 m)

## SULPHUR SPRINGS WALK-IN

Klamath NF (916) 493-2243
State map: B3
From HAPPY CAMP, go S on Elk
Creek Rd 14 miles (22.4 k). Walk
about 100 ft to sites.
FREE but choose a chore.
Open All Year.
7 scattered, open tent sites.
Pit toilets, tables, grills.
On creek with trails into wilderness.
Take a hike. Swim and fish in stream.
NO water/trash facilities. 14-day limit.
2300 ft (690 m)

## SUMMIT CAMP

Sierra NF (209) 467-5155
State map: J4
From WANONA, go W on
CR 5S092 for 5 miles (8 k).
FREE but choose a chore.
Open May-Oct.
10 close, open sites.
Water, pit toilets, tables, fire rings.
Near Yosemite NP.
Create base for exploring area.
14-day/22-ft limits.
5800 ft (1740 m)

## SUNSET POINT

Mountain Home SF
(209) 539-2855
State map: M4
From SPRINGVILLE, go W for
22 miles (35.2 k) on Bear Creek
Rd-steep and winding. (Also see Frasier
Mill, Hedrick Pond, Hidden Falls, Moses
Gulch, and Shake Camp.)
FREE but choose a chore.
Open May-Nov; dry camping
off-season.
13 close, open sites.
Water, pit toilets, tables, fire rings.
In open area with tall trees.
Explore magnificent region. View
wildlife. Fish.
14-day limit. Crowded and noisy.
Hunting in season.
6500 ft (1950 m)

## SWANSON MEADOW

Sierra NF (209) 893-2111
State map: K4
From SHAVER LAKE, go 3 miles
(4.8 k) E on Dinkey Creek Rd.
FREE but choose a chore.
Open All Year.
12 scattered, open sites.
Pit toilets, tables, fire rings.
In dense woods about 2 miles (3.2 k)
from Shaver Lake.
At lake swim, boat, ski, and fish. Hike
trails. Snow ski in winter.
NO water/trash arrangements.
14-day/25-ft limits. Crowded holidays.
Hunting in season.
5600 ft (1680 m)

▲ ▲ ▲ ▲ ▲ ▲ ▲ ▲ ▲ ▲ ▲ ▲ ▲ ▲ ▲ ▲ ▲ ▲ ▲ ▲ ▲ ▲ ▲ ▲ ▲

## SWEET WATER

Sierra NF (209) 467-5155
State map: J4
From NORTH FORK, go SE on
CR 225 for 4.5 miles (7.2 k). Turn
Left (NE) on FR 81 (Minarets). Go
33 miles (52.8 k). Turn Right on FR 6S25
and pass **Placer Camp** (fee charged). (See
Little Jackass and Soda Springs.)
FREE. Open Apr–Oct.
10 (5 tent-only) close, open sites.
Pit toilets, tables, fire rings.
On creek near Mammoth Pool Reservoir.
Wade, fish, and relax.
NO water. 14-day/16-ft limits.
3800 ft (1140 m)

## SYCAMORE #2

COE (209) 787-2589
State map: K4
From PIEDRA, take Trimmer
Springs Rd E about 20 miles
(32 k)–just past Sycamore Creek.
Find $10 alternative at **Island Park**.
FREE. Open Mar–Sep.
24 (2 RV-only, 4 tent-only) close,
open sites. &
Pit toilets, tables, grills.
On Pine Flat Lake in pine-oak belt of
Sierra Nevada foothills.
Enjoy spring wildflowers. Swim, boat,
and fish in lake. Spot wildlife: deer,
coyote, bobcat, and golden eagle.
NO water. 14-day limit. Crowded
Memorial Day. Quiet hours.
1100 ft (330 m)

## TABOOSE CREEK

Inyo County Parks
(619) 878-2411
State map: K5
From BIG PINE, go S on US 395
for 12.5 miles (20 k). Turn Right
(W) on Taboose Creek Rd and drive
2.5 miles (4 k). (Also see Tinnemaha.)
$5. Open All Year.
55 scattered, open sites.
Water, pit toilets, tables, grills, fire rings.
Along shady creek in semidesert area.
Hike to John Muir Trail. Fish or picnic.
14-day limit. Holidays crowded.
4200 ft (1260 m)

## TALBOT

Tahoe NF (916) 367-2224
State map: G4
From FORESTHILL, go E on
FR 96 (Mosquito Ridge Rd) for
45.5 miles (72.8 k).
FREE. Open May 25–Nov 30; camping
allowed off-season.
5 close, open sites. River water must be
purified, pit toilets, tables.
On Middle Fork of American River.
Take trail to Granite Chief Wilderness
for backpacking trip. View wildlife
(you're in game refuge), and fish.
14-day limit. Saddle and pack animals.
5600 ft (1680 m)

## THOMAS MOUNTAIN

San Bernardino NF
(714) 659-2117
State map: R5
Take CA 74 E from MOUNTAIN
CENTER about 11 miles (17.6 k).
Turn Right on FR 6S13 and drive about
7 miles (11.2 k). Sister camp, **Tool Box
Springs**, is another 2 miles.
FREE but choose a chore. Open All Year.
6 close, open tent sites.
Pit toilets, tables, grills.
In forest with hiking trails. Relax too.
NO water/trash arrangements (pack it
out). 14-day limit. Small vehicles only.
6500 ft (1950 m)

## THORNE MEADOWS

Los Padres NF (805) 683-6711
State map: O3
From FRAZIER PARK, go W on
FH 95 (Frazier Mountain Park
Rd) for 3.5 miles (5.6 k). Bear Left
(SW) in Lake of the Woods on CR 9N03
(Lockwood Valley Rd). Drive 10.5 miles
(16.8 k). Turn Left (S) on FR 7N03. Go
7 miles (11.2 k). Bear Right (W) on
FR 7N03B and go 1 mile (1.6 k). A
couple of isolated camps are up trail.
(Also see Half Moon and Pine Spring.)
FREE. Open May 15–Nov 15.
5 close, open sites.
Pit toilets, tables, fire rings.
Along remote, beautiful creek.
Enjoy seclusion with biking, hiking, and

fishing possibilities. Find Pacific views at Thorne Point, a steep 3-mile (4.8-k) trail. NO water/trash arrangements (pack it out). 14-day/16-ft limits.
5000 ft (1500 m)

## THREE PRONG

Mendocino NF (916) 824-5196
State map: E2
From PASKENTA, take FR 23N01 (Toomes Camp) W to FR 24N13. Turn Left to camp–total of 25 miles (40 k). (See Kingsley Glade.)
FREE. Open Jun 1–Oct 31; dry camping off-season.
6 close, open sites.
Water, pit toilets, tables, fire rings.
Amidst fir and pine next to large meadow, enjoy getaway.
No trash arrangements (pack it out). 14-day limit. Hunting in season.
5800 ft (1740 m)

## TINNEMAHA

Inyo County Parks
(619) 878-2411
State map: K5
From BIG PINE, go S on US 395 for 7 miles (11.2 k). Turn Right (W) on Fish Springs Rd and go .5 mile (800 m). Turn onto Tinnemaha Rd. Drive 2 miles (3.2 k). (Also see Taboose Creek.)
$5. Open All Year.
55 scattered, open sites.
Water, pit toilets, tables, grills, fire rings.
Along shaded creek in semidesert area.
Picnic, fish, and relax.
14-day limit. Crowded at fishing season opening.
4100 ft (1230 m)

## TOAD LAKE WALK-IN

Shasta-Trinity NF (916) 926-4511
State map: C4
From MT SHASTA, take Barr Rd SW for 3.5 miles (5.6 k) to FR 41N53. Turn Right (N), jog to Morgan Meadow Rd. Take Morgan Meadow W about 12 miles (19.2 k) to parking. Walk in .25 mile (400 m).
FREE but choose a chore.
Open Jun 1–Oct 1; camping off-season.

6 close, open tent sites.
Pit toilets, tables, fire rings.
On small scenic lake.
Take advantage of photo taking and hiking opportunities. Try fishing, canoeing, or even swimming for hardy.
NO water. 14-day limit.
7000 ft (2100 m)

## TOAD SPRING

Los Padres NF (805) 683-6711
State map: N2
From MARICOPA, go S on CA 166 for 9 miles (14.4 k). Turn Left (SE) on FH 95 and drive 15 miles (24 k). (Also see Caballo, Campo Alto, and Valle Vista.)
FREE but choose a chore.
Open May 15–Nov 15.
7 close, open sites.
Pit toilets, tables, fire rings.
On road to Mt Abel.
Fair hiking plus peace and quiet.
NO water/trash arrangements (pack it out). 14-day/16-ft limits.
5700 ft (1710 m)

## TOMHEAD SADDLE

Shasta-Trinity NF (916) 352-4211
State map: D2
Rangers advise obtaining forest map for this one. From RED BLUFF, go W on CA 36 for 13 miles to Cannon Rd. Turn Left (SW) and continue about 5 miles (8 k) to CR 146. Turn Right, go about 24 miles (38.4 k)–jog Left about 5 miles (8 k) out.
FREE. Open May 15–Oct 31; camping allowed off-season.
5 close, open sites.
Pit toilets, tables, corral.
Explore Yolla Bolly Wilderness–by horse or foot. Enjoy solitude.
NO water. 14-day limit.
5600 ft (1680 m)

## TRAIL CREEK

Klamath NF (916) 468-5351
State map: C3
From CALLAHAN, take road to CECILVILLE (CR FH93) SW for 16.5 miles (26.4 k). Camp is

.25 mile (400 m) off road on FR 39N08. (Also see Shadow Creek.)
**$4**. Open Memorial Day–Oct 15; dry camping off-season.
12 close, open sites.
Water, pit toilets, tables, grills, fire rings.
Near several streams and lakes with desirable summer shade and activities.
Access lake trails into Trinity Alps Wilderness for day hikes. Fish. Cross-country ski in winter.
Bears are regular visitors. 14-day limit for humans. Little parking area.
5000 ft (1500 m)

## TRINITY RIVER

Shasta-Trinity NF (916) 623-2121
State map: C3
Go N on CA 3 from TRINITY CENTER for 9.5 miles (15.2 k).
**$5**. Open All Year.
7 close, open sites.
Water, pit toilets, tables, fire rings.
Near river with access to north section of Trinity Wilderness.
Fishing, hiking, and relaxing here.
14-day/32-ft limits.
2500 ft (750 m)

## TROUT CREEK

Shasta-Trinity NF (916) 964-2184
State map: C4
From MCCLOUD, go 3 miles (4.8 k) E on CA 89 to FR 42N13. Turn Left (N) and drive 25 miles (40 k) to FR 42N09. Turn, continuing N for .75 mile (1.2 k) to FR 43N44. Turn Left (W) and proceed .2 mile (300 m).
**FREE** but choose a chore.
Open May 1–Nov 1; camping off-season.
10 sites. Pit toilets.
NO water. 14-day/22-ft limits.
5100 ft (1530 m)

## TROY MEADOW

Sequoia NF (619) 376-3781
State map: M5
From INYOKERN, take US 395 N for 15 miles (24 k). Turn Left (NW) on CR 152 (Nine Mile Canyon) and go 23.5 miles (37.6 k). Take FR 21S02 NW for 10 miles (16 k). (See

Fish Creek and Kennedy.)
**FREE** but choose a chore.
Open Jun 1–Nov 15.
73 close, open sites.
Water, pit toilets, tables, fire rings.
On creek in remote, scenic area.
Mountain bike or take extended trek into backcountry. Fish and picnic too.
No trash facilities. 14-day/22-ft limits.
7800 ft (2340 m)

## TUNNEL ROCK

Shasta-Trinity NF (916) 623-2121
State map: C3
From LEWISTON, take Buckeye Creek Rd (CR 105) N for 7 miles (11.2 k).
**FREE**. Open May 15–Oct 1; camping allowed off-season.
6 close, open sites.
Pit toilets, tables, fire rings.
In rolling hills around Lewiston Lake.
Try fishing, boating, or swimming.
NO water. 14-day limit.
2000 ft (600 m)

## TUTTLE CREEK

BLM (619) 256-8313
State map: L5
From LONE PINE, take Whitney Portal Rd (CR 15S02) W for 3.5 miles (5.6 k). Go SW on Horseshoe Meadow (CR 15S01) for 1.5 miles (2.4 k). Turn onto Tuttle Creek Rd. (Also see Road's End.)
**FREE**. Open May 1–Nov 15.
85 close, open sites.
Pit toilets, tables, fire rings.
On creek near Mt Whitney.
Make base while exploring area.
NO water/trash facilities. 14-day limit.
5100 ft (1530 m)

## TWIN PINES

Los Padres NF (805) 683-6711
State map: O2
From GORMAN, take Hungry Valley Rd (CR 1048) S about 9 miles (14.4 k). At fork, take rough, dirt Alamo Mountain Rd to Right. Drive 12 miles (19.2 k). For alternative, check out more primitive **Dutchman**

Camp about a mile farther.
**FREE**. Open May 15–Oct 31; camping allowed off-season.
5 close, open tent sites.
Pit toilets, tables, fire rings.
Remote spot for relaxing and hiking.
NO water/trash facilities. 14-day limit.
6600 ft (1980 m)

## UPPER CARLTON FLAT

Tahoe NF (916) 288-3231
State map: F4
From CAMPTONVILLE, go NE on CA 49 about 9.5 miles (15.2 k). Site is off Cal Ida Rd.
**FREE** but choose a chore. Open All Year.
Undesignated, undeveloped sites. Stream water only (must purify), pit toilets.
Behind Indian Valley outpost with access to Yuba River.
Pan for gold, fish, swim, and hike.
14-day limit.
2200 ft (660 m)

## UPPER CHIQUITO

Sierra NF (209) 467-5155
State map: J4
Just E of NORTH FORK, take CR 274 (Mallum Ridge) N for 9 miles (14.4 k). Turn Right (N) at Bass Lake on FR 7 and drive about 24 miles (38.4 k). Camp is on your Left.
**FREE** but choose a chore. Open Jun–Oct.
20 close, open sites.
Pit toilets, tables, fire rings.
Beside creek.
Wade, fish, walk nature trails, and relax.
NO water. 14-day/22-ft limits.
6800 ft (2040 m)

## UPPER RUSH CREEK

Modoc NF (916) 299-3215
State map: D5
From ADIN, go 7.5 miles (12 k) NE on CA 299 to FR 40N39. Turn Right (E). Drive 2.3 miles (3.7 k).
(RVers, see Lower Rush Creek.)
**$5**. Open May–Oct.
13 close, open sites.
Water, pit toilets, tables, grills, fire rings.
With creek at your feet and large conifers over your head.

Nice fishing and relaxing.
14-day/22-ft limits.
5000 ft (1500 m)

## UPPER TENMILE

Sequoia NF (209) 338-2251
State map: L4
From GRANT GROVE, take CA 180 N for 6 miles (9.6 k). Turn Right (SE) on Hume Lake Rd (FR 13S01) and go 8 miles (12.8 k). (Also see Landslide.)
**FREE**. Open May 15–Oct 15.
8 close, open sites.
Pit toilets, tables, fire rings.
On Tenmile Creek near Hume Lake and Kings Canyon NP.
Enjoy excellent exploring and hiking.
NO water. 14-day/22-ft limits.
5800 ft (1740 m)

## VALLE VISTA

Los Padres NF (805) 683-6711
State map: N2
From MARICOPA, go S on CA 166 for 9 miles (14.4 k). Turn Left (SE) on FH 95 and drive 12 miles (19.2 k). (Also see Caballo, Campo Alto, and Toad Spring.)
**FREE** but choose a chore. Open All Year.
10 close, open sites.
Pit toilets, tables, fire rings.
On road to Mt Abel with views of Bakersfield Valley.
Enjoy nice spot to picnic and relax.
NO water. 14-day/22-ft limits.
4800 ft (1440 m)

## VALLEY FORGE

Angeles NF (818) 578-1079
State map: P4
From I-10, take CA 2 NE for 14 miles (22.4 k) to unpaved Red Box-Rincon Rd. Turn Right and drive (walk in winter) 2.5 miles (4 k). (Also see West Fork.)
**FREE** but choose a chore. Open All Year.
8 scattered, open sites.
Stream water (must purify), pit toilets, tables, grills, fire rings.
In canyon riparian setting on West Fork of San Gabriel River.

▲ ▲ ▲ ▲ ▲ ▲ ▲ ▲ ▲ ▲ ▲ ▲ ▲ ▲ ▲ ▲ ▲ ▲ ▲ ▲ ▲ ▲ ▲ ▲ ▲ ▲

Nearby trails lead to Mt Wilson and high country. Fish and mountain bike too. 14-day limit. Hunting in season.
3500 ft (1050 m)

**WAGON FLAT**

Los Padres NF (805) 683-6711
State map: N1
From SANTA MARIA, head N on US 101 for 3 miles (4.8 k). Take CA 166 E for 15 miles (24 k). Turn Right (S) on Buckhorn Canyon Rd and drive 8.5 miles (13.6 k). Turn Left (E) on steep, dirt FR 11N04 (Colson Canyon Rd). Go 10 miles (16 k), bearing Left at fork. For more remote, check out **Lazy Camp** to NE. (Also see Barrel Springs and Colson Canyon.)
FREE but choose a chore. Open All Year.
5 close, open tent sites.
Pit toilets, tables, fire rings.
In secluded, scenic area.
Make base for hiking and biking.
NO water/trash facilities (pack it out). 14-day/16-ft limits. Road impassible when wet. Hot summers.
1400 ft (420 m)

**WAKALUMI**

COE (209) 673-5151
State map: K3
From MADERA, take CR 400 E for 12 miles (19.2 k) to CR 603. Turn Left and cross river to CR 407. Turn Right (E) and go another .5 mile (800 m).
FREE but choose a chore.
Open Mar 1–Sep 30.
10 close, open sites.
Chemical toilets, tables, grills, fire rings. Below Hidden Dam on Fresno River. Fish a bunch. Watch the birdies too. NO water. 14-day limit. Quiet hours. Rattlesnakes.
500 ft (150 m)

**WALKER**

Imperial County Parks
(619) 339-4384
State map: T6
From HOLTVILLE, go W for .5 mile (800 m). On S side of

CA 11. (Also see Heber Dunes.)
FREE but choose a chore.
Open All Year.
10 scattered, open sites.
Flush toilets, tables, grills, fire rings.
On Alamo River, make overnight stop. NO water. 3-day limit. Hot summers.

**WALKER PASS**

BLM (805) 861-4191
State map: N5
From ONYX, head E on CA 178 for 14 miles (22.4 k).
FREE but choose a chore.
Open All Year.
10 close, open tent sites.
Water, pit toilets, tables, fire rings.
Hike on Pacific Crest Trail.
14-day limit.
5200 ft (1560 m)

**WARD LAKE**

Sierra NF (209) 893-2111
State map: K5
From LAKESHORE (above Huntington Lake), take FR 80 (Kaiser Pass Rd) E for 10.5 miles (14.4 k). Take dirt FR 7S01 (Florence turnoff) for 4 miles (6.4 k). (Also see Bolsillo, Florence Lake, Portal Foreboy, and Sample Meadow.)
FREE. Open May 15–Oct 15; camping allowed off-season.
17 close, open tent sites.
Pit toilets, tables, fire rings.
Next to area's only natural lake with lots of rocks and trees.
Hike, fish, canoe, raft, and swim.
NO water/trash facilities. 14-day/25-ft limits. Crowded holidays. Hunting in season. Bears.
7300 ft (2190 m)

**WARNER CREEK**

Lassen NF (916) 258-2141
State map: E4
From CHESTER, go 8 miles (12.8 k) N on Warner Valley Rd.
FREE but choose a chore.
Open May 1–Nov 1; camping off-season.
15 scattered, open sites. Water (must treat), pit toilets, tables, grills, fire rings.

▲ ▲ ▲ ▲ ▲ ▲ ▲ ▲ ▲ ▲ ▲ ▲ ▲ ▲ ▲ ▲ ▲ ▲ ▲ ▲ ▲ ▲ ▲ ▲

Along creek in nice setting with fishing possibilities. Visit Lassen Volcanic NP.
14-day limit.
5000 ft (1500 m)

## WATTS LAKE PRIMITIVE AREA

Six Rivers NF (707) 574-6233
State map: D2
From ZENIA (E of Garverville), go E on unpaved CR about 17 miles (27.2 k), then N for 4 miles (6.4 k) on FR.
FREE but choose a chore. Open All Year.
6 scattered, open tent sites.
Pit toilets, fire rings.
In hard-to-find location on lake.
Enjoy quiet when hunting season is over.
NO water/trash facilities (pack it out).

## WELLS CABIN

Mendocino NF (916) 824-5196
State map: E2
From COVELLO, drive NE on CA 162 for 2.5 miles (4 k). Turn Right (E) on CR 338. Go 11 miles (17.6 k). Go E on dirt FH 7 for 12 miles (19.2 k). Turn Left (N) toward Anthony Peak on CR 23N69. Go 4 miles (6.4 k).
FREE. Open Jun 15–Oct 1; dry camping off-season.
25 close, open sites.
Water, pit toilets, tables, grills, fire rings.
In red fir with stunning scenery.
On clear days, walk up Anthony Peak to view Pacific Ocean. Take photos.
No trash facilities. 21-day/22-ft limits.
6300 ft (1890 m)

## WEST BRANCH

Klamath NF (916) 493-2243
State map: A3
From HAPPY CAMP, take unpaved O'Brian-Grayback Rd N for 12 miles (19.2 k).
FREE but choose a chore.
Open May 1–Nov 1.
12 scattered, screened sites.
Water, pit toilets, tables, fire rings.
In wooded, uncrowded setting (except for forest work center).
Good hiking and photo taking opportunities plus wildlife viewing and fishing.

No trash arrangements (pack it out).
14-day limit. No large vehicles.
1300 ft (390 m)

## WEST FORK

Angeles NF (818) 578-1079
State map: P4
From I-10, take CA 2 NE for 14 miles (22.4 k) to unpaved Red Box-Rincon Rd. Turn Right and go 4 miles (6.4 k). For more privacy, take trail about 1.2 miles (1.9 k) to DeVore Camp. (Also see Valley Forge.)
FREE but choose a chore.
Open All Year (walk-in during winter).
7 scattered, open tent sites.
Pit toilets, tables, fire rings.
On stream near national recreation trails.
Get away and hike.
NO water/trash arrangements.
3000 ft (900 m)

## WEST KAISER

Sierra NF (209) 877-3138
State map: K4
From BIG CREEK, take FR 8S01 NE for 15 miles (24 k).
FREE. Open May 15–Oct 15; camp off-season.
10 close, open tent sites.
Pit toilets, tables, fire rings.
In trees with short walks to creeks.
Choose from several hikes. Fish nearby lakes and streams.
NO water/trash facilities. 14-day limit.
Crowded holidays. Hunting in season. Bears.
7400 ft (2220 m)

## WHISKERS

Sierra NF (209) 467-5155
State map: J4
From NORTH FORK, go SE on CR 225 for .5 mile (800 m). Turn Left (N) on CR 274 (Mallum Ridge) and drive about 4.2 miles (6.7 k). Turn Right (E) on twisting FR 6S42 (Central Camp) and go about 8 miles (12.8 k). (Also see Gaggs Camp.)
FREE but choose a chore.
Open Apr–Oct.
8 (5 tent-only) close, open sites.

▲ ▲ ▲ ▲ ▲ ▲ ▲ ▲ ▲ ▲ ▲ ▲ ▲ ▲ ▲ ▲ ▲ ▲ ▲ ▲ ▲ ▲ ▲ ▲ ▲

Pit toilets, tables, fire rings.
On Sand Timber Creek.
Wade, fish, and relax.
NO water. 14-day/16-ft limits.
5300 ft (1590 m)

## WHISKEY FALLS

Sierra NF (209) 467-5155
State map: J4
Go E from NORTH FORK on
CR 225 for 1.5 miles (2.4 k). Turn
Left on CR 233 for 1.5 miles
(2.4 k). Turn Left (N) on FR 8S09 and
drive about 7 miles (11.2 k). Turn Right
(E) on FR 8S70 for 1 mile (1.6 k).
FREE but choose a chore. Open Jun–Oct.
15 close, open sites.
Pit toilets, tables, fire rings.
Beside creek perfect for wading and
fishing near plunge pool.
NO water. 14-day/22-ft limits.

## WHISKEYTOWN NRA-Brandy Creek

(916) 241-6584
State map: D3
From REDDING, drive 8 miles
(12.8 k) W on CA 299. Turn Left
(S) on Kennedy Dr. Go 5 miles
(8 k).
FREE. Also, free backcountry permits
available at headquarters or ranger
stations. Open All Year.
36 RV sites.
Water, dump station, boat ramp.
At parking lot for self-contained units.
(Regular sites and walk-ins at Oak
Bottom cost $10).
Boat, swim, and fish on Whiskeytown
Lake. Hike to escape crowds.
No toilets. 14-day/25-ft limits.
1200 ft (360 m)

## WHITE ROCK

Shasta-Trinity NF (916) 352-4211
State map: D2
From PLATINA, take CA 36 NW
for 5 miles (8 k). Turn Left (SW)
on unpaved FR 29N13 (Stuart
Gap Rd) and go 14.5 miles (23.2 k) to
FR 29N19. Turn and continue about
5.5 tough miles (8.8 k).
FREE. Open May 15–Oct 31; dry

camping off-season.
3 sites.
Water, pit toilets, tables, fire rings.
At remote place to relax and walk. Fish
nearby stream.
14-day limit.
4800 ft (1440 m)

## WHITLOCK

Mendocino NF (916) 824-5196
State map: E2
From PASKENTA, take FR 23N01
(Toomes Camp) NW for
14.5 miles (23.2 k). Turn Right on
FR 24N41. (Also see Rocky Cabin.)
FREE. Open May 1–Oct 31; dry camping
off-season.
5 close, open sites.
Water, pit toilets, tables, grills, fire rings.
Among large oaks and ponderosa pines.
Picnic and relax at this getaway.
No trash arrangements (pack it out).
14-day limit. Hunting in season.
4300 ft (1290 m)

## WILDCAT

COE (916) 557-5285
State map: J3
From CHOWCHILLA, go E on
Ave 26 for 17 miles (27.2 k) then
N on CR 29 for 7 miles (11.2 k).
FREE but choose a chore.
Open All Year.
19 close, open sites.
Water, pit toilets, tables, fire rings.
On Eastman Lake irrigation project with
swimming, waterskiing, and boating.
14-day limit.
600 ft (180 m)

## WILLOW

Inyo NF (619) 873-2500
State map: K5
From BISHOP, head W on
CA 168 for 13 miles (20.8 k). Bear
Left on unpaved FR 8S01 (South
Lake) and drive 5 miles (8 k).
FREE. Open May 1–Oct 15; camping
allowed off-season.
7 close, open sites. Stream water only
(must purify), chemical toilets, tables.
In beautiful Bishop Canyon.

Superb hiking with Tyee/George Trailhead at bridge across road. Fish or relax. NO water/trash facilities. 7-day limit. 9000 ft (2700 m)

## WOODCHUCK

Tahoe NF (916) 265-4538
State map: G4
Exit off I-80 at CISCO GROVE.
Go W on North frontage road.
Turn Right (N) on Rattlesnake
Rd. Drive 3 miles (4.8 k) on steep, winding road. (Also see Lake Sterling.)
**FREE** but choose a chore.
Open Jun 15–Sep 30; camping allowed off-season.
8 close, open tent sites. Stream water only (must purify), pit toilets, tables.
In lightly-used spot with hiking and fishing possibilities.
No trash arrangements. 14-day limit.
Limited parking area (no trailers).
7000 ft (2100 m)

## YOSEMITE NP

(209) 372-0301
State map: J4
Savor spectacular scenery of granite domes, waterfalls, lakes, high-country meadows as well as giant trees and delicate wildflowers.
$5 entrance fee (or pass). Also, **free** backcountry permits available at visitor centers and ranger stations. (Reserve in advance, if coming summer weekend.)
Must often struggle with crowds (especially in valley).

▲ **Porcupine Flat**
Drive about 38 miles (60.8 k) E from YOSEMITE VALLEY on CA 120.
$4. Open Memorial Day–Labor Day.
55 close, open sites with some screening and few RV spaces (in front area only).
Stream water (purify), pit toilets, tables, fire rings, food storage, pay phone.
Near Yosemite Creek in high country (sometimes space available).
Walk nice trails.
14-day limit.
8100 ft (2430 m)

▲ **Sunnyside Walk-In**
Find in YOSEMITE VALLEY near lodge

behind Chevron station. About 100-yard (100-m) walk.
$2/person. Open Apr–Nov.
35 close, open tent sites.
Water, flush toilets, tables, grills, food storage, pay phone.
Though first-come, first-serve policy, share site with 4 or 5 strangers.
Enjoy great hiking as well as informative Visitor Center and museums–all nearby.
7-day limit.
4000 ft (1200 m)

▲ **Tamarack Flat**
Travel about 23 miles (36.8 k) from YOSEMITE VALLEY on CA 120 E. Turn on campground road and go 2.5 miles (4 k). Access road is steep and winding–not suitable for large vehicles.
$4. Open Memorial Day–Labor Day.
52 close, open sites. Stream water (must purify), pit toilets, tables, fire rings.
In woods near good hiking and away from most crowds.
14-day limit.
6331 ft (1899 m)

▲ **Yosemite Creek**
Go about 35 miles (56 k) from YOSEMITE VALLEY on CA 120 E. Turn on 4.6-mile (7.4-k) dirt access road–not for large vehicles.
$4. Open Memorial Day–Labor Day.
75 close, open sites (for tents and pickup campers). Stream water (must purify), pit toilets, tables, fire rings.
On Yosemite Creek among granite boulders and pines.
Revel in hiking this part of Yosemite.
14-day limit. Pets in sites 1-40 only.
7530 ft (2259 m)

## YUBA PASS

Tahoe NF (916) 288-3231
State map: F4
From SIERRA CITY, go 11 miles (17.6 k) E on CA 49.
$5. Open Jun 1–Nov 1; camping allowed off-season.
20 close, open sites. Water (should be purified), pit toilets, tables, grills.
In winter ski area with hiking or fishing.
14-day limit.
6700 ft (2010 m)

# Colorado

Grid conforms to official state map. For your copy, call (800) 433-2656
or write Colorado Tourism Board, 1625 Broadway, Suite 1700, Denver, CO 80202.

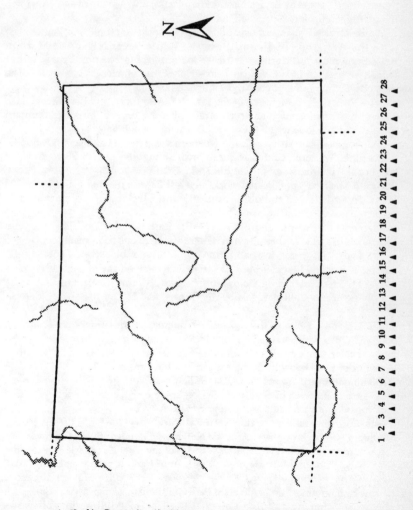

The US Forest Service administers most of the $5-or-less camping opportunities in Colorado. Find these sites in the state's mountainous regions.

In addition to developed campgrounds, the **Roosevelt National Forest** (NF) offers backpacking in Cache la Poudre, Indian Peaks, and Rawah wilderness areas. With Arapaho NF, it manages Cache la Poudre Wild and Scenic River. As in most Colorado forests, watch for bighorn sheep, black bear, and elk near alpine lakes.

Straddling the Continental Divide, **Routt NF** highlights include Flat Tops, Mount Zirkel (and the rugged Parks Range), Neota, and Never Summer wilderness areas. Here observe bobcat and mule deer.

In the **Arapaho NF**, find Arapaho National Recreation Area (NRA), Mount Goliath Natural Area, abandoned-town Alice and nearby St Mary's Glacier, and more wilderness areas: Eagles Nest, Indian Peaks, and Mount Evans. In winter, the ptarmigan flock to Guanella Pass.

**White River NF** shares unusual Flat Tops with the Routt NF and Eagles Nest with the Arapaho NF. In addition, the White River NF sports Maroon Bells-Snowmass Wilderness with its incomparable Maroon Peaks. Other wilderness areas include Collegiate Peaks, Holy Cross, Hunter-Fryingpan, and The Raggeds. Sight mountain goat and mountain lion too.

Pikes Peak is the centerpiece of the **Pike NF**. Also there, find Lost Creek, Lake Abyss, and Bristlecone Pine scenic areas plus the rugged Tarryall Mountain Range. Add antelope to the list of frequent wildlife sightings.

Look for mountain sheep instead of bighorn sheep in the **Gunnison NF**. See the Timberline Overlook, Gothic Natural Area, Slumgullion Earth Flow, and two additional wilderness areas: West Elk and La Garita.

**Grand Mesa NF** contains the world's largest flat-top mountain and about 300 lakes. In addition to the ubiquitous elk and black bear, see marmot and golden-mantled ground squirrel.

Segments of **Uncompahgre NF** offer Big Blue, Mount Sneffels (America's Switzerland), and Lizard Head wilderness areas. Here one occasionally spots lynx.

San Isabel NF provides habitation for antelope, black bear, bobcat, elk, mountain goat and lion plus bighorn sheep. Find them on any of the twenty peaks over 14000 feet, including Colorado's highest, Mount Elbert. On foot or by horseback, access Collegiate Peaks, Holy Cross, and Mount Massive wilderness areas.

**Rio Grande NF** shares the La Garita Wilderness with Gunnison NF and the South San Juan with San Juan NF. In addition, it holds the Weminuche Wilderness and Wheeler Geological Area. Besides unusual rocks, Rio Grande NF offers sightings of two showy birds, ptarmigan and blue grouse.

Continuations of Lizard Head, South San Juan, and Weminuche wilderness areas are administered by **San Juan NF**. See Chimney Rock Archeological Site and look for nesting bald eagle and peregrine falcon.

For $5-or-less camping, the **National Park Service** (NPS) offers: Rocky Mountain NP (backcountry), Dinosaur National Monument (NM,) Colorado NM (backcountry), Curecanti NRA, Black Canyon of the Gunnison (backcountry), and Great Sand Dunes NM (backcountry). **Bureau of Land Management** (BLM), **US Army Corps of Engineers** (COE), and **US Fish & Wildlife** provide numerous notable campgrounds. Colorado State Parks (SPs) are too expensive ($3 daily pass plus $6-$10 camping fee). The **Colorado Division of Wildlife** does offer free, primitive camping in many areas; seven State Wildlife Areas (SWAs) are

▲ ▲ ▲ ▲ ▲ ▲ ▲ ▲ ▲ ▲ ▲ ▲ ▲ ▲ ▲ ▲ ▲ ▲ ▲ ▲ ▲ ▲ ▲ ▲ ▲ ▲

highlighted. On the city-county level, noteworthy entries include the City of Wray's Beecher Island Battleground and Larimer County's four reservoirs.

Coloradoans take their recreation seriously in every season. Take advantage of the many opportunities.

▲ ▲ ▲ ▲ ▲ ▲ ▲ ▲ ▲ ▲ ▲ ▲ ▲ ▲ ▲ ▲ ▲ ▲ ▲ ▲ ▲ ▲ ▲ ▲ ▲ ▲

## ALAMOSA

Rio Grande NF
(719) 274-5193
State map: O11
From MONTE VISTA, take CO 15 S for 12 miles (19.2 k) to end of pavement at junction with FR 250 (Alamosa River Rd). Drive another 17.5 miles (28 k) W. (Other camping areas include La Jara Reservoir SWA and Stunner.)
**FREE** but choose a chore.
Open May 25–Sep 15.
10 scattered, screened sites. Hand water pump, pit toilets, tables, fire rings.
In stand of pine next to river.
Hike and view nature.
No trash arrangements (pack it out).
14-day/20-ft limits. No fishing.
8600 ft (2580 m)

## ANTONE SPRING

Uncompahgre NF
(303) 874-7691
State map: K4
From MONTROSE, drive 24 miles (38.4 k) SW via CO 90 then 1 mile (1.6 k) W on FR 402.
**FREE** but choose a chore.
Open Jun 1–Sep 30.
9 sites. Pit toilets, tables, grills.
Near spring.
Relax in peace and quiet here.
NO water. 22-ft limit.
9700 ft (2910 m)

## AVERY PEAK

Gunnison NF (303) 641-0471
State map: I9
From CRESTED BUTTE, head N approximately 7 miles (11.2 k) on CR 3 (Gothic Rd) then continue 1.5 miles (2.4 k) N on gravel FR 317. (Pass Gothic on CR 3.)
**FREE** but choose a chore.
Open May 1–Sep 30; camping allowed off-season.

10 close, screened sites.
Pit toilets, tables, grills, fire rings.
In heart of Colorado Rockies with spectacular views and lush vegetation, including incredible wildflowers.
Hike and photograph nature. Explore old Gothic townsite. Enjoy fishing in East River.
NO water/trash facilities. 14-day/16-ft limits. Changing weather/road conditions. Crowded. Hunting in season.
Flies in July.
9600 ft (2880 m)

## BALDY

Pike NF (303) 236-7386
State map: G15
From BUFFALO CREEK, go .5 mile (800 m) SE on CO 126 then 4 miles (6.4 k) SW on gravel FR 543. (Also see Green Mountain.)
**FREE** but choose a chore.
Open May 1–Oct 15; dry camping off-season.
Close, screened tent sites. Hand water pump, pit toilets, tables, grills, fire rings.
In scattered lodgepole pine along Buffalo Creek near Baldy Peak.
Fish!
14-day limit. Crowded Jul 4–Aug 15.
7400 ft (2220 m)

## BEAVER CREEK

Pike NF (719) 545-8737
State map: H13
From FAIRPLAY, drive 3 miles (4.8 k) NW on CR 1 then 2 miles (3.2 k) N on FR 413.
**FREE** but choose a chore.
Open May 15–Labor Day.
3 sites. Pit toilets, tables, fire rings.
On creek in mountain meadow setting.
Fishing popular here.
22-ft limit.
10900 ft (3270 m)

▲ ▲ ▲ ▲ ▲ ▲ ▲ ▲ ▲ ▲ ▲ ▲ ▲ ▲ ▲ ▲ ▲ ▲ ▲ ▲ ▲ ▲ ▲ ▲ ▲ ▲ ▲

## BEECHER ISLAND BATTLEGROUND
Wray City Parks
(303) 332-4431
State map: E28
Go 5 miles (8 k) S of WRAY on US 385
then 13 miles (20.8 k) SE on CR 61.
**FREE** but choose a chore.
Open All Year.
30 sites. Flush toilets, showers, tables,
fire rings, playground.
At site of one of last white man vs
Indian battles, Sep 17–18, 1868.
Tour battlefield. Observe wildlife.

## BIG BLUE
Gunnison NF (303) 641-0471
State map: L7
Between GUNNISON and
LAKE CITY, take steep, winding, dirt
FR 868 (Alpine Rd) from CO 149 for
12 miles (19.2 k)–slick when wet. (Other
campgrounds in area include Red Bridge
and The Gate.)
**FREE** but choose a chore.
Open May 31–Oct 15; camping allowed
off-season.
11 scattered with choice of open or
screened sites.
Pit toilets, tables, grills, fire rings.
In secluded area.
Hike into Big Blue Wilderness. Fish in
stream or beaver ponds.
NO water/trash arrangements–come
prepared. 14-day/16-ft limits. No trailers.
2 vehicles/campsite.
9800 ft (2940 m)

## BIG CIMARRON
Uncompahgre NF
(303) 249-3711
State map: L6
From MONTROSE, drive E on US 50
approximately 20 miles (32 k) to gravel
FR 858. Turn Right (S) and go 20 miles
(32 k). Over-$5 **Beaver Lake** is nearby.
**FREE** but choose a chore.
Open Jun 15–Sep 15; camping allowed
off-season.
15 sites. Pit toilets, tables, fire rings.
Along Cimarron River in cottonwood,
aspen, and spruce.
Hike and photograph nature. Fish in

river or canoe in nearby lakes.
NO water/trash facilities. 14-day/22-ft
limits. Hunting in season.
8800 ft (2640 m)

## BIG CREEK
Grand Mesa NF
(303) 487-3534
State map: H5
From COLLBRAN, proceed 15 miles
(24 k) S on FR 121 (Bonham Rd) then
1 mile (1.6 k) W on FR 121A. (Also see
Cottonwood Lake and Twin Lake.)
**FREE** but choose a chore.
Open Jun 15–Sep 15; dry camping
off-season. (Scheduled to be closed in
1993 for dam work).
26 close, screened sites.
Central water faucet, pit toilets, tables,
fire rings, boat ramp.
In spruce-fir forest near one of many
lakes and reservoirs on Grand Mesa.
Boat and fish. Observe and photograph
nature.
14-day/24-ft limits. Frequent, cooling
evening showers. Quiet 10pm–6am.
10100 ft (3030 m)

## BIG DOMINGUEZ
BLM (303) 244-3000
State map: I2
Drive about 20 miles (32 k)
SW from GRAND JUNCTION via US 6,
US 50, and paved scenic byway CO 141.
Turn Left on unsurfaced FR 402 (Divide
Rd) and travel 4 miles (6.4 k) to
Dominguez sign. Turn Left on dirt road
and continue another 4 miles
(6.4 k)–difficult when wet. (Also see
Carson Hole and Divide Fork.)
**FREE** but choose a chore.
Open May 1–Oct 30.
9 sites. Pit toilets, tables, fire rings.
In red-sandstone-walled canyon along
creek among cottonwood, ponderosa
pine, juniper, pinyon, and aspen.
Hike or bike along Tabaguache Trail.
Enjoy viewing and taking photos of
scenery and wildlife.
NO water/trash facilities. 14-day/30-ft
limits.
7500 ft (2250 m)

▲ ▲ ▲ ▲ ▲ ▲ ▲ ▲ ▲ ▲ ▲ ▲ ▲ ▲ ▲ ▲ ▲ ▲ ▲ ▲ ▲ ▲ ▲ ▲ ▲

## BIG SOUTH

Roosevelt NF (303) 498-1375
State map: B13
From LAPORTE, travel
4 miles (6.4 k) N on US 287 then
51 miles (81.6 k) W on scenic CO 14.
(Other campgrounds along CO 14
include Stevens Gulch, Narrows Co-op,
and Stove Prairie Landing.)
**FREE** but choose a chore.
Open May 15–Nov 15.
3 sites. Pit toilets, tables, fire rings.
At Joe Wright Creek and Big South Fork
of Cache la Poudre River. Fish.
14-day/32-ft limits.
8400 ft (2520 m)

## BIG TURKEY

Pike NF (303) 236-7386
State map: H16
From WOODLAND PARK,
drive 11.5 miles (18.4 k) NW on CO 67.
Turn Left (SW) and go .75 mile (1.2 k) on
FR 200 then 3.75 miles (6 k) SW on
gravel FR 360.
**FREE** but choose a chore.
Open May 20–Sep 15; camping allowed
off-season.
10 close, screened sites.
Pit toilets, tables, grills, fire rings.
Among lodgepole pine on Turkey Creek
(no live water) near Turkey Rock.
Hike or bike to view nature.
NO water/trash arrangements.
14-day/16-ft limits. Hunting in season.
8000 ft (2400 m)

## BISHOP

BLM (303) 824-4441
State map: A2
Off US 40 from MAYBELL,
travel NW on CO 318 for 45 miles (72 k).
Turn Right and continue N on CR 10
about 16 miles (25.6 k). Drive another
9 miles (14.4 k) and choose Bishop,
**Calloway**, or **Rocky Reservoir**
(high-clearance vehicle recommended).
**FREE** but choose a chore.
Open May 15–Nov 1; camping allowed
off-season.
3 scattered, screened sites.
Pit toilet, table, fire ring.

In three remote mountaintop locations
among aspen.
Enjoy solitude. Backpack or hike to view
antelope, deer, and elk. Mountain bike or
horseback ride.
NO water/trash facilities. 14-day limit.
Hunting in season.
8500 ft (2550 m)

## BLACK CANYON OF THE GUNNISON NM-Backcountry

(303) 249-7036
State map: J6
From MONTROSE, proceed
15 miles (24 k) E on CO 347.
**FREE** but $3 entrance fee (or pass).
(North and South Rim campgrounds cost
over $5.) Inquire about backcountry
permits at Visitor Center or ranger
stations.
Open Apr 15–Oct 31.
This dark, sheer-walled canyon of
ancient origin offers many scenic
overlooks. Backcountry campers can stay
in 2000-ft-deep gorge carved by
Gunnison River.
Walk with care near canyon rim. No
campfires or firewood gathering–cook
on grills or campstoves.
8200 ft (2460 m)

## BLANCO

San Juan NF (303) 247-4874
State map: P9
From PAGOSA SPRINGS,
travel 13 miles (20.8 k) SE on US 84 then
1.75 miles (2.8 k) E on FR 656.
**$5.** Open May 15–Nov 15.
18 sites. Pit toilets, tables, fire rings.
In Blanco River Canyon.
Fish, hike, or enjoy community
recreation facilities (baseball, volleyball,
and horseshoes).
NO water. 14-day/16-ft limits.
7200 ft (2160 m)

## BROWNS PARK

Roosevelt NF (303) 498-1375
State map: B13
From LAPORTE, drive
4 miles (6.4 k) N on US 287; 55 miles
(88 k) W on scenic CO 14; then 21 miles

▲ ▲ ▲ ▲ ▲ ▲ ▲ ▲ ▲ ▲ ▲ ▲ ▲ ▲ ▲ ▲ ▲ ▲ ▲ ▲ ▲ ▲ ▲ ▲ ▲ ▲ ▲ ▲

(33.6 k) N on FR 190.
FREE but choose a chore.
Open May 15–Nov 12.
28 sites. Pit toilets, tables, grills.
In alpine scenery along Jinks Creek.
Hike into Rawah Wilderness in Medicine
Bow Mountains. Fish in creeks and lakes.
NO water. 14-day/32-ft limits.
8400 ft (2520 m)

## BROWNS PARK NWR
(303) 365-3613
State map: A1
Head 65 miles (104 k) NW of
MAYBELL on CO 318.
FREE but choose a chore.
Open All Year.
65 sites at Crook and Swinging Bridge.
Pit toilets, fireplaces, boat ramp.
In cottonwood habitat along Green
River. Uplands support juniper in arid,
mountain environment.
View and photograph waterfowl and
river runners.
NO water/trash facilities in camps—
water at refuge headquarters. 16-day
limit. Fishing and hunting regulations.
5300 ft (1590 m)

## BUCKEYE
Manti-LaSal NF
(801) 259-7155
State map: K1
Off CO 90 from PARADOX, go
11.75 miles (18.8 k) NW on FR 071.
FREE but choose a chore.
Open Jun 1–Sep 30.
16 sites. Pit toilets, tables, fire rings.
On Buckeye Reservoir in setting of open
ponderosa pine with meadows plus
views of LaSal Mountains.
Boat (only trolling motors), swim, and
fish for trout. Hike on logging roads.
NO water/trash arrangements—handle
responsibly. 22-ft limit.
7600 ft (2280 m)

## BUFFALO PASS
Rio Grande NF
(719) 655-2547
State map: L11
From SAGUACHE, take CO 114 NW for

27.5 miles (44 k). Turn onto campground
access road (FR 775) and drive S another
1.5 miles (2.4 k).
FREE but choose a chore.
Open May 25–Sep 30.
30 scattered, screened sites. Hand water
pump, pit toilets, tables, fire rings.
In ponderosa pine stand said to be site
of Indian camps and stagecoach stops.
View and photograph nature.
14-day/22-ft limits. Hunting in season.
9100 ft (2730 m)

## BUFFALO SPRINGS
Pike NF (719) 836-2031
State map: H13
From FAIRPLAY, go
14.5 miles (23.2 k) S on US 285 then
7 miles (11.2 k) W on gravel CR 18.
FREE but choose a chore.
Open May 1–Oct 30; dry camping
off-season.
13 close, screened sites. Hand water
pump, pit toilets, tables, grills, fire rings.
In flat, lodgepole-pine area.
Hike and rockhound.
14-day/16-ft limits. Hunting in season.
10800 ft (3240 m)

## BURNING BEAR
Pike NF (303) 236-7386
State map: G14
From GRANT, proceed
5.25 miles (8.4 k) NW on gravel FR 118.
FREE but choose a chore.
Open May 1–Sep 15; camping allowed
off-season.
13 close, screened sites.
Pit toilets, tables, grills, fire rings.
On Geneva Creek in mixed species trees.
Hike or fish.
NO water. 14-day/16-ft limits.
9500 ft (2850 m)

## CARSON HOLE
Uncompahgre NF
(303) 242-8211
State map: J2
From WHITEWATER, drive 24 miles
(38.4 k) SW on paved scenic byway
CO 141 then another 7 miles (11.2 k) SW
on unsurfaced FR 402 (Divide Rd)–road

varies with weather. (Also see Big Dominguez and Divide Fork.)
**FREE** but choose a chore.
Open May 20–Nov 1; camping allowed off-season.
5 sites. Pit toilets, tables, fire rings.
Underneath canopy of ponderosa pine and aspen.
Hike Carson Hole Trail to observe and photograph nature.
NO water/trash facilities. 16-ft/14-day limits. Hunting in season. ATVs.
8400 ft (2520 m)

## CARTER LAKE

Larimer County Parks
(303) 679-4570
State map: C16
From LOVELAND, drive W on US 34; S on CO 29; W on CR 18E; then S on CR 31 to foothills lake.
$4/night weekdays, $5/night weekends (annual passes for vehicles and boats).
Open All Year.
175 sites scattered around three sides of lake in open settings.
Central water faucet, flush/pit toilets, dump station, tables, grills, fire rings, grills, fire rings, pay phone, store with ice and rentals, swimming beach, boat ramp, marina.
Water enthusiasts boat, waterski, swim, and fish. Landlubbers hike to observe and photograph nature.
Crowded weekends. 14-day limit. Quiet hours.
5760 ft (1728 m)

## CATARACT CREEK

White River NF
(303) 945-2521
State map: E11
From KREMMLING, go .25 mile (400 m) E on US 40; 12.25 miles (19.6 k) S on CO 9; 4.75 miles (7.6 k) SE on CR 30; then 2 miles (3.2 k) SW on CR 1725–high-clearance vehicles. (Also see Davis Springs, Elliot Creek, and Willows.)
**FREE** but choose a chore.
Open Jun 1–Sep 30.
4 sites.
Water, pit toilets, tables, grills.

Fish in creek. Hike into Gore Range. Watch for eagles.
10-day/16-ft limits.
8600 ft (2580 m)

## CATHEDRAL

Rio Grande NF
(719) 657-3321
State map: N10
From DEL NORTE, take US 160 W for almost 9 miles (14.4 k). Turn on CR 18 (Embargo Creek) and drive another 5.5 miles (8.8 k). Turn N on FR 650 and go 11 miles (17.6 k)–slippery when wet.
**FREE** but choose a chore.
Open May 25–Sep 15.
33 scattered, screened sites. Hand water pump, pit toilets, tables, fire rings.
In aspen grove near creek with beautiful view of Cathedral Rock.
Hike. View and photograph nature. Fish in area creeks.
14-day/22-ft limits. Hunting in season.
9500 ft (2850 m)

## CHEROKEE PARK SWA

CO Wildlife (303) 484-2836
State map: B16
From FORT COLLINS, drive 10 miles (16 k) N on US 287 to Red Feather Lakes Rd then 8 miles (12.8 k) to unit–road varies with weather.
**FREE** but choose a chore.
Open–call about special restrictions.
Undesignated, scattered sites. Pit toilets.
Among evergreens in mountain setting.
Hike to view and photograph wildlife.
Fish according to regulations.
NO water/trash arrangements–be responsible. 14-day limit.
7000 ft (2100 m)

## COALDALE WALK-IN

San Isabel NF (719) 539-3591
State map: K13
From COALDALE, drive 4 miles (6.4 k) SW on gravel FR 249.
**FREE** but choose a chore.
Open May 18–Nov 1.
11 close, screened tent sites. Hand water pump, pit toilets, tables, grills, fire rings.
Across Hayden Creek.

Hike or fish.
14-day limit. Hunting in season.
7800 ft (2340 m)

## COFFEE POT SPRING

White River NF
(303) 945-2521
State map: F8

From GLENWOOD SPRINGS, head
17 miles (27.2 k) E on US 6; 2 miles
(3.2 k) N on CR 301; then 20.5 miles
(32.8 k) NW and uphill on unpaved
FR 600. (Deep Lake and Supply Basin
are 6–7 miles up road.)
FREE but choose a chore.
Open Jun 15–Nov 15; dry camping
off-season.
15 scattered, open sites. Water, pit toilets,
tables, fire rings.
In alpine-like setting with grassy
meadow surrounded by aspen.
Observe wildflowers, birds, and clouds.
No trash pickup. 14-day/22-ft limits.
Rapidly changing weather/road
conditions. ATVs.
10000 ft (3000 m)

## COLD SPRINGS

Gunnison NF (303) 641-0471
State map: J10
From GUNNISON, travel
11 miles (17.6 k) N on CO 135 to
ALMONT. Continue NE on FR 742 for
16 miles (25.6 k). (Off this road are
several other campgrounds with water
and fees.)
FREE but choose a chore.
Open May 1–Oct 31; camping allowed
off-season.
7 sites. Pit toilets, tables, grills, fire rings.
In picturesque Taylor River Canyon.
Enjoy scenery and fish.
NO water/trash facilities (pack it out).
14-day/16-ft limits. Crowded.
9000 ft (2700 m)

## COLORADO NM-Backcountry

(303) 858-3617
State map: H2
From GRAND JUNCTION,
drive 4 miles (6.4 k) W on CO 340.
FREE but $3 entrance fee (or pass).

(Saddlehorn costs over $5.) Inquire about
free backcountry permit at Visitor
Center. Open All Year.
In this colorful sandstone country, find
rugged canyons, unusual rock
formations, remains of prehistoric Indian
cultures, and ancient dinosaur fossils.
Pack out trash. No open fires or
firewood gathering–cook with
campstove. No ATVs or pets.
5800 ft (1740 m)

## COLUMBINE

Uncompahgre NF
(303) 874-7691
State map: K3

Off CO 348 out of DELTA, drive
30 miles (48 k) SW on CR 214 then
2.5 miles (4 k) S on FR 402.
FREE but choose a chore.
Open Jun 10–Sep 30.
6 sites. Pit toilets, tables, fire rings.
At Columbine Pass on plateau.
Enjoy peace and quiet here.
NO water. 14-day/22-ft limits.
8700 ft (2610 m)

## COMMISSARY

Gunnison NF (303) 641-0471
State map: K7
From GUNNISON, travel
26 miles (41.6 k) W on US 50; .5 mile
(800 m) NW on CO 92; and 9.25 miles
(14.8 k) N on FR 721–not recommended
for trailers or large RVs. (Over-$5 Soap
Creek is nearer highway.)
FREE but choose a chore.
Open May 1–Labor Day; camping
allowed off-season.
7 sites. Pit toilets, tables, grills, fire rings.
Among spectacular rock cliffs, creek, and
old-growth forest.
Hike to observe and photograph wildlife.
Fish in Soap Creek.
NO water/trash facilities (pack it out).
14-day limit. Crowded.
7900 ft (2370 m)

## COMSTOCK

Rio Grande NF
(719) 657-3321
State map: O11

▲ ▲ ▲ ▲ ▲ ▲ ▲ ▲ ▲ ▲ ▲ ▲ ▲ ▲ ▲ ▲ ▲ ▲ ▲ ▲ ▲ ▲ ▲ ▲

From MONTE VISTA, take CO 15 S for 2 miles (3.2 k). Turn W on CR 25 and proceed 14 miles (22.4 k) to forest boundary. Continue W on FR 265 and travel another 2 miles (3.2 k). (2 more miles to Rock Creek.)
FREE but choose a chore.
Open Jun 1–Sep 15.
8 scattered, screened sites.
Pit toilets, tables, fire rings.
In stand of mixed conifers near North Fork of Rock Creek.
Hike in area or fish in waters.
NO water/trash facilities. 14-day/20-ft limits. Hunting in season.
9500 ft (2850 m)

## COTTONWOOD LAKE

▲  Grand Mesa NF
(303) 487-3534
State map: H5

Travel approximately 12 miles (19.2 k) S of COLLBRAN by way of paved then graveled FR 121 (Bonham Rd). Continue another 5 miles (8 k) W on gravel FR 257–moderately difficult road for RVs. (Nearby campgrounds include Fish Hawk and Twin Lake.)
$5. Open Jun 15–Sep 15; dry camping off-season.
42 sites. Central water faucet, pit toilets, tables, fire rings, boat ramp.
Next to mountain lake in spruce forest.
Boat and fish on largest lake in area.
Hike to Bull Basin reservoir. Observe and photograph nature.
14-day/24-ft limits. Quiet 10pm–6am. Crowded July 4. Frequent thundershowers. July mosquitos. Hunting in season.
10100 ft (3030 m)

## CRAG CREST

▲  Grand Mesa NF
(303) 242-8211
State map: H5

From CEDAREDGE, drive 16 miles (25.6 k) N on paved CO 65 then 3.5 miles (5.6 k) E on FR 121. (Other alternatives around Eggleston Lake include Trickle Park and Kiser Creek as well as Eggleston Lake.)

$5. Open Jun 20–Sep 15.
11 close, open sites. Hand water pump, pit toilets, tables, fire rings.
Near lake among spruce and fir.
Hike Crag Crest National Recreation Trail. Observe and photograph nature.
Boat and fish on Eggleston Lake.
14-day/22-ft limits. Changing weather/road conditions.
10300 ft (3090 m)

## CROSHO

▲  Routt NF (303) 879-1722
State map: D9
5 miles (8 k) off CR 16 (Flat Tops Trail Scenic Byway) leading from YAMPA. (Another free campground off byway is Sheriff.)
FREE but choose a chore.
Open May 15–Sep 15.
7 sites. Pit toilets, tables, fire rings.
Canoe and fish Crosho Lake.
14-day/20-ft limits.
8960 ft (2688 m)

## CROWN POINT-PINGREE

▲  Roosevelt NF (303) 482-3822
State map: B14
From LAPORTE, drive 4 miles (6.4 k) N on US 287; 27 miles (43.2 k) W on CO 14; then 8 miles (12.8 k) S on CR 131. (Tom Bennett Campground is off CR 131 too.)
FREE but choose a chore.
Open May 1–Oct 31.
12 sites. Pit toilets, tables, fire rings.
In forest, off scenic drive along Cache la Poudre River.
Admire natural beauty and fish.
NO water. 14-day/32-ft limits.
8000 ft (2400 m)

## CURECANTI NRA-Gateview

▲  (303) 641-2337
State map: K8
Go 7 miles W of POWDER-HORN via CO 149 then 6 miles N on improved but narrow gravel road.
FREE but choose a chore.
Open Memorial Day–Labor Day; camping allowed off-season.
7 scattered, screened tent sites.

▲ ▲ ▲ ▲ ▲ ▲ ▲ ▲ ▲ ▲ ▲ ▲ ▲ ▲ ▲ ▲ ▲ ▲ ▲ ▲ ▲ ▲ ▲ ▲ ▲ ▲ ▲

Pit toilets, tables, grills.
At southern end of Lake Fork Arm of
Blue Mesa Reservoir in deep, narrow
canyon with shade trees.
Fish, observe wildlife, and take pictures.
NO water. 14-day limit. Crowded. Quiet
10pm–6am. Ticks Apr–Jul.
7520 ft (2256 m)

## DAVIS SPRINGS

White River NF
(303) 945-2521
State map: E12
From DILLON, travel 30.25 miles (48.4 k)
NW on CO 9 then 3 miles (4.8 k) NW on
CR 30. (Cataract Creek, Elliot Creek, and
Willow are accessible from CR 30.)
FREE but choose a chore.
Open May 23–Sep 30.
7 sites. Pit toilets, tables, fire rings.
In hardwood forest on Green Mountain
Reservoir with good fishing.
NO water. 14-day/16-ft limits.
8200 ft (2460 m)

## DEEP LAKE

White River NF
(303) 945-2521
State map: F8
From GLENWOOD SPRINGS, drive E
on US 6 about 17 miles (27.2 k); 2 miles
(3.2 k) N on CR 301; then 26.5 miles
(42.4 k) NW on FR 600. (Pass Coffee Pot
Spring.)
FREE but choose a chore.
Open Jun 1–Oct 31.
21 sites. Pit toilets, tables, grills.
Boat (no motors) and fish in lake.
NO water. 14-day/22-ft limits.
10500 ft (3150 m)

## DELANEY BUTTE LAKES SWA

CO Wildlife (303) 484-2836
State map: B11
From WALDEN, drive
.5 mile (800 m) W on CO 14. Go
4.5 miles (7.2 k) W on CR 18 then 1 mile
(1.6 k) N on CR 5.
FREE but choose a chore.
Open All Year.
Undesignated, scattered sites.
Pit toilets, shade shelters, boat ramp.

In open area among three lakes in high
mountain valley.
Boat and fish in lakes. Hike, view and
photograph wildlife.
NO water/trash pick-up. Changing
weather/road conditions. Hunting in
season.
8000 ft (2400 m)

## DINOSAUR NM

(303) 374-2216
State map: B1-C2
Locate in NW corner of CO
with primary access via US 40.
FREE but $5 entrance fee (or pass). Also,
free backcountry permits available at
Visitor Center or ranger stations.
While much attention focuses on
dinosaur research in UT section of
monument, great natural beauty and
uncrowded opportunities are accessible
along Green and Yampa rivers in CO.
▲ Deerlodge Park
Find 53 miles (84.8 k) E of Headquarters
near DINOSAUR. From Visitor Center,
continue on US 40 about 39 miles
(62.4 k). Turn Left (N) on 14-mile (22.4 k)
access road to E section of monument.
Open May 15–Nov 15, snow decides.
8 sites. Pit toilets, picnic tables, fire rings,
boat ramp.
Beside Yampa River.
Float (with permit) or fish river.
NO water. 15-day limit.
5600 ft (1680 m)
▲ Echo Park
From Visitor Center near DINOSAUR,
continue 25 miles (40 k) N on Harpers
Corner Scenic Dr. Turn Right onto Echo
Park Rd (steep, narrow road for
high-clearance vehicles) and go another
13 miles (20.8 k)–impassable when wet.
Open Jun 1–Nov 1, snow decides.
14 sites. Water, pit toilets, tables, fire
rings, boat ramp.
At union of Yampa and Green rivers.
Float (with permit) or fish rivers. Hike to
view and photograph rock art.
NO water–come prepared. 15-day limit.
5000 ft (1500 m)
▲ Gates of Lodore
On CO 318 from MAYBELL, go 52 miles

▲ ▲ ▲ ▲ ▲ ▲ ▲ ▲ ▲ ▲ ▲ ▲ ▲ ▲ ▲ ▲ ▲ ▲ ▲ ▲ ▲ ▲

(82 k) to 10-mile (16-k) access road–
106 miles (169.6 k) from Visitor Center.
Open All Year.
17 sites. Water, pit toilets, tables, fire
rings, boat ramp.
On Green River near Browns Park NWR
in northern section of monument.
Float (with permit) or fish river. Walk
nature trail.
15-day limit.
5300 ft (1590 m)

▲ **Rainbow Park**
From JENSEN, take CO 149 for 3 miles
(4 k) N. Turn Left (NW) on Brush Creek
Rd and continue 5 miles (8 k). Turn
Right on unpaved road following Brush
Creek 4 miles (7 k) N. Turn Right (E) on
Island Park Rd and go another 12 miles
(19 k)–for high-clearance vehicles only;
primitive road impassable when wet.
Open Jun 1–Nov 1, snow decides.
4 tent sites.
Pit toilets, tables, fire rings, boat ramp.
On Green River.
Float (with permit) or fish river. Drive
5 miles (8 k) of remaining road to Island
Park area and Ruple Ranch.
NO water–come prepared. 15-day limit.

## DIVIDE FORK
Uncompahgre NF
(303) 242-8211
State map: J2
From WHITEWATER, go 24 miles
(38.4 k) SW on paved CO 141 then
10 miles (16 k) on unpaved FR 402, also
called Divide Rd. (Other nearby choices
are Big Dominguez and Carson Hole.)
FREE but choose a chore.
Open May 20–Nov 1; dry camping
off-season.
11 scattered, screened sites. Central
water faucet, pit toilets, tables, fire rings.
Among aspen.
Hike trails to observe nature.
14-day/16-ft limits. Changing
weather/road conditions. ATVs. Horses.
Hunting in season.
9200 ft (2760 m)

## DOME LAKE SWA
CO Wildlife (303) 641-0088
State map: K10
From GUNNISON, go
8 miles (12.8 k) E on US 50 then 22 miles
(35.2 k) SE on CO 114.
FREE. Open All Year.
Undesignated, scattered sites. Pit toilets.
Among wildflowers and sagebrush with
mountains in background.
Hike to view and photograph scenery
and wildlife. Boat (no motors) and fish
in Dome Lake.
NO water/trash arrangements–be
responsible. 14-day limit. Changing
weather/road conditions.
9017 ft (2703 m)

## DRY LAKE
Routt NF (303) 879-1722
State map: B10
Drive 4 miles (6.4 k) N of
STEAMBOAT SPRINGS on CR 36
(Strawberry Park Rd) then 3.6 miles
(5.8 k) E on FR 60 (Buffalo Pass Rd).
(Summit Lake is also in area.)
FREE but choose a chore.
Open Jul 15–weather closure.
8 close, open sites.
Pit toilets, tables, fire rings.
At base of Buffalo Pass.
Hike or bike trails. View wildlife and
take photographs.
NO water/trash arrangements.
14-day/16-ft limits. Crowded.
8000 ft (2400 m)

## EAST MAROON
White River NF
(303) 945-2521
State map: H9
From ASPEN, head approximately
1 mile (1.6 k) NW on CO 82 then
9.5 miles (15.2 k) SW on FR 125.
FREE but choose a chore.
Open Jun 1–Oct 1.
13 sites. Pit toilets, tables, fire rings.
Near impressive Maroon Bells.
Hike in nearby wilderness. Take lots of
photos. Fish in numerous lakes.
NO water. 10-day limit.
8700 ft (2610 m)

▲ ▲ ▲ ▲ ▲ ▲ ▲ ▲ ▲ ▲ ▲ ▲ ▲ ▲ ▲ ▲ ▲ ▲ ▲ ▲ ▲ ▲ ▲ ▲ ▲ ▲

## EGGLESTON LAKE

▲ Grand Mesa NF
(303) 242-8211
State map: H5

From CEDAREDGE, drive 16 miles (25.6 k) N on paved CO 65 then 3.5 miles (5.6 k) E on gravel FR 121. (See Crag Crest, Kiser Creek, or Trickle Park.)
$5. Open Jun 20–Sep 15.
6 close, open sites. Hand water pump, pit toilets, tables, fire rings.
In spruce and fir trees beside lake on top of Grand Mesa.
Boat and fish in lake. Observe and photograph nature.
Changing weather/road conditions. 14-day/30-ft limits. Quiet 10pm–6am. Mosquitos.
10100 ft (3030 m)

## ELK WALLOW

▲ White River NF
(303) 945-2521
State map: G9

From BASALT, drive 23 miles (36.8 k) E on CR 105 then 3.25 miles (5.2 k) E on FR 501 to North Fork of Frying Pan River.
FREE but choose a chore.
Open May 25–Nov 1.
7 sites. Pit toilets, tables, fire rings.
Fish in river.
NO water. 14-day/30-ft limits.
8900 ft (2670 m)

## ELLIOT CREEK

▲ White River NF
(303) 945-2521
State map: E12

From DILLON, proceed NW on CO 9 for 30.25 miles (48.4 k) then 3 miles (4.8 k) SW on CR 30. (Also see Cataract Creek, Davis Springs, and Willow.)
FREE but choose a chore.
Open May 25–Oct 31.
64 sites. Pit toilets, tables, fire rings.
On creek at Green Mountain Reservoir in grassy setting with mountain views.
Boat, waterski, swim, or fish.
NO water. 10-day/22-ft limits.
8200 ft (2460 m)

## FISH HAWK

▲ Grand Mesa NF
(303) 242-8211
State map: H5

From CEDAREDGE, drive 16 miles (25.6 k) N on paved CO 65 then 6 miles (9.6 k) E on FR 121. (Also see Cottonwood Lake and Twin Lake.)
FREE but choose a chore.
Open Jun 20–Sep 30; camping allowed off-season.
5 sites. Pit toilets, tables, fire rings.
On Eggleston Lake in spruce and fir.
Boat and fish lake. Watch hawks.
NO water/trash arrangements (pack it out). 14-day/16-ft limits. Changing weather/road conditions. Mosquitos.
Hunting in season. 14-day limit.
10200 ft (3060 m)

## FIVE POINTS

▲ BLM (719) 539-7289
State map: K15
Travel 16 miles (25.6 k) W of
CANON CITY via US 50.
$2. Open All Year.
12 sites. Pit toilets, tables, grills, fire rings, wildlife viewing area.
In oasis-like corridor of Arkansas River in Colorado's high desert next to McIntyre Hills Wilderness Study Area.
Hike or climb in canyon. Observe and photograph wildlife. Fish or run river in rafts or kayaks.
NO water/trash arrangements–come prepared. Hunting in season.
6000 ft (1800 m)

## FLATIRON RESERVOIR

▲ Larimer County Parks
(303) 679-4570
State map: C16

From LOVELAND, drive W on US 34; S on CR 29; then W on CR 18E.
$4/night weekdays, $5/night weekends (annual passes for vehicles and boats).
Open All Year.
60 sites in two loops on one side of reservoir. Central water faucet, pit toilets, tables, grills, fire rings.
Fishing, hiking, birdwatching, and photography at this foothills reservoir.

▲ ▲ ▲ ▲ ▲ ▲ ▲ ▲ ▲ ▲ ▲ ▲ ▲     ▲ ▲ ▲ ▲ ▲ ▲ ▲ ▲ ▲ ▲ ▲ ▲

14-day limit. Crowded weekends. Quiet hours.
5500 ft (1650 m)

## FREEMAN

Routt NF (303) 879-1722
State map: B7
Head 13 miles (20.8 k) N of CRAIG on CO 13 then 8.5 miles (13.6 k) NE on FR 112-2B and CR 11.
$5. Open Jun 15–Nov 15, snow decides. 17 close, open sites. ♿
Hand water pump, pit toilets, tables, grills, fire rings, boat ramp.
Next to shore on Freeman Reservoir.
Boat (no motors) and fish. Watch the birdies. Hike.
Changing weather conditions. 14-day/22-ft limits.
8800 ft (2640 m)

## GENEVA PARK

Pike NF (303) 236-7386
State map: G14
From GRANT, go 7 miles (11.2 k) NW on FR 118 then .25 mile (400 m) NW on gravel FR 119.
FREE but choose a chore.
Open May 1–Oct 15; camping allowed off-season.
26 close, screened sites.
Pit toilets, tables, grills, fire rings.
Off Guanella Pass Scenic Byway at Geneva Creek in mixed species trees.
Hike, fish, or relax and enjoy scenery.
NO water. 14-day/16-ft limits.
9800 ft (2940 m)

## GOLD CREEK

Gunnison NF (303) 641-0471
State map: J10
From OHIO, head 8 miles (12.8 k) N on gravel FR 771.
FREE but choose a chore.
Open Jun 1–Nov 30.
6 sites.
Pit toilets, tables, grills, fire rings.
At end of road in isolated area of lodgepole pine next to creek.
Fish in creek and high-country lakes.
Hike and bike to observe or photograph scenery and wildlife.

NO water/trash facilities. 14-day limit. Crowded July 4. ATVs. Hunting in season.
10000 ft (3000 m)

## GOOSE CREEK

Pike NF (303) 236-7386
State map: H15
From WOODLAND PARK, drive 24 miles (38.4 k) NW on CO 67; 3 miles (4.8 k) SW on CR 126; then 12 miles (19.2 k) SW on gravel FR 211.
FREE but choose a chore.
Open May 1–Oct 15 (snow decides).
10 close, screened sites. Hand water pump, pit toilets, tables, grills, fire rings.
Among lodgepole pine along Goose Creek, next to Lost Creek Wilderness.
Take a hike or go fishing.
Crowded summers. 14-day/16-ft limits.
8100 ft (2430 m)

## GOTHIC

Gunnison NF (303) 641-0471
State map: I9
From CRESTED BUTTE, travel approximately 6 miles (9.6 k) on CR 3 (Gothic Rd). (Avery Peak is close.)
FREE but choose a chore.
Open May 1–Oct 31.
4 sites. Pit toilets, tables.
With incomparable mountain scenery near old mining townsite.
Hike (don't miss Copper Creek Trail) or bike to see and photograph area. Fish in high-country streams and lakes. Climb nearby mountains.
NO water/trash facilities. 14-day limit.
Crowded. Changing weather/road conditions. Hunting in season.
9600 ft (2880 m)

## GRAND VIEW

Roosevelt NF (303) 498-1375
State map: C13
From LAPORTE, drive 4 miles (6.4 k) N on US 287; 61 miles (97.6 k) W on CO 14; then 11 miles (17.6 k) SE on FR 156. (Pass Long Draw.)
FREE but choose a chore.
Open Jun 15–Sep 30.
9 tent sites. Pit toilets, tables, grills.

▲ ▲ ▲ ▲ ▲ ▲ ▲ ▲ ▲ ▲ ▲ ▲ ▲ ▲ ▲ ▲ ▲ ▲ ▲ ▲ ▲ ▲ ▲ ▲

On Long Draw Reservoir at boundary to scenic Rocky Mountain NP.
Fish on reservoir. Hike trails to observe and photograph nature.
NO water. 14-day limit.
10400 ft (3120 m)

## GRANITE

Routt NF (303) 879-1722
State map: B10
Head N of STEAMBOAT SPRINGS for 4 miles (6.4 k) on CR 36 (Strawberry Park Rd). Continue 12 miles (19.2 k) E on FR 60 (Buffalo Pass Rd) then 5 miles (8 k) S to FR 310 (Fish Creek Reservoir Rd).
FREE but choose a chore.
Open Jul 15–Oct 1, weather decides.
6 close, open sites.
Pit toilets, tables, fire rings, boat ramp.
Boat (no gasoline motors) and fish in reservoir. Hike or bike to observe and photograph nature.
NO water/trash facilities. 14-day/18-ft limits. Changing weather. Insects. ATVs. Hunting in season.
9000 ft (2700 m)

## GREAT SAND DUNES NM
**Backcountry**

(719) 378-2312
State map: N14
From ALAMOSA, follow US 160 E to CO 150 and monument.
FREE but $3 entrance fee (or pass).
(Pinyon Flats costs over $5.) Inquire about backcountry permits at Visitor Center. Open Apr–Oct.
Camp near or among windblown, 700-ft-high sand dunes at base of 14000-ft, snow-topped Sangre de Cristo Mountains.
No firewood gathering or open fires–cook with campstoves. Wear shoes to protect feet from hot sand. In thunderstorm, seek low ground.
8200 ft (2460 m)

## GREEN MOUNTAIN

Pike NF (719) 545-8737
State map: G15
From BUFFALO CREEK,

travel .5 mile (800 m) SE on CR 126 then 7.75 miles (12.4 k) SW on gravel FR 543. (Pass Baldy.)
FREE but choose a chore.
Open May 1–Oct 15.
6 sites.
Water, pit toilets, tables, fire rings.
Within mile of Wellington Lake and trail into Lost Creek Wilderness.
Fish or hike.
14-day limit. Crowded late summer.
7000 ft (2100 m)

## GRIZZLY CREEK

Routt NF (303) 879-1722
State map: B11
From WALDEN, go 13 miles (20.8 k) SW on CO 14 to HEBRON; 10.5 miles (16.8 k) W on CR 24; then .25 mile (400 m) W on FR 60.
$5. Open Jun 15–Nov 1, weather decides.
12 (6 tent-only) sites. Hand water pump, pit toilets, tables, fire rings.
Near Mt Zirkel Wilderness.
Fish in creek. Hike or bike to view and photograph nature.
14-day/18-ft limits–minimal parking. ATVs.
8500 ft (2550 m)

## GYPSUM RS

BLM (303) 244-3000
State map: F9
From GYPSUM, go 1.5 miles (2.4 k) W on US 6.
FREE but choose a chore.
Open May 30–Oct 31.
10 sites. Pit toilets, tables.
On Eagle River.
Fish or run river.
NO water. 14-day/22-ft limits.
6200 ft (1860 m)

## HALL VALLEY & HANDCART

Pike NF (303) 236-7386
State map: G14
From GRANT, head 3 miles (4.8 k) W on US 285 then 4.5 miles (7.2 k) NW on gravel FR 120. (Handcart is .5 mile farther.)
FREE but choose a chore.

▲ ▲ ▲ ▲ ▲ ▲ ▲ ▲ ▲ ▲ ▲ ▲ ▲ ▲ ▲ ▲ ▲ ▲ ▲ ▲ ▲ ▲ ▲ ▲ ▲ ▲ ▲ ▲ ▲ ▲

Open May 1–Oct 15; camping allowed off-season.
9 sites at Hall Valley, 10 at Handcart.
Pit toilets, tables, grills, fire rings.
In dense, mixed conifers along Hall Valley Creek near Kenosha Pass and headwaters of North Fork of South Platte River.
Hiking and fishing.
NO water/trash facilities–come prepared. 14-day/16-ft limits.
9800 ft (2940 m)

## HAY PRESS

Uncompahgre NF
(303) 242-8211
State map: I2
From GRAND JUNCTION, drive 10 miles (16 k) SW on CO 340; then 20 miles (32 k) S on FR 400. (Also see BLM's Miracle Rock and Mud Springs.)
FREE but choose a chore.
Open May 20–Nov 1; camping allowed off-season.
11 scattered, open sites.
Pit toilets, tables, fire rings.
In aspen on Hay Press Creek near Fruita Reservoir #3 and Colorado NM.
Fish in creek or lake. Observe wildlife.
NO water. 14-day/16-ft limits. Changing weather/road conditions. ATVs. Horses. Hunting in season.
9300 ft (2790 m)

## HAYDEN CREEK

San Isabel NF (719) 539-3591
State map: K13
From COALDALE, head 5 miles (8 k) SW on gravel FR 249. (Coaldale Walk-In is another option.)
FREE but choose a chore.
Open May 18–Oct 15.
11 (3 tent-only) sites. Hand water pump, pit toilets, tables, grills, fire rings.
On Hayden Creek with Rainbow Trail.
Hike a lot or fish a bunch.
No trash arrangements (pack it out).
14-day/16-ft limits. Hunting in season.
8000 ft (2400 m)

## HECLA JUNCTION

BLM (719) 539-7289
State map: J12
9 miles (14.4 k) N of SALIDA via US 285, watch for sign to turn Right (NE) then go 3 miles (4.8 k) on CR 129.
$2. Open All Year.
20 sites. Pit toilets, tables, grills, fire rings, changing room.
In oasis corridor of Arkansas River in high desert near Browns Canyon Wilderness Study Area as well as D&RGW Railroad.
Boat (raft or kayak), swim, or fish. Climb canyon walls. Hike to observe and photograph nature.
NO water/trash arrangements–be responsible. 14-day limit.
7300 ft (2190 m)

## HIGHWAY SPRINGS

Rio Grande NF
(719) 657-3321
State map: N10
From SOUTH FORK, take US 160 for 4 miles (6.4 k) SW. (See Beaver Creek.)
FREE but choose a chore.
Open May 25–Sep 15.
11 scattered, screened sites.
Pit toilets, tables, fire rings.
In stand of ponderosa pine on South Fork of Rio Grande.
Fish and observe nature.
NO water. 14-day/25-ft limits.
8400 ft (2520 m)

## HILL CREEK

White River NF
(303) 945-2521
State map: E6
From MEEKER, travel 2 miles (3.2 k) E on CO 13; 23 miles (36.8 k) E on CR 8; 8 miles (12.8 k) SE on CR 12; then .5 mile (800 m) NE on FR 228.
FREE but choose a chore.
Open May 25–Nov 1.
10 sites. Pit toilets, tables, fire rings.
On creek near scenic Flat Tops Wilderness with good fishing and excellent hiking opportunities.
NO water.
8100 ft (2430 m)

## HIMES PEAK

White River NF
(303) 945-2521
State map: E7

From MEEKER, proceed 2 miles (3.2 k) E
on CO 13; 41 miles (65.6 k) E on CR 8;
then 5 miles (8 k) SE on FR 205.
$5. Open Jun 15–Nov 15.
11 sites.
Water, pit toilets, tables, fire rings.
On North Fork of White River with trail
into Flat Tops Wilderness.
Fishing, hiking, and horseback riding.
14-day/36-ft limits.
8800 ft (2640 m)

## HINMAN

Routt NF (303) 879-1722
State map: B9
From CLARK, go 1 mile
(1.6 k) N on CR 129; 6 miles (9.6 k) NE
on FR 400 (Seedhouse Rd); then .5 mile
(800 m) SW on FR 440.
$5. Open Jun 15–Labor Day.
13 close, open sites. Hand water pump,
pit toilets, tables, fire rings.
On Elk River with trails to Hinman Lake
and Mt Zirkel Wilderness.
Fishing, hiking, cycling, and
photography.
14-day/22-ft limits. Crowded. ATVs.
7600 ft (2280 m)

## HORSETOOTH RESERVOIR

Larimer County Parks
(303) 679-4570
State map: C16

From FORT COLLINS, drive W on
CR 38E to foothills reservoir.
$4/night weekdays, $5/night weekends
(annual passes for vehicles and boats).
Open All Year.
120 scattered, open sites. Central water
faucet, dump station, pit toilets, tables,
grills, fire rings, pay phone, marina with
ice and rentals, boat ramp, beach.
Water enthusiasts boat, waterski, scuba
dive, swim and fish. Landlubbers hike,
observe wildlife, and take photos.
14-day limit. Crowded weekends. Quiet
hours.
5430 ft (1629 m)

## IRISH CANYON

BLM (303) 824-4441
State map: A2
From US 40 in MAYBELL,
travel NW on CO 318 about 45 miles
(72 k). Turn Right (N) on gravel CR 10
and continue 8 miles (12.8 k).
FREE but choose a chore.
Open All Year.
3 (2 tent-only) scattered, screened sites.
Pit toilets, tables, fire rings.
In colorful, semiarid canyon with
interesting geology and rock art.
Share trails with hikers, mountain bikers,
and horseback riders. View and
photograph scenery as well as wildlife.
NO water/trash facilities. 14-day limit.
6500 ft (1950 m)

## IVY CREEK

Rio Grande NF
(719) 658-2556
State map: N9

From CREEDE, head W on CO 149 for
6 miles (9.6 k). Turn onto FR 523 (Middle
Creek Rd) and proceed 4 miles (6.4 k).
Turn onto FR 528 (Lime Creek Rd) and
continue 3 miles (4.8 k). Turn again on
rough FR 526 for another 3 miles (4.8 k).
FREE but choose a chore.
Open May 25–Sep 15.
4 sites suitable for tents or pop-up
trailers. Pit toilets, fire rings.
Near open grassland but in stand of
Engelmann spruce on Ivy Creek near
Weminuche Wilderness.
Fish on creek. Hike to observe nature or
to rockhound.
NO water/trash facilities–come
prepared. 14-day limit.
9200 ft (2760 m)

## KISER CREEK

Grand Mesa NF
(303) 242-8211
State map: H5

From CEDAREDGE, travel 16 miles
(25.6 k) N on paved CO 65; 3 miles
(4.8 k) E on FR 121; then S on FR 123.
FREE but choose a chore.
Open Jun 20–Sep 30.
12 sites. Hand water pump, pit toilets,

tables, fire rings.
Near Eggleston and Baron Reservoirs in spruce and fir setting.
Boat and fish reservoirs. Observe and photograph nature.
14-day/16-ft limits. Changing weather/road conditions. ATVs. Hunting in season.
10100 ft (3030 m)

## KITE LAKE

Pike NF (719) 836-2031
State map: G12
Drive 6 miles (9.6 k) NW of ALMA on CR 8 then Road of Ten—for 4WD vehicles.
FREE but choose a chore.
Open Jun 30–Sep 30; camping allowed off-season.
7 tent sites. Pit toilets, tables, fire rings.
Above-timberline with access to three 14000-ft peaks.
Fish in lake. Hike and mountain climb to observe and photograph nature.
NO water/trash provisions—handle responsibly. 14-day limit.
11000 ft (3300 m)

## KLINES FOLLY

White River NF
(303) 945-2521
State map: F6
From GLENWOOD SPRINGS, head 17 miles (27.2 k) E on US 6; 2 miles (3.2 k) N on CR 301; then 25.5 miles (40.8 k) NW on FR 600.
FREE but choose a chore.
Open Jul 1–Oct 31.
4 sites. Pit toilets, tables, fire rings.
In historic area, near lake in forest.
See if you can discover how this campground got its name.
NO water. 14-day/22-ft limits.
10200 ft (3060 m)

## LA JARA RESERVOIR SWA

CO Wildlife (303) 249-3431
State map: P11
From MONTE VISTA, drive 20 miles (32 k) S on CO 15; .5 mile (800 m) on FR 255; then 10 miles (16 k) W on FR 240. (Alamosa and Stunner are nearby.)
FREE but choose a chore.
Open All Year.
Undesignated, scattered sites. Hand water pump, pit toilets, boat ramp.
On shoreline of rock and grass, pine and aspen.
Boating and fishing. Hiking to observe and photograph wildlife.
Changing weather/road conditions. Hunting in season.
9000 ft (2700 m)

## LAKE HASTY

COE (719) 336-3476
State map: L25
Go 3 miles (4.8 k) S of HASTY via CR 24.
$4, $2 for electrical hook-up.
Open Apr 15–Sep 15; dry camping off-season.
64 sites scattered in open and screened settings. ₵
Water, flush/chemical toilets, dump station, electric hook-ups, tables, grills, fire rings, boat ramp, wading pool, playground, store with ice, pay phone.
With trees, grass, and beach on Lake Hasty near John Martin Dam and Reservoir.
Boat, ski, swim, or fish on reservoir.
Observe and photograph nature. Attend ranger programs. Tour dam facilities.
14-day limit. Crowded holiday weekends. Hunting in season.
3800 ft (1140 m)

## LINCOLN GULCH

White River NF
(303) 945-2521
State map: H10
From ASPEN, drive 12 miles (19.2 k) SE on CO 82; .5 mile (800 m) SW on FR 106; then .25 mile (400 m) on access road. (See Lostman, Portal, and Weller.)
$5. Open Jul 1–Sep 15.
7 sites. Pit toilets, tables, fire rings.
Near Lincoln Creek and Roaring Fork River plus Collegiate Peaks Wilderness.
Fish or hike.
16-ft limit.
9700 ft (2910 m)

## LONG DRAW

Roosevelt NF (303) 498-1375
State map: C13
From LAPORTE, go 4 miles (6.4 k) N on US 287; 61 miles (97.6 k) W on CO 14; then 9 miles (14.4 k) SE on FR 156. (Also see Grand View.)
FREE but choose a chore.
Open Jun 15–Sep 30.
31 sites. Pit toilets, tables, grills.
Near Long Draw Reservoir on scenic boundary to Rocky Mountain NP.
Fish in reservoir. Hike Corral Creek Trail into national park trail system.
NO water. 14-day/32-ft limits.
10000 ft (3000 m)

## LOST LAKE

Gunnison NF (303) 527-4131
State map: I8
From CRESTED BUTTE, go W on Kebler Pass Rd–difficult for RVs. (From PAONIA, go NE on CO 133 then E on Kebler Pass Rd.) Off Kebler Pass Rd, continue 3 miles (4.8 k) S on FR 706.
FREE but choose a chore.
Open Jun 10–Oct 15.
11 close, screened sites.
Pit toilets, tables, grills.
On scenic lake at base of East Beckwith Mountain near West Elk Wilderness.
Hike on trail to three lakes. Observe and photograph scenery and wildlife. Canoe and fish in lakes.
NO water/trash facilities. 14-day limit.
Crowded. Hunting in season.
9200 ft (2760 m)

## LOST PARK

Pike NF (719) 836-2031
State map: G14
From JEFFERSON, proceed 1.25 miles (2 k) NE on US 285 then 20 miles (32 k) E on gravel FR 127.
FREE but choose a chore.
Open May 15–Oct 15; dry camping off-season.
10 close, screened sites. Hand water pump, pit toilets, tables, grills, fire rings.
Among lodgepole pine next to Lost Creek and Lost Creek Wilderness.
Fish in creek. Hike on wilderness trails.
Climb nearby mountains.
14-day/22-ft limits. No trash arrangements. Hunting in season.
10000 ft (3000 m)

## LOST TRAIL

Rio Grande NF
(719) 658-2556
State map: N7
From CREEDE, drive CO 149 SW for 20 miles (32 k). Turn onto FR 520 (Rio Grande Reservoir Rd) and proceed 18 miles (28.8 k).
FREE but choose a chore.
Open May 15–Sep 15.
7 sites. Hand water pump, pit toilets, tables, fire rings.
In Engelmann spruce stand above upper Rio Grande Reservoir.
Fish in reservoir. Hike to observe and photograph scenery and wildlife.
14-day/25-ft limits. No trash arrangements. Changing weather/road conditions. ATVs. Hunting in season.
9500 ft (2850 m)

## LOSTMAN

White River NF
(303) 945-2521
State map: H10
From ASPEN, travel 14.25 miles (22.8 k) SE on CO 82. (Also see Lincoln Gulch, Portal, and Weller.)
$5. Open Jul 1–Sep 30.
9 sites. Pit toilets, tables, fire rings.
Near confluence of Lostman Creek and Roaring Fork River.
Fish or hike to observe and photograph natural beauty.
10-day/22-ft limits.
10700 ft (3210 m)

## LOWER PIEDRA

San Juan NF (303) 247-4874
State map: P7
From CHIMNEY ROCK, go 1 mile (1.6 k) N of US 160 on FR 621 to Piedra River.
FREE but choose a chore.
Open May 1–Nov 1.
17 sites. Pit toilets, tables, grills.
Fish or hike.

14-day/32-ft limits.
6600 ft (1980 m)

## LUDERS

Rio Grande NF
(719) 655-2547
State map: L10
From SAGUACHE, go 22 miles (35.2 k)
NW on CO 114. Turn on FR 750 and
continue 11 miles (17.6 k) NW.
**FREE** but choose a chore.
Open May 25–Sep 30.
6 scattered, screened sites.
Pit toilets, tables, fire rings.
In mixed conifers or open meadow along
Luders Creek near Continental Divide at
Cochetopa Pass.
Hike along old Ute Trail.
14-day/25-ft limits. NO water/trash
arrangements. Hunting in season.
10000 ft (3000 m)

## MARVINE & EAST MARVINE

White River NF
(303) 945-2521
State map: E7
From MEEKER, proceed 2 miles (3.2 k) E
on CO 13; 29 miles (46.4 k) E on CR 8
(Flat Tops Trail Scenic Byway); then
4.5 miles (7.2 k) SE on FR 12. (See North
Fork & Overflow.)
**$5.** Open May 25–Nov 15.
25 sites.
Water, pit toilets, tables, fire rings.
On Marvine Creek near Marvine Lake in
Flat Tops Wilderness.
Fish in creek or lake. Hike in wilderness.
14-day/22-ft limits. Horses.
8100 ft (2430 m)

## MEADOW LAKE

White River NF
(303) 945-2521
State map: F7
From NEW CASTLE, travel about
8 miles (12.8 k) NE on CR 245 (Elk Circle
Rd); 20.5 miles (32.8 k) N on FR 244;
3.5 miles (5.4 k) E on FR 601; then
3 miles (4.8 k) S on FR 823.
**$5.** Open Memorial Day–Labor Day.
10 sites. Water, pit toilets, tables, grills.
Fish in lake.

16-ft limit. ATVs.
9600 ft (2880 m)

## MERIDIAN

Pike NF (303) 236-7386
State map: G14
From BAILEY, go 2.25 miles
(3.6 k) N on US 285; 6.5 miles (10.4 k)
NW on FR 100; 1 mile (1.6 k) N on
gravel FR 102.
**FREE** but choose a chore.
Open May 1–Oct 15; camping allowed
off-season.
18 close, screened sites.
Pit toilets, tables, grills, fire rings.
In mixed-conifers on Deer Creek,
adjoining Mt Evans Wilderness.
Fish in creek or hike in wilderness.
NO water/trash arrangements.
14-day/16-ft limits.
9000 ft (2700 m)

## MESA

Gunnison NF (303) 874-7691
State map: J6
From CRAWFORD, drive
18 miles (28.8 k) SE on CO 92.
**FREE** but choose a chore.
Open Jun 1–Nov 15.
5 sites.
Water, pit toilets, tables, fire rings.
Near Black Canyon of Gunnison NM's
North Rim entrance.
View canyon and area panoramas.
14-day/32-ft limits.
9000 ft (2700 m)

## MIDDLE QUARTZ

Gunnison NF (303) 641-0471
State map: J11
From PITKIN, travel
1.5 miles (2.4 k) on FR 765. Turn E on
FR 767 for another 5.5 miles (8.8 k).
**FREE** but choose a chore.
Open Jun 1–Nov 30; camping allowed
off-season.
7 sites. Pit toilets, tables, fire rings.
In deep glacial valley with creek and
beaver ponds.
Hike to observe and photograph nature.
Fish in Middle Quartz Creek. Climb
nearby mountains.

▲ ▲ ▲ ▲ ▲ ▲ ▲ ▲ ▲ ▲ ▲ ▲ ▲ ▲ ▲ ▲ ▲ ▲ ▲ ▲ ▲ ▲ ▲ ▲

NO water/trash arrangements–come prepared. 14-day/16-ft limits. Crowded July 4. ATVs. Hunting in season.
10200 ft (3060 m)

## MILL CREEK

BLM (303) 249-7791
State map: M7
From LAKE CITY, proceed 2.5 miles (4 k) S on CO 149. Turn Right on road to Lake San Cristobal and continue 4 miles (6.4 k) on pavement then 6 miles (9.6 k) on gravel.
$5. Open Jun 1–Oct 30; dry camping off-season.
22 scattered sites in choice of open or screened settings. Hand water pump, pit toilets, tables, grills, fire rings.
On Lake Fork of Gunnison River amid spectacular San Juan Mountains.
Fish, hike, mountain climb, mountain bike, and explore ghost towns. Bring your camera.
14-day/22-ft limits. Noisy weekends. ATVs. Hunting in season.
9400 ft (2820 m)

## MIRACLE ROCK

BLM (303) 244-3000
State map: I2
From GRAND JUNCTION, take Monument Rd into Colorado NM. Turn onto East Glade Park Rd which becomes DS Rd. Turn Left on 9.8 Rd and proceed to site. (Also see Hay Press and Mud Springs.)
FREE but choose a chore.
Open May 1–Oct 30.
4 sites.
Pit toilets, tables, grills, fire rings.
In upland juniper growing among interesting rocks.
Hike to observe and photograph scenery and wildlife.
NO water/trash provisions–be responsible. 14-day/30-ft limits.
7000 ft (2100 m)

## MIRAMONTE RESERVOIR SWA

CO Wildlife (303) 249-3431
State map: M3
From NORWOOD, drive 1.5 miles (2.4 k) E on CO 145 then 17 miles (27.2 k) S on FR 610 (Dolores–Norwood Rd).
FREE but choose a chore.
Open All Year.
Undesignated, scattered sites.
Hand water pump, pit toilets, dump station, boat ramp.
In sagebrush around reservoir.
Windsurf, boat, waterski, or fish on reservoir. Hike. Observe and photograph waterfowl.
No trash arrangements. Noisy power boats and jet skis. Hunting in season.
7600 ft (2280 m)

## MOLLY GULCH

Pike NF (303) 236-7386
State map: H15
From WOODLAND PARK, drive 24 miles (38.4 k) NW on CO 67; 2.75 miles (4.4 k) SW on CR 126; then about 9.5 miles (15.2 k) SW on gravel FR 211.
FREE but choose a chore.
Open May 1–Oct 15; camping allowed off-season.
15 close, screened sites.
Pit toilets, tables, grills, fire rings.
In mixed-conifer setting along Goose Creek near mountainous Lost Creek Wilderness.
Fish in creek or hike in wilderness.
NO water/trash facilities. 14-day/16-ft limits.
7500 ft (2250 m)

## MOUNTAIN SHEEP POINT

BLM (303) 247-4082
State map: N1
From eastern edge of DOVE CREEK, follow signs from US 666 along steep and narrow, gravel and dirt roads.
FREE but choose a chore.
Open Apr 1–Oct 31; camping allowed off-season.
3 scattered, screened sites. Pit toilets, tables, grills, fire rings, boat ramp.
In 1000-ft deep Dolores River Canyon, surrounded by boxelder, oakbrush, willow, pine, and cottonwood.
Boat (canoe, kayak, or raft) as well as

▲ ▲ ▲ ▲ ▲ ▲ ▲ ▲ ▲ ▲ ▲ ▲ ▲ ▲ ▲ ▲ ▲ ▲ ▲ ▲ ▲ ▲ ▲ ▲ ▲ ▲ ▲ ▲ ▲

fish river. Hike to observe and photograph nature.
NO water/trash pickup (pack it out).
14-day limit. 4-wheeling and hunting.
Crowded July 4 weekend.
6100 ft (1830 m)

## MUD SPRINGS

BLM (303) 244-3000
State map: I2
From GRAND JUNCTION,
take Monument Rd into Colorado NM.
Turn on East Glade Park Rd which
becomes DS Rd. Turn Left (S) onto
16.5 Rd and follow for 6 miles (9.6 k).
(Also see Hay Press and Miracle Rock.)
FREE but choose a chore.
Open May 1–Oct 30.
10 scattered, screened sites.
Central water faucet, pit toilets, tables,
grills, fire rings.
In aspen grove in Glade Park.
Hike to rockhound or to take photos.
No trash facilities. 14-day/30-ft limits.
8000 ft (2400 m)

## NARROWS CO-OP

Roosevelt NF (303) 482-3822
State map: B15
From LAPORTE, travel
4 miles (6.4 k) N on US 287 then
23.5 miles (37.6 k) W on CO 14. (Stevens
Gulch is nearby.)
FREE but choose a chore.
Open All Year.
4 sites. Pit toilets, dump station, tables,
fire rings.
Just off picturesque drive along Cache la
Poudre River.
Fish this wild and scenic river.
NO water. 14-day/32-ft limits.
6500 ft (1950 m)

## NORTH FORK (& OVERFLOW)

White River NF
(303) 945-2521
State map: D7
From MEEKER, go 2 miles (3.2 k) E on
CO 13 then 31 miles (49.6 k) E on CR 8
(Flat Tops Trail Scenic Byway). (Also see
two Marvines and Himes Peak.)
$5. Open May 15–Nov 15.

47 sites.
Water, pit toilets, tables, fire rings.
On North Fork of White River.
Fish and hike.
14-day/22-ft limits.
8000 ft (2400 m)

## NORTH FORK POUDRE

Roosevelt NF (303) 498-1375
State map: B14
From RED FEATHER
LAKES, travel 1 mile (1.6 k) S on CR 4
then 7 miles (11.2 k) W on FR 162.
FREE but choose a chore.
Open Jun 1–Nov 15.
9 sites. Pit toilets, tables, grills.
Fish or hike along river.
NO water. 14-day/30-ft limits.
9100 ft (2730 m)

## NORTH FORK RESERVOIR

San Isabel NF (719) 539-3591
State map: J11
From SALIDA, drive
10 miles (16 k) W on US 50 then 11 miles
(17.6 k) NW on dirt FR 214.
FREE but choose a chore.
Open Jun 18–Sep 20; camping allowed
off-season.
8 close, screened sites.
Pit toilets, tables, grills, fire rings.
On North Fork Reservoir in Colorado
"High Country." Fish!
NO water/trash facilities–camp with
care. 14-day limit.
11000 ft (3300 m)

## OAK CREEK

San Isabel NF (719) 275-4119
State map: K15
Head 12 miles (19.2 k) SW of
CANON CITY on gravel CR 143.
FREE but choose a chore.
Open May 22–Sep 15; dry camping
off-season.
15 sites. Hand water pump, pit toilets,
tables, grills, fire rings.
On creek in mixed conifers and
oakbrush.
Fish in Oak Creek. Hike in Lion Canyon.
14-day/16-ft limits. Hunting in season.
7600 ft (2280 m)

## PINE RIVER

San Juan NF (303) 247-4874
State map: O6
From BAYFIELD, travel
25 miles (40 k) NE on CR 501 then FRs
600, 603, and 602.
FREE but choose a chore.
Open May 1–Nov 1.
9 sites.
Water, pit toilets, tables, grills.
At trailhead to Weminuche Wilderness.
Fish area streams and lakes. Hike into
wilderness.
14-day/22-ft limits.
8100 ft (2430 m)

## PINEWOOD LAKE

Larimer County Parks
(303) 679-4570
State map: C16
From LOVELAND, drive W on US 34; S
on CR 29; then W on CR 18E.
$4/night weekdays, $5/night weekends
(annual passes for vehicles and boats).
Open All Year.
42 open sites in three areas.
Central water faucet, pit toilets, tables,
grills, fire rings, boat ramp.
On mountain lake.
Boat (wakeless), swim, fishing, hike,
observe nature, and take photographs.
14-day limit. Crowded weekends. Quiet
hours.
6200 ft (1860 m)

## PLATTE RIVER

Pike NF (303) 236-7386
State map: G16
From BUFFALO CREEK,
head 16.75 miles (26.8 k) SE on CR 126
then 4 miles (6.4 k) N on gravel CR 67.
FREE but choose a chore.
Open All Year.
10 tent sites. Hand water pump, pit
toilets, tables, grills, fire rings.
Fish river and numerous other creeks.
14-day limit. Crowded summers.
6400 ft (1920 m)

## PORTAL

White River NF
(303) 945-2521
State map: H10
From ASPEN, travel 10.5 miles (16.8 k)
SE on CO 82; then 6.5 miles (10.4) SE on
FR 106–4WD road. (Also see Lincoln
Gulch, Lostman, and Weller.)
FREE but choose a chore.
Open Jul–Labor Day.
7 tent sites. Pit toilets, tables, fire rings.
On shore of Grizzly Reservoir near
Collegiate Peaks Wilderness.
Fish in reservoir or hike into wilderness.
NO water. 16-ft limit.
10700 ft (3210 m)

## POSO

Rio Grande NF
(719) 655-2547
State map: M11
From MONTE VISTA, drive US 285 N
for 18 miles (28.8 k). Take La Garita Rd
6 miles (9.6 k). Proceed NW on FR 690
(Carnero Creek Rd) for 10 miles (16 k).
Turn W on FR 675 for additional
1.5 miles (4 k). (Stormking is alternative.)
FREE but choose a chore.
Open May 25–Sep 30.
11 scattered, screened sites. Hand water
pump, pit toilets, tables, fire rings.
Within stand of Engelmann spruce on
South Fork of Carnero Creek.
Fish. Observe and photograph nature.
Rockhound.
No trash arrangements (pack it out).
14-day/16-ft limits.
9000 ft (2700 m)

## PUMPHOUSE RS

BLM (303) 724-3437
State map: E10
From KREMMLING, drive S
2 miles (3.2 k) on CO 9. Turn W on
gravel CR 1 (Trough Rd) and travel
14 miles (22.4 k). Pass Inspiration Point
and turn right on 1.5-mile (4-k) access
road. (Radium is nearby option.)
FREE but choose a chore.
Open May 15–Sept 15.
14 close, open sites. &
Central water faucet, pit toilets, tables,

grills, fire rings, boat ramp.
On Upper Colorado River, at put-in
point for float trips.
Boat (canoe, kayak, raft) or fish on river.
Mountain bike or hike to observe and
photograph nature.
No trash arrangements (pack it out).
14-day limit. Hunting in season.
7000 ft (2100 m)

## RADIUM

BLM (303) 724-3437
State map: E10
Located about 25 miles (40 k)
from KREMMLING–first, drive S
2 miles (3.2 k) on CO 9. Turn W on
gravel CR 1 (Trough Rd) and continue
14 miles (22.4 k). (Pass Inspiration Point
and Pumphouse RS.)
**FREE** but choose a chore.
Open Apr 1–Oct 30.
4 scattered, open sites. &
Pit toilets, tables, grills, fire rings, boat
ramp.
On Upper Colorado River.
Boat (canoe, kayak, raft) or fish.
Mountain bike. Observe and photograph
nature.
NO water/trash facilities (pack it out).
14-day limit. Hunting in season.
7000 ft (2100 m)

## RADIUM SWA

CO Wildlife (303) 248-7175
State map: E10
From KREMMLING, drive
2 miles (3.2 k) S on CO 9. Turn on gravel
CR 1 (Trough Rd) and continue to State
Bridge then 12 miles (19.2 k) SW to
property around town of RADIUM.
**FREE** but choose a chore.
Open All Year.
Undesignated, scattered sites. Pit toilets.
Among mountain meadows, rolling hills,
canyons, and Colorado River bottom.
Hike to observe and photograph wildlife.
Fish. Rockclimb in summer and
snowmobile in winter.
NO water/trash arrangements–camp
with care. Changing weather. Hunting in
season.
7000 ft (2100 m)

## RAINBOW LAKES

Roosevelt NF (303) 444-6600
State map: E14
From NEDERLAND, drive
6.5 miles (10.4 k) N on CO 72 then
5 miles (8 k) W on very rough CR 116.
**FREE** but choose a chore.
Open Jun 20–Oct 15.
18 sites. Pit toilets, tables.
Amidst little lakes.
Hike to Glacier Rim. Fish in lakes.
NO water. 7-day/16-ft limits.
10000 ft (3000 m)

## RED BRIDGE

BLM (303) 249-7791
State map: L8
From LAKE CITY, drive N
on CO 149 for 20 miles (32 k). Turn on
well-maintained, gravel Gateview Rd
and continue 2 miles (3.2 k). (Also see
Big Blue and The Gate.)
**FREE** but choose a chore.
Open Apr–Nov.
5 close, open sites.
Pit toilets, tables, grills, fire rings.
Along Lake Fork of Gunnison River.
Fish or run river. Explore nearby
historical sites.
NO water/trash arrangements–handle
responsibly. 14-day limit.
7800 ft (2340 m)

## RINCON

BLM (719) 539-7289
State map: K13
Via US 50–from SALIDA,
drive 9 miles (14.4 k) SE; from
HOWARD, travel 3 miles (4.8 k) NW.
**$2.** Open All Year.
10 sites. Pit toilets, tables, grills, fire
rings, boat ramp.
On Arkansas River banks.
Boat, swim, and fish in river. Hike and
bike to observe and photograph geology
and wildlife.
NO water/trash facilities.
6750 ft (2025 m)

## RIO GRANDE

Rio Grande NF
(719) 658-2556
State map: N9
From CREEDE, take CO 149 SW for
8.4 miles (13.4 k). Turn on FR 529 ("Rio
Grande Fisherman's Rd") and drive S for
1 mile (1.6 k).
FREE but choose a chore.
Open May 20–Sep 30.
4 scattered, open sites.
Hand water pump, pit toilets, tables.
In open area next to Rio Grande.
Fish!
No trash pickup. 14-day limit.
8900 ft (2670 m)

## ROAD CANYON

Rio Grande NF
(719) 658-2556
State map: N8
From CREEDE, take CO 149 SW for
20 miles (32 k). Turn on FR 520 (Rio
Grande Reservoir Rd). Go W for 6 miles
(9.6 k).
FREE but choose a chore.
Open May 20–Sep 30.
6 scattered, open sites.
Pit toilets, tables, fire rings.
On upper end of Road Canyon
Reservoir.
Fish. Observe and photograph wildlife.
NO water/trash facilities–come
prepared. 14-day limit. No shade.
Changing weather/road conditions.
9300 ft (2790 m)

## ROCK CREEK

Rio Grande NF
(719) 657-3321
State map: O11
From MONTE VISTA, drive S on CO 15
for 2 miles (3.2 k). Turn W on CR 25 and
proceed 14 miles (22.4 k) to forest
boundary. Continue on FR 265 for
4 miles (6.4 k) SW. (Pass Comstock.)
FREE but choose a chore.
Open May 25–Sep 30.
13 (2 tent-only) sites in scattered layout
with natural screening.
Pit toilets, tables, fire rings.
In Engelmann spruce near Rock Creek.

Hike and take photographs of nature.
Fish in creek.
NO water/trash arrangements–be
responsible. 14-day/16-ft limits.
Changing weather/road conditions.
9400 ft (2820 m)

## ROCKY MOUNTAIN NP-Backcountry

(303) 586-2371
State map: C14
From DENVER, travel
65 miles (104 k m) NW via US 36.
FREE but $5 entrance fee (or pass).
(All developed campgrounds cost over
$5.) Inquire about backcountry permits
at park headquarters, west unit office, or
most ranger stations.
Open Jun 1–Sep 30.
Escape crowds on 355 miles of trails into
remote sections of park. Choose your
elevation (and ecology). Visit subalpine
forests, alpine lakes, tundra, and glaciers.
No open fires. No ATVs or pets. No
harassing or feeding of wildlife.
8000-14255 ft (2400-4276 m)

## RUBY MOUNTAIN

BLM (719) 539-7289
State map: J12
Located 7 miles (11.2 k) S of
BUENA VISTA via US 285. Turn at
Fisherman's Bridge and follow signs.
$2. Open All Year.
12 sites.
Pit toilets, tables, grills, fire rings.
Beside Arkansas River.
Boat (raft, canoe, kayak), swim, and fish
in river. Hike, mountain climb,
rockhound, and take photographs.
NO water/trash provisions.
7700 ft (2310 m)

## SELKIRK

Pike NF (719) 836-2031
State map: G13
From COMO, drive 3.5 miles
(5.6 k) NW on CR 33; .5 mile (800 m)
NW on CR 50; then 1.75 miles (2.8 k)
NW on gravel FR 406.
FREE but choose a chore.
Open Jun 1–Oct 15; camping allowed
off-season.

▲ ▲ ▲ ▲ ▲ ▲ ▲ ▲ ▲ ▲ ▲ ▲ ▲ ▲ ▲ ▲ ▲ ▲ ▲ ▲ ▲ ▲ ▲ ▲ ▲ ▲ ▲ ▲

15 close, screened sites.
Pit toilets, tables, grills, fire rings.
In dense woods near Tarryall Creek.
Fishing and photography two of quiet
activities enjoyed here.
NO water/trash arrangements–handle
responsibly. 14-day/22-ft limits.
10500 ft (3150 m)

## SEYMOUR LAKE SWA

CO Wildlife (303) 484-2836
State map: B10
From WALDEN, travel
14 miles (22.4 k) SW on CO 14. Turn S
on CR 28 for 1 mile (1.6 k). Turn S on
CR 11 for another 3 miles (4.8 k). Turn
W on CR 228 for final .5 mile (800 m).
FREE but choose a chore.
Open All Year.
Undesignated, scattered sites.
Pit toilets, boat ramp.
In high mountain meadow.
Boat and fish in lake. Observe and
photograph wildlife.
NO water/trash facilities.

## SHERIFF

Routt NF (303) 879-1722
State map: D8
From YAMPA, take CR 16 W
(the Flat Tops Trail Scenic Byway) then
FR 959 S. (Also see Crosho.)
FREE but choose a chore.
Open Jun 15–Nov 1.
6 sites.
Pit toilets, tables, fire rings, boat ramp.
On Trout Creek and small lake.
Boat and fish in lake. Hike on trails.
NO water/trash pickup. Changing
weather/road conditions. Horses.
14-day/20-ft limits.
9800 ft (2940 m)

## SIG CREEK

San Juan NF (303) 247-4874
State map: N5
From SILVERTON, drive
21 miles (33.6 k) SW on US 550 then
6 miles (9.6 k) W on FR 578.
FREE but choose a chore.
Open May 15–Nov 1.
9 sites. Pit toilets, tables, fire rings.

On East Fork of Hermosa Creek.
Fish or hike.
NO water. 14-day limit.
9400 ft (2820 m)

## SNOWBLIND

Gunnison NF (303) 874-7691
State map: J11
From PITKIN, travel 1 mile
(1.6 k) NE on US 50 then 7 miles (11.2 k)
N on FR 888.
FREE but choose a chore.
Open Jun 15–Oct 31.
23 (12 tent-only) sites.
Pit toilets, tables, fire rings.
On Canyon Creek.
Fish. Hike along Canyon and Horseshoe
creeks and explore old mining remains.
Photograph area scenery. Climb nearby
mountains.
NO water. 14-day/22-ft limits. ATVs.
9800 ft (2940 m)

## SOUTH FORK

White River NF
(303) 945-2521
State map: E7
From MEEKER, head 2 miles (3.2 k) E on
CO 13. Continue E for 23 miles (36.8 k)
on CR 8. Turn Right (S) and go 9.5 miles
(15.2 k) on CR 12 then .5 mile (800 m) SE
on FR 200.
$5. Open May 15–Nov 15.
17 sites. ♿
Water, pit toilets, tables, grills, fire rings.
On South Fork of White River near
Spring Cave.
Fish and swim in river. Hike into Flat
Tops Wilderness.
14-day/16-ft limits.
8000 ft (2400 m)

## SPRUCE GROVE

Grand Mesa NF
(303) 487-3534
State map: H4
From GRAND JUNCTION, drive
approximately 46 miles (73.6 k) E via
I-70 then CO 65 (12 miles or 19.2 k from
MESA, near Jumbo Campground).
$5. Open Jun 15–Sep 15; dry camping
off-season.

16 close, screened sites. Central water faucet, pit toilets, tables, fire rings.
In dense forest of spruce and fir.
Hike to observe and photograph nature.
Fish.
14-day/24-ft limits. Quiet 10pm–6am.
Cool evenings with frequent showers.
Crowded July 4. Mosquitos in July.
10000 ft (3000 m)

## STEVENS GULCH

Roosevelt NF (303) 482-3822
State map: B15
From LAPORTE, head
4 miles (6.4 k) N on US 287 then
20 miles (32 k) W on CO 14. (Another option is Narrows Co-op.)
FREE but choose a chore.
Open Apr 1–Dec 31.
4 sites. Pit toilets, tables, fire rings.
Along Cache la Poudre River.
Drive scenic byway. Fish river.
NO water. 32-ft limit.
8600 ft (2580 m)

## STONE CELLAR

Rio Grande NF
(719) 655-2547
State map: M10
From SAGUACHE, take CO 114 NW for
22 miles (35.2 k). Turn W on FR 750 for
18.75 miles (30 k) over Cochetopa Pass.
Turn S on FR 787 for additional
16.5 miles (26.4 k).
FREE but choose a chore.
Open Jun 10–Sep 30.
5 sites. Hand water pump, pit toilets, tables, fire rings.
In open area in Saguache Park next to North Fork of Saguache Creek.
Fish!
No trash arrangements (pack it out).
14-day limit. Changing weather/road conditions. Hunting in season.
9500 ft (2850 m)

## STORMKING

Rio Grande NF
(719) 655-2547
State map: M11
From MONTE VISTA, drive N for
18 miles (28.8 k) on US 285. On La

Garita Rd, proceed W for 6 miles (9.6 k).
At FR 690 (Carnero Creek Rd), continue
NW 14.5 miles (23.2 k). (Also see Poso.)
FREE but choose a chore.
Open May 25–Sep 30.
11 (3 tent-only) scattered, screened sites.
Hand water pump, pit toilets, tables, fire rings.
Within mixed conifer stand on Middle Fork of Carnero Creek at base of Stormking Mountain.
Observing nature and rockhounding.
14-day/25-ft limits. Hunting in season.
Changing weather/road conditions.
9200 ft (2760 m)

## STOVE PRAIRIE LANDING

Roosevelt NF (303) 482-3822
State map: B15
From LAPORTE, travel
4 miles (6.4 k) N on US 287 then
17 miles (27.2 k) W on CO 14. (Upper Landing with 6 tent sites is 2 miles farther.)
FREE but choose a chore.
Open All Year.
7 sites. Pit toilets, tables, fire rings.
On Cache la Poudre River.
Fish a bunch.
NO water. 14-day/30-ft limits.
6000 ft (1800 m)

## STUNNER

Rio Grande NF
(719) 274-5193
State map: O10
From MONTE VISTA, drive CO 15 S for
12 miles (19.2 k). Turn on FR 250
(Alamosa–Conejos Rd) and proceed
27 miles (43.2 k). (Also see Alamosa and La Jara Reservoir SWA.)
FREE but choose a chore.
Open May 25–Sep 20.
10 sites. Pit toilets, tables, fire rings.
In aspen and Engelmann spruce stand of upper Alamosa drainage near Stunner Pass.
Fish, observe and photograph nature.
NO water/trash facilities. 14-day/16-ft limits. Changing weather/road conditions. ATVs. Hunting in season.
9800 ft (2940 m)

## SUMMIT LAKE

Routt NF (303) 879-1722
State map: B10
Drive 4 miles (6.4 k) N of STEAMBOAT SPRINGS on CR 36 (Strawberry Park Rd) then 11.5 miles (18.4 k) E on FR 60 (Buffalo Pass Rd). (Also see Dry Lake.)
**FREE** but choose a chore.
Open Jul 1–Oct 31, weather decides.
17 (8 tent-only) close, open sites.
Pit toilets, tables, fire rings.
On Summit Lake near Buffalo Pass and Mt Zirkel Wilderness.
Fish in lake. Hike and cycle to observe and photograph nature.
NO water/trash arrangements–come prepared. 14-day/22-ft limits. Changing weather/road conditions. ATVs.
10300 ft (3090 m)

## SUPPLY BASIN

White River NF
(303) 945-2521
State map: F8
From GLENWOOD SPRINGS, head 17 miles (27.2 k) E on US 6; 2 miles (3.2 k) N on CR 301; 25.5 miles (40.8 k) NW on FR 600; then 1.75 miles (2.8 k) W on FR 601 (Also see Coffee Pot Spring and Deep Lake.)
**FREE** but choose a chore.
Open Jul 1–Oct 31.
6 sites. Pit toilets, tables, fire rings.
Boat and fish on Heart Lake. Explore area for early history.
NO water. 14-day/22-ft limit. ATVs.
10800 ft (3240 m)

## THE CRAGS

Pike NF (719) 636-1602
State map: I16
From DIVIDE, go 4.5 miles (7.2 k) S on CO 67 then 3.5 miles (5.6 k) E on gravel FR 1094.
**FREE** but donations appreciated.
Open May 15–Oct 1; dry camping off-season.
17 close, screened sites. Hand water pump, pit toilets, tables, grills, fire rings.
In relatively flat area on Fourmile Creek with stands of mixed conifers and scattered large boulders.
Hike to The Crags (750-ft rise in 1.5 miles). Fish in Fourmile Creek.
No trash pickup. 14-day/22-ft limits.
10100 ft (3030 m)

## THE GATE

BLM (303) 249-7791
State map: L8
Drive approximately 16 miles (25.6 k) N of LAKE CITY on CO 149. (See Big Blue and Red Bridge.)
**FREE** but choose a chore.
Open Apr–Nov.
8 sites, close together with choice of open or screened settings.
Pit toilets, tables, fire rings.
On banks of Lake Fork of Gunnison.
Fish, raft, or kayak river. Observe and photograph nature.
NO water/trash facilities (pack it out).
14-day/35-ft limits. Hunting in season.
8400 ft (2520 m)

## THREE FORKS

White River NF
(303) 945-2521
State map: F6
From RIFLE, head 3 miles (4.8 k) N on CO 13; 11.25 miles (18 k) NE on CO 325; 2.25 miles (3.6 k) N on CR 217; then 20 miles (32 k) N on FR 825.
**FREE** but choose a chore.
Open Jun 1–Oct 31.
4 sites. Pit toilets, tables, fire rings.
In geologically interesting, scenic area.
Fish in streams or rockhound.
10-day/16-ft limits.
7600 ft (2280 m)

## TOM BENNETT

Roosevelt NF (303) 482-3822
State map: B14
From LAPORTE, travel 4 miles (6.4 k) N on US 287; 27 miles (43.2 k) W on CO 14; 11 miles (17.6 k) S on CR 131; then 5 miles (8 k) W on CR 145. (See Crown Point-Pingree.)
**FREE** but choose a chore.
Open May 15–Oct 31.
12 sites. Pit toilets, tables, grills.
Near Cache la Poudre River.

▲ ▲ ▲ ▲ ▲ ▲ ▲ ▲ ▲ ▲ ▲ ▲ ▲ ▲ ▲ ▲ ▲ ▲ ▲ ▲ ▲ ▲ ▲ ▲ ▲ ▲ ▲

Fish in creek or river. Hike Beaver Creek Trail into Comanche Peak Wilderness or Stormy Peaks into Rocky Mountain NP. NO water. 14-day/16-ft limits.
9000 ft (2700 m)

## TOP OF THE WORLD
Pike NF (303) 236-7386
State map: G16
From BUFFALO CREEK, drive 2 miles (3.2 k) S on CR 126 then 1.75 miles (2.8 k) N on gravel FR 538. (Another option is Wigwam.)
FREE but choose a chore.
Open May 1–Oct 15; camping allowed off-season.
7 close, screened sites.
Pit toilets, tables, grills, fire rings.
In area that feels higher than surroundings.
Hike to enjoy views.
NO water/trash arrangements-be responsible. 14-day/16-ft limits. Hunting in season.
7500 ft (2250 m)

## TRAIL CREEK
Pike NF (719) 636-1602
State map: H16
From WOODLAND PARK, proceed 12 miles (19.2 k) NW on CO 67 then 3 miles (4.8 k) S on gravel CR 3. (Big Turkey Campground is off CO 67.)
FREE but choose a chore.
Open May 25–Oct 1; camping allowed off-season.
7 close, screened sites.
Pit toilets, tables, grills, fire rings.
On creek in relatively flat area with lodgepole pine.
Hike or fish.
NO water/trash facilities (pack it out).
14-day/16-ft limits.
7800 ft (2340 m)

## TRAMWAY WALK-IN
Pike NF (303) 236-7386
State map: G15
From BUFFALO CREEK, drive .5 mile (800 m) SE on CR 126 then 4.75 miles (7.6 k) SW on gravel FR 543.
(Also see Baldy.)

FREE but choose a chore.
Open May 1–Oct 15; camping allowed off-season.
6 tent sites in close together, screened settings 50-100 ft from parking area.
Pit toilets, tables, grills, fire rings.
On Buffalo Creek near Hoosier Pass and Continental Divide.
Hike a lot and fish a bunch.
NO water/trash provisions–camp with care. 14-day limit.
7200 ft (2160 m)

## TRANSFER
San Juan NF (303) 247-4874
State map: O4
From MANCOS, head .25 mile (400 m) N on CO 184 then 11.75 miles (18.8 k) NE on FR 561.
$5. Open May 24–Oct 15.
13 sites.
Water, pit toilets, tables, grills.
In secluded location on Mancos River.
Fish in river. Hike trails to lakes.
30-day/16-ft limits.
8500 ft (2550 m)

## TRICKLE PARK
Grand Mesa NF
(303) 242-8211
State map: H5
From CEDAREDGE, travel 16 miles (25.6 k) N on paved CO 65 then 8 miles (12.8 k) E on FR 121. (Also see Crag Crest and Kiser Creek.)
FREE but choose a chore.
Open Jun 20–Sep 30; camping allowed off-season.
5 close, open sites.
Pit toilets, tables, fire rings.
Near Vela Reservoir in spruce and fir.
Boat and fish on reservoir.
NO water/trash arrangements–come prepared. 14-day/22-ft limits.
10100 ft (3030 m)

## TWIN LAKE
Grand Mesa NF
(303) 242-8211
State map: H5
From CEDAREDGE, drive 16 miles (25.6 k) N on CO 65; 10 miles (16 k) E on

▲▲▲▲▲▲▲▲▲▲▲▲▲▲▲▲

FR 121; then 2 miles (3.2 k) E on FR 126.
(Also see Cottonwood and Fish Hawk.)
**FREE** but choose a chore.
Open Jun 20–Sep 30; camping allowed
off-season.
13 sites. Pit toilets, tables, fire rings.
Among spruce and fir on Twin
Lake #1–boat (no motors) and fish.
NO water/trash facilities. 14-day/22-ft
limits. Changing weather/road
conditions. Hunting in season.
10300 ft (3090 m)

**VAUGHN LAKE**
Routt NF (303) 879-1722
State map: D8
Proceed 6 miles (9.6 k) NW
of YAMPA on CR 132 then 28.25 miles
(45.2 k) on FR 16 (Flat Tops Trail Scenic
Byway). (See Himes Peak and Sheriff.)
**FREE** but choose a chore.
Open Jun 15–Nov 1.
8 close, open sites.
Pit toilets, tables, fire rings.
On Vaughn Lake near Flat Tops
Wilderness.
Hike to observe and photograph nature.
Boat (no motors) and fish for brown or
rainbow trout.
NO water/trash facilities. 14-day/18-ft
limits. Changing weather/road
conditions. Hunting in season.
9500 ft (2850 m)

**WAGON TONGUE**
Pike NF (719) 836-2031
State map: I15
From LAKE GEORGE, drive
6.5 miles (10.4 k) S on FR 245 then 1 mile
(1.6 k) S on gravel FR 393.
**FREE** but choose a chore.
Open May 1–Oct 30; camping allowed
off-season.
5 close, open tent sites.
Pit toilets, tables, grills, fire rings.
On open hillside under mixed conifers.
Hike, rockhound, fish, or attend ranger
programs.
NO water/trash provisions. 14-day/16-ft
limits.
8400 ft (2520 m)

**WEIR & JOHNSON**
Grand Mesa NF
(303) 242-8211
State map: H5
From CEDAREDGE, go 16 miles (25.6 k)
N on paved CO 65; 11 miles (17.6 k) E
on FR 121; then 3 miles (4.8 k) E on
FR 126 to end of road. (See Big Creek
and Cottonwood Lake.)
**FREE** but choose a chore.
Open Jun 20–Sep 30; camping allowed
off-season.
12 close, open sites.
Pit toilets, tables, fire rings.
Among spruce and fir trees between two
reservoirs, Weir & Johnson and Sackette.
Boat and fish popular lakes. Hike trail to
view and photograph nature.
NO water/trash facilities–act
responsibly. 14-day/22-ft limits.
10500 ft (3150 m)

**WELLER**
White River NF
(303) 945-2521
State map: H10
From ASPEN, drive 11 miles (17.6 k) SE
on CO 82 then .25 mile (400 m) S. (See
Portal, Lincoln Gulch, and Lostman.)
**$5.** Open Jun 15–Sep 30.
11 sites.
Water, pit toilets, tables, fire rings.
On Roaring Fork River with views of
Collegiate Peaks.
Fish or hike.
5-day/16-ft limits.
9200 ft (2760 m)

**WESTON PASS**
Pike NF (719) 836-2031
State map: H12
From FAIRPLAY, travel
5 miles (8 k) S on US 285; 7 miles
(11.2 k) SW on CR 5; then 4 miles (6.4 k)
SW on gravel CR 22 (Weston Pass
Rd–former toll road).
**FREE** but choose a chore.
Open May 25–Oct 30; dry camping
off-season.
14 close, screened sites. Hand water
pump, pit toilets, tables, grills, fire rings.
In dense woods on South Fork of South

▲ ▲ ▲ ▲ ▲ ▲ ▲ ▲ ▲ ▲ ▲ ▲ ▲ ▲ ▲ ▲ ▲ ▲ ▲ ▲ ▲ ▲ ▲ ▲ ▲ ▲

Platte River.
Hike or fish.
14-day/22-ft limits. Hunting in season.
10200 ft (3060 m)

## WHITE OWL

White River NF
(303) 945-2521
State map: E8
From GLENWOOD SPRINGS, proceed
17 miles (27.2 k) E on US 6; 2 miles
(3.2 k) N on CR 301; then 25.5 miles
(40.8 k) NW on FR 600.
FREE but choose a chore.
Open Jul 1–Oct 31.
5 sites. Pit toilets, tables, fire rings.
Near Sweetwater Creek and Lake.
Boat and fish. Photograph scenery.
NO water. 22-ft limit.
10200 ft (3060 m)

## WHITESIDE

Pike NF (303) 236-7386
State map: G14
From GRANT, head 2.5 miles
(4 k) NW on gravel CR 62.
FREE but choose a chore.
Open May 1–Oct 25; camping allowed
off-season.
5 close, screened tent sites.
Pit toilets, tables, grills, fire rings.
On Geneva Creek in dense conifers.
Fish or hike.
NO water/trash facilities. 14-day limit.
8900 ft (2670 m)

## WIGWAM

Pike NF (303) 236-7386
State map: G15
From BUFFALO CREEK,
drive 14.25 miles (22.8 k) S on paved
CR 126–not maintained in winter.
FREE but choose a chore.
Open All Year but weather dependent.
10 open tent sites. Hand water pump, pit
toilets, tables, grills, fire rings.
Along Sixmile Creek near junction of
Wigwam Creek.
Hike or fish.
14-day limit. Hunting in season.
6600 ft (1980 m)

## WILDHORN

Pike NF (719) 636-1602
State map: H15
From LAKE GEORGE, go
10 miles (16 k) NE on gravel CR 3.
FREE but donations appreciated.
Open May 25–Oct 1; camping allowed
off-season.
9 sites.
Pit toilets, tables, grills, fire rings.
In mixed woods on Trail Creek.
Fish, hike, and rockhound.
NO water/trash facilities–camp with
care. 14-day/22-ft limits.
9100 ft (2730 m)

## WILLOWS

White River NF
(303) 945-2521
State map: E12
From DILLON, go 30.25 miles (48.4 k)
NW on CO 9 then 1 mile (1.6 k) SW on
CR 30. (Options include Cataract Creek,
Davis Springs, and Elliot Creek.)
FREE but choose a chore.
Open May 25–Sep 30.
35 sites. Pit toilets, tables.
On Green Mountain Reservoir in grassy
area with mountain views.
Boat, waterski, swim, and fish.
NO water. 10-day/32-ft limits.
8200 ft (2460 m)

# Hawaii

N

Hawaii

Maui

Molokai

Lanai

Oahu

Kauai

Niihau

▲ ▲ ▲ ▲ ▲ ▲ ▲ ▲ ▲ ▲ ▲ ▲ ▲ ▲ ▲ ▲ ▲ ▲ ▲ ▲ ▲ ▲ ▲ ▲ ▲ ▲ ▲ ▲ ▲ ▲

Yes, there's camping in Hawaii, the exotic land and culture that has made familiar to the world: hulas, leis, wahines, kahunas, pupu platters, and ukuleles.

When you plan to camp Hawaii, come as free-spirited as Pele, the Hawaiian goddess of fires and volcanoes. You need to travel light for security as well as for convenience and be prepared to move frequently. A positive attitude helps you conform to regulations that protect this harsh yet lush environment, full of rare plants and animals.

Most camping on the Hawaiian islands is now tent camping. RVs and trailers encounter too many difficulties with tight spaces and dramatic elevation changes in this volcanic ecology. You can pitch a tent, however, and enjoy the outdoors any time of year thanks to the balmy climate.

Think of each island as a county offering campgrounds run by the National Park Service (NPS), state of Hawaii, or island government. Well in advance, contact appropriate administrators about any necessary permits and reservations.

**Hawaii,** the Big Island, showcases Hawaii Volcanoes NP, MacKenzie State Recreation Area (SRA), and over a dozen county-operated beach parks. The national park works on a first-come, first-serve basis. For camping in the state area, write the district office at 75 Aupuni Street (PO Box 936), Hilo, HI 96721, or call (808) 933-4200. For registration information at county parks, write Hawaii Department of Parks and Recreation at 25 Aupuni Street, Hilo, HI 96720, or call (808) 961-8311.

On the Garden Isle, **Kauai,** camp at such beautiful and remote locations as the Na Pali Coast and Waimea Canyon or at a half dozen beach parks administered by Kauai Parks and Recreation. Write the county parks administrator at 4193 Hardy Street, Lihue, HI 96766, or call (808) 245-8821. For information on the Na Pali Coast and two other state parks (Kokee and Polihale), write Kauai District Office at 3060 Eiwa Street (PO Box 1671), Lihue, HI 96766, or call (808) 241-3444. Use the same address to contact the state's Division of Forestry for Waimea Canyon information. The phone number, however, is (808) 241-3433.

The Valley Isle, **Maui,** offers a national park (Haleakala), two state camping areas (Polipoli Spring and Wainapanapa), as well as two county parks. Most of these sites are upcountry on Mount Haleakala rather than on the beach. Again, at the national park, it is first come, first serve. Additional specifics on state parks can be gathered at 54 South High Street, Wailuku, HI 96793; call (808) 243-5354. Contact the County of Maui Department of Parks and Recreation at War Memorial Gym, 1580 Kaahumanu Avenue, Wailuku, HI 96793; call (808) 243-7383.

Only three public-land camping locations exist on the Friendly Isle, **Molokai:** Palaau State Park (SP) and county-operated One Alii and Papohaku beaches. For the free state park, write the district office at PO Box 153, Kaunakakai, HI 96748, or call (808) 567-6083. For county parks, write Molokai Department of Parks and Recreation, Kaunakakai, HI 96748, or call (808) 553-5141.

**Oahu,** the Gathering Place, has the most county and state parks available for camping, plus a botanical garden. To protect the environment, Oahu campgrounds are closed often—at least two days a week (check listings for specifics). Write the state district office at 1151 Punchbowl Street (PO Box 621), Honolulu, HI 96809, or call (808) 548-7455. City and County of Honolulu campground reservations can be made at satellite city halls or the main one at 650 S King Street, Honolulu, HI 96813; call (808) 523-4525. A cultivated site is Honolulu Botanical Gardens. Write at 50 N Vineyard Boulevard, Honolulu, HI 96817, or call at (808) 235-6636.

▲ ▲ ▲ ▲ ▲ ▲ ▲ ▲ ▲ ▲ ▲ ▲ ▲ ▲ ▲ ▲ ▲ ▲ ▲ ▲ ▲ ▲ ▲ ▲

These $5-and-under listings are grouped by island to help you make your plans. It does take planning to camp Hawaii's islands but as you read the descriptions in these listings, you realize it can be one of your most rewarding camping trips. Aloha!

▲ ▲ ▲ ▲ ▲ ▲ ▲ ▲ ▲ ▲ ▲ ▲ ▲ ▲ ▲ ▲ ▲ ▲ ▲ ▲ ▲ ▲ ▲ ▲

## HAWAII–"The Big Island"

## HAWAII VOLCANOES NP
(808) 967-7311
Find Kilauea Visitor Center (park head-quarters) 29 miles (46.4 k) SW of HILO–off HI 11.
**FREE** but $5/vehicle or $2/person entrance fee (or pass). Also, **free** backcountry permits and safety recommendations for backpack trips are available at Kilauea Visitor Center.
Open All Year.
See volcanoes at work here. (Kilauea, most active volcano on earth, has blocked recent roads.) Park preserves varied ecologies of Mauna Loa and Kilauea as well as creates refuge of lush vegetation providing homes and food for numerous animals including Hawaii's state bird, the nene.
Drive scenic roads with overlooks. Hike along still-steaming Kilauea crater or up snowcapped Mauna Loa (stay on trails for safety). Take lots of photographs. Attend ranger programs.
Stay on approved roads and trails.
▲ **Kamoamoa**
Drive 28 miles (44.8 k) from park headquarters–off Chain of Craters Rd.
7 first-come, first-serve tent sites.
Pit toilets, tables, fire pits.
In shady sites near open, grassy areas.
No swimming here. Bring your own drinking water–availability varies.
10 ft (3 m)
▲ **Kipuka Nene**
Travel 11 miles (17.6 k) from park headquarters–on Hilina Pali Rd.
First-come, first-serve tent sites. Water, pit toilets, fireplace pavilion.
In open, grassy area.
No dogs or open fires here.
2900 ft (870 m)

▲ **Namakani Paio**
Proceed 3 miles (4.8 k) from park headquarters on HI 11 at mile 31.5.
First-come, first-serve tent sites.
Water, flush toilets, fire pits, 2 fireplace pavilions.
In shady, grassy area.
Keep away from ground cracks.
4000 ft (1200 m)

## HO'OKENA BEACH PARK
Hawaii Parks and Recreation
(808) 961-8311
In South Kona District off HI 11, look for turnoff to 2.25-mile (3.6-k) narrow road–between mile markers 101 and 102.
$1/adult, $.50/teenager.
Open All Year. Reservations required.
22 gravel tent sites.
Flush toilets, tables, grills.
On lava cliffs and black sand beach–once thriving fishing community described by Robert Louis Stevenson as typical Hawaiian village.
Swim, snorkel around reef, surf, or fish.
NO water. Bugs can be a problem. Be careful of strong ocean currents. Follow Hawaii County Parks rules, including length of stay (7 days in summer; 14 days remainder of year).
10 ft (3 m)

## ISAAC HALE BEACH PARK
Hawaii Parks and Recreation
(808) 961-8311
From PAHOA (on Pohoiki Bay in Puna District), go 9 miles (14.4 k) SE on HI 132 then 7 miles (11.2 k) W on HI 137.
$1/adult, $.50/teenager.
Open All Year. Reservations required.
22 tent sites.
Central water faucet, flush and pit toilets, showers, tables, grills, boat ramp.
On gravel and grass among heavy vegetation next to ocean. Fishing!
Conform to all Hawaii County Park

Rules, including 7-day stay during summer and 14 days rest of year. Mosquitos and other insects can be pests.
10 ft (3 m)

## JAMES KEALOHA BEACH PARK

Hawaii Parks and Recreation
(808) 961-8311
Locate in HILO on "Four-Mile Beach" (distance down beach to Hilo post office), across Kalanianaole Ave from Lokowaka Pond.
$1/adult, $.50/teenager.
Open All Year. Reservations required.
22 ocean-front, grassed-paved, tent sites. Central water faucet, flush toilets, showers, tables, grills.
On urban beach.
Fishing. Some swimming and surfing though strong rip currents.
Obey all Hawaii County Park Rules, including 7-day stays during summer and 14-day stays during rest of year. Mosquitos and other insects can be prolific due to heavy rainfalls.
10 ft (3 m)

## KALOPA SRA

(808) 933-4200
Travel 5 miles (8 k) SE of HONOKAA– 3 miles (4.8 k) inland from Mamalahoa Hwy (HI 19) at end of Kalopa Rd.
FREE but choose a chore.
Open All Year. Reservations required.
4 tent sites. Central water faucet, flush toilets, tables, grills.
In forest on lower Mauna Kea.
Walk nature trail through native ohia forest. Hike other trails. Ride 2-mile (3.2-k) loop horse trail. Enjoy viewing nature and taking photographs.
5-day limit.
2000 ft (600 m)

## KAPA'A BEACH PARK

Hawaii Parks and Recreation
(808) 961-8311
Find in North Kohala District, 1.25 miles (2 k) N of MAHUKONA and about 1 mile (1.6 k) off HI 270.
$1/adult, $.50/teenager.
Open All Year. Reservations required.

22 open tent sites. Central water faucets (treat drinking water), flush toilets, showers, electric hookups, tables, grills.
In grassy park (no sandy beach) with view of Maui. Fish!
Be familiar with all Hawaii County Park regulations, including 7-day summer stays and 14-day stays in other seasons. Be prepared for rains and insects.
10 ft (3 m)

## KEOKEA BEACH PARK

Hawaii Parks and Recreation
(808) 961-8311
In North Kohala District past intersection of 250 and 270 heading toward Pololu Valley, look for signed turnoff to park about 1.5 miles (2.4 k) before Pololu Valley Lookout.
$1/adult, $.50/teenager.
Open All Year. Reservations required.
22 ocean-front, grassed-paved, tent sites. Central water faucets, flush toilets, showers, electric hookups, tables, grills.
On secluded rocky coast–scenic but unsuitable for water sports.
Fish. Drive to Pololu Valley Lookout.
Follow all Hawaii County Park regulations, including 7-day summer stays and 14-day stays remainder of year.
10 ft (3 m)

## KOLEKOLE BEACH PARK

Hawaii Parks and Recreation
(808) 961-8311
From HILO, drive 12 miles (19.2 k) N on HI 19 then about .25 mile (400 m) W on Beach Rd (near HAKALAU in North Hilo District).
$1/adult, $.50/teenager.
Open All Year. Reservations required.
45 grassed-paved, tent sites. Central water faucets (must treat), flush toilets, showers, electric hookups, tables, grills.
With river as well as ocean access.
Fish or swim.
Prepare for lots of rain and lots of insects. Obey all Hawaii County Park regulations, including 7-day stays in summer, 14-days in other seasons.
10 ft (3 m)

## LAUPAHOEHOE POINT PARK

Hawaii Parks and Recreation
(808) 961-8311
Drive 2 miles (3.2 k) NE of
LAUPAHOEHOE–off HI 19 (halfway
between HONOKAA and HILO in North
Hilo District).
$1/adult, $.50/teenager.
Open All Year. Reservations required.
45 ocean-front grassy tent sites.
Central water faucets, flush toilets,
showers, electric hookups, tables, grills,
playground, boat ramp.
At Laupahoehoe, scenic "leaf of lava"
was landing site of immigrant sugar
cane workers. Off-highway seclusion
good for camping and too-frequent
partying.
Fish. (Water too rough for swimming).
Conform to all Hawaii County Park
regulations, including stay limits of
7 days in summer and 14 days during
rest of year. Prepare for steep winding
road down to point as well as lots of
bugs and rain.
10 ft (3 m)

## MACKENZIE SRA

(808) 933-4200
Locate on Kalapana-Kapoho Beach Rd
(HI 137)–9 miles (14.4 k) NE of KAIMU.
FREE but choose a chore.
Open All Year. Reservations required.
4 tent sites. Central water faucet (treat
for drinking), pit toilets, tables, grills.
On low-cliffed, wild, volcanic coastline
with an ironwood grove.
Hike along old Hawaiian coastal trail.
Take photographs. Boat and fish.
No fence on edge of cliff. 5-day limit.
25 ft (6 m)

## MAHUKONA BEACH PARK

Hawaii Parks and Recreation
(808) 961-8311
In North Kohala District, travel 1 mile
(1.6 k) N of LAPAKAHI–.5 mile (800 m)
off HI 270.
$1/adult, $.50/teenager.
Open All Year. Reservations required.
22 grassed-paved, tent sites. Central
water faucet (treat water), flush toilets,

showers, electric hookups, tables, grills.
At site of old railroad link to sugar mills.
Coral bed and ship remains off shore.
Snorkeling and diving good, except in
rough winter waters. Swimming and
fishing popular, too.
Prepare for bugs and obey all Hawaii
County Park rules, including 7-day
summer stays and 14 days rest of year.
10 ft (3 m)

## MANUKA STATE WAYSIDE

(808) 933-4200
From NAALEHU, drive 19.3 miles
(30.9 k) W on Mamalahoa Hwy (HI 11).
FREE but choose a chore.
Open All Year. Reservations required.
1 site, shelter. Central water faucet (treat
for drinking), flush toilets, tables.
In botanical garden of tropical trees.
View nature and take photographs.
1800 ft (540 m)

## MILOLI'I BEACH PARK

Hawaii Parks and Recreation
(808) 961-8311
In South Kona District, turn off HI 11
at mile marker 88 in PAPA. Find village
of MILOLI'I at end of steep, winding,
one-lane, 5-mile (8-k) road.
$1/adult, $.50/teenager.
Open All Year. Reservations required.
22 ocean-front, gravel, sand tent sites.
Pit toilets, tables, grills, picnic shelter.
With beach, tidal pools, coral bed, and
lava flow, but right in village.
Explore lava flow, snorkel, swim, or fish.
NO water. Bring insect repellant.
Conform to Hawaii County Park rules,
including length of stay (7 days summer;
14 days during other seasons).
10 ft (3 m)

## ONEKAHAKAHA BEACH PARK

Hawaii Parks and Recreation
(808) 961-8311
In HILO, locate park .25 mile (400 m) off
Kalanianaole Ave.
$1/adult, $.50/teenager.
Open All Year. Reservations required.
45 grassed-paved, tent sites.
Central water faucet, flush toilets,

showers, electric hookups, tables, grills, pay phone.
With natural wading pool and cove.
Fish, swim, or snorkel inside breakwater.
Bring your insect repellant and rain gear.
Follow all Hawaii County Parks regulations, including stays of 7 days in summer and 14 days rest of year.
10 ft (3 m)

## PUNALU'U BEACH PARK
Hawaii Parks and Recreation
(808) 961-8311
In Kau District, drive 4 miles (6.4 k) SW on HI 11 then 1.5 miles (2.4 k) E on Beach Rd.
$1/adult, $.50/teenager.
Open All Year. Reservations required.
22 ocean-front, grassed-paved, tent sites.
Central water faucets, flush toilets, showers, electric hookups, tables, grills, pay phone.
On strip of black-sand beach protected by coral reef–believed to be landing site of first Polynesians.
Swim and fish.
Prepare to battle bugs. Be careful of strong currents. Obey all Hawaii County Parks rules, including length of stay (7 days in summer and 14 days remainder of year).
10 ft (3 m)

## R H WHITTINGTON BEACH PARK
Hawaii Parks and Recreation
(808) 961-8311
In Kau District on Honuapo Bay, find turnoff approximately 3 miles (4.8 k) NE of NAALEHU–1 mile (1.6k) beyond scenic overlook of Honuapo Bay.
$1/adult, $.50/teenager.
Open All Year. Reservations required.
22 ocean-front, grassed-paved, tent sites.
Flush toilets, electric hookups, tables, grills, picnic shelters.
On Honuapo Bay with remains of pier once used to ship sugar and hemp.
Explore tidal pools or fish. (Ocean too rough here for swimming).
NO water. Be prepared to fight off bugs.
Follow all Hawaii County Park regulations, including stay of 7 days in

summer and 14 days in other seasons.
10 ft (3 m)

## SAMUEL SPENCER BEACH PARK
Hawaii Parks and Recreation
(808) 961-8311
From intersection of HI 270 and HI 19 in South Kohala District near KAWAIHAE, go 1 mile (1.6 k) W–below Puukohola Heiau National Historic Site.
$1/adult, $.50/teenager.
Open All Year. Reservations required.
68 grass-gravel tent sites.
Central water faucets, flush toilets, showers, electric hookups, tables, grills, picnic pavilion, pay phone.
On sandy beach protected by jetty as well as reef. Swim and snorkel. Fish.
Prepare for lots of bugs and people.
Obey all Hawaii County Parks regulations, including length of stay (7 days in summer; 14 days rest of year).
10 ft (3 m)

## KAUAI–"The Garden Isle"

## ANINI ("WANINI") BEACH PARK
Kauai Parks and Recreation
(808) 245-8821
On north shore, take Kalihiwai Rd (Hanalei side). Bear Left onto Anini Rd for 1.5 miles (2 k). Park is "makai" (toward ocean) of ANINI.
$3/person. Reservations required.
Open All Year.
Tent sites. Water, changing rooms, tables, shelters, pay phones.
On long beach with almond trees.
Swim, snorkel, windsurf. Explore shallow reef at Anini Flats.
4-day limit.
10 ft (3 m)

## HAENA BEACH PARK
Kauai Parks and Recreation
(808) 245-8821
Locate in HAENA at end of HI 560.
$3/person; electrical hook-up extra.
Open All Year. Reservations required.

▲ ▲ ▲ ▲ ▲ ▲ ▲ ▲ ▲ ▲ ▲ ▲ ▲ ▲ ▲ ▲ ▲ ▲ ▲ ▲ ▲ ▲ ▲ ▲ ▲ ▲ ▲ ▲

4 tent sites. Water, flush toilets, showers, tables, grills.

On curved beach of white sand along north shore for beachcombing. Snorkel in Tunnels Reef. Dive in large underwater caves. Hike on nearby Kalalau Trail.

4-day limit. Beware of rip tides.

10 ft (3 m)

## HANALEI BEACH PARK
Kauai Parks and Recreation
(808) 245-8821
Find in north-shore town of HANALEI at end of Weke Rd on peninsula where Hanalei River flows into Hanalei Bay.
$3/person. Reservations required.
Open All Year.
Tent sites. Water, flush toilets, showers, tables, grills.
In ironwood trees on long beach around crescent-shaped bay.
Swim, surf, and snorkel.
Camping allowed only weekends and holidays.
10 ft (3 m)

## HANAMAULU BEACH PARK
Kauai Parks and Recreation
(808) 245-8821
Off HI 56 in HANAMAULU, turn E ("makai"–toward the ocean) on Hanamaulu Rd then turn Right (S) on Hehi Rd.
$3/person; electrical hook-up extra.
Reservations required. Open All Year.
4 tent sites. Water, flush toilets, showers, tables, grills.
On Hanamaulu Bay near abandoned railroad trestle.
Swim behind breakwater. Fish too.
4-day limit.
10 ft (3 m)

## KOKEE SP
(808) 241-3444
Travel 15 miles (24 k) N of KEKAHA on Kokee Rd (HI 550).
FREE but choose a chore. Reservations required. Open All Year.
10 scattered, open tent sites Central water faucet, flush toilets, cold showers, tables, grills, fire rings, pay phone.

Near Waimea Canyon SP, with commanding views of Kalalau Valley. Hike in rain forest and Waimea Canyon. Study nature and take photographs. Pick wild plums or hunt pig in season. Fish for trout. Swim too.
5-day limit. Crowded.
3600 ft (1080 m)

## LUCY WRIGHT PARK
Kauai Parks and Recreation
(808) 245-8821
Locate on west side of town of WAIMEA on Ala Wai Rd, just past Waimea Bridge.
$3/person. Reservations required.
Open All Year.
Tent sites. Water, flush toilets, showers, tables, grills.
In flat, grassy area at side of road in village where Captain Cook landed in 1778 and first missionaries disembarked in 1820.
Walk around historic town. Catch a town ball game.
4-day limit.
10 ft (3 m)

## NA PALI COAST SP
(808) 241-3444
FREE but choose a chore
Open All Year. Reservations required.
▲ Kalalau Trail
Trail begins at end of Kuhio Hwy (HI 560) in Haena Beach Park. Kalalau Valley is accessible by boat (commercial boats run May–Sep).
Tent sites. Pit toilets, fire rings.
Along 13-mile (20.8 k) trail (one way) with scenic sea cliffs, valleys, remote wildlands, and beach.
While hiking, enjoy views, streams, and waterfalls. Pause for lots of photos. Fish or hunt for wild goats. Try tropical fruits. Boat and swim near beach.
No 2 consecutive nights may be spent at Hanakaipiai Valley (at 4 miles) or at Hanakoa Valley (at 7.5 miles). Find primitive Kalalau Beach campsite at 13 miles. Plan maximum of 5-nights along this exceptional trail. Travel light. Treat drinking water.
10–400 ft (3–120 m)

## ▲ Miloli'i Boat-In Section

Private and commercial boats can access area in summer when ocean is calm.
Tent sites. Pit toilets.
In major valley on Na Pali Coast–once sizable settlement, now wilderness.
Enjoy colorful sunsets. Fish.
Inquire about boat landing restrictions.
Unpredictable ocean currents. Treat water. 3-night maximum stay.
10 ft (3 m)

## POLIHALE SP

(808) 241-3444
From village of MANA, take 5-mile (8-k) dirt road off Kaumualii Hwy (HI 50).
FREE but choose a chore. Reservations required. Open All Year.
Undesignated sites. Central water faucet, flush toilets, cold showers, tables, grills, fire rings, picnic shelters, pay phone.
In hot, dry, wild coastline with broad sandy beach with dunes. Good views of Na Pali Coast and colorful sunsets.
Swim and boat in summer. Hike to observe and photograph nature. Fish too.
5-day limit.
10 ft (3 m)

## SALT POND BEACH PARK

Kauai Parks and Recreation
(808) 245-8821
From HANAPEPE at 17-mile marker on HI 50, turn Left onto Lele Rd. Turn Right onto Lokokai Rd.
$3/person. Reservations required.
Open All Year.
Tent sites. Water, flush toilets, showers, tables.
On west-side sandy beach near salt ponds where natives evaporate sea water then add iron-rich earth to make red alae salt.
Swim (lifeguard on duty).
4-day limit.
10 ft (3 m)

## WAIMEA CANYON

Hawaii Division of Forestry
(808) 245-3433
From LIHUE, drive 27 miles (43.2 k) SW on HI 50 to KEKAHA town. Turn Right

on HI 55. From where HI 55 and 550 join–8 miles (12.8 k) uphill, continue 2 miles (3.2 k) to Kukui Trailhead on right side of road.
FREE but choose a chore.
Open All Year. Reservations required.
4 hike-in tent sites, scattered along Waimea and Koaie canyons (**Wiliwili, Kaluahaulu, Hipalau,** and **Lonomea**).
Pit toilets, tables, trail shelters.
In "Grand Canyon of the Pacific" known for its depth, breadth, and color. Kukui Trail is 2.5 miles (4 k) down west side of canyon. Trail makes 2000-ft (610-m) elevation drop to canyon floor at Wiliwili Camp. Kaluahaulu is located .5 mile (800 m) north and across Waimea River. Koaie Trail starts about .5 mile (800 m) up Waimea River from end of Kukui Trail. This trail takes 3-mile (4.8-k) route along south side of Koaie Canyon, another scenic canyon with good swimming holes. There are two campsites along trail, Hipalau and Lonomea.
Photograph scenery and wildlife.
NO water. Pack out trash. No access to Koaie Trail during stormy weather due to flash floods. Seasonal hunting. Stays limited to 4 nights within 30-day period.
800 ft (240 m)

## MAUI–"The Valley Isle"

## BALDWIN BEACH PARK

Maui Parks and Recreation
(808) 243-7383
Travel 1 mile (1.6 k) W of PAIA (E of KAHULUI) on HI 36.
$3/person, $.50 under age 18.
Open All Year. Reservations required.
Tent sites. Water, flush toilets, showers, tables, ball fields.
In fenced, flat, grassy spot by road on long, sandy beach.
Bodysurf here. Catch a local ball game.
See town sights, including sugar mill and Buddhist temple.
3-day limit. Safety problems in past.
10 ft (3 m)

▲ ▲ ▲ ▲ ▲ ▲ ▲ ▲ ▲ ▲ ▲ ▲ ▲ ▲ ▲ ▲ ▲ ▲ ▲ ▲ ▲ ▲ ▲

## HALEAKALA NP
(808) 572-9306

To Haleakala Crater section of park is 1.5-hour trip from KAHULUI via HI 36, 37, 377, and 378. To Kipahulu District is 3.5–4-hour trip from KAHULUI via HI 360 to HANA then HI 31 toward KIPAHULU.

FREE but $3 entrance fee (or pass). Also, free backcountry permits available at Visitor Center. Open All Year.

Dominating island is massive, volcanic mountain full of rainforests, streams, waterfalls, and pools.

Hike across barren but surprisingly colorful landscape of world's largest volcanic crater (25 square miles with drop of 3000 feet). Experience mystical sunrise at this kahuna-touted power source. Take lots of photographs.

No off-trail hiking.

### ▲ 'Ohe'o Stream
In Kipahulu District, travel 62 miles (99.2 k) SE of KAHULUI Airport via Hana Hwy (HI 36 and 360). In HANA, take HI 31 to KIPAHULU. (It's 3-hour drive one way on narrow, rugged roads with no gas available in Kipahulu area.)

First-come, first-serve tent sites.

Chemical and pit toilets, some picnic tables and grills.

In secluded field near ocean.

NO water. Do NOT use detergents in stream–it kills rare aquatic life. Pets are allowed. Fires in grills only. No food or other lodging in Kipahulu area. Camping limited to 3 nights/month.

10 ft (3 m)

### ▲ Holua
From KAHULUI, take HI 37 S past PUKALANI. Turn Left on HI 377 and Left again on HI 378. (It's 32 miles (51.2 k) from Kahului to Visitor Center.)

Hike-in tent sites (limit of 25 first-come, first-serve individuals–permit required).

Central water faucet, chemical toilets.

On grassy flat with lava rocks at bottom of 1200-ft (366-m) volcano crater cliff.

No trash receptacles (pack it out). No fires. 2-consecutive-night limit at either crater campground with limit of 3 nights/month. Prepare for rapid weather changes.

7000 ft (2100 m)

### ▲ Hosmer Grove
From KAHULUI, go S on HI 37 past PUKALANI. Take Left on HI 377 then another Left on HI 378. (It's 32 miles (51.2 k) from Kahului to Visitor Center.)

Close, open tent sites.

Central water faucet, chemical toilets, tables, grills, picnic shelter.

Near park entrance.

View wildlife here.

Weather changes rapidly–be prepared. Often crowded. 3-nights/month limit.

6800 ft (2040 m)

### ▲ Paliku
From KAHULUI, drive S on HI 37. Just beyond PUKALANI, turn left on HI 377 then left again on HI 378. (It's 32 miles (51.2 k) from Kahului to Visitor Center.)

Tent sites (maximum of 25 first-come, first-serve individuals–permit required).

Central water faucet, chemical toilets.

On grassy area inside east end of crater–9.8 miles (15.6 k) to nearest road.

No trash receptacles (pack it out). Be prepared for rain (average of 200 inches/year).

7000 ft (2100 m)

## POLIPOLI SPRING SRA
(808) 243-5354

Drive 9.75 miles (15.6 k) upland from KULA on Waipoli Rd off Kekaulike Ave (HI 377). 4WD recommended for last 5 miles (8 k) of unpaved road up slope of Haleakala.

FREE but choose a chore.

Open All Year. Reservations required.

Tent sites. Central water faucet, pit toilets, tables, grills, 2 picnic shelters.

In fog belt of Kula Forest Reserve, reminiscent of Pacific Northwest conifer forests. Sweeping view of Maui, Kahoolawe, Molokai, and Lanai.

Hike on extensive trail system. Photograph scenery and wildlife.

Treat drinking water. 5-day limit. Seasonal pig and bird hunting. Frequent freezes on winter nights.

6200 ft (1860 m)

▲ ▲ ▲ ▲ ▲ ▲ ▲ ▲ ▲ ▲ ▲ ▲ ▲ ▲ ▲ ▲ ▲ ▲ ▲ ▲ ▲ ▲ ▲ ▲ ▲ ▲ ▲ ▲

## RAINBOW
Maui Parks and Recreation
(808) 243-7383
Find near upcountry village of
HALIIMAILE–off Kula Hwy (HI 37).
$3/person, $.50 under age 18.
Open All Year. Reservations required.
Tent sites. Water, flush toilets.
Inland and more off-the-beaten path.
Relax or use as base to visit Kahula Bay
and Haleakala NP sights.
3-day limit.

## WAIANAPANAPA SP
(808) 243-5354
On Hana Hwy (HI 360) 4.5 miles (7.2 k)
E of HANA, locate access road .5 mile
(800 m) S of HANA airport turnoff. (It's
52.8 miles (84.5 k) E of KAHULUI
Airport, a 3-hour drive on winding,
paved road.)
FREE but choose a chore.
Open All Year. Reservations required.
Walk-in tent sites. Central water faucet,
flush toilets, showers, tables, grills,
picnic shelters, pay phone.
On small black-sand beach along scenic,
low-cliffed volcanic coastline. Lava arch,
sea stacks, anchialine pools, and blow
holes on this remote, rocky bay.
Sunbathe, swim, snorkel, or fish in beach
area. Hike along ancient Hawaiian
coastal trail (through hala forest, into a
heiau (place of worship), and inside
lava-tube caves). Birdwatching and
photography too.
Lots of rain, insects, and people as well
as rip tides. 5-day limit.
100 ft (30 m)

## MOLOKAI–"The Friendly Isle"

## ONE ALII BEACH PARK
Molokai Parks and Recreation
(808) 553-5141
Go 3 miles (4.8 k) E of KAUNAKAKAI–
off Kamehameha Hwy (HI 450).
$3/person. Reservations required.
Open All Year.
Tent sites. Water, flush toilets, showers,
BBQ pits.
Near coconut grove and fish pond.
Enjoy beach activities. See Japanese
immigration memorials.
3-day limit.
10 ft (3 m)

## PALAAU SP
(808) 567-6083
Drive 12 miles (19.2 k) NE of KAUN-
AKAKAI to end of Kalae Hwy (HI 47).
FREE but choose a chore.
Open All Year. Reservations required.
6 tent sites. Central water faucet, flush
toilets, tables, grills.
In ironwood trees with scenic overlook
of historic Kalaupapa leprosy colony.
Hike for cliff-top views of peninsula as
well as feeling of ironwood forest. Visit
phallic stone. Take lots of pictures.
No showers at this state park. 5-day
limit. Frequent cold winds and rains.
2500 ft (750 m)

## PAPOHAKU BEACH PARK
Molokai Parks and Recreation
(808) 553-5141
Take Magnolia Hwy (HI 460) to
Kaluakoi Rd then access road to this
west end beach.
$3/person. Reservations required.
Open All Year.
Tent sites. Water, flush toilets, showers,
changing rooms, BBQ pits.
In grassy, landscaped park on Hawaii's
largest white sand beach.
Walk 2.5-mile (4-k) beach.
Perilous swimming. Windy. 3-day limit.
10 ft (3 m)

▲ ▲ ▲ ▲ ▲ ▲ ▲ ▲ ▲ ▲ ▲ ▲ ▲ ▲ ▲ ▲ ▲ ▲ ▲ ▲ ▲ ▲ ▲ ▲ ▲ ▲

**OAHU–"The Gathering Place"**

**BELLOWS FIELD BEACH PARK**
City-County of Honolulu (808) 523-4525
Find S of KAILUA and NE of
WAIMANALO on beach by Bellows Air
Force Base off Kalanianaole Hwy (HI 72).
FREE but choose a chore.
Open All Year. Reservations required.
50 tent sites.
Flush toilets, tables, pay phones.
In ironwood trees on windward coast.
Swim and body/board surf (lifeguard on
duty). Windsurf and sail too.
Camping allowed weekends only.
City-County Parks make "kapu"
(forbidden) alcohol, dogs, campfires, and
litter.
10 ft (3 m)

**HALE'IWA BEACH PARK**
City-County of Honolulu (808) 523-4525
From HALE'IWA, locate off
Kamehameha Hwy (HI 83)–across
Anahulu River bridge.
FREE but choose a chore.
Open All Year. Reservations required.
4 tent sites. Water, flush toilets, tables,
pay phones, playground, ball fields,
night security.
On north shore's Waialua Bay with view
of island points.
Swim behind breakwater.
Closed Wednesday–Thursday. City-
County Parks make "kapu" (forbidden)
alcohol, dogs, campfires, and litter.
10 ft (3 m)

**HAU'ULA BEACH PARK**
City-County of Honolulu (808) 523-4525
Proceed .5 mile (800 m) from HAU'ULA
on Kamehameha Hwy (HI 83).
FREE but choose a chore.
Open All Year. Reservations required.
12 tent sites.
Water, flush toilets, showers, tables,
grills, shelter, pay phones.
On windward-shore beach popular with
locals.

Fishing and lobstering (coral reef makes
swimming poor). Hiking on forest trails
behind town.
Closed Wednesday–Thursday. City-
County Parks make "kapu" (forbidden)
alcohol, dogs, campfires, and litter.
10 ft (3 m)

**HO'OMALUHIA BOTANICAL
GARDENS**
(808) 235-6636
Luluku Rd turns toward mountains from
Kahekili Hwy (HI 83) near intersection
of HI 83 and HI 63.
FREE but choose a chore.
Open All Year. Reservations required.
500 tent sites. Water in every site, flush
toilets, showers, tables, grills, fire rings,
pay phone.
In large areas with tropical trees from
around the world. With spectacular view
of surrounding mountains and ocean.
Hiking, wildlife viewing, taking photographs, and attending nature programs.
Stay Thursday through Monday (closed
Tuesday–Wednesday, Christmas, and
New Years Day). No tying or using
trees. No generators. No swimming,
boating, or fishing in reservoir.
Mosquitos.
150 ft (45 m)

**KAHANA BAY BEACH PARK**
City-County of Honolulu (808) 523-4525
Locate on Kamehameha Hwy (HI 83)
between Ka'a'awa and Punalu'u parks.
FREE but choose a chore.
Open All Year. Reservations required.
4 tent sites. Flush toilets, showers, tables,
pay phones.
In scenic area on windward shore with
breadfruit, mango, and bamboo indicating site of old Hawaiian village.
Enjoy swimming, body/windsurfing,
sailing, and fishing.
Closed Wednesday–Thursday. City-
County Parks make "kapu" (forbidden)
alcohol, dogs, campfires, and litter.
10 ft (3 m)

▲ ▲ ▲ ▲ ▲ ▲ ▲ ▲ ▲ ▲ ▲ ▲ ▲ ▲ ▲ ▲ ▲ ▲ ▲ ▲ ▲ ▲ ▲ ▲ ▲ ▲ ▲ ▲

## KAHE POINT

City-County of Honolulu (808) 523-4525
S of NANAKULI, access point from
Farrington Hwy (HI 93).
**FREE** but choose a chore.
Open All Year. Reservations required.
4 tent sites. Water, flush toilets, showers,
tables, pay phones.
Near cliffs of point but view of power
plant intrudes.
Fish here year-round. Good nearby
places to swim, surf, snorkel, and scuba.
Closed Wednesday–Thursday. City-
County Parks make "kapu" (forbidden)
alcohol, dogs, campfires, and litter.

## KAIAKA BEACH PARK

City-County of Honolulu (808) 523-4525
In HALE'IWA, take either Hale'iwa Rd
just NE of Hale'iwa Elementary School
off Kamehameha Hwy (HI 83) or follow
Waialua Beach Rd on north shore.
**FREE** but choose a chore.
Open All Year. Reservations required.
Tent sites. Central water faucet, flush
toilets, cold showers, tables, grills.
In landscaped, former state park with
fine views and small, sandy beach.
Enjoy full range of beach activities,
including shore fishing.
Closed Wednesday–Thursday. City-
County Parks make "kapu" (forbidden)
alcohol, dogs, campfires, and litter.
10 ft (3 m)

## KAIONA BEACH PARK

City-County of Honolulu (808) 523-4525
Take Kalanianaole Hwy (HI 72) SE of
WAIMANALO.
**FREE** but choose a chore.
Open All Year. Reservations required.
Tent sites. Water, flush toilets, showers,
tables, grills, pay phones.
On windward shore.
Sail, windsurf, bodysurf, swim, and fish.
Closed Wednesday–Thursday. City-
County Parks make "kapu" (forbidden)
alcohol, dogs, campfires, and litter.
10 ft (3 m)

## KAKELA BEACH PARK

City-County of Honolulu (808) 523-4525

Find off Kamehameha Hwy (HI 83)
between towns of HAU'ULA and LAIE.
**FREE** but choose a chore.
Open All Year. Reservations required.
Tent sites. Flush toilets, tables.
On windward shore known for sailing.
Windsurf, bodysurf, and swim too.
Closed Wednesday–Thursday. City-
County Parks make "kapu" (forbidden)
alcohol, dogs, campfires, and litter.
10 ft (3 m)

## KEA'AU BEACH PARK

City-County of Honolulu (808) 523-4525
Drive 10 miles (16 k) N of MAKAHA on
Farrington Hwy (HI 93).
**FREE** but choose a chore.
Open All Year. Reservations required.
55 tent sites. Water, flush toilets,
showers, tables, pay phones.
In grassy area on rocky leeward shore.
Fish year-round. Swim and surf near
small, sandy beach to north. Snorkel and
scuba reef when calm.
Closed Wednesday–Thursday. City-
County Parks make "kapu" (forbidden)
alcohol, dogs, campfires, and litter.
10 ft (3 m)

## KEAIWA HEIAU SRA

(808) 548-7455
Locate approximately 12 miles (19.2 k)
from WAIKIKI.
**FREE** but choose a chore.
Open All Year. Reservations required.
Tent sites. Central water faucet, flush
toilets, cold showers, tables, grills, fire
rings, pay phone.
Along wooded ridge known as "Aiea
Heights."
Hiking 4.8-mile (7.7-k) loop trail, viewing
remains of healing temple and specimens of medicinal plants, watching
wildlife, and taking photos.
Open Friday–Tuesday. Obey all rules,
including gate hours, stay limits, and
generator use. Often crowded.
600 ft (180 m)

## KUALOA PARK

City-County of Honolulu (808) 523-4525
Find off Kamehameha Hwy (HI 83) at

▲ ▲ ▲ ▲ ▲ ▲ ▲ ▲ ▲ ▲ ▲ ▲ ▲ ▲ ▲ ▲ ▲ ▲ ▲ ▲ ▲ ▲ ▲ ▲ ▲

Kualoa Point.
FREE but choose a chore.
Open All Year. Reservations required.
36 tent sites. Flush toilets, tables, pay
phones, night security.
In grassy park with palms near once-
sacred point where mountains rise
vertically.
Swim (lifeguard on duty) or surf
(body/wind). Sail too.
Closed Wednesday–Thursday. City-
County Parks make "kapu" (forbidden)
alcohol, dogs, campfires, and litter.
10 ft (3 m)

## LUALUALEI BEACH PARK
City-County of Honolulu (808) 523-4525
Locate 7 miles (11.2 k) N of MAILI–off
Farrington Hwy (HI 93).
FREE but choose a chore.
Open All Year. Reservations required.
15 tent sites. Flush toilets, showers,
tables, pay phones.
On leeward-shore, white-sand beach.
Fish. When calm, snorkel or scuba reef.
Closed Wednesday–Thursday. City-
County Parks make "kapu" (forbidden)
alcohol, dogs, campfires, and litter.
10 ft (3 m)

## MAKAPU'U BEACH PARK
City-County of Honolulu (808) 523-4525
Discover in WAIMANALO, easternmost
part of island.
FREE but choose a chore.
Open All Year. Reservations required.
7 tent sites. Water, flush toilets, tables,
pay phones.
In visually-pleasing setting on windward
shore with waves of 12 ft and higher.
Bodysurfing is primary activity here
(boards and motorboats prohibited).
Enjoy swimming when calm (lifeguard).
Dangerous currents despite breakwater.
Closed Wednesday–Thursday. City-
County Parks make "kapu" (forbidden)
alcohol, dogs, campfires, and litter.
20 ft (6 m)

## MALAEKAHANA SRA
(808) 548-7455
Turn off Kamehameha Hwy (HI 83)

1.3 miles (2.1 k) N of LAIE town.
FREE; group cabins available at
$2.50/adult; reservations required.
Open All Year.
40 walk-in tent sites, approximately
300 ft (90 m)from parking area.
Water in every site, flush toilets,
showers, tables, fire rings, pay phone,
aquatic equipment rentals, night security.
In wooded beach park.
Body surf, swim, and shore fish at beach.
While hiking, take camera for scenery
and wildlife.
Open Friday–Tuesday. Obey all rules,
including gate hours, stay limits, and
generator use. Often crowded.
20 ft (6 m)

## MOKULE'IA BEACH PARK
City-County of Honolulu (808) 523-4525
Locate near Dillingham Air Force Base–
off Farrington Hwy (HI 93).
FREE but choose a chore.
Open All Year. Reservations required.
15 tent sites. Flush toilets, showers,
tables, pay phones.
In grassy area on north shore.
Windsurfing in spring and fall. Swim-
ming in summer calm (winter brings
dangerous currents).
Closed Wednesday–Thursday. City-
County Parks make "kapu" (forbidden)
alcohol, dogs, campfires, and litter.
10 ft (3 m)

## NANAKULI BEACH PARK
City-County of Honolulu (808) 523-4525
Find in NANAKULI–off Farrington
Hwy (HI 93).
FREE but choose a chore.
Open All Year. Reservations required.
19 tent sites. Water, flush toilets,
showers, tables, pay phones, ball fields.
On leeward-shore, broad, sandy beach.
Swim (lifeguard on duty). Snorkel and
scuba too (be aware of winter currents).
Closed Wednesday–Thursday. City-
County Parks make "kapu" (forbidden)
alcohol, dogs, campfires, and litter.
10 ft (3 m)

▲ ▲ ▲ ▲ ▲ ▲ ▲ ▲ ▲ ▲ ▲ ▲ ▲ ▲ ▲ ▲ ▲ ▲ ▲ ▲ ▲ ▲ ▲ ▲ ▲ ▲ ▲ ▲ ▲ ▲

## SAND ISLAND SRA

(808) 548-7455
Drive to end of Sand Island Access Rd,
off Nimitz Hwy (HI 92)–3 miles (4.8 k)
from HONOLULU on south shore.
FREE but choose a chore.
Open All Year. Reservations required.
32 tent sites. Central water faucet, flush
toilets, showers, tables, fire rings, pay
phone, night security.
In landscaped park with small, sandy
beach. Good view of Honolulu Harbor
and sunset.
Swimming, board surfing, boating (boat
ramp nearby), and fishing. Walk beach
and nature trail to view wildlife.
Open Friday through Tuesday.
10 ft (3 m)

## SWANZY BEACH PARK

City-County of Honolulu (808) 523-4525
Discover near KA'A'AWA off
Kamehameha Hwy (HI 83).
FREE but choose a chore.
Open All Year. Reservations required.
20 tent sites.
Flush toilets, showers, tables, grills, pay
phones, playground, ball fields.
On windward shore. Fish. (Exposed
coral, rocks, and currents dangerous for
swimming.) Catch a ball game.
Camp weekends only. City-County Parks
make "kapu" (forbidden) alcoholic bever-
ages, dogs, campfires, and litter.
10 ft (3 m)

## WAIMANALO BAY BEACH PARK

City-County of Honolulu (808) 523-4525
Locate on Kamehameha Hwy (HI 83),
between Bellows Air Force Base and
Aloiloi St in WAIMANALO.
FREE but choose a chore.
Open All Year. Reservations required.
33 tent sites. Central water faucet, flush
toilets, showers, tables, fire rings, pay
phones, night security.
In ironwood grove near one of Hawaii's
largest sandy beaches (part of park that
was formerly a state park).
Try windward-shore location for
body/board surfing, swimming, fishing,
and other beach-related activities.
Closed Wednesday–Thursday. Frequently crowded. City-County Parks
make "kapu" (forbidden) alcohol, dogs,
campfires, and litter.
10 ft (3 m)

# Idaho

Grid conforms to official state map. For your copy, call (800) 635-7820
or wite Idaho Travel Council, 700 W State St, Boise, ID 83720.

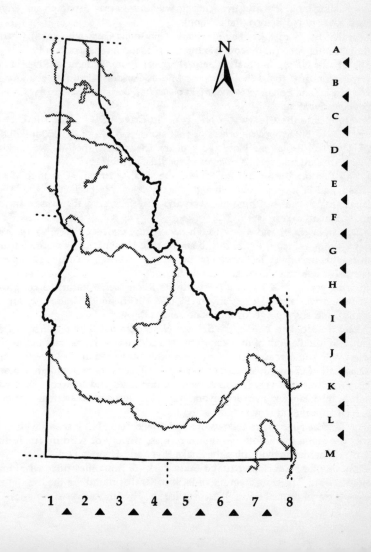

Idaho boasts the two deepest canyons in the United States, portions of the most rugged mountain ranges, rivers with incredible whitewater rapids, and a wide variety of wildlife. Interspersed among these untamed lands are agricultural valleys and rolling prairies.

Camping opportunities cluster due to topography and, consequently, few roads in vast territories. Often you'll find several alternatives under each entry.

The **National Park Service** (NPS) offers two possibilities: City of Rocks National Reserve and Craters of the Moon NM (Backcountry). The **Bureau of Land Management** (BLM) administers many qualifying camps in the state's lower sections, while the US Forest Service claims the mountains.

**Boise National Forest** (NF) possesses ghost towns, alpine lakes, reservoirs, hot springs, summer habitat for big game, and hundreds of miles of hiking or cross-country skiing trails. It shares two fantastic wilderness areas: Sawtooth and Frank Church River of No Return (the Salmon).

Near the Utah border, **Caribou NF** offers Minnetonka Cave (with tours), Cherry Springs Nature Area (near Scout Mountain), plus mountain-lake beauty.

The **Challis NF** typifies Idaho's natural appeal. From wilderness (River of No Return) to unusual rivers (Lost River or Middle Fork of Salmon) to abandoned towns (Custer and Bonanza) to mountain peaks (tall Boriah or spectacular Castle), pick your adventure.

To appreciate the **Clearwater NF**, you can drive US 12 along the Lochsa River/Selway Bitterroot Wilderness or trek along portions of the 150-mile Lolo Trail. That still leaves the North Fork of the Clearwater, the Mallard-Larkins Pioneer Area, and thousands of acres of roadless territory.

**Idaho Panhandle NF** consolidates three smaller forests–Coeur d'Alene, Kaniksu, and St Joe–into one. Though heavily logged (especially in the St Joe area), the region boasts picturesque rivers and waterfalls, several groves of ancient trees, and many lakes.

Aside from ID 14 and a few rough backroads, the **Nez Perce NF** remains isolated from vehicles. Walk, raft, boat, or ride horseback to explore natural features that include Hells Canyon on the west as well as the Gospel Hump and River of No Return wilderness areas on the east.

Moving south, find **Payette NF** with the River of No Return, a couple of incredible drives along Hells Canyon (FR 050–Kleinschmidt Grade only for the intrepid), and some gorgeous mountain ranges thrown in.

Along the Montana border, the **Salmon NF** is dominated by the effects of the Lemhi and Middle Fork of the Salmon rivers. It displays wild, remote, and rugged scenery with summer access to many spots often measured in weeks not months.

Over half of the northern part of **Sawtooth NF** consists of Sawtooth National Recreation Area (NRA) with countless mountain lakes and snowcovered peaks. South of Interstate 84, there are several disjointed, less-visited sections that offer a special appeal (and winter sport activities).

The **Targhee NF** borders Yellowstone and Grand Teton NP. It shares with those parks the same incredible mountain ranges, variety of wildlife (including grizzlies), thermal activity, plus the Snake River and Henry's Fork.

Only one, less-developed **Idaho State Park** (SP) qualifies price-wise; most charge $7–$12. There are a couple of local parks that round out the list.

As the travel council states, "Discover Idaho–The Undiscovered America."

▲ ▲ ▲ ▲ ▲ ▲ ▲ ▲ ▲ ▲ ▲ ▲ ▲ ▲ ▲ ▲ ▲ ▲ ▲ ▲ ▲ ▲

## ABBOT

Sawtooth NF (208) 737-3200
State map: J3
From FEATHERVILLE, head E
on FR 227 for 2 miles (3.2 k).
First in series of eight
camps–go 1 mile (1.6 k) to **Chaparral**
(7 sites), then 1 mile (1.6 k) to **Bird
Creek** (5 sites), then 2 miles (3.2 k) to
**Willow Creek** (5 sites), then 3.5 miles
(5.6 k) to **Baumgartner** (29 sites), then
3 miles (4.8 k) to **Skeleton Creek**
(5 sites), then 10 miles (16 k) to **Bounds**
(12 sites), then Left (N) and 2 miles
(3.2 k) up FR 085 to **Canyon** (6 sites).
**FREE** but choose a chore.
Open May 20–Sep 30.
7 close, open sites.
Pit toilets, tables, fire rings.
Along South Fork of Boise River.
Float, tube, and fish on river. Soak in
various hot springs.
NO water (except at Baumgartner,
Bounds, and Canyon). 14-day limit.
4600 ft (1380 m)

## AGENCY CREEK RS

BLM (208) 756-5401
State map: H5
From TENDOY, go E on Lemhi
Pass Rd for 6 miles (9.6 k).
**FREE**. Open All Year.
4 close, open sites.
Pit toilets, tables, fire rings.
On small creek in mountain valley near
Continental Divide. Some rock art on
east side of site (do not deface).
Fish or hike. Take photographs. Cross-
country ski and snowmobile.
NO water/trash arrangements.
5000 ft (1500 m)

## ANDERSON RANCH RESERVOIR

Boise NF (208) 334-1516
State map: K3
From MOUNTAIN HOME, go
24 miles (38.4 k) NE on US 20.
Turn Left (N) on FR 134 and
go 5 miles (8 k). Turn Right (NE) on
FR 113. Find series of 5 camps next
6 miles (9.6 k)–**Elk Creek** (10 sites),
**Little Wilson** (2 sites), **Evans Creek**
(12 sites), **Castle Creek** (2 sites), and **Fall
Creek** (20 sites). (Also see Ice Springs,
Deer Creek, and Little Camas.)
**FREE** but choose a chore.
Open Jun 1–Sep 30.
46 sites. Pit toilets, tables, fire rings, boat
launch (Fall Creek and Elk Creek).
Fish, boat, waterski, or swim large lake.
NO water. No trash arrangements at
Little Wilson.
4200 ft (1260 m)

## BANNER CREEK

Challis NF (208) 838-2201
State map: I3
From STANLEY, head W on
ID 21 for 21.5 miles (34.4 k).
For alternatives, go 2 miles
(3.2 k) to **Bench Creek** (5 sites) then take
FR 520 SW for 2 miles (3.2 k) to **Bull
Trout Lake** (19 sites–no power boats).
**FREE** but choose a chore.
Open Jun 15–Sep 15.
3 sites.
Water, pit toilets, tables, fire rings.
On creek with fishing, hiking, and
relaxing possibilities.
No trash facilities. 14-day/22-ft limits.
6500 ft (1950 m)

## BAYHORSE LAKE

Challis NF (208) 838-2201
State map: I4
From CHALLIS, go 9 miles
(14.4 k) S on ID 75 to BLM's
fee-charged **Bayhorse** Camp
(9 sites). Turn Right (W) on steep,
narrow FR 051 and go 8 miles (12.8 k).
**FREE** but choose a chore.
Open Jul 1–Sep 10.
7 sites.
Water, pit toilets, tables, fire rings.
Fish here or on Little Bayhorse. Hike.
No trash arrangements. 14-day limit.
8600 ft (2580 m)

## BEAR CREEK

Targhee NF (208) 523-1412
State map: K8
From PALISADES DAM, go
2.5 miles (4 k) S on US 26.
Turn Right (SW) on FR 076. Go

▲ ▲ ▲ ▲ ▲ ▲ ▲ ▲ ▲ ▲ ▲ ▲ ▲ ▲ ▲ ▲ ▲ ▲ ▲ ▲ ▲ ▲ ▲ ▲

1.5 miles (2.4 k). Continue on FR 058 for 4.5 miles (7.2 k).
FREE but choose a chore.
Open May 25–Sep 15.
6 close, open sites. Water, pit toilets, tables, grills, horse ramp.
At trailhead to scenic area.
Hike Bear Creek Trail. Ride horses. Fish.
No trash arrangements (pack it out).
16-day/22-ft limits.
5800 ft (1740 m)

## BEAR GULCH

Sawtooth NF (208) 737-3200
State map: M4
From HOLLISTER, go S on US 93 for 7.5 miles (12 k). Turn Left (E) on CR and go 4 miles (6.4 k). Turn Right (S) on Foot Hill Rd and go 14 miles (22.4 k), always bearing Left. Turn Left (N) on FR 513 and continue 1 mile (1.6 k).
FREE but choose a chore.
Open May 15–Oct 15.
13 close, open sites. &
Water, pit toilets, tables, fire rings.
In secluded canyon near historic Shoshone Cabin.
Walk, picnic, and relax.
14-day limit.
5200 ft (1560 m)

## BEAVER CREEK

Caribou NF (208) 847-0375
State map: M8
From ST CHARLES, go W on FR 411 (Green Canyon) about 11 miles (17.6 k). For larger, more developed alternative **Cloverleaf** (fee charged) near Minnetonka Cave, take 412 out of St Charles.
FREE but choose a chore.
Open May 15–Sep 15.
5 close, open sites.
Water, pit toilets, tables, grills.
In woods along quiet creek with access to High Line National Recreation Trail.
Relax, take rewarding hikes, and fish.
14-day limit.

## BELL BAY

Idaho Panhandle NF
(208) 765-7381
State map: D1
From COEUR D'ALENE, go E on I-90 for 7 miles (11.2 k). Take Exit 22 and head S on ID 97 for 25 miles (40 k)–N of Harrison. Turn Right (W) on CR 314 and go 3 miles (4.8 k).
FREE but choose a chore.
Open May 1–Oct 1.
26 close, open sites.
Pit toilets, tables, fire rings, boat dock.
On east side of lake.
Swim, boat, and waterski.
NO water. 14-day limit. No boat launching on-site.
2600 ft (780 m)

## BERLIN FLAT

Idaho Panhandle NF
(208) 752-1221
State map: C2
From PRICHARD, go N on CR 208 for 14 miles (22.4 k). Pass fee-charged **Kit Price** (52 sites) and **Devil's Elbow** (20 sites). Turn Right (NE) on FR 412 and go 7 miles (11.2 k).
FREE but choose a chore.
Open May 15–Oct 15.
9 close, open sites.
Water, pit toilets, tables, fire rings.
In woods next to Shoshone Creek.
Enjoy this peaceful getaway.
14-day limit.
2600 ft (780 m)

## BIG CREEK

Idaho Panhandle NF
(208) 245-2531
State map: D2
From CALDER, head E on Northside Rd for 5 miles (8 k). Turn Left (NW) on FR 537 (Big Creek) and go 3 miles (4.8 k).
FREE but choose a chore.
Open May 15–Oct 15.
8 close, open sites.
Pit toilets, tables, fire rings.
In woods along creek.
Hike on national recreation trails.

▲ ▲ ▲ ▲ ▲ ▲ ▲ ▲ ▲ ▲ ▲ ▲ ▲ ▲ ▲ ▲ ▲ ▲ ▲ ▲ ▲ ▲ ▲ ▲ ▲ ▲ ▲

Explore remnants of mining and logging activities. Pick berries. Relax.
NO water. 14-day limit. Hunting in season.
2400 ft (720 m)

## BIG CREEK

Challis NF (208) 879-4321
State map: I5
From PATTERSON, head S on CR (Pahsimeroi) for 7 miles (11.2 k). Turn Left (E) on FR 097 (Big Creek). Go 3 miles (4.8 k).
FREE. Open Jun 15–Sep 30.
3 close, open sites.
Pit toilets, tables, fire rings.
On secluded creek.
Hike South or North Fork trails.
NO water. 14-day limit. No trailers.
Hunting in season.
6600 ft (1980 m)

## BIG EIGHTMILE

Salmon NF (208) 768-2371
State map: I5
From LEADORE, head W on CR about 6.5 miles (10.4 k). Turn Left (SW) on FR 096 and drive about 2.5 miles (4 k).
FREE but choose a chore.
Open May 15–Oct 15.
4 close, open sites.
Water, pit toilets, tables, fire rings.
On creek near alpine meadow.
Hike, fish, or picnic.
No trash arrangements. 14-day/24-ft limits. Motorcycles.

## BIG SPRINGS

Targhee NF (208) 558-7301
State map: I8
From MACKS INN, go 4.5 miles (7.2 k) E on ID 84.
$5. Open May 25–Sep 15.
17 close, open sites. Water, pit toilets, tables, grills, fire rings.
Next to constant 52°F spring (that means rainbow trout year-round) at headwaters of Henry's Fork of Snake River.
Swim (brrr) and float or boat but no fishing. Walk interpretive trail.
16-day limit. Crowded holidays.

## BLACK ROCK

Boise NF (208) 334-1516
State map: J3
From IDAHO CITY, go NE on ID 21 for 3 miles (4.8 k). Turn Right (E) on FR 327 and go 15 miles (24 k).
FREE but choose a chore.
Open Jun 1–Oct 15.
11 (4 tent-only) sites.
Water, pit toilets, tables, fire rings.
On North Fork of Boise River.
Hike and fish in remote locale.
No trash arrangements (pack it out).
4200 ft (1260 m)

## BOILING SPRINGS

Boise NF (208) 334-1516
State map: I2
From CROUCH, head N on FR 698 about 22 miles (35.2 k). (Also see Tie Creek.)
FREE but choose a chore.
Open Jun 1–Oct 15.
9 sites. Pit toilets, tables, fire rings.
On Middle Fork of Payette River.
Hike upstream to several hot springs.
Relax. Fish.
NO water/trash arrangements.
4000 ft (1200 m)

## BONNEVILLE

Boise NF (208) 334-1516
State map: J3
From LOWMAN, go E on ID 21 for 18 miles (28.8 k). Turn Left just beyond Warm Springs airstrip.
FREE. Open May 15–Sep 30.
9 sites. Pit toilets, tables, fire rings.
On Warm Springs Creek near South Fork of Payette. Raft, kayak, or fish river.
Soak in several nearby hot springs.
NO water/trash arrangements.
4700 ft (1410 m)

## BOUNDARY

Sawtooth NF (208) 737-3200
State map: J4
From KETCHUM, head NE on FR 408 just beyond Sawtooth NF boundary.

**FREE** but choose a chore.
Open May 15–Nov 15.
6 close, open sites.
Water, pit toilets, tables, fire rings.
On stream behind Sun Valley.
Relax or hike Morgan Ridge Trail.
14-day limit.
6000 ft (1800 m)

## BOX CANYON
Targhee NF (208) 558-7301
State map: I8
From ISLAND PARK, go S on
US 20 to Ponds Lodge.
Continue S for 2.25 miles
(3.6 k). Turn Right (SW) on CR 134 and
go .75 mile (1.2 k). Turn Right (NW) on
FR 135 and go 1 mile (1.6 k).
**$5.** Open May 25–Sep 15.
19 close, open sites. Water, pit toilets,
tables, grills, fire rings.
On banks of Henry Fork of Snake River,
considered one of world's best fly
fishing streams. Fish. Walk nature trail.
Observe Rocky Mountain birds that
winter here.
16-day limit. Crowded holidays.
6200 ft (1860 m)

## BRIDGE CREEK
Nez Perce NF (208) 842-2255
State map: G3
From ELK CITY, go 3 miles
(4.8 k) S on ID 14. Go SE on
CR 222 for 14 miles (22.4 k)
reaching Red River Ranger Station. Head
NE on FR 234 for 10 miles (16 k). (Also
see Ditch Creek and Red River.)
**FREE** but choose a chore.
Open Jun 1–Oct 31; camping allowed
off-season.
5 close, open sites.
Pit toilets, tables, grills.
Within .5 mile (800 m) of Red River Hot
Springs. Soak and relax. Also, swim, fish,
hike, or cross-country ski.
NO water/trash facilities. Crowded.
Limited parking. 14-day/16-ft limits.
4800 ft (1440 m)

## BROWNLEE
Payette NF (208) 634-4100
State map: I1
From CAMBRIDGE, head NW
on ID 71 for 18 miles (28.8 k).
Turn Right (NE) on FR 044
and go 1.5 miles (2.4 k).
**$3.** Open May 15–Oct 15.
12 (7 tent-only) sites.
Water, pit toilets, tables, fire rings.
Fish. Explore along creek.
14-day/16-ft limits.
4400 ft (1320 m)

## BURGDORF

Payette NF (208) 634-4100
State map: H2
From MCCALL, go N on
CR 21 (Warren Wagon) for
30 miles (48 k) to BURGDORF.
Pass fee-charged **Upper Payette Lake**
(9 sites). Check out **Burgdorf Junction**
(5 sites) before turning NW on FR 246.
Drive 2 miles (3.2 k). (Also see Chinook.)
**FREE** but choose a chore.
Open Jun 1–Sep 30.
6 close, open sites.
Pit toilets, tables, grills, fire rings.
Next to private Burgdorf Hot Springs.
Hike or mountain bike. Fish or relax.
NO water/trash arrangements (pack it
out). 14-day limit.
6100 ft (1830 m)

## CASTLE CREEK

Nez Perce NF (208) 983-1963
State map: G2
From GRANGEVILLE, go
14 miles (22.4 k) E on ID 14–
heavy logging traffic. (See
Meadow Creek and South Fork.)
**$5;** fee may increase. Open All Year; dry
camping off-season.
8 (2 tent-only) close, screened sites. &
Water, pit toilets, tables, fire rings.
In shade on South Fork of Clearwater.
Swim and fish. Birdwatch.
14-day limit. Crowded weekends.
2300 ft (690 m)

▲ ▲ ▲ ▲ ▲ ▲ ▲ ▲ ▲ ▲ ▲ ▲ ▲ ▲ ▲ ▲ ▲ ▲ ▲ ▲ ▲ ▲ ▲ ▲ ▲

## CCC

Nez Perce NF (208) 926-4258
State map: F3
At LOWELL, cross bridge
heading SE on Selway River
Rd. Drive about 6.5 miles
(10.4 k). (Also see Johnson Bar, O'Hara,
and Rackliff.)
FREE but choose a chore.
Open All Year.
Undesignated, open sites.
Pit toilets, beach.
On river underneath western larch.
Canoe, float, swim, or fish.
NO water/trash facilities. 14-day limit.
Crowded weekends/holidays. Hunting
in season.
1400 ft (420 m)

## CEDAR CREEK

Idaho Panhandle NF
(208) 245-2531
State map: D2
From CLARKIA, go N on ID 3
for 3 miles (4.8 k).
FREE but choose a chore.
Open Jun 1–Oct 15.
3 close, open sites.
Pit toilets, tables, fire rings.
On banks of St Maries River.
Fish, picnic, or do nothing.
NO water. 14-day limit.
2800 ft (840 m)

## CEDARS

Clearwater NF (208) 476-4541
State map: E3
Just S of PIERCE off ID 11,
take FR 250 E-NE for 73 miles
(116.8 k). Alternatives are fee-
based: Kelly Forks (14 sites) at mile 47
(75.2 k) and Hidden Creek (13 sites)
at mile 55 (88 k).
FREE but choose a chore.
Open May 15–Nov 15.
5 close, open sites.
Pit toilets, tables, fire rings.
Along river near Montana Border.
Take trails into remote locations. Watch
for moose and deer. Fish and relax.
NO water/trash facilities. 14-day limit.
3700 ft (1110 m)

## CHERRY CREEK

Caribou NF (208) 766-4743
State map: M7
From DOWNEY, go SW on
Aspen Creek CR about
3.5 miles (5.6 k). Continue
straight (S) on FR 047 (Cherry Creek)
about 5.5 miles (8.8 k).
FREE but choose a chore.
Open May 15–Sep 15.
4 close, open sites.
Water, pit toilets, tables, grills.
In woods along creek.
Fish. Hike trails, including Oxford Peak.
No trash arrangements. 14-day limit.
5800 ft (1740 m)

## CHINOOK

Payette NF (208) 634-4100
State map: H2
Go 39 miles (62.4 k) N of
MCCALL on CR 21 (Warren
Wagon). (Also see Burgdorf.)
FREE but choose a chore.
Open Jun 1–Sep 30.
9 close, open sites.
Pit toilets, tables, grills, fire rings.
Near Secesh River.
Hike Loon Lake Trail (to beautiful
spot–5 miles one-way). Fish and relax.
NO water/trash arrangements (pack it
out). 14-day limit.
5900 ft (1770 m)

## CITY OF ROCKS
## NATIONAL RESERVE

(288) 824-5519
State map: M5
From ALMO, drive 3 miles on
SW gravel road.
FREE but choose a chore.
Open Mar 1–Oct 1; dry camping
off-season.
100 scattered, open sites. Hand water
pump, pit toilets, some tables and grills.
Among fantastic rock spires formed by
erosion of 2.5 billion-year-old rocks.
Climb or watch climbers. Absorb history
of 1840's California Trail. Hike,
birdwatch, and take photos.
14-day limit. Crowded weekends
May–Aug. Snow closes road in winter.

▲ ▲ ▲ ▲ ▲ ▲ ▲ ▲ ▲ ▲ ▲ ▲ ▲ ▲ ▲ ▲ ▲ ▲ ▲ ▲ ▲ ▲ ▲ ▲

Generator and pet leash rules. No wood cutting or off-road vehicle travel.
7000 ft (2100 m)

## COLD SPRINGS

Caribou NF (208) 847-0375
State map: M8
From SODA SPRINGS, go S on CR (past airport) about 6 miles (9.6 k). Turn Right (S) on FR 425 (Eightmile) and drive about 5 miles (8 k). (Also see Eightmile.)
FREE but choose a chore.
Open May 15–Sep 15.
3 close, open sites.
Water, pit toilets, tables, grills.
Along wooded creek.
Relax, hike, and, perhaps, fish.
14-day limit.
6200 ft (1860 m)

## CONRAD CROSSING

Idaho Panhandle NF
(208) 245-4517
State map: D3
From AVERY, head E on CR 50 (St Joe River) for 28 miles (44.8 k). Alternatives are larger, fee-charged **Turner** and **Tin Can Flat**. (Also see Fly Flat.)
FREE but choose a chore.
Open Jun 1–Oct 15.
8 scattered, open sites.
Water, pit toilets, tables, fire rings.
On wild and scenic river (3 sites) or above road (5 sites).
Besides fishing in wild trout waters, enjoy historic Montana Trail.
14-day limit.
3300 ft (990 m)

## COPPER CREEK

Idaho Panhandle NF
(208) 267-5561
State map: A2
From EASTPORT, head S on US 95 for 1 mile (1.6 k). Turn Left on FR 2517 and go 1 more mile (1.6 k). For fee-charged, lake camp, check out nearby **Robinson Lake**.
FREE but choose a chore.
Open May 15–Oct 15.

16 close, open sites.
Water, pit toilets, tables, fire rings.
In Moyie River woods near Canada.
Visit Copper Falls (a couple of miles S) plus float, fish, and hike.
14-day limit.
2500 ft (750 m)

## COPPER CREEK

Sawtooth NF (208) 737-3200
State map: K5
From CAREY, head N on CR around Little Wood River Reservoir–about 12 miles (19.2 k). Turn Right (E) on CR/FR 134 along Muldoon Creek and go about 15 miles (24 k).
FREE but choose a chore.
Open May 15–Oct 15.
5 sites. Pit toilets, tables, fire rings.
On Garfield Creek.
Fish and hike (from trailhead up FR 130) into area known for mining.
NO water. 14-day limit.
6400 ft (1920 m)

## COTTONWOOD

Boise NF (208) 334-1516
State map: J3
From BOISE, take ID 21 E about 16 miles (25.6 k). Turn Right (NE) on FR 268 along shore of Arrowrock Reservoir and drive 15 miles (24 k). (See Willow Creek.)
FREE but choose a chore.
Open May 15–Sep 30.
3 tent sites. Pit toilets, tables, fire rings.
On Cottonwood Creek near reservoir.
Boat, waterski, hike, explore, or fish.
NO water/trash arrangements.
3300 ft (990 m)

## COTTONWOOD RS

BLM (208) 756-5401
State map: I4
From CHALLIS, head N on US 93 for 16 miles (25.6 k)–2 miles (3.2 k) S of ELLIS. Farther S on 93 is **Spring Gulch** (10 sites) with water and fees.
FREE but choose a chore.
Open All Year.

▲ ▲ ▲ ▲ ▲ ▲ ▲ ▲ ▲ ▲ ▲ ▲ ▲ ▲ ▲ ▲ ▲ ▲ ▲ ▲ ▲ ▲ ▲ ▲ ▲ ▲ ▲ ▲

6 scattered, open sites.
Pit toilets, tables, fire rings.
In large, grassy meadow on banks of
Salmon River known for its fishing.
NO water/trash arrangements.
5000 ft (1500 m)

## CRATERS OF THE MOON NM
**Backcountry**

(208) 527-3257
State map: K5
Find monument 18 miles SW
of ARCO on US 20/26/93.
**FREE** but $3 entrance fee.
Explore volcanic phenomena: cones,
craters, flows, caves, fissures. Study
plant communities: grass, sagebrush,
pine, fir. In winter, cross-country ski.
Snow closes road and determines season.

## CROOKED RIVER #2 & #3

Nez Perce NF (208) 842-2245
State map: G3
From ELK CITY, go W on
ID 14 for 6 miles (9.6 k). Turn
Left (S) on CR 233 and go
2 miles (3.2 k).
**FREE** but choose a chore.
Open May 15–Sep 15.
8 (4 tent-only at #3) sites. Pit toilets.
Fish in river. Explore mining remains.
NO water/trash arrangements. Hunting
in season.

## CURLEW

BOR (208) 382-4258
State map: I2
From CASCADE, head S on
Lakeshore Dr. Turn Right on
West Side Rd and drive about
20 miles (32 k). (Also see Poison Creek.)
$2; reservations accepted.
Open May–Sep.
25 close, open tent sites.
Water, chemical toilets, tables, fire rings.
On western shore near north end of
Cascade Reservoir.
Swimming, boating, waterskiing, and
fishing. Good hiking nearby.
14-day limit. No ATVs. Subject to
monsoon-like winds (4-ft waves).
5000 ft (1500 m)

## CUSTER 1

Challis NF (208) 838-2201
State map: I4
From SUNBEAM (13 miles E of
STANLEY), go N on FR 013 for
8 miles (12.8 k). Turn Right
(NE) on FR 070 and go 3 miles (4.8 k).
For alternative camp (no water), go
4 miles (6.4 k) to **Eightmile** (2 sites).
**FREE** but choose a chore.
Open Jun 15–Sep 10.
6 sites.
Water, pit toilets, tables, fire rings.
On Yankee Fork of Salmon River near
Custer museum and old gold dredge.
Visit historic mining ruins. Explore.
14 day limit.
6600 ft (1980 m)

## DAGGER FALLS #1

Challis NF (208) 879-5204
State map: I3
From LOWMAN, head NE on
FR 668 for 34.1 miles (54.6 k).
Fee-charged **Boundary**
(14 sites) is another .7 mile (1.1 k).
**FREE** but choose a chore.
Open Jun 1–Sep 15.
10 close, open sites.
Pit toilets, tables, fire rings.
In woods by creek in canyon.
Picnic, fish, and hike–nature trails and
wilderness access. Enjoy 15-ft falls.
NO water. 14-day/22-ft limits.
5800 ft (1740 m)

## DEADMAN HOLE RS

BLM (208) 756-5401
State map: I4
From CLAYTON, head N on
ID 75 about 10 miles (16 k).
Pass **East Fork** (fee charged)
at mile 4 (6.4 k).
**FREE** but choose a chore.
Open All Year.
11 close, open sites.
Water, pit toilets, tables, fire rings.
In open area along Salmon River.
Fish for steelhead, boat, or hike.
No trash arrangements (pack it out).

▲ ▲ ▲ ▲ ▲ ▲ ▲ ▲ ▲ ▲ ▲ ▲ ▲ ▲ ▲ ▲ ▲ ▲ ▲ ▲ ▲ ▲ ▲

## DEADWOOD RESERVOIR AREA

Boise NF (208) 334-1516
State map: I3
From STANLEY, head W on
ID 21 for 21 miles (33.6 k).
Turn Right (W) on FR 082/579
and go 21 miles (33.6 k). Turn Left (S) on
FR 555 and go 7 miles (11.2 k). Find
4 camps on east side of lake: **Riverside**
(9 sites), **Barneys** (6 sites), **Howers**
(5 sites), and **Cozy Cove** (9 sites).
**FREE** but choose a chore.
Open Jul 1–Sep 15.
29 sites. Pit toilets, tables, fire rings.
On secluded Deadwood Reservoir.
Boat, fish, and hike.
NO water/trash arrangements.
5300 ft (1590 m)

## DEEP CREEK

Bitterroot NF (406) 821-3269
State map: G4
From DARBY, MT, go 4 miles
(6.4 k) S on US 93. Turn Right
(SW) on scenic CR 473. Drive
14.5 miles (23.2 k). Turn Right (W) on
FR 468 and go about 32 miles (51.2 k).
(Also see Paradise and Poet Creek.)
**FREE** but choose a chore.
Open Jun 15–Sep 6.
3 close, open sites. Pit toilets, tables.
Fish creek. Enjoy natural surroundings.
Hike into Selway Bitterroot or River of
No Return wilderness areas. Drive
FR 468 to Magruder Saddle.
10-day/16-ft limits.

## DEEP CREEK RS

BLM (208) 756-5401
State map: J4
From MACKAY, head NW on
US 93 for 15 miles (24 k). Turn
Left (SW) on Trail Creek Rd.
Drive 19 miles (30.4 k). Area alternatives
include **Phi Kappa** (21 sites) in about
6 miles (9.6 k) then **Park Creek** (17 sites).
Or bear Left in .5 mile (800 m) on FR 136
and in 7 miles (11.2 k), find **Wildhorse**
(15 sites). (Also see Garden Creek.)
**FREE** but choose a chore.
Open All Year.
2 scattered, open sites.

Pit toilets, tables, fire rings.
At confluence of East and North Forks of
Big Lost River.
Fish, hike, and rockhound.
NO water/trash arrangements.

## DEER CREEK

Boise NF (208) 334-1516
State map: K3
From PINE, go SE on FH 61
for 3 miles (4.8 k). Alternatives
are fee-charged **Curlew Creek**
(25 sites) another 1.5 miles (2.4 k) S; or
from PINE, fee-charged **Dog Creek**
(12 sites) 3 miles (4.8 k) N and another
free camp, **Pine** (12 sites) 2 miles S on
FR 128. (Also see Anderson Ranch.)
**FREE** but choose a chore.
Open Jun 1–Sep 30.
30 sites. Pit toilets, tables, fire rings, boat
launch, pay phone.
On northeastern shore of Anderson
Ranch Reservoir.
Swim, waterski, boat, or fish. Hike up
Deer Creek.
NO water.
4200 ft (1260 m)

## DEER FLAT

Boise NF (208) 334-1516
State map: I3
From STANLEY, head W on
ID 21 for 21 miles (33.6 k).
Turn Right (W) on FR 082/579
and go 17 miles (27.2 k).
**FREE** but choose a chore.
Open Jul 1–Sep 15.
5 sites. Pit toilets, tables, fire rings.
Beneath pass on Deer Creek.
Hike or relax in quiet atmosphere.
NO water/trash arrangements.
6300 ft (1890 m)

## DITCH CREEK

Nez Perce NF (208) 842-2255
State map: G3
From ELK CITY, go 3 miles
(4.8 k) S on ID 14. Go SE on
CR 222 for 14 miles (22.4 k)
reaching Red River Ranger Station. Head
NE on FR 234 for 5 miles (8 k). (Also see
Bridge Creek and Red River.)

▲ ▲ ▲ ▲ ▲ ▲ ▲ ▲ ▲ ▲ ▲ ▲ ▲ ▲ ▲ ▲ ▲ ▲ ▲ ▲ ▲ ▲ ▲ ▲

**FREE** but choose a chore.
Open Jun 1–Oct 31; camping allowed
off-season.
4 close, open sites.
Pit toilets, tables, grills, fire rings.
In open flat across road from river.
Make base for fishing, hiking, cross-
country skiing.
NO water/trash arrangements (pack it
out). 14-day limit. Hunting in season.
4500 ft (1350 m)

## DRY CANYON

Caribou NF (208) 766-4743
State map: M7
From WESTON, go W on
CR heading up Weston Creek
toward reservoir about
4.5 miles (7.2 k). Turn Left (W) on
FR 053 (Dry Canyon). Go about 3.5 miles
(5.6 k). Take Left fork (FR 224) and go
1 mile (1.6 k).
**FREE** but choose a chore.
Open May 15–Sep 15.
3 close, open sites.
Water, pit toilets, tables, grills.
In quiet, isolated section of woods.
Enjoy series of trails. Take time for
observation and reflection.
No trash arrangements (pack it out).
14-day limit.

## DUTCHMAN FLAT

Sawtooth NF (208) 737-3200
State map: I4
From SUNBEAM (13 miles E of
STANLEY), go E on ID 75 for
1 mile (1.6 k). More developed
(fee-charged) alternatives are **Upper** and
**Lower O'Brien** (10 sites each) 1.5 miles
(4 k) E or head N from SUNBEAM on
FR 013 and find within 4 miles (6.4 k)
**Blind Creek** (5 sites), **Flat Rock** (9 sites),
and **Pole Flat** (17 sites).
**FREE** but choose a chore.
Open Jun 15–Sep 15.
5 sites. Pit toilets, tables, fire rings.
Raft or kayak Salmon River. Hike or fish.
NO water. 14-day limit.
5800 ft (1740 m)

## EBENEZAR BAR

Salmon NF (208) 865-2383
State map: G4
From NORTH FORK, head W
on FR 030 for 34.4 miles (55 k).
Another 13 miles (20.8 k) to
**Corn Creek** (fee charged).
**FREE** but choose a chore.
Open Mar 15–Nov 15.
4 close, open sites.
Pit toilets, tables, fire rings.
Along Salmon River.
Fish, even swim, in river. Explore.
NO water/trash arrangements (pack it
out). 14-day limit.

## EIGHTMILE

Caribou NF (208) 847-0375
State map: M8
From SODA SPRINGS, go S on
CR (past airport) about 6 miles
(9.6 k). Turn Right (S) on
FR 425 (Eightmile). Drive about 6.5 miles
(10.4 k). (Also see Cold Springs.)
**FREE** but choose a chore.
Open May 15–Sep 15.
3 close, open sites.
Water, pit toilets, tables, grills.
On wooded creek.
Relax, hike, and, perhaps, fish.
14-day limit.
6300 ft (1890 m)

## ELK SUMMIT

Clearwater NF (208) 476-4541
State map: E4
From POWELL, take FR 360 S
for 17 miles (27.2 k). Looking
for fishing and spectacular
Lochsa River, check out string of
8 camps along US 12 W of POWELL–all
have fees.
**FREE** but choose a chore.
Open May 15–Nov 15.
16 close, open sites.
Pit toilets, tables, fire rings.
Near Elk Summit Guard Station at major
access to Selway Bitterroot Wilderness.
Hike to Hidden or Big Sand lakes.
NO water/trash arrangements (pack it
out). 14-day limit.
5756 ft (1725 m)

## FIR CREEK

Boise NF (208) 334-1516
State map: I3
From STANLEY, head W on
ID 21 for 21 miles (33.6 k).
Turn Right (W) on FR 082/579
and go 7 miles (11.2 k). Turn Right (N)
on FR for .5 mile (800 m). Continue on
FR 579 another 4 miles (6.4 k) for **Bear
Valley** (10 sites).
FREE but choose a chore.
Open Jun 15–Sep 15.
5 sites. Pit toilets, tables, fire rings.
On Bear Valley Creek.
Hike Blue Bunch Mountain Trail. Raft,
canoe, or relax.
NO water/trash arrangements.
6400 ft (1920 m)

## FISH CREEK

Nez Perce NF (208) 983-1963
State map: G2
From GRANGEVILLE, go
1 mile (1.6 k) E on ID 13. Turn
Right (E) on CR 17 and drive
1 mile (1.6 k). Turn Right (SE) on FR 221
and go about 5 miles (8 k).
$5; fee under review.
Open May 15–Sep 30; dry camping
off-season.
11 close, open sites.
Water, pit toilets, tables, fire rings.
In shade adjacent to meadow and
timbered area. Near Snowhaven ski area.
On trails, hike, bike, and horseback ride
in summer; snowmobile and cross-
country ski in winter.
No trash arrangements. 14-day limit.
5200 ft (1560 m)

## FISH CREEK RESERVOIR

BLM (208) 886-2206
State map: K5
From CAREY, go E on US 93
for 6 miles (9.6 k). Turn Left
(N) on gravel CR and go
5 miles (8 k).
FREE but choose a chore.
Open Apr–Nov; camping allowed
off-season.
Undesignated, scattered sites. Pit toilets,
tables (2), fire rings, boat ramp.

Fish in lake or picnic.
NO water/trash arrangements. 14-day
limit. Hot summers. Water level
fluctuates drastically.
5300 ft (1590 m)

## FLY FLAT

Idaho Panhandle NF
(208) 245-4517
State map: D3
From AVERY, head E on
CR 50 (St Joe River) for
33 miles (52.8 k). Continue straight on
FR 218 (Red Ives Work Center) for
5 miles (8 k). (Also see Conrad Crossing
and Spruce Tree.)
FREE but choose a chore.
Open Jun 1–Oct 15.
14 close, open sites.
Water, pit toilets, tables, fire rings.
On wild and scenic river.
Fish river and walk Fly Creek Trail.
14-day limit. Water on from Jul–Oct.
3500 ft (1050 m)

## FOUR MILE

Boise NF (208) 334-1516
State map: J3
From LOWMAN, go S on
scenic ID 21 for 11 miles
(17.6 k). Turn Left (E) on
FR 384 and go 12 miles (19.2 k). Turn
Left (W) on FR 327 and go 1.5 miles
(2.4 k). **Robert E Lee** (6 sites) and **Deer
Park** (3 sites) within next 4 miles (6.4 k).
FREE but choose a chore.
Open Jun 1–Oct 15.
5 sites. Pit toilets, tables, fire rings.
On North Fork of Boise.
Enjoy remote feeling. Explore.
NO water/trash arrangements.
4300 ft (1290 m)

## GARDEN CREEK RS

BLM (208) 756-5401
State map: J4
From MACKAY, head NW on
US 93 for 15 miles (24 k). Turn
Left (SW) on Trail Creek Rd.
Go 10 miles (16 k). (See Deep Creek.)
FREE but choose a chore.
Open All Year.

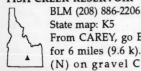

▲ ▲ ▲ ▲ ▲ ▲ ▲ ▲ ▲ ▲ ▲ ▲ ▲ ▲ ▲ ▲ ▲ ▲ ▲ ▲ ▲ ▲ ▲ ▲

3 close, open sites.
Pit toilets, tables, fire rings.
In aspen next to Big Lost River.
Fish, hike, or relax.
NO water/trash facilities. 14-day limit.
6200 ft (1860 m)

## GRAHAM BRIDGE

Boise NF (208) 334-1516
State map: J3
From LOWMAN, go S on
scenic ID 21 for 11 miles
(17.6 k). Turn Left (E) on
FR 384 and go 3 miles (4.8 k). Turn Left
(NW) on difficult, rough FR 312 and go
about 30 miles (48 k). **Johnson Creek**
(3 sites) is 2 more miles (3.2 k).
**FREE** but choose a chore.
Open Aug 1–Oct 15.
4 sites. Pit toilets, tables, fire rings.
On North Fork of Boise River near
Sawtooth Wilderness.
Enjoy remoteness. Hike into wilderness.
NO water/trash facilities. Hunting in
season.
5600 ft (1680 m)

## GRANDJEAN

Sawtooth NF (208) 737-3200
State map: I3
From LOWMAN, go 21 miles
(33.6 k) NE on ID 21. Turn
Right (E) on FR 524 and go
6 miles (9.6 k) to end.
**FREE** but choose a chore.
Open Jun 15–Sep 15.
34 sites. Pit toilets, tables, fire rings.
At trailheads for Sawtooth Wilderness.
Hike to several beautiful mountain lakes.
Fish South Fork of Payette River.
NO water. 14-day/22-ft limits.
5060 ft (1518 m)

## GRANDVIEW

Targhee NF (208) 652-7442
State map: I8
From ASHTON, go E on ID 47
(Mesa Falls Scenic Byway)
about 15 miles (24 k). (Also see
Pole Bridge and Warm River.)
**FREE** but choose a chore.
Open May 25–Sep 15.

5 close, open sites.
Pit toilets, tables, grills.
With view of Lower Mesa Falls.
Explore scenic area on western edge of
Yellowstone ecosystem.
NO water/trash arrangements (pack it
out). 16-day/22-ft limits.
6200 ft (1860 m)

## GRANITE SPRINGS

Nez Perce NF (208) 842-2255
State map: G3
From ELK CITY, go 3 miles
(4.8 k) S on ID 14. Go SE on
CR 222 for 14 miles (22.4 k)
reaching Red River Ranger Station. Head
E up Magruder Carricker Rd (FR 468) for
16 miles (25.6 k). (Also see Poet Creek.)
**FREE** but choose a chore.
Open Jul 15–Oct 15; dry camping
off-season.
4 close, open sites.
Water, pit toilets, fire rings.
Hike, as well as ride, trails.
No trash arrangements. 14-day/16-ft
limits. Crowded hunting season.
6700 ft (2010 m)

## GREEN BAY

Idaho Panhandle NF
(208) 263-5111
State map: B2
From GARFIELD BAY, head E
on FR 532 for 2 miles
(3.2 k)–option to larger, fee-charged
**Garfield Bay.**
**FREE** but choose a chore.
Open May 15–Oct 15.
3 close, open tent sites.
Pit toilets, tables, fire rings, beach.
On western shore of Lake Pend Oreille.
Swim, boat, and waterski lake. Walk
interpretive trail.
NO water. 14-day limit.
2000 ft (600 m)

## GROUSE

Payette NF (208) 634-4100
State map: H2
From MCCALL, head NW on
ID 55 for 5 miles (8 k). Turn
Right (N) on FR 768 (Brundage

Ski Area) and go 7 miles (11.2 k). Bear Left (N) on FR 257 and go 4 miles (6.4 k). For alternative, go N for 11 miles (19.2 k) to **Hazard Lake** (13 sites). $3. Open May 15–Oct 15.
6 sites.
Water, pit toilets, tables, fire rings.
On Goose Lake.
Swim, boat (no motors), and fish.
14-day limit.
6500 ft (1950 m)

## HALFWAY HOUSE

Nez Perce NF (208) 842-2255
State map: G3
From ELK CITY, go 3 miles (4.8 k) S on ID 14. Go SE on CR 222 for 14 miles (22.4 k) reaching Red River Ranger Station. Continue S on CR 222I for 20 miles (32 k). (Also see Sam's Creek.)
**FREE**. Open Jun 15–Oct 31; dry camping off-season.
4 close, open sites. Water (needs treating), pit toilets, tables, grills.
At end of road next to Crooked Creek. Hike into Gospel Hump Wilderness. Fish. Ski in winter.
No trash arrangements. 14-day/16-ft limits. Crowded. Hunting in season.
5000 ft (1500 m)

## HAMMER CREEK

BLM (208) 962-3245
State map: G2
From WHITE BIRD, take signed paved/gravel road N for 1.5 miles (2.4 k).
$4. Open All Year.
8 close, open sites. Water, pit toilets, tables, grills, dump station, boat launch.
In deep canyon on Salmon River.
Whitewater raft, boat, fish, explore.
14-day/21-ft limits. Rattlesnakes.
1440 ft (432 m)

## HAWKINS RESERVOIR

BLM (208) 678-5514
State map: L7
5 miles (8 k) S of ARIMO, take DOWNEY Exit off I-15. Head W on oil-surfaced CR for 10 miles (16 k).
**FREE** but choose a chore.
Open Apr–Dec; camping allowed off-season.
7 scattered, open sites. &
Pit toilets, tables, grills, fire rings.
Above reservoir (full in spring, low in fall) in sparse vegetation, some juniper.
Boat (small) and fish reservoir. Picnic.
NO water/trash arrangements. 14-day limit. Crowded Memorial Day. Hunting in season.
5142 ft (1542 m)

## HAWLEY CREEK

Salmon NF (208) 768-2371
State map: I5
From LEADORE, head E on ID 29 for .5 mile (800 m). Turn Right (SE) on CR. Drive about 6.5 miles (10.4 k). Turn Left on FR 275 for 2 miles (3.2 k). If occupied, go 1 mile (1.6 k) to site at **Big Bear**.
**FREE** but choose a chore.
Open May 15–Oct 15.
1 site. Water, pit toilets, tables, fire rings. Hike, fish, picnic along creek.
No trash facilities. 14-day/24-ft limit.

## HAYDEN CREEK

Salmon NF (208) 768-2371
State map: I5
From LEMHI, head N on ID 28 almost 1 mile (1.6 k). Make hard Left (SW) on CR/FR 008 and drive about 8 miles (12.8 k). If occupied go W on FR 009 about 4 miles (6.4 k) to **Bear Valley Trailhead** (2 sites plus water).
**FREE** but choose a chore.
Open May 15–Oct 15.
1 site. Pit toilets, tables, fire rings. Hike, fish, picnic along creek.
NO water/trash arrangements (pack it out). 14-day/24-ft limits.

## HELLER CREEK

Idaho Panhandle NF
(208) 245-4517
State map: D3
From SUPERIOR, MT, head SW on CR 350 for 33 miles

▲ ▲ ▲ ▲ ▲ ▲ ▲ ▲ ▲ ▲ ▲ ▲ ▲ ▲ ▲ ▲ ▲ ▲ ▲ ▲ ▲ ▲ ▲ ▲ ▲

(52.8 k). Alternate access from AVERY, ID via 350 not suitable for cars.
**FREE** but choose a chore.
Open Jun 1–Oct 15.
4 close, open sites. ♿
Pit toilets, tables, fire rings.
On St Joe River.
Fish wild trout waters. Visit Heller gravesite. Enjoy seclusion.
NO water. 14-day limit.
4700 ft (1410 m)

## HELLS CANYON NRA
**Seven Devils/Windy Saddle**

Wallowa-Whitman NF
(503) 426-4978
State map: G1
From just S of RIGGINS, take rough, steep FR 517 SW for 17 miles (27.2 k).
**FREE** but choose a chore.
Open All Year.
14 close, open sites. ♿
Pit toilets, tables, grills.
On canyon rim next to Seven Devils Mountains.
Explore from Heavens Gate Overlook.
NO water/trash arrangements (pack it out). 14-day limit.

## HERD LAKE RS

BLM (208) 756-5401
State map: J4
From CLAYTON, head E on ID 75 about 5 miles (8 k). Turn Right (S) on East Fork Rd and drive to Herd Lake Rd. Go SE on Herd Lake for 10 miles (16 k). For more primitive, wilderness camp, go about 5 miles (8 k) to **Upper Lake Creek**.
**FREE** but choose a chore.
Open All Year.
3 close, open sites.
Pit toilets, tables, fire rings.
In scenic area below lake–walk to water.
Explore rock slide that created lake. Do some fishing and canoeing.
NO water/trash arrangements.

## HONEYSUCKLE

Idaho Panhandle NF
(208) 765-7381
State map: C2
From COEUR D'ALENE, go E on FR 268 (Fernan Lake) for 11 miles (17.6 k). Bear Left at intersection on FR 612 and drive 11 miles (17.6 k).
**FREE** but choose a chore.
Open Jun 1–Sep 30.
8 close, open sites. ♿
Water, pit toilets, tables, fire rings.
In woods next to Sands Creek.
Take time away for picnicking and reflecting. Relax.
14-day limit. Hunting in season.
2800 ft (840 m)

## HORSE CREEK HOT SPRINGS

Salmon NF (208) 865-2383
State map: G4
From NORTH FORK, head W on FR 030 about 12 miles (19.2 k)–just before Shoup.
Turn Right (N) on FR 038 and go about 8 miles (12.8 k). Turn Left (W) on FR 044 and meander 12 miles (19.2 k). Turn Left (SW) on FR 065 and go 2 miles (3.2 k).
**FREE** but choose a chore.
Open May 15–Oct 15.
6 close, open sites.
Water, pit toilets, tables, fire rings.
Relax in this remote creek setting.
No trash pickup. 14-day/22-ft limits.
6000 ft (1800 m)

## HUCKLEBERRY

BLM (208) 769-5000
State map: D2
From CALDER, head S on bridge across river. Turn Left (E) on CR 350 (St Joe River Rd) and go 4 miles (6.4 k).
**$4**. Open Apr 1–Nov 15; dry camping off-season.
23 close, open sites. Water, pit toilets, tables, fire rings, dump station.
On grassy flat beneath cottonwood in river canyon.
Hike, boat, or fish.
14-day limit. Crowded summer.
2240 ft (672 m)

## ICE SPRINGS

Boise NF (208) 334-1516
State map: K3
From MOUNTAIN HOME, go
24 miles (38.4 k) NE on US 20.
Turn Left (N) on FR 134 and
go 5 miles (8 k). Turn Right (NE) on
FR 113 and go 5 miles (8 k). Continue N
on FR 123 for 5 miles (8 k). (See
Anderson Ranch and Deer Creek.)
**FREE** but choose a chore.
Open Jun 1–Sep 30.
7 sites. Pit toilets, tables, fire rings.
On Fall Creek near Anderson Ranch
Reservoir.
Fish, hike, or relax.
NO water/trash arrangements.
5000 ft (1500 m)

## INDIAN CREEK

Bitterroot NF (406) 821-3269
State map: G4
From DARBY, MT, go 4 miles
(6.4 k) S on US 93. Turn Right
(SW) on scenic CR 473 and
drive 14.5 miles (23.2 k). Turn Right (W)
on FR 468 and go 36.5 miles (58.4 k) to
FR 6223. Turn Right (N) and continue
5 miles (8 k). (Also see Deep Creek,
Raven Creek, Paradise, or Poet
Creek–reached from ELK CITY.)
**FREE** but choose a chore.
Open Jun 15–Sep 15; camping allowed
off-season.
8 close, open sites. Pit toilets, tables.
Hike into Selway Bitterroot Wilderness
or fish this remote creek.
10-day/16-ft limits.
3600 ft (1080 m)

## IRON BOG

Challis NF (208) 588-2224
State map: J5
From MACKAY, head SE on
US 93 for 12 miles (19.2 k).
Turn Right (SW) on Antelope
Creek Rd. Go 25 miles (40 k)–road
becomes FR 137.
**$4.** Open Jun 30–Sep 15.
20 sites. Water, pit toilets, tables, grills,
fire rings.
On Antelope Creek.

Hike on Iron Bog Lakes Trail. Fish.
No trash facilities. 14-day/24-ft limits.
6500 ft (1950 m)

## IRON LAKE

Salmon NF (208) 756-3724
State map: H4
From SALMON, head S on
US 93 for 5 miles (8 k). Turn
Right (W) on FR 021 (Williams
Creek). Drive about 14 miles (22.4 k) to
Williams Summit. Turn Left (S) on
rough, scenic FR 020. Go 20 miles (32 k).
**$3.** Open Jun 15–Sep 15.
6 close, open sites.
Water, pit toilets, tables, fire rings.
At beautiful spot in woods by lake.
Boat (no motors), fish, even swim if you
dare. Hike and enjoy scenery.
No trash arrangements. 14-day limit.
8800 ft (2640 m)

## JOHNSON BAR

Nez Perce NF (208) 926-4258
State map: F3
At LOWELL, cross bridge
heading SE on Selway River
Rd. Drive about 4 miles (6.4 k).
(See CCC, O'Hara, and Rackliff.)
**FREE** but choose a chore.
Open All Year.
Undesignated, open sites with some
screening. Water, pit toilets, tables, grills,
fire rings, beach.
On large river flat.
Float, canoe, swim, and fish.
14-day limit. Crowded summer
weekends. Hunting in season.
1430 ft (429 m)

## KENNALLY CREEK

Payette NF (208) 634-4100
State map: H2
From MCCALL, head S on
US 95 for 10 miles (16 k). Turn
Left (E) on FR 338 (Paddy Flat)
and drive 19 miles (30.4 k). Nearby less-
developed choices are **Paddy Flat** and
**Rapid Creek.**
**FREE** but choose a chore.
Open Jun 1–Sep 30.
11 (2 tent-only) close, open sites.

▲ ▲ ▲ ▲ ▲ ▲ ▲ ▲ ▲ ▲ ▲ ▲ ▲ ▲ ▲ ▲ ▲ ▲ ▲ ▲ ▲ ▲ ▲ ▲

Pit toilets, tables, grills, fire rings, horse facilities.
Hike easy (and pretty) Kennally Creek Trail. Fish too.
NO water/trash facilities. 14-day limit.

## KILLARNEY LAKE

BLM (208) 769-5000
State map: D1
From ROSE LAKE, head SW on ID 3 for 5 miles (8 k). Turn on gravel Killarney Lake Rd and go 4 miles (6.4 k).
FREE but choose a chore.
Open All Year.
12 close, open sites. Water, pit toilets, tables, fire rings, boat ramp.
On gravel in forest river valley next to 480-acre lake. Swim, canoe, and fish.
14-day limit. Hunting in season.
2160 ft (468 m)

## KIRKHAM

Boise NF (208) 334-1516
State map: J3
From LOWMAN, go E on ID 21 for 5 miles (8 k). Fee-charged **Helende** (10 sites) is another 4 miles (6.4 k).
FREE but choose a chore.
Open May 10–Sep 20.
16 sites. Pit toilets, tables, fire rings.
On South Fork of Payette.
Whitewater raft. Soak in hot springs.
NO water.
4000 ft (1200 m)

## LAFFERTY

Payette NF (208) 634-4100
State map: H1
From COUNCIL, head NW on CR/FR 002 for 20 miles (32 k)–bear Right at Hornet Guard Station. For alternative, continue 10 miles (16 k) past Bear Guard Station to **Huckleberry** (10 sites).
$3. Open May 15–Oct 15.
12 sites.
Water, pit toilets, tables, fire rings.
Explore secluded area on Crooked River.
14-day limit.
4300 ft (1290 m)

## LAKE FORK

Payette NF (208) 634-4100
State map: H2
From MCCALL, go E on Lick Creek Rd for 8 miles (12.8 k).
$3. Open May 15–Sep 15.
9 sites.
Water, pit toilets, tables, grills, fire rings.
On creek at beginning of scenic drive.
Hike and explore.
No trash arrangements. 14-day limit.
5600 ft (1680 m)

## LITTLE BOULDER CREEK

BLM (208) 756-5401
State map: J4
From CLAYTON, head E on ID 75 about 5 miles (8 k). Turn Right (S) on East Fork Rd and drive 20 miles (32 k).
FREE but choose a chore.
Open All Year.
3 close, open sites.
Pit toilets, tables, fire rings.
Adjacent to Sawtooth NRA.
Excellent hiking.
NO water/trash arrangements.

## LITTLE CAMAS

Boise NF (208) 334-1516
State map: K3
From MOUNTAIN HOME, go 26 miles (41.6 k) NE on US 20. Turn Left (N) on FR 160 and go 2.5 miles (4 k). (See Anderson Ranch.)
FREE but choose a chore.
Open Jun 1–Sep 30.
16 sites. &
Pit toilets, tables, fire rings, boat launch.
On reservoir.
Boat, fish, waterski, or swim.
NO water.
5000 ft (1500 m)

## LITTLE ROARING RIVER

Boise NF (208) 334-1516
State map: K3
From MOUNTAIN HOME, go 24 miles (38.4 k) NE on US 20. Turn Left (N) on FR 134 and go 5 miles (8 k). Turn Right (NE) on FR 113 and go 5 miles (8 k). Continue N

▲ ▲ ▲ ▲ ▲ ▲ ▲ ▲ ▲ ▲ ▲ ▲ ▲ ▲ ▲ ▲ ▲ ▲ ▲ ▲ ▲ ▲ ▲ ▲ ▲

on FR 123 for 19 miles (30.4 k). Within 1 mile (1.6 k) find **Little Trinity** (3 sites) or fee-charged **Big Roaring River** (10 sites) and **Big Trinity** (15 sites).
**FREE** but choose a chore.
Open Jul 1–Sep 15.
4 sites. Pit toilets, tables, fire rings.
On one of four alpine lakes in vicinity. Fish and canoe. Hike from Trinity Mountain to six more, private lakes.
NO water/trash arrangements.
7900 ft (2370 m)

## LITTLE SMOKY

Sawtooth NF (208) 737-3200
State map: K4
From FAIRFIELD, head N on FR 093/094 toward Soldier Mountain and Couch Summit–about 11 miles (17.6 k). Bear Right on FR 094 and go 9 miles (14.4 k)–just beyond Five Points area.
**FREE** but choose a chore.
Open Jun 1–Sep 30.
2 close, open sites.
Pit toilets, tables, fire rings.
On creek.
Enjoy seclusion. Picnic, walk, relax.
NO water. 14-day limit.
5600 ft (1680 m)

## LITTLE WOOD RESERVOIR

BOR (208) 678-0461
State map: K5
From CAREY, take CR NW for 11 miles (17.6 k).
**FREE** but choose a chore.
Open May 15–Sep 30.
25 close, open sites. &
Water, flush toilets, tables, grills, boat ramp.
On lakeshore in high-mountain setting. Swim, boat, or fish. Picnic and relax.
14-day limit. Hunting in season.
5000 ft (1500 m)

## LOLO

Clearwater NF (208) 476-4541
State map: F2
Just S of PIERCE off ID 11, continue straight (S) on FR 100 for 18 miles (28.8 k).

**FREE** but choose a chore.
Open May 15–Nov 15.
5 close, open sites.
Pit toilets, tables, fire rings.
On creek by Lewis & Clark Trail.
Walk historic path. Fish and relax.
NO water/trash arrangements (pack it out). 14-day limit.
2600 ft (780 m)

## LUD DREXLER PARK

BLM (208) 678-5514
State map: M4
From ROGERSON, go 8 miles (12.8 k) W on Jarbidge CR.
**$4.** Open All Year.
20 (14 with ramadas) scattered, open sites. Free RV camping for about 60 units near high water mark. &
Water, pit toilets, dump station, tables, grills, fire rings, boat ramp.
On Salmon Falls Creek Reservoir.
Fish for 9 different game fish. Waterski, swim, and boat. Hike and birdwatch.
14-day limit. Crowded holidays. Generator rules.
5000 ft (1500 m)

## MACKAY BAR

Nez Perce NF (208) 842-2255
State map: G3
From ELK CITY, go 3 miles (4.8 k) S on ID 14. Go SE on CR 222 for 14 miles (22.4 k) reaching Red River Ranger Station. Continue S on CR 222 for 44 miles (70.4 k)–check with Ranger before driving. Difficult access road may require 4WD (no trailers).
**FREE** but choose a chore.
Open Jun 15–Oct 31; dry camping off-season.
3 scattered, open sites.
Water (needs treating), pit toilets, tables, grills, boat launch.
On Salmon River in remote setting.
Swimming, canoeing or kayaking, and fishing plus hiking into wilderness.
No trash arrangements. 14-day limit.
2300 ft (690 m)

▲ ▲ ▲ ▲ ▲ ▲ ▲ ▲ ▲ ▲ ▲ ▲ ▲ ▲ ▲ ▲ ▲ ▲ ▲ ▲ ▲ ▲ ▲ ▲ ▲

## MACKAY RESERVOIR

BLM (208) 756-5401
State map: J5
From MACKAY, head NW on
US 93 for 5 miles (8 k).
$5. Open All Year.
59 close, open sites.
Water, pit toilets, tables, grills, fire rings,
dump station, boat ramp.
On lake with Lost River Range views.
Boat, waterski, swim, or fish.
14-day limit.
5700 ft (1710 m)

## MAGIC MOUNTAIN AREA

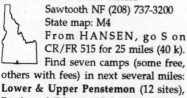

Sawtooth NF (208) 737-3200
State map: M4
From HANSEN, go S on
CR/FR 515 for 25 miles (40 k).
Find seven camps (some free,
others with fees) in next several miles:
**Lower & Upper Penstemon** (12 sites),
**Pettit** and **Diamondfield Jack** (8 sites
each) then on FR 500: **Porcupine Spring,
Fathers & Sons**, and **Bostetter** (40 sites).
FREE but choose a chore.
Open Jun 1–Oct 15.
68 close, open sites.
Water, pit toilets, tables, fire rings.
Among springs in ski area.
Hike, fish, or take photos. Ski winters.
14-day limit.
7000 ft (2100 m)

## MAGIC RESERVOIR

BLM (208) 886-2206
State map: K4
From SHOSHONE, head N on
ID 75 for 18 miles (28.8 k).
Turn Left (NW) on CR and go
9 miles (14.4 k).
FREE but choose a chore.
Open All Year.
Several informal camping areas.
Pit toilets, tables, fire rings, boat ramp.
On lake and Wood River.
Windsurf, waterski, swim, or fish.
NO water/trash arrangements (clean it
up and pack it out). Water fluctuates
drastically. Be careful with fires.
4800 ft (1440 m)

## MAMMOTH SPRINGS

Idaho Panhandle NF
(208) 245-4517
State map: D3
From AVERY, head E on
CR 50 (St Joe River) for
22 miles (35.2 k). Turn Right (SW) on
FR 509 (Bluff Creek) for 14 miles (22.4 k).
Bear Right on FR 201 (Avery Timber
Creek) for 2.5 miles (4 k).
FREE but choose a chore.
Open Jun 1–Oct 15.
6 close, open sites.
Water, pit toilets, tables, fire rings.
In woods only 1 mile (1.6 k) down 201
from Dismal Lake.
Relax, observe wildlife, and fish.
14-day limit. Water on Jul–Oct.
5700 ft (1710 m)

## MANN CREEK

BOR (208) 344-1461
State map: I1
About 13 miles (20.8 k) N of
WEISER, take US 95 about
10 miles (16 k). Watch for Left
turn on reservoir access road.
FREE but choose a chore.
Open May 25–Oct 10.
7 close, screened tent sites. Water, pit
toilets, tables, fire rings, boat ramp.
Boat, waterski, swim or fish reservoir.
14-day limit.
2500 ft (750 m)

## MCFARLAND

BLM (208) 756-5401
State map: H5
From LEADORE, go N on
ID 28 for 13 miles (20.8 k).
FREE but choose a chore.
Open All Year.
10 close, open sites.
Water, pit toilets, tables, grills, fire rings.
On Lemhi River with views of Bitterroot
Mountains.
Fish, watch birds, and take photos.
No trash facilities. 14-day limit.

▲ ▲ ▲ ▲ ▲ ▲ ▲ ▲ ▲ ▲ ▲ ▲ ▲ ▲ ▲ ▲ ▲ ▲ ▲ ▲ ▲ ▲

## MEADOW CREEK

Idaho Panhandle NF
(208) 267-5561
State map: A2
N of BONNERS FERRY at
intersection of US 95 and US 2,
head E on US 2 for 2 miles (3.2 k). Turn
Left (N) on FR 229 (Meadow Creek) and
go 11 miles (17.6 k). (See Smith Lake.)
**FREE** but choose a chore.
Open May 15–Oct 15.
22 close, open sites.
Water, pit toilets, tables, fire rings.
In woods on Moyie River.
Besides floating, fishing, and hiking, pick
huckleberries in season.
14-day limit.
2400 ft (720 m)

## MEADOW CREEK

Nez Perce NF (208) 983-1950
State map: G2
From GRANGEVILLE, go
17 miles (27.2 k) E on ID 14–
heavy logging traffic. (Also see
Castle Creek and South Fork.)
**FREE** but choose a chore.
Open All Year; camping allowed
off-season.
2 close, screened sites.
Pit toilets, tables, fire rings.
Next to South Fork of Clearwater near
Cougar and Johns Creek trailheads.
Swim and fish. Hike and birdwatch.
NO water. 14-day limit.
2300 ft (690 m)

## MEADOW LAKE

Salmon NF (208) 768-2371
State map: I5
From LEADORE, head SE on
ID 28 about 16 miles (25.6 k).
Turn Right (W) on CR/FR 002
and go 6 miles (9.6 k).
**$4**. Open Jun 15–Sep 15.
7 sites.
Water, pit toilets, tables, fire rings.
Next to beautiful, mountain lake.
Swim, boat, fish, or hike. Enjoy views of
Portland Mountain and Sheephorn Peak.
14-day/24-ft limits.
9200 ft (2760 m)

## MIDDLE FORK PEAK

Salmon NF (208) 756-3221
State map: H4
From SALMON, head S on
US 93 for 5 miles (8 k). Turn
Right (W) on FR 021 (Williams
Creek). Go about 16 miles (25.6 k). Turn
Left on FR 055. Go 10 miles (16 k)–about
5 miles past ranger station. Turn Right
on FR 112. Go about 24 miles (38.4 k).
**FREE** but choose a chore.
Open Jul 1–Oct 15.
3 close, open sites.
Pit toilets, tables, fire rings.
In remote area with wilderness access.
Hike and explore. Savor solitude.
NO water/trash arrangements (pack it
out). 14-day limit.
9100 ft (2730 m)

## MOKINS BAY

Idaho Panhandle NF
(208) 765-7381
State map: C1
From COEUR D'ALENE, go N
on US 95 for 6 miles (9.6 k).
Turn Right (E) on Lancaster Rd for
.5 mile (800 m). Turn on southern loop
road and drive around Hayden Lake for
11 miles (17.6 k) to "Public Camp" sign.
**FREE** but choose a chore.
Open May 1–Oct 1.
16 close, open sites.
Water, pit toilets, tables, fire rings.
On lakeshore with beach.
Enjoy swimming, boating, waterskiing.
14-day limit.
2300 ft (690 m)

## MONTOUR WILDLIFE RA

BOR (208) 344-1461
State map: J2
From EMMETT, head N then
E, on US 52 for 15 miles (24 k).
**FREE** but choose a chore.
Open May 30–Oct 13.
17 close, open sites. &
Water, flush toilets, tables, grills, fire
rings.
Among rolling hills and valleys.
Enjoy fantastic birdwatching and wildlife
observation. Relax and explore.

▲ ▲ ▲ ▲ ▲ ▲ ▲ ▲ ▲ ▲ ▲ ▲ ▲ ▲ ▲ ▲ ▲ ▲ ▲ ▲ ▲ ▲ ▲ ▲

14-day limit.
3000 ft (900 m)

## MORGAN CREEK RS

BLM (208) 756-5401
State map: I4
From CHALLIS, head N on
US 93 about 7 miles
(11.2 k)–informal **Spring
Gulch** is another 3 miles (4.8 k). Turn
Left (NW) on Morgan Creek Rd and
drive 4 miles (6.4 k). Another 5 miles
(8 k) bearing Left on FR 057 is **Little
West Fork** (2 sites).
FREE but choose a chore.
Open All Year.
5 close, open sites.
Pit toilets, tables, grills, fire rings.
On creek near Salmon NF.
Fish, hike, or relax. Hunt for agates,
geodes, and, perhaps, opals.
NO water/trash arrangements.
6200 ft (1860 m)

## MORSE CREEK

Challis NF (208) 879-4321
State map: I5
From MAY, head E on
CR/FR 094 for 6.5 miles
(10.4 k).
FREE but choose a chore.
Open Jun 15–Sep 15.
2 close, open sites.
Pit toilets, tables, fire rings.
Hike East Fork or Morse Creek trails.
Enjoy seclusion of creekside site.
NO water. 14-day/16-ft limits. Hunting
in season.
6500 ft (1950 m)

## MURDOCK

Sawtooth NF (208) 737-3200
State map: J4
From KETCHUM, head N on
ID 75 for 7 miles (11.2 k). Turn
Right (N) on FR 146 and go
1 mile (1.6 k). **Caribou** and **Cougar** (each
with 10 sites) are 2 more miles (3.2 k).
FREE but choose a chore.
Open Jun 1–Oct 15.
10 sites. Pit toilets, tables, fire rings.
At confluence of North Fork of Big

Wood River and Murdock Creek.
Fish. Explore Sawtooth NRA.
NO water. 14-day/22-ft limits.
5900 ft (1770 m)

## NEWSOME

Nez Perce NF (208) 842-2245
State map: F3
From ELK CITY, head W on
ID 14 about 11 miles (17.6 k).
Turn Right (N) on FR 1858. Go
5 miles (8 k) pass **Sing Lee** (5 sites), **Bear
Creek** (4 sites), and **Ox Bow** (2 sites).
FREE but choose a chore.
Open Jun 15–Sep 30.
6 sites. Pit toilets, tables, fire rings.
On creek near historic Newsome
townsite. Explore old mining remains.
Fish. Hike trails from Sing Lèe.
NO water/trash arrangements. Hunting
in season.
3200 ft (960 m)

## NORTH FORK SLATE CREEK

Nez Perce NF (208) 839-2211
State map: G2
About 10 miles (16 k) S of
WHITE BIRD on US 95, look
for gravel Slate Creek Rd
(FR 233) heading E. Turn and go about
10 miles (16 k). (Also see Rocky Bluff.)
FREE but choose a chore.
Open All Year.
5 close, open sites.
Chemical toilets, tables, fire rings.
In cool, woods along scenic Slate Creek.
Get away to picnic, hike, and fish.
NO water/trash arrangements (pack it
out). 14-day limit.
2800 ft (840 m)

## O'HARA

Nez Perce NF (208) 926-4258
State map: F3
At LOWELL, cross bridge
heading SE on Selway River
Rd. Drive about 7 miles
(11.2 k). (Also see CCC, Johnson Bar, and
Rackliff.)
$4. Open May 24–Oct 1.
33 close, screened sites.
Water, pit toilets, tables, grills, fire rings.

▲ ▲ ▲ ▲ ▲ ▲ ▲ ▲ ▲ ▲ ▲ ▲    ▲ ▲ ▲ ▲ ▲ ▲ ▲ ▲ ▲ ▲ ▲ ▲

Along river with secluded spots.
Take hikes on national recreation trails.
Float, swim, canoe, and fish.
14-day limit. Crowded holiday
weekends. Hunting in season.
1400 ft (420 m)

## PALISADES

Targhee NF (208) 523-1412
State map: K8
From PALISADES DAM, go N
on FR 80255 for 2 miles (3.2 k).
$4. Open May 25–Sep 15.
7 close, open sites.
Water, pit toilets, tables, grills.
At trailhead with outstanding scenery.
Hike and ride horseback to upper lake
then south to Waterfall Canyon. Fish.
16-day/22-ft limits.

## PAPOOSE CREEK

Nez Perce NF (208) 839-2211
State map: G2
From RIGGINS, go just S of
town and take Squaw Creek
Rd (#517) about 5 miles (8 k)
until you just enter NF.
**FREE** but choose a chore.
Open All Year.
Undesignated, scattered sites.
Chemical toilets, 1 table, fire rings.
In shady creekside location.
Pack a picnic.
NO water/trash arrangements. 14-day
limit. Crowded hunting season.
4000 ft (1200 m)

## PARADISE

Payette NF (208) 634-4100
State map: I1
From WEISER, head N on
US 95 for 13 miles (20.8 k).
Turn Left (NW) on CR/FR 009
(Upper Mann Creek Rd) and drive
14 miles (22.4 k)–always bear Right.
Also check out **Justrite** (4 sites) or
2 miles (3.2 k) farther, fee-charged **Lower
Springs Creek** (12 sites).
**FREE** but choose a chore.
Open Jun 1–Sep 30.
4 close, open tent sites.
Pit toilets, tables, fire rings.

Fish, hike, or picnic along creek.
NO water/trash arrangements (pack it
out). 14-day limit.
4200 ft (1260 m)

## PARADISE

Bitterroot NF (406) 821-3269
State map: G4
From DARBY, MT, go 4 miles
(6.4 k) S on US 93. Turn Right
(SW) on scenic CR 473 and
drive 14.5 miles (23.2 k). Turn Right (W)
on FR 468 and go 36.5 miles (58.4 k) to
FR 6223. Turn Right (N) and continue
11.5 miles (18.4 k). (See Deep Creek,
Indian Creek, and Raven Creek.)
**FREE** but choose a chore.
Open Jun 1–Sep 15; camping allowed
off-season.
11 (7 tent-only) close, open sites.
Pit toilets, tables.
In remote, scenic area near wild Selway
River near Selway Bitterroot Wilderness.
Hike trails, float river, or fish.
10-day/16-ft limits.
3200 ft (960 m)

## PEN BASIN

Boise NF (208) 334-1516
State map: I3
From WARM LAKE, go E on
FR 579, passing **Summit Lake**
(3 sites), for 7.5 miles (12.8 k)
to Landmark Work Center. Continue on
FR 579 for 2.5 miles (4 k) to Pen Basin.
Or, alternatively, turn Left (N) on FR 413
and go 2 miles (3.2 k) to **Buck Mountain**
(4 sites).
**FREE** but choose a chore.
Open Jun 1–Oct 15.
6 sites. Pit toilets, tables, fire rings.
On secluded Johnson Meadows Creek.
Walk Rock Creek Trail. Fish. Explore.
NO water/trash arrangements.
6700 ft (2010 m)

## PENNY SPRINGS

Boise NF (208) 334-1516
State map: I2
From WARM LAKE (all 5
camps next to lake charge
fees), go W on FR 579 for

3 miles (4.8 k). Turn Right (N) on FR 474 and go 5 miles (8 k).
**FREE** but choose a chore.
Open May 15–Oct 15.
4 sites. Pit toilets, tables, fire rings.
On South Fork of Salmon near Nickel and Dime creeks, across river from Two-Bit, Six-Bit, and Dollar creeks.
Boat, fish, or hike. Seek small fortune.
NO water/trash arrangements.
5200 ft (1560 m)

## PINE BAR RS

BLM (208) 962-3245
State map: F2
From COTTONWOOD, head S on Graves Creek Rd for 11 miles (17.6 k) turning Left when road parallels river.
**FREE** but choose a chore.
Open All Year.
6 close, screened sites.
Water, pit toilets, tables, grills.
On Salmon River at Pine Bar Rapids.
Swim, boat, fish, hike, or relax.
14-day/16-ft limits. Rattlesnakes.
1360 ft (408 m)

## PINE CREEK

Targhee NF (208) 354-2312
State map: J8
From VICTOR, go 5.3 miles (8.5 k) W on ID 31.
**$5.** Open Jun 1–Sep 30.
11 close, open sites.
Water, pit toilets, tables, grills.
Hike, fish, or relax along stream.
No trash arrangements. 16-day limit.
6600 ft (1980 m)

## PINEBAR

Caribou NF (208) 547-4356
State map: L8
From FREEDOM, WY, go W on ID 34 (FH 40) for 10.5 miles (16.8 k). (See Tincup.)
**FREE** but choose a chore.
Open May 15–Sep 15.
5 close, open sites.
Water, pit toilets, tables, grills.
Along wooded creek near Tincup Hwy.
Fish or picnic.

No trash arrangements. 14-day limit.
6000 ft (1800 m)

## PIONEER

Sawtooth NF (208) 737-3200
State map: K4
From FAIRFIELD, head N on FR 093/094 toward Soldier Mountain about 11 miles (17.6 k).
**FREE** but choose a chore.
Open Jun 1–Sep 30.
5 close, open sites.
Water, pit toilets, tables, fire rings.
On Soldier Creek next to Soldier Mountain Ski Area.
Picnic, strut, and relax.
14-day limit.
6500 ft (1950 m)

## PIPELINE

BLM (208) 678-5514
State map: L6
From AMERICAN FALLS, take ROCKLAND Exit off I-86 and go 2 miles (3.2 k) W.
**FREE** but choose a chore.
Open Mar–Oct.
5 (2 tent-only) close, open sites.
Pit toilets, tables, fire rings, boat ramp.
On Snake River.
Enjoy excellent birdwatching in spring and fall. Catch trophy-size trout.
NO water/trash arrangements (pack it out). 14-day limit. Crowded holidays.
4750 ft (1425 m)

## POET CREEK

Nez Perce NF (208) 842-2255
State map: G3
From ELK CITY, go 3 miles (4.8 k) S on ID 14. Go SE on CR 222 for 14 miles (22.4 k) reaching Red River Ranger Station. Head E up FR 468 (Magruder Carricker Rd) for 26 miles (41.6 k).
**FREE** but choose a chore.
Open Jul 15–Oct 15; dry camping off-season.
4 close, open sites. Water (needs treating), pit toilets, grills, stock facilities.
Make base for wilderness exploration.

▲ ▲ ▲ ▲ ▲ ▲ ▲ ▲ ▲ ▲ ▲ ▲ ▲ ▲ ▲ ▲ ▲ ▲ ▲ ▲ ▲ ▲ ▲ ▲ ▲ ▲ ▲

Hike and ride horses.
No trash arrangements. 14-day/16-ft
limits. Crowded hunting season.
5100 ft (1530 m)

## POISON CREEK

BOR (208) 382-4258
State map: I2
From CASCADE, head S on
Lakeshore Dr. Turn Right on
West Side Rd and drive about
15 miles (24 k). (Also see Curlew.)
**$2**; reservations accepted.
Open May – Sep; camping allowed
off-season.
20 close, open sites.
Water, flush and pit toilets, tables, grills,
fire rings, boat ramp, beach, pavilion.
On western shore near north end of
Cascade Reservoir.
Boat, waterski, swim, and fish. Hike
nearby trails.
14-day limit. No ATVs. Subject to
monsoon-like winds (4-ft waves).
5000 ft (1500 m)

## POLE BRIDGE

Targhee NF (208) 652-7442
State map: I8
From ASHTON, go E on ID 47
(Mesa Falls Scenic Byway)
about 17 miles (27.2 k) –
becomes FR 294. Turn Right (E) on
FR 150 and go 7 miles (11.2 k). (Also see
Grandview.)
**FREE** but choose a chore.
Open Jun 1 – Oct 31.
10 close, open sites. Water, pit toilets.
Fish, relax, or picnic along stream.
No trash facilities. 14-day/22-ft limits.
6300 ft (1890 m)

## PONDEROSA

Payette NF (208) 634-4100
State map: H2
From MCCALL, head E on
scenic FH 48 (Lick Creek Rd)
for 31 miles (49.6 k).
**$3**. Open May 25 – Sep 15.
14 (7 tent-only) sites.
Water, pit toilets, tables, fire rings.
On Lick Creek.

Enjoy great hiking on several trails. No
trash arrangements. 14-day limit.
4000 ft (1200 m)

## PORCUPINE LAKE

Idaho Panhandle NF
(208) 263-5111
State map: B2
From CLARK FORK, take
CR 419 (Lightning Creek) N for
9 miles (14.4 k). Turn Left (W) on FR 632
(Porcupine Creek). Drive 6 miles (9.6 k).
**FREE** but choose a chore.
Open May 15 – Oct 15.
5 close, open sites.
Pit toilets, tables, fire rings.
On wooded lakeshore.
Enjoy remote fishing and getaway spot.
NO water. 14-day limit.
4800 ft (1440 m)

## POWER PLANT

Boise NF (208) 334-1516
State map: J3
From historic ghost town
ATLANTA, go 1 mile (1.6 k) E
on FR 268. For alternate choice,
find **Riverside** (7 sites) just N of town.
**FREE** but choose a chore.
Open May 1 – Nov 1.
24 sites. Pit toilets, tables, fire rings.
Near Middle Fork of Boise at southern
boundary of Sawtooth Wilderness.
Explore old mining remains. Trek into
pristine region.
NO water/trash arrangements.
5800 ft (1740 m)

## PRAIRIE CREEK

Sawtooth NF (208) 737-3200
State map: J4
From KETCHUM, go 18 miles
(28.8 k) NW on ID 75.
**FREE** but choose a chore.
Open Jun 1 – Oct 15.
10 sites. Water, flush and pit toilets,
tables, fire rings.
Fish on creek. Hike from end of FR 179
to Prairie or Miner lakes. Ski in winter.
16-day limit.
6850 ft (2055 m)

▲ ▲ ▲ ▲ ▲ ▲ ▲ ▲ ▲ ▲ ▲ ▲ ▲ ▲ ▲ ▲ ▲ ▲ ▲ ▲ ▲ ▲ ▲ ▲

## PRIEST LAKE SP-Dickensheet

(208) 443-2200
State map: A1
From PRIEST RIVER, take
ID 57 N for 22.5 miles (36 k).
Turn Right (E) at major
intersection (see park sign) and travel
1 mile (1.6 k) E toward COOLIN.
$5, $2/extra vehicle.
Open Apr 15–Oct 31; camping allowed
off-season.
11 close, open sites.
Pit toilets, trash cans, tables, and grills.
In forest next to Priest River.
Fish or raft. Birdwatch. Take photos.
NO water. 10-day/25-ft limits. Crowded
weekends.
2400 ft (720 m)

## RACE CREEK

Nez Perce NF (208) 983-1950
State map: F3
From LOWELL, head SE on
FR 223 to end – 21 miles
(33.6 k). Within 1 mile (1.6 k)
find **Racetrack** (13 sites), **Slims** (3 sites),
and fee-charged **Selway Falls** (7 sites).
FREE but choose a chore.
Open Jun 15–Sep 15.
3 sites. Pit toilets, tables, fire rings.
On creek at major access point to Selway
Bitterroot Wilderness.
Take a trek. View beautiful area.
NO water.

## RACKLIFF

Nez Perce NF (208) 926-4258
State map: F3
At LOWELL, cross bridge
heading SE on Selway River
Rd. Drive about 8 miles
(12.8 k)–last 1 mile is gravel. Many other
possibilities if you continue SE. (See
O'Hara and Twenty Mile Bar.)
**$4**. Open May 24–Oct 1; camping
allowed off-season.
6 close, screened sites.
Water, pit toilets, tables, grills, fire rings.
On quiet Rackliff Creek (2 sites on west
or 4 sites on east).
Enjoy hiking and wildlife observation.
Float, canoe, swim, or fish too.

14-day/25-ft limits. Crowded holiday
weekends. Hunting in season.
1450 ft (435 m)

## RAVEN CREEK

Bitterroot NF (406) 821-3269
State map: G4
From DARBY, MT, go 4 miles
(6.4 k) S on US 93. Turn Right
(SW) on beautiful CR 473 and
drive 14.5 miles (23.2 k). Turn Right (W)
on FR 468 and go 36.5 miles (58.4 k) to
FR 6223. Turn Right (N) and continue
5 miles (8 k). (Also see Deep Creek,
Indian Creek, Paradise, or Poet
Creek–reached from ELK CITY.)
FREE but choose a chore.
Open Jun 1–Sep 15; camping off-season.
2 close, open tent sites. Pit toilets, tables.
In remote forest on creek.
Drive scenic FR 468 SW from Magruder
Crossing toward Magruder Saddle. Hike
to 19th-century massacre site. Fish.
10-day/16-ft limits.
3800 ft (1140 m)

## RED RIVER

Nez Perce NF (208) 842-2255
State map: G3
From ELK CITY, go 3 miles
(4.8 k) S on ID 14. Go SE on
CR 222 for 14 miles (22.4 k)
reaching Red River Ranger Station. Head
NE on FR 234 for 7 miles (11.2 k). (Also
see Bridge Creek and Ditch Creek.)
**$5**; reservations accepted.
Open Jun 1 – Oct 31; dry camping
off-season.
44 close, open sites.
Water, pit toilets, tables, grills.
Enjoy nature and hiking trails plus river
for fishing and relaxing.
14-day/24-ft limits. No horses. Noisy.
Hunting in season.
4600 ft (1380 m)

## RIVERFRONT CITY PARK

Kamiah City Parks
(208) 935-2672
State map: F2
In KAMIAH, at intersection of
US 12 and Mill Rd.

▲ ▲ ▲ ▲ ▲ ▲ ▲ ▲ ▲ ▲ ▲ ▲ ▲ ▲ ▲ ▲ ▲ ▲ ▲ ▲ ▲ ▲ ▲ ▲ ▲

**FREE** or $5 for electricity.
Open All Year.
6 sites.
Water, flush and pit toilets, tables,
electric hookups, boat ramp, beach.
In shade with beautiful view of
Clearwater River.
Take nature trail to explore area. Swim,
boat, waterski, and fish.
2-day limit.
1250 ft (375 m)

## ROCKY BLUFF

Nez Perce NF (208) 839-2211
State map: G2
About 10 miles (16 k) S of
WHITE BIRD on US 95, look
for gravel Slate Creek Rd
(FR 233) heading E. Turn and go about
14 miles (22.4 k). Turn on FR 641 and go
1 mile (1.6 k). Sites are 10-30 yards from
parking. (See North Fork Slate Creek.)
**FREE** but choose a chore.
Open May – Nov; camping allowed
off-season.
4 (2 tent-only) close, open sites.
Chemical toilets, tables, fire rings.
In scenic spot next to Gospel Hump
Wilderness.
Explore lots of trails (horse and foot).
Fish plus cross-country ski when snow.
NO water/trash arrangements (pack it
out). 14-day/16-ft limits.
5000 ft (1500 m)

## ROCKY RIDGE LAKE

Clearwater NF (208) 476-4541
State map: E3
Just S of PIERCE off ID 11,
take FR 250 E-NE for 5 miles
(8 k). When 250 forks Left,
continue straight on FR 555 about
16 miles (25.6 k). Turn Left on FR 500.
Go about 4 miles (6.4 k).
**FREE** but choose a chore.
Open May 15 – Nov 15.
3 close, open sites.
Pit toilets, tables, fire rings.
In remote, quiet spot.
Hike, including trail up Weitas Butte.
NO water/trash arrangements (pack it
out). 14-day limit.

## SAM'S CREEK

Nez Perce NF (208) 842-2255
State map: G3
From ELK CITY, go 3 miles
(4.8 k) S on ID 14. Go SE on
CR 222 for 14 miles (22.4 k)
reaching Red River Ranger Station.
Continue S on CR 222I for 19 miles
(30.4 k). (Also see Halfway House.)
**FREE** but choose a chore.
Open Jun 15 – Oct 31; dry camping
off-season.
3 close, open sites. Water (needs
treating), pit toilets, tables, grills.
With fishing access near town of Dixie.
Enjoy trail into Gospel Hump
Wilderness and berries in season.
No trash arrangements (pack it out).
14-day/16-ft limits. No stock.
5200 ft (1560 m)

## SAWMILL

Sawtooth NF (208) 737-3200
State map: K4
From HAILEY, head S on ID
75 for 6 miles (9.6 k). Turn Left
(E) on FR 118 (toward
Triumph). Go 11 miles (17.6 k). **Federal
Gulch** (3 sites) is another .5 mile (800 m).
**FREE** but choose a chore.
Open May 15 – Oct 15.
3 sites. Pit toilets, tables, fire rings.
On East Fork of Wood River.
Fish. Take trails from Federal Gulch.
NO water. 14-day limit.
6700 ft (2010 m)

## SCHIPPER

Sawtooth NF (208) 737-3200
State map: M4
From HANSEN, go S on
CR/FR 515 for 15 miles (24 k).
**Steer Basin** is another 3 miles
(4.8 k). (Also see Magic Mountain.)
**FREE** but choose a chore.
Open May 15 – Oct 15.
7 close, open sites.
Water, pit toilets, tables, fire rings.
Fish, walk, explore along Rock Creek.
14-day limit.
4600 ft (1380 m)

▲ ▲ ▲ ▲ ▲ ▲ ▲ ▲ ▲ ▲ ▲ ▲ ▲ ▲ ▲ ▲ ▲ ▲ ▲ ▲ ▲

## SHEEP SPRING

BLM (208) 769-5000
State map: D2
From COEUR D'ALENE, take
I-90 E to CATALDO Exit. Go S
on gravel Latour Creek/
Rochat Divide Rd for 21 miles (33.6 k).
FREE but choose a chore.
Open Jun 15–Oct 15; dry camping
off-season.
2 scattered, open sites. Water, pit toilets,
tables, fire rings.
At timber line.
Walk 2-mile (3.2-k) trail to alpine lake.
14-day limit. Hunting in season.
5520 ft (1656 m)

## SHIEFER

Payette NF (208) 634-4100
State map: H3
Go 77 miles (123.2 k) NE of
MCCALL on CR 21/FR 340
(Warren Wagon Rd over
Warren Summit)–unsuitable for trailers.
FREE but choose a chore.
Open Jun 1–Sep 30.
4 close, open sites.
Pit toilets, tables, grills, fire rings.
Near River of No Return Wilderness.
Create base for day hikes.
NO water/trash arrangements. 14-day
limit. No firewood.
6100 ft (1830 m)

## SHOUP BRIDGE RS

BLM (208) 756-5401
State map: H5
From SALMON, head S on
US 93 for 5 miles (8 k).
FREE. Open All Year.
6 sites.
Pit toilets, tables, fire rings, boat ramp.
Launch a boat and fish Salmon River.
NO water.
4000 ft (1200 m)

## SILVER CREEK
BLM (208) 886-2206
State map: K4
From RICHFIELD, go NE on
US 93 for 13 miles (20.8 k).
Turn Left at Silver Creek sign.

FREE but choose a chore.
Open Mar–Nov; camping allowed
off-season.
2 (1 "North," 1 "South") sites.
Pit toilets, tables, grills, fire rings.
Fish and picnic along creek.
NO water. 14-day limit.
4700 ft (1410 m)

## SILVER CREEK

Boise NF (208) 334-1516
State map: I2
From CROUCH, head N on
FR 698 about 15 miles (24 k).
Bear Right (NE) on FR 671 and
go 8 miles (12.8 k). Pass fee-based **Silver
Plunge**. (Also see Tie Creek.)
FREE but choose a chore.
Open Jun 1–Oct 15.
4 sites. Pit toilets, tables, fire rings.
On creek near guard station.
Hike trail along Peace Creek. Discover
hot springs. Relax and, maybe, fish.
NO water/trash arrangements.
4600 ft (1380 m)

## SLATE CREEK RS

BLM (208) 962-3245
State map: G2
From WHITE BIRD, head S on
US 95 for 9 miles (14.4 k).
$4. Open All Year.
5 close, open sites. Water, pit toilets,
tables, grills, pay phone, boat launch.
Boat, fish, and explore Salmon River.
14-day/21-ft limits. Rattlesnakes.
1500 ft (450 m)

## SLAUGHTER GULCH

Payette NF (208) 634-4100
State map: H2
From NEW MEADOWS, head
SW on US 95 for 8 miles
(12.8 k). Continue W toward
Lost Valley Reservoir on FR 50257 for
5 miles (8 k). Alternative is fee-charged
**Cold Springs**.
FREE but choose a chore.
Open Jun 1–Sep 30.
18 close, open sites.
Pit toilets, tables, fire rings.
On north shore of lake.

▲ ▲ ▲ ▲ ▲ ▲ ▲ ▲ ▲ ▲ ▲ ▲ ▲ ▲ ▲ ▲ ▲ ▲ ▲ ▲ ▲ ▲ ▲ ▲ ▲ ▲

Boat and fish. Pick berries when ripe.
NO water/trash arrangements (pack it
out). 14-day limit.
4800 ft (1440 m)

## SMITH LAKE

Idaho Panhandle NF
(208) 267-5561
State map: A2
From BONNERS FERRY, head
N on US 95 for 5 miles (8 k).
Turn Right (NE) on dirt FR 1005 and go
2 miles (3.2 k). (See Meadow Creek.)
FREE but choose a chore.
Open May 15–Oct 15.
7 close, open sites. ♿
Water, pit toilets, tables, fire rings, boat
ramp.
On wooded lakeshore.
Boat and fish. Picnic and relax.
14-day limit.
3000 ft (900 m)

## SMOKEY'S CUBS RS

BLM (208) 756-5401
State map: I5
From LEADORE, head N on
ID 29 (Railroad Canyon Rd)
toward Bannock Pass about
4 miles (6.4 k).
FREE but choose a chore.
Open All Year.
8 close, open sites.
Pit toilets, tables, fire rings, boat ramp.
Fish in Canyon Creek or nearby Lemhi
River. Hike and explore.
NO water/trash arrangements (pack it
out). Crowded in fall.
5000 ft (1500 m)

## SOUTH FORK

Nez Perce NF (208) 983-1963
State map: G2
From GRANGEVILLE, go
15 miles (24 k) E on
ID 14–heavy logging traffic.
See Castle Creek and Meadow Creek.)
$5; fee may increase.
Open All Year; dry camping off-season.
8 close, screened sites. ♿
Water, pit toilets, dump station, tables,
fire rings.

In partly timbered area with large grassy
meadow adjacent to South Fork of
Clearwater.
Swim and fish. Birdwatch and relax.
14-day limit. Crowded weekends.
2300 ft (690 m)

## SOUTH FORK CAMAS

Challis NF (208) 879-2285
State map: I4
About .5 mile (800 m) W of
US 93 in CHALLIS, take CR N
for 3.5 miles (5.6 k). Bear Left
(NW) on same road (becomes FR 083)
and drive about 33 miles (52.8 k) passing
Mahoney Creek (2 sites). At end of road
in another 4 miles (6.4 k) is Sleeping
Deer (4 sites).
FREE but choose a chore.
Open Jul–Sep.
3 sites. Pit toilets, tables, fire rings.
Explore beautiful, remote area on trail.
Fish in river.
NO water/trash facilities. No trailers.
9200 ft (2760 m)

## SPRING BAR

Nez Perce NF (208) 839-2211
State map: G2
From RIGGINS, go just S of
town then turn Left (E) on
FR 1614 and drive 10.5 miles
(16.8 k). (Also see Van Creek.)
$4. Open All Year.
15 close, open sites.
Water, chemical toilets, tables, grills, fire
rings, boat ramp, beach.
Within walking distance of Salmon River
for delightful rafting, kayaking, and
swimming.
14-day/16-ft limits.
1800 ft (540 m)

## SPRUCE TREE-LINE CREEK

Idaho Panhandle NF
(208) 245-4517
State map: D3
From AVERY, head E on
CR 50 (St Joe River) for
33 miles (52.8 k). Continue straight on
FR 218 (Red Ives Work Center) about
11 miles (17.6 k)–2 miles (3.2 k) beyond

▲ ▲ ▲ ▲ ▲ ▲ ▲ ▲ ▲ ▲ ▲ ▲ ▲ ▲ ▲ ▲ ▲ ▲ ▲ ▲ ▲ ▲ ▲ ▲ ▲ ▲ ▲ ▲ ▲

Work Center. (Also see Fly Flat.)
**FREE** but choose a chore.
Open Jun 1–Oct 15.
5 close, open sites.
Water, pit toilets, tables, fire rings.
At beginning of wild portion of St Joe
Wild and Scenic River.
Fish. Walk St Joe River Trail.
14-day limit. Water on Jul–Oct.
3800 ft (1140 m)

## SQUAW CREEK

Idaho Panhandle NF
(208) 245-4517
State map: D2
From AVERY, head N on
FR 456 (Moon Pass) for 5 miles
(8 k). Turn on Old Moon Pass. Fee-
charged alternatives include **Turner** and
**Tin Can Flat** on main river.
**FREE** but choose a chore.
Open May 15–Oct 15.
7 sites. Pit toilets, tables, fire rings.
Along wooded creek on North Fork of St
Joe River. Access Nelson Peak Recreation
Trail. Fish too.
NO water/trash arrangements (pack it
out). 14-day limit. No trailers.
2600 ft (780 m)

## STAGGER INN

Idaho Panhandle NF
(208) 443-2512
State map: A1
From NORDMAN, head N on
FR 302 for 12 miles (19.2 k).
**FREE** but choose a chore.
Open May 15–Sep 15.
4 sites. Pit toilets, tables, fire rings.
In woods near Granite Falls and
Roosevelt Grove of Ancient Cedars.
Explore both upper and lower grove of
cedars. View falls (best in spring).
NO water/trash arrangements.
3200 ft (960 m)

## STARHOPE

Challis NF (208) 588-2224
State map: J5
From MACKAY, head SE on
US 93 for 12 miles (19.2 k).
Turn Right (SW) on Antelope

Creek Rd. Go about 20 miles (32 k) to
Antelope Guard Station. Turn Right
(NW) on FR 135. Go 15 miles (24 k) to
Copper Basin Guard Station. Turn Left
(SW) on FR 138. Go 8 miles (12.8 k).
**$4.** Open Jun 30–Sep 15.
21 sites.
Water, pit toilets, tables, grills, fire rings.
In Pioneer Mountains among spruce and
pine trees.
Hike Bear Canyon Trail. Explore.
No trash arrangements (pack it out).
14-day/32-ft limits.
8000 ft (2400 m)

## STODDARD CREEK

Targhee NF (208) 374-5422
State map: I7
From SPENCER, head N on
I-15 for 3.5 miles (5.6 k). Turn
Left (NW) on FR 003 and go
1.25 miles (2 k).
**$5.** Open May 25–Sep 15.
16 sites. Water, pit toilets, tables, grills,
fire rings.
Fish in creek. Hike loop trail to Van Noy
Canyon. Relax.
16-day/22-ft limits.
6200 ft (1860 m)

## SUBLETT

Sawtooth NF (208) 737-3200
State map: M6
From MALTA, head E on
Sublett Rd for 20 miles (32 k).
Around 18 mile mark, **Lake
Fork** (3 sites) is just to Left on FR 564.
**FREE** but choose a chore.
Open Jun 1–Oct 31.
7 sites. Pit toilets, tables, fire rings.
On creek near reservoir. Boat, waterski,
and fish at lake. Picnic and relax.
NO water.
5600 ft (1680 m)

## SUMMIT CREEK RS

BLM (208) 756-5401
State map: J6
From HOWE, head NW on CR
(Pahsimeroi) 41 miles (65.6 k).
**FREE** but choose a chore.
Open All Year.

9 close, open sites.
Pit toilets, tables, fire rings, boat ramp.
Along creek in Pahsimeroi Valley with
Barney Hot Springs across road.
Relax and soak.
NO water/trash arrangements.

## SWINGING BRIDGE

Boise NF (208) 334-1516
State map: J2
From BANKS, go N on ID 55
for 7.25 miles (11.6 k).
Alternatives within 3 miles
(4.8 k) N are **Canyon** (7 sites), **Cold
Springs** (5 sites), and **Big Eddy** (3 sites).
$3. Open May 10–Sep 30.
11 (8 tent-only) sites.
Water, pit toilets, tables, fire rings.
On North Fork Payette River.
Fish, hike, or relax.
14-day/22-ft limits.
3700 ft (1110 m)

## TABLE MEADOWS

Nez Perce NF (208) 842-2245
State map: F3
From ELK CITY, head NW on
CR 199 for 8 miles (12.8 k).
Turn Right (N) on FR 471 and
go 2 miles (3.2 k). Turn Right (NE) on
FR 464 and go 3 miles (3.2 k). Turn Right
(S) on FR 283 and go 1.5 miles (2.4 k).
**FREE** but choose a chore.
Open Jun 1–Sep 15.
6 sites. Pit toilets, fire rings.
Beneath Ericson Ridge on West Fork of
American River.
Hike several trails. Enjoy seclusion.
NO water/trash arrangements. Hunting
in season.
5000 ft (1500 m)

## TABLE ROCK

Targhee NF (208) 523-1412
State map: J8
From HEISE, go E for 5 miles
(8 k) on FR 218.
$5. Open May 25–Sep 15.
9 close, open sites.
Water, pit toilets, tables, grills.
At Hawley trailhead.
Hiking and horseback riding here.

No trash arrangements (pack it out).
16-day/22-ft limits.
5800 ft (1740 m)

## TEN MILE

Boise NF (208) 334-1516
State map: J3
From IDAHO CITY, go NE on
scenic ID 21 for 9.75 miles
(15.6 k). **Bad Bear** (8 sites) and
**Hayfork** (6 sites) within next 2 miles
(3.2 k).
$3. Open Jun 1–Oct 15.
14 (4 tent-only) sites.
Water, pit toilets, tables, fire rings.
At confluence of Mores Creek and
Tenmile Creek.
Fish. Hike to Mores Creek Summit.
14-day/22-ft limits.
5000 ft (1500 m)

## THOMPSON FLAT

Sawtooth NF (208) 737-3200
State map: M5
From ALBION, head SE on
ID 77 for 5.5 miles (8.8 k). Turn
Right (W) on FR 549 and go
8 miles (12.8 k). In 1 more mile (1.6 k),
find **Brackenbury** (9 sites) and **Lake
Cleveland** (8 sites).
$3. Open Jun 15–Oct 10.
16 sites.
Water, pit toilets, tables, fire rings.
In quiet location.
Hike and picnic. Fishing nearby.
14-day/22-ft limits.
8000 ft (2400 m)

## THORN CREEK RESERVOIR

BLM (208) 886-2206
State map: K4
From GOODING, head N on
ID 46 for 17 miles (27.2 k).
Turn Right (E) on access road
and go 4 miles (6.4 k).
**FREE** but choose a chore.
Open Mar–Nov.
Undesignated, scattered, open sites.
Pit toilets, tables, grills, fire rings.
On small reservoir.
Good fishing in non-drought years.
NO water/trash arrangements. 14-day

▲ ▲ ▲ ▲ ▲ ▲ ▲ ▲ ▲ ▲ ▲ ▲ ▲ ▲ ▲ ▲ ▲ ▲ ▲ ▲ ▲ ▲ ▲ ▲ ▲ ▲

limit. Water level fluctuates.
5500 ft (1650 m)

## TIE CREEK

Boise NF (208) 334-1516
State map: I2
From CROUCH, head N on
FR 698 about 9 miles (14.4 k).
Within 4 miles (6.4 k) N, find
**Hardscrabble** (6 sites), **Rattlesnake**
(10 sites), and **Trail Creek** (11 sites). (See
Boiling Springs and Silver Creek.)
**FREE** but choose a chore.
Open May 15–Oct 15.
6 sites. Pit toilets, tables, fire rings.
On Middle Fork of Payette River.
Hike and fish. Relax.
No trash arrangements (pack it out).
3200 ft (960 m)

## TIN CUP

Challis NF (208) 879-5204
State map: I4
From SUNBEAM (13 miles E of
STANLEY), go N on FR 013 for
8 miles (12.8 k). Continue N on
narrow (trailers not advised) FR 172 for
17 miles (27.2 k). Stay Right on FR 007
along Loon Creek for 4 miles (6.4 k).
**FREE** but choose a chore.
Open Jun 15–Sep 30.
17 sites. Pit toilets, tables, fire rings.
On Loon Creek at trailhead in historic
remote mining district.
Hike to explore mining ruins.
NO water. 14 day limit.
5600 ft (1680 m)

## TINCUP

Caribou NF (208) 547-4356
State map: L8
From FREEDOM, WY, go W
on ID 34 (FH 40) for 3.5 miles
(5.6 k). (Also see Pinebar.)
**FREE** but choose a chore.
Open May 15–Sep 15.
5 close, open sites.
Water, pit toilets, tables, grills.
In woods by creek along Tincup Hwy.
Fish or picnic.
No trash arrangements. 14-day limit.
6000 ft (1800 m)

## TIPTON FLAT

Boise NF (208) 334-1516
State map: J3
From BOISE, take ID 21 E
about 15 miles (24 k). Turn
Right (NE) on FR 268 along
shore of Arrowrock Reservoir and drive
about 23 miles (36.8 k)–just past **Willow
Creek**. Turn Right (SE) on FR 113 and go
8 miles (12.8 k). Bear Left on FR 217 and
continue 4 miles (6.4 k).
**FREE** but choose a chore.
Open Jun 15–Sep 15.
7 sites. Pit toilets, tables, fire rings.
At confluence of remote Tipton and
Rattlesnake creeks.
Hike to Rattlesnake Mountain. Fish.
NO water/trash arrangements.
4900 ft (1470 m)

## TOWER ROCK

BLM (208) 756-5401
State map: G5
From SALMON, head N on
US 93 for 11 miles (17.6 k).
**FREE** but choose a chore.
Open All Year.
6 close, open sites.
Pit toilets, tables, grills.
Fish and boat on Salmon River at Lewis
& Clark expedition campsite.
NO water/trash arrangements.
4000 ft (1200 m)

## TWENTY MILE BAR

Nez Perce NF (208) 983-1950
State map: F3
From LOWELL, head SE on
FR 223 for 10 miles (16 k).
Within 5 more miles (8 k), find
**Slide Creek** (6 sites), **Boyd Creek**
(7 sites), and **Twentyfive Mile Bar**
(9 sites). (See Rackliff and Race Creek.)
**FREE** but choose a chore.
Open Jun 15–Sep 15.
3 sites. Pit toilets, tables, fire rings.
On Selway River.
Fish. Explore beautiful area.
NO water.

▲ ▲ ▲ ▲ ▲ ▲ ▲ ▲ ▲ ▲ ▲ ▲ ▲ ▲ ▲ ▲ ▲ ▲ ▲ ▲ ▲ ▲

## TWIN SPRINGS

Caribou NF (208) 766-4743
State map: M6
From HOLBROOK, go NW on
ID 37 for 8.5 miles (13.6 k). For
lake camp, check out fee-
charged **Curlew** S of HOLBROOK.
FREE but choose a chore.
Open May 15–Sep 15.
5 close, open sites.
Water, pit toilets, tables, grills.
In pastoral spot of Curlew National
Grassland near Hudspeth Cutoff Trail.
Walk, picnic, and relax.
14-day limit.
4700 ft (1410 m)

## VAN CREEK

Nez Perce NF (208) 839-2211
State map: G2
From RIGGINS, go just S of
town then turn Left (E) on
FR 1614 and drive 11 miles
(17.6 k). (Also see Spring Bar.)
FREE but choose a chore.
Open All Year.
2 close, open sites.
Chemical toilets, tables, fire rings.
Along Salmon River.
Rafting, kayaking, and swimming. Gold
prospecting too.
NO water/trash arrangements (pack it
out). 14-day/16-ft limits.
1800 ft (540 m)

## WALLACE LAKE

Salmon NF (208) 756-3724
State map: H5
From SALMON, head N on
US 93 for 3 miles (4.8 k). Turn
Left (W) on FR 023 and drive
about 11 miles (17.6 k). Turn Left (S) on
FR 020 and go 5 miles (8 k).
$3. Open Jun 15–Sep 15.
12 close, open sites.
Water, pit toilets, tables, fire rings.
In woods by lake.
Hike. Boat (no motors), fish, or swim if
you dare. Enjoy remote, beautiful spot.
No trash arrangements. 14-day limit.
8800 ft (2640 m)

## WARM RIVER

Targhee NF (208) 652-7442
State map: I8
From ASHTON, go E on ID 47
(Mesa Falls Scenic Byway)
about 9 miles (14.4 k). (Also
see Grandview.)
$4; for additional $6, reservations
accepted at (800) 283-2267.
Open May 1–Oct 31.
23 close, open sites. Water, flush and pit
toilets, tables, grills, fire rings.
Explore scenic western edge of
Yellowstone ecosystem. Float, swim, or
fish river.
14-day/22-ft limits.
5200 ft (1560 m)

## WEBBER

Targhee NF (208) 374-5422
State map: I6
From DUBOIS, head NW on
CR A3 for 25 miles (40 k). Turn
W on FR 196 about 4 miles
(6.4 k).
FREE but choose a chore.
Open May 25–Sep 15; camping allowed
off-season.
5 close, open sites.
Pit toilets, tables, grills, fire rings.
Fish and relax along stream. Hike
Webber Creek/Divide Creek Trail.
16-day/16-ft limits.
7000 ft (2100 m)

## WEITAS

Clearwater NF (208) 476-4541
State map: E3
Just S of PIERCE off ID 11,
take FR 250 E-NE for 35 miles
(56 k). In another 5 miles (8 k),
find fee-charged **Noe Creek** (6 sites).
FREE but choose a chore.
Open May 15–Nov 15.
6 close, open sites.
Pit toilets, tables, fire rings.
At confluence of Weitas Creek and
North Fork of Clearwater.
Hike Trail 20 S to historic log structures.
View wildlife and fish.
NO water/trash facilities. 14-day limit.
2600 ft (780 m)

▲ ▲ ▲ ▲ ▲ ▲ ▲ ▲ ▲ ▲ ▲ ▲ ▲ ▲ ▲ ▲ ▲ ▲ ▲ ▲ ▲ ▲ ▲ ▲ ▲ ▲ ▲ ▲ ▲ ▲ ▲ ▲ ▲

## WEST END

Targhee NF (208) 558-7301
State map: I8
From ASHTON, go N on
US 20 for 18 miles (28.8 k).
Turn Right (NW) on FR 167
and drive 15 miles (24 k).
FREE but choose a chore.
Open May 25–Sep 15.
19 close, open sites. Water, pit toilets,
tables, grills, boat ramp.
On shores of Island Park Reservoir.
Swim, waterski, boat, and fish.
16-day/22-ft limits.
6200 ft (1860 m)

## WHISKEY ROCK BAY

Idaho Panhandle NF
(208) 263-5111
State map: C2
From CLARK FORK, head SW
across bridge. Turn Right on
FR 278 and drive 30 miles (48 k).
FREE but choose a chore.
Open Jun 1–Nov 15.
9 close, open sites. Pit toilets, tables, fire
rings, beach, dock.
On eastern shore of Lake Pend Oreille.
Swim, boat, waterski. Walk nature trail.
NO water. 14-day limit.
2000 ft (600 m)

## WHITEWATER

Boise NF (208) 334-1516
State map: J3
From LOWMAN, go W on
CR 17 for 3 miles (4.8 k).
Alternative, fee-charged Pine
Flats (27 sites) is another 2 miles (3.2 k).
Two other fee-charged options are
Mountain View (14 sites) E of
LOWMAN and Park Creek (26 sites)
3 miles (4.8 k) N on FR 582.
FREE but choose a chore.
Open May 15–Sep 30.
5 sites. Pit toilets, tables, fire rings.
At confluence of Deadwood and South
Fork of Payette rivers.
Whitewater rafting, hiking, or relaxing.
NO water/trash arrangements.
3700 ft (1110 m)

## WILDHORSE LAKE

Nez Perce NF (208) 842-2255
State map: G3
About 10 miles (16 k) W of
ELK CITY on ID 14, take
unpaved CR 233I SW for
25 tough miles (40 k).
FREE but choose a chore.
Open Jul 1–Sep 30; dry camping
off-season.
6 close, screened sites. Water (needs
treating), pit toilets, tables, grills.
On high, remote lakeshore.
Access Gospel Hump Wilderness for
hiking and exploring. Swimming (for
brave), fishing, canoeing or rowing.
No trash arrangements. 14-day/16-ft
limits. Crowded. Hunting in season.
7500 ft (2250 m)

## WILLIAMS LAKE

BLM (208) 756-5401
State map: H5
From SALMON, head S on
US 93 for 5 miles (8 k). Turn
Right (W) on signed road
(becomes FR 028).
FREE but choose a chore.
Open All Year.
11 close, screened sites.
Pit toilets, tables, fire rings.
In pine trees near north side of lake.
Swim, boat, or fish. Watch birds. Walk
Thunder Mountain Historic Trail. Take
photographs.
NO water/trash arrangements (come
prepared and pack out trash).
5500 ft (1650 m)

## WILLOW CREEK

Boise NF (208) 334-1516
State map: J3
From BOISE, take ID 21 E
about 16 miles (25.6 k). Turn
Right (NE) on FR 268 along
shore of Arrowrock Reservoir and drive
about 23 miles (36.8 k). Series of four
camps–in 3 miles find Badger Creek
(5 sites), 6 more miles (9.6 k) Troutdale
(4 sites), and another 4 miles (6.4 k)
Ninemeyer (8 sites). (Also see
Cottonwood and Tipton Flat.)

**FREE** but choose a chore.
Open May 15–Sep 30.
10 sites.
Water, pit toilets, tables, fire rings.
On banks of Middle Fork of Boise.
Hike, explore, or fish.
No trash arrangements (pack it out).
3200 ft (960 m)

## WILLOW CREEK

Boise NF (208) 334-1516
State map: J3
From **LOWMAN**, go S on
scenic ID 21 for 11 miles
(17.6 k) to alternative, fee-
charged **Edna Creek** (9 sites). Turn Left
(E) on FR 384 and go 5 miles (8 k).
**FREE** but choose a chore.
Open Jun 1–Oct 15.
4 sites. Pit toilets, tables, fire rings.
Enjoy remote creek. Explore.
NO water/trash arrangements.
5400 ft (1620 m)

## WOLFTONE CAMP

Sawtooth NF (208) 737-3200
State map: K4
From HAILEY, go N on ID 75
for 2 miles (3.2 k). Turn Left
(W) on CR/FR 097 (Deer
Creek) and go 8.5 miles (13.6 k). **Bridge**
(3 sites) is 1 more mile (1.6 k).
**FREE** but choose a chore.
Open May 15–Oct 15.
3 sites. Pit toilets, tables, fire rings.
At confluence of Wolftone and Deer
creeks. Fish. Hike trails in side canyons.
NO water. 14-day limit.
5500 ft (1650 m)

## YELLOW PINE

Boise NF (208) 334-1516
State map: H3
From YELLOW PINE, go S on
FR 413 for 1 mile (1.6 k). For
alternative, continue S 1 mile
(1.6 k) to **Golden Gate** (9 sites) or
3 miles (4.8 k) to **Ice Hole** (10 sites).
**FREE** but choose a chore.
Open Jun 1–Oct 15.
14 sites.
Water, pit toilets, tables, fire rings.
On Johnson Creek.
Walk up Golden Gate Hill. Fish and
swim at Ice Hole.
14-day/22-ft limits.
4800 ft (1440 m)

## YELLOWJACKET LAKE

Salmon NF (208) 756-3221
State map: H4
From SALMON, head S on
US 93 for 5 miles (8 k). Turn
Right (W) on FR 021 (Williams
Creek) and drive about 16 miles (25.6 k)
passing **Cougar Point** (12 sites). Turn
Left on FR 055, pass **Deep Creek**
(3 sites), and go 10 miles (16 k)–about
2 miles (3.2 k) past **McDonald Flat**. Turn
Right on FR 112 and go 6 miles (9.6 k).
Bear Right on rough FR 113 and go
15 miles (24 k). For better wilderness
access, try fee-charged **Crags** (turn off
FR 113 onto FR 114) with incredible
trails into Bighorn Crags.
**FREE** but choose a chore.
Open Jun 15–Oct 15.
6 close, open sites.
Water, pit toilets, tables, fire rings.
In woods by lake at edge of wilderness.
Boat (no motors), fish, even swim if you
dare. Walk and enjoy remote spot.
No trash arrangements. 14-day limit.
8200 ft (2460 m)

# Montana

Grid conforms to official state map. For your copy, call (800) 541-1447
or write Travel Montana, 1424 9th Avenue, Helena, MT 59620.

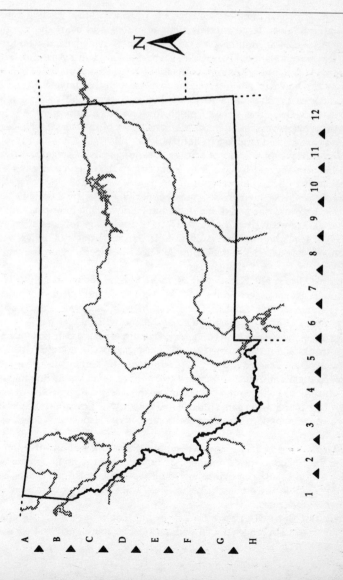

▲ ▲ ▲ ▲ ▲ ▲ ▲ ▲ ▲ ▲ ▲ ▲ ▲ ▲ ▲ ▲ ▲ ▲ ▲ ▲ ▲ ▲ ▲ ▲ ▲ ▲

Montana, the "Big Sky" state, sports hundreds of camping choices. The eastern 60 percent consists of Great Plains broken by large manmade reservoirs. The west dramatically changes into rugged, snowtopped mountains. The range of inexpensive campgrounds is as diverse as the state's topography.

In the plains, find your camp near water—either river or reservoir. The **US Army Corps of Engineers** (COE) possesses the perfect example with its Fort Peck Reservoir. The **Bureau of Land Management** (BLM) also contributes with sites in the central and southern portions of the state. The **Bureau of Reclamation** (BOR) adds multiple possibilities at three major projects: Clark Canyon, Fresno Reservoir, and Lake Elwell.

When most people think of Montana, the picture includes rushing streams, remote alpine lakes, large animals such as moose and bear, and gorgeous wildflower meadows. Find this type of scenery in the national and state forests.

The **Beaverhead National Forest** (NF) shares the spectacular Anaconda-Pintler Wilderness. In fact, over 70 percent of the forest is roadless. Appreciate mountain beauty by car, however, when taking the loop through the Gravelly Range.

In addition to a portion of the Anaconda-Pintler, **Bitterroot NF** claims two other excellent wilderness areas—Frank Church River of No Return and the Selway-Bitterroot. While several sites are in Montana, most of the camps for accessing these areas are located (and listed) in Idaho.

While not heavy on wilderness acreage, **Deerlodge NF** boasts huge mountain ranges like Sapphire and Tobacco Root. View glaciers, lakes, and panoramic vistas plus fascinating Elkhorn ghost town.

Parts of the **Custer NF** include a grasshopper-filled glacier; Granite Peak (the state's highest); and one end of the Beartooth Highway, the most beautiful road in America according to Charles Kuralt. Indeed, this forest's segmented jurisdiction spreads from the South Dakota border almost 500 miles west to Yellowstone National Park. Discover the Absaroka-Beartooth region and you'll be impressed.

Bordering Glacier NP, **Flathead NF** offers a couple of choices: beautiful 34-mile long Hungry Horse Reservoir or some of the country's most fantastic wilderness areas. The premier Bob Marshall, Great Bear, Mission Mountains, and Scapegoat provide close to one million acres of seclusion and wildlife viewing.

Lying along the Yellowstone NP border, **Gallatin NF** has a petrified forest with upright trunks and a lake created by a 1959 earthquake. In addition, there's the pristine Spanish Peaks Wilderness where dense fir and spruce give way to subalpine vegetation. You can also view two very different mountain ranges—one gentle, the other awe-inspiring—both compose the Absaroka-Beartooth Wilderness.

Lots of trails and roads gain entrance into **Helena NF**. Best known for its Gates of the Mountain, opportunities for seclusion include Scapegoat Wilderness and Figure 8 Loop.

Bordering Canada and Idaho, **Kootenai NF** has one scenic attraction after another. Find hoodoo rock formations at Tobacco River's mouth, alpine flower gardens in Ten Lakes Scenic Area, incredible waterfalls, giant red cedars, crystal clear lakes in Northwest Peak Scenic Area, and, certainly not least, Cabinet Mountains Wilderness.

**Lewis and Clark NF** is two forests in one. The Jefferson division has six accessible mountain ranges dotted with abandoned mines, gentle streams, even

▲ ▲ ▲ ▲ ▲ ▲ ▲ ▲ ▲ ▲ ▲ ▲ ▲ ▲ ▲ ▲ ▲ ▲ ▲ ▲ ▲ ▲ ▲ ▲ ▲ ▲ ▲

an ice cave. The Rocky Mountain division claims half the spectacular Bob Marshall and Scapegoat wilderness areas.

**Lolo NF** is known for beautiful mountains, elk on grassy slopes, 2000 miles of trails, and winter skiing. In addition to the popular Rattlesnake Wilderness, explore the Welcome Creek alternative.

The **National Park Service** (NPS) makes two additions to the book–Bighorn National Recreation Area (NRA) and Glacier NP. Both rate spectacular and offer incredible backcountry experiences.

The state of Montana offers free camping in three **State Forests** (SFs) plus the complex of facilities administered by **Fish, Wildlife & Parks** (FWP). Although the state parks prove too expensive with a $5 camping fee plus a $3 daily use fee, the agency does provide several hundred, mostly free, Fishing Access Sites (FAS) plus recreation areas and monuments. Choice sites have been selected.

Many of Montana's smaller communities provide free city-county parks. Several are listed. If you find yourself in need of an overnight spot, be sure to ask about additional possibilities.

Wander wide-open, wild, and wonderful Montana.

▲ ▲ ▲ ▲ ▲ ▲ ▲ ▲ ▲ ▲ ▲ ▲ ▲ ▲ ▲ ▲ ▲ ▲ ▲ ▲ ▲ ▲ ▲ ▲ ▲ ▲ ▲

## ABBOT

Gallatin NF
(406) 587-6701
State map: G5

From BOZEMAN, head S on CR 243 for 8 miles (12.8 k). Turn Left (SE) on FR 64 and go 5 miles (8 k). (Also see Blackmore and Palace Butte.)
**FREE** but choose a chore.
Open Jun 15–Sep 15.
3 close, open sites.
Pit toilets, tables, fire rings.
On creek in Hyalite Canyon.
Explore along forest roads and trails.
NO water or trash arrangements (pack it out). 14-day limit.
6400 ft (1920 m)

## ALTA

Bitterroot NF
(406) 821-3269
State map: F2

From DARBY, go 4 miles (6.4 k) S on US 93. Turn Right (SW) on CR 473 and drive 21.5 miles (34.4 k). Turn S on CR 96 and go 6 more miles (9.6 k). (Also see Slate Creek.)
**FREE** but choose a chore.
Open Jun 25–Sep 6.
15 close, open sites.
Water, pit toilets, tables.
Near West Fork of Bitterroot River, home

of historic Hughes Creek placer gold mining.
Hiking (trail passes through camp), plus fishing and panning for gold dust.
10-day/22-ft limits.
5000 ft (1500 m)

## ASPEN

Gallatin NF
(406) 932-5155
State map: G6

From BIG TIMBER, head S on US 298 for 33.5 miles (53.6 k)–last 8.5 miles (13.6 k) are gravel. (Also see Big Beaver, Chippy Park, Falls Creek, Hell's Canyon, and Hick's Park.)
**FREE** but choose a chore.
Open All Year.
8 scattered, screened sites. &
Water, pit toilets, tables, grills.
Adjacent to Boulder River for fishing.
No trash arrangements (pack it out).
Camp only in designated sites.
15-day/32-ft limits. Crowded weekends.
Often inaccessible in winter.
5300 ft (1590 m)

## BAD MEDICINE

Kootenai NF
(406) 882-4451
State map: B1

From TROY, head SE on US 2 about

▲ ▲ ▲ ▲ ▲ ▲ ▲ ▲ ▲ ▲ ▲ ▲ ▲ ▲ ▲ ▲ ▲ ▲ ▲ ▲ ▲ ▲

3 miles (4.8 k) to MT 56. Turn Right (S) and go 18.7 miles (30 k). Turn Right (W) on FR 398 (Ross Creek Cedars) and after 1 mile (1.6 k) Right again for another mile on FR 8019. (Also see Dorr Skeels.)

$5. Open May 20–Sep 30; dry camping off-season.

16 close, open sites. Water, pit toilets, tables, fire rings, boat ramp.

With beach on scenic Bull Lake.

Ski and swim, if you like cool water, or fish and boat. Picnic at Ross Creek Scenic Area. Walk mile-long Giant Cedars Nature Trail. View rock spires.

14-day limit. Crowded weekends.

2300 ft (690 m)

## BALANCED ROCK

Beaverhead NF
(406) 842-5432
State map: G4

From SHERIDAN, follow dirt road E with "Mill Creek Recreation Area" sign. Go 10 miles (16 k) on narrow, very rough road. (Also see Branham Lakes and Mill Creek.)

FREE but choose a chore.

Open May 15–Nov 1; camping allowed off-season.

2 close, open tent sites.

Pit toilets, tables, fire rings.

In stand of lodgepole pine between road and Mill Creek.

Relax and picnic or try a bit of fishing and birdwatching.

NO water/trash arrangements (pack it out). 14-day limit.

7320 ft (2196 m)

## BARRETTS PARK

BOR (406) 657-6202
State map: G3

Go 9 miles (14.4 k) S of DILLON off I-15. (Also see Clark Canyon Reservoir.)

FREE but choose a chore.

Open All Year.

Undesignated, scattered sites. &

Water, pit toilets, tables, grills, fire rings. On Red Rock River with boating and fishing possibilities. Relaxing too.

14-day limit. Generator rules.

5520 ft (1656 m)

## BARRON CREEK

Kootenai NF
(406) 293-7773
State map: B1

From LIBBY, head E on MT 37 for 14 miles (22.4 k). Turn Left (N) on FR 228 and go about 13 miles (20.8 k).

FREE but choose a chore.

Open Apr 1–Dec 31; camping allowed off-season.

15 close, open sites. &

Pit toilets, tables, fire rings, boat launch (small boats).

On western shore of 50-mile-long Lake Koocanusa.

Canoe, kayak, swim, or fish.

NO water/trash arrangements (pack it out). 14-day/24-ft limits.

4000 ft (1200 m)

## BASIN

Custer NF (406) 446-2103
State map: G7

From RED LODGE, go 7 miles (11.2 k) W on paved FR 71. (Also see Cascade.)

$5. Open May 25–Sep 15; dry camping off-season.

30 scattered, open sites. Water, pit toilets, tables, fire rings, paved road and spurs.

In flat, sandy area with mature lodgepole pine next to West Fork of Rock Creek.

Walk up Rock Creek National Recreation Trail a few miles to Absaroka Wilderness. Fish or do nothing.

10-day limit. Crowded weekends.

6900 ft (2070 m)

## BASIN CANYON

Deerlodge NF
(406) 287-3223
State map: E4

From BASIN, head N on dirt FR 172 for 4.5 miles (7.2 k).

FREE but choose a chore.

Open May 22–Sep 15.

2 sites. Pit toilets, tables, fire rings.

On quiet creek with fishing, hiking, and

relaxing opportunities.
NO water. 14-day/16-ft limits.
5800 ft (1740 m)

## BATTLE RIDGE
Gallatin NF
(406) 587-6701
State map: F5
From BOZEMAN, head N on MT 86/293
(becomes FR 74) for 21 miles (33.6 k).
(Also see Fairy Lake.)
FREE but choose a chore.
Open Jun 10–Sep 30.
13 close, open sites.
Water, pit toilets, tables, fire rings.
At Battle Ridge Pass.
Hike, take photos, or relax.
No trash pickup. 14-day/16-ft limits.
6400 ft (1920 m)

## BEAN LAKE FAS
MT FWP (406) 454-3441
State map: D4
From AUGUSTA, head S
on MT 434 for 10 miles (16 k).
FREE but choose a chore.
Open All Year.
25 scattered, open sites.
Pit toilets, tables, fire rings, boat ramp.
On high plains reservoir with beautiful
views of Rocky Mountains.
Swim, boat, or fish lake. Hike into
nearby forest. Observe wildlife.
NO water. Water drawn in summer.

## BEAR CREEK
COE (406) 526-3411
State map: C10
From FORT PECK, take
oiled road S for 15 miles (24 k)–check at
office before driving. (See Flat Lake,
Nelson Creek, and Rock Creek SRA.)
FREE but choose a chore.
Open All Year.
6 close, open sites.
Pit toilets, tables, grills.
On Fort Peck Reservoir.
Fishing, fishing, fishing.
NO water/trash arrangements (pack it
out). 14-day limit. Hunting in season.
2250 ft (675 m)

## BEAR CREEK
Gallatin NF
(406) 848-7375
State map: G6
From GARDINER, take gravel Jardine
Rd past JARDINE for 3 miles (4.8 k).
(See Eagle Creek and Timber Camp.)
FREE but choose a chore.
Open Jun 15–Sep 15; camping allowed
off-season.
5 scattered, screened sites.
Pit toilets, fire rings.
On Bear Creek drainage 1 mile (1.6 k)
from Absaroka-Beartooth Wilderness.
Create base for hiking or backpacking.
NO water/trash arrangements.
14-day/16-ft limits. Severe winters.
8200 ft (2460 m)

## BEAR CREEK PASS
Bitterroot NF
(406) 821-3913
State map: F2
From DARBY, take US 93 N for 7.3 miles
(11.7 k). Turn Left (W) on CR 17 and go
1.4 miles (2.2 k). Continue W on rough,
dirt FR 429 for 17 tough miles (27.2 k).
FREE but choose a chore.
Open Jul 15–Sep 15; camping allowed
off-season.
7 close, open sites.
Pit toilets, tables.
At head of Lost Horse Creek.
Make base for excellent exploring and
hiking during short season.
10-day/22-ft limits.
6200 ft (1860 m)

## BEAVERDAM
Deerlodge NF
(406) 494-2147
State map: F4
From BUTTE, take I-15 S for 17 miles
(27.2 k) to Feeley Exit. Go W on Divide
Creek Rd (FR 961) for 8 miles (12.8 k).
FREE but choose a chore.
Open May 22–Sep 15.
15 sites.
Water, pit toilets, tables, fire rings.
On South Fork Creek.
Walk nature trails. Fish, picnic, relax.
14-day/22-ft limits.

▲ ▲ ▲ ▲ ▲ ▲ ▲ ▲ ▲ ▲ ▲ ▲ ▲ ▲ ▲ ▲ ▲ ▲ ▲ ▲

## BENCHMARK

Lewis & Clark NF
(406) 791-7700
State map: C3

From AUGUSTA, go W on CR/FR 235 for 29.5 miles (47.2 k). Pass **Wood Lake** (9 sites). For another alternative, go 1 mile (1.6 k) to **South Fork** (7 sites).
$5. Open Jun 20–Nov 25.
25 sites.
Water, pit toilets, tables, fire rings.
On creek near Scapegoat Wilderness.
Hike to Scapegoat Mountain with its vertical limestone wall. View double falls off road 1 mile (1.6 k) N of Wood Lake.
Fish creeks or nearby Wood Lake.
14-day/22-ft limits.
5200 ft (1560 m)

## BIG BEAVER

Gallatin NF
(406) 932-5155
State map: G6

From BIG TIMBER, head S on US 298 for 33 miles (52.8 k). Last 8 miles (12.8 k) are gravel. (See Aspen, Chippy Park, Falls Creek, Hell's Canyon, and Hick's Park.)
FREE but choose a chore.
Open All Year.
5 close, open sites with some screening.
Pit toilets, tables, grills.
Fish or explore along Boulder River.
NO water/trash arrangements. Camp only in designated sites. 15-day/32-ft limits. Crowded weekends. Often inaccessible in winter.
5300 ft (1590 m)

## BIG CREEK

Flathead NF
(406) 892-4372
State map: B2

From COLUMBIA FALLS, head N on CR 486 (North Fork Rd) for 20 miles (32 k).
$5. Open May–Sep; dry camping off-season.
22 close, open sites. Water, pit toilets, tables, grills, fire rings.
At confluence of Big Creek and North Fork of Flathead River. Across river from Glacier NP.

Float the Flathead. Create base for exploring Glacier. View wildlife and fish. In grizzly country–store food carefully and pack out trash. 14-day limit.
3300 ft (990 m)

## BIG EDDY

Kootenai NF
(406) 827-3534
State map: B1

Find on N side of Cabinet Reservoir, opposite HERON off MT 200.
FREE but choose a chore.
Open Apr 23–Oct 30; camping allowed off-season.
4 close, open sites. &
Pit toilets, tables, fire rings, boat launch.
In beautiful area with Cabinet and Bitterroot mountains around lake.
Enjoy water by fishing or boating.
Explore neighboring mountains.
NO water/trash arrangements (pack it out). 14-day limit.
2200 ft (660 m)

## BIG NELSON

Lolo NF (406) 329-3750
State map: D3

From OVANDO, take MT 200 SE for 7 miles (11.2 k). Turn Left (N) on gravel CR 500 (North Fork Blackfoot Rd). Drive 12 miles (19.2 k).
FREE but choose a chore.
Open Jun 15–Sep 15.
4 sites. Pit toilets, tables, fire rings, small boat launch area.
On shores of Coopers Lake.
Explore area or plan longer trip into Scapegoat Wilderness. Fish and canoe.
NO water. 14-day limit.
4200 ft (1260 m)

## BIG THERRIAULT LAKE

Kootenai NF
(406) 882-4451
State map: A1

Take US 93 NW from FORTINE for 2.8 miles (4.5 k). Turn Right (NE) on CR 114 (Graves Creek) and drive 3.2 miles (5.1 k) to FR 114. Continue NE another 10.6 miles (17 k). Turn Left (W) on FR 319 (Therriault Lakes) and drive

▲ ▲ ▲ ▲ ▲ ▲ ▲ ▲ ▲ ▲ ▲ ▲ ▲ ▲ ▲ ▲ ▲ ▲ ▲ ▲ ▲ ▲ ▲ ▲

13 miles (20.8 k). For more seclusion, there's 1 site on Little Bluebird Creek about a mile (1.6 k) back up FR 319. (Also see Little Therriault Lake.)
FREE but choose a chore.
Open Jul 1 – Nov 15; dry camping off-season.
9 close, open sites. &
Water, pit toilets, tables, grills, boat launch (small boats).
On lake with easy access to Ten Lakes Scenic Area.
Hiking excellent and fishing acceptable.
Row your boat or try cold swimming.
No trash arrangements (pack it out).
14-day limit. Crowded.
5700 ft (1710 m)

## BIGHORN CANYON NRA-Afterbay

(406) 689-3155
State map: G9
From FORT SMITH, go NW on CR.
FREE but $3 entrance fee (or pass). Also, free backcountry permits available at Visitor Center.
Open All Year.
30 close, open sites. Water (Apr–Oct), flush toilets, tables, grills, dump station.
On scenic, semiarid canyon lake created by damming Bighorn River. Lake measures 71 miles; canyon walls reach 1500 ft.
Fish and boat. Search for fossils. See Visitor Center. Attend ranger program.
14 day/20-ft limits. Extreme heat.
3200 ft (960 m)

## BITTERROOT FLAT

Lolo NF (406) 329-3814
State map: E3
From CLINTON, take I-90 E for 5 miles (8 k). Exit onto FR 102 (Rock Creek Rd) S and drive 23 miles (36.8 k)–rough last 11 miles (17.6 k)–to fifth of six camps along Rock Creek. (Also see Dalles, Grizzly, Harry's Flat, Norton, and Siria.)
FREE but choose a chore.
Open May 1 – Nov 1; dry camping off-season.
15 scattered-open tent sites.

Water, pit toilets, tables, fire rings.
Beneath large ponderosa pine.
Relax and fish blue-ribbon stream. Hike nearby trails (Alder Creek).
14-day limit.
4200 ft (1260 m)

## BLACK BEAR

Bitterroot NF
(406) 821-3913
State map: E2
From HAMILTON, take US 93 S for 3 miles (4.8 k) to MT 38. Turn Left (E) and drive 12.9 miles (20.6 k).
FREE but choose a chore.
Open Jun 1 – Sep 15.
6 close, open sites.
Water, pit toilets, tables.
In scenic location along creek.
Hiking quite good; fishing acceptable; relaxing fantastic.
10-day/22-ft limits.

## BLACKMORE

Gallatin NF
(406) 587-6701
State map: G5
From BOZEMAN, head S on CR 243 for 8 miles (12.8 k). Turn Left (SE) on FR 64 and go 9 miles (14.4 k). (Also see Abbot and Palace Butte.)
FREE but choose a chore.
Open Jun 15 – Sep 15.
10 close, open sites.
Water, pit toilets, tables, fire rings.
Next to Hyalite Reservoir.
Boat and fish. Hike to Blackmore Lake.
14-day limit.
6600 ft (1980 m)

## BONE TRAIL

COE (406) 526-3411
State map: C9
From FORT PECK, go 5 miles (8 k) NW on oiled road, 50 miles (80 k) W on gravel Willow Creek Rd.
FREE but choose a chore.
Open All Year.
Undesignated, open sites.
Tables, boat ramp.
In remote location with great fishing and abundant wildlife.

Swim, boat, and fish reservoir plus practice nature photography.
NO water/toilet/trash arrangements (come prepared). 14-day limit.
2250 ft (675 m)

## BOULDER CITY PARK

(406) 225-4381
State map: F4
Find on MT 69 N of BOULDER.
**FREE** but choose a chore.
Open May 1–Sep 30.
10 open sites. Water, flush toilets, tables, grills, dump station.
Picnic and relax near river.
16-ft limit.
5000 ft (1500 m)

## BRANHAM LAKES

Beaverhead NF
(406) 842-5432
State map: G4
From SHERIDAN, follow dirt road E with "Mill Creek Recreation Area" sign. Go 13 miles (20.8 k) on steep, narrow, very rough road. (Also see Balanced Rock and Mill Creek.)
**FREE** but choose a chore.
Open Jul 1–Oct 1; dry camping off-season.
6 close, screened tent sites.
Water, pit toilets, tables, fire rings.
Among scenic meadows and spruce-fir stands of mountain basin with two lakes encircled by massive peaks.
Wonderful area to explore and photograph. Also fishing possibilities.
No trash facilities. 14-day limit.
8600 ft (2580 m)

## CABIN CITY

Lolo NF (406) 329-3750
State map: D1
From DE BORGIA, go E on I-90 to Exit 22. Drive 2 miles (3.2 k) NE on Camel's Hump Rd. Turn Left (N) on FR 352 and go .25 mile (400 m).
**$4.** Open May 23–Sep 6.
24 sites.
Water, pit toilets, tables, fire rings.
Along Twelvemile Creek, fish or hike.

14-day/22-ft limits.
3200 ft (960 m)

## CABLE MOUNTAIN

Deerlodge NF
(406) 859-3211
State map: F3
From PHILIPSBURG, take MT 1 S for 12 miles (19.2 k). Turn Left on FR 65 (Discovery Basin Rd) and go 3 miles (4.8 k). Find primitive camping at nearby **Echo Lake.** (Also see Flint Creek.)
**FREE** but choose a chore.
Open May 22–Sep 15.
11 sites.
Water, pit toilets, tables, fire rings.
Along North Fork of Flint Creek with several lakes nearby.
Mountain bike, hike, or fish.
14-day/22-ft limits.
6500 ft (1950 m)

## CAMP 32

Kootenai NF
(406) 296-2536
State map: A1
From REXFORD, go S on MT 37 for 2.5 miles (4 k). Turn Left (SE) on FR 856 and drive 2 miles (3.2 k). Turn Right (SW) on FR 7182 (Rondo) and continue another 1.5 miles (2.4 k).
**FREE** but choose a chore.
Open Apr 15–Nov 15.
4 close, open tent sites.
Pit toilets, tables, grills.
On Pinkham Creek near falls in secluded forest meadow.
Hike, relax, watch birds. Fish creek or head down to lake.
NO water/trash arrangements (pack it out). 14-day limit.
3200 ft (960 m)

## CAMP CREEK

BLM (406) 538-7461
State map: C8
From ZORTMAN, head E for 1 mile (1.6 k) on CR.
**FREE** but choose a chore.
Open May 1–Nov 30.
21 sites.
Water, pit toilets, tables, fire rings.

Hike, fish, or relax along creek. 14-day limit.

## CANYON CREEK

Beaverhead NF
(406) 832-3178
State map: F3

Just S of MELROSE on US 91, turn Right (W) on CR 187/FR 2701. Drive 10.2 miles (16.3 k) to end, bearing Right then Left (trailers not advised).

FREE but choose a chore.

Open Jun 15–Sep 30; camping allowed off-season.

4 close, open sites.

Pit toilets, tables, fire rings.

In pretty, timbered valley with steep side slopes.

Hike to six lakes, spot mountain goats, fish for trout, look for charcoal kilns.

NO water/trash arrangements (pack it out). 14-day/22-ft limits. Crowded holiday weekends.

7400 ft (2220 m)

## CARIBOU

Kootenai NF
(406) 295-4693
State map: A1

From YAAK, take FH 92 NE for 38 miles (60.8 k).

FREE but choose a chore.

Open Jun 1–Sep 30; camping allowed off-season.

3 tent sites. Pit toilets, tables.

Along stream in remote location.

Fish and relax.

NO water/trash arrangements. 14-day limit. Watch out for logging trucks.

3600 ft (1080 m)

## CASCADE

Custer NF (406) 446-2103
State map: G7
From RED LODGE, go

10 miles (16 k) W on paved then graveled FR 71. (Also see Basin.)

$5. Open May 25–Sep 15; dry camping off-season.

30 scattered, open sites.

Water, pit toilets, tables, fire rings.

Among lodgepole pine and underbrush

on sloping bench above West Fork of Rock Creek.

Hiking and exploring along trails in beautiful area. Fishing too.

10-day/32-ft limits. Crowded weekends.

7800 ft (2340 m)

## CEDAR CREEK

Swan River SF
(406) 754-2301
State map: C2

Take MT 83 S from SWAN LAKE for 12 miles (19.2 k). Turn Right (W) on Fatty Creek Rd. Drive about .5 mile (800 m).

FREE but choose a chore.

Open Apr–Nov; camping allowed off-season.

6 scattered, screened sites.

Stream water (must be treated), pit toilets, tables, grills, fire rings.

At confluence of Cedar Creek and Swan River in heavily timbered area.

Good fishing plus swimming, boating, and hiking possibilities.

No trash pickup. Hunting in season.

3400 ft (1020 m)

## CHARLES WATERS

Bitterroot NF
(406) 777-5461
State map: E2

From STEVENSVILLE, take CR 269 NW for 1.5 miles (2.4 k) to US 93. Turn Right (N) and go 4 miles (6.4 k) to CR 22. Turn Left (W) and drive 1.7 miles (2.7 k). Turn on FR 1316 and go .5 mile (800 m).

$4. Open May 25–Sep 10.

18 close, open sites.

Water, pit toilets, tables.

Near Bass Creek in scenic region.

Take short walks or extended treks along fitness, nature, and hiking trails.

14-day/22-ft limits.

3800 ft (1140 m)

## CHIEF LOOKING GLASS FAS

MT FWP (406) 542-5500
State map: E2
From MISSOULA, go S

14 miles (22.4 k) on US 93 to milepost 77. Turn E on CR and go 2 miles (3.2 k).

▲ ▲ ▲ ▲ ▲ ▲ ▲ ▲ ▲ ▲ ▲ ▲ ▲ ▲ ▲ ▲ ▲ ▲ ▲ ▲ ▲ ▲ ▲ ▲ ▲ ▲ ▲ ▲

$5. Open May 1–Nov 30.
25 scattered, open sites.
Hand water pump, pit toilets, tables, grills, fire rings.
Among cottonwood on Bitterroot River.
Fish, birdwatch, and take photos.
7-day/25-ft limits. Quiet hours.
3900 ft (1170 m)

## CHIEF JOSEPH

Gallatin NF
(406) 848-7375
State map: G6
From COOKE CITY, go E on US 212 about 5 miles (8 k). Turn Right. (Also see Colter and Fox Creek, WY.)
$5. Open Jun 23–Sep 1.
6 close, screened sites. Water, pit toilets, tables, fire rings, food storage.
In woods on scenic route to Yellowstone and across from major trailhead into Absaroka-Beartooth Wilderness.
Make stop-over for sightseeing or backpacking. Attend ranger programs.
15-day/20-ft limits. Generator rules.
8000 ft (2400 m)

## CHIPPY PARK

Gallatin NF
(406) 932-5155
State map: G6
From BIG TIMBER, head S on US 298 for 35 miles (56 k)–gravel last 10 miles (16 k). (Also see Aspen, Big Beaver, Falls Creek, Hell's Canyon, and Hick's Park.)
FREE but choose a chore.
Open All Year.
7 (5 RV-only, 2 tent-only) scattered, screened sites. &
Water, pit toilets, tables, grills.
Next to Boulder River for easy fishing.
No trash arrangements (pack it out).
Camp only in designated sites.
15-day/32-ft limits. Crowded weekends.
Often inaccessible in winter.
5300 ft (1590 m)

## CHOTEAU CITY PARK

(406) 466-2510
State map: C4
Find in town on US 221.
FREE but choose a chore.

Open May 10–Nov 1.
75 sites. Water, flush toilets, tables, grills, dump station.
Picnic and relax near river.
3-day limit.
3810 ft (1143 m)

## CLARK CANYON RESERVOIR

BOR (406) 657-6202
State map: H3
Drive 20 miles (32 k) S of DILLON on I-15.
FREE but choose a chore. Open All Year.
Undesignated, scattered sites.
Swim, boat, and fish.
14-day limit. Generator rules.
5545 ft (1662 m)

▲ Beaverhead
Water, pit toilets, tables, grills, fire rings, boat ramp. &
With beach on lakeshore.

▲ Beaverhead Marina
Reservations accepted at (406) 683-5556.
Water, flush toilets, showers, tables, grills, fire rings, full hook-ups for RVs, dump station, pay phone, beach, boat ramp, dock with gas, store with ice and rentals. &
On most developed part of reservoir.

▲ Cameahwait
Water, pit toilets, tables, grills, fire rings.
At one of nicer locations on reservoir.

▲ Fishing Access
Water, pit toilets, tables, grills, fire rings.
Below dam on beautiful Beaverhead River with good boating and fishing, plus self-guided nature trail. Swimming in reservoir.

▲ Hap Hawkins
Individuals: first-come, first-serve.
Groups: reserve at (406) 683-6472.
Water, pit toilets, tables, grills, fire rings, large group pavilion with fireplace.

▲ Horse Prairie
Water, pit toilets, tables, grills, fire rings, boat ramp. &
With beach on reservoir shore.

▲ Lewis & Clark
Water, pit toilets, tables, grills, fire rings, beach.
Next to marina and store.

▲ **Lone Tree**
Water, pit toilets, tables, grills, fire rings, beach.
On west shore of reservoir.

▲ **West Cameahwait**
Water, pit toilets, tables, grills, fire rings, beach.
On northwest shore of reservoir.

**CLARK MEMORIAL**
Lolo NF (406) 329-3750
State map: C1
From THOMPSON
FALLS, take MT 200 E for 5 miles (8 k).
Turn Left (N) on Thompson River Rd.
Go 5 miles (8 k). (Also see Copper King.)
**FREE** but choose a chore.
Open Jun 1–Sep 30.
5 sites. Pit toilets, tables, fire rings.
Picnic and fish on river.
NO water. 14-day limit.
2700 ft (810 m)

**CLEARWATER CROSSING**
Lolo NF (406) 329-3750
State map: D2
Take Exit 66 S off I-90 (E
of TARKIO) onto Fish Creek Rd. Drive
10 miles (32 k) to West Fork Rd. Follow
it to end.
**FREE** but choose a chore.
Open Jun 1–Nov 30.
2 sites. Pit toilets, tables, fire rings.
At Upper Fish Creek RA in deep woods
on stream.
Hike, fish, or relax.
NO water. 14-day limit.
3900 ft (1170 m)

**CLOVER MEADOWS**
Beaverhead NF
(406) 842-5432
State map: G4
First, obtain map from SHERIDAN
Ranger Station. From ALDER, go S on
gravel FR 100 (Ruby River Rd) about
32 miles (51.2 k.)–1 mile (1.6 k) before
Vigilante Guard Station. Turn Left (E) on
FR 163 and go 7 twisting miles (11.2 k).
Turn Right (SE) on FR 290 and go
3 miles (4.8 k). (Also see Cottonwood.)
**FREE** but choose a chore.

Open Jul 1–Oct 15; camping allowed
off-season.
Undesignated sites (officially, picnic area
but camping allowed). Pit toilets, tables.
On top of Gravelly Range with
spectacular mountain views.
Photograph, watch wildlife, relax.
NO water/trash arrangements (pack it
out). Flies in summer.
8700 ft (2610 m)

**COLTER**
Gallatin NF
(406) 848-7375
State map: G6
From COOKE CITY, go E on US 212
about 3.5 miles (5.6 k). Turn Left. (Also
see Chief Joseph and Fox Creek, WY.)
**$5.** Open Jun 15–Sep 1.
23 scattered, open sites with some
screening. Water, pit toilets, tables, fire
rings, food storage.
Close to jeep roads and wilderness. On
scenic route to Yellowstone NP.
Make base for sightseeing and backpacking. Attend ranger programs.
15-day/22-ft limits. Generator rules.
7900 ft (2370 m)

**COPPER CREEK**
Deerlodge NF
(406) 859-3211
State map: F3
From PHILIPSBURG, take MT 1 S for
6 miles (9.6 k). Turn Right on MT 38. Go
8.5 miles (13.6 k). Turn S on FR 5106
(Middle Ford Rd). Go 10 miles (16 k).
Turn on FR 80 and go .25 mile (400 m).
**FREE** but choose a chore.
Open May 22–Sep 30.
7 close, open sites. &
Water, pit toilets, tables, fire rings.
On isolated, remote creek.
Reflect at this getaway. Hike and fish.
14-day/22-ft limits.

**COPPER KING**
Lolo NF (406) 329-3750
State map: C1
From THOMPSON
FALLS, take MT 200 E for 5 miles (8 k).
Turn Left (N) on Thompson River Rd.

Go 4 miles (6.4 k). (See Clark Memorial.)
FREE but choose a chore.
Open Jun 1–Sep 30.
5 sites. Pit toilets, tables, fire rings.
On Thompson River.
Fish or walk up Buckeye Canyon.
NO water. 14-day limit.
2700 ft (810 m)

## COTTONWOOD

Beaverhead NF
(406) 842-5432
State map: G4
From ALDER, go S on gravel FR 100
(Ruby River Rd) about 36 miles (57.6 k).
Watch for sign. (Also see Clover
Meadows.)
FREE but choose a chore.
Open Jun 1–Nov 1; camping allowed
off-season.
10 close, open sites.
Pit toilets, tables, fire rings.
Under cottonwood and willow near
Ruby River with scenic views of
Snowcrest Mountains.
Relax and picnic or try a bit of fishing
and birdwatching.
NO water/trash arrangements (pack it
out). 14-day limit. Crowded holidays and
hunting season. Biting flies.
6364 ft (1908 m)

## COW BELL

Musselshell County
(406) 323-1104
State map: E8
Locate in ROUNDUP just off Main St on
2nd Ave E.
FREE but donations requested.
Open All Year.
20 sites. Water, flush toilets, tables, grills,
playground.
Swim and fish in Musselshell River.
Walk and bike in Bull Mountains.
Crowded July.
3500 ft (960 m)

## COW CREEK

Custer NF (406) 784-2344
State map: G10
Take US 312 E from
ASHLAND for 3 miles (4.8 k) to Cotton

Creek Rd. Turn Right (S) and drive
20 miles (32 k). Turn Right (W) on
unpaved FR 95 and go 4 miles (6.4 k).
FREE but choose a chore.
Open May 15–Nov 1; camping allowed
off-season.
8 scattered, screened sites.
Pit toilets, tables, fire rings.
In secluded setting along stream with
willow and ponderosa pine.
Get away to relax. Perhaps birdwatch.
NO water/trash arrangements (pack it
out). 14-day/30-ft limits. Crowded in
hunting season. Ticks and rattlesnakes.
3800 ft (1140 m)

## CRAZY CREEK

Bitterroot NF
(406) 821-3201
State map: F2
From SULA, take US 93 N for 4.75 miles
(7.6 k) to CR 100. Turn Left (SW) and go
1 mile (1.6 k). Turn SW on FR 370 and
drive 3 miles (4.8 k). About .5 mile
(800 m) before camp, find area for
unloading stock with feed bunkers and
tie racks. (Also see Warm Springs.)
FREE but choose a chore.
Open Jun 1–Sep 15.
16 close, open sites.
Water, pit toilets, tables.
Besides fishing in creek, try hiking and
horseback riding in Warm Springs Area.
(Horses allowed in lower loop).
14-day/22-ft limits.
5000 ft (1500 m)

## CRYSTAL CREEK

Deerlodge NF
(406) 859-3211
State map: F3
From PHILIPSBURG, take MT 1 S for
6 miles (9.6 k). Turn Right on MT 38
(Skalkaho Hwy). Go 30.75 miles (49.2 k).
FREE but choose a chore.
Open May 22–Sep 30.
7 close, open sites. &
Pit toilets, tables, fire rings.
Along remote creek near Mud Lake via
fascinating mountain road in beautiful
Sapphire Range.
Get away to reflect and relax. Hike too.

NO water. 14-day/16-ft limits.
7100 ft (2130 m)

## DAILEY LAKE FAS

MT FWP (406) 994-4042
State map: G5
From EMIGRANT, go E
across Yellowstone River to CR 540.
Turn Right (SW) and drive until sign for
gravel road to Dailey Lake–about
8 total miles (12.8 k).
FREE but choose a chore.
Open All Year.
30 scattered, open sites.
Pit toilets, tables, boat ramp.
Around shore of 200-acre lake with no
trees or other shade.
Fish, swim, boat, even windsurf.
NO water (though may be added).
14-day limit. Crowded summer week-
ends. High winds at times–hot and dry.
4500 ft (1350 m)

## DALLES

Lolo NF (406) 329-3814
State map: E3
From CLINTON, take
I-90 E for 5 miles (8 k). Exit onto FR 102
(Rock Creek Rd) S and drive 13.5 miles
(21.6 k)–rough last 1.5 miles (2.4 k)–to
third of six free camps along Rock Creek.
(Also see Bitterroot Flat, Grizzly, Harry's
Flat, Norton, and Siria.)
FREE but choose a chore.
Open May 1–Nov 1; dry camping
off-season.
10 scattered, screened tent sites.
Water, pit toilets, tables, fire rings.
In lodgepole pine.
Relax and fish. Hike Welcome Creek
Trail to wilderness. Spot bighorn sheep.
14-day limit.
4100 ft (1230 m)

## DELMOE LAKE

Deerlodge NF
(406) 287-3223
State map: F4
From BUTTE, head E on I-90 to Home-
stake Pass Exit. Take FR 222 for 10 miles
(16 k) following signs.
FREE but choose a chore.

Open May 22–Sep 15.
25 close, open sites. &
Water, pit toilets, tables, fire rings.
On lake.
Swim, boat, fish, hike, or picnic.
14-day limit.

## DEVIL CREEK

Flathead NF
(406) 387-5243
State map: B3
From HUNGRY HORSE, go 44.6 miles
(71.4 k) E on US 2.
$5. Open Jun 1–Sep 15; dry camping
off-season.
12 RV (hard side) sites.
Water, pit toilets, tables, grills.
Adjacent to Glacier NP in mountainous
setting of woods near Maria Pass on
Continental Divide.
Try hiking Devil Creek Trail.
In grizzly country–store food carefully
and pack out trash. 14-day limit.
4360 ft (1308 m)

## DEVILS CORKSCREW

Flathead NF
(406) 387-5243
State map: B3
From MARTIN CITY, take gravel
logging road (FR 38) SE for 37 miles
(59.2 k). (Also see Murray Bay.)
FREE but choose a chore.
Open Jun 1–Sep 15; camping allowed
off-season.
4 close, screened tent sites. Pit toilets,
tables, grills, fire rings, boat ramp.
In woods on east side of Hungry Horse
Reservoir surrounded by mountains.
Swimming and boating. Hiking, berry
picking, wildlife and wildflower viewing
and photo taking opportunities.
NO water/trash arrangements (pack it
out). 14-day limit.
3570 ft (1071 m)

## DICKIE BRIDGE

BLM (406) 494-5059
State map: F3
From WISE RIVER, take
MT 43 W for 7 miles (11.2 k). (Also see
East Bank.)

▲ ▲ ▲ ▲ ▲ ▲ ▲ ▲ ▲ ▲ ▲ ▲ ▲ ▲ ▲ ▲ ▲ ▲ ▲ ▲ ▲ ▲ ▲ ▲

FREE but choose a chore.
Open All Year.
8 scattered, open sites.
Pit toilets, tables, grills, boat ramp.
In lodgepole pine across gravel road
from Big Hole River.
Picnic and fish. Try birdwatching.
NO water/trash arrangements (pack it
out). 14-day limit.
5714 ft (1713 m)

## DINNER STATION

Beaverhead NF
(406) 683-3900
State map: G3
From DILLON, go N on I-15 for 12 miles
(19.2 k) to Apex Exit. Go W on Birch Rd
11.5 miles (18.4 k).
FREE but choose a chore.
Open May 15–Sep 15; dry camping
off-season.
7 sites.
Water, pit toilets, tables, fire rings.
In mature lodgepole pine next to Birch
Creek. Trail to Deerhead Lake in narrow
rock canyon at south end of camp. Hike,
fish, and enjoy Thief Creek-Birch Creek
Scenic Drive.
No trash arrangements (pack it out).
14-day limit. Crowded holidays. Not
suitable for RVs.
7200 ft (2160 m)

## DIVIDE BRIDGE

BLM (406) 494-5059
State map: F4
From DIVIDE, take
MT 43 W for 1 mile (1.6 k).
FREE but choose a chore.
Open All Year.
35 (10 tent-only) scattered, open sites.
Water, pit toilets, tables, fire rings, boat
ramp.
In aspen along creek .5 mile (800 m)
downstream from day-use area.
Besides boating and fishing, walk nature
and hiking trails. Picnic, birdwatch, and
relax.
No trash arrangements (pack it out).
14-day limit. Crowded May–Jun.
5400 ft (1620 m)

## DORR SKEELS

Kootenai NF
(406) 295-4693
State map: B1
From TROY, head SE on US 2 about
3 miles (4.8 k). Turn Right (S) on MT 56.
Go 12.5 miles (20 k). Watch for Right
(W) turn to entrance. (Also see Bad
Medicine.)
FREE but choose a chore.
Open May 20–Sep 15; camping allowed
off-season.
6 close, open sites. Pit toilets, tables, fire
rings, boat ramp, beach.
On shores of Bull Lake.
Waterskiing and swimming for cold-
natured plus fishing and boating.
NO water/trash arrangements. 14-day
limit. Crowded weekends.
2200 ft (660 m)

## EAGLE CREEK

Gallatin NF
(406) 848-7375
State map: G6
From GARDINER, take gravel Jardine
Rd NE for 3.5 miles (5.4 k). (Also see
Bear Creek and Timber Camp.)
FREE but choose a chore.
Open All Year.
10 close, open sites.
Pit toilets, tables, fire rings.
In Yellowstone River Valley overlooking
northeast entrance to park.
Hike, take photographs, or fish. Visit
Yellowstone NP.
NO water/trash arrangements (pack it
out). 14-day limit. Severe winters.
6800 ft (2040 m)

## EAST BANK

BLM (406) 494-5059
State map: F3
From WISE RIVER, take
MT 43 W for 8 miles (12.8 k). (Also see
Dickie Bridge.)
FREE but choose a chore.
Open All Year.
5 scattered, open sites.
Pit toilets, tables, grills, boat ramp.
Among lodgepole pine adjacent to Big
Hole River.

Picnic and fish. Watch the birdies.
NO water/trash arrangements (pack it out). 14-day limit.
5740 ft (1722 m)

## EAST BOULDER

Gallatin NF
(406) 932-5155
State map: G6
From BIG TIMBER, head S on US 298 for 19 miles (30.4 k) to East Boulder Turnoff. Turn Left (E) and drive 6 miles (9.6 k) on gravel road.
FREE but choose a chore.
Open All Year.
2 close, open sites with some screening.
Pit toilets, tables, fire rings.
Next to East Boulder River.
Make base for extended hikes. Fish.
NO water/trash arrangements (pack it out). Camp only in designated sites. 15-day limit. Crowded weekends. Often inaccessible in winter.
5625 ft (1686 m)

## EAST CREEK

Beaverhead NF
(406) 683-3900
State map: H3
From DILLON, go S on I-15 for 50 miles (80 k) to Lima Exit. Go W and follow signs for 8.5 miles (13.6 k) on narrow dirt road.
FREE but choose a chore.
Open May 15–Oct 1; dry camping off-season.
4 close, open sites.
Water, pit toilets, tables, fire rings.
In narrow valley with aspen and fir, creek, and Lima Peaks to south.
Relaxing place for nature enthusiasts.
No trash arrangements (pack it out). 14-day limit. Smaller vehicles only.
7000 ft (2100 m)

## EAST FORK

Deerlodge NF
(406) 859-3211
State map: F3
From PHILIPSBURG, take MT 1 S for 6.25 miles (10 k). Turn Right (SW) on MT 38 and drive 6 miles (9.6 k). Turn

Left (SE) on FR 672 (East Fork Rd) and go 4.5 miles (7.2 k). (Also see Spillway.)
FREE but choose a chore.
Open May 22–Sep 30.
7 sites.
Water, pit toilets, tables, fire rings.
On scenic creek.
Splash in water, fish, or hike.
14-day/22-ft limits.
6000 ft (1800 m)

## EAST ROSEBUD FAS

MT FWP (406) 232-4365
State map: E10
Locate on NE side of FORSYTH.
$5. Open All Year.
12 scattered, screened sites.
Water, pit toilets, tables, pay phone, boat ramp, beach.
On Yellowstone River in cottonwood/mixed hardwood forest.
Fishing, boating, and relaxing.
Crowded during early Aug (Rosebud County Fair). 14-day limit.
2515 ft (753 m)

## EKALAKA PARK

Custer NF (605) 797-4432
State map: F12
From EKALAKA, take MT 323 S for 3 miles (4.8 k) to CR/FR 813. Turn Right (W) and go 6 miles (9.6 k).
FREE but choose a chore.
Open May 1–Nov 15; camping allowed off-season.
9 scattered, screened sites. Spring water, pit toilets, tables, grills, fire rings.
On flat with green ash, cottonwood, elm, and lots of grass.
Use as getaway.
No trash arrangements (pack it out). 14-day limit. Crowded hunting season.
3800 ft (1140 m)

## ELKO

Lewis & Clark NF
(406) 791-7700
State map: C4
From CHOTEAU, go 5.5 miles (8.8 k) N on US 89. Turn Left (W) on CR 144 and

drive 23 miles (36.8 k). Turn Right (N) on FR 144 and go 2.5 miles (4 k). (Also see Mills Falls and West Fork.)
**FREE** but choose a chore.
Open Jun 1–Nov 15.
3 sites. Pit toilets, tables, fire rings.
On Teton River near Bob Marshall Wilderness.
Hike, fish, or picnic.
NO water/trash arrangements (pack it out). 14-day limit.
5500 ft (1650 m)

## EMERALD LAKE

Custer NF (406) 446-2103
State map: G7
From FISHTAIL, go SW on MT 425 for 6 miles (9.6 k) to FR 72. Go S for 12 rough miles (19.2 k). (Also see Pine Grove.)
**$5.** Open May 25–Sep 15; dry camping off-season.
30 sites–some close, others scattered with screening. Water, pit toilets, tables, grills, fire rings.
On steep, north-facing timbered slope close to West Rosebud Creek and West Rosebud Reservoir.
Swim, fish, or put in small boat. Hike up to Mystic Lake or saunter to West Rosebud Lake. Explore.
No trash pickup (pack it out to dumpster 10 miles up road). 10-day limit. Crowded weekends.
6400 ft (1920 m)

## ENNIS FAS

MT FWP (406) 994-4042
State map: G4
From ENNIS, drive SW on MT 287 for .5 mile (800 m).
**$5.** Open All Year.
25 scattered, open sites. Water, pit toilets, tables, fire rings, boat ramp.
On Madison River in cottonwood.
Fish, boat, swim, and birdwatch.
14-day limit. Crowded summers. Mosquitos. Ice prevents access Dec–Mar.
4500 ft (1350 m)

## FAIRY LAKE

Gallatin NF
(406) 587-6701
State map: F5
From BOZEMAN, head N on MT 86/293 (becomes FR 74) for 22 miles (35.2 k). Turn Left (NW) just beyond Battle Ridge Pass. Go 6 miles (9.6 k). (Also see Battle Ridge.)
**FREE** but choose a chore.
Open Jun 15–Sep 15.
9 close, open tent sites.
Water, pit toilets, tables, fire rings.
On quiet lake.
Canoe, picnic, fish, relax. Hike up to Sacagawea and over to Hardscrabble.
No trash arrangements. 14-day limit.
7600 ft (2280 m)

## FALLS CREEK

Gallatin NF
(406) 932-5155
State map: G6
From BIG TIMBER, head S on US 298 for 30 miles (48 k)–gravel last 5 miles (8 k). (Also see Aspen, Big Beaver, Chippy Park, Hell's Canyon, and Hick's Park.)
**FREE** but choose a chore.
Open All Year.
8 close tent sites with some screening. Water, pit toilets, tables, grills, fire rings.
Adjacent to Boulder River and Froze to Death Creek with trail access into Absaroka-Beartooth Wilderness.
Base camp for extended hikes or exploring immediate area. Fishing.
No trash arrangements (pack it out). Camp only in designated sites. 15-day/16-ft limits. Crowded weekends. Often inaccessible in winter.
5200 ft (1560 m)

## FIREMEN'S MEMORIAL PARK

Libby City Parks
(406) 293-2731
State map: B1
Find on US 2 in LIBBY.
**FREE** but donations requested.
Open Apr 1–Nov 1.
20 close, open sites. Water, flush toilets, tables, pay phone, dump station.
In trees near shopping area.

▲ ▲ ▲ ▲ ▲ ▲ ▲ ▲ ▲ ▲ ▲ ▲ ▲ ▲ ▲ ▲ ▲ ▲ ▲ ▲ ▲ ▲ ▲ ▲ ▲ ▲

Take advantage of nature trail plus swim, boat, and fish.
3-day limit.

## FISHTRAP CREEK

Lolo NF (406) 329-3750
State map: C1
From THOMPSON FALLS, take MT 200 E for 5 miles (8 k). Turn Left (N) on Thompson River Rd and drive 13 miles (20.8 k). Turn Left (NW) on FR 516 (Fishtrap Creek Rd) and go about 9 miles (14.4 k). (Also see Fishtrap Lake.)
FREE but choose a chore.
Open Jun 1–Sep 30.
4 sites.
Water, pit toilets, tables, fire rings.
On creek for picnicking and fishing. Hiking nearby.
14-day limit.
4200 ft (1260 m)

## FISHTRAP LAKE

Lolo NF (406) 329-3750
State map: C1
From THOMPSON FALLS, take MT 200 E for 5 miles (8 k). Turn Left (N) on Thompson River Rd and drive 13 miles (20.8 k). Turn Left (NW) on FR 516 (Fishtrap Creek Rd) and go about 11 miles (17.6 k). Turn Left (W) on FR 7593 and go about 2 miles (3.2 k). (Also see Fishtrap Creek.)
FREE but choose a chore.
Open Jun 1–Sep 30.
11 sites.
Water, pit toilets, tables, fire rings.
Walk lake trail or take more extensive hikes into backcountry. Canoe and fish.
14-day limit.
4200 ft (1260 m)

## FLAT LAKE

COE (406) 526-3411
State map: C10
Take MT 24 S from FORT PECK for 6 miles (9.6 k). Turn Right on gravel road for 1 mile (1.6 k). (See Bear Creek and Fort Peck West RA.)
FREE but choose a chore.
Open All Year.

15 close, open sites.
Pit toilets, tables, fire rings, boat ramp.
On east side of Fort Peck Reservoir with few trees and little shade.
Swimming, skiing, boating, and fishing plus good birdwatching too.
NO water. 14-day limit.
2250 ft (675 m)

## FLINT CREEK

Deerlodge NF
(406) 859-3211
State map: F3
From PHILIPSBURG, take MT 1 S for 8 miles (12.8 k). Turn Left on FR 1090. For developed, fee-charged camps continue S on MT 1 for 2 miles (3.2 k) and find **Lodgepole**, **Philipsburg Bay**, and **Piney**. (Also see Cable Mountain.)
FREE but choose a chore.
Open May 22–Sep 30.
7 close, open sites. ⅃
Pit toilets, tables, fire rings.
On creek (closest free camp to Georgetown Lake).
Hike and fish on creek. Drive to nearby Georgetown Lake.
NO water. 14-day/16-ft limits.
5800 ft (1740 m)

## FORT PECK WEST RA

COE (406) 526-3411
State map: C10
Locate just outside FORT PECK. Follow signs. (Also see Bear Creek and Flat Lake.)
FREE but choose a chore.
Open All Year.
21 scattered, open sites. Water, flush and pit toilets, tables, grills, fire rings, shelters with electric grills.
On overlook above Fort Peck Lake.
Boating and fishing. Plenty of room for land-base recreation.
14-day limit.
2250 ft (675 m)

## FOURCHETTE CREEK

COE (406) 526-3411
State map: C9
From MALTA, take gravel roads S about 50 miles (80 k).

▲ ▲ ▲ ▲ ▲ ▲ ▲ ▲ ▲ ▲ ▲ ▲ ▲ ▲ ▲ ▲ ▲ ▲ ▲ ▲ ▲ ▲ ▲ ▲

Follow signs.
FREE but choose a chore.
Open All Year.
Undesignated sites.
Pit toilets, tables, fire rings, boat ramp.
On Fort Peck Lake in remote area.
Fishing, waterskiing, and boating.
NO water/trash arrangements (pack it
out and clean it up). 14-day limit.
2250 ft (675 m)

## FRESNO RESERVOIR

BOR (406) 657-6202
State map: B6
FREE but choose a chore.
Open All Year.
On shores of reservoir.
Swim, boat, and fish.
NO water/trash arrangements. Stay on
roads to prevent erosion.
2580 ft (774 m)

▲ Kiehns Bay
From HAVRE, go 12 miles (19.2 k) W on
US 2. Turn Right (N) on gravel road and
drive 3 miles (4.8 k). Turn Left (NW) and
continue .5 mile (800 m).
Undesignated, open sites.
Pit toilets, tables, fire rings, beach.

▲ Kremlin Bay
From HAVRE, go 15 miles (24 k) W on
US 2. Go N on dirt road for 4 miles
(6.4 k) then Right (E) for 1 mile (1.6 k).
8 close, open sites.
Pit toilets, tables, fire rings.

▲ River Run
From HAVRE, go 12 miles (19.2 k) W on
US 2. Turn Right (N) on gravel road and
drive 1.5 miles (2.4 k), bearing Left. At
bottom of hill, turn Left.
Undesignated, open sites.
Pit toilets, tables, fire rings.

## GLACIER NP-Cut Bank

(406) 888-5441
State map: B3
Head S on US 17 from ST
MARYS about 15 miles (24 k) to Cut
Bank Rd. Turn Right (W) on dirt road
and drive 4 miles (56.4 k) to only free
drive-to camp in park. Road unsuitable
for any vehicle over 22 ft.
FREE but $5 entrance fee (or pass). Also,

free backcountry permits available at
any ranger station.
Open May 23–Sep 14 (snow decides);
dry camping off-season.
19 close, open sites.
Water, pit toilets, tables, grills.
On creek nicely situated for hikes–both
day and backpack.
Explore this natural treasure of glacier-
carved landscapes that join Canada's
Waterton Lakes NP. Find over 200 lakes,
streams, waterfalls, wildflower meadows,
and forests. Sight mountain goats and
grizzly bears among wildlife.
Bear country–store food carefully.
5200 ft (1560 m)

## GOLD CREEK

Bitterroot NF
(406) 777-5461
State map: E2
From STEVENSVILLE, go S on CR 269
for 1 mile (1.6 k). Turn Left (E) on
CR 372. Go 11 miles (17.6 k) to FR 312.
Turn Right (S) and go 4 difficult miles
(6.4 k).
FREE but choose a chore.
Open Jun 1–Sep 15.
5 close, open sites.
Water, pit toilets, tables.
Fish, hike, or relax along stream.
14-day/22-ft limits.
4800 ft (1440 m)

## GOLD RUSH

Lolo NF (406) 329-3750
State map: C1
From THOMPSON
FALLS, head S on East Fork of Dry
Creek Rd for 9 miles (16.3 k).
FREE but choose a chore.
Open Jun 1–Oct 31.
7 sites.
Water, pit toilets, tables, fire rings.
On creek near excellent hiking trails.
Fish and relax.
14-day limit.
3000 ft (900 m)

▲ ▲ ▲ ▲ ▲ ▲ ▲ ▲ ▲ ▲ ▲ ▲ ▲ ▲ ▲ ▲ ▲ ▲ ▲ ▲ ▲ ▲ ▲ ▲ ▲ ▲ ▲ ▲ ▲

## GRASSHOPPER

Beaverhead NF
(406) 683-3900
State map: G3

From intersection of MT 278 and Wise River–Polaris Rd, head N toward POLARIS for 12.5 miles (20 k). Camp is off road to left about .5 mile (800 m).
FREE but choose a chore.
Open Jun 16–Sep 15; dry camping off-season. (Water available behind group picnic area until Nov.)
24 close, open sites.
Water, pit toilets, tables, fire rings.
Next to Grasshopper Creek on gentle slope under spruce and lodgepole pine.
Explore scenic area. Swim or fish. Visit Elkhorn Hot Springs Resort north of camp.
No trash arrangements. 14-day limit.
Crowded holiday weekends.
6900 ft (2070 m)

## GRASSHOPPER CREEK

Lewis & Clark NF
(406) 791-7700
State map: E6

From WHITE SULPHUR SPRINGS, head E on US 12 for 7 miles (11.2 k). Turn Right (S) on FR 211. Drive 4.25 miles (6.8 k). (See Richardson Creek.)
FREE but choose a chore.
Open Jun 1–Oct 15.
12 sites.
Water, pit toilets, tables, fire rings.
Hike, fish, or picnic along creek.
No trash arrangements. 14-day limit.
6000 ft (1800 m)

## GRAVE CREEK

Kootenai NF
(406) 882-4451
State map: A1

Take US 93 NW from FORTINE for 2.8 miles (4.5 k). Turn Right (NE) on CR 114 and drive 2.1 miles (3.4 k) to FR 7019. Turn Right (E) and go about .5 mile (800 m) down to creek.
FREE but choose a chore.
Open Jul 1–Nov 15; camping off-season.
3 close, open sites.
Pit toilets, tables, grills.

On quiet creek.
Fish stream. Picnic and relax.
NO water/trash arrangements (pack it out). 14-day/20-ft limits.
3500 ft (1050 m)

## GRAVES BAY

Flathead NF
(406) 387-5243
State map: B2

From HUNGRY HORSE, take gravel FR 895 SE for 35 miles (56 k) crossing dam to western side of reservoir. (Also see Handkerchief Lake, Lake View, and Lid Creek.)
FREE but choose a chore.
Open Jun 1–Sep 15; camping allowed off-season.
10 (6 tent-only) close, screened sites.
Pit toilets, tables, grills, fire rings.
On Hungry Horse Reservoir side of road (tent sites with 50-ft walk-in) or open wooded area to Right (W) of bridge along Graves Creek.
Swim, fish, boat, hike up creek to falls, and just relax.
NO water/trash arrangements (pack it out). No large vehicles. 14-day limit.
3600 ft (1080 m)

## GRIZZLY

Lolo NF (406) 329-3814
State map: E3

From CLINTON, take I-90 E for 5 miles (8 k). Exit onto FR 102 (Rock Creek Rd) S and drive 11.5 miles (18.4 k). Turn Left (E) on Ranch Creek Rd and go 1 mile (1.6 k). (Also see Bitterroot Flat, Dalles, Harry's Flat, Norton, and Siria.)
FREE but choose a chore.
Open May 1–Nov 1; dry camping off-season.
9 scattered, screened tent sites.
Water, pit toilets, tables, fire rings.
Among old-growth ponderosa pine surrounded by talus slopes along Ranch Creek.
Play volleyball and horseshoes plus hike great trails leading out of remote spot.
14-day limit.
4100 ft (1230 m)

## HALFMOON

Gallatin NF
(406) 932-5155
State map: F6

From BIG TIMBER, take US 191 N for
11 miles (17.6 k). Turn Left (W) on Big
Timber Canyon Rd. In 2 miles (3.2 k)
watch for turnoff sign and continue
another 10 miles (16 k).
FREE but choose a chore.
Open All Year.
8 close, open sites with some screening.
Water, pit toilets, tables, grills, fire rings.
At end of road on Big Timber Creek.
Excellent hiking and reasonable fishing.
No trash arrangements (pack it out).
15-day limit. Use designated sites only.
Crowded weekends. Road often inac-
cessible in winter.
6400 ft (1920 m)

## HANDKERCHIEF LAKE

Flathead NF
(406) 387-5243
State map: B2

From HUNGRY HORSE, take gravel
FR 895 SE for 35 miles (56 k) to FR 879.
Turn Right (W), go 2 miles (3.2 k). (See
Graves Bay, Lake View, and Lid Creek.)
FREE but choose a chore.
Open Jun 1 – Sep 15; camping allowed
off-season.
9 close, screened tent sites.
Pit toilets, tables, grills, fire rings.
Over bank from parking area (about
100 ft) near small lake in mountainous
setting with cool nights.
Fish for Arctic Grayling or access Jewel
Basin Hiking Area–trailhead at end of
FR 879, 1 mile (1.6 k) from camp.
NO water/trash arrangements (pack it
out). No large vehicles. 14-day limit.
3920 ft (1176 m)

## HARPERS LAKE FAS

MT FWP (406) 542-5500
State map: D3
From SEELEY LAKE,
travel 14 miles (22.4 k) S on MT 83.
$4. Open All Year.
15 close, open sites. Pit toilets, tables,
grills, fire rings, boat ramp.

In conifers along Clearwater River.
Boat, swim, and fish. Observe and
photograph wildlife, particularly birds.
NO water. 7-day/25-ft limits. Quiet
10pm–7am.
4000 ft (1200 m)

## HARRISON LAKE FAS

MT FWP (406) 994-4042
State map: G5
From HARRISON, go E
on CR for 4 miles (6.4 k).
$4. Open All Year.
30 scattered, open sites.
Water (needs treating), pit toilets, tables,
fire rings, boat ramp.
On west side of 400-acre lake.
Fish, swim, boat, or ride ATVs.
14-day limit. Crowded weekends. High
winds and hot at times; harsh winters.
4500 ft (1350 m)

## HARRY'S FLAT

Lolo NF (406) 329-3814
State map: E3
From CLINTON, take
I-90 E for 5 miles (8 k). Exit onto FR 102
(Rock Creek Rd) S and drive 17 miles
(27.2 k)–rough last 5 miles (8 k)–to
fourth of six free camps along Rock
Creek. (Also see Bitterroot Flat, Dalles,
Grizzly, Norton, and Siria.)
FREE but choose a chore.
Open May 1 – Nov 1; dry camping
off-season.
18 scattered, screened tent sites.
Water, pit toilets, tables, fire rings.
Among ponderosa pine and talus.
Watch for bighorn sheep. Relax and fish.
14-day limit
4200 ft (1260 m)

## HAY CANYON

Lewis & Clark NF
(406) 791-7700
State map: E6

From UTICA, take SW gravel CR along
Judith River 12 miles (19.2 k). Continue
SW on FR 487 for 4.5 miles (7.2 k). (Also
see Indian Hill.)
FREE but choose a chore.
Open All Year.

▲ ▲ ▲ ▲ ▲ ▲ ▲ ▲ ▲ ▲ ▲ ▲ ▲ ▲ ▲ ▲ ▲ ▲ ▲ ▲ ▲ ▲ ▲ ▲ ▲

9 sites. Pit toilets, tables, fire rings.
On quiet creek.
Relax, picnic, walk, perhaps fish.
NO water/trash arrangements (pack it
out). 14-day limit.
5250 ft (1575 m)

## HELL'S CANYON

Gallatin NF
(406) 932-5155
State map: G6

From BIG TIMBER, head S on US 298 for
35.5 miles (64.8 k). Last 10.5 miles
(16.8 k) are gravel. (See Aspen, Big
Beaver, Chippy Park, Falls Creek, and
Hick's Park.)
**FREE** but choose a chore.
Open All Year.
11 close, open sites with some screening.
Pit toilets, tables, grills.
Within walking distance of Boulder
River and trail access to Absaroka-
Beartooth Wilderness.
Base camp for extended hikes or
exploring immediate area. Fishing too.
NO water/trash arrangements. Camp
only in designated sites. 15-day/16-ft
limits. Crowded weekends. Often inac-
cessible in winter.
6000 ft (1800 m)

## HICKS PARK

Gallatin NF
(406) 932-5155
State map: G6

From BIG TIMBER, head S on US 298 for
46 miles (73.6 k)–gravel last 19 miles
(30.4 k). (See Aspen, Big Beaver, Chippy
Park, Falls Creek, and Hell's Canyon.)
**FREE** but choose a chore.
Open All Year.
16 close, open sites with some screening.
Water, pit toilets, tables, grills.
Next to Boulder River with trail to
Absaroka-Beartooth Wilderness.
Make base for extended hiking or
fishing. Also, sight harlequin duck.
No trash facilities. Camp only in
designated sites. 15-day/32-ft limits.
Crowded weekends. Often inaccessible
in winter.
6400 ft (1920 m)

## HOME GULCH

Lewis & Clark NF
(406) 791-7700
State map: C3

From AUGUSTA, drive NW on
CR 1081/FR 108 for 21.5 miles (34.4 k).
**Mortimer Gulch** (23 sites, no water but
$5) is another 2.5 miles (4 k).
**$4.** Open May 15–Nov 25.
15 sites. Water, pit toilets, tables, fire
rings, boat ramp.
On Sun River with several trails.
Walk nature trail or trek into Bob
Marshall Wilderness. Boat, swim, or fish.
14-day/16-ft limits.
4400 ft (1320 m)

## HOWARD LAKE

Kootenai NF
(406) 293-7741
State map: B1

From LIBBY, take US 2 S for 12 miles
(19.2 k). Turn Right (W) on FR 231 and
drive 12 miles (19.2 k). (Also see Lake
Creek.)
**$5.** Open May 20–Oct 1.
10 (2 tent-only) close, open sites. &
Water, pit toilets, tables, fire rings, boat
launch (small boats), beach.
Beside picture-pretty lake a few miles
from Cabinet Mountains Wilderness.
Use as base for extensive exploration of
wilderness or as pleasant getaway.
14-day limit.
4120 ft (1236 m)

## INDIAN HILL

Lewis & Clark NF
(406) 791-7700
State map: E6

From UTICA, take SW gravel CR along
Judith River about 12 miles (19.2 k).
Continue SW on FR 487 for 5.5 miles
(8.8 k). (Also see Hay Canyon.)
**FREE** but choose a chore.
Open All Year.
7 sites.
Water, pit toilets, tables, fire rings.
On quiet creek in Little Belt Mountains.
Relax, picnic, walk, and perhaps, fish.
No trash arrangements. 14-day limit.
5300 ft (1590 m)

▲ ▲ ▲ ▲ ▲ ▲ ▲ ▲ ▲ ▲ ▲ ▲ ▲ ▲ ▲ ▲ ▲ ▲ ▲ ▲ ▲ ▲ ▲

## INDIAN TREES

Bitterroot NF
(406) 821-3201
State map: F2
From SULA, head 6 miles (9.6 k) S on
US 93. Turn Right (SW) on FR 729 and
go 1 mile (1.6 k).
$5. Open Jun 15–Sep 15.
18 close, open sites.
Water, pit toilets, tables.
On creek near several hot springs and
historic Indian trees.
Swim, fish, hike, or soak.
14-day/22-ft limits.
5000 ft (1500 m)

## INTAKE FAS

MT FWP (406) 232-4365
State map: D12
From GLENDIVE, take
MT 16 N for 17 miles (27.2 k). Turn
Right (E) on CR and go 2 miles (3.2 k).
$5. Open All Year.
75 scattered sites in choice of open or
screened settings. Water, pit toilets, ta-
bles, pay phone, boat ramp, seasonal
store with ice and rentals.
With beach on Yellowstone River in
mixed hardwood river bottom.
Discover Montana's best paddlefish spot.
Also, boat and relax.
Crowded during paddlefish season
(May 15–Jun 30). 14-day limit.
2000 ft (600 m)

## ITCH-KEP-PE CITY PARK

Columbus City Parks
(406) 322-5313
State map: G7
Go 1 mile (1.6 k) S on MT 78 from Exit
408 of I-90 in COLUMBUS.
FREE but donations appreciated.
Open Mar–Nov.
49 scattered, open sites.
Water, flush and pit toilets, tables, grills,
fire rings, boat ramp, firewood.
Under cottonwood along banks of
Yellowstone River in pine-covered hills
with views of Beartooth Mountains.
Boat and fish river or just relax.
10-day limit. Mosquitos.
3575 ft (1071 m)

## JAMES KIPP

BLM (406) 538-7461
State map: C8
From LEWISTON, head
NE on US 191 for 63 miles (100.8 k).
FREE but choose a chore.
Open All Year.
15 sites.
Pit toilets, tables, fire rings, boat ramp.
On Missouri River in Charles Russell
NWR.
Fish, boat, watch wildlife, or hike.
NO water.

## J C WEST PARK

Glendive City Parks
State map: D12
Find in GLENDIVE.
FREE but choose a chore.
Open May 1–Sep 30.
20 sites. Water, flush toilets, tables, grills,
boat ramp, tennis courts, playground,
dump station.
On Yellowstone River.
Fish, boat, play, or relax.
2-day/24-ft limits.

## JENNINGS CAMP

Bitterroot NF
(406) 821-3201
State map: F2
From SULA, go 1 mile (1.6 k) W on
US 93. Turn Right (NE) on CR 472. Go
10 miles (16 k). (See Martin Creek.)
FREE but choose a chore.
Open Jun 15–Sep 15.
5 close, open sites.
Water, pit toilets, tables.
On East Fork of Bitterroot River.
Explore area or just relax.
14-day/22-ft limits.
5000 ft (1500 m)

## JIMMY JOE

Custer NF (406) 657-6361
State map: G7
From ROSCOE, head SW
on CR 177 for 7 miles (11.2 k). Continue
SW on FR 177 for 3 miles (4.8 k). In
3 more miles (4.8 k), find **East Rosebud
Camp** with water and fees.
FREE but choose a chore.

Open May 27–Sep 5.
10 close, screened sites.
Pit toilets, tables, fire rings.
In woods along creek.
Use as base for hiking trails around East Rosebud Lake. Take advantage of lake activities. Relax in camp.
NO water. 14-day limit.
5600 ft (1680 m)

## JUDITH LANDING SRA

MT FWP (406) 454-3441
State map: B6
From BIG SANDY, take CR 236 SE for 44 miles (70.4 k).
FREE but choose a chore.
Open May 15–Oct 15.
5 sites.
Water, pit toilets, tables, fire rings.
On Wild and Scenic Missouri River.
Fish and relax.
14-day limit.

## KADING

Helena NF (406) 449-5490
State map: E4
From ELLISTON, go about 1 mile (1.6 k) E on MT 12 to Little Blackfoot Rd. Turn Right (S). Go 15 miles (24 k).
FREE but choose a chore.
Open Jun 1–Sep 15.
16 close, open sites. Water, pit toilets, tables, fire rings, corral.
Next to Little Blackfoot River.
Hike Upper Little Blackfoot Trail with beaver ponds and nice picnic spot 5 miles upstream. Fish at camp.
No trash pickup. 14-day/25-ft limits.
6000 ft (1800 m)

## KILBRENNEN LAKE

Kootenai NF
(406) 295-4693
State map: A1
From TROY, go NW on US 2 for 2.7 miles (4.3 k) to FR 2394. Turn Right (NE) and continue 9.8 miles (15.7 k). (Also see Yaak Falls and Yaak River.)
FREE but choose a chore.
Open May 20–Sep 30; camping allowed off-season.

5 close, open sites.
Pit toilets, tables, fire rings.
On pretty lake.
Put in a canoe or drop a line. Explore secluded region.
NO water/trash arrangements (pack it out). 14-day limit.
2900 ft (870 m)

## LADYSMITH

Deerlodge NF
(406) 494-2147
State map: F4
From BUTTE, take I-15 N for 20 miles (32 k) to Bernice Exit. Drive W on FR 82 for 4 miles (6.4 k). (Also see Mormon Creek and Whitehouse.)
FREE but choose a chore.
Open May 22–Sep 15.
Undesignated sites.
Pit toilets, tables, fire rings.
Fish, picnic, or relax along creek.
NO water. 14-day/16-ft limits.
5500 ft (1650 m)

## LAKE CREEK

Kootenai NF
(406) 293-7741
State map: B1
From LIBBY, take US 2 S for 24 miles (38.4 k) Turn Right (W) on FR 231 and drive about 7 miles (11.2 k). (Also see Howard Lake.)
FREE but choose a chore.
Open May 20–Oct 1; dry camping off-season.
4 close, open sites.
Water, pit toilets, tables, fire rings.
Along secluded, scenic Lake and Bramlett creeks near Cabinet Mountains Wilderness.
Use as base for extensive exploration of wilderness (4 trails) or as pleasant getaway. Pick berries in late summer; ski and snowmobile in winter.
No trash arrangements. 14-day limit.
3360 ft (1008 m)

▲ ▲ ▲ ▲ ▲ ▲ ▲ ▲ ▲ ▲ ▲ ▲ ▲ ▲ ▲ ▲ ▲ ▲ ▲ ▲ ▲ ▲ ▲ ▲ ▲ ▲ ▲

## LAKE ELWELL

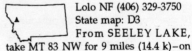

BOR (406) 657-6202
State map: B5
**FREE** but choose a chore.
Open All Year.
Undesignated, scattered sites.
14-day limit. Mosquitos and rattlesnakes.

### ▲ Island RA

From CHESTER, go S on gravel roads
about 18 miles (28.8 k) to marina, which
offers water, dump station, flush toilets,
showers, hot tub, store with ice and
rentals, boat ramp, pay phone.
Pit toilets, tables, grills, fire rings.
In open prairie setting with some trees
and shrubs.
Swimming, boating, river floating,
fishing—even derbies. Ice fishing and
snowmobiling in winter.
High winds at times. Crowded.
3016 ft (903 m)

### ▲ North Bootlegger

From SHELBY, go E on US 2 about
25 miles (40 k). Turn Right (S) on gravel
road (Left takes you to Galata).
Pit toilets, tables, fire rings, grills, boat
ramp.
In secluded-feeling, open prairie setting
with few trees and native grasses.
Access lake to swim, boat, ski, or fish.
Ice fish and snowmobile in winter.
No trash pickup. High winds.
3051 ft (915 m)

### ▲ Sanford Park

From CHESTER, go S on gravel roads
about 18 miles (28.8 k)–below Tiber
Dam.
37 (34 tent-only), scattered, open sites.
Water, pit toilets, tables, grills, fire rings,
boat ramp (to river), ball fields,
playground.
Below dam and Lake Elwell on Marias
River with cottonwood and grass areas.
Enjoy full range of water and land
sports, including swimming, boating,
fishing, and hiking.
Crowded.
2836 ft (849 m)

### ▲ South Bootlegger

From LEDGER, go E on 366. Watch for
signs and gravel road to N–site on S
side of lake.

Pit toilets, tables, fire rings, boat ramp,
beach.
In open prairie setting with no trees but
native grasses.
Enjoy lake by swimming, boating, skiing,
and fishing. Ice fishing and snowmobiling in winter.
High winds. Crowded.
3016 ft (903 m)

### ▲ VFW

From CHESTER, go S on gravel roads
about 18 miles (28.8 k)–by Tiber Dam.
Pit toilets, tables, grills, fire rings, boat
ramp, beach, picnic shelters.
Close to river among trees and scrub
with scenic views of Marias Rim and
Mushroom Rock formations.
Find range of water sports nearby.
3023 ft (906 m)

### ▲ Willow Creek

From LOTHAIR, go S of US 2 on gravel
road to area.
Pit toilets, tables, fire rings, boat ramp.
In open prairie setting with no trees as
yet but native grasses.
Access lake to swim, boat, waterski, or
fish. Ice fish and snowmobile in winter.
High winds. Crowded.
3016 ft (903 m)

## LAKE INEZ

Lolo NF (406) 329-3750
State map: D3
From SEELEY LAKE,
take MT 83 NW for 9 miles (14.4 k)–on
N end of lake.
**FREE** but choose a chore.
Open All Year (when snow gone).
3 scattered, open sites.
Pit toilets, tables, fire rings, boat ramp.
On lakeshore midway between Lake Ala
and Seeley Lake.
Swim, waterski, boat, fish, or hike.
NO water/trash arrangements (pack it
out). 14-day limit.
4100 ft (1230 m)

## LAKE VIEW

Flathead NF
(406) 387-5243
State map: B2
From HUNGRY HORSE, take FR 895 SE

▲ ▲ ▲ ▲ ▲ ▲ ▲ ▲ ▲ ▲ ▲ ▲ ▲ ▲ ▲ ▲ ▲ ▲ ▲ ▲ ▲ ▲ ▲ ▲

for 19 miles (30.4 k). Look for small "camping" sign on Left (E). (See Graves Bay, Handkerchief Lake, and Lid Creek.)
**FREE** but choose a chore.
Open Jun 1–Sep 15; camping allowed off-season.
5 close, open sites.
Pit toilets, tables, grills, fire rings.
In cool mountainous woods on west side of Hungry Horse Reservoir.
Swim, fish, boat, and ski lake. Explore by foot, canoe, or mountain bike.
NO water/trash arrangements (pack it out). 14-day limit. No large vehicles.
3620 ft (1086 m)

## LANTIS SPRING

Custer NF (605) 797-4432
State map: F12
From CAMP CROOK, SD, take Tie Creek Rd W for 11 miles (17.6 k) then 8 miles (12.8 k) N on rough FRs.
**FREE** but choose a chore.
Open May 1–Nov 15; camping allowed off-season.
5 scattered, open sites. Spring water, pit toilets, tables, sun shelters, fire rings.
With sun shelters substituting for burned trees after devastating 1988 fire.
Enjoy secluded getaway and observe renewal after fire. Find Capitol Rock.
No trash facilities. 14-day/30-ft limits.
3900 ft (1170 m)

## LEE CREEK

Lolo NF (406) 329-3814
State map: E2
From LOLO, head W on US 12 for 26 miles (41.6 k). (Also see Lewis & Clark.)
**$5.** Open Memorial Day-Labor Day; dry camping off-season.
22 scattered, open sites with some screening.
Water, pit toilets, tables, fire rings.
Next to creek in mature pine-spruce.
Walk nature or hiking trails. Soak in nearby hot springs. Fish.
14-day limit. Quiet hours.
4400 ft (1320 m)

## LEWIS & CLARK

Lolo NF (406) 329-3814
State map: E2
From LOLO, go W on US 12 for 15 miles (24 k). (Also see Lee Creek.)
**$5.** Open Memorial Day-Labor Day; dry camping off-season.
22 scattered, open sites with some screening.
Water, pit toilets, tables, fire rings.
Next to Lolo Creek in mature larch-pine-spruce forest.
Hike trails. Fish creek. Mountain bike.
14-day limit. Crowded summer weekends. Quiet hours.
4400 ft (1320 m)

## LID CREEK

Flathead NF
(406) 387-5243
State map: B2
From HUNGRY HORSE, take FR 895 SE for 15 miles (24 k). Take winding gravel road on Left (E) 1.5 miles (2.4 k). (If camp too crowded, check out first road after you turn off FR 895. Also see Graves Bay, Handkerchief Lake, and Lake View)
**FREE** but choose a chore.
Open Jun 1–Sep 15; camping allowed off-season.
23 close, open sites. Pit toilets, tables, grills, fire rings, boat ramp dependent on water level.
In open woods on Hungry Horse Reservoir with scenic views of Great Bear Wilderness.
Swim, fish, boat, and ski lake. Explore area by canoe, foot, or mountain bike.
NO water/trash arrangements (pack it out). 14-day limit.
3570 ft (1071 m)

## LITTLE JOE

Beaverhead NF
(406) 832-3178
State map: G3
From WISE RIVER, take FR 484 (Wise River–Polaris Scenic Byway) S for 19.6 miles (31.4 k). (Also see Mono Creek and Willow.)

▲ ▲ ▲ ▲ ▲ ▲ ▲ ▲ ▲ ▲ ▲ ▲ ▲ ▲ ▲ ▲ ▲ ▲ ▲ ▲ ▲ ▲ ▲

FREE but choose a chore.
Open Jun 1 – Sep 30; dry camping
off-season.
4 close, open tent sites. Water (rusty), pit
toilets, tables, fire rings.
On bench among lodgepole pine above
scenic Wise River.
Explore, hike, fish, or relax.
No trash arrangements (pack it out).
14-day/22-ft limits. Crowded holidays.
7000 ft (2100 m)

## LITTLE THERRIAULT LAKE

Kootenai NF
(406) 882-4451
State map: A1

Take US 93 NW from FORTINE for
2.8 miles (4.5 k). Turn Right (NE) on
CR 114 and drive 3.2 miles (5.1 k).
Continue NE on FR 114 another
10.6 miles (17 k). Turn Left (W) on
FR 319 and drive 13.2 miles (21.1 k).
(Also see Big Therriault Lake.)
FREE but choose a chore.
Open Jul 1 – Nov 15; dry camping
off-season.
6 close, open sites. &
Water, pit toilets, tables, grills.
Near lake (carry small boats) and Ten
Lakes Scenic Area.
Excellent hiking and acceptable fishing.
No trash arrangements. 14-day limit.
5800 ft (1740 m)

## LOON LAKE

Kootenai NF
(406) 293-7741
State map: B1

From LIBBY, head E on MT 37 for only
.5 mile (800 m). Turn Left (N) on FR 68
(Pipe Creek Rd) and go about 18 miles
(28.8 k). Turn Left (W) on FR 471 and
drive another 3 miles (4.8 k).
FREE but choose a chore.
Open May 20 – Oct 1; camping allowed
off-season.
4 close, open sites.
Pit toilets, tables, fire rings, boat ramp.
On small, secluded lake at base of
mountains.
Canoe and fish. Watch for moose. Hike
along Seventeen mile Creek or to Tom

Poole Lake.
NO water/trash arrangements (pack it
out). 14-day/20-ft limits.
3600 ft (1080 m)

## LOST JOHNNY CAMP

Flathead NF
(406) 387-5243
State map: B2

From HUNGRY HORSE, take FR 895 SE
for 9 miles (14.4 k) across dam. (Also see
Lost Johnny Point.)
$5. Open Jun 1 – Sep 15; dry camping
off-season.
5 close, screened sites. Water, pit toilets,
tables, grills, fire rings.
In grass and woods on beautiful Hungry
Horse Reservoir.
Swim, fish, boat, and ski lake. Relax.
No trash pickup. 14-day/22-ft limits.
3600 ft (1080 m)

## LOST JOHNNY POINT

Flathead NF
(406) 387-5243
State map: B2

From HUNGRY HORSE, take FR 895 SE
for 10 miles (16 k) across dam. (Also see
Lost Johnny Camp.)
$5. Open Jun 1 – Sep 15; dry camping
off-season.
21 close, screened sites. &
Water, pit toilets, tables, grills, fire rings,
paved pads, gravel boat ramp.
In woods on Hungry Horse Reservoir.
Swim, fish, boat, and ski lake. Walk
nature and Jimmy Ridge trails.
No trash facilities. 14-day/30-ft limits.
3570 ft (1071 m)

## LOWLAND

Deerlodge NF
(406) 494-2147
State map: F4

From BUTTE, take I-15 N for 8 miles
(12.8 k) to Elk Park Exit. Drive W on
FR 442 for 8 miles (12.8 k). Turn Left on
FR 9485 and go 1.5 miles (2.4 k).
FREE but choose a chore.
Open May 22 – Sep 15.
7 close, open sites. &
Water, pit toilets, tables, fire rings.

▲ ▲ ▲ ▲ ▲ ▲ ▲ ▲ ▲ ▲ ▲ ▲ ▲ ▲ ▲ ▲ ▲ ▲ ▲ ▲ ▲ ▲ ▲ ▲ ▲ ▲ ▲ ▲

Fish, picnic, or relax on quiet creek.
14-day/22-ft limits.
6000 ft (1800 m)

## MANY PINES

Lewis & Clark NF
(406) 791-7700
State map: D6

From NEIHART, drive S on US 89 for
3.5 miles (5.6 k). **Kings Hill** (14 sites,
same fees) is another 5.5 miles (8.8 k) or
there's **Aspen** (6 sites, same fees) 4 miles
(6.4 k) N of NEIHART.
$5. Open May 15–Dec 1.
25 (4 RV-only) sites.
Water, pit toilets, tables, fire rings.
On Belt Creek in scenic area.
Hike, mountain bike, and explore.
14-day/22-ft limits.
6000 ft (1800 m)

## MARTEN CREEK

Kootenai NF
(406) 827-3534
State map: B1

From NOXON, go SE about 10 miles
(16 k) on CR/FR 2231. (Also see North
Shore.)
FREE but choose a chore.
Open Apr 23–Oct 30; camping allowed
off-season.
4 close, open sites. &
Pit toilets, tables, fire rings, boat ramp.
On western shore of beautiful lake.
Boat, fish, enjoy scenery, and relax.
NO water/trash facilities. 14-day limit.
2200 ft (660 m)

## MARTIN CREEK

Bitterroot NF
(406) 821-3201
State map: F2

From SULA, go 1 mile (1.6 k) W on
US 93. Turn Right (NE) on CR 472. Drive
4 miles (6.4 k) to FR 80. Turn NE and go
12 miles (19.2 k). (See Jennings Camp.)
FREE but choose a chore.
Open Jun 15–Sep 15.
7 close, open sites.
Water, pit toilets, tables.
Explore, fish, or picnic on creek.
14-day/22-ft limits.

## MARTINSDALE RESERVOIR FAS

MT FWP (406) 454-3441
State map: E6
Follow signs off US 12 E

of MARTINSDALE.
FREE but choose a chore.
Open All Year.
Undesignated, scattered sites. &
Pit toilets, tables in 2 picnic shelters.
Next to lake with views of surrounding
hills and mountains.
Swim, boat, or fish lake. Hike and
birdwatch.
NO water/trash arrangements (pack it
out). 14-day limit. Extreme water draw-
down in summer.
3500 ft (1050 m)

## MAY CREEK

Beaverhead NF
(406) 689-3243
State map: F2

From WISDOM, take MT 43 W for
18 miles (28.8 k).
$4. Open Jun 20–Sep 1; dry camping
off-season.
21 close, screened sites. Water, pit toilets,
tables, grills, fire rings.
In northern West Big Hole Mountains.
Enjoy several nearby hiking trails.
14-day limit. Crowded holidays.
6300 ft (1890 m)

## MCGREGOR LAKE

Kootenai NF
(406) 293-7773
State map: B2

From KALISPELL, go 32 miles (51.2 k)
W on US 2.
$4. Open May 15–Sep 30; dry camping
off-season.
15 close, open sites.
Water, pit toilets, tables, fire rings, boat
launch (small boats).
On lake surrounded by mountains.
Waterskiing, boating, fishing, and swimming in summer; ice fishing, skiing, and
snowmobiling in winter.
14-day limit.
3900 ft (1170 m)

## MILL CREEK

Beaverhead NF
(406) 842-5432
State map: G4

From SHERIDAN, take narrow, dirt road
with "Mill Creek Recreation Area" sign
for 6 rough miles (9.6 k) E. (See Balanced
Rock and Branham Lakes.)

FREE but choose a chore.

Open May 15 – Nov 1; dry camping
off-season.

9 scattered, open sites.

Water, pit toilets, tables, fire rings.

In quiet canyon bottom near creek under
large lodgepole pine.

Relaxing, picnicking, or fishing.

No trash arrangements. 14-day limit.
Crowded holiday weekends.

6430 ft (1929 m)

## MILLS FALLS

Lewis & Clark NF
(406) 791-7700
State map: C4

From CHOTEAU, go 5.5 miles (8.8 k) N
on US 89. Turn Left (W) on CR 144 and
drive about 19 miles (30.4 k). Turn Left
(S) on CR 109 then Right (W) as road
changes to FR 109–total of about 9 miles
(14.4 k). (Also see Elko.)

FREE but choose a chore.

Open Jun 1–Sep 15.

4 sites. Pit toilets, tables, fire rings.

Beneath Bear Top Mountain near
waterfalls.

Reflect, hike, fish, or picnic.

NO water/trash arrangements (pack it
out). 14-day limit.

## MINER LAKE

Beaverhead NF
(406) 689-3243
State map: G3

From JACKSON, take FR 182 SW for
14 miles (22.4 k).

$4. Open Jun 20–Sep 1; dry camping
off-season.

17 close, screened sites.

Water, pit toilets, tables, fire rings.

On shore of lake in heart of West Big
Hole Mountains.

Canoe and swim. Fish and hike. Explore

backroads.

14-day limit. Crowded holidays.

7000 ft (2100 m)

## MISSOURI RIVER
## RECREATION ROAD FAS

MT FWP (406) 454-3441
State map: D4

Find road 30 miles (48 k)
N of HELENA (E and parallel to I-15).

FREE but choose a chore.

Open All Year.

Scattered spots along road for
several miles. One developed site near
CRAIG with $5 fee.

Pit toilets, tables, fire rings, boat ramp.

On scenic section of Missouri River.

Boat. Fish for world-class trout. Hike
about Helena or Lewis & Clark NF,
Beartooth Game Range, or Holter Lake.

NO water. Crowded holiday weekends.

## M–K

Custer NF (406) 446-2103
State map: G7

Take US 212 S from RED
LODGE for 12 miles (19.2 k) to FR 421.
Turn Right (SW) and go 4 miles (6.4 k).
Pass series of 3 more developed
alternatives, known as **Rock Creek
Camps**, with fees.

FREE but choose a chore.

Open May 25–Sep 5; camping allowed
off-season.

10 scattered, open sites.

Pit toilets, tables, fire rings.

Along south side of Rock Creek on
glacial moraine with pine.

Excellent hiking by entering Absaroka
Wilderness. Fishing too.

NO water/trash arrangements (pack it
out). 10-day/20-ft limits.

7500 ft (2250 m)

## MONO CREEK

Beaverhead NF
(406) 832-3178
State map: G3

From WISE RIVER, take FR 484 (Wise
River–Polaris Scenic Byway) S for
23 miles (36.8 k). Turn Left (E) on dirt
access road and go 1 mile (1.6 k). (Also

see Little Joe and Willow.)
**FREE** but choose a chore.
Open Jun 1–Sep 30; dry camping off-season.
5 close, open sites.
Water, pit toilets, tables, fire rings.
Along Happy Creek in wooded valley.
Explore East Pioneer Mountains or nearby ghost town. Hike to Four Lakes. Dig for gems at Crystal Park.
No trash arrangements. 14-day/16-ft limits. Crowded Jun–Aug weekends.
7000 ft (2100 m)

## MONTANA GULCH

BLM (406) 538-7461
State map: C8
From LANDUSKY, go NW on CR for .5 mile (800 m).
**FREE** but choose a chore.
Open May 1–Nov 30.
5 sites. Pit toilets, tables, fire rings.
On creek in hills.
Hike, bike, or relax.
NO water. 14-day limit.

## MONTURE

Lolo NF (406) 329-3750
State map: D3
From OVANDO, take Monture Rd (FR 89) N 9 miles (14.4 k).
**FREE** but choose a chore.
Open Jun 15–Sep 30.
5 sites. Pit toilets, tables, fire rings.
On creek.
Access Bob Marshall and Scapegoat Wildernesses for extended hiking. Fish.
NO water (1 mile away). 14-day limit.
4200 ft (1260 m)

## MOOSE CREEK

Helena NF (406) 449-5490
State map: E4
From HELENA, go about 8 miles (12.8 k) W on MT 12. Turn Left (S) on gravel Ten Mile Rd toward Rimini and drive 5 miles (8 k).
**FREE** but choose a chore.
Open Jun 1–Sep 15.
10 close, open sites.
Water, pit toilets, tables, fire rings.
Along Ten mile Creek.

Enjoy hiking Continental Divide Trail and picnicking at Ten mile Picnic Area (1 mile up road) with Environmental Education Trail and field for games.
No trash pickup. 14-day/20-ft limits.
4880 ft (1464 m)

## MOOSE CREEK

Lewis & Clark NF
(406) 791-7700
State map: E6
From WHITE SULPHUR SPRINGS, take US 89 N for 18 miles (28.8 k). Turn Left (W) on FR 119 and drive 5.5 miles (8.8 k). Turn Right (N) on FR 204 for 3 miles (4.8 k). For developed **Jumping Creek** (15 sites with fees), continue on US 89 N past 119 cutoff for another 4 miles (6.4 k).
**FREE** but choose a chore.
Open Jun 1–Oct 15.
9 sites.
Water, pit toilets, tables, fire rings.
Fish on quiet creek. Walk up Moose Mountain or along Allen Creek.
No trash arrangements. 14-day limit.
5250 ft (1575 m)

## MOOSE LAKE DISPERSED CAMPING AREA

Flathead NF
(406) 892-4372
State map: B2
From COLUMBIA FALLS, head N on CR 486 (North Fork Rd) for 20 miles (32 k) to Big Creek Rd. Turn Left (W) on FR 316 (Big Creek) and go 17.5 miles (28 k) turning Right first on FR 315 (Hallowat) then FR 5207 (Kletomus).
**FREE** but choose a chore.
Open May-Sep; camping allowed off-season.
1 site with pit toilet, table; other sites scattered along road.
Next to Moose Lake.
Fishing and canoeing popular (carry craft about 150 ft to lake). Hike to Moose Peak or into Deadhorse Basin. Pick wild berries in season.
NO water/trash arrangements (pack it out–remember this is grizzly country).
Keep vehicles away from shoreline. No

▲ ▲ ▲ ▲ ▲ ▲ ▲ ▲ ▲ ▲ ▲ ▲ ▲ ▲ ▲ ▲ ▲ ▲ ▲ ▲ ▲ ▲

trailer space.
5655 ft (1695 m)

## MORMON CREEK

Deerlodge NF
(406) 494-2147
State map: F4
From BUTTE, take I-15 N for 20 miles
(32 k) to Bernice Exit. Drive W on FR 82
for 2 miles (3.2 k). (Also see Ladysmith
and Whitehouse.)
FREE but choose a chore.
Open May 22–Sep 19.
16 sites. Pit toilets, tables, fire rings.
Fish, picnic, and relax along creek.
NO water. 14-day/16-ft limits.
5500 ft (1650 m)

## MURRAY BAY

Flathead NF
(406) 387-5243
State map: B2
From MARTIN CITY, take gravel
logging road, FR 38, SE for 22 miles
(35.2 k). (Also see Devils Corkscrew.)
FREE but choose a chore.
Open Jun 1–Sep 15; camping allowed
off-season.
46 close, screened sites.
Pit toilets, tables, grills.
In woods on eastern banks of Hungry
Horse Reservoir.
Swimming, boating and fishing. Hiking
with wildlife/wildflower viewing and
photo taking opportunities nearby.
NO water/trash arrangements (pack it
out). 14-day limit.
3570 ft (1071 m)

## MUSSIGBROD

Beaverhead NF
(406) 689-3243
State map: F3
From WISDOM, take MT 43 W for
1 mile (1.6 k). Turn Right (N) on Lower
North Fork Rd. Drive 8 miles (12.8 k). At
sign, turn Left (NW) on rough FR 573
and go about 10 miles (16 k).
FREE but choose a chore.
Open Jul 5–Sep 1; dry camping
off-season.
5 close, screened sites.

Water, pit toilets, tables, fire rings.
On shore of 100-acre lake with great
access to Anaconda-Pintler Wilderness.
Take a hike or swim in cool waters. Boat
and fish.
No trash arrangements (pack it out).
14-day limit. No large vehicles.
6500 ft (1950 m)

## NELSON CREEK

COE (406) 526-3411
State map: C10
Take MT 24 S from
FORT PECK about 45 miles (72 k). Turn
Right on gravel road. (Also see Flat Lake
and Rock Creek SRA.)
FREE but choose a chore.
Open All Year.
20 close, open sites.
Pit toilets, tables, fire rings, boat ramp.
On east side of Fort Peck Lake.
Boat, fish, observe wildlife (especially
birds), and relax.
NO water/trash arrangements (pack it
out–clean it up). 14-day limit.
2250 ft (675 m)

## NELSON RESERVOIR

BOR (406) 657-6202
State map: B9
From MALTA, go E on
US 2 for 15 miles (24 k). Turn Left (N) at
Sleeping Buffalo turnoff. Drive 2 miles
(3.2 k).
FREE but choose a chore.
Open All Year.
10 scattered, open sites. Water, pit toilets,
tables, fire rings, boat ramp.
On shore of reservoir.
Swim, boat, fish, and ski, or just relax.
Birdwatch here and at Bowdoin NWR.
14-day limit.
2450 ft (735 m)

## NORTH DICKEY LAKE

Kootenai NF
(406) 296-2536
State map: A1
From STRYKER, go 4.7 miles (7.5 k) NW
on US 93. Turn Left.
$5. Open May 16–Sep 15; dry camping
off-season.

25 (4 tent-only), close, open sites.
Water, pit toilets, tables, grills, boat launch (small boats).
With beach on lake but near highway (more desirable South Dickey camp presently closed to camping).
Enjoy opportunities for swimming, waterskiing, boating, and fishing.
14-day limit.
3100 ft (930 m)

## NORTH SHORE

Kootenai NF
(406) 827-3534
State map: B1
On North side of Noxon Rapids Reservoir. Take MT 200 NW from TROUT CREEK about 2.5 miles (4 k) to MT 10A. Turn Left (NW) and go .5 mile (800 m). (Also see Marten Creek.)
$5. Open Apr 23–Oct 30.
12 close, open sites.
Water, flush and pit toilets, tables, fire rings, boat ramp.
On scenic lake, fish, boat, waterski, and swim (for cool water buffs). Hike too.
14-day limit.
2400 ft (720 m)

## NORTH VAN HOUTEN

Beaverhead NF
(406) 689-3243
State map: G3
From JACKSON, take FR 181 (Bloody Dick Rd) S for 12 miles (19.2 k). (Also see South Van Houten.)
FREE but choose a chore.
Open Jun 15–Oct 1; camping allowed off-season.
3 close, open sites.
Pit toilets, tables, fire rings.
On northern shore of Van Houten Lake with beautiful mountain views.
Swim in cool waters or fish and canoe.
NO water/trash facilities. 14-day limit.
6700 ft (2010 m)

## NORTON

Lolo NF (406) 329-3814
State map: E3
From CLINTON, take
I-90 E for 5 miles (8 k). Exit onto FR 102

(Rock Creek Rd) S and drive 10.5 miles (16.8 k) – first of six free camps with tent sites along Rock Creek. (Also see Bitterroot Flat, Dalles, Grizzly, Harry's Flat, and Siria.)
FREE but choose a chore.
Open All Year.
10 (5 tent-only), close, screened sites.
Water, pit toilets, tables, fire rings.
On valley bottom near creek.
Relax and fish.
14-day limit.
4100 ft (1230 m)

## OROFINO

Deerlodge NF
(406) 846-1770
State map: E4
From DEER LODGE, take FR 82 SE for 13 miles (20.8 k).
FREE but choose a chore.
Open May 22–Sep 15.
10 sites.
Water, pit toilets, tables, fire rings.
In quiet woods with excellent hiking.
14-day/22-ft limits.
6600 ft (1980 m)

## PALACE BUTTE

Gallatin NF
(406) 587-6701
State map: G5
From BOZEMAN, head S on CR 243 for 8 miles (12.8 k). Turn Left (SE) on FR 64 and go 15 miles (24 k). (Also see Abbot and Blackmore.)
FREE but choose a chore.
Open Jun 15–Sep 15.
3 close, open sites.
Pit toilets, tables, fire rings.
On Hyalite Creek at base of The Mummy.
Take trail up creek. Fish and relax.
NO water/trash arrangements (pack it out). 14-day limit.
6700 ft (2010 m)

## PALISADES

Custer NF (406) 446-2103
State map: G7
From south side of RED LODGE, take FR 71 W for 1 mile (1.6 k)

▲ ▲ ▲ ▲ ▲ ▲ ▲ ▲ ▲ ▲ ▲ ▲ ▲ ▲ ▲ ▲ ▲ ▲ ▲ ▲ ▲ ▲ ▲ ▲ ▲

to FR 3010. Drive another 2 miles (3.2 k).
FREE but choose a chore.
Open May 25–Sep 5; camping allowed
off-season.
7 sites. Pit toilets, tables, fire rings, group
picnic area.
Beneath aspen, spruce, and pine in
narrow canyon.
Enjoy nice getaway.
NO water/trash arrangements (pack it
out). 10-day/20-ft limits.
6400 ft (1920 m)

## PARK LAKE

Helena NF (406) 449-5490
State map: E4
From CLANCY, go about
1 mile (1.6 k) N on CR 426. Turn Left
(W) on CR 4000 and drive 8 miles
(12.8 k). Continue 6 miles (9.6 k) W on
FR 4009 (Lump Gulch Rd).
FREE but choose a chore.
Open Jun 1–Sep 15.
22 (7 tent-only) close, open sites.
Water, pit toilets, tables, fire rings.
On lake with no motors allowed.
Canoe, fish, hike, or picnic.
No trash facilities. 14-day/20-ft limits.
6360 ft (1908 m)

## PETE CREEK

Kootenai NF
(406) 295-4693
State map: A1
From YAAK, go 2 miles (3.2 k) SW on
FH 92. (See Red Top and White Tail.)
FREE but choose a chore.
Open Jun 1–Sep 30; dry camping
off-season.
13 close, open sites.
Water, pit toilets, tables, fire rings.
At Yaak River and Pete Creek.
Scenic relaxing and fishing.
No trash arrangements. 14-day limit.
3000 ft (900 m)

## PIGEON CREEK

Deerlodge NF
(406) 287-3223
State map: F4
From WHITEHALL, head W on MT 2
for 15 miles (24 k). Turn Left (S) on dirt

FR 668 for 5 miles (8 k). (Also see Toll
Mountain.)
FREE but choose a chore.
Open May 22–Sep 15.
6 sites.
Water, pit toilets, tables, fire rings.
Hike, explore, or fish along creek.
14-day limit. No trailers.
5900 ft (1770 m)

## PIKES GULCH

Helena NF (406) 449-5201
State map: E5
From YORK, head N on
FR 138 about 18 miles (28.8 k).
FREE but choose a chore.
Open Jun 1–Sep 15.
5 close, open sites.
Pit toilets, tables, fire rings.
In remote, isolated spot.
Good hiking in area (pick up hiking
packet from Helena Ranger District).
Locate old sapphire mines.
NO water/trash arrangements (pack it
out). 14-day/25-ft limits.
6200 ft (1860 m)

## PINE GROVE

Custer NF (406) 446-2103
State map: G7
From FISHTAIL, go SW
on MT 425 for 6 miles (9.6 k) to FR 72.
Go S for 8 rough miles (12.8 k). (Also see
Emerald Lake.)
$5. Open May 25–Sep 5; dry camping
off-season.
45 sites (some close, others scattered) in
open setting. Water, pit toilets, tables,
grills, fire rings.
On both sides of West Rosebud Creek.
Fishing popular here but take trail leading to more remote spots.
No trash facilities (pack it out to dumpster 8 miles up road). 10-day limit.
5800 ft (1740 m)

## PINTLER

Beaverhead NF
(406) 832-3178
State map: F3
From WISDOM, go N on MT 43 for
16 miles (25.6 k). Turn Left (W) on

▲ ▲ ▲ ▲ ▲ ▲ ▲ ▲ ▲ ▲ ▲ ▲ ▲ ▲ ▲ ▲ ▲ ▲ ▲ ▲ ▲ ▲ ▲ ▲ ▲ ▲

gravel CR 1251 (North Big Hole Rd). Go
5.5 miles (8.8 k). Turn Right (N) on
FR 185 (Pintler Creek Rd). Go 5 miles
(8 k).
FREE but choose a chore.
Open Jun 1–Sep 30; dry camping
off-season.
4 close, open sites.
Water, pit toilets, fire rings.
In lodgepole pine, along soothing creek
next to small, shallow Pintler Lake.
Make day hike past waterfalls, to Pintler
Meadows, beside Pintler Peaks, to Pintler
Pass. Watch for elk and mountain goat.
Fish and boat (no motors). Watch birds
and relax.
14-day limit. Crowded holidays.
6300 ft (1890 m)

## PISHKUN RESERVOIR FAS

MT FWP (406) 454-3441
State map: C4
From CHOTEAU, head
SW on CR for 17 miles (27.2 k).
FREE but choose a chore.
Open All Year.
Undesignated, scattered, open sites.
Pit toilets, tables, fire rings, boat ramp.
On high plains reservoir with beautiful
views of Rocky Mountains.
Swim, boat, waterski, or fish lake. Hike
and watch birds.
NO water. 14-day limit. Water draw-
down in summer.

## POINT PLEASANT

Swan River SF
(406) 754-2301
State map: C2
Take MT 83 S from SWAN LAKE for
6 miles (9.6 k). Turn Right (W) on dirt
road and drive about .25 mile (400 m).
FREE but choose a chore.
Open Apr–Nov; camping allowed
off-season.
12 close, screened sites.
Stream water (must be treated), pit
toilets, tables, grills, fire rings.
In dense woods near Swan River.
Enjoy scenic views. Fish, swim, boat,
raft, and hike in summer. Cross-country
ski in winter.

No trash pickup. Hunting in season.
3300 ft (990 m)

## POTOSI

Beaverhead NF
(406) 682-4253
State map: F4
From PONY, take CR 1601 SE for 3 miles
(4.8 k). Continue SW on FR 1501 for
5 miles (8 k).
FREE but choose a chore.
Open Jun 1–Sep 30.
15 sites.
Water, pit toilets, tables, fire rings.
On pretty South Willow Creek near
Potosi Hot Springs.
Hike to nearby lakes. Fish or relax.
14-day limit.
6200 ft (1860 m)

## RACETRACK

Deerlodge NF
(406) 846-1770
State map: E4
From DEER LODGE, take I-90 S for
11 miles (17.6 k) to Racetrack Exit. Head
W 1 mile (1.6 k) then turn Left (S) for
.75 mile (1.2 k). Turn Right (W) on
FR 169 and continue 1.5 miles (2.4 k).
FREE but choose a chore.
Open May 22–Sep 15.
13 close, open sites. &
Pit toilets, tables, fire rings.
Fishing on creek plus hiking nearby.
NO water. 14-day/16-ft limits.

## RATINE

Custer NF (406) 446-2103
State map: G7
From RED LODGE, take
US 212 S for 8 miles (12.8 k) to FR 379.
Turn Left (E) on gravel road and go
1 mile (1.6 k). (Also see Sheridan.)
FREE but choose a chore.
Open May 25–Sep 5; dry camping
off-season.
7 close, screened sites.
Water, pit toilets, tables, grills, fir rings.
In shade of willow and cottonwood
along Rock Creek.
Good choice for hiking and fishing.
Pack trash to ranger station. 10-day/22-ft

▲ ▲ ▲ ▲ ▲ ▲ ▲ ▲ ▲ ▲ ▲ ▲ ▲ ▲ ▲ ▲ ▲ ▲ ▲ ▲ ▲ ▲ ▲ ▲ ▲

limits. Crowded around holidays. Wet early in season.
6400 ft (1920 m)

## RED MEADOWS LAKE DISPERSED CAMPING AREA

Flathead NF
(406) 892-4372
State map: B2

From COLUMBIA FALLS, head N on CR 486 (North Fork Rd) about 42 miles (67.2 k). Turn Left (W) on CR 115 (Red Meadows Creek Rd). Go 11.5 miles (18.4 k).
FREE but choose a chore.
Open May-Sep; camping allowed off-season.
1 site with pit toilet and table.
Along road next to lake.
Fishing and canoeing. Hike to Nasukoin Mountain, Chain and Link Lakes, or along Whitefish Divide Trail.
NO water/trash arrangements (pack it out and remember this is grizzly country). Limited trailer space.
5540 ft (1662 m)

## RED MOUNTAIN

BLM (406) 494-5059
State map: G5
From NORRIS, take MT 84 E for 8 miles (12.8 k). Turn on gravel Bear Trap Rd. Go .25 mile (400 m).
FREE but choose a chore.
Open All Year.
11 scattered, open sites.
Water, pit toilets, tables, fire rings.
On loop next to Madison River.
Fishing and boating with some hiking possible (wilderness area to south).
No trash arrangements. 14-day limit.
4450 ft (1335 m)

## RED SHALE

Custer NF (406) 784-2344
State map: G11
From ASHLAND, go 6 miles (9.6 k) E on US 212.
FREE but choose a chore.
Open May 1-Nov 15.
14 scattered, open sites.

Pit toilets, tables, fire rings.
In sloping, piney setting with grass understory.
NO water–fee if restored. 14-day limit.
Crowded in hunting season. Ticks and snakes.
3000 ft (900 m)

## RED TOP

Kootenai NF
(406) 295-4693
State map: A1

From TROY, go 10.2 miles (16.3 k) NW on US 2 to MT 508. Turn Right (NE) and drive another 12.8 miles (20.5 k). (Also see Pete Creek and Whitetail.)
FREE but choose a chore.
Open Jun 1–Sep 30; camping allowed off-season.
3 close, open sites.
Pit toilets, tables, fire rings.
On Yaak River in private location.
Hike up Red Top or fish.
NO water/trash arrangements (pack it out). 14-day/22-ft limits.
3000 ft (900 m)

## RESERVOIR LAKE

Beaverhead NF
(406) 683-3900
State map: G3

From GRANT, go W on MT 324 for 7 miles (11.2 k) to Bloody Dick Rd. Turn Right (N) and drive 19 miles (30.4 k) on gravel road.
FREE but choose a chore.
Open Jun 16–Sep 15; dry camping off-season.
16 close, open sites. Water, pit toilets, tables, fire rings, boat ramp.
On pine-covered flat overlooking Reservoir Lake.
Fish and boat lake (no motors). Hike several trails in area.
No trash arrangements (pack it out). 14-day limit. Crowded holidays and weekends. Suitable for small vehicles.
7000 ft (2100 m)

▲ ▲ ▲ ▲ ▲ ▲ ▲ ▲ ▲ ▲ ▲ ▲ ▲ ▲ ▲ ▲ ▲ ▲ ▲ ▲ ▲ ▲ ▲ ▲ ▲ ▲

## RICHARDSON CREEK

Lewis & Clark NF
(406) 791-7700
State map: E6

From WHITE SULPHUR SPRINGS, head E on US 12 for 7 miles (11.2 k). Turn Right (S) on FR 211. Drive 5 miles (8 k). (Also see Grasshopper Creek.)
FREE but choose a chore.
Open Jun 1–Oct 15.
4 sites. Pit toilets, tables, fire rings.
Hike, fish, or picnic along creek.
NO water/trash arrangements (pack it out). 14-day limit.
6000 ft (1800 m)

## ROCK CREEK SRA

MT FWP (406) 228-9347
State map: C10
From FORT PECK, head S on MT 24 for 28 miles (44.8 k). Turn Right (W) on CR and go 7 miles (11.2 k). (Also see Bear Creek and Nelson Creek.)
FREE but choose a chore.
Open May 1–Sep 30.
20 sites. Water, pit toilets, tables, fire rings, boat ramp.
On eastern shore of Fort Peck Lake.
Boat, waterski, fish, or swim.
14-day limit.

## ROCK LAKE

Kootenai NF
(406) 882-4451
State map: A1

Leaving EUREKA, cross bridge at electric office and travel to top of hill. Go straight at gravel junction then 1 mile (1.6 k). Turn Left on FR 3656 and follow signs about 5 miles (8 k).
FREE but choose a chore.
Open May 16–Sep 15; camping allowed off-season.
6 close, open sites.
Pit toilets, tables, fire rings.
On small foothills lake.
Hike to several other lakes with acceptable fishing (Rock Lake has turned alkaline). Carry-in boats.
NO water/trash arrangements (pack it out). 14-day/20-ft limits.
3000 ft (900 m)

## ROMBO

Bitterroot NF
(406) 821-3269
State map: F2

From DARBY, go 4 miles (6.4 k) S on US 93. Turn Right (SW) on CR 473 and drive 18 miles (28.8 k).
$5. Open Jun 25–Sep 6.
16 close, open sites. &
Water, pit toilets, tables.
Near Rombo Creek and West Fork of Bitterroot River.
Fishing opportunities.
10-day/22-ft limits.
4400 ft (1320 m)

## RUBY RESERVOIR

BLM (406) 494-5059
State map: G4
From ALDER, take paved road SW to Reservoir–about 9 miles (14.4 k).
FREE but choose a chore.
Open All Year.
Undesignated, scattered, open sites.
Pit toilets, tables.
Along willow-lined shore.
Fish or gather rubies.
NO water/trash arrangements (pack it out). 14-day limit.
5400 ft (1620 m)

## SACAJAWEA MEMORIAL

Beaverhead NF
(406) 683-3900
State map: H3

From GRANT, go W on MT 324 for 10 miles (16 k). Turn Right and go 2 miles (3.2 k) to fork. Take Left fork and drive 10 more miles (16 k)–treacherous when wet.
FREE but choose a chore.
Open Jun 16–Sep 15; camping allowed off-season.
2 close, open tent sites plus parking for self-contained campers.
Spring water (must be treated), pit toilets, tables, fire rings.
Beneath Lemhi Pass where Lewis & Clark expedition crossed Continental Divide in 1805.
Retrace expedition's steps to headwaters

of Missouri River. Enjoy profusion of wildflowers.
No trash arrangements. 14-day limit.
7400 ft (2220 m)

## RUSSELL GATES FAS

MT FWP (406) 542-5500
State map: D3
From BONNER, drive 35 miles (56 k) E on MT 200.
$4. Open All Year.
12 close, open sites. Hand water pump, pit toilets, tables, grills, fire rings.
In mature pines on Blackfoot River.
Fish or run river. Birdwatch and take photographs.
14-day/20-ft limits.
3900 ft (1170 m)

## SALMON FLY FAS

MT FWP (406) 994-4042
State map: F4
From MELROSE, cross bridge and go .5 mile (800 m) W.
FREE but choose a chore.
Open All Year.
8 close, open sites.
Pit toilets, tables, boat ramp.
On Big Hole River.
Fishing, swimming, and boating.
14-day limit. Small vehicles only.
Crowded, noisy summers. Mosquitos.
5000 ft (1500 m)

## SAM BILLINGS MEMORIAL

Bitterroot NF
(406) 821-3269
State map: F2
From DARBY, go 4 miles (6.4 k) S on US 93. Turn Right (SW) on CR 473 and drive 13 miles (20.8 k). Turn Right (NW) on FR 5631 and go 1 mile (1.6 k).
FREE but choose a chore.
Open Jun 1–Sep 15; camping off-season.
11 close, open sites. Pit toilets, tables.
On creek near West Fork of Bitterroot River and wilderness.
Good hiking opportunities include adventuresome backpacking (Boulder Creek Trailhead). Fishing and relaxing.
10-day/22-ft limits.
4400 ft (1320 m)

## SCHUMAKER

Bitterroot NF
(406) 821-3913
State map: E2
From DARBY, head N on US 93 for 7 miles (11.2 k). Turn Left (W) on CR 76. Go 2 miles (3.2 k). Turn W on FR 429. Drive 16 miles (25.6 k). Turn Right on FR 5505 and go another 2 miles (3.2 k).
FREE but choose a chore.
Open Jul 15–Sep 15.
5 close, open sites. Pit toilets, tables.
Near Twin Lakes.
Hike into Selway Wilderness. Fish area streams and lakes.
10-day/22-ft limits.
6800 ft (2040 m)

## SEYMOUR CREEK

Beaverhead NF
(406) 832-3178
State map: F3
From WISE RIVER, take MT 43 W for 12 miles (19.2 k). Turn Right (N) on CR 274 and drive 3 miles (4.8 k). Turn Left (NW) on FR 934 (Seymour Creek Rd) and go 7 miles (11.2 k).
FREE but choose a chore.
Open Jun 1–Sep 30; dry camping off-season.
17 close, open sites.
Water, pit toilets, tables, fire rings.
In small stand of lodgepole pine along creek within .25 mile (400 m) of lake.
Hike into Anaconda-Pintler Wilderness.
Fish or do nothing.
No trash arrangements. 14-day/16-ft limits. Crowded holidays.
6800 ft (2040 m)

## SHERIDAN

Custer NF (406) 446-2103
State map: G7
From RED LODGE, take US 212 S for 8 miles (12.8 k) to FR 379. Turn Left (E) on gravel road and go 2 miles (3.2 k). (Also see Ratine.)
$5. Open May 25–Sep 5; dry camping off-season.
8 scattered, screened sites. Water, pit toilets, tables, grills, fire rings.
In valley bottom shaded by willow and

▲ ▲ ▲ ▲ ▲ ▲ ▲ ▲ ▲ ▲ ▲ ▲ ▲ ▲ ▲ ▲ ▲ ▲ ▲ ▲ ▲ ▲ ▲

cottonwood along Rock Creek.
Hike and fish.
Pack out trash to ranger station.
10-day/22-ft limits. Crowded holidays.
6300 ft (1890 m)

## SIRIA

Lolo NF (406) 329-3750
State map: E3
From CLINTON, take
I-90 E for 5 miles (8 k). Exit onto FR 102
S and drive 28 miles (44.8 k)–rough last
16 miles (25.6 k)–last of six free camps
in area. (See Bitterroot Flat, Dalles,
Grizzly, Harry's Flat, Norton, and Squaw
Rock.)
FREE but choose a chore.
Open All Year.
4 sites. Pit toilets, tables, fire rings.
Relax and fish along Rock Creek.
NO water. 14-day limit.
4400 ft (1320 m)

## SKIDWAY

Helena NF (406) 266-3425
State map: E5
From TOWNSEND, head
E on US 12 for 21 miles (33.6 k). Turn
Right (S) on FR 4042. Go 2 miles (3.2 k).
FREE but choose a chore.
Open Jun 1–Sep 15.
13 close, open sites.
Water, pit toilets, tables, fire rings.
In quiet spot with scenic vistas.
Take 3 mile (4.8 k) walk up Grassy
Mountain. Picnic and relax.
14-day/20-ft limits. Hunting in season.
5800 ft (1740 m)

## SLATE CREEK

Bitterroot NF
(406) 821-3269
State map: F2
From DARBY, go 4 miles (6.4 k) S on
US 93. Turn Right (SW) on CR 473 and
drive 21.5 miles (34.4 k). Turn S on
CR 96 and go 2 more miles (3.2 k). (Also
see Alta.)
FREE but choose a chore.
Open Jun 25–Sep 6.
13 close, open sites. ♿
Water, pit toilets, tables, fire rings,

nearby boat ramp.
On Slate Creek as it flows into lake.
Besides hiking and gold panning, ski,
boat, and fish Painted Rocks Lake.
10-day/22-ft limits.
4800 ft (1440 m)

## SODA BUTTE

Gallatin NF
(406) 848-7375
State map: G6
From COOKE CITY, go E on US 212
about 2 miles (3.2 k). Turn Right. (Also
see Chief Joseph and Colter.)
$5. Open Jun 15–Oct 15.
21 close, open sites with some screening.
Water, pit toilets, tables, fire rings, food
storage.
Along Soda Butte Creek on scenic route
to Yellowstone. Near trails into
Absaroka-Beartooth Wilderness.
Make base for sightseeing or backpacking. Attend ranger programs.
15-day/22-ft limits. Generator rules.
7800 ft (2340 m)

## SOUP CREEK

Swan River SF
(406) 754-2301
State map: C2
Take MT 83 S from SWAN LAKE for
5 miles (8 k). Turn Left (E) on dirt road
and drive about 4 miles (6.4).
FREE but choose a chore.
Open Apr--Nov; camping allowed
off-season.
12 close, screened sites.
Stream water (must be treated), pit
toilets, tables, grills, fire rings.
In heavily timbered area with scenic
views along small creek.
Try your hand at fishing. Hike too.
No trash facilities. Hunting in season.
3500 ft (1050 m)

## SOUTH MADISON RA

BLM (406) 494-5059
State map: H5
From ENNIS, take
MT 287 S for 20 miles (32 k). At sign,
turn Right (W) and go 1 mile (1.6 k).
(Also see West Madison RA.)

▲ ▲ ▲ ▲ ▲ ▲ ▲ ▲ ▲ ▲ ▲ ▲ ▲ ▲ ▲ ▲ ▲ ▲ ▲ ▲ ▲ ▲ ▲ ▲ ▲ ▲ ▲ ▲

$5. Open All Year.
11 scattered, open sites. Water, pit toilets, tables, grills, fire rings, boat ramp.
Along fantastic Madison River.
Enjoy excellent fishing and boating.
No trash arrangements. 14-day limit.
5600 ft (1680 m)

## SOUTH VAN HOUTEN

Beaverhead NF
(406) 689-3243
State map: G3
From JACKSON, take FR 181 (Bloody Dick Rd) S for 12 miles (19.2 k). (Also see North Van Houten.)
**FREE** but choose a chore.
Open Jun 15–Oct 1; camping allowed off-season.
3 close, open sites. Spring water, pit toilets, tables, fire rings.
On southern shore of Van Houten Lake with beautiful mountain views.
Swim cool waters, canoe, or fish. Hike.
No trash arrangements. 14-day limit.
6700 ft (2010 m)

## SPANISH CREEK

Gallatin NF
(406) 587-6701
State map: G5
From GALLATIN GATEWAY, head S on US 191 for 8 miles (12.8 k). Turn Right (W) on CR (Spanish Creek) and go 3.5 miles (5.6 k). Turn Left (S) on FR 982 and drive to end. (Also see Spire Rock.)
**FREE** but choose a chore.
Open Jun 15–Sep 15.
6 close, open sites.
Water, pit toilets, tables, fire rings.
On creek at edge of Lee Metcalf Wilderness.
Create base for taking treks.
No trash arrangements. 14-day limit.
6000 ft (1800 m)

## SPAR LAKE

Kootenai NF
(406) 295-4693
State map: B1
From TROY, go SE on US 2 about 3 miles (4.8 k) to Lake Creek Rd. Turn Right (S) and drive 8 miles (12.8 k) to

FR 384 (Spar Lake Rd). Continue 12 miles (19.2 k).
**FREE** but choose a chore.
Open May 20–Sep 30; dry camping off-season.
8 close, open sites.
Water, pit toilets, tables, fire rings, boat ramp (small boats).
On nice, remote, little lake.
Picnic, read a book. Watch for wildlife.
Fish or boat.
No trash arrangements. 14-day limit.
3300 ft (990 m)

## SPILLWAY

Deerlodge NF
(406) 859-3211
State map: F3
From PHILIPSBURG, take MT 1 S for 6.25 miles (10 k). Turn Right (SW) on MT 38 and drive 6 miles (9.6 k). Turn Left (SE) on FR 672 (East Fork Rd) and go 5 miles (8 k). (Also see East Fork.)
**FREE** but choose a chore.
Open May 22–Sep 30.
13 sites.
Water, pit toilets, tables, fire rings.
Splash or fish on creek. Hike.
14-day/22-ft limits.
6400 ft (1920 m)

## SPIRE ROCK

Gallatin NF
(406) 587-6701
State map: G5
From GALLATIN GATEWAY, head S on US 191 for 11.5 miles (18.4 k). Turn Left (E) on FR 132 and go 3.5 miles (5.6 k). (Also see Spanish Creek.)
**FREE** but choose a chore.
Open Jun 15–Sep 15.
17 close, open sites.
Pit toilets, tables, fire rings.
Along Squaw Creek.
Unwind and picnic. Explore backroads.
NO water/trash arrangements (pack it out). 14-day limit.
5600 ft (1680 m)

▲ ▲ ▲ ▲ ▲ ▲ ▲ ▲ ▲ ▲ ▲ ▲ ▲ ▲ ▲ ▲ ▲ ▲ ▲ ▲ ▲ ▲ ▲ ▲ ▲ ▲ ▲ ▲

## SPOTTED BEAR

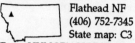

Flathead NF
(406) 752-7345
State map: C3

From HUNGRY HORSE, go S on gravel
FR 38 for 55 miles (88 k).
$3. Open Jun 25-Labor Day; dry camping
off-season.
13 close, open sites with some screening.
Water, pit toilets, tables, fire rings, dump
station.
In woods at Spotted Bear and South Fork
rivers next to ranger station.
Wonderful hiking (Deans Falls) and
good fishing.
Grizzly country. 14-day limit. Crowded
Jul–Aug in warm, dry summers.
3600 ft (1080 m)

## SPRING CREEK

Gallatin NF
(406) 587-6701
State map: H5

From WEST YELLOWSTONE, go W on
US 20 about 8 miles (12.8 k). Turn Right
(N) on Hebgen Lake Rd (will become
FR 167) and go 8 miles (12.8 k). Pass free
alternative **Rumbaugh Ridge** (5
tent sites) and developed, fee-charged
**Lonsomehurst** (23 sites).
FREE but choose a chore.
Open May 15–Sep 30.
10 sites. Pit toilets, tables, fire rings.
On west shore of Hebgen Lake.
Fish, boat, or swim.
NO water. 14-day limit.

## SPRING CREEK

Stillwater SF
(406) 881-2371
State map: B2

From OLNEY, take MT 93 N for
7.5 miles (12 k)–on Left (W) just before
creek (no signs).
FREE but choose a chore.
Open All Year.
6 scattered, open sites.
Stream water (must be treated), pit
toilets, tables, fire rings.
On both sides of creek in open stand of
lodgepole pine. Area logged in 1980s
(replanted but still small).

Hike creek to Duck Lake or over to
Stillwater River. Try a bit of fishing.
No trash arrangements (pack it out).
Spring insects. 14-day limit. Please keep
water clean (no soap).

## SPRING GULCH

Bitterroot NF
(406) 821-3201
State map: F2

From SULA, head N on US 93 for
4 miles (6.4 k).
$4. Open Jun 1–Sep 15.
10 (1 bicycle group) close, open sites.
Water, pit toilets, tables.
On Bitterroot River.
Picnic, relax, bike, hike, swim, and fish.
10-day/22-ft limits.

## SPRING HILL

Deerlodge NF
(406) 846-1770
State map: E4

From ANACONDA, take MT 1 W for
10.75 miles (17.2 k). (Also see Warm
Springs.)
FREE but choose a chore.
Open Jun 15–Sep 5.
16 sites.
Water, pit toilets, tables, fire rings.
Fish, hike, or picnic along creek.
14-day/22-ft limits.
6400 ft (1920 m)

## SQUAW ROCK

Deerlodge NF
(406) 859-3211
State map: F3

From PHILIPSBURG, take CR 348 W for
14 miles (22.4 k). Turn West on Rock
Creek Rd (FR 102). Go 4.6 miles (7.4 k).
Turn again on FR 9346. (Also see Siria.)
FREE but choose a chore.
Open May 22–Sep 30.
10 close, open sites.
Water, pit toilets, tables, fire rings.
Hike and fish along remote creek.
14-day limit.
5200 ft (1560 m)

## STEEL CREEK

Beaverhead NF
(406) 689-3243
State map: G3

From WISDOM, take Steel Creek Rd W
for 9 miles (14.4 k).
FREE but choose a chore.
Open Jun 15–Sep 20; dry camping
off-season. Scheduled for refurbishment.
9 (2 tent-only) close, screened sites.
Water, pit toilets, tables, fire rings.
Along creek beneath lodgepole pine.
Walking, fishing, and picnicking.
No trash arrangements. 14-day limit.
6200 ft (1860 m)

## SYLVAN LAKE

Kootenai NF
(406) 293-7773
State map: C1

From TROUT CREEK, take MT 200 W
for 1 mile (1.6 k) to FR 154 (Vermilion
River Rd). Turn Right (N) and go
17 miles (27.2 k). (See Willow Creek.)
FREE but choose a chore.
Open May 15–Oct 1; camping allowed
off-season.
5 close, open sites.
Pit toilets, tables, fire rings.
On one of area's small lakes.
Hiking but mainly good fishing.
NO water/trash arrangements (pack it
out). 14-day/20-ft limits.
3600 ft (1080 m)

## THE PINES AREA

COE (406) 526-3411
State map: C10

Go 6 miles (9.6 k) NW
from FORT PECK on MT 24. Turn Left
on oiled road. Follow signs about
30 miles (48 k)–road tricky when wet.
FREE but choose a chore.
Open All Year.
12 close, open sites.
Water, pit toilets, tables, grills, fire rings,
pay phone, boat ramp.
On peninsula in Fort Peck Lake with
great view and, naturally, lots of pines.
Swim, ski, boat, and fish lake.
14-day limit.
2250 ft (675 m)

## TIMBER CAMP

Gallatin NF
(406) 848-7375
State map: G6

From GARDINER, take gravel Jardine
Rd past JARDINE another 2 miles
(3.2 k). (Also see Bear Creek and Eagle
Creek.)
FREE but choose a chore.
Open Jun 15–Sep 5; camping allowed
off-season.
6 scattered, screened sites.
Pit toilets, fire rings.
In meadow or woods along Bear Creek
drainage, close to Absaroka-Beartooth
Wilderness.
Use as base for hiking, backpacking, or
mountain biking.
NO water/trash arrangements (pack it
out). Severe winters.
8000 ft (2400 m)

## TOBACCO RIVER

Kootenai NF
(406) 296-2536
State map: A1

From REXFORD, go 2 miles (3.2 k) E on
MT 37 to river. Camp is .5 mile (800 m)
W on primitive FR along river.
FREE but choose a chore.
Open Apr 15–Oct 15; camping allowed
off-season.
4 close, open sites.
Pit toilets, tables, fire rings.
On river near Lake Koocanusa.
Fish adjacent Tobacco Inlet. Explore
nearby hoodoos.
NO water/trash facilities. 14-day limit.
2500 ft (750 m)

## TOLL MOUNTAIN

Deerlodge NF
(406) 287-3223
State map: F4

From WHITEHALL, head W on MT 2
for 15 miles (24 k). Turn Right (N) on
dirt FR 240 for 3 miles (4.8 k). (Also see
Pigeon Creek.)
FREE but choose a chore.
Open May 22–Sep 15. Scheduled to
reopen in 1993.
5 sites. Pit toilets, tables, fire rings.

▲ ▲ ▲ ▲ ▲ ▲ ▲ ▲ ▲ ▲ ▲ ▲ ▲ ▲ ▲ ▲ ▲ ▲ ▲ ▲ ▲ ▲ ▲ ▲

Hike, explore, or fish along creek.
NO water. 14-day/22-ft limits.
5900 ft (1770 m)

## TOM MINER

Gallatin NF
(406) 848-7375
State map: G5

From GARDINER, take US 89 NW for
16 miles (25.6 k). Turn Left (SW) on
gravel CR 63 and go 12 miles (19.2 k).
Continue on dirt FR 63 for 3.5 miles
(5.6 k).
$5. Open Jun 15–Sep 5; dry camping
off-season.
16 close sites with some screening.
Water, pit toilets, tables, fire rings.
In remote, high mountain valley near
Gallatin Petrified Forest (camp's old
name was Petrified Forest).
Hike interpretive and other trails in
fascinating area. (Ramshorn Peak great
for rock enthusiasts–fee permit).
15-day/22-ft limits.

## TOSTON DAM

BLM (406) 494-5059
State map: F5

From TOSTON, go S on
MT 287 for 2 miles (3.2 k) Turn Left (SE)
on gravel road. Go about 5 miles (8 k).
FREE but choose a chore.
Open All Year.
7 scattered, open sites.
Pit toilets, tables, fire rings, boat ramp.
In two areas–one on reservoir and other
below dam next to river.
Boat and fish.
NO water/trash facilities. 14-day limit.
3855 ft (1155 m)

## TRAFTON PARK

Malta City Parks
(406) 654-1251
State map: B8

Locate in MALTA, N of intersection of
US 2 and US 191.
$3. Open All Year.
25 sites. Water, pit toilets, tables, grills,
playground.
Picnic and relax.
7-day limit.

## TROUT CREEK

Lolo NF (406) 329-3750
State map: D1

From SUPERIOR, head
SE on MT 269 about 4.5 miles (7.2 k).
Turn Right on Trout Creek Rd (CR 257)
and go 2.5 miles (4 k).
FREE but choose a chore.
Open All Year.
12 sites.
Water, pit toilets, tables, fire rings.
Picnic and fish along creek.
No trash arrangements. Water cut off
after Labor Day. 14-day limit.
3000 ft (900 m)

## TUCHUCK

Flathead NF
(406) 892-4372
State map: A2

From COLUMBIA FALLS, take CR 486
(North Fork Rd) N almost to Canadian
border about 54 miles (86.4 k). Turn Left
(W) on FR 114 (Trail Creek Rd) and go
9 miles (14.4 k).
FREE but choose a chore.
Open Jun 15–Sep 15; camping allowed
off-season.
7 close, open sites.
Pit toilets, tables, fire rings.
Next to Seemo, Tuchuck, and Yakinikak
creeks with four trailheads, beaver
ponds, and wild berry patches.
Become a nature enthusiast. Hike,
explore, and indulge your senses.
NO water/trash arrangements (pack it
out). Small vehicles only.
4645 ft (1392 m)

## TWIN LAKES

Beaverhead NF
(406) 689-3243
State map: G2

From WISDOM, take MT 278 S for
7 miles (11.2 k) to FR 945. Turn Right
(W) and follow directional signs closely
another 21 miles (33.6 k).
FREE but choose a chore.
Open Jun 20–Sep 1; dry camping
off-season.
21 close, screened sites.
Water, pit toilets, tables, fire rings.

▲ ▲ ▲ ▲ ▲ ▲ ▲ ▲ ▲ ▲ ▲ ▲ ▲ ▲ ▲ ▲ ▲ ▲ ▲ ▲ ▲ ▲ ▲ ▲ ▲

On shore with great views of West Big Hole Mountains.
Swim, boat (no motors), and fish. Hike.
No trash arrangements (pack it out).
14-day limit. Crowded holidays.
6200 ft (1860 m)

## VIGILANTE

Helena NF (406) 449-5490
State map: E5
From YORK, head NE on a CR for 5 miles (8 k) along Trout Creek.
FREE but choose a chore.
Open Jun 1–Sep 15.
22 scattered, screened sites. &
Water, pit toilets, tables, fire rings.
Along Trout Creek with meadow for games plus wooded, private sites.
Take rewarding walk up Trout Creek Canyon with spectacular rock formations. Connect with Hanging Valley National Scenic Trail.
No trash pickup. 14-day/20-ft limits.
4400 ft (1320 m)

## WARM SPRINGS

Bitterroot NF
(406) 821-3201
State map: F2
From SULA, take US 93 N for 4.75 miles (7.6 k) to CR 100. Turn Left (SW) and go 1 mile (1.6 k). (Also see Crazy Creek.)
$5. Open May 25–Sep 10.
13 close, open sites.
Water, pit toilets, tables.
Along Warm Springs Creek.
Swim, fish, and take nature walks.
14-day/22-ft limits.
4400 ft (1320 m)

## WARM SPRINGS

Deerlodge NF
(406) 846-1770
State map: E4
From ANACONDA, take MT 1 W for 10.5 miles (16.8 k). Turn Right (N) on FR 170 and drive 2.5 miles (4 k). (Also see Spring Hill.)
FREE but choose a chore.
Open May 22–Sep 25.
6 sites.
Water, pit toilets, tables, fire rings.

Fish, hike, or picnic along creek.
14-day/16-ft limits.
6600 ft (1980 m)

## WEST BOULDER

Gallatin NF
(406) 932-5155
State map: G6
From BIG TIMBER, head S on US 298 for 16 miles (25.6 k). Turn Right (W) on West Boulder Rd and go 7.5 miles (12 k). Turn Left (S) and continue additional 7 miles (11.2 k).
FREE but choose a chore.
Open All Year.
10 close, open sites with some screening.
Water, pit toilets, tables, grills.
Next to West Boulder River with trail to Absaroka-Beartooth Wilderness.
Use as base camp for extended hikes or exploring immediate area. Fish too.
No trash arrangements. Camp only in designated sites. 15-day/20-ft limits.
Crowded weekends. Often inaccessible in winter.
5500 ft (1650 m)

## WEST FORK

Lewis & Clark NF
(406) 791-7700
State map: C4
From CHOTEAU, go 5.5 miles (8.8 k) N on US 89. Turn Left (W) on CR 144 and drive 23 miles (36.8 k). Turn Right (N) on FR 144 and go 10 miles (16 k). (Also see Elko.)
FREE but choose a chore.
Open Jun 1–Sep 15.
6 sites.
Water, pit toilets, tables, fire rings.
Next to river at Teton Peak with trail into Bob Marshall Wilderness.
Observe and reflect. Take a long walk.
No trash arrangements. 14-day limit.
5500 ft (1650 m)

## WEST MADISON RA

BLM (406) 494-5059
State map: H5
From ENNIS, take MT 287 S for 17 miles (27.2 k). At sign, turn Right (W) and go 1 mile (1.6 k)

▲ ▲ ▲ ▲ ▲ ▲ ▲ ▲ ▲ ▲ ▲ ▲ ▲ ▲ ▲ ▲    ▲ ▲ ▲ ▲ ▲ ▲ ▲ ▲ ▲ ▲ ▲ ▲ ▲ ▲

across bridge. Turn Left (S) on paved
road and go 3 miles (4.8 k). (Also see
South Madison RA.)
$5. Open All Year.
22 scattered, open sites. Water, pit toilets,
tables, grills, fire rings.
On either side of Ruby Creek near
Madison River.
Fish, picnic, or relax.
No trash arrangements. 14-day limit.
5500 ft (1650 m)

## WHITEHOUSE
Deerlodge NF
(406) 494-2147
State map: F4
From BUTTE, take I-15 N for 20 miles
(32 k) to Bernice Exit. Drive W on FR 82
for 6 miles (9.6 k). (Also see Ladysmith
and Mormon Creek.)
FREE but choose a chore.
Open May 22-Sep 15.
5 plus scattered area sites.
Water, pit toilets, tables, fire rings.
Along Boulder River.
Hike, fish, picnic, or relax.
14-day/22-ft limits.
5500 ft (1650 m)

## WHITETAIL
Kootenai NF
(406) 295-4693
State map: A1
From YAAK, go 5 miles (8 k) SW on
FH 92. (See Pete Creek and Red Top.)
FREE but choose a chore.
Open Jun 1 - Sep 30; dry camping
off-season.
12 close, open sites.
Water, pit toilets, tables, fire rings.
On wonderful spot beside Yaak River.
Hiking trails abound as do fishing holes
and relaxing spots.
No trash arrangements. 14-day limit.
3000 ft (900 m)

## WILLOW
Beaverhead NF
(406) 832-3178
State map: F3
From WISE RIVER, take FR 484 (Wise
River-Polaris Scenic Byway) S for

13.4 miles (21.4 k). **Boulder, Fourth of
July,** and **Lodgepole** offer fee-charged
options. (Also see Little Joe and Mono
Creek.)
FREE but choose a chore.
Open Jun 1-Sep 30.
5 close, open sites.
Water, pit toilets, tables, fire rings.
On small flat next to Wise River,
surrounded by steep mountains.
Photograph scenic region. Explore, hike,
or fish.
No trash pickup. 14-day/16-ft limits.
Crowded weekends and holidays.
Mosquitos.
6600 ft (1980 m)

## WILLOW CREEK
Kootenai NF
(406) 827-3534
State map: C1
From TROUT CREEK, take MT 200 W
for 1 mile (1.6 k) to FR 154 (Vermilion
River Rd). Turn Right (N) and go
14 miles (22.4 k). (Also see Sylvan Lake.)
FREE but choose a chore.
Open May 15-Oct 10; camping allowed
off-season.
4 close, open sites.
Pit toilets, tables, fire rings.
At peaceful spot on Vermilion River.
Daydream. Maybe catch a fish.
NO water/trash facilities. 14-day/20-ft
limits. Hunting in fall.
2750 ft (825 m)

## WILLOW CREEK RESERVOIR FAS
MT FWP (406) 454-3441
State map: C4
From AUGUSTA, head
NW on CR 108 about 5 miles (8 k).
FREE but choose a chore.
Open All Year.
Undesignated, scattered, open sites.
Pit toilets, tables, fire rings, boat ramp.
On high plains reservoir with beautiful
views of Rocky Mountains.
Swim, boat, or fish lake. Hike and view
wildlife at Sun River Game Refuge-
gateway to Bob Marshall Wilderness.
NO water.

▲ ▲ ▲ ▲ ▲ ▲ ▲ ▲ ▲ ▲ ▲ ▲ ▲ ▲ ▲ ▲ ▲ ▲ ▲ ▲ ▲ ▲ ▲ ▲ ▲ ▲ ▲

## WOODBINE

Custer NF (406) 446-2103
State map: G6
From NYE, take MT 419
for 8 miles (12.8 k) SW.

$5. Open May 25–Sep 5; dry camping off-season.

45 scattered, open sites with some screening. Water, pit toilets, tables, grills, fire rings.

On gentle slope to Stillwater River.

Enjoy nice hikes, nearby waterfall, wilderness access, rockhounding opportunities, plus seclusion.

10-day limit. Windy.

5300 ft (1590 m)

## YAAK FALLS

Kootenai NF
(406) 295-4693
State map: A1

From TROY, go NW on US 2 for 10.2 miles (16.3 k) to MT 508 (Yaak River). Turn Right (NE) and continue 6.5 miles (10.4 k). (Also see Kilbrennen Lake and Yaak River.)

FREE but choose a chore.

Open May 20–Sep 30; camping allowed off-season.

7 close, open sites.

Pit toilets, tables, fire rings.

Near several waterfalls (best in early spring) and scenic river canyon.

Explore!

NO water/trash arrangements (pack it out). 14-day limit.

2500 ft (750 m)

## YAAK RIVER

Kootenai NF
(406) 295-4693
State map: A1

From TROY, go NW on US 2 for 7.5 miles (12 k). (Also see Kilbrennen Lake and Yaak Falls.)

$5. Open May 20–Sep 30; dry camping off-season.

43 close, open sites. Water, pit toilets, tables, fire rings, small boat put-in.

Near road at confluence of Yaak and Kootenai rivers.

Use pretty spot popular for fishing, hiking, boating, and mountain biking.

14-day limit.

1800 ft (540 m)

## YANKEE JIM CANYON

Gallatin NF
(406) 848-7375
State map: G5

From GARDINER, take US 89 NW for 17 miles (27.2 k). Turn Left.

FREE but choose a chore.

Open All Year.

9 sites. Pit toilets, tables, fire rings.

Next to Yellowstone River.

Fish or hike.

NO water/trash arrangements (pack it out). 15-day/25-ft limits.

5000 ft (1500 m)

# Nevada

Grid conforms to official state map. For your copy, call (800) Nevada-8 or write Commission on Tourism, Capitol Complex, Carson City, NV 89710.

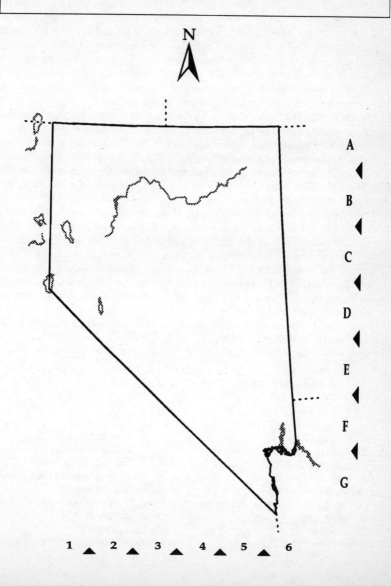

▲ ▲ ▲ ▲ ▲ ▲ ▲ ▲ ▲ ▲ ▲ ▲ ▲ ▲ ▲ ▲ ▲ ▲ ▲ ▲ ▲ ▲ ▲ ▲ ▲ ▲ ▲ ▲

There's far more to Nevada than gambling casinos. $5-or-less camping opportunities are diverse–from tall peaks, to man-made reservoirs, to flat deserts, even to interstate rest stops in an emergency.

The **Nevada State Parks** (SPs) qualify, since prices begin at $4 per site. The strategically situated parks reflect the state's geological and historical variety.

Huge tracts of land belong to the US Department of the Interior's agencies. Find numerous **Bureau of Land Management** (BLM) developed campsites scattered throughout the state, providing choices in a wide variety of natural settings. **US Fish and Wildlife Service** offers incredible chances for wildlife observation with Sheldon National Wildlife Refuge (NWR) in northwestern Nevada, Stillwater NWR in the central area of the state, and Desert NWR in the southern section. The **National Park Service** (NPS) administers the massive Lake Mead National Recreation Area (NRA) as well as Great Basin NP, the nation's newest. Located in the central part of Nevada near the Utah border, Explorer John Fremont gave the area its name because rivers and streams flow inland, without outlet to the ocean. Here scenery ranges from mountains to caverns. Camping opportunities reflect the different above-ground ecologies within the basin.

The Department of Agriculture's **US Forest Service** controls the Humboldt and Toiyabe national forests. In the **Humboldt National Forest (NF)**, find the following wilderness areas: Current Mountain, East Humboldt, Grant Range, Jarbidge, Mount Moriah, Quinn Canyon, Ruby Mountain, and Santa Rose-Paradise Peak. View stands of ancient bristlecone pine, glacial activity in Lamoille Canyon, the threatened bald eagle species as well as golden eagle, elk, mountain lion, and Rocky Mountain bighorn sheep.

The **Toiyabe NF** stretches intermittently along the California border toward the tip of Nevada. It's one of the largest national forests with features that vary from forest-surrounded lakes (Lake Tahoe) to Joshua-tree-studded deserts (Mohave). Too, there are numerous wilderness areas to explore within the Toiyabe: Alta Toquima, Arc Dome, Carson-Iceberg, Hoover, Mokelumne, Mount Charleston, Mount Rose, and Table Mountain. In addition to the common mule deer, observe black bear, bobcat, wild burro, elk, and mountain lion. Less seldom seen are antelope and desert bighorn sheep.

Experience Nevada's diversity firsthand or, as the state tourism commission says, "Discover Both Sides of Nevada."

▲ ▲ ▲ ▲ ▲ ▲ ▲ ▲ ▲ ▲ ▲ ▲ ▲ ▲ ▲ ▲ ▲ ▲ ▲ ▲ ▲ ▲ ▲ ▲ ▲ ▲ ▲ ▲

**ANGEL CREEK**

Humboldt NF (702) 752-3357
State map: A5
Take NV 231 SW from WELLS for 9 miles (14.4 k). (Also see Angel Lake.)
**$5; for additional $6, reservations** accepted at (800) 283-2267.
Open May 20–Sep 30; dry camping off-season.
18 scattered, screened sites. Water, pit toilets, tables, grills, fire rings.
In shady aspen.
Hike into Humboldt Mountains.

No trash arrangements. 14-day limit. 6800 ft (2040 m)

**ANGEL LAKE**
Humboldt NF (702) 752-3357
State map: A5
From WELLS, go SW on NV 231 for 13 miles (20.8 k)– steep mountain access road.
(Also see Angel Creek.)
**$5; for additional $6, reservations** accepted at (800) 283-2267.
Open Jun 14–Sep 14.
26 scattered, open sites. Water, pit toilets,

tables, grills, fire rings.
Next to high mountain lake.
Do some exploring. Drop a line to fish.
No trash arrangements. 14-day limit.
8500 ft (2550 m)

## BARLEY CREEK/COTTONWOOD

Toiyabe NF (702) 482-6286
State map: D4
From TONOPAH, go E on
US 6 for 5 miles (8 k). Turn
Left (N) on NV 376 and drive
13 miles (20.8 k). Continue N on CR 82
about 31 miles (49.6 k). Turn Right (E)
on FR 005 and go 11 miles (17.6 k). (Also
see Pine Creek.)
FREE but choose a chore.
Open May–Oct.
10 close, open sites.
Pit toilets, tables, fire rings.
On stream at edge of Table Mountain
Wilderness.
Fish, hike, and explore.
NO water. 14-day limit.
7800 ft (2340 m)

## BEAVER DAM SP

(702) 728-4467
State map: E6
From CALIENTE, go N on
US 93 for 6 miles (9.6 k) to
gravel road. Turn Right (E)
and drive 32 miles (51.2 k)–long, rough
access not advisable for RVs or trailers.
$4. Open All Year.
33 scattered, open sites. Water,
chemical/pit toilets, tables, fire rings.
With deep canyons, meandering streams,
and small reservoir within pinyon-
juniper forest near Utah border.
Superb hiking for nature enthusiast.
Fishing and boating (no motors).
14-day limit. Leash pets and keep quiet
hours. Severe winters.
5100 ft (1530 m)

## BERLIN-ICHTHYOSAUR SP

(702) 964-2440
State map: D3
From GABBS, take NV 844 E
for 22 miles (35.2 k). Go
2 miles (3.2 k) E on gravel

road.
$4, $1 for fossil tours. Open All Year.
14 scattered, screened sites.
Water, chemical/pit toilets, dump
station, tables, grills, fire rings.
In central Nevada mountains among
pinyon-juniper woodlands.
Observe ancient fossils (ichthyosaurs)
and recent ghost town (Berlin).
Attend ranger programs. Ski winters.
14-day limit. Rattlesnakes. Quiet hours.
Bad roads in winter.
7000 ft (2100 m)

## BIG BEND

Humboldt NF (702) 763-6691
State map: A5
From ELKO, take NV 225 N
for 65 miles (104 k) to sign.
Turn Right (E) on unpaved
CR 145 and continue 10 miles (16 k).
$4. Open Jun 16–Oct 15.
15 scattered, screened sites. Water, pit
toilets, tables, grills, fire rings.
In aspen patch.
Observe and photograph nature.
14-day limit. Hunting in season.
6900 ft (2070 m)

## CATHEDRAL GORGE SP

(702) 728-4467
State map: E6
From PIOCHE, take US 93 S
for 10 miles (16 k). Watch for
well-marked turnoff on Left
(W). Take access road 1.5 miles
(2.4 k)–not plowed in winter.
$5. Open All Year.
22 close, open sites with some screening.
Water, flush/pit toilets, dump station,
showers, tables, fire rings, pay phone.
Under shade trees in high-desert canyon
among impressive badlands.
Follow trails through ancient geologic
formations as well as evidence of area's
10000-year human use. Take photographs. Birdwatch.
14-day limit. Crowded summer holidays.
No ATVs.
4970 ft (1491 m)

▲ ▲ ▲ ▲ ▲ ▲ ▲ ▲ ▲ ▲ ▲ ▲ ▲ ▲ ▲ ▲ ▲ ▲ ▲ ▲ ▲ ▲ ▲ ▲

## CAVE LAKE SRA

State Parks and Wildlife
(702) 728-4467
State map: C6
From ELY, take US 6 S for
8 miles (12.8 k). Turn Left (E)
on NV 486 (Success Summit). Go 6 miles
(9.6 k)–impassable when wet.
$4. Open All Year.
36 close, open sites. Water, flush toilets,
showers, tables, fire rings, boat ramp.
Fish, boat, or swim on lake. Picnic.
Cross-country ski and snowmobile.
14-day/23-ft limits. Crowded holidays.
7000 ft (2100 m)

## CLEVE CREEK

BLM (702) 289-4865
State map: C6
From MAJOR'S PLACE near
intersection of NV 893 and
US 6/50 (SE of ELY), take
NV 893 N for 12.2 miles (19.5 k). Turn
Left (W) on graded road.
FREE but choose a chore.
Open All Year.
12 scattered, open sites. Pit toilets, tables.
In lush, green Spring Valley at mouth of
narrow canyon with constant stream.
Within Schell Creek Range.
Hike–short walks or extended treks.
Fish, birdwatch, or relax.
NO water. 14-day/24-ft limits.
6233 ft (1869 m)

## COLUMBINE

Toiyabe NF (702) 482-6286
State map: D3
From IONE, go NE on CR 91
for a couple of miles to ranger
station. Take FR 119 SE for
9 miles (14.4 k).
FREE but choose a chore.
Open May–Oct.
4 close, open sites.
Pit toilets, tables, fire rings.
In high country along Stewart Creek at
base of Arc Dome and wilderness.
Trails, streams, beauty, seclusion–you
figure out what to do.
NO water. 14-day limit.
9000 ft (2700 m)

## CURRANT CREEK

Humboldt NF (702) 738-5171
State map: D5
From CURRANT, head NE on
US 6 about 7 miles (11.2 k).
FREE but choose a chore.
Open May 15–Sep 15.
7 close, open sites.
Water, pit toilets, tables, grills.
Walk, fish, or relax in high country.
14-day limit.
6300 ft (1890 m)

## DAYTON SP

(702) 687-5678
State map: C1
Located just off US 50 near
DAYTON.
$4. Open All Year.
10 scattered, screened sites.
Water, flush toilets, dump station, tables,
grills, fire rings.
With beach on Carson River amidst
sagebrush and cottonwood at Nevada's
first white settlement.
Relax, picnic, and wander.
No wading in irrigation ditch. 7-day
limit. Crowded weekends. No fires in
dry conditions. Highway noise.
4200 ft (1260 m)

## DESERT CREEK

Toiyabe NF (619) 932-7070
State map: D1
From WELLINGTON, travel
SE on NV 338 about 5 miles
(8 k). Continue S on FR 20027
for 6.25 miles (10 k).
FREE but choose a chore.
Open May 1–Oct 30.
12 close, open sites.
Pit toilets, tables, grills.
Beneath 9000-ft peak.
Explore area. Fish in creek.
NO water/trash arrangements (pack it
out). 14-day/22-ft limits.
6300 ft (1890 m)

## DESERT NWR-Backcountry
(702) 646-3401
State map: F5
From LAS VEGAS, head N on
US 95 for 23 miles (36.8 k) to
sign for Corn Creek Station.
Turn Right (E) on gravel road for 4 miles
(6.4 k) to enter Refuge.
**FREE** but choose a chore.
Open All Year.
Undesignated, scattered sites.
NO facilities (come prepared to be self
sufficient; leave trace-free camp).
With remote, primitive roadside camping
within 100 ft of roads but at least
.25 mile (400 m) from waterholes or
springs.
Observe wildlife: desert bighorn sheep,
deer, coyote, badger, bobcat, fox, and,
even, a mountain lion or two. Watch
multitudes of birds.
Extreme summer temperatures. Snakes.
Nellis Air Force Base Bombing Range in
west portion (stay out).
2500 ft (750 m)

## EAST CREEK
Humboldt NF (702) 738-5171
State map: C6
Take US 93 N from MCGILL
for 5 miles (8 k). Turn Right
(E) on NV 486 (Duck Creek).
After about 4 miles (6.4 k), continue
straight (E) on FR 564 for 5 miles (8 k).
(Also see Timber Creek.)
**FREE** but choose a chore.
Open May 15–Sep 30.
3 sites. Pit toilets, tables, fire rings.
Hike in woods along creek.
NO water. 14-day limit.
7400 ft (2220 m)

## ECHO CANYON SP
(702) 962-5103
State map: E6
From PIOCHE, take CR 323 E
for 11 miles (17.6 k). (Also see
Meadow Valley and Spring
Valley SP.)
**$4.** Open All Year.
33 close, open sites. Water, flush toilets,
dump station, tables, grills, fire rings,

pay phone, boat ramp.
In sagebrush and juniper near 65-acre
lake among rolling hills.
Walk, boat, and fish. Attend ranger
programs.
14-day limit. Crowded long weekends.
5600 ft (1680 m)

## FORT CHURCHILL SHP
(702) 577-2345
State map: C1
From SILVER SPRINGS, go S
on US 95A for 8 miles (12.8 k).
Turn Right (W) on Old Fort
Churchill Rd and continue 1 mile (1.6 k).
**$4.** Open All Year.
20 scattered, screened sites.
Water, pit toilets, dump station, tables,
grills, fire rings, pay phone.
Beneath large cottonwoods near ruins of
old Army post, modern Visitor Center,
as well as Carson River.
Wander trails. Absorb history. Star gaze.
Boat, swim, and fish on Lahontan Reservoir–8 miles (12.8 k) away.
14-day/30-ft limits. Crowded holidays.
Spring gnats. Quiet hours.
3600 ft (1080 m)

## GAP MOUNTAIN
BLM (702) 289-4865
State map: C6
SW of ELY, take NV 318 S to
Nye milepost 11.9. Turn Right
(W) on southern access road to
Kirch Wildlife Area.
**FREE** but choose a chore.
Open All Year.
6 scattered, open sites.
Pit toilets, tables. (Coming soon,
more sites, water, and electricity).
Picnicking and relaxing. Fishing too.
NO water. 14-day/24-ft limits.
5220 ft (1566 m)

## GREAT BASIN NP
(702) 234-7331
State map: C6
No entrance fee. In addition to
following campgrounds, **free**
backcountry permits available
at Visitor Center.

▲ ▲ ▲ ▲ ▲ ▲ ▲ ▲ ▲ ▲ ▲ ▲ ▲ ▲ ▲ ▲ ▲ ▲ ▲ ▲ ▲ ▲ ▲ ▲ ▲ ▲

Above desert, find mountain terrain dominated by 13000-ft Wheeler Peak, forests with 3000-year-old bristlecone pines, glacial lakes and streams, as well as limestone caverns.

▲ **Baker Creek**
From BAKER, go 5 miles (8 k) W on NV 488. Turn Left at sign and follow gravel road 3 miles (4.8 k).
FREE. Open May 1–Oct 15.
34 scattered, open sites. Water (must treat), pit toilets, tables, grills, fire rings.
In riparian area, including meadows and shade-providing spruce and aspen.
Hike trails to Baker Lake and Johnson Lake (no pets on trails). Fish.
14-day limit. Crowded holidays and weekends. Quiet hours.
7300 ft (2190 m)

▲ **Lower & Upper Lehman Creek**
From BAKER, go 5 miles (8 k) W on signed NV 488.
$5. Open All Year.
35 sites (11 at Lower, 24 at Upper with 10 tent-only). Water, pit toilets, tables, grills, fire rings.
Next to running creek with tall pine and aspen plus beautiful mountain views.
Make base for exploring and hiking newest NP. Birdwatch and fish. Tour Lehman Caves (90 minutes).
14-day/30-ft limits. Quiet hours. Crowded summers. No pets on trails.
7300 ft (2190 m)

▲ **Wheeler Peak**
From BAKER, go 5 miles (8 k) W on NV 488. Turn Right on Wheeler Peak Rd. After passing Upper Lehman, go 12 miles (19.2 k) on 8 per cent grade–no large RVs.
FREE. Open May–Oct.
37 scattered, screened sites. Water, pit toilets, tables, grills, fire rings.
Beneath aspen next to running creek at base of Wheeler Peak.
Take trails to Bristlecone Grove, Glacier Ice Field, and Alpine Lakes (no pets on trails). Take photographs. Attend ranger-led activities. Ski in winter.
14-day limit. Crowded holidays and weekends. Quiet hours.
9900 ft (2970 m)

## HICKISON PETROGLYPH RS

BLM (702) 635-4000
State map: C4
Take US 50 E from AUSTIN for 24 miles (38.4 k). Turn Left (N) on gravel entrance road and proceed .8 mile (1.3 k).
FREE but choose a chore.
Open All Year.
21 (5 tent-only) sites. Pit toilets, tables, grills, fire rings, 16 sun shelters.
In sagebrush, pinyon, and juniper.
Thrust yourself back several thousand years to imagine life for inhabitants of that time. Walk interpretive trail to petroglyphs (do not deface).
NO water. 14-day limit. Hot summers with storms. Heavy winter snows.
6500 ft (1950 m)

## ILLIPAH RESERVOIR

BLM (702) 289-4865
State map: C5
From ELY, take US 50 W for 38 miles (60.8 k). Turn Left (S) on dirt road.
FREE but choose a chore.
Open All Year.
17 scattered, open sites. &
Pit toilets, tables, fire rings, wind breaks.
At popular fishing spot on reservoir.
Relax, fish, and picnic.
NO water. 14-day limit.
6840 ft (2052 m)

## JACK CREEK

Humboldt NF (702) 763-6691
State map: A4
From ELKO, take NV 225 N for 27 miles (43.2 k). Turn Left (NW) on NV 226. Go 35 miles (56 k). Turn Right (E) on unpaved CR 732 (Jack Creek). Go 3 miles (4.8 k).
FREE but choose a chore.
Open May 23–Oct 15; camping allowed off-season.
6 scattered, open sites.
Pit toilets, tables, fire rings.
Spread along creek in cottonwood.
Fish or hunt in season.
NO water/trash facilities. 14-day limit.
6400 ft (1920 m)

## JARBIDGE

Humboldt NF (208) 543-4129
State map: A5
From JARBIDGE, go S on
unpaved CR 752 for 1 mile
(1.6 k). (Also see Pine Creek.)
**FREE** but choose a chore.
Open Jun 1 – Oct 31; dry camping
off-season.
5 scattered, screened sites.
Water, pit toilets, tables, fire rings.
Under cottonwood on Jarbidge River.
Fish in river or do nothing.
No trash arrangements. 14-day limit.
6300 ft (1890 m)

## LAHONTAN SRA

(702) 867-3500
State map: C1
From FALLON, take US 50 W
for 18 miles (28.8 k). Another
option is 41-site **Silver Springs
Beach Unit** (S of SILVER SPRINGS and
E on Fir Ave).
**$4.** Open All Year.
53 close, open sites.
Water, flush toilets, showers, tables, fire
rings, dump station, boat ramp.
With beach on shores of Carson River
and huge Lahontan Reservoir.
Enjoy full range of water activities–boat,
waterski, swim, or fish.
14-day limit.
4200 ft (1260 m)

## LAKE MEAD NRA-Backcountry

(702) 293-8906
State map: F6
From LAS VEGAS, drive
27 miles (43.2 k) SE on US 93
**FREE** and no entrance fee. All
developed campgrounds cost more than
$5. At no cost, you can boat, ride
horseback, or walk to set up camp away
from developed or ecologically-sensitive
areas. To take your vehicle, obtain map
of approved roads and recommendations
from any ranger (most car camping
opportunities in AZ).
Open All Year.
NRA contains all of Lake Mead and
Lake Mohave plus surrounding desert.

Travel scenic drives. Hike to observe
wildlife and view petroglyphs. Boat, fish,
or swim.
Extreme summer temperatures. Thunderstorms cause flashfloods. Take care
around mine shafts, scorpions,
rattlesnakes, and Gila monsters.
2000 (600 m)

## LIKES LAKE

Stillwater NWR (702) 423-5128
State map: C2
Take US 50 E from FALLON
to Cemetery Rd. Turn Left (N)
and go .4 mile (650 m) to
Indian Lakes Rd. Follow this partially
paved road 10 miles (16 k).
**FREE** but choose a chore.
Open All Year.
Undesignated, open sites.
Chemical toilet (Apr 1–Sep 30).
Swim and fish 75-acre lake. Enjoy out-
standing birdwatching opportunities.
NO water. 8-day limit. Crowded
holidays. Insects, scorpions, and cows.
No ATVs.
3950 ft (1185 m)

## LYE CREEK

Humboldt NF (702) 623-5025
State map: A3
From PARADISE VALLEY,
drive N on paved-then-dirt
NV 792 for 18 miles (28.8 k)
up and over Hinkey Summit. Turn Left
(W) on FR 087 and go 2 miles (3.2 k).
**$4.** Open Jul 1–Oct 31; dry camping
off-season.
7 scattered, screened sites.
Water, pit toilets, tables, fire rings.
Savor solitude of remote aspen patch.
No trash arrangements (pack it out).
14-day limit. Hunting in season.
7400 ft (2220 m)

## MEADOW VALLEY

BLM (702) 289-4865
State map: D6
Find just North of URSINE on
Left (W) of NV 322. If you see
Spring Valley SP sign, you're
.8 mile (1.3 k) too far–no large vehicles.

# NEVADA

246

(See Echo Canyon or Spring Valley SPs.)
FREE but choose a chore.
Open All Year.
6 scattered, screened sites.
Pit toilets, tables.
Enjoy valley hiking–short walks or
extended treks. Fish, birdwatch, or relax.
NO water. 14-day limit.
6233 ft (1869 m)

## MILL CREEK

BLM (702) 635-4000
State map: B3
From BATTLE MOUNTAIN,
go S on NV 305 for 23 miles
(36.8 k). Turn Left (E) on
signed, gravel road. Go 4 miles (6.4 k).
FREE but choose a chore.
Open All Year.
10 (3 tent-only) sites.
Pit toilets, tables, grills, fire rings.
Under large cottonwood by small trout
stream in sagebrush desert.
Enjoy quiet getaway for fishing,
birdwatching, or doing nothing.
NO water. 14-day limit. Hot summer
temperatures; frequent thunderstorms.
4500 ft (1350 m)

## NORTH WILDHORSE

BLM (702) 753-0200
State map: A4
From ELKO, go 70 miles
(112 k) N on NV 225. (Also see
Wildhorse SRA and Wildhorse
Crossing.)
$3. Open Memorial Day–Nov 15.
18 close, screened sites. Water, pit toilets,
tables, grills, fire rings.
On north shore of Wildhorse Reservoir
in shady aspen grove.
Boat, fish, or birdwatch.
14-day/20-ft limits. Crowded holidays
and weekends. Jets break tranquility.
6200 ft (1860 m)

## PEAVINE CREEK

Toiyabe NF (702) 482-6286
State map: D3
From MANHATTAN, take
NV 377 E for 7 miles (11.2 k).
Turn Left (S) on NV 376 and

drive 2 miles (3.2 k). Turn Right (NW)
on FR 020 and go 10 miles (16 k).
FREE but choose a chore.
Open May–Oct.
7 close, open sites.
Pit toilets, tables, fire rings.
On stream near southern end of Arc
Dome Wilderness.
Explore scenic area on long hikes.
NO water. 14-day limit.
6700 ft (2010 m)

## PINE CREEK

Humboldt NF (208) 543-4129
State map: A5
From JARBIDGE, go S on
unpaved CR 752 for 3 miles
(4.8 k). (Also see Jarbidge.)
FREE but choose a chore.
Open Jun 1–Oct 31; dry camping
off-season.
6 scattered, screened sites.
Water, pit toilets, tables, fire rings.
Among cottonwood at confluence of
Pine Creek and Jarbidge River.
Fishing and hiking.
No trash arrangements (pack it out to
keep this place clean). 14-day limit.
6300 ft (1890 m)

## PINE CREEK

Toiyabe NF (702) 355-5301
State map: D4
From TONOPAH, go E on
US 6 for 5 miles (8 k). Turn
Left (N) on NV 376 and drive
13 miles (20.8 k). Continue N on CR 82
for 43.5 miles (69.6 k). Turn Left (W) on
FR 009 and continue 2.5 miles (4 k).
(Also see Barley Creek/Cottonwood.)
FREE but choose a chore.
Open May–Oct.
22 close, open sites.
Pit toilets, tables, fire rings.
On stream at base of Mt Jefferson on
edge of Alta Toquima Wilderness.
Fish and hike this remote area.
NO water. 14-day limit.
7600 ft (2280 m)

▲ ▲ ▲ ▲ ▲ ▲ ▲ ▲ ▲ ▲ ▲ ▲ ▲ ▲ ▲ ▲ ▲ ▲ ▲ ▲ ▲ ▲ ▲ ▲ ▲ ▲

## RUBY MARSH

Humboldt NF (702) 752-3357
State map: B5
From ELKO, take NV 227 SE
for 6 miles (9.6 k) to Jiggs
Turnoff (NV 228). Turn Right
(S) on 228 and drive 30 miles (48 k) to
pavement end. Take dirt CR 718 E for
15 miles (24 k) over Harrison Pass. Turn
Right (S) on CR 788 and continue
10 miles (16 k).
**$5**; for additional $6, reservations
accepted at (800) 283-2267.
Open May 20–Oct 15.
35 scattered, screened sites. Water, pit
toilets, dump station, tables, fire rings.
In secluded pinyon-juniper setting next
to Ruby Lake Wildlife Refuge.
Observe birds and other wildlife. Follow
fishing regulations.
No trash arrangements. 14-day limit.
6200 ft (1860 m)

## RYE PATCH SRA

(702) 538-7321
State map: B2
From LOVELOCK, take I-80
NE 21 miles (33.6 k). Exit W
for 1 mile (1.6 k).
**$5**. Open All Year.
44 close, open sites. Water, flush toilets,
dump station, showers, tables, grills, fire
rings, pay phone, boat ramp.
With beach and grassy area along shore
of large Rye Patch Reservoir.
Enjoy walking nature trails in addition
to swimming, boating, and fishing.
14-day limit.
4100 ft (1230 m)

## SAULSBURY WASH

Toiyabe NF (702) 355-5301
State map: D4
From TONOPAH, take US 6 E
for 34 miles (54.4 k).
FREE but choose a chore.
Open All Year.
12 close, open sites.
Water, pit toilets, tables, fire rings.
Picnic and relax in this foothills camp.
14-day limit.
5500 ft (1650 m)

## SHELDON NWR

(503) 947-3315
State map: A1
From DENIO JUNCTION, take
NV 140 W for 34 miles (54.4 k)
to 8A.
**FREE** but choose a chore.
Open All Year.
Undesignated, open sites. Pit toilets.
Observe wildlife from deer to bighorn
sheep to over 180 bird species. Find
ancient petroglyphs and artifacts (leave
undisturbed). Enjoy hot springs.
NO potable water (must be treated). No
trash arrangements (pack it out). Roads
deteriorate in bad weather.
4100 ft (1230 m)
For first 8 camps below, follow basic
directions plus:

### ▲ Badger
Turn Left (S) on 8A and go about
15 miles (24 k) to Summit Lake Rd. Turn
Left (SE). Badger will be on your Right
in about 5 miles (8 k).

### ▲ Bateman Spring
Turn Left (S) on 8A and go about
15 miles (24 k) to Summit Lake Rd. Turn
Left (SE). Bateman Spring will be on
your Right in 10 miles (16 k).

### ▲ Big Spring
Drive 2 miles (3.2 k) E of 8A on NV 140.
Look for unpaved road to N and Big
Spring Reservoir. Camp is about 2 miles
(3.2 k) up road.

### ▲ Catnip Reservoir
Turn Left (S) on 8A and go about 5 miles
(8 k) to fork. Bear Right (W) on 34A
about 13 miles (20.8 k).

### ▲ Fish Spring
Turn Left (S) on 8A and go about
15 miles (24 k). Camp is on Left (E).

### ▲ Gooch Spring
Turn Left (S) on 8A and drive about
5 miles (8 k).

### ▲ Horse Canyon Spring
Turn Left (S) on 8A and go about
10 miles (16 k). Camp is on Right (W).

### ▲ West Rock Spring
Turn Left (S) on 8A and go about 5 miles
(8 k) to fork. Go Right (W) on 34A and
continue about 5 miles (8 k) to camp on
Left (S).

▲ ▲ ▲ ▲ ▲ ▲ ▲ ▲ ▲ ▲ ▲ ▲ ▲ ▲ ▲ ▲ ▲ ▲ ▲ ▲ ▲ ▲ ▲ ▲ ▲ ▲ ▲

▲ **Virgin Valley**
Ignore above directions. From DENIO
JUNCTION, take NV 140 W for 25 miles
(40 k) to Duferrena headquarters. Turn
Left (S).

## SPORTSMAN'S BEACH

BLM (702) 882-1631
State map: D2
From HAWTHORNE, head N
on US 95 about 16 miles
(25.6 k). A couple of miles
north, another BLM camp, **Tamarack
Point**, may also be open.
**FREE** but choose a chore.
Open All Year.
17 close, open sites.
Pit toilets, tables, fire rings, boat ramp.
On western shore of Walker Reservoir.
Enjoy full range of water activities –
swimming, boating, fishing.
NO water. 14-day limit.
4500 ft (1350 m)

## SPRING VALLEY SP
**Horsethief Gulch**

(702) 962-5102
State map: D6
From PIOCHE, take NV 322 E
for 20 miles (32 k). (Nearby
options are Echo Canyon SP
and Meadow Valley.)
**$5.** Open All Year.
42 (6 tent-only) sites in open setting with
some screening. Water, flush/chemical
toilets, showers, dump station, tables,
grills, fire rings, pay phone, boat ramp.
Next to 65-acre lake nestled in steep
canyon. Upstream of lake, land opens to
wet meadow surrounded by rolling hills
and sandstone rock formations. Boat and
fish. Hike and ride horses.
14-day limit. Crowded holidays/summer
weekends. Noise/pet rules.
5800 ft (1740 m)

## TABOR CREEK

BLM (702) 753-0200
State map: A6
From WELLS, take US 93 N
for 12 miles (19.2 k). Turn on
gravel road for 10 miles

(16 k) – not designed for muddy use.
**FREE** but choose a chore.
Open May 1 – Nov 15; camping allowed
off-season.
10 scattered, screened sites.
Pit toilets, tables, fire rings.
Beside meandering creek with willow
and sage providing screening. In
foothills of Snake Mountains.
Fish creek or stroll area for bird and
other wildlife viewing.
NO water/trash arrangements. 14-day
limit. Crowded during hunting season.
6300 ft (1890 m)

## THOMAS CANYON

Humboldt NF (702) 752-3357
State map: B5
From ELKO, take NV 227 E
for 20 miles (32 k) to Lamoille
Canyon turnoff. Turn Right (S)
on paved FR 660. Go 8 miles (12.8 k).
**$5; for additional $6, reservations**
accepted at (800) 283-2267.
Open May 20 – Sep 14.
42 scattered, screened sites.
Water, tables, grills, fire rings.
Under aspen on Lamoille Canyon creek.
Hike on nature and longer trails.
Observe birds and wildlife. Fish in creek.
No trash arrangements (pack it out).
14-day limit. Crowded.
7600 ft (2280 m)

## TIMBER CREEK

Humboldt NF (702) 289-3031
State map: C6
Take US 93 N from MCGILL
for 5 miles (8 k). Turn Right
(E) on NV 486 (Duck Creek)
and go 8 miles (12.8 k). Turn Left (E) on
unpaved FR 425 (Timber Creek Rd) and
go 4 miles (6.4 k). (See East Creek.)
**$4.** Open Jun 1 – Sep 15.
6 sites.
Water, flush toilets, tables, fire rings.
Among conifers along Timber Creek.
Hike and take photographs.
14-day limit.
8200 ft (2460 m)

▲ ▲ ▲ ▲ ▲ ▲ ▲ ▲ ▲ ▲ ▲ ▲ ▲ ▲ ▲ ▲ ▲ ▲ ▲ ▲ ▲ ▲ ▲ ▲ ▲

## VALLEY OF FIRE SP

(702) 397-2088
State map: F6
Take I-15 NE from LAS
VEGAS for 34 miles (54.4 k) to
Exit 75 (NV 169). Turn E and
drive 18 miles (28.8 k).
**$4. Open All Year.**
51 close, open sites.
Water, flush toilets, dump station,
showers, tables, grills, fire rings, pay
phone, Visitor Center.
Among red sandstone formations in
Mohave Desert. Near ancient trees and
petroglyphs of prehistoric man.
Take photographs as you explore park's
many features. Enjoy water sports on
nearby Lake Mead.
Desert environment requires common
sense for survival. Crowded spring and
fall weekends. Generator rules.
2000 feet (600 m)

## WARD MOUNTAIN

Humboldt NF (702) 289-3031
State map: C5
Take US 6 W out of ELY for
7 miles (11.2 k).
**$4. Open May 21 – Oct 15; dry
camping off-season.**
29 scattered, screened sites.
Water, pit toilets, tables, fire rings.
Located in pinyon-juniper woodland.
Relax and walk.
14-day limit.
7400 ft (2220 m)

## WASHOE LAKE SRA

(702) 687-4319
State map: C1
From CARSON CITY, take
US 395 N for 7 miles (11.2 k)
to East Lake Blvd Exit. Follow
signs.
**$5. Open All Year.**
49 scattered, open sites with some
screening. Water, flush toilets, showers,
tables, grills, fire rings, pay phone, dump
station, boat ramp.
With beach on lake among sagebrush.
Hike trails. When droughts break, enjoy
swimming, boating, and fishing.

14-day limit (7-day limit when lake up).
Crowded weekends. Quiet hours.
5020 ft (1506 m)

## WHITE RIVER

Humboldt NF (702) 289-3031
State map: C6
From ELY, take US 6 W for
38 miles (60.8 k). Turn Right
(N) on dirt CR 1163 and drive
10 miles (16 k).
**FREE but choose a chore.**
Open Jun 1 – Sep 15; dry camping
off-season.
8 scattered, screened sites.
Water, pit toilets, tables, fire rings.
In pinyon-juniper ecology.
Get away and relax here.
No trash arrangements (pack it out).
14-day limit. Hunting in season.
7000 ft (2100 m)

## WILDHORSE CROSSING

Humboldt NF (702) 763-6691
State map: A4
Take NV 225 N from ELKO
for 70 miles (112 k). (Also see
North Wildhorse and Wild-
horse SRA.)
**$4. Open May 23 – Oct 15.**
20 scattered, open sites. Water, pit toilets,
tables, grills, fire rings.
In sagebrush along Owyhee River.
Fish!
14-day limit.
5900 ft (1770 m)

## WILDHORSE SRA

(702) 758-6493
State map: A5
Take NV 225 N from ELKO
for 67 miles (107.2 k). (Other
options are North Wildhorse
and Wildhorse Crossing.)
**$5. Open All Year.**
33 scattered, open sites. Water, flush/pit
toilets, dump station, showers, tables,
fire rings, pay phone, boat ramp.
In high-desert environment dominated
by sagebrush with access to lake in
scenic mountains.
Hiking plus swimming, boating, and

▲ ▲ ▲ ▲ ▲ ▲ ▲ ▲ ▲ ▲ ▲ ▲ ▲ ▲ ▲ ▲ ▲ ▲ ▲ ▲ ▲ ▲ ▲ ▲ ▲ ▲

fishing in reservoir.
14-day limit. Generator rules. Harsh
winters.
6226 ft (1866 m)

## WILLOW CREEK RA

Toiyabe NF (702) 355-5301
State map: F5
From INDIAN CREEK, take
Willow Canyon Rd (off US 95)
SE for 14 miles (22.4 k).
**FREE** but choose a chore.
Open Mar–Nov.
7 scattered, open sites.
Pit toilets, tables, fire rings.
On stream at northern edge of Mt
Charleston Wilderness.
Fish, picnic, and relax.
NO water. 14-day limit.
5800 ft (1740 m)

## WILSON RESERVOIR RA

BLM (702) 753-0200
State map: A4
From ELKO, take NV 225 N
for 27 miles (43.2 k). Turn Left
(NW) on NV 226 and go
40 miles (64 k). Watch signs. Last
16 miles (25.6 k) unpaved–impassable
when wet.
**FREE** but choose a chore.

Open Apr 1 – Sep 30; dry camping
off-season.
15 scattered, open sites.
Water, pit toilets, tables, fire rings, dump
station, small boat ramp. (Scheduled for
reconstruction and fees).
In sagebrush setting with views of Bull
Run Mountains.
Enjoy scenery. Fish and boat.
14-day/30-ft limits. Crowded holidays.
5300 ft (1590 m)

## ZUNINO RESERVOIR

BLM (702) 753-0200
State map: B5
From ELKO, go 7 miles
(11.2 k) E on NV 227. Turn
Right (S) on NV 228 and drive
additional 23 miles (36.8 k).
**FREE** but choose a chore.
Open All Year.
22 (2 tent-only) sites scattered in open
setting.
Pit toilets in picnic area, tables, grills.
On north and south shores of reservoir
with views of ranch hay fields and Ruby
Mountains to east.
Fish, boat, birdwatch, or just relax.
14-day limit. Reservoir dry by mid-
summer in drought).
5600 ft (1680 m)

# New Mexico

Grid conforms to official state map. For your copy, call (800) 545-2040
or write Department of Tourism, 1100 St Francis Dr, Santa Fe, NM 87503.

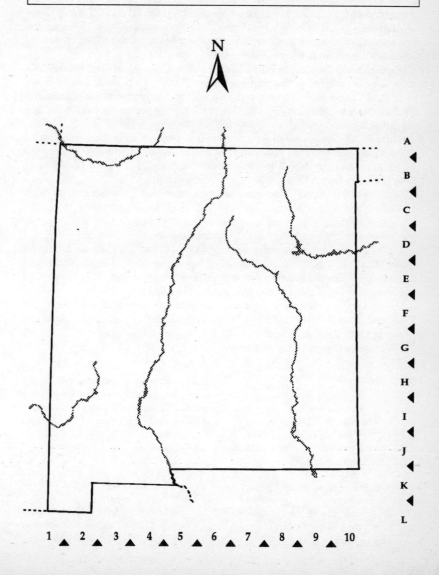

▲ ▲ ▲ ▲ ▲ ▲ ▲ ▲ ▲ ▲ ▲ ▲ ▲ ▲ ▲ ▲ ▲ ▲ ▲ ▲ ▲ ▲ ▲ ▲ ▲ ▲ ▲ ▲

New Mexico campsites are concentrated in the scenic mountainous regions of the state. Also here are picturesque Spanish villages, Indian pueblos, prehistoric ruins, modern-day art colonies, and renowned winter sports areas.

In the $5-or-less camping category, the **National Park Service** (NPS) offers camping opportunities in the following areas: Chaco Culture National Historical Park (NHP), Bandelier National Monument (NM) (backcountry), El Malpais National Conservation Area (backcountry-joint administration with BLM), El Morro NM, White Sands NM (backcountry), Carlsbad Caverns NP (backcountry). Campgrounds near the Gila Cliff Dwellings NM are actually run by the Gila National Forest. Other federal agencies offering additional camping opportunities include **Bureau of Land Management** (BLM) and **US Army Corps of Engineers** (COE). On one hand, the New Mexico State Parks (SPs) are too expensive ($6 and up for any campsite). On the other hand, the US Forest Service administers numerous $5-or-less campsites in New Mexico.

In addition to the developed campsites in the **Carson National Forest** (NF), there are five wilderness designations: Wheeler Peak, Latir Peak, Cruces Basin, Pecos, and Chama River Canyon, plus two wild and scenic rivers: Rio Chama and the Rio Grande. When at high-altitude, look for the returning bald eagle and peregrine falcon.

**Santa Fe NF** lists as special attractions four wilderness areas (Pecos, San Pedro Parks, Chama, and Dome) plus two wild and scenic rivers (the East Fork of the Jemez River and the Pecos). Wildlife include bald eagle, peregrine falcon, mule deer, bighorn sheep, elk, black bear, and Abert squirrel.

Segmented **Cibola NF** offers more tall mountains with panoramic views (such as Sandia) and four wilderness areas (Apache Kid, Sandia Mountain, Manzano Mountain, Withington). Wildlife reports list antelope, black bear, elk, gray fox, mountain lion, bighorn sheep, and, of course, coyote.

The Gila Cliff Dwellings and a suspended trail called The Catwalk are found in the **Gila NF**. Too, there are three wilderness areas (Gila, Aldo Leopold, and Blue Range). Unique wildlife viewing opportunities include Gila trout, Gila topminnow, spotted bat, hooded skunk, and a banded rattlesnake.

In the **Lincoln NF**, see the Smokey Bear Museum near Capitan and the limestone caves in the Guadalupe Mountains. Wilderness areas include White Mountain and Capitan Mountain.

Welcome to the land of enchantment.

▲ ▲ ▲ ▲ ▲ ▲ ▲ ▲ ▲ ▲ ▲ ▲ ▲ ▲ ▲ ▲ ▲ ▲ ▲ ▲ ▲ ▲ ▲ ▲ ▲ ▲ ▲ ▲

**ABIQUIU DAM**

COE (505) 685-4371
State map: B5
From ABIQUIU, proceed 67 miles (107.2 k) NW on US 84 then 2 miles (3.2 k) SW on NM 96. $3. Open Apr 15–Sep 15.
63 sites around lake. Water, flush and pit toilets, dump station, tables, grills, fire rings, boat ramp.
On Rio Chama among mesas, canyons, pinyons, and junipers in Georgia O'Keeffe country.

Water enthusiasts boat, waterski, swim, and fish. Landlubbers hike or tour nearby Ghost Ranch Living Museum. 14-day limit. Hunting for waterfowl during season.
6200 ft (1860 m)

**AGUA PIEDRA**

Carson NF (505) 758-6200
State map: C6
Drive 1.5 miles (2.4 k) NW of TRES RITOS on NM 518 then Left on FR 708. (3-site **South Agua**

Piedra is up road. Duran Canyon and
Flechado are off NM 518.)
**FREE** but choose a chore.
Open May–Oct.
10 sites.
Flush and pit toilets, tables, fire rings.
Hike on national recreational trail. Fish
in Agua Piedra Creek.
NO water. 14-day/22-ft limits.
8100 ft (2430 m)

**AGUIRRE SPRING**
BLM (505) 525-8228
State map: J5
Take US 70 for 3.5 miles
(5.6 k) E of ORGAN to
Aguirre Spring Rd. Follow curvy road
approximately 5 miles (8 k)–ices quickly
in mid-winter. Entrance gate locks 6pm
winters and 8pm summers.
$3. Open All Year.
55 scattered, open or screened sites. Pit/
chemical toilets, tables, grills, fire rings.
On lower, eastern slope of Organ Mountains in pinyon-juniper transition
between Chihuahuan Desert and pine-
oak life zones.
Enjoy hiking, rock climbing, wildlife
watching, and photography. View White
Sands missile range activities below and
mountain climbers above.
NO water. 7-day/20-ft limits. Quiet
hours. Crowded weekends except
winter. Rattlesnakes. No firearms or
fireworks.
5500 ft (1650 m)

**ANGEL PEAK**
BLM (505) 327-5344
State map: B3
Proceed S of BLOOMFIELD
on paved NM 44 for 15 miles
(24 k). Turn Left (E) on gravel road at
sign and continue another 5 miles (8 k).
**FREE** but choose a chore.
Open All Year.
10 scattered, open or screened sites.
Pit toilets, tables, grills, fire rings, sun
shelters.
On rim of Kutz Canyon, with stunning
views of "badlands" plus La Plata and
San Juan Mountains.

Walk nature trail; hike into badlands;
and take photographs of scenery.
NO water. 14-day limit.
6000 ft (1800 m)

**ANGOSTURA**
Carson NF (505) 758-6200
State map: C7
Travel 3 miles (4.8 k) SE of
TRES RITOS by way of
NM 518. (Agua Piedra and Duran
Canyon are in vicinity.)
**FREE** but choose a chore.
Open May–Sep.
11 sites. Pit toilets.
On Angostura Creek.
Fish in creek or walk nature trail.
NO water. 14-day/16-ft limits.
9200 ft (2760 m)

**ARGENTINA/BONITO TRAILHEAD**
Lincoln NF (505) 257-4095
State map: H6
Follow NM 48 for 9 miles
(14.4 k) N out of RUIDOSO.
Turn Left (W) onto NM 37 for 1.5 miles
(2.4 k). Turn Left (SW) on FR 107. Follow
to end–5 miles (8 k) past South Fork.
**FREE** but choose a chore.
Open All Year.
Undesignated, scattered sites–open or
screened. Pit toilets and horse corrals.
At end of Bonito Canyon with access to
Bonito Lake and White Mountain
Wilderness–a good base for hiking,
horseback riding, fishing, birdwatching,
and taking photographs.
NO water/trash arrangements. Crowded
holidays. 14-day limit. Hunting nearby.
7800 ft (2340 m)

**ASPEN BASIN**
Santa Fe NF (505) 753-7331
State map: C6
From SANTA FE, drive
approximately 15 miles (24 k)
NE on paved scenic byway NM 475
(Hyde Park Rd). (Pass Big Tesuque.)
**FREE** but choose a chore.
Open All Year.
10 (9 best for tents, 5 best for RVs) close,
open sites. Pit toilets, tables, fire rings.

Among mixed conifers and aspens next to Santa Fe ski area and near major trailhead into Pecos Wilderness.

Skiing, hiking, birdwatching, and taking photographs favorite pastimes. Fishing opportunities nearby.

NO water. Crowded during fall color and winter ski seasons. 14-day/16-ft limits. Generators frowned upon. Hunting nearby.

10300 ft (3090 m)

## BANDELIER NM-Backcountry

(505) 672-3861
State map: C5
From SANTA FE, take US 84/285 N for 16 miles (25.6 k). Turn Left (W) on NM 502 and go 12 miles (19.2 k). Go SW on NM 4 toward WHITE ROCK another 8 miles (12.8 k) to entrance.

FREE but $5/car entrance fee (or pass). (Juniper Campground costs over $5.) Inquire about free backcountry permit at Visitor Center.

Open All Year.

Though named after explorer Adolf Bandelier, native Americans inhabited this region for centuries. See remnants of their homes in cliff dwellings and pueblos in canyons and mesas. Enjoy same mountain vistas filled with pinyon, juniper, and ponderosa pine forests.

No wood fires.

7000 ft (2100 m)

## BEARTRAP

Cibola NF (505) 854-2281
State map: G3
From MAGDALENA, head W for 12 miles (19.2 k) on US 60 then Left (S) for 15 miles (24 k) on FR 549. Watch for signs. (Also see Hughes Mill.)

FREE but choose a chore.

Open May 1–Oct 31; camping allowed off-season.

4 scattered, open sites.

Pit toilets, tables, grills.

In open meadow surrounded by spruce and fir in mountain canyon with spring and small stream.

Quietly enjoy hiking, birdwatching, and photography.

NO water/trash arrangements. Do not pollute stream or spring. 14-day/30-ft limits. Hunting in season. ATVs.

8600 ft (2580 m)

## BEN LILLY

Gila NF (505) 388-8201
State map: H2
Go 31 miles (49.6 k) NE of GLENWOOD via US 180 then NM 159. (Bursum, Gillita, and Willow Creek are off NM 159 too.)

FREE but choose a chore.

Open Apr–Nov.

6 sites. Pit toilets, tables, grills.

In Mogollon Mountains not far from Snow Lake. Fish there.

NO water. 30-day/17-ft limits.

8100 ft (2430 m)

## BIG TESUQUE WALK-IN

Santa Fe NF (505) 753-7331
State map: C6
Proceed 12 miles (19.2 k) NE of SANTA FE on paved scenic byway NM 475 (Hyde Park Rd). Aspen Basin is another 3 miles (4.8 k).

FREE but choose a chore.

Open May–Oct.

7 scattered, relatively open sites.

Pit toilets, tables, fire rings.

In mixed conifer and aspen setting.

Hiking, birdwatching, and photo opportunities. 2-3 miles (4 k) to fishing and 5 miles (8 k) to skiing.

NO water. Crowded during fall color. 14-day limit. Concerns: highway exhaust fumes and stray bullets from hunters.

9700 ft (2910 m)

## BIGHORN

Gila NF (505) 539-2481
State map: H1
Find N of GLENWOOD town limits on US 180. "The Catwalk" is nearby.

FREE but choose a chore.

Open All Year; camping allowed off-season.

6 close, open sites.

Pit toilets, tables, grills.
Among pinyons and junipers.
Hiking, birdwatching, and fishing.
NO water. Hunting in season.
4800 ft (1440 m)

## BLACK CANYON-LOWER & UPPER

Gila NF (505) 536-2250
State map: I3
From MIMBRES, go 4 miles
(6.4 k) N on NM 61. Turn
Right (N) on FR 150 for another 26 miles
(41.6 k). (Pass Rocky Canyon.)
FREE but choose a chore.
Open All Year.
5 sites (3 sites-Lower; 2 sites-Upper).
Pit toilets, tables, fire rings.
Near constantly running water, lots of
grass, and ponderosa pine.
Fish, hike, observe/photograph nature.
Treat water and pack out trash. Roads
subject to closure in bad weather.
Hunting in season.
6700 ft (2010 m)

## BORREGO MESA

Santa Fe NF (505) 753-7331
State map: C6
Travel 1 mile (1.6 k) N of
Santa Cruz Reservoir on
NM 4 then Right (E) for 9 miles (14.4 k)
on dirt FR 430.
FREE but choose a chore.
Open May-Oct.
8 scattered, open sites.
Pit toilets, tables, fire rings.
On NW edge of Pecos Wilderness in
stand of large ponderosa pine.
Hiking, birdwatching and photography
on site. Fishing about 1 mile (1.6 k) S on
Rio Medio.
NO water. 14-day/16-ft limits. Hunting
in season. Vandalism problems in past.
8400 ft (2520 m)

## BURSUM

Gila NF (505) 539-2481
State map: H2
Drive 22 miles (35.2 k) NE of
GLENWOOD via US 180 then
NM 159. (Also see Ben Lilly, Gillita, and
Willow Creek.)

FREE but choose a chore.
Open May-Nov; camping allowed
off-season.
2 sites. Pit toilets, tables, grills.
In mixed conifer and aspen zone.
Hike, birdwatch, take photos, or fish.
NO water. Hunting in season. Check
weather-road conditions.
9100 ft (2730 m)

## BUZZARD PARK

Carson NF (505) 758-6200
State map: B4
Head 35 miles (56 k) NE of
BLANCO on US 64. (Also see
Cedar Springs.)
FREE but choose a chore.
Open May-Nov.
4 sites. Pit toilets.
Try to relax here.
NO water. 14-day/32-ft limits.
7300 ft (2190 m)

## CABRESTO LAKE

Carson NF (505) 758-6200
State map: B7
Proceed 8 miles (12.8 k) NE
of QUESTA via NM 38, Left
on FR 134, and Left again on FR 134A, a
2-mile (3.2 k) dirt roadbed not recom-
mended for trailers or RVs. (Also see
Goat Hill.)
FREE but choose a chore.
Open May-Sep.
9 sites. Pit toilets, tables, fire rings.
Along lakeshore.
Fishing and boating (no motors).
NO water. 14-day limit.
9500 ft (2850 m)

## CANJILON CREEK

Carson NF (505) 758-6200
State map: B5
Above ABIQUIU off US 84,
find town of CANJILON.
Travel 9 miles (14.4 k) E by way of
NM 110/FR 559 then 1 mile (1.6 k) N on
dirt FR 130–not for trailers or RVs. (Pass
FR 129 that leads to Canjilon Lakes
complex.)
FREE but choose a chore.
Open Jun-Sep.

▲ ▲ ▲ ▲ ▲ ▲ ▲ ▲ ▲ ▲ ▲ ▲ ▲ ▲ ▲ ▲ ▲ ▲ ▲ ▲ ▲ ▲ ▲ ▲

4 sites. Pit toilets.
On creek with "good" fishing.
NO water. 14-day limit.
9300 ft (2790 m)

## CANJILON LAKES

Carson NF (505) 758-6200
State map: B5
Drive 7 miles (11.2 k) E of
CANJILON via NM 110/
FR 559 then Left (N) for 4 miles (6.4 k)
uphill on curvy FR 129. (Turnoff to
Canjilon Creek is couple miles farther on
FR 559.)
$5. Open May 20–Sep 30.
40 sites in three different areas (Lower,
Middle, and Upper). &
Water, pit toilets, tables, fire rings.
Among lakes at base of Canjilon Moun-
tain. Choose a lake to boat and fish.
14-day/16-ft limits.
9900 ft (2970 m)

## CAPILLA PEAK

Cibola NF (505) 847-2990
State map: F5
From MANZANO, go W up
FR 245–not the best of roads.
(Pass New Canyon.)
FREE but choose a chore.
Open May–Sep.
10 scattered sites in meadow.
Pit toilets, tables, fire rings.
On mountain designated for National
Eyes on Wildlife viewing. HawkWatch
International conducts annual fall raptor
migration count here.
Hike. Enjoy watching wildlife, wild-
flowers, clouds, and stars.
NO water at this time–fee when added.
14-day/16-ft limits. Hunting in season.
9200 ft (2760 m)

## CAPULIN

Carson NF (505) 758-6200
State map: B7
Head 7 miles (11.2 k) SE of
TAOS on US 64. (Near La
Sombra and Las Petacas.)
FREE but choose a chore.
Open May–Oct.
10 sites. &

Pit toilets, tables, fire rings.
On stream.
Fish in Rio Fernando de Taos and its
tributaries.
NO water. 14-day/16-ft limits.
7900 ft (2370 m)

## CARLSBAD CAVERNS NP
Backcountry

(505) 785-2232
State map: J8
From CARLSBAD, drive
20 miles (32 k) SW on
US 62/180. Visitor Center is 7 miles
(11.2 k) W of WHITES CITY on NM 7.
FREE. No campground here; inquire
about backcountry permit and safety
recommendations at Visitor Center.
Open All Year.
There's more to Carlsbad than caverns.
Explore rugged backcountry full of
desert flora (numerous cacti) and fauna
(from deer to rattlesnake).
Prepare for extreme weather changes at
any time of year.
3100 ft (930 m)

## CEBOLLA MESA

Carson NF (505) 758-6200
State map: B6
Proceed 8 miles (12.8 k) SW
of QUESTA on NM 522 then
dirt FR 29–slick when wet.
FREE but choose a chore.
Open May–Sep.
5 sites. Pit toilets, tables.
Hike into Rio Grande Wild and Scenic
River Area. Fish too.
No water. 14-day/32-ft limits.
7300 ft (2190 m)

## CEDAR SPRINGS

Carson NF (505) 758-6200
State map: B4
Travel 30 miles (48 k) NE of
BLANCO via US 64. (Buzzard
Peak is nearby option off this highway.)
FREE but choose a chore.
Open May–Nov.
4 sites. Pit toilets.
NO water. 14-day/32-ft limits.
7300 ft (2190 m)

▲ ▲ ▲ ▲ ▲ ▲ ▲ ▲ ▲ ▲ ▲ ▲ ▲ ▲ ▲ ▲ ▲ ▲ ▲ ▲ ▲ ▲ ▲ ▲ ▲ ▲ ▲

## CHACO CULTURE NHP-Gallo

(505) 786-7014
State map: C3
Call (505) 988-6767 or 6716
about road conditions.
From **North**, turn off NM 44 at NAGEEZI and follow CR 7800 for 22 miles (35.2 k) to NM 57. Visitor Center is 15 miles (24 k) ahead.
From **South**, turn N onto NM 371/NM 57 from I-40 at THOREAU and travel 44 miles (70.4 k) on paved road. 2 miles (3.2 k) N of CROWN-POINT, NM 57 turns to Right. Continue E on NM 57 to marked turnoff. From here, 20-mile (32-k) stretch of unpaved road leads to Visitor Center.
$5 plus $3 entrance fee (or pass).
Open All Year.
64 close, open sites.
Flush toilets, tables, fire rings, grills, pay phone, dump station.
In high-desert canyon environment with steep mesas and cliff dwelling ruins. See ruins of Anasazi-built major structures such as Pueblo Bonito and several outliers such as Pueblo Alto on mesa. Take great care with these major national treasures. Hike, attend ranger programs, study archeology and archeoastronomy. Water available only at Visitor Center. Very little shade. In summer, wear hats, cool clothing, and sunscreen.
6200 ft (1860 m)

## CHERRY CREEK

Gila NF (505) 538-2771
State map: I2
Take NM 15 N from SILVER CITY about 14 miles (22.4 k) -4.5 miles (7.2 k) past PINOS ALTOS. (McMillan is 1 mile (1.6 k) farther.)
**FREE** but choose a chore.
Open Apr 1–Nov 15.
6 close, open sites.
Pit toilets, tables, grills.
In riparian zone along stream.
Hike, observe and photograph natural surroundings.
NO water. 22-ft limit. Pets allowed.
Hunting in season.
7000 ft (2100 m)

## CIMARRON

Carson NF (505) 758-6200
State map: A7
Drive 30 miles (48 k) SW of COSTILLA (near CO border) via NM 196, FR 1950, and FR 1910. (McCrystal not far as crow flies.)
$5. Open May–Nov.
32 sites. &
Pit toilets, tables, fire rings, horse corrals.
In Sangre de Cristo Mountains.
Enjoy fishing or horseback riding.
14-day/32-ft limits.
9400 ft (2820 m)

## CLEAR CREEK

Santa Fe NF (505) 289-3264
State map: C5
Go 12 miles (19.2 k) E of CUBA on NM 126–last 10 miles (16 k) unpaved but scheduled for improvement during 1993–94. If temporarily closed, check Rio Las Vacas. (Also see Seven Springs.)
$5. Open May–Oct.
14 scattered , screened sites. &
Hand water pump, pit toilets, tables, grills, fire rings.
Along clear creek in ponderosa pine and mixed conifer stands.
Fish. Observe and photograph nature.
14-day/16-ft limits. Crowded weekends.
Hunting in season.
8500 ft (2550 m)

## COAL MINE

Cibola NF (505) 287-8833
State map: E3
Head 10 miles (16 k) NE of GRANTS on NM 547. (Lobo Canyon is nearby.)
$5; for additional $6, reservations accepted at (800) 282-2267.
Open May 15–Sep 30.
17 close, screened, paved units.
Central water faucet, flush toilets, tables, grills, fire rings.
Among pinyon and juniper in canyon below Mt Taylor.
Walk nature trail. Identify birds.
14-day/22-ft limits. Quiet hours.
7600 ft (2280 m)

▲ ▲ ▲ ▲ ▲ ▲ ▲ ▲ ▲ ▲ ▲ ▲ ▲ ▲ ▲ ▲ ▲ ▲ ▲ ▲ ▲ ▲ ▲ ▲ ▲

## COMALES

Carson NF (505) 758-6200
State map: C6
From PENASCO, go 7 miles
(11.2 k) E via NM 75 then
NM 578. (See Agua Piedra or Flechado.)
FREE but choose a chore.
Open May–Oct.
2 sites. Pit toilets, tables, fire rings.
Hike into canyons or fish in Rio Pueblo.
NO water. 14-day/16-ft limits.
7800 ft (2340 m)

## COTTONWOOD CANYON

Gila NF (505) 547-2612
State map: G1
13 miles (20.8 k) SW of
RESERVE via NM 12 and
US 180. (Pueblo Park is nearby.)
FREE but choose a chore.
Open Apr–Nov.
2 sites. Pit toilets, fire rings.
In Tularosa Mountains.
Relax and indulge in birdwatching.
NO water. 30-day/22-ft limits.
6000 ft (1800 m)

## COW CREEK

Santa Fe NF (505) 757-6121
State map: D6
Travel 10 miles (16 k) NE of
PECOS on gravel/dirt FR 86
then dirt FR 92. Narrow road frequently
creates right-of-way problems–not
recommended for trailers.
FREE but choose a chore.
Open May–Oct.
5 scattered, open sites.
Pit toilets, tables, fire rings.
Along Cow Creek in ponderosa pine and
riparian vegetation.
Fish and observe wildlife. Tour nearby
Pecos NM.
NO water/trash arrangements. Crowded
summer weekends. 14-day limit.
8200 ft (2460 m)

## CUCHILLA DEL MEDIO

Carson NF (505) 758-6200
State map: B6
Drive 5 miles (8 k) N of
TAOS via US 64/NM 522
then Right (NE) for 9 miles (14.4 k) on
NM 150. (Nearby free camps include
Lower Hondo, Twining, and Upper
Italianos.)
FREE but choose a chore.
Open May–Sep.
3 sites. Pit toilets.
In Hondo Canyon below Taos Ski Valley
and Bull-of-the-Woods Mountain.
Fish in mountain streams.
NO water. 14-day/16-ft limits.
7800 ft (2340 m)

## DATIL WELL

BLM (505) 835-0412
State map: G3
Find 1 mile (1.6 k) W of
DATIL with access from
NM 12 or US 60.
$5. Open Apr–Oct; dry camping
off-season.
22 scattered, relatively open sites.
Central water, pit toilets, tables, grills,
fire rings, some sun shelters, firewood.
At one of water wells along historic
Magdalena Livestock Driveway.
Hike along ridges to view San Augustine
Plains and surrounding mountains. Look
for wildlife.
Prohibitions on woodcutting tools,
firearms, and trail bikes. Rules on pets
and generators. Speed limits. Park in
specified places only. 7-day limit.
7000 ft (2100 m)

## DIPPING VAT

Gila NF (505) 388-8201
State map: H2
From RESERVE, drive 6 miles
(9.6 k) S on NM 435; 28 miles
(44.8 k) SE on FR 141; 8 miles (12.8 k)
SW on FR 78; then another 7 miles
(11.2 k) E on FR 142.
$5. Open May 1–Nov 25.
40 sites. &
Water, chemical/pit toilets, tables, grills,
fire rings, boat launch.
On remote lake.
Boat or fish. Walk nature trail or hike
into Gila Wilderness.
30-day/22-ft limits.
7300 ft (2190 m)

▲ ▲ ▲ ▲ ▲ ▲ ▲ ▲ ▲ ▲ ▲ ▲ ▲ ▲ ▲ ▲ ▲ ▲ ▲ ▲ ▲ ▲ ▲ ▲

## DURAN CANYON

Carson NF (505) 758-6200
State map: C7
Head .5 mile (800 m) SE of
TRES RITOS on NM 518; Left
(NE) for 2 miles (3.2 k) on FR 76; then
Right (SE) for .5 mile (800 m) on FR 76A.
(Also see Agua Piedra, Comales, and
Flechado.)
$5. Open May–Sep.
12 sites.
Water, pit toilets, tables, fire rings.
Near one of three little rivers, Rito la
Presa. Walk nature trail or fish.
Access sometimes blocked during high
water. 14-day/22-ft limits.
9100 ft (2730 m)

## ECHO AMPHITHEATER

Carson NF (505) 758-6200
State map: B5
Travel 15 miles (24 k) NW of
ABIQUIU by way of NM 84.
$4. Open All Year.
10 sites.
Water, pit toilets, tables, fire rings.
Set in Georgia O'Keeffe country.
Enjoy nature trail. Tour nearby Ghost
Ranch Living Museum.
14-day/32-ft limits.
6600 ft (1980 m)

## EL MALPAIS NATIONAL
## CONSERVATION AREA-Backcountry

(505) 285-5406
State map: E3
Find S of GRANTS off I-40
and NM 117 or NM 53.
FREE. Inquire about backcountry
permits at Visitor Center (temporarily at
624 East Santa Fe Ave in Grants) or at
BLM ranger station on NM 117 (4 miles
S of Grants).
Open All Year.
Among rugged lava flows, sandstone
mesas, and pinyon-juniper forests.
Hike and climb rocks.
Hunting in season.

## EL MORRO NM

(505) 783-4226
State map: E2
From GALLUP, go 56 miles
(89.6 k) via NM 602 and
NM 53. From GRANTS, drive 42 miles
(67.2 k) SW on NM 53.
$5 plus $1/person or $3/car entrance fee
(or pass). Open All Year.
9 scattered sites with some screening.
Central water, pit toilets, tables, grills.
In pinyon-juniper forest near pioneer
trail landmark, Inscription Rock.
Walk trails and take photos of rock
carvings and prehistoric Indian ruins
(treat with care). Tour Visitor Center and
attend ranger programs.
No large trailers and motorhomes. No
generators. Ice and snow in winter.
7200 ft (2160 m)

## EL RITO

Carson NF (505) 758-6200
State map: B5
Head 5 miles (8 k) NW of
village of EL RITO by way of
NM 110/FR 559.
FREE but choose a chore.
Open Apr–Oct.
11 sites. Pit toilets, tables, fire rings.
Fish in little river, El Rito.
NO water. 14-day/22-ft limits.
7600 ft (2280 m)

## FLECHADO

Carson NF (505) 758-6200
State map: C6
Travel 3 miles (4.8 k) NW of
TRES RITOS on NM 518.
(Also see Agua Piedra, Comales, and
Duran Canyon.)
FREE but choose a chore.
Open May–Sep.
8 sites. Pit toilets, tables, fire rings.
In canyon below Gallegos Peak.
Hike or fish along this mountain stream.
NO water. 14-day/16-ft limits.
8400 ft (2520 m)

▲ ▲ ▲ ▲ ▲ ▲ ▲ ▲ ▲ ▲ ▲ ▲ ▲ ▲ ▲ ▲ ▲ ▲ ▲ ▲ ▲ ▲ ▲ ▲

## FORKS

Gila NF (505) 536-9461
State map: H2
Proceed 38 miles (60.8 k) N of
SILVER CITY on NM 15.
(Also see Grapevine and Scorpion.)
**FREE** but choose a chore.
Open All Year.
20 scattered sites. Pit toilets.
Near Gila Forks confluence.
Tour and photograph Gila Cliff
Dwellings as well as soak in area hot
springs. Hike, fish, and birdwatch too.
Treat water before drinking. Pack out
trash. Hunting in season. Roads ice in
winter. Crowded summer holidays.
Raccoons and skunks. Quiet hours and
generator rules. 30-day limit.
5700 ft (1710 m)

## FOURTH OF JULY

Cibola NF (505) 847-2990
State map: E5
From MOUNTAINAIR, travel
5 miles (8 k) N on NM 542;
15 miles (24 k) NW on NM 55 to
TAJIQUE; then Left (W) for 8 miles
(12.8 k) on FR 55. (Pass Tajique camp.)
**FREE** but choose a chore.
Open Apr–Oct; camping allowed
off-season.
26 sites. &
Pit toilets, tables, fire rings.
In Manzano Mountains near springs.
Hike. View and photograph scenery and
wildlife. Fish. Cross-country ski.
NO water at this time–fee when added.
14-day/22-ft limits. Hunting in season.
7500 ft (2250 m)

## GILLITA

Gila NF (505) 388-8201
State map: H2
32 miles (51.2 k) NE of
GLENWOOD via US 180 then
NM 159. (See Ben Lilly, Bursum, and
Willow Creek.)
**FREE** but choose a chore.
Open Apr–Nov.
6 sites. Pit toilets, tables, fire rings.
In Mogollon Mountains, approaching
continental divide at Elk Mountain.

Hike into Gila Wilderness. Fish streams.
NO water. 30-day/17-ft limits.
8100 ft (2430 m)

## GOAT HILL

Carson NF (505) 758-6200
State map: B6
Take NM 38 for 4 miles
(6.4 k) E of QUESTA. (An
alternative is Cabresto Lake.)
**FREE** but choose a chore.
Open May–Sep.
3 sites. Pit toilets.
At Goat Hill Gulch on Red River.
"Good" fishing here.
NO water. 14-day/32-ft limits.
7500 ft (2250 m)

## GRAPEVINE

Gila NF (505) 536-9461
State map: H2
Travel 37.7 miles (60.3 k) N
from SILVER CITY on
NM 15. (Also see Forks and Scorpion.)
**FREE** but choose a chore.
Open All Year.
20 sites. Pit toilets.
At two forks of Gila River.
Hike to Gila Cliff Dwellings and hot
springs. Fish and watch for wildlife.
Take lots of photos.
Treat water before drinking. Pack out
trash. Generator rules. Quiet hours.
30-day limit. Crowded summer
weekends and holidays. Raccoons.
Skunks. Hunting in season. Roads ice.
5700 ft (1710 m)

## HODGES

Carson NF (505) 758-6200
State map: C6
From PENASCO, drive
1.5 miles (2.4 k) SE on NM 73
then Left (SE) for 4 miles (6.4 k) on
FR 116. (Continue a couple miles to
Santa Barbara.)
**FREE** but choose a chore.
Open May–Oct.
14 sites. Pit toilets, tables, fire rings.
Fish on Rio Santa Barbara.
NO water on-site. 14-day/22-ft limits.
8200 ft (2460 m)

▲ ▲ ▲ ▲ ▲ ▲ ▲ ▲ ▲ ▲ ▲ ▲ ▲ ▲ ▲ ▲ ▲ ▲ ▲ ▲ ▲ ▲ ▲ ▲ ▲ ▲

## HOPEWELL LAKE

Carson NF (505) 758-6200
State map: B6
Go 20 miles (32 k) NW of
TRES PIEDRAS on US 64.
FREE but choose a chore.
Open May–Oct.
6 sites. Pit toilets.
On lakeshore. Enjoy fishing and boating
(electric motors).
NO water. 14-day/16-ft limits.
9800 ft (2940 m)

## HORSESHOE SPRINGS

Santa Fe NF (505) 829-3535
State map: C5
Head 9 miles (14.4 k) N of
JEMEZ SPRINGS on NM 4;
Left (NW) for 1 mile (1.6 k) on NM 126;
then Left (W) for 1 mile (1.6 k) on dirt
FR 12–muddy after rain.
FREE but choose a chore.
Open May–Oct.
3 sites. Central water faucet, pit toilets,
tables, fire rings.
Among ponderosa pine.
Relax and, maybe, do some fishing in
stream .75 mile (1.2 k) away.
Generator rules. 14-day limit.
7800 ft (2340 m)

## HUGHES MILL

Cibola NF (505) 854-2281
State map: G4
From MAGDALENA, go W
12 miles (19.2 k) on US 60
then S on NM 168/FR 549 for 17 miles
(27.2 k) into Beartrap Canyon. (Pass
Beartrap.)
FREE but choose a chore.
Open May 1–Oct 31; camping allowed
off-season.
2 scattered, open sites.
Pit toilets, tables, grills.
In large meadow in canyon.
Explore and take photos.
NO water/trash arrangements–come
prepared. Hunting in season. ATVs.
14-day/20-ft limits.
8000 ft (2400 m)

## IRON CREEK

Gila NF (505) 536-2250
State map: I3
Proceed 12 miles (19.2 k) W
of KINGSTON on NM 152.
FREE but choose a chore.
Open May 1–Oct 15; camping allowed
off-season.
15 sites.
Pit toilets, tables, grills, fire rings.
In ponderosa pine and fir with running
water all year.
Enjoy nearby hiking trail for bird-
watching and photo opportunities.
Treat water before drinking. 14-day/22-ft
limits. Hunting in season. ATVs.
7000 ft (2100 m)

## IRON GATE

Santa Fe NF (505) 757-6121
State map: C6
Travel 19 miles (30.4 k) N of
PECOS on paved NM 63 then
4 miles (6.4 k) NE on FR 223–very rough
road not recommended after rains or for
low-clearance vehicles.
FREE but choose a chore.
Open May–Oct.
15 (1 tent-only) scattered, open sites.
Pit toilets, tables, fire rings, horse corrals.
In mixed conifer and aspen stands near
Pecos Wilderness.
Hiking and horseback riding in wilder-
ness as well as photography.
NO water/trash arrangements.
14-day/16-ft limits. Hunting in season.
9400 ft (2820 m)

## JAMES CANYON

Lincoln NF (505) 687-3411
State map: I6
From MAYHILL, take US 82
NW for 2 miles (3.2 k).
FREE but choose a chore.
Open Apr–Nov.
5 sites. Pit toilets, tables, group ramada.
Near highway for easy access.
Birdwatch here.
NO water. Generator rules. 14-day limit.
Crowded during holidays.
6800 ft (2040 m)

## JOHN F KENNEDY

Cibola NF (505) 847-2990
State map: F5
Drive 25 miles (40 k) E of
BELEN via NM 47, CR 68,
then FR 33.
**FREE** but choose a chore.
Open Apr–Nov; camping allowed
off-season.
18 sites. Pit toilets, tables, fire rings.
In Canyon del Trigo below Gallo Peak.
Hike, view, and photograph nature.
NO water at this time–fee when added.
14-day limit. Hunting in season.
6200 ft (1860 m)

## KINGSTON

Gila NF (505) 894-6677
State map: I3
From HILLSBORO, go about
9 miles (14.4 k) W on
NM 152–near town of KINGSTON.
**FREE** but choose a chore.
Open All Year.
Undesignated sites.
Chemical toilets, tables, grills.
On Percha Creek in well-shaded area.
Hiking and birdwatching.
NO water. Hunting in season. 30-day
limit in 45-day period.
6200 ft (1860 m)

## LA SOMBRA

Carson NF (505) 758-6200
State map: B7
Proceed 7.5 miles (12 k) SE of
TAOS on US 64. (Also see
Capulin and Las Petacas.)
**$4**. Open May–Oct.
13 sites. &
Water, pit toilets, tables, fire rings.
Fish on Rio Fernando de Taos.
14-day/16-ft limits.
7800 ft (2340 m)

## LAGUNA LARGA

Carson NF (505) 758-6200
State map: A5
From TRES PIEDRAS, travel
9 miles (14.4 k) N on US 285;
Left (NW) for 9 miles (14.4 k) on FR 87;
then Right (N) for 4 miles (6.4 k) on

FR 78–rough roads. (Lagunitas is
12-13 miles farther on FR 87.)
**FREE** but choose a chore.
Open May–Oct.
4 sites. Pit toilets.
Between two lakes. Boat and fish.
NO water. 14-day limit.
9000 ft (2700 m)

## LAGUNITAS

Carson NF (505) 758-6200
State map: A5
Drive 9 miles (14.4 k) N of
TRES PIEDRAS on US 285
then 21-22 miles (34.4 k) NW on
FR 87–rough road.
**FREE** but choose a chore.
Open Jun–Oct 15.
12 sites. Pit toilets, tables, fire rings.
In scenic area of little lakes.
Fishing opportunities galore.
NO water. 14-day/16-ft limits.
10400 ft (3120 m)

## LAS CONCHAS WALK-IN

Santa Fe NF (505) 829-3535
State map: C5
Go 25 miles (40 k) NE of
JEMEZ SPRINGS on NM 4.
Alternative route is 21 miles (33.6 k) SW
of LOS ALAMOS on NM 4. Walk
100–500 ft (30–150 m).
**FREE** but choose a chore.
Open May–Oct.
8 scattered, open sites.
Pit toilets, tables, fire rings.
Next to highway and East Fork of Jemez
(Wild and Scenic River) in mixed conifer
and riparian vegetation.
Fish, hike, and take photographs here.
Crowded weekends. 14-day limit.
8400 ft (2520 m)

## LAS PETACAS

Carson NF (505) 758-6200
State map: B7
Head 4 miles (6.4 k) SE of
TAOS on US 64. (Also see
Capulin and La Sombra.)
**FREE** but choose a chore.
Open Apr–Nov.
9 sites. &

Pit toilets, tables, fire rings.
Fish in Rio Fernando de Taos.
Tour Kit Carson Memorial. Hike too.
NO water. 14-day/16-ft limits.
7400 ft (2220 m)

## LOBO CANYON

Cibola NF (505) 287-8833
State map: E3
From GRANTS, travel
10 miles (16 k) NE on
NM 547/FR 239 then Right on
FR 193–too rough for trailers or RVs.
(Also see Coal Mine.)
**FREE** but choose a chore.
Open May–Sep.
8 close, open tent sites.
Pit toilets, tables, grills, 1 shelter.
Among ponderosa pine, pinyon, and
juniper.
Enjoy quiet activities–birdwatching and
photography.
NO water. 14-day limit.
7400 ft (2220 m)

## LOWER HONDO

Carson NF (505) 758-6200
State map: B6
Proceed 4 miles (6.4 k) N of
TAOS on US 64/NM 522 then
8 miles (12.8 k) NE on NM 150. (Cuchilla
del Medio is just up canyon.)
**FREE** but choose a chore.
Open May–Sep.
4 sites. Pit toilets.
Fish a bunch on Rio Hondo.
NO water. 14-day/16-ft limits.
7700 ft (2310 m)

## LUNA PARK

Cibola NF (505) 854-2281
State map: G3
From MONTICELLO, go
7.5 miles (12 k) N on FR 139
then 4.6 miles (7.4 k) N on FR 225.
**FREE** but choose a chore.
Open Apr 1–Nov 15; camping allowed
off-season.
3 close, open sites.
Pit toilets and tables.
At unique rock formation with vista of
Rio Grande Valley.

Find Apache Kid's grave.
NO water/trash arrangements–camp
with care. 14-day/30-ft limits. Hunting
in season. ATVs.
6800 ft (2040 m)

## MCCRYSTAL

Carson NF (505) 758-6200
State map: B7
Travel 5 miles (8 k) NE of
CIMARRON via US 64. Turn
Left (NW) on FR 1950 and go about
31 miles (49.6 k). (Also see Cimarron.)
**$5**. Open May–Nov.
60 sites. &
Water, pit toilets, tables, fire rings, horse
corrals.
Enjoy fishing or horseback riding.
14-day/32-ft limits.
8100 ft (2430 m)

## MCGAFFEY

Cibola NF (505) 287-8833
State map: D2
From I-40, take Exit 33. Drive
S on NM 400 for 10 miles
(16 k) through FT WINGATE toward
MCGAFFEY. (Camp scheduled for
re-construction in 1993; Quaking Aspen
is alternative.)
**$5**; for additional **$6**, reservations
accepted at (800) 283-2273.
Open May 15–Sep 30.
25 close, screened sites. Central water,
flush toilets, tables, grills, fire rings.
In ponderosa pine within walking
distance to McGaffey Lake.
Walking nature trail, fishing, identifying
birds, and taking photos rate as favorite
pastimes here.
14-day/22-ft limits. Quiet hours.
8000 ft (2400 m)

## MCMILLAN

Gila NF (505) 538-2771
State map: I2
Take NM 15 N from SILVER
CITY for approximately
7 miles (11.2 k). Continue past PINOS
ALTOS another 5.5 miles (8.8 k). (Also
see Cherry Creek.)
**FREE** but choose a chore.

▲ ▲ ▲ ▲ ▲ ▲ ▲ ▲ ▲ ▲ ▲ ▲ ▲ ▲ ▲ ▲ ▲ ▲ ▲ ▲ ▲ ▲ ▲ ▲

Open Apr 1–Nov 15.
2 close, open sites.
Pit toilets, tables, grills.
In riparian zone of stream.
Hike, birdwatch, and take photos.
NO water. Crowded holiday travel
times. Not recommended for large
vehicles. Hunting in season.
7000 ft (2100 m)

## MONJEAU

Lincoln NF (505) 257-4095
State map: H6
Follow NM 48 N for 4 miles
(6.4 k) out of RUIDOSO. Turn
Left (W) onto NM 532. Go 1 mile (1.6 k).
Turn Right (N) on FR 117 and drive
another 5 miles (8 k). (See Oak Grove
and Skyline.)
**FREE** but choose a chore.
Open May 1–Sep 1.
4 close, screened sites.
Pit toilets, tables, grills, fire rings.
Surrounded by conifers and aspen with
breathtaking view of White Mountain
Wilderness.
Visit old Monjeau lookout tower, hike
into wilderness, identify birds, and take
photographs.
NO water/trash facilities. Generator
rules. Crowded holidays. 14-day limit.
9500 ft (2850 m)

## NEW CANYON

Cibola NF (505) 847-2990
State map: F5
Drive 8 miles (12.8 k) W of
MANZANO via NM 55 then
FR 245. (Capilla Peak is up road.)
**FREE** but choose a chore.
Open Apr–Oct; camping allowed
off-season.
10 sites. Pit toilets, tables, fire rings.
At base of Capilla and Gallo peaks.
Relax and watch for wildlife.
NO water at this time–fee when added.
14-day/22-ft limits. Hunting in season.
7800 ft (2340 m)

## OAK GROVE

Lincoln NF (505) 257-4095
State map: H6
Take NM 48 N out of
RUIDOSO for 4 miles (6.4 k).
Turn Left (W) on NM 532 and go 5 miles
(8 k). (Monjeau and Skyline are nearby.)
**FREE** but choose a chore.
Open May 15–Sep 15.
29 close, screened or open sites. Pit
toilets, tables, fire rings.
In open meadow surrounded by oak and
conifers in mountainous setting.
Enjoy quiet activities–birdwatching and
taking photographs.
NO water. 16-ft limit. Generator rules.
Crowded holidays. 14-day limit.
8400 ft (2520 m)

## OJO REDONDO

Cibola NF (505) 287-8833
State map: E3
26 miles (41.6 k) S of
THOREAU, take NM 412
then FR 178 and FR 480.
**FREE** but choose a chore.
Open Apr–Nov; camping allowed
off-season.
19 sites. Pit toilets, tables, grills.
In isolated spot among ponderosa pine
and Douglas fir.
Relax in this setting.
NO water/trash arrangements.
14-day/22-ft limits. Hunting in season.
8900 ft (2670 m)

## ORILLA VERDE RA

BLM (505) 758-8851
State map: B6
Take NM 68 S from TAOS for
12 miles (19.2 k). Turn W on
NM 570 and watch for sign. Go another
1.5 miles (2.4 k) to RA.
**$5** primitive, **$7** developed.
Open All Year.
25 developed sites in 5 camps plus
undesignated primitive sites scattered
throughout–selection of screened or
open settings.
Water in developed sites. Flush/pit
toilets, tables, grills, fire rings, some sun
shelters, handicapped fishing platform,

pay phone.
Along Rio Grande with beach.
Boat, swim, or fish. Hike to view wildlife
and photograph petroglyphs. Attend
ranger programs too.
Crowded holidays. 14-day limit. Leash
pets. No ATVs, firearms, or fireworks.
6000 ft (1800 m)

## PUEBLO PARK

Gila NF (505) 547-2612
State map: H1
18 miles (28.8 k) SW of
RESERVE via NM 12, US 180,
then FR 232. (Check out Cottonwood
Canyon too.)
FREE but choose a chore.
Open Apr–Nov.
6 sites. Pit toilets, tables, grills.
Birdwatching.
NO water. 14-day limit.
7000 ft (2100 m)

## QUAKING ASPEN

Cibola NF (505) 287-8833
State map: D2
From I-40, take Exit 33 then
drive 8 miles (12.8 k) S on
NM 400. (McGaffey is a bit farther.)
$5. Open May 15–Sep 30.
20 close, screened sites. Central water,
pit toilets, tables, grills.
In ponderosa pine (no quaking aspen?).
Walk nature trail, look for wildlife, take
photos, and fish.
14-day/22-ft limits. Quiet hours. Hunting
in season.
7600 ft (2280 m)

## QUEMADO LAKE

Gila NF (505) 773-4678
State map: G2
23 miles (36.8 k) S of
QUEMADO via US 60,
NM 32 then FR 13.
FREE but choose a chore.
Open All Year.
12 sites. Pit toilets, tables, grills, paved
boat launch.
On lake, so boat and fish.
NO water arrangements. 7-day limit.
8000 ft (2400 m)

## RED CANYON

Cibola NF (505) 847-2990
State map: F5
From MANZANO, head
12 miles (19.2 k) W via
NM 55 then FR 253.
FREE but choose a chore.
Open Apr–Oct.
19 sites. Pit toilets, tables, fire rings.
On stream near Manzano Peak.
Hike, view, and photograph nature.
NO water at this time–fee when added.
14-day/22-ft limits. Hunting in season.
8000 ft (2400 m)

## RED CLOUD

Cibola NF (505) 847-2990
State map: G6
From CORONA, head 8 miles
(12.8 k) SW on US 54; Right
(W) for 1 mile (1.6 k) on FR 161; then
Right (NW) for 6 miles (9.6 k) on FR 99.
FREE but choose a chore.
Open Apr–Oct; camping off-season.
7 sites. Pit toilets, tables, fire rings.
At base of Rough Mountain in Red
Cloud Canyon.
Observe wildlife here.
NO water/trash arrangements.
14-day/22-ft limits. Hunting in season.
7600 ft (2280 m)

## RESUMIDERO

Santa Fe NF (505) 638-5526
State map: C5
Go W of COYOTE for 6 miles
(9.6 k) on NM 96; Left (SW)
for 5 miles (8 k) on gravel FR 172; Left
(S) for 5 miles (8 k) on FR 103; then
Right (W) for 2.5 miles (4 k) on gravel
FR 93. (Rio Puerco is down FR 103.)
FREE but choose a chore.
Open May–Oct.
4 scattered, open sites.
Portable toilets, tables, fire rings.
Close to creek in large open meadow
ringed by mixed conifers.
Hiking, fishing, birdwatching, and taking
photographs.
Treat water. Pack out trash. Hunting in
season.
9000 ft (2700 m)

▲ ▲ ▲ ▲ ▲ ▲ ▲ ▲ ▲ ▲ ▲ ▲ ▲ ▲ ▲ ▲ ▲ ▲ ▲ ▲ ▲ ▲ ▲ ▲ ▲ ▲

## RIO CHIQUITO

Carson NF (505) 758-6200
State map: C7
Travel 2 miles (3.2 k) S of
RANCHOS DE TAOS via
NM 518 then 12 miles (19.2 k) E on
FR 437.
FREE but choose a chore.
Open May–Oct.
1 site. Pit toilet.
By river near Paradise Park. Fish.
NO water. 14-day/16-ft limits.
9000 ft (2700 m)

## RIO DE LOS PINOS

Carson NF (505) 758-6200
State map: A5
Off US 285, take CONEJOS,
CO county road leading W,
paralleling railroad tracks and river–
turns into FR 284.
FREE but choose a chore.
Open May–Sep.
4 sites. Pit toilets.
On Rio de Los Pinos (River of Pines).
Fishing.
NO water. 14-day/16-ft limits.
8000 ft (2400 m)

## RIO LAS VACAS

Santa Fe NF (505) 289-3264
State map: C5
Drive 13 miles (20.8 k) E of
CUBA on NM 126–last
11 miles (17.6 k) unpaved but to be
improved during 1993-94. (If temporarily
closed, Clear Creek and Seven Springs
are nearby.)
FREE in 1993; $5 in 1994.
Open May–Oct.
20 sites. &
Hand water pump, pit toilets, tables,
grills, fire rings.
Along Rio Las Vacas in ponderosa pine,
mixed conifer, and riparian vegetation.
Within 3 miles (4.8 k) of main trailhead
into San Pedro Parks Wilderness.
Fishing, wildlife watching, taking photographs, and hiking.
14-day/16-ft limits. Crowded weekends.
Hunting in season.
8200 ft (2460 m)

## RIO PUERCO

Santa Fe NF (505) 638-5526
State map: C5
Go 11 miles (17.6 k) W of
COYOTE on paved NM 96
then 9.5 miles (15.2 k) S on gravel
FR 103. (Also see Resumidero.)
FREE but choose a chore.
Open May–Oct.
6 scattered, open sites. Pit toilets.
Along Rio Puerco in mixed conifer and
riparian vegetation.
Fishing. Also, hiking, birdwatching, and
taking photographs.
NO water/trash facilities. Generator
rules. Hunting in season.
8200 ft (2460 m)

## ROCKY CANYON

Gila NF (505) 536-2250
State map: I3
From MIMBRES, go 4 miles
(6.4 k) N on NM 61 then turn
Right (N) and continue 15 miles (24 k)
on FR 150–subject to closure in bad
weather. (Black Canyon campgrounds
are bit farther.)
FREE but choose a chore.
Open All Year.
2 scattered, open sites.
1 pit toilet, tables, fire rings.
Surrounded by ponderosa pine and
grass plus stream.
Hike, fish, and photograph nature.
Treat water and pack out trash. Quiet
hours. Hunting in season.
6800 ft (2040 m)

## SANTA BARBARA

Carson NF (505) 758-6200
State map: C6
Head 1.5 miles (2.4 k) SE of
PENASCO on NM 73 then
Left (SE) for 6 miles (9.6 k) on FR 116.
(Pass Hodges.)
$5. Open May–Sep.
29 sites. Pit toilets, tables, fire rings.
On Rio Santa Barbara.
Explore nature on trails. Fish.
14-day/32-ft limits. Horses on trails.
8900 ft (2670 m)

▲ ▲ ▲ ▲ ▲ ▲ ▲ ▲ ▲ ▲ ▲ ▲ ▲ ▲ ▲ ▲ ▲ ▲ ▲ ▲ ▲ ▲ ▲

## SAPILLO

Gila NF (505) 536-2250
State map: I3
Proceed 9.5 miles (15.2 k) N
of MIMBRES on NM 35.
FREE but choose a chore.
Open All Year.
Undesignated, open, scattered sites.
Pit toilets.
Among ponderosa pine and juniper.
Enjoy hiking, fishing, birdwatching, and
photography.
NO water. Often used by large groups,
ATVers, and hunters in season. Quiet
hours.
6200 ft (1860 m)

## SCORPION

Gila NF (505) 536-9461
State map: H2
Travel 43 miles (68.8 k) N
from SILVER CITY on
NM 15–road ices in winter. (Also see
Forks and Grapevine.)
FREE but choose a chore.
Open All Year.
20 sites with walk-ins (100 ft) for tents
and overflow parking for RVs.
Central water faucet. Flush toilets and
dump station in summer; pit toilets in
winter. Tables, grills, fire rings.
Picnic area adapted to camping.
Hike to Gila Cliff Dwellings and hot
springs. Watch for wildlife. Fish in
nearby streams. Attend ranger programs.
Take lots of photos.
No trash arrangements (pack it out).
Quiet hours. Crowded summer holidays.
22-ft/30-day limits. Skunks and
raccoons.
5700 ft (1710 m)

## SEVEN SPRINGS

Santa Fe NF (505) 829-3535
State map: C5
Go 9 miles (14.4 k) N of
JEMEZ SPRINGS on NM 4;
Left (NW) for 14 miles (22.4 k) on
NM 126; then Right (E) for 1.5 miles
(2.4 k) on FR 314–muddy after summer
rains. (Also off NM 126, are Clear Creek
and Rio Las Vacas.)

FREE but choose a chore.
Open May–Oct.
6 scattered, open sites.
Pit toilets, tables, grills, fire rings.
Along Rio Cebolla within mixed conifer
and riparian vegetation.
Fishing and photography.
NO water. Generator rules. 14-day limit.
Hunting in season.
8000 ft (2400 m)

## SIMON CANYON

BLM (505) 327-5344
State map: B3
Approximately 12 miles
(19.2 k) E of BLOOMFIELD
on US 63, turn Left (N) on NM 511. In
another 7 miles (11.2 k), turn Left (W) on
NM 173. Within 1 mile (1.6 k), turn at
sign to Simon Canyon RA and Cotton-
wood. Travel 3 miles (4.8 k) to end of
dirt road–impassable when wet.
FREE but choose a chore.
Open All Year.
Only tents along north bank of San Juan
River (RV camping at **Cottonwood SP**).
Pit toilets and a couple of tables.
In Simon Canyon (dry most of year).
Explore Simon Pueblito Ruin (circa 1720)
or fish for blue ribbon trout (special
regulations apply).
Treat water before drinking. Pack out
trash. 14-day limit.
5700 ft (1710 m)

## SKYLINE

Lincoln NF (505) 257-4095
State map: H6
Follow NM 48 N out of
RUIDOSO for 4 miles (6.4 k).
Turn Left (W) on NM 532 and travel
1 mile (1.6 k). Turn Right (N) on FR 117
and drive another 4 miles (6.4 k). (See
Monjeau and Oak Grove.)
FREE but choose a chore.
Open May–Sep.
17 sites. Pit toilets, tables, fire rings.
Among conifers and aspen with panor-
amas of Eagle Creek.
Enjoy hiking, birdwatching, and
photography.
NO water/trash arrangements (pack it

out). 16-ft limit. Generator rules.
Crowded holidays.
9000 ft (2700 m)

## SPRINGTIME

Cibola NF (505) 854-2281
State map: H3
From MONTICELLO, go N
on FR 139 to FR 225 for total
of 12.5 miles (20 k). Or from I-25 Inter-
change 115, head S on NM 1 for 12 miles
(19.2 k) to FR 225 then Right (W) another
12 miles (19.2 k). FR 225 is unsuitable for
vehicles larger than pick-ups.
FREE but choose a chore.
Open Apr 15–Nov 15; camping allowed
off-season.
6 scattered, screened sites.
Pit toilets, tables, grills, lean-to shelters.
Near Apache Kid Wilderness.
Hiking, wildlife viewing, and taking
photographs.
NO water/trash arrangements. 14-day
limit. Hunting in season.
7400 ft (2220 m)

## TAJIQUE

Cibola NF (505) 847-2990
State map: E5
Go 5 miles (8 k) W of
TAJIQUE via NM 55/FR 55.
(Fourth of July is farther up canyon.)
FREE but choose a chore.
Open Apr–Oct; camping allowed
off-season.
6 sites. Pit toilets, tables, fire rings.
Fish a bunch.
NO water at this time–fee when added.
14-day/22-ft limits. Hunting in season.

## THREE RIVERS

Lincoln NF (505) 257-4095
State map: H6
Drive 17 miles (27.2 k) N
from TULAROSA or 28 miles
(44.8 k) S from CARRIZOZO on US 54 to
village of THREE RIVERS. Proceed
13 miles (20.8 k) E on CR 830/FR 579.
(Check out BLM's Three Rivers
Petroglyph Site too.)
FREE but choose a chore.
Open All Year.

6 scattered, screened sites.
Pit toilets, tables, fire rings.
At western entrance to White Mountain
Wilderness.
Hike, fish, view wildlife, and practice
photography.
NO water. Generator rules. Crowded
holidays. 14-day limit. Hunting in
season.
6400 ft (1920 m)

## THREE RIVERS PETROGLYPH SITE

BLM (505) 525-8228
State map: H6
Drive 17 miles (27.2 k) N
from TULAROSA or 28 miles
(44.8 k) S from CARRIZOZO on US 54 to
village of THREE RIVERS. Drive 4 miles
(6.4 k) E on CR 830, another paved road.
$3, $3 for day-users too.
Open All Year.
6 close, open sites.
Central water faucet, pit toilets, sun
shelters, tables, grills.
Within walking distance of 20000
examples of prehistoric native American
rock art–please respect this outstanding
archeological site.
View and photograph petroglyphs.
14-day limit.
4992 ft (1497 m)

## TRAMPAS-DIAMANTE, MEDIO &
## TRAILHEAD

Carson NF (505) 758-6200
State map: C6
Head 6 miles (9.6 k) S of
PENASCO on NM 76. Turn
W on FR 207, before reaching town of
LAS TRAMPAS. Follow road to three
different areas.
FREE but choose a chore.
Open May–Sep.
5 sites in each of three campgrounds.
Pit toilets, tables, fire rings.
In Spanish land grant, Las Trampas.
Hike on major trail. Fish too.
NO water. 14-day/16-ft limits.
8900 ft (2670 m)

▲ ▲ ▲ ▲ ▲ ▲ ▲ ▲ ▲ ▲ ▲ ▲ ▲ ▲ ▲ ▲ ▲ ▲ ▲ ▲ ▲ ▲ ▲ ▲ ▲ ▲

## TROUT LAKES

Carson NF (505) 758-6200
State map: B5
Proceed 10 miles (16 k) NE of
CEBOLLA via US 84 and
FR 125–slick when wet.
**FREE** but choose a chore.
Open May–Sep.
12 sites. Pit toilets, tables, fire rings.
Among scenic lakes.
Try fishing or photography.
NO water. 14-day/16-ft limits.
9300 ft (2790 m)

## TWINING

Carson NF (505) 758-6200
State map: B7
Drive 4 miles (6.4 k) N of
TAOS on US 64/NM 522 then
16 miles (25.6 k) on NM 150. (Also see
Cuchilla del Medio, Lower Hondo, and
Upper Italianos.)
**FREE** but choose a chore.
Open May–Sep.
4 sites. Pit toilets.
At foot of Bull-of-the-Woods Mountain
in Taos Ski Valley.
Hike on trail or fish in Rio Hondo.
NO water. 14-day/16-ft limits.
9300 ft (2790 m)

## UPPER END

Gila NF (505) 536-2250
State map: I2
Proceed 20 miles (32 k) N
from SILVER CITY on NM 15
then 4 (6.4 k) miles E on NM 35.
**$5.** Open All Year.
10 sites. Central water faucets, 1 pit
toilet, tables, grills, fire rings.
In ponderosa pine ecology.
Hiking on two trails. Fishing and
boating on lake (boat rentals and ramp
nearby on Lake Roberts). Birdwatching
and photography also.
7-day/22-ft limits. Quiet hours. Hunting
in season.
6000 ft (1800 m)

## UPPER FRISCO

Gila NF (505) 547-2612
State map: G1
2 miles (3.2 k) W of LUNA.
**FREE** but choose a chore.
Open Apr–Nov.
2 sites. Pit toilet.
Near San Francisco River.
Fishing "good".
NO water. 30-day limit.
7100 ft (2130 m)

## UPPER ITALIANOS

Carson NF (505) 758-6200
State map: B7
From TAOS, head 4 miles
(6.4 k) N on US 64/NM 522
then 12.5 miles (20 k) NE on NM 150.
(See Cuchilla del Medio and Twining.)
**FREE** but choose a chore.
Open May–Oct.
1 tent site. Pit toilet.
In Hondo Canyon in Taos Ski Valley.
Hiking and fishing here.
NO water. 14-day limit.
8600 ft (2580 m)

## UPPER LA JUNTA

Carson NF (505) 758-6200
State map: C7
Go 4 miles (6.4 k) NE of
TRES RITOS by way of
FR 76. (Duran Canyon is close.)
**FREE** but choose a chore.
Open May–Sep.
8 sites. Pit toilets, tables, fire rings.
Fish or hike along Rito la Presa.
NO water. 14-day/16-ft limits.
9400 ft (2820 m)

## VALLEY OF FIRES RA

BLM (505) 624-1790
State map: H6
From CARRIZOZO, take
NM 380 W for 4 miles (6.4 k).
**$5** primitive, **$7** developed, **$11** electricity. Open All Year.
25 (5 tent-only) scattered, open sites.
Water in every site, flush toilets, dump
station, tables, grills.
In one of nation's youngest lava fields
(900–1000 years old).

▲ ▲ ▲ ▲ ▲ ▲ ▲ ▲ ▲ ▲ ▲ ▲ ▲ ▲ ▲ ▲ ▲ ▲ ▲ ▲ ▲ ▲ ▲ ▲ ▲

Walk nature trail onto lava flow for close-up view. Take photos and observe birds.

Generator rules. 21-day limit. Hunting in season. Extremely hot summers.

6294 ft (1887 m)

## WATER CANYON

Cibola NF (505) 854-2281
State map: G4
Take US 60 13 miles (20.8 k) W from SOCORRO or 13 miles (20.8 k) E from MAGDALENA. Sign at FR 235 indicates turn S for another 4.5 miles (7.2 k).

FREE but choose a chore.

Open Mar 15-Dec 15.

15 scattered sites with choice of open or screened settings.

Pit toilets, tables, grills.

In large canyon with small stream used by early mining community named Water Canyon.

Explore canyon. Look for wildlife. Take pictures.

NO water – pollution of drainage lingering concern. Crowded Jul–Aug. 14-day limit.

6800 ft (2040 m)

## WHITE SANDS NM-Backcountry

(505) 479-6124
State map: I5
From ALAMOGORDO, Visitor Center is 15 miles (24 k) SW on US 70.

FREE but $3/car entrance fee (or pass).

Open All Year.

No campground here; inquire at Visitor Center about backcountry permits and safety recommendations.

Dunes of blowing white gypsum sand rise 10-45 ft above desert floor.

Explore ecology. Discover animals which have adapted to this harsh environment.

4700 ft (1410 m)

## WILLOW CREEK

Gila NF (505) 388-8201
State map: H2
31 miles (49.6 k) NE of GLENWOOD via US 180 then NM 159. (Ben Lilly, Bursum, and Gillita are along this road too.)

FREE but choose a chore.

Open Apr–Nov.

6 sites. Pit toilets, tables, fire rings.

Fish on creek near Gila Wilderness.

NO water. 30-day limit.

8000 ft (2400 m)

# Oregon

Grid conforms to official state map. For your copy, call (800) 547-7842
or write Tourism Division, 775 Summer St NE, Salem, OR 97310.

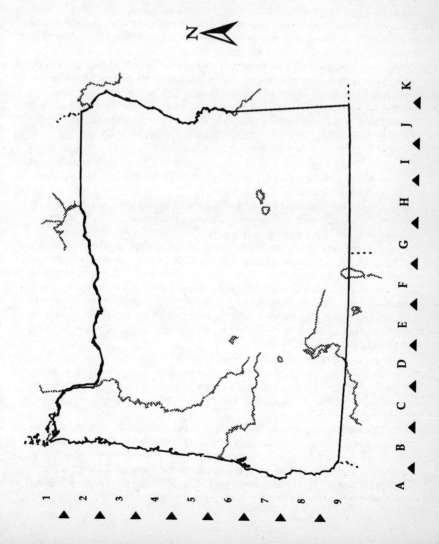

Hit the trail to discover Oregon. Indeed, you can follow in tracks left by pioneers 150 years ago. Today you can drive on established routes, hike along trails, and examine in depth ruts left by wagon wheels.

There's much to discover in Oregon. The spectacular Pacific coastline stretches from the Columbia River down to the California border. Complete with sea stacks, sand dunes, and spruce forests stretching to ocean edge, the seascape suggests the variety of the state. Two dramatic and parallel mountain ranges dominate the western part of the state, the Coast and the Cascade. In between lies the peaceful Willamette Valley known for its agriculture. Traveling east, Crater Lake beautifully attests to geologically recent volcanic activity. When massive Mazama blew her top and created the lake, she also changed much of the landscape and climate of the area now known as Oregon. The southeast section has become semiarid, filled with dry lake beds and marshes. Along the Idaho border, however, find Hells Canyon. This aptly named gash stretches 200 miles and averages 5500 feet deep. It's one of the deepest gorges on the North American continent, cut through basalt by the Snake River.

Oregon camping allows you to sample its diversity. There are camps pitched among sand dunes, others nestled in forests, some situated along wild and scenic rivers, one located in a sagebrush-covered bowl with a hot spring. Administrators offering these campgrounds in the $5-and-less range include the National Park Service (NPS), US Forest Service, Bureau of Land Administration (BLM), Bureau of Reclamation (BOR), US Fish and Wildlife, a few counties and cities.

Crater Lake is probably Oregon's best-known **NPS** site. The Oregon Sand Dunes and Hells Canyon national recreation areas (NRAs) are jointly administered by the national park and forest services, specifically the Siuslaw and Wallowa-Whitman national forests.

The **Deschutes National Forest** (NF), around Bend, finds itself extremely popular year-round with sightseers, fishermen, hikers, rockhounds, mountain climbers, and skiers for its easy access to its forested volcanic landscapes.

Also in south-central Oregon, the **Fremont NF** stretches from sagebrush to pine ecologies with weather conditions to match. Often a low elevation experiences summer while at the same time a high elevation feels winter. A special attraction of the Fremont is the Gearhart Mountain wilderness area's picturesque rock formations and wildflower meadows.

In central Oregon, the **Malheur NF** offers the Strawberry Mountain Wilderness as well as the headwaters for the John Day River. Other attractions include fossils and abandoned gold mines.

Near the Columbia River Gorge, **Mount Hood NF** claims majestic Mount Hood, Oregon's highest point in the Cascade Range. Find glaciers, lakes, streams, waterfalls, hot springs, and alpine meadows in these wilderness areas: Badger Creek, Bull of the Woods, Columbia, Mount Hood, Mount Jefferson, and Salmon-Huckleberry.

The **Ochoco NF** is practically in the center of the state despite its three sections, including the Crooked River National Grassland. This forest has three wilderness areas: Black Canyon, Bridge Creek, and Mill Creek. The Ochoco is known for its wild horses and its thundereggs, a geode containing agate or opal.

**Rogue River NF**, in the southwest part of the state, contains Mount Ashland as well as the headwaters of the Applegate and Rogue rivers. It's a rugged area popular for its mountain scenery and recreational pursuits, including hiking the Pacific Crest Trail.

On the southern coast, the **Siskiyou NF** contains numerous rare plants in the heath, cedar, pine, and spruce families. Wilderness areas include Grassy Knob, Kalmiopsis, Red Buttes, and Wild Rogue.

As mentioned before, the **Siuslaw NF** administers Oregon Dunes National Recreation Area (NRA), a forty-mile stretch of sand with dunes as tall as 200 feet. Also in this forest, find such interesting coastal phenomena as the Devil's Churn.

The **Umatilla NF**, in northeast Oregon, offers the Blue Mountain National Scenic Byway and the Vinegar Hill-Indian Rock Scenic Area as well as the Wenaha-Tucannon Wilderness.

Wilderness areas in the **Umpqua NF** include Boulder Creek, Mount Thielsen, Rogue-Umpqua Divide. This Cascade Range scenery provides something for every outdoors enthusiast, including Diamond Lake Recreation Area (RA) and part of the Pacific Crest Trail.

Hells Canyon NRA is administered by **Wallowa-Whitman NF**. The forest also offers the Eagle Cap Wilderness, supplying a range of scenery from barren canyon to snowcovered mountain.

The **Willamette NF** in the Cascade Range offers access to eight wilderness areas: Bull of the Woods, Diamond Peak, Menagerie, Middle Santiam, Mount Jefferson, Mount Washington, Three Sisters, and Waldo Lake. Again, the Pacific Crest Trail winds its way among the peaks as does the McKenzie Pass Scenic Highway. (The Pacific Crest Trail travels through the Cascade Range and the following Oregon forests: Rogue River, Winema, Umpqua, Deschutes, Willamette, and Mount Hood.)

East of Crater Lake, the **Winema NF** extends from the high mountains to the Klamath Basin. Popular wilderness areas include Mount Thielsen, Mountain Lakes, and Sky Lakes.

In Oregon's natural areas, find large animals such as pronghorn antelope, black bear, black-tailed deer, elk, mountain goat, mountain lion, moose, bighorn sheep. Birds include bald eagle, osprey, and Wallowa gray-crowned rosy finch.

**BLM** sites can be found around mountains, forest reserves, rivers, and reservoirs. At this time, the **BOR** still administers Prineville Reservoir. The **National Wildlife Refuges** (NWRs) are primarily for migratory birds and antelope though some camping is permitted. Counties such as Columbia, Coos, Hood River, and Morrow as well as cities such as Corvallis offer campsites too.

Pretend you're a Sacajawea, Lewis, or Clark. Discover Oregon!

## ABBOT CREEK
Deschutes NF (503) 549-2111
State map: 4D
From SISTERS, drive NW about 13 miles (20.8 k) on US 20/ OR 126. Turn on FR 12 and drive about 10 miles (16 k).
**FREE** but choose a chore.
Open Apr 15–Oct 15.
4 sites. Pit toilets, tables, fire rings.
Fish or hike along creek.

NO water/trash arrangements.
14-day/16-ft limits.
3100 ft (930 m)

## ABBOTT CREEK
Rogue River NF
(503) 560-3623
State map: 8C
From town of PROSPECT, travel 6.75 miles (10.8 k) N on OR 62. Turn W on FR 68 and go 3.75 miles (6 k).

▲ ▲ ▲ ▲ ▲ ▲ ▲ ▲ ▲ ▲ ▲ ▲ ▲ ▲ ▲ ▲ ▲ ▲ ▲ ▲ ▲ ▲ ▲ ▲ ▲ ▲

$4/vehicle, $2/extra vehicle.
Open mid May–Oct 30.
28 scattered sites in open or screened
settings. Hand water pump, pit toilets,
tables, fire rings, horse facilities.
In expansive-feeling meadows between
Abbott and Woodruff creeks.
Fish or birdwatch.
14-day/22-ft limits. Crowded holidays.
Hunting in season.
3100 ft (930 m)

## ALDER FLAT WALK-IN

Mt Hood NF (503) 630-4256
State map: 3D
From ESTACADA, drive
OR 224 SE about 26 miles (41.6 k). Park
near Ripplebrook Ranger Station. Hike
.75 mile (1.2 k).
FREE but choose a chore.
Open Apr 23–Sep 30.
6 tent sites. &
Pit toilets, tables, grills.
Hike or fish along Clackamas River.
NO water/trash arrangements (pack it
out). 14-day limit.
1300 ft (390 m)

## ALDER GLEN

BLM (503) 375-5610
State map: 3B
From CARLTON, take BLM 32
(Nestucca River Rd) W about 22 miles
(35.2 k). For alternative, continue 3 miles
(4.8 k) to NF **Rocky Bend** (10 sites).
(Also see Fan Creek.)
FREE but choose a chore.
Open All Year.
11 close, screened sites. Hand water
pump, pit toilets, tables, fire rings.
In forest next to Nestucca River in
Oregon's Coast Range.
Play in water or fish. Birdwatch and take
photos.
Pack out trash. 14-day/30-ft limits.
Frequent rain. Hunting in season.
800 ft (240 m)

## ALDER SPRINGS

Willamette NF (503) 822-3381
State map: 5D
From MCKENZIE BRIDGE,

drive 4.5 miles (7.2 k) E on OR 126 then
9 miles (14.4 k) E on OR 242, one of
state's most narrow and steep highways–not recommended for trailers or
RVs over 35 ft.
FREE but choose a chore.
Open late Apr–late Nov; camping
allowed off-season.
6 close, open tent sites.
Pit toilets, tables, fireplaces.
In scenic area off Old McKenzie Hwy.
Enjoy hiking and taking photos.
NO water/trash arrangements. 14-day
limit. No trailers or RVs recommended.
3600 ft (1080 m)

## ALPINE

Mt Hood NF (503) 622-3191
State map: 3D
From GOVERNMENT CAMP,
drive US 26 E .8 mile (1.3 k) then take
road to Mt Hood/Timberline Lodge ski
area for 4.5 miles (7.2 k.)
FREE but choose a chore.
Open Jul–Sep.
16 tent sites.
Water, pit toilets, tables, grills.
On southern slope of Mt Hood.
Tour nearby Timberline Lodge National
Historic Site. Hike along Pacific Crest
Trail or into Mount Hood Wilderness.
No trailers recommended.
5400 ft (1620 m)

## ALSEA FALLS

BLM (503) 375-5610
State map: 5B
From ALSEA, head SE on
South Fork Alsea Rd for 7 miles (11.2 k).
$5. Open May 15–Oct 1.
16 close, screened sites. Central water
faucets, pit toilets, tables, fire rings.
In woods next to South Fork Alsea River
in Oregon's Coast Range.
Play in water or fish. Study wildlife and
geology. Take pictures.
14-day limit. Very rainy off-season.
Hunting in season.
800 ft (240 m)

## ANSON WRIGHT PARK

Morrow County Parks
(503) 676-9061
State map: 3G
Proceed 27 miles (43.2 k) S of HEPPNER on OR 207.
**$5**, extra $3 for hookups, extra $2 for second vehicle. Open May 20–Nov 15.
25 sites. Water in every site, flush toilets, showers, optional electric hookups, tables, fire rings.
In foothills of Blue Mountains with big pine trees for shade.
Relax and enjoy mountains–hiking, viewing nature, taking photographs, and fishing.
10-day/30-ft limits. Quiet 10pm–7am. Crowded in hunting season.
3000 ft (900 m)

## ANTELOPE RESERVOIR

Ochoco NF (503) 447-9641
State map: 5F
From PRINEVILLE, drive 29 miles (46.4 k) SE on Hwy 380 then 11 miles 17.6 k) SE on FR 17.
**$5**. Open May 15–Oct 15.
25 sites. Hand water pump, pit toilets, tables, fire rings, boat ramp.
In mixed-conifer, high-elevation forest on lake.
Fish, boat, or swim. Hike to observe wildlife and take photos.
14-day/32-ft limits. No trash facilities. Hunting in season.
4600 ft (1380 m)

## APPLE CREEK

Umpqua NF (503) 496-3532
State map: 6C
From IDLEYLD PARK, head E on OR 138 for 23 miles (36.8 k). (Also see Boulder Flat and Island.)
**FREE** but choose a chore.
Open All Year.
8 sites. Pit toilets, tables, fire rings.
On North Umpqua River.
Fly fishing, whitewater boating, hiking (Panther Trail).
NO water. 14-day limit.
1365 ft (408 m)

## BARLOW CREEK

Mt Hood NF (503) 328-6211
State map: 3D
From GOVERNMENT CAMP, drive 2 miles (3.2 k) E on US 26; 4.5 miles (7.2 k) E on OR 35; then 4 miles (6.4 k) SE on FR 3530. (Also see Devil's Half Acre and Grindstone.)
**FREE** but choose a chore.
Open May–Sep.
5 tent sites. Pit toilets, tables, grills.
Beside creek on pioneer wagon road.
Hike along wagon road and trails. Fish in creek.
NO water. No trailers recommended. Hunting in season.
3100 ft (930 m)

## BARLOW CROSSING

Mt Hood NF (503) 328-6211
State map: 3D
From GOVERNMENT CAMP, drive US 26 E for 2 miles (3.2 k); 6 miles (9.6 k) E on OR 35; then 9 miles (14.4 k) S on FR 48. (Also see White River Station.)
**FREE** but choose a chore.
Open May 15–Sep 30.
5 tent sites. Pit toilets, tables, grills.
Also on Barlow Creek, but not as popular as Barlow Creek Campground.
Enjoy seclusion. View and photograph nature. Fish.
NO water. No trailers recommended.
14-day limit.

## BASSER DIGGINS

BLM (503) 473-3144
State map: 4J
Drive 15 miles (24 k) E of DURKEE on gravel/dirt road in fair weather only–not recommended for large RVs or trailers.
**FREE** but choose a chore.
Open All Year.
Undesignated, close, open sites. Central water faucet, pit toilets, tables, fire rings.
Near Lookout Mountain with dense woods, lush meadows, running streams, and variety of wildlife.
Take photos of scenery and wildlife. Hike too.

▲ ▲ ▲ ▲ ▲ ▲ ▲ ▲ ▲ ▲ ▲ ▲ ▲ ▲ ▲ ▲ ▲ ▲ ▲ ▲ ▲ ▲ ▲ ▲ ▲ ▲

14-day limit. Quiet 10pm–7am. Hunting in season.
5980 ft (1794 m)

## BEAR WALLOW CREEK

Umatilla NF (503) 427-3231
State map: 3H
From UKIAH, head NE on OR 244 for 10 miles (16 k). Pass **Lane Creek** (4 sites). (Also see Frazier.)
**FREE** but choose a chore.
Open Jun 1–Nov 1; camping off-season.
6 (1 tent-only) sites.
Pit toilets, tables, fire rings.
In woods near Camas Creek.
Hike or fish.
NO water. 14-day limit. Hunting in season.
3900 ft (1170 m)

## BEAVER DAM

Rogue River NF
(503) 482-3333
State map: 9C
Drive 22 miles (35.2 k) E of ASHLAND via Dead Indian Rd then 1.5 miles (3.2 k) N on FR 37.
$3 donation requested.
Open Apr 28–Nov 15.
4 (2 tent-only) scattered, open sites.
Water needs treating, tables, grills, fire rings.
In quiet riparian zone with beaver dams and wildflowers.
Study nature and take photos. Fish or hike too.
No trash arrangements. 14-day limit.
4600 ft (1380 m)

## BEAVER-SULPHUR

Rogue River NF
(503) 889-1812
State map: 9C
From MEDFORD, travel 13 miles (20.8 k) SW on OR 238; 9 miles (14.4 k) S on CR 10; then 3 miles (4.8 k) E on FR 20.
$3/vehicle, $1.50/extra vehicle.
Open Apr–Oct; dry camping off-season.
10 scattered, open tent sites.
Central water faucet, chemical toilets, tables, grills, fire rings.
Along quiet, peaceful Beaver Creek.

Hike to observe nature. Fish too.
14-day limit. Hunting in season.
2100 ft (630 m)

## BEECH CREEK

Malheur NF (503) 575-2110
State map: 4H
From FOX, head S on US 395 for 6 miles (9.6 k).
**FREE** but choose a chore.
Open May 30–Oct 15.
5 (2 tent-only) sites.
Water, pit toilets, tables, fire rings.
Enjoy this creekside getaway.
No trash arrangements (pack it out).
4500 ft (1350 m)

## BENNETT COUNTY PARK

Coos County Parks
(503) 396-3121
State map: 7A
Find campground 8 miles (12.8 k) NE from MYRTLE POINT on Dora–Sitkum Hwy near GRAVELFORD on North Fork of Coquille River.
$3. Closed in winter.
18 sites.
Pit toilets, fire rings, wading pool.
Hike and rockhound. Wade in pool or fish in river.
NO water. Call (503) 396-3121 ext 355 about opening/closing dates, vehicle lengths, and limit of stay.

## BESSON

Deschutes NF (503) 388-5664
State map: 5E
About 11 miles (17.6 k) S of BEND on US 97, turn Right (W) and travel 2.5 miles (4 k) on FR 40 (at blinking light to SUNRIVER) and cross Deschutes River. In about a mile, turn Right on FR 41. In another mile, turn Right again into campground entrance.
**FREE** but choose a chore.
Open Apr 15–Sep 30.
2 sites. Chemical toilets, tables, fire rings.
On oxbow of Deschutes River.
Boating and fishing. Hiking.
NO water/trash arrangements.
14-day/16-ft limits. Crowded.
4100 ft (1230 m)

## BIG BEN

Rogue River NF
(503) 865-3581
State map: 8C

From BUTTE FALLS, travel .5 mile (800 m) E. Turn Left (NE) on CR/FR 34 and go 13 miles (20.8 k). Turn right on FR 37 and continue 1 mile (1.6 k). (Also see South Fork.)
FREE but choose a chore.
Open May–Oct; camping allowed off-season.
2 scattered, open sites.
Pit toilets, tables, grills, fire rings.
In creekside seclusion among tall trees.
Fish, hike, birdwatch, and take photos.
NO water. 14-day/15-ft limits. Crowded during hunting season.
4000 ft (1200 m)

## BIG BEND

BLM (503) 447-4115
State map: 4G

From KIMBERLY, drive Hwy 402 N about 2.5 miles (4 k).
FREE but choose a chore.
Open All Year.
4 close, open sites. &
Pit toilets, tables, fire rings, boat ramp.
In scenic high-desert surroundings along North Fork of John Day River.
Boat, swim, and fish in river. View and photograph nature. Hike trails and attend NPS ranger programs at nearby John Day Fossil Beds NM.
NO water/trash facilities. 14-day limit.
Rattlesnakes. Hunting in season.
1200 ft (360 m)

## BIG CREEK

Umatilla NF (503) 427-3231
State map: 3H

From UKIAH, head SE on FR 52 for 22 miles (35.2 k). Pass Drift Fence (3 sites).
FREE but choose a chore.
Open Jun 1–Nov 1; camping allowed off-season.
2 sites. Pit toilets, tables, fire rings.
On creek between two sections of North Fork John Day Wilderness.
Make base for extended treks. Fish.

NO water. 14-day limit. Hunting in season.
5200 ft (1560 m)

## BIG CREEK

Malheur NF (503) 820-3311
State map: 5H

From SENECA, head E on FR 16 for 21 miles (33.6 k). Turn Left (N) on FR 815 and go .5 mile (800 m). For alternative, retrace route W for 1.5 miles (2.4 k) on FR 16 and turn Right (N) on FR 924 and drive 2.5 miles (4 k) to Murray (6 sites).
FREE but choose a chore.
Open May 30–Oct 15.
14 sites.
Water, pit toilets, tables, fire rings.
Enjoy creekside solitude. Fish. Explore nearby Strawberry Wilderness.
No trash arrangements (pack it out).
5100 ft (1530 m)

## BIG ELK

Siuslaw NF (503) 487-5811
State map: 4B

From HARLAN, head W on CR 538 for 1.5 miles (2.4 k).
$3. Open All Year.
10 sites.
Water, pit toilets, tables, fire rings.
Swim and fish in creek. Hike.
20-ft limit.
500 ft (150 m)

## BIG POOL

Willamette NF (503) 937-2129
State map: 5C

From LOWELL, travel 2 miles (3.2 k) N on CR 6220,;10 miles (16 k) E on CR 6240; then 1.5 miles (2.4 k) N on FR 181 (Fall Creek Rd).
FREE but choose a chore.
Open May–Sep 15.
Undesignated (3 tent-only) sites.
Pit toilets, tables, fireplaces.
On Fall Creek, fish or swim. Hike Fall Creek National Recreation Trail.
NO water at this time – fee when repaired. 10-day/16-ft limits.
1000 ft (300 m)

▲ ▲ ▲ ▲ ▲ ▲ ▲ ▲ ▲ ▲ ▲ ▲ ▲ ▲ ▲ ▲ ▲ ▲ ▲ ▲ ▲ ▲ ▲ ▲

## BIG RIVER

Deschutes NF (503) 388-5664
State map: 5E
From BEND, go 16.5 miles
(26.4 k) S on US 97. Turn Right (W) onto
FR 40. (Do not turn right into town of
SUNRIVER or continue straight to cross
river at this point.) Turn Left on road
that parallels Little Deschutes River.
Turn Right on CR 42 to cross Little
Deschutes then Deschutes rivers.
Immediately find campground on Right.
(Also see Fall River.)
**FREE** but choose a chore.
Open May 1–Oct 15.
13 (5 tent-only, 3 RV-only) sites.
Pit toilets, tables, fire rings, boat ramp.
In pleasant spot along Deschutes River.
Fish, hike, and observe nature.
NO water/trash arrangements.
14-day/22-ft limits. Hunting in season.
4200 ft (1260 m)

## BLACK PINE SPRING

Deschutes NF (503) 549-2111
State map: 5E
From SISTERS, drive about
9 miles (14.4 k) S on FR 16.
**FREE** but choose a chore.
Open May 15–Oct 15.
4 sites. Pit toilets, tables, fire rings.
Relax here.
NO water/trash facilities. 16-ft limit.
4300 ft (1290 m)

## BLAIR LAKE

Willamette NF (503) 782-2291
State map: 6C
From OAKRIDGE and OR 58,
turn E and drive 1 mile (1.6 k) on
CR 149. Turn NE onto FR 24 (Salmon
Creek Rd) and continue 9 miles (14.4 k).
Turn onto FR 1934 (Wall Creek
Rd–narrow gravel road not recommended for RVs or trailers) and drive
7.5 miles (12 k). Turn Right onto FR 733
and proceed 2 miles (3.2 k).
$3/vehicle, $1.50/extra vehicle.
Open Jun 15–Oct 1; dry camping
off-season.
8 close, open tent sites. Hand water
pump, pit toilets, tables, fire rings.

With wildflower meadow on small lake.
Canoe (no motorboats), swim, and fish.
Hike area trails to observe and
photograph nature. Cross-country ski.
14-day limit. Quiet 10pm–7am. Crowded
summers. Erect tents in designated areas
only–meadow fragile. Road not plowed
in winter.
4800 ft (1440 m)

## BOLAN LAKE

Siskiyou NF (503) 592-2166
State map: 9B
From O'BRIEN, take CR 5560
E for 4 miles (6.4 k). Continue E on
CR 5828/FR 48 about 10 twisting miles
(16 k). Turn Left (NE) on FR 4812 and go
8 miles (12.8 k).
**FREE** but choose a chore.
Open May 30–Sep 10; dry camping
off-season.
12 tent sites.
Water, pit toilets, tables, fire rings.
On remote lake beneath Grizzly Peak.
Swim, fish, or boat (no motors). Hike.
14-day limit.
5400 ft (1620 m)

## BONNEY CROSSING

Mt Hood NF (503) 467-2291
State map: 3E
From WAMIC, travel 6 miles
(9.6 k) W on CR 226; 1 mile (1.6 k) W on
FR 48; then short access road.
**FREE** but choose a chore.
Open Apr 20–Oct 15.
8 sites. Pit toilets, tables, grills.
On Badger Creek.
Hike trail into Badger Creek Wilderness.
View and photograph scenery and
wildlife. Fish too.
NO water. 14-day/16-ft limits.
2200 ft (660 m)

## BOULDER CREEK

Umpqua NF (503) 825-3201
State map: 7C
From TILLER, take
CR 28/FR 46 (South Umpqua Rd) NE for
14 miles (22.4 k). Pass free **Dumont
Creek** (5 sites). Too, across road is free
**Annex** (4 sites). (Also see Camp

▲ ▲ ▲ ▲ ▲ ▲ ▲ ▲ ▲ ▲ ▲ ▲ ▲ ▲ ▲ ▲ ▲ ▲ ▲ ▲ ▲ ▲ ▲ ▲

Comfort.)
**FREE** but choose a chore.
Open May 20–Oct 31; camping allowed off-season.
8 sites.
Pit toilets, tables, grills, fire rings.
In mixed-age conifers on South Umpqua River near creek.
Fish and hike.
**NO water (pump broken) or trash arrangements.** 14-day limit.
1400 ft (420 m)

## BOULDER FLAT

Umpqua NF (503) 496-3532
State map: 6C
From IDLEYLD PARK, head E on OR 138 for 31 miles (49.6 k). Pass fee-charged options: **Horseshoe Bend** (24 sites) and **Eagle Rock** (25 sites). (Also see Apple Creek and Toketee Lake.)
**FREE** but choose a chore.
Open All Year.
11 sites. Pit toilets, tables, fire rings.
On North Umpqua River with outstanding scenery.
Fly fishing and whitewater boating. Hiking on Boulder Creek or North Umpqua trails.
NO water. 14-day limit.
1600 ft (480 m)

## BOULDER LAKE WALK-IN

Mt Hood NF (503) 467-2291
State map: 3E
From WAMIC, drive 6 miles (9.6 k) S on CR 226; 12.25 miles (19.6 k) SW on FR 408; then 5.75 miles (9.2 k) N on FR 446. Hike .5 mile (800 m) W on Trail 463.
**FREE** but choose a chore.
Open Jul 1–Sep 10.
4 tent sites. Pit toilets, tables, fire rings.
On quiet lake.
Canoe, fish, or swim.
NO water.
4600 ft (1380 m)

## BOUNDARY

Hells Canyon NRA
(503) 426-4978
State map: 2I

From WALLOWA, head S on CR/FR 6250-040 for 9 miles (14.4 k).
**FREE** but choose a chore.
Open May 15–Nov 1; camping allowed off-season.
8 tent sites. Pit toilets, tables, fire rings.
On Doc Creek.
Fish. Hike into Eagle Cap Wilderness.
NO water. 10-day limit.
3600 ft (1080 m)

## BROKEN BOWL

Willamette NF (503) 937-2129
State map: 5C
12 miles (19.2 k) NE of LOWELL, access via OR 58 then FR 18 (Fall Creek Rd).
**FREE** but choose a chore.
Open May–Sep 15.
9 (3 tent-only) sites. &
Pit toilets, tables, fireplaces.
Fish, swim or hike.
**NO water at this time – fee when repaired.** 14-day limit.
1000 ft (300 m)

## BUCKHORN OVERLOOK

Hells Canyon NRA
(503) 426-4978
State map: 2J
From JOSEPH, head N on OR 82 for 3 miles (4.8 k). Bear Right at fork for 1 mile (1.6 k). Turn Right (NE) on CR 697/FR 46 (Zumwalt Rd) and drive 40 rough miles (64 k).
**FREE** but choose a chore.
Open Jul 1–Oct 31; camping allowed off-season.
6 tent sites. Spring water, pit toilets, tables, fire rings.
In remote setting overlooking Hells Canyon.
Sightsee and explore. Pick berries when ripe.
10-day limit.
5200 ft (1560 m)

## BULL BEND

Deschutes NF (503) 388-5664
State map: 6D
From LA PINE, drive N on US 97 for 2 miles (3.2 k). Turn Left (W)

▲ ▲ ▲ ▲ ▲ ▲ ▲ ▲ ▲ ▲ ▲ ▲ ▲ ▲ ▲ ▲ ▲ ▲ ▲ ▲ ▲ ▲ ▲ ▲

on CR 43 and continue 8 miles (12.8 k).
Turn Left on FR 4370 and go 1.5 miles
(2.4 k). (Pringle Falls and Wyeth are
nearby.)
FREE but choose a chore.
Open Apr 15–Sep 30.
8 sites. Pit toilets, tables, fire rings.
On bend of Deschutes River good for
floating downstream.
Fish, relax, and observe nature.
NO water/trash arrangements. 14-day
limit. Crowded. Hunting in season.

## BUTLER BAR

Siskiyou NF (503) 439-3011
State map: 8A
From PORT ORFORD, head N
on US 101 for 2.5 miles (4 k). Turn Right
(E) on CR 208/FR 5325 and go about
14 miles (22.4 k).
FREE but choose a chore.
Open May 30–Sep 10; camping allowed
off-season.
8 (3 tent-only) sites.
Pit toilets, tables, fire rings.
On Elk River at edge of Grassy Knob
Wilderness.
Hike or fish. Relax.
NO water. 14-day limit.

## CABIN LAKE

Deschutes NF (503) 388-5664
State map: 6E
From FORT ROCK, take CR 18
N for 10 miles (16 k.)
FREE but choose a chore.
Open May 15–Oct 31.
14 sites. Hand water pump, pit toilets,
tables, fire rings.
Observe birds from nearby blind. Relax.
No trash facilities. 14-day/32-ft limits.
4500 ft (1350 m)

## CAMP COMFORT

Umpqua NF (503) 825-3201
State map: 7C
From TILLER, take
CR 28/FR 46 (South Umpqua Rd) NE for
26 miles (41.6 k). (Also see Boulder
Creek.)
FREE but choose a chore.
Open May 20–Oct 31; camping allowed

off-season.
5 sites.
Pit toilets, tables, grills, fire rings.
Under large, old-growth cedar and fir
near headwaters of South Umpqua.
Fish and hike. Near trailheads for
Rogue-Umpqua Divide Wilderness.
NO water/trash arrangements (pack it
out). 14-day limit.
2000 ft (600 m)

## CAMP TEN

Mt Hood NF (503) 630-4256
State map: 4D
From ESTACADA, drive SE
on OR 224 for 27 miles (43.2 k); S on
FR 46 for 22 miles (35.2 k); SE on
FR 4690 for 8 miles (12.8 k); then S on
FR 4220 for another 6 miles (9.6 k). Pass
Lower Lake Walk-In (9 sites). Other
options on Olallie Lake include fee-
charged Peninsula (35 sites) and Paul
Dennis (15 sites). For more remote
setting, continue 2 miles (3.2 k) to
Horseshoe Lake (4 sites). (Also see
Olallie Meadows.)
FREE but choose a chore.
Open Jun 15–Sep 15.
7 sites. Pit toilets, tables, grills.
On lakeshore surrounded by scenic
mountains.
Canoe, kayak, and sail on Olallie Lake.
Make wonderful hikes to other small
lakes.
NO water. 14-day/16-ft limits.
5000 ft (1500 m)

## CAMPBELL LAKE

Fremont NF (503) 943-3114
State map: 8F
From PAISLEY, drive 1 mile
(1.6 k) W on CR 28. Turn Right on
FR 3315 and go 22.5 miles (36 k). Turn
Left on FR 28 and go 3 miles (4.8 k) S.
Turn Right on FR 033 and go 3.5 miles
(5.6 k) W. Deadhorse Lake is 1 mile
farther. (Also see Lee Thomas.)
FREE but choose a chore.
Open Apr–Oct; dry camping off-season.
15 sites. Hand water pump, pit toilets,
tables, grills.
Among lodgepole pine around lake.

Swim, boat, and fish. Hike or relax at this get-away.
No trash arrangements. 14-day limit.
7195 ft (2157 m)

## CAMPERS FLAT
Willamette NF (503) 782-2283
State map: 6C
From OAKRIDGE and OR 58, turn Right on CR 360 (Kitson Springs Rd) and drive .5 mile (800 m). Turn Right on FR 21. Go 18 miles (28.8 k). (Also see Sacandaga and Secret.)
$3. Open Apr 15–Sep 30; dry camping off-season.
5 close, open sites. Hand water pump, pit toilets, tables, fire rings.
On flat next to Middle Fork Willamette River. River sounds drown out noise. Hike on Young's Rock and Middle Fork trails. Try hand at fishing. Take photographs of animals and scenery.
10-day/21-ft limit.
2000 ft (600 m)

## CANAL CREEK
Siuslaw NF (503) 563-3211
State map: 4B
From WALDPORT, head E on OR 34 for 7 miles (11.2 k). Turn Right (S) on FR 3462 and go 4 miles (6.4 k).
FREE but choose a chore.
Open All Year.
9 sites.
Water, pit toilets, tables, fire rings.
Fish, hike, and relax along creek.
22-ft limit.

## CANDLE CREEK
Deschutes NF (503) 549-2111
State map: 4E
From SISTERS, travel N on US 20 about 7 miles (11.2 k). Turn on CR/FR 14 and proceed about 13 miles (20.8 k) to end of road.
FREE but choose a chore.
Open Apr 15–Oct 15.
8 (1 tent-only) sites.
Chemical toilets, tables, fire rings.
On creek at edge of forest and Warm Springs Indian Reservation.
Fish or hike.

NO water/trash facilities.
2800 ft (840 m)

## CANYON MEADOWS
Malheur NF (503) 575-2110
State map: 5H
From JOHN DAY, head S on US 395 for 10 miles (16 k). Turn Left (SE) on CR 65 and go 8 miles (12.8 k) Pass **Wickiup** (9 sites). Turn Left (NE) on FR 1520 and go 3 miles (4.8 k). (Also see Parish Cabin.)
FREE but choose a chore.
Open May 30–Oct 15.
18 sites.
Water, pit toilets, tables, fire rings.
Fish on small reservoir. Drive to end of FR 1520 and take trail from Buckhorn Meadow into Strawberry Wilderness.
No trash arrangements (pack it out).
5100 ft (1530 m)

## CARTER BRIDGE
Mt Hood NF (503) 467-2291
State map: 3D
From ESTACADA, travel 16 miles (25.6 k) SE on OR 224.
$5. Open Apr 24–Sep 11.
15 sites. &
Water, pit toilets, dump station, picnic tables, fire rings.
Fish on Clackamas River.
14-day/22-ft limits.
800 ft (240 m)

## CASTLE ROCK
Siuslaw NF (503) 392-3161
State map: 3B
From HEBO, take OR 22 SE for 4 miles (6.4 k).
FREE but choose a chore.
Open All Year.
4 tent sites.
Water, pit toilets, tables, fire rings.
On Three Rivers.
Use as base to explore coast.
10-day limit.

▲ ▲ ▲ ▲ ▲ ▲ ▲ ▲ ▲ ▲ ▲ ▲ ▲ ▲ ▲ ▲ ▲ ▲ ▲ ▲ ▲ ▲ ▲ ▲ ▲ ▲ ▲ ▲

## CASTLE ROCK

BLM (503) 447-4115
State map: 5E
From PRINEVILLE, drive paved OR 27 that parallels Crooked River about 12 miles (19.2 k). For alternatives, choose from **Stillwater** (8 sites), **Lone Pine** (8 sites), **Lower Palisades** (12 sites), **Chimney Rock** (16 sites), **Cobble Rock** (6 sites), **Post Pile** (7 sites), and **Poison Butte** (5 sites).
$3/vehicle, $1/additional vehicle.
Open All Year.
5 scattered, open sites.
Pit toilets, some tables.
In high-desert environment within rugged Crooked River canyon walls.
Boat, swim, and fish on river. Observe and photograph nature.
NO water (at Chimney Rock). 14-day limit. Quiet 10pm-7am. Crowded summer weekends. Extreme fire danger summers. Hunting in season.
2960 ft (888 m)

## CEDAR CREEK

Umpqua NF (503) 942-5591
State map: 6C
From DISSTON, head SE on CR 2470 (Brice Creek) for 4 miles (6.4 k). For alternatives, continue another 3 miles (4.8 k) to either **Hobo** (2 sites) or **Lund** (2 sites). For more developed, fee-charged, option take CR 17 NE from DISSTON for 2 miles (3.2 k) to **Rujada** (10 sites).
FREE but choose a chore.
Open May 25-Nov 30; camping allowed off-season.
8 sites. Pit toilets, tables, fire rings.
In open stand of old-growth Douglas fir on banks of Brice Creek.
Fish. Pan for gold. Walk Brice Creek Trail.
NO water. 14-day limit.
1520 ft (456 m)

## CHERRY CREEK COUNTY PARK

Coos County Parks
(503) 396-3121
State map: 7B
Find .75 mile (1.2 k) E of MCKINLEY on Old Wagon Rd (16 miles from COQUILLE and 20 miles from MYRTLE POINT).
$3. Closed in winter.
11 sites. Pit toilets, tables, fireplaces, shelter with electric stove, wading pool.
On Cherry Creek.
Wade in pool, fish in creek, or rock-hound grounds.
Call (503) 396-3121 ext 355 for opening/closing dates, vehicle lengths, and stay limits.

## CHINA HAT

Deschutes NF (503) 388-5664
State map: 6E
From BEND, travel S on US 97 for 3 miles (4.8 k). Turn Left (SE) on CR/FR 18 (at flags) and drive about 28 miles (44.8 k). Turn Right on FR 800 and continue .25 mile (400 m).
FREE but choose a chore.
Open May 16-Oct 15.
14 sites. Hand water pump, pit toilets, tables, fire rings.
Near China Hat volcanic formation.
Drive up China Hat. Examine flows.
14-day limit.
5100 ft (1530 m)

## CHUKAR PARK

BLM (503) 473-3144
State map: 6I
Find 6 miles (9.6 k) N of JUNTURA off US 20 on graded, gravel road. Look for signs at turnoff-road unsuitable for large RVs.
$3 when water on May-Oct; FREE rest of year.
Undesignated, close, screened sites.
Central water faucets, pit toilets, tables, grills, fire rings.
In sagebrush-juniper canyon with access to Malheur River.
Fishing, wading, wildlife watching, and taking photographs.
Quiet 10pm-7am. 14-day limit.
3200 ft (960 m)

▲ ▲ ▲ ▲ ▲ ▲ ▲ ▲ ▲ ▲ ▲ ▲ ▲ ▲ ▲ ▲ ▲ ▲ ▲ ▲ ▲ ▲ ▲ ▲ ▲ ▲

## CLACKAMAS LAKE

Mt Hood NF (503) 328-6211
State map: 3D
From GOVERNMENT CAMP,
take US 26 SE for 15 miles (24 k). Turn
Right on FR 42 S and go 8 miles (12.8 k).
Turn Left on FR 4270 E for .5 mile
(800 m).
$4. Open May 15–Oct 15.
47 sites. &
Well water, pit toilets, tables, grills.
On rather small, shallow lake near
Clackamas River and Timothy Lake.
Hike along Pacific Crest Trail among
others. Bicycle. Canoe Clackamas Lake.
Motorboat and fish (various trout as well
as kokanee salmon) at Timothy Lake. See
historic ranger station.
14-day/22-ft limits.
3400 ft (1020 m)

## CLAY CREEK

BLM (503) 683-6600
State map: 5B
Find 28 miles (44.8 k) W of
LORANE along Siuslaw River Rd, a
paved but narrow, winding road.
$5. Open May 15–Nov 30.
20 scattered, screened sites.
Hand water pump, chemical toilets,
tables, grills, and fire rings.
Under dense canopy of Douglas fir with
understory of maple and sword fern.
Near beach-like area where Clay Creek
joins Siuslaw River.
Swim and fish. View wildlife and take
photos.
14-day limit. Hunting in season.
1400 ft (420 m)

## CLEAR CREEK

Mt Hood NF (503) 328-6211
State map: 3E
From MAUPIN, travel
28 miles (44.8 k) W on OR 216. Pass fee-
charged **Bear Springs** (21 sites). Turn
Right on FR 2130 and go 3 miles (4.8 k)
N. Turn Right (E) on FR 260 for .5 mile
(800 m)–not recommended for trailers or
RVs. (Also see Keeps Mill.)
FREE but choose a chore.
Open May–Oct.

5 tent sites. Pit toilets, tables, grills.
At quiet location on Clear Creek.
Enjoy seclusion. Make base for recreation
in Mt Hood area.
NO water.

## CLEARWATER FALLS

Umpqua NF (503) 498-2531
State map: 7D
From IDLEYLD PARK, head E
on OR 138 for 48 miles (76.8 k) to closest
free camp to Diamond Lake. Pass free
**Whitehorse Falls** (8 sites). (Also see
Toketee Lake.)
FREE but choose a chore.
Open Jun 1–Oct 31; camping allowed
off-season.
9 sites. Pit toilets, tables, fire rings.
On Clearwater River near falls.
Hike or do nothing.
NO water. 14-day limit.
4200 ft (1260 m)

## CONTORTA POINT

Deschutes NF (503) 433-2234
State map: 6D
From CRESCENT, take US 97
S for 9 miles (14.4 k). Turn Right onto
OR 58 and continue 7 miles (11.2 k).
Turn Left on FR 6020 for additional
7 miles (11.2 k). (Also see Summit Lake.)
FREE but choose a chore.
Open Jun 1–Sep 30.
15 sites. Pit toilets, tables, fire rings.
On south end of Crescent Lake.
Boat, waterski, windsurf, swim or fish.
Bike too.
NO water/trash arrangements.
14-day/22-ft limits.
4800 ft (1440 m)

## COOLWATER

Umpqua NF (503) 496-3532
State map: 6C
From GLIDE, head E on CR 17
(Little River Rd) for 15.5 miles (24.8 k).
Pass fee-charged **Wolf Creek** (8 sites)
and BLM's free **Emile** (4 sites). If
occupied, go 1.5 miles (2.4 k) and turn
Right to free **White Creek** (4 sites).
FREE but choose a chore.
Open May 20–Oct 31; dry camping

▲ ▲ ▲ ▲ ▲ ▲ ▲ ▲ ▲ ▲ ▲ ▲ ▲ ▲ ▲ ▲ ▲ ▲ ▲ ▲ ▲ ▲ ▲ ▲

off-season.
7 sites.
Water, pit toilets, tables, fire rings.
In forest along Little River.
Swim and fish. Hike (within 5 miles are
Grotto Falls, Overhang, and Wolf Creek
Falls trails).
14-day/24-ft limits.
1300 ft (390 m)

## CORRAL CREEK

Fremont NF (503) 353-2427
State map: 8E
From BLY, take OR 140 E for
1 mile (1.6 k) then turn Left (N). In about
.5 mile (800 m), turn Right (E) on FR 34
and go 18 miles (28.8 k) before turning
Left on FR 012.
FREE but choose a chore.
Open May–Oct; camping allowed
off-season.
5 sites. Pit toilets, tables, fire rings.
In secluded spot on Corral Creek
within mile of Gearhart Wilderness.
Hike and view wildlife here. Take trail
to The Dome with fascinating rock
formations along way.
NO water/trash facilities. 14-day limit.
6080 ft (1824 m)

## CORRAL SPRING

Winema NF (503) 365-2229
State map: 7D
From CHEMULT, travel N on
US 97 about 3 miles (4.8 k). Turn Left
(W) on FR 9774 and go 2 miles (3.2 k).
FREE but choose a chore.
Open May 15–Oct 31.
7 tent sites.
Pit toilets, tables, grills, fire rings.
At spring NE of Crater Lake NP.
Relax.
NO water. 14-day/22-ft limits.
4900 ft (1470 m)

## COTTONWOOD MEADOWS

Fremont NF (503) 947-3334
State map: 8F
From LAKEVIEW, travel
24 miles (38.4 k) W on OR 140 then
8 miles (12.8 k) NE on FR 3870.
FREE but choose a chore.

Open Jun–Oct; dry camping off-season.
21 close, open sites. Central faucet/ hand
water pump, pit toilets, tables, grills, fire
rings, boat ramp.
In scenic area on small lake.
Swim or fish in lake. Hike on three trails
or ride horseback on another trail. View
scenery and wildlife.
No trash arrangements. 14-day limit.
6100 ft (1830 m)

## COVER

Umpqua NF (503) 825-3201
State map: 7C
From TILLER, take CR 46
(South Umpqua Rd) NE for 5 miles (8 k).
Turn Right (SE) on FR 29 (Jackson Creek
Rd) and drive 13 miles (20.8 k).
FREE but choose a chore.
Open May 20–Oct 31; camping allowed
off-season.
7 sites.
Pit toilets, tables, grills, fire rings.
Under Douglas firs on Jackson Creek.
Fish and hike.
NO water/trash arrangements (pack it
out). 14-day limit. Hunting in season.
1700 ft (510 m)

## COW MEADOW

Deschutes NF (503) 388-5664
State map: 6D
From BEND, 43 miles (68.8 k)
SW on OR 46 (Cascade Lakes Hwy) then
2 miles (3.2 k) E on FR 620.
FREE but choose a chore.
Open May 1–Sep 30.
19 (3 tent-only) sites.
Pit toilets, tables, fire rings, boat ramp.
Near northern end of Crane Prairie
Reservoir on Deschutes River.
Boat and fish.
NO water/trash arrangements.
14-day/22-ft limits.
4500 ft (1350 m)

## COYOTE

Hells Canyon NRA
(503) 426-4978
State map: 2J
From ENTERPRISE, go N on OR 3 for
15 miles (24 k). Turn Right (NE) on

▲ ▲ ▲ ▲ ▲ ▲ ▲ ▲ ▲ ▲ ▲ ▲ ▲ ▲ ▲ ▲ ▲ ▲ ▲ ▲ ▲ ▲ ▲ ▲ ▲ ▲

FR 46 and go 25 twisting miles (40 k). For alternative, continue another 6.5 miles (10.4 k) to **Dougherty Springs** (6 sites). (Also see Vigne.)
**FREE** but choose a chore.
Open May 15–Nov 30; camping allowed off-season.
21 (13 tent-only) sites.
Pit toilets, tables, fire rings.
At remote spring.
Hike and explore.
NO water. 10-day/21-ft limits.
4800 ft (1440 m)

## CRATER LAKE NP-Lost Creek
(503) 594-2511
State map: 7D
Find in SE part of park along road to Pinnacles, about 14 miles (22.4 k) from headquarters.
**$5** plus $5 entrance fee (or pass) until snow. Also, **free** backcountry permits available from park rangers.
Open Jul–Sep.
16 tent sites. Central water faucet, flush toilets, tables, grills, and fire rings.
In wooded setting.
Create base to view sapphire-blue Crater Lake (deepest lake in US at 1932 ft) and surrounding virgin forests of ponderosa and lodgepole pine, red fir, and mountain hemlock. Hike (Cleetwood Trail to lake). Birdwatch. Attend ranger-led activities.
No accommodations and few services for winter snowmobiling and cross-country skiing (OR 62 open all year).
6000 ft (1800 m)

## CRESCENT CREEK
Deschutes NF (503) 433-2234
State map: 6D
From CRESCENT, take CR 61 approximately 8 miles (12.8 k) W.
**$4**/vehicle, $2/extra vehicle.
Open May 15–Oct 31.
10 sites. Hand water pump, pit toilets, tables, fire rings, boat ramp.
On creek near Odell Butte.
Swim and fish in creek.
14-day/22-ft limits.
4800 ft (1440 m)

## CUTSFORTH PARK
Morrow County Parks
(503) 676-9061
State map: 3G
Find 22 miles (35.2 k) SW of HEPPNER, following Blue Mountain Scenic Byway then Willow Creek Rd. (Also see Penland Lake.)
**$5** for space, $3 for hookups, $2 for second vehicle.
Open May 20–Nov 15.
34 close, open sites. Water in every site, flush toilets, showers, electric hookups, tables, fire rings.
In quiet, cool place in Blue Mountains.
Hike or fish. Relax and enjoy nature.
10-day/30-ft limits. Quiet 10pm–7am.
Hunting in season.
4000 ft (1200 m)

## DAIRY POINT
Fremont NF (503) 943-3114
State map: 8F
From PAISLEY, head W on CR 28/FR 33 (Mill Rd) for 15 miles (24 k). Turn Left on FR 28 for 2 miles (3.2 k). Turn Left again on FR 3428. (Also see Happy Camp.)
**FREE** but choose a chore.
Open Apr–Oct; dry camping off-season.
4 close, open sites.
Hand water pump, pit toilets, tables.
In popular spot on hot days.
Wade or fish.
No trash arrangements. 14-day limit.
5800 ft (1740 m)

## DALEY CREEK
Rogue River NF (503) 482-3333
State map: 8C
Travel 22 miles (35.2 k) E of ASHLAND via CR 364 (Dead Indian Rd) then 1 mile (1.6 k) N on FR 37.
**$3** donation requested.
Open Apr 15–Nov 15; camping allowed off-season.
8 (2-handicapped, 3 tent-only) sites.
Drinking water needs treating, pit toilets, tables, grills, fire rings.
In quiet riparian area with wildflowers.
Fish in creek. Hike trails to observe and photograph nature. Cross-country ski in

▲ ▲ ▲ ▲ ▲ ▲ ▲ ▲ ▲ ▲ ▲ ▲ ▲ ▲ ▲ ▲ ▲ ▲ ▲ ▲ ▲ ▲ ▲ ▲ ▲ ▲ ▲ ▲

winter.
No trash facilities. 14-day/16-ft limits.
4600 ft (1380 m)

## DAVIS LAKE-East & West

Deschutes NF (503) 433-2234
State map: 6D
From CRESCENT, take CR 61
W for 9 miles (14.4 k). To access East
section, turn Right on FR 46 and go
6.5 miles (10.4 k) N then 1.5 miles (2.4 k)
W on FR 855. To access West section,
turn Right on FR 46 and go 3.25 miles
(5.2 k) N; 3.75 miles (6 k) W on FR 4660;
then 2 miles (3.2 k) E on FR 4669. (Also
see Lava Flow.)
$5/vehicle, $3/extra vehicle.
Open May–Oct.
58 sites. Hand water pump, pit toilets,
tables, fire rings.
Boat and fish on Davis Lake. Hike.
14-day/24-ft limits.
4400 ft (1320 m)

## DEAD HORSE LAKE

Fremont NF (503) 943-3114
State map: 8F
From PAISLEY, drive 1 mile
(1.6 k) W on CR 28. Turn Right on
FR 3315 and go 22.5 miles (36 k). Turn
Left on FR 28 and go 3 miles (4.8 k) S.
Turn Right on FR 033 and go 4.5 miles
(7.2 k) W. (Pass companion campground,
Campbell Lake.)
FREE but choose a chore.
Open Apr–Oct; dry camping off-season.
18 (6 tent-only) sites in close, open
setting. ♿
Hand water pump, pit toilets, tables, fire
rings.
In lodgepole pine beside lake where
fifty-year-old dugout canoes still float.
Fish and boat (no motors) on lake. Hike
in forest.
No trash arrangements (pack it out).
14-day/22-ft limits. Hunting in season.
7372 ft (2211 m)

## DEEP CREEK

Fremont NF (503) 947-3334
State map: 9F
From LAKEVIEW, drive

6 miles (9.6 k) N on US 395. Turn Right
and go 8 miles (12.8 k) E on OR 140.
Turn Right and go 14 miles (22.4 k) SE
on FR 3915; then Right again for 1 mile
(1.6 k) SW on FR 4015. (Also see Willow
Creek.)
FREE but choose a chore.
Open Jun–Oct; camping allowed
off-season.
8 (3 tent-only) close sites.
Pit toilets, tables, fire rings.
Along Deep Creek with tent sites on
other side offering more solitude.
Commune with nature or fish.
NO water/trash arrangements (pack it
out). 14-day limit. Hunting in season.
5600 ft (1680 m)

## DEER CREEK

Wallowa-Whitman NF
(503) 523-6391
State map: 4I
From SUMPTER, head SE on
CR 410/OR 7 for 5 miles (8 k). Turn Left
(N) on FR 6550 and go 4 miles (6.4 k).
(Also see Southwest Shore.)
FREE but choose a chore.
Open May 1–Nov 15.
6 sites. Pit toilets, tables, fire rings.
Fish and hike along creek.
NO water. 10-day limit.
4600 ft (1380 m)

## DELINTMENT LAKE

Ochoco NF (503) 573-7292
State map: 5G
From HINES, travel 1 mile
(1.6 k) S on US 20/395; 16 miles (25.6 k)
NW on FR 47; then 30 miles (48 k) NW
on FR 41.
$4. Open Jun 16–Oct 15; dry camping
off-season.
24 (5 tent-only) sites. Hand water pump,
pit toilets, tables, fire rings, boat ramp.
In ponderosa pine on 65-acre lake.
Boat, swim, and fish. Observe and
photograph nature.
14-day limit. Quiet 10pm–6am. Leash
pets. Crowded holidays.
5600 ft (1680 m)

▲ ▲ ▲ ▲ ▲ ▲ ▲ ▲ ▲ ▲ ▲ ▲ ▲ ▲ ▲ ▲ ▲ ▲ ▲ ▲ ▲ ▲ ▲ ▲ ▲ ▲ ▲ ▲

## DEVIL'S HALF ACRE

Mt Hood NF (503) 328-6211
State map: 3D
From GOVERNMENT CAMP,
travel 2 miles (3.2 k) E on US 26;
4.5 miles (7.2 k) N on OR 35; then 1 mile
(1.6 k) SE on FR 3530–not recommended
for trailers or RVs. (Also see Barlow
Creek, Barlow Crossing, and
Grindstone.)
FREE but choose a chore.
Open May 15–Oct 1.
5 tent sites. Pit toilets, tables, grills.
On old wagon road along Barlow Creek.
Hike along Old Barlow Rd (pioneer
wagon trail) or Pacific Crest Trail.
NO water.
3600 ft (1080 m)

## DEVILS FLAT

Umpqua NF (503) 825-3201
State map: 7C
From AZALEA, take CR 36 E
for 17 miles (27.2 k).
FREE but choose a chore.
Open May 20–Oct 31; camping allowed
off-season.
3 tent sites.
Pit toilets, tables, grills, fire rings.
Across from 1915 ranger cabin on Cow
Creek.
Walk to Cow Creek Falls and along
gorge. Fish.
NO water/trash arrangements (pack it
out). 14-day limit.
2200 ft (660 m)

## DEVILS LAKE WALK-IN

Deschutes NF (503) 388-5664
State map: 5D
From BEND, drive W on
CR 46 (Cascade Lakes Hwy) to Devils
Lake–about 27 miles (43.2 k). Walk 200
yds. (Also see Soda Creek.)
FREE but choose a chore.
Open Jul 1–Sep 15.
6 tent sites.
Pit toilets, tables, fire rings, boat ramp.
Boat (no motors) or fish on scenic lake.
Hike into Three Sisters Wilderness.
NO water/trash arrangements.
5500 ft (1650 m)

## DIVIDE WELL

Umatilla NF (503) 427-3231
State map: 3G
From UKIAH, head W on
FR 53 for 15 miles (24 k). Turn Left (SE)
on FR 5327 and go 8 miles (12.8 k).
FREE but choose a chore.
Open All Year.
3 sites. Pit toilets, tables.
Get away in this remote setting.
NO water. 14-day limit. ATVs.
4700 ft (1410 m)

## DIXIE

Malheur NF (503) 575-2110
State map: 4H
From PRAIRIE CITY, head E
on US 26/OR 7 for 8 miles (12.8 k)–just
beyond Dixie Pass. Turn Left (N) on
FR 848 and continue .25 mile (400 m).
FREE but choose a chore.
Open May 30–Oct 15.
11 sites.
Water, pit toilets, tables, fire rings.
Beneath pine trees near creek.
Pick berries. Hike. Explore (superb views
from Dixie Butte).
No trash arrangements. 22-ft limit.
5000 ft (1500 m)

## DOG LAKE

Fremont NF (503) 947-3334
State map: 9F
From LAKEVIEW, travel
10 miles (16 k) W on OR 140; Turn Left
(S) and go 4.5 miles (7.2 k) on CR 1-13
and 1-11; Turn Right (W) and go
12 miles (19.2 k) on CR 1-11D and
FR 4017. (Also see Drews Creek.)
FREE but choose a chore.
Open Jun–Oct; camping allowed
off-season.
8 sites. Pit toilets, tables, grills, fire rings,
boat ramp.
In two areas–one by lake, other over-
looking lake.
Watch Canadian Geese. Boat and fish.
NO water/trash facilities. 14-day limit.
5100 ft (1530 m)

▲ ▲ ▲ ▲ ▲ ▲ ▲ ▲ ▲ ▲ ▲ ▲ ▲ ▲ ▲ ▲ ▲ ▲ ▲ ▲ ▲ ▲ ▲ ▲

## DOVRE

BLM (503) 375-5610
State map: 3B
From CARLTON, take BLM 32
(Nestucca River Rd) W about 13 miles
(20.8 k). (Also see Fan Creek.)
**FREE** but choose a chore. May add fee.
Open All Year; dry camping off-season.
10 close, screened sites. Hand water
pump, pit toilets, tables, fire rings.
Next to Nestucca River in forested area
of Coast Range.
Play or fish in water. View and take
photos of animals and scenery.
14-day/30-ft limits. Rainy springs.
1500 ft (450 m)

## DREWS

Fremont NF (503) 947-3334
State map: 9F
From LAKEVIEW, travel
10 miles (16 k) W on OR 140; Turn Left
(S) and go 4.5 miles (7.2 k) on CR 1-13
and 1-11; Turn Right (W) and go 5 miles
(8 k) on CR 1-11D and FR 4017. (Also
see Dog Lake.)
**FREE** but choose a chore.
Open Jun–Oct; dry camping off-season.
5 sites. Central water faucet, pit toilets,
tables, grills, and fire rings.
On creek in hills.
Walk nature trail, fish, play baseball or
horseshoes.
No trash arrangements (pack it out).
4900 ft (1470 m)

## DRIFTWOOD

Deschutes NF (503) 549-2111
State map: 5D
From SISTERS, drive FR 16
about 17 miles (27.2 k) S to end of road.
(Also see Three Creeks Lake.)
**FREE** but choose a chore.
Open Jun 15–Oct 15.
15 (6 tent-only) sites.
Chemical toilets, tables, fire rings.
In woods on Three Creeks Lake.
Boat (no motors). Fish. Hike trails.
**NO water/trash arrangements.**
14-day/16-ft limits.
6400 ft (1920 m)

## DUCK LAKE

Hells Canyon NRA
(503) 426-4978
State map: 3J
From HALFWAY, go N on
CR 733/FR 66 for 39 rough miles
(62.4 k). Pass **Twin Lakes** (6 sites). Turn
Left on access road.
**FREE** but choose a chore.
Open Jul 1–Oct 31; camping allowed
off-season.
2 tent sites. Pit toilets, tables, fire rings.
On lake near Eagle Cap Wilderness.
Fish. Enjoy solitude. Take a hike.
NO water. 10-day limit.
5200 ft (1560 m)

## DUNCAN RESERVOIR

BLM (503) 947-2177
State map: 7E
From SILVER LAKE, travel E
5 miles (8 k) on OR 31. Turn Right (S) on
CR 4-14 for 1 mile (3.2 k). Turn on
BLM 6197 and travel S 4 miles (6.4 k).
**FREE** but choose a chore.
Open All Year (weather decides);
camping allowed off-season.
5 close, open sites.
Pit toilets, boat ramp.
Beside lake in high-desert sagebrush and
juniper with sweeping vistas.
Boat and fish. Observe wildlife.
NO water/trash arrangements.
4832 ft (1449 m)

## EAGLE FORKS

Wallowa-Whitman NF
(503) 742-7511
State map: 3J
From RICHLAND, head 10 miles (16 k)
NW on FR 7735 (Eagle Creek Rd).
**FREE** but choose a chore.
Open Jun 1–Oct 31.
7 sites.
Water, pit toilets, tables, fire rings.
Fish and hike along creek.
10-day limit.
3000 ft (900 m)

## EAST BAY

Fremont NF (503) 947-2107
State map: 7E
From SILVER LAKE, travel
.5 mile (800 m) W on OR 31. Turn Left
(S) on CR 4-12/FR 28 and go 13 miles
(20.8 k). Turn Right (W) on FR 014 and
go 1 mile (1.6 k).
$3. Open May 1–Nov 15; dry camping
off-season.
18 close, open sites. &
Hand water pump, pit toilets, tables,
grills, fire rings, boat ramp.
In ponderosa pine trees overlooking
Thompson Reservoir.
Fish, walk nature trail, ride bicycles, and
watch birds.
14-day/22-ft limits. No water in
reservoir during drought. Hunting in
season.
5000 ft (1500 m)

## EAST SHORE

BLM (503) 756-0100
State map: 6B
From REEDSPORT, drive
13 miles (20.8 k) E on OR 38 then 7 miles
(11.2 k) S on Ash Rd in Elliott State
Forest.
$5. Open All Year.
8 scattered, screened tent sites.
Pit toilets, tables, fire rings.
With beach on Loon Lake.
Boat, waterski, swim, and fish. Hike
trails to view and photograph nature.
Attend ranger programs.
NO water. Quiet 10pm-6am. Crowded
Aug.
310 ft (93 m)

## EIGHTMILE CROSSING

Mt Hood NF (503) 467-2291
State map: 3E
From DUFUR, drive 12 miles
(19.2 k) SW on CR 1. Continue W on
FR 44 until junction of FR 4430 and
**Underhill Site**. Proceed another .5 mile
(800 m) on 4430. If you continue on 44,
find **Pebble Ford** (3 sites). (Also see
Lower Crossing and Knebal Springs.)
$4. Open Jun–Oct 15.
24 sites. Pit toilets, tables, grills.

Along Eightmile Creek.
Hike on area trails.
NO water. 30-ft limit.
4200 ft (1260 m)

## ELDERBERRY FLAT

BLM (503) 770-2200
State map: 8B
From I-5, take Exit 48 at
ROGUE RIVER. Travel N on Evans
Creek Rd 20 miles (32 k). Turn Left on
West Fork Evans Creek Rd and travel
another 9 miles (14.4 k).
FREE but choose a chore.
Open May 1–Nov 1; camping allowed
off-season.
10 scattered, open sites.
Pit toilets, tables, fire rings.
Along West Fork of Evans Creek in
forested foothills of Cascade Range.
Fish in creek or play in swimming hole
(4 miles E). Pick berries when ripe.
NO water. 14-day/30-ft limits. Summers
hot. Crowded holiday weekends.
1500 ft (450 m)

## ELK LAKE

Willamette NF (503) 854-3366
State map: 4D
From DETROIT, drive
4.5 miles (7.2 k) NE on FR 46. Bear Left
on FR 4696 for .75 mile (1.2 k). Turn Left
(NW) on FR 2209 and go 6 miles (9.6 k).
Turn Left for .5 mile (800 m) – last
2 miles not recommended for low-
clearance cars, trailers, or RVs.
FREE but choose a chore.
Open Jun–Oct; camping allowed
off-season.
12 scattered, open tent sites.
Pit toilets, tables, fireplaces, substandard
boat launch.
At high-elevation lake with views of Bull
of Woods Wilderness as well as Cascade
Range.
Swim, boat, and fish on lake. Hike, view
wildlife, and take lots of photographs.
Drinking water needs treating. No trash
arrangements. 14-day limit. Quiet hours.
Hunting in season.
4200 ft (1260 m)

## ELKHORN VALLEY

BLM (503) 375-5610
State map: 4D
From SALEM, drive 24 miles
(38.4 k) E on OR 22 then 10 miles (16 k)
NE on Elkhorn Rd.
$5/vehicle, $3/extra vehicle.
Open May 15–Oct 1.
23 close, screened sites. Hand water
pump, pit toilets, tables, fire rings.
In woods near Little North Santiam
River in foothills to Cascade Range.
Play in water, swim, fish, view nature,
and take photos.
14-day/18-ft limits.
1000 ft (300 m)

## EMIGRANT

Ochoco NF (503) 573-7292
State map: 6G
From HINES, drive 1 mile
(1.6 k) S on US 20; 20 miles (32 k) NW
on FR 47; then 12 miles (19.2 k) W on
FR 43. (Also see Falls.)
$3. Open Jun 1–Oct 15; dry camping
off-season.
5 scattered, open sites. Central water
faucet, pit toilets, tables, fire rings.
In ponderosa pine forest with stream,
beaver ponds, and meadows.
View and photograph nature. Swim and
fish.
14-day/32-ft limits. Quiet 10pm-6am.
Leash pets. Crowded holidays.
5400 ft (1620 m)

## FAIRVIEW

Umatilla NF (503) 676-9187
State map: 3G
From HARDMAN, head S on
OR 207 for 15 miles (24 k). For fee-
charged option, go NE on FR 2039 for
2 miles (3.2 k) to **Bull Prairie** (28 sites).
FREE but choose a chore.
Open Jun 1–Nov 1; dry camping
off-season.
5 (1 tent-only) sites.
Water, pit toilets, tables, fire rings.
In woods near spring.
Hike. Explore.
14-day limit. Hunting in season.
4300 ft (1290 m)

## FALL RIVER

Deschutes NF (503) 388-5664
State map: 6D
From BEND, go 16.5 miles
(26.4 k) S on US 97. Turn Right (W) onto
FR 40. (Do not turn right into town of
SUNRIVER or continue straight to cross
river at this point.) Turn Left on road
that parallels Little Deschutes River.
Turn Right on CR 42 to cross Little
Deschutes then Deschutes rivers. Go
9 miles (14.4 k). (Also see Big River.)
FREE but choose a chore.
Open Apr 15–Sep 30.
12 sites. Pit toilets, tables, fire rings.
Fly fish or hike along river.
NO water/trash facilities. 22-ft limit.
4000 ft (1200 m)

## FALLS

Ochoco NF (503) 573-7292
State map: 6G
From HINES, drive S 1 mile
(1.6 k) on US 20; 20 miles NW (32 k) on
FR 47; then 10 miles W (16 k) on FR 43.
(Also see Emigrant.)
$3. Open Jun 1–Oct 15; dry camping
off-season.
5 scattered, open sites. Central water
faucet, pit toilets, tables, fire rings.
In ponderosa pine near Emigrant Creek,
waterfalls, beaver ponds, and meadows.
Observe and photograph wildlife. Fish
and swim too.
14-day/30-ft limits. Quiet 10pm-7am.
Crowded holidays. Hunting in season.
5300 ft (1590 m)

## FAN CREEK

BLM (503) 375-5610
State map: 3B
From CARLTON, take BLM 32
(Nestucca River Rd) W about 15 miles
(24 k). For alternative, check out **Elk
Bend** in about 2 miles (3.2 k). (Also see
Alder Glen and Dovre.)
FREE but choose a chore—may add fee
in 1993. Open All Year.
12 close, screened sites. Hand water
pump, pit toilets, tables, fire rings.
In woods along Nestucca River in Coast
Range.

▲ ▲ ▲ ▲ ▲ ▲ ▲ ▲ ▲ ▲ ▲ ▲ ▲ ▲ ▲ ▲ ▲ ▲ ▲ ▲ ▲ ▲ ▲ ▲ ▲ ▲

Dabble in water play, fishing, landscape and wildlife photography.
No trash arrangements (pack it out).
14-day/30-ft limits. Rainy off-season.
1200 ft (360 m)

## FERNVIEW

Willamette NF (503) 367-5168
State map: 4D
Travel 20.25 miles (32.4 k) E of SWEET HOME via US 20.
$4. Open Apr 15-Nov 15.
11 (9 tent-only) sites. Water, pit toilets, tables, fireplaces.
On Santiam River at Boulder Creek.
Fish, swim, or hike.
14-day/18-ft limits.
1400 ft (420 m)

## FIFTEENMILE

Mt Hood NF (503) 467-2291
State map: 3E
From DUFUR, drive 2 miles (3.2 k) S on OR 197. Bear Right (SW) on CR 118 (Mays Canyon) for 14 miles (22.4 k)–eventually heading W. Bear Right (NW) on FR 2630 and continue 9 miles (14.4 k).
FREE but choose a chore.
Open Jul 1-Sep 10.
3 sites. Pit toilets, tables, grills.
On creek at edge of Badger Creek Wilderness. Fish. Hike. Explore.
NO water. 16-ft limit.
4600 ft (1380 m)

## FISH LAKE

Wallowa-Whitman NF (503) 742-7511
State map: 3J
From HALFWAY, go N on CR 733/FR 66 for 29 miles (46.4 k). For alternative, go N 6 more miles (9.6 k) to Twin Lakes (6 sites). (See Duck Lake.)
FREE but choose a chore.
Open Jul 1-Oct 31; camping off-season.
21 sites. Spring water, pit toilets, tables, fire rings, boat launch.
On lake near Eagle Cap Wilderness.
Swim, boat, or fish. Excellent hiking.
10-day/22-ft limits.
6600 ft (1980 m)

## FISH LAKE

Willamette NF (503) 822-3381
State map: 4D
Proceed 22.5 miles (36 k) NE of MCKENZIE BRIDGE via OR 126.
(Also see Ice Cap Creek.)
$5. Open Apr-Oct (weather decides); dry camping off-season.
8 sites. Central water faucet, pit toilets, tables, fire rings, interpretive display.
On lava flow beside lake disappearing early summer and reappearing late fall. Explore area geology. Obey special fishing regulations. Hike along old Santiam wagon trail and McKenzie River National Recreation Trail.
14-day limit.
3200 ft (960 m)

## FOREST CREEK

Mt Hood NF (503) 467-2291
State map: 3E
From WAMIC, travel 6 miles (9.6 k) W CR 226; 12.5 miles (20 k) SW on FR 48; 1 mile (1.6 k) SE on FR 4885; then .25 mile (400 m) S on FR 3530. (Also see Keeps Mill, Post Camp, and White River Station.)
$2. Open Jul 1-Sep 10.
8 sites. Pit toilets, tables, grills.
On Forest Creek site used by early settlers on Old Barlow Wagon Trail.
Hike and explore.
NO water. 22-ft limit.

## FOURBIT FORD

Rogue River NF (503) 865-3581
State map: 8C
From BUTTE FALLS, take CR 821/FR 30 for 9 miles (14.4 k). Turn Left at sign and continue 1 mile (1.6 k) NE on FR 3065. (Pass Whiskey Spring.)
$4/vehicle, $2/extra vehicle.
Open May-Oct.
7 scattered, open sites. Hand water pump, pit toilets, tables, grills, fire rings.
On Fourbit Creek with great fishing.
14-day limit. Crowded, noisy holidays.
3200 ft (960 m)

▲ ▲ ▲ ▲ ▲ ▲ ▲ ▲ ▲ ▲ ▲ ▲ ▲ ▲ ▲ ▲ ▲ ▲ ▲ ▲ ▲ ▲ ▲

## FOURTH CREEK

Wallowa-Whitman NF
(503) 446-3351
State map: 4I

From WHITNEY, head SE on CR 507 for
4 miles (6.4 k).
**FREE** but choose a chore.
Open May 1–Nov 15.
2 sites. Pit toilets, tables, fire rings.
On creek near Burnt River.
Fish. Hike. Enjoy solitude.
NO water. 10-day limit.
4100 ft (1230 m)

## FRAZIER

Umatilla NF (503) 427-3231
State map: 3H
From UKIAH, head NE on
OR 244 for 16 miles (25.6 k). Turn Right
(S) on FR 5226 and go .5 mile (800 m).
(Also see Bear Wallow Creek.)
**FREE** but choose a chore.
Open Jun 1–Nov 1; camping allowed
off-season.
32 (5 tent-only) sites.
Pit toilets, tables, fire rings.
Hike in woods or fish in Frazier Creek.
NO water. 14-day limit. ATVs. Hunting
in season.
4300 ft (1290 m)

## FRAZIER

Ochoco NF (503) 477-3713
State map: 5G
About 3 miles (4.8 k) E of
PAULINA, take Left fork of CR 113. In
another 1.5 miles (2.4 k), turn Right on
CR 135 leading to FR 58. Turn Right on
FR 58 and drive approximately 5 miles
(8 k). Turn Left on FR 500 and proceed
to FR 511 and campground.
**FREE** but choose a chore.
Open May 15–Oct 31.
6 (3 tent-only) sites. Central water faucet,
pit toilets, tables, fire rings.
In mixed conifers beside Frazier Creek.
Birdwatch. Mountain bike and ride
horses on area roads.
No trash arrangements (pack it out).
14-day/22-ft limits. Hunting in season.
5000 ft (1500 m)

## FRENCH GULCH WALK-IN

Rogue River NF
(503) 889-1812
State map: 9B

From JACKSONVILLE, proceed 8 miles
(12.8 k) SW on OR 238; 14 miles (22.4 k)
SW on CR/FR 10 leading from RUCH to
Applegate Lake; then 1 mile (1.6 k) on
FR 1075. **Stringtown Walk-In** at $3 is
two miles farther.
**$4.** Open All Year.
9 scattered, open tent sites. Central water
faucet, pit toilets, tables, fire rings.
Fish, swim, and boat on Applegate Lake.
Hike and birdwatch.
14 day limit.
2000 ft (600 m)

## FRENCH PETE

Willamette NF (503) 822-3317
State map: 5D
From BLUE RIVER, travel
3.5 miles (5.6 k) E on US 126; then about
12 miles (19.2 k) S along FR 19
(Aufderheide National Scenic Byway).
(Also see Homestead, Twin Springs,
Frissell Crossing, and Slide Creek.)
**$5/single site, $10/multiple site.**
Open All Year.
17 close, open sites. Hand water pumps,
pit toilets, tables, fireplaces.
Along South Fork of McKenzie River
and French Pete Creek in grove of fir,
hemlock, and cedar.
Hike French Pete Trail into Three Sisters
Wilderness. Boat, swim, and fish in
nearby Cougar Reservoir. Photograph
scenery and wildlife. Cross-country ski
in winter.
14-day/18-ft limits. Hunting in season.
FR 19 not maintained for snow and ice.
1800 ft (540 m)

## FRISSELL CROSSING

Willamette NF (503) 822-3317
State map: 5D
From BLUE RIVER, 3.5 miles
(5.6 k) E on US 126; then 27.5 miles
(44 k) S on FR 19 (Aufderheide Scenic
Byway). (Pass French Creek, Homestead,
and Twin Springs.)
**$5/single site, $10/multiple site.**

Open All Year.
12 close, open sites. Hand water pump,
pit toilet, tables, fireplaces.
In grove of fir and maple along South
Fork of McKenzie River.
Hike into Three Sisters Wilderness via
Olallie Trail. Boat, swim, and fish at
nearby Cougar Reservoir. Photograph
wildlife and scenery. In winter, cross-
country ski.
14-day/18-ft limits. FR 19 not maintained
during winter.
2600 ft (780 m)

**FRONA PARK**
Coos County Parks
(503) 396-3121
State map: 7A
Proceed .25 mile (400 m) E of DORA or
18 miles (28.8 k) NE of MYRTLE POINT
on Dora-Sitkum Hwy.
$3. Closed in winter.
17 scattered, open sites.
Pit toilets, tables, fire rings.
On East Fork of Coquille River.
Wade, fish or rockhound.
NO water. Call (503) 396-3121 ext 355
about opening/closing dates, vehicle
length, and limit of stay.

**GERBER RESERVOIR**
BLM (503) 947-2177
State map: 9E
From BONANZA, travel
11 miles (17.6 k) E on Langell Valley Rd.
Turn Left on Gerber Rd and continue
8 miles (12.8 k).
$4. Open May 1–Oct 15; dry camping
off-season.
50 scattered, open sites in two areas.
Central water faucets, "clean-smelling"
pit toilets, dump station, tables, grills,
fire rings, boat ramps, boat dock, fish
cleaning station.
On reservoir in mixed juniper and
ponderosa pine forest.
Fish and boat. Hike to view and
photograph high-desert wildlife and
scenery.
14-day/30-ft limits. Cool at night.
Hunting in season.
4700 ft (1410 m)

**GOLD DREDGE**
Umatilla NF (503) 427-3231
State map: 3H
From DALE, head NE on
FR 5506 for 7 miles (11.2 k). Pass
**Tollbridge** (7 sites). For more remote
camp with wilderness access, continue
another 5 miles (8 k) to **Oriental Creek**
(5 sites).
FREE but choose a chore.
Open Jun 1–Nov 1; camping allowed
off-season.
5 sites. Pit toilets, tables, fire rings.
On North Fork John Day River.
Hike or fish.
NO water. 14-day limit. ATVs. Hunting
in season.
4300 ft (1290 m)

**GRANDE RONDE LAKE**
Wallowa-Whitman NF
(503) 523-6391
State map: 3I
From NORTH POWDER, head SW on
CR 102/FR 7312 (Pilcher Creek) for
3.5 miles (5.6 k). Turn Left (S) on
CR 1146/FR 73 (Elkhorn Scenic Byway)
and go about 15 miles (24 k). Pass fee-
charged **Anthony Lakes** (47 sites) and
**Mud Lake** (7 sites).
$3. Open Jul 1–Sep 30; dry camping
off-season.
8 sites.
Water, pit toilets, tables, fire rings.
On mountain lake.
Swim or fish. Hike. Enjoy winter sports.
10-day limit.
6800 ft (2040 m)

**GRANDVIEW**
Wallowa-Whitman NF
(503) 963-7186
State map: 3I
From NW side of LA GRANDE, head N
toward Mt Emily on CR/FR 3120 for
14 miles (22.4 k). Turn Right.
FREE. Open Jun 1–Oct 31.
4 sites. Spring water, pit toilets, tables,
fire rings.
Sightsee and hike around Mt Emily.
10-day limit.
6000 ft (1800 m)

## GREEN MOUNTAIN

BLM (503) 947-2177
State map: 6F
From CHRISTMAS VALLEY,
follow county and BLM roads 8 miles
(12.8 k) N.
FREE but choose a chore.
Open All Year (weather decides).
Undesignated, close, open sites.
Tables, fire rings.
In juniper near summit of Green
Mountain with dramatic views of desert
landscapes.
Observe and take photos of scenery and
wildlife.
NO water, trash, or toilet facilities.
Extreme fire danger summers.

## GRINDSTONE

Mt Hood NF (503) 328-6211
State map: 3D
From GOVERNMENT CAMP,
drive 2 miles (3.2 k) E on US 26;
4.5 miles (7.2 k) E on OR 35; then 2 miles
(3.2 k) SE on FR 3530. (Also see Devil's
Half Acre.)
FREE but choose a chore.
Open May–Oct.
5 sites. Pit toilets, tables, grills.
Above Barlow Creek on old wagon road.
Hike along road. Enjoy seclusion.
Photograph scenery and wildlife.
NO water. 22-ft limit.

## HAMAKER

Rogue River NF
(503) 560-3623
State map: 7C
From PROSPECT, drive 12 (19.2 k) miles
N on OR 62; 11 miles (17.6 k) N on
OR 230; .5 mile (800 m) SE on FR 6530;
then another .5 mile (800 m) S on
FR 900.
$4/vehicle, $2/extra vehicle.
Open Memorial Day–Oct 31.
10 sites scattered in open or screened
settings. Hand water pump, pit toilets,
tables, fire rings.
Under Douglas fir near headwaters of
Rogue River.
Fish. Hike to study and photograph
nature.

14-day/16-ft limits. Crowded holidays.
Hunting in season.
4000 ft (1200 m)

## HAPPY CAMP

Fremont NF (503) 943-3114
State map: 8F
From PAISLEY, head W on
CR 28/FR 33 (Mill Rd) for 15 miles
(24 k). Turn Left on FR 28 for 2 miles
(3.2 k). Bear Right on FR 047. (Also see
Dairy Point.)
FREE but choose a chore.
Open Apr–Oct; dry camping off-season.
9 close, open sites.
Hand water pump, pit toilets, tables,
grills, CCC-built picnic shelters.
Relax and fish along Dairy Creek.
No trash arrangements (pack it out).
14-day/16-ft limits. Hunting in season.
5289 ft (1584 m)

## HART MOUNTAIN NATIONAL
## ANTELOPE REFUGE-Hot Springs

(503) 947-3315
State map: 8G
From LAKEVIEW, go N on
US 395 for 5 miles (8 k). Turn Right on
OR 140 and go 16 miles (25.6 k). Turn
Left (N) on CR to Plush and go 19 miles
(30.4 k). Continue N bearing Right along
mesa until road switchbacks and climbs
to top–about 15 unpaved miles (24 k)
impassable in rain or snow.
FREE but choose a chore.
Open All Year.
Undesignated, scattered, open sites.
Pit toilets, some tables, open-air shelter
around hot spring.
In bowl-like setting with aspen and
willow, surrounded by sagebrush-
covered hills and mountains.
Soak, hike, view and take photographs
of scenery and wildlife.
NO water/trash arrangements (pack it
out). 14-day/20-ft limits. Crowded
holidays. Quiet hours.
5800 ft (1740 m)

## HART-TISH PARK

Rogue River NF
(503) 889-1812
State map: 9B

From JACKSONVILLE, drive 8 miles
(12.8 k) SW on OR 238 then 15 miles
(24 k) SW on CR/FR 10. For free walk-in
camps on Applegate Lake, look at
French Gulch listing plus inquire at
Applegate Ranger District about **Harr
Point** (no water), **Latgawa Cove** (no
water or toilets), or **Tipsu Tyee** (no
water). With basics, find $3 walk-in
camping at **Carberry** (3 miles from
Hart-Tish) and $4 walk-in camping at
**Watkins** (2 miles from Hart-Tish).
$2/vehicle, $1/extra vehicle.
Open Apr–Oct.
4 RV sites scattered in open setting.
Central water faucet, flush toilets, tables,
boat ramp.
Boat, swim, or fish on Applegate Lake.
Hike and watch birds.
14-day limit. Crowded.
2000 ft (600 m)

## HAT POINT

Hells Canyon NRA
(503) 426-4978
State map: 3J

From IMNAHA, go SE on FR 4240 for 25
exciting miles (40 k)–no trailers. Pass
**Saddle Creek** (4 sites). Turn Right (E) on
FR 4240-315 and go 1.5 miles (2.4 k).
Find another alternative 1 mile
farther–**Sacajawea** (8 sites).
FREE but choose a chore.
Open Jun 15–Nov 15; camping allowed
off-season.
6 sites. Pit toilets, tables, fire rings.
At incredible overlook of Hells Canyon.
Sightsee. Enjoy view.
NO water. 10-day limit.
6982 ft (2094 m)

## HAYSTACK RESERVOIR

Crooked River National
Grassland (503) 447-9640
State map: 4E

From MADRAS, travel approximately
9.5 miles (15.2 k) S on US 97; 3 miles
(4.8 k) SE on CR 6; then .5 mile (800 m)

N on FR 1275.
$5. Open May 1–Oct 15.
24 sites. Central water faucet, flush
toilets, tables, fire rings, boat ramp.
On 250-acre lake in juniper-sagebrush
hills with red cliffs and views of Mt
Jefferson.
Boat, waterski, swim, and fish. Birdwatch too.
14-day/22-ft limits. Hunting in season.
2500 ft (750 m)

## HEAD OF THE RIVER

Winema NF (503) 783-2221
State map: 8D

From CHILOQUIN, travel E
on CR 858 about 12 miles (19.2 k). Turn
Left on CR 600 (Williamson River Rd)
for almost 14 miles (22.4 k) NE. Turn
Left and go .5 mile (800 m) N on
FR 4668.
FREE but choose a chore.
Open Jun 1–Oct 15.
6 sites. Pit toilets, tables, fire rings.
At headwaters of Williamson River.
Fish!
NO water. 14-day/30-ft limits.
4400 ft (1320 m)

## HEMLOCK LAKE

Umpqua NF (503) 496-3532
State map: 6C

From GLIDE, head E on CR 17
(Little River Rd) for 32 miles (51.2 k).
Pass fee-charged **Lake in the Woods**
(11 sites).
FREE but choose a chore.
Open Jun 1–Oct 31; camping allowed
off-season.
13 (3 tent-only) sites.
Pit toilets, tables, fire rings.
On 28-acre lake.
Boat (no motors). Swim and fish. Hike
5-mile (8 k) Yellow Jacket Loop.
NO water. 14-day limit.
4400 ft (1320 m)

## HIDEAWAY LAKE

Mt Hood NF (503) 630-4256
State map: 3D

From ESTACADA, drive
27 miles (43.2 k) SE on OR 224; Left (E)

▲ ▲ ▲ ▲ ▲ ▲ ▲ ▲ ▲ ▲ ▲ ▲ ▲ ▲ ▲ ▲ ▲ ▲ ▲ ▲ ▲ ▲ ▲

for 7.5 miles (12 k) on FR 57; Left (N) for 3 miles (4.8 k) on FR 58; then Left (NW) for 5.5 miles (8.8 k) on FR 5830.
**$5. Open Jun 15-Sep 30.**
9 scattered sites.
Water, pit toilets, tables, grills.
Around gem of a lake.
Fish for trout. Hike loop to other lakes. 16-ft limit.
3800 ft (1140 m)

## HIGHROCK SPRING
Mt Hood NF (503) 630-4256
State map: 3D
From ESTACADA, go 27 miles (43.2 k) SE on OR 224; Left (E) for 7.5 miles (12 k) on FR 57; Left (N) for 10.5 miles (16.8 k) on FR 58 – not recommended for trailers or RVs.
**FREE but choose a chore.**
**Open Jun 15-Sep 30.**
7 tent sites. Pit toilets, tables, grills.
In area of large rocks with lakes.
Climb to High Rock for views, including Mt Hood. Enjoy fishing in lakes. Pick berries when ripe.
NO water.

## HOMESTEAD
Willamette NF (503) 822-3317
State map: 5D
From BLUE RIVER, travel 3.5 miles (5.6 k) E on US 126; then approximately 23 miles (36.8 k) S along FR 19 (Aufderheide National Scenic Byway). (Other campgrounds along this road include French Pete, Twin Springs, and Frissell Crossing.)
**FREE. Open All Year.**
7 scattered, screened sites.
Pit toilets, some tables and fireplaces.
On South Fork of McKenzie River.
Hike, view wildlife, and photograph scenery in Three Sisters Wilderness. Boat, swim, and fish in nearby Cougar Reservoir. Cross-country ski in winter. NO water/trash pick-up (nearby Frissell Crossing offers water). Facilities need upgrading. 14-day limit. Hunting in season. FR 19 not maintained for snow or ice.
2200 ft (660 m)

## HUCKLEBERRY MOUNTAIN
Rogue River NF
(503) 560-3623
State map: 7C
From PROSPECT, proceed 17 miles (27.2 k) N on OR 62. Turn Right on FR 60 and go 3 miles (4.8 k) up steep, narrow road – not recommended for trailers or large RVs.
**FREE but choose a chore.**
Open Memorial Day-Oct 31 (weather decides); dry camping off-season.
27 sites. Hand water pump, pit toilets, tables, fire rings.
In isolated wildflower meadow surrounded by Douglas fir trees.
Hike to view and photograph nature as well as pick berries when ripe.
No trash pick-up (pack it out).
14-day/22-ft limits.
5400 ft (1620 m)

## HURRICANE CREEK
Hells Canyon NRA
(503) 426-4978
State map: 3J
From JOSEPH, head W for 2 miles (3.2 k) past airport. Turn Left (S) on FR 8205 and go 2 miles (3.2 k).
**FREE but choose a chore.**
**Open Jun 15-Nov 1.**
10 tent sites.
Pit toilets, tables, fire rings.
On creek at edge of Eagle Cap Wilderness.
Fish, hike, and explore.
NO water. 10-day limit.
5400 ft (1620 m)

## HYATT LAKE SOUTH OVERFLOW
BLM (503) 770-2200
State map: 9C
From ASHLAND on I-5, take Exit 14 then drive OR 66 E 20 miles (32 k). Turn Left on Eastshore Hyatt Lake Rd and travel another 5 miles (8 k). Also find primitive sites on nearby **Little Hyatt Lake.**
**$4. Open May 15-Nov 1; camping** allowed off-season.
10 scattered, open sites.
Pit toilets, tables, grills.

▲ ▲ ▲ ▲ ▲ ▲ ▲ ▲ ▲ ▲ ▲ ▲ ▲ ▲ ▲ ▲ ▲ ▲ ▲ ▲ ▲ ▲ ▲ ▲ ▲ ▲ ▲

Beside forest lake in Siskiyou Mountains. Boat and fish. Hike along Pacific Crest National Scenic Trail. View and photograph wildlife.
NO water. Crowded holidays. 14-day limit.
5200 ft (1560 m)

## ICE CAP CREEK
Willamette NF (503) 822-3381
State map: 5D
From MCKENZIE BRIDGE, take US 126 N for 19 miles (30.4 k) then short distance NE on FR 14071. (Also see Fish Lake and Trail Bridge.)
$5. Open May 1 - Oct 31 (weather decides).
22 (6 tent-only) close, screened sites.
Central water faucet, flush/pit toilets, tables, grills, fire ring.
Near Koosah and Sahalie Falls with access to McKenzie River and Carmen Reservoir.
Fish and boat (no motors) in reservoir. Hike on McKenzie River National Recreation Trail to waterfalls. Visit nearby Clear Lake.
14-day/16-ft limits.
3000 ft (900 m)

## IDLEWILD
Malheur NF (503) 573-7292
State map: 6H
From BURNS, head N on US 395 for 17 miles (27.2 k).
FREE but choose a chore.
Open May 30-Oct 15.
24 sites.
Water, pit toilets, tables, fire rings.
Explore Devine Canyon. Relax.
No trash arrangements (pack it out).
5300 ft (1590 m)

## IMNAHA
Rogue River NF
(503) 865-3581
State map: 8C
From BUTTE FALLS, take CR 992 SE. Turn Right on FR 34 (which becomes FR 37) and go 17.5 miles (28 k).
FREE but choose a chore.
Open May-Oct.

4 scattered, open sites.
Pit toilets, tables, grills, fire rings.
Near springs on creek in very green, cool setting.
Observe and photograph nature. Hike trails into Sky Lakes Wilderness. Tour old guard station.
NO water. 14-day limit.
3800 ft (1140 m)

## INDIAN CROSSING
Hells Canyon NRA
(503) 426-4978
State map: 3J
From JOSEPH, go E on OR 350 for 7.5 miles (12 k). Turn Right (S) on FR 39 and go 28.75 miles (46 k). Continue straight (SW) on FR 3960 for 8.75 miles (14 k). On way, options include Lick Creek (10 sites) at top of canyon, Blackhorse (17 sites), Ollokot (12 sites), and Hidden (10 sites).
FREE but choose a chore.
Open Jun 15-Nov 15; dry camping off-season.
15 sites.
Water, pit toilets, tables, fire rings.
On wild and scenic Imnaha River at edge of Eagle Cap Wilderness.
Excellent hiking possibilities (such as Blue Hole). Fish too.
10-day limit.
4500 ft (1350 m)

## INDIGO SPRINGS
Willamette NF (503) 782-2283
State map: 6C
From OAKRIDGE, take OR 58 E. Turn Right (S) onto CR 360 (Kitson Springs Rd) and drive .5 mile (800 m). Turn Right onto FR 21 and proceed 26 miles (41.6 k).
FREE but choose a chore.
Open Apr 15-Sep 30; camping allowed off-season.
3 sites. Pit toilets, tables, fireplaces.
Under old-growth Douglas fir with secluded remnant of historic Oregon Central Military Wagon Road and nearby cold water spring.
Hike, take photographs, and enjoy relative peace and quiet.

NO water/trash arrangements.
16-day/16-ft limits.
2800 ft (840 m)

## INLET

Umpqua NF (503) 498-2531
State map: 7D
From IDLEYLD PARK, head E
on OR 138 for 50 miles (80 k). Turn Left
(N) on FR 2610. Go 3 miles (4.8 k). Turn
Right (E) on FR 400. Go 2 miles (3.2 k).
Pass **East Lemolo** (6 sites), or continue
around lake 2 miles (3.2 k) to **Bunker
Hill** (8 sites), or proceed additional
1 mile (1.6 k) to fee-charged **Poole Creek**
(59 sites).
FREE but choose a chore.
Open May 15–Sep 30; camping allowed
off-season.
14 (3 tent-only) sites.
Pit toilets, tables, fire rings.
On E side of Lemolo Lake.
Swim, waterski, boat, or fish. Hike to
Lemolo Falls.
NO water. 14-day limit.
4200 ft (1260 m)

## IRISH & TAYLOR

Deschutes NF (503) 388-5664
State map: 6D
From BEND, take OR 46
(Cascade Lakes Hwy) for 43 miles
(68.8 k) SW. Turn on FR 4630 for
3.5 miles (5.6 k) SW toward Cultus Lake.
Jog Left on 640 then turn right for
5 miles (8 k) on FR 600 – for high
clearance vehicles.
FREE but choose a chore.
Open Jun 15–Sep 15.
5 tent sites. Tables, fire rings.
Near Pacific Coast Trail between Irish
and Taylor lakes (wilderness permit for
Irish Lake Hike-In).
Hike and fish.
NO water, trash, or toilet facilities.
5700 ft (1710 m)

## ISLAND

Umpqua NF (503) 496-3532
State map: 6C
From IDLEYLD PARK, head E
on OR 138 for 19 miles (30.4 k). Pass fee-
charged options: BLM's **Susan Creek**
(33 sites) and NF's **Bogus Creek**
(15 sites). (Also see Apple Creek and
Steamboat Falls.)
FREE but choose a chore.
Open All Year.
7 sites. ♿
Pit toilets, tables, fire rings.
On North Umpqua River.
Fly fish, whitewater boat. Hike Canton
Creek Falls, Mott, and Panther trails.
NO water. 14-day/24-ft limits.
1189 ft (354 m)

## JACK CREEK

Deschutes NF (503) 549-2111
State map: 4D
From SISTERS, travel US 20
NW for 8.5 miles (13.6 k). Turn Right (N)
on FR 12 and go 3.5 miles (5.6 k). Turn
Left (W) on FR 1230.
FREE but choose a chore.
Open Apr 15–Oct 15.
15 sites.
Chemical toilets, tables, fire rings.
Fish in creek or hike into Mt Jefferson
Wilderness.
NO water/trash arrangements.
14-day/22-ft limits.
3100 ft (930 m)

## JACK LAKE

Deschutes NF (503) 549-2111
State map: 4D
From SISTERS, travel US 20
NW for 8.5 miles (13.6 k). Turn Right (N)
on FR 12 and go 3.5 miles (5.6 k). Turn
Left (W) on FR 1230 and go 1.5 miles
(2.4 k). Turn Left on FR 1234 and drive
to end of road – about 3.5 miles (5.6 k).
FREE but choose a chore.
Open Jun 15–OCT 15.
2 sites.
Chemical toilets, tables, fire rings.
On edge of Mt Jefferson Wilderness.
Boat, swim, and fish. Hike or ride horses
to Wasco Lake.
NO water (OK for stock). 14-day limit.
5700 ft (1710 m)

## JACKSON CREEK

Winema NF (503) 365-2229
State map: 7E
From CHEMULT, drive
24.5 miles (39.2 k) S on US 97. Turn Left
(NE) for 22 miles (35.2 k) on CR 676
(Silver Lake Hwy); then Right (SE) for
5 miles (8 k) on FR 49.
FREE but choose a chore.
Open May 1–Nov 15.
12 sites. Pit toilets, tables, fire rings.
Between Klamath Marsh and Yamsay
Mountain.
Watch birds. Fish.
NO water. 14-day/22-ft limits.
4600 ft (1380 m)

## JEAN LAKE

Mt Hood NF (503) 467-2291
State map: 3E
From WAMIC, travel 6 miles
(9.6 k) SW on CR 226; 10.5 miles (16.8 k)
SW on FR 48. Turn Right (N) on FR 4890
and go 2 miles (3.2 k). Continue Straight
(N) on FR 4891 for 5 miles (8 k). Turn
Right (NE) on FR 3550 and go 2.5 miles
(4 k). Pass **Bonny Meadows** and **Camp
Windy** (both closed at last report).
FREE but choose a chore.
Open Jul 1–Sep 10.
4 tent sites. Pit toilets, fire rings.
At quiet lake next to Badger Creek
Wilderness.
Boat (no motors), swim, or fish.
NO water. No trailers or RVs.
4800 ft (1440 m)

## KEEPS MILL

Mt Hood NF (503) 328-6211
State map: 3E
From WAMIC, drive 6 miles
(9.6 k) W on CR 226; 12.5 miles (20 k)
SW on FR 48; 3 miles (4.8 k) SE on
FR 4885; then .25 mile (400 m). (Also see
Clear Creek and Forest Creek.)
FREE but choose a chore.
Open May 15–Oct 1.
5 tent sites. Pit toilets, tables, fire rings.
On old mill site at confluence of Clear
Creek and White River.
Hike on area trails.
NO water. 14-day limit. No trailers or
RVs.
2600 ft (780 m)

## KLAMATH RIVER

BLM (503) 947-2177
State map: 9D
From KLAMATH FALLS,
travel 3 miles (4.8 k) S on 97. Drive
OR 66 about 16.5 miles (26.4 k) W to
powerplant sign. Turn Left and follow
gravel road 4 miles (6.4 k) to powerhouse. Go 3 miles (4.8 k) S on primitive
road for high-clearance vehicles only.
FREE but choose a chore.
Open All Year (weather decides).
2 scattered, screened sites.
Pit toilets, tables, fire rings.
Under large ponderosa pine and oak
trees along Upper Klamath River.
Study nature. View birds and other
wildlife. Fish or run river (contact BLM
for whitewater rafting info). Mountain
bike. Enjoy scenery. Find solitude.
NO water/trash arrangements. Hunting
in season.
3200 ft (960 m)

## KNEBAL SPRINGS

Mt Hood NF (503) 467-2291
State map: 3E
From DUFUR, proceed
12 miles (19.2 k) SW on CR 1; 4.25 miles
(6.8 k) SW on FR 44; 4 miles (6.4 k) N on
FR 4430; then 1 mile (1.6 k) SW on
FR 1720. (Also see Eightmile Crossing.)
FREE but choose a chore.
Open Jul 1–Sep 10.
4 sites.
Pit toilets, tables, grills, horse facilities.
Near erratic spring.
Hike or ride horseback on area trails.
NO water. 22-ft limit.

## LAKE HARRIET

Mt Hood NF (503) 630-4256
State map: 3D
From ESTACADA, drive
27 miles (43.2 k) SE on OR 224; 6.5 miles
(10.4 k) E on FR 57; then 1.2 miles (1.9 k)
W on FR 4630.
$5. Open Apr 30–Sep 30.
13 sites. &

Well water, pit toilets, tables, grills, boat launch.
On lake formed by dam on Oak Grove Fork of Clackamas River.
Boating (up to small motors) and fishing (for several varieties trout).
30-ft limit. No horses allowed.
2100 ft (630 m)

## LAVA CAMP LAKE
Deschutes NF (503) 549-2111
State map: 5D
From SISTERS, take OR 242 approximately 12 miles (19.2 k) W.
FREE but choose a chore.
Open Jun 15–Oct 31.
12 (2 tent-only) sites.
Pit toilets, tables, fire rings.
In forest near McKenzie Pass and Pacific Coast Trail.
Swim, fish, hike, or relax.
NO water/trash arrangements.
14-day/22-ft limits.
5200 ft (1560 m)

## LAVA FLOW
Deschutes NF (503) 433-2234
State map: 6D
From BEND, take paved Cascade Lakes Hwy (FR 46) then FR 850 to Davis Lake–about 75 miles (120 k). (At first snow, road closes at Mt Bachelor). (Also see Davis Lake.)
FREE but choose a chore.
Open May–Oct.
12 sites. Central water faucet, pit toilets, tables, fire rings, boat ramp.
On eastern shore of Davis Lake.
Boat and fish.
14-day/22-ft limits. Hunting in season.
4400 ft (1320 m)

## LEE THOMAS
Fremont NF (503) 943-3114
State map: 8F
From PAISLEY, drive 1 mile (1.6 k) W on CR 28. Turn Right on FR 3315 and go 22.5 miles (36 k). Turn Left on FR 28 and go 1 mile (1.6 k) S. Turn Right on FR 3411 for additional 5 miles (8 k). (Also see Campbell Lake and Sandhill Crossing.)

FREE but choose a chore.
Open Apr–Oct; dry camping off-season.
7 close, open sites. Hand water pump, pit toilets, tables, grills, fire rings.
With overlooks of large meadow and deep woods near North Fork of Sprague River.
Good birdwatching and fishing here.
No trash facilities. 14-day/16-ft limits.
6260 ft (1878 m)

## LESLIE GULCH
BLM (503) 473-3144
State map: 6J
From JORDAN, head N on US 95 for 18 miles (28.8 k). Turn Left (N) at Malloy Ranch on Leslie Gulch-Succor Creek National Backcountry Byway, a graded gravel road. Go 9 miles (14.4 k). Turn Left (W) and go 13 miles (20.8 k). Use caution in wet weather–watch for flash floods in canyon.
FREE but choose a chore.
Open All Year.
Undesignated, scattered, open sites.
Pit toilets, tables.
With picturesque rock formations and excellent desert wildlife viewing in side canyon of Owyhee Canyon and its reservoir.
Hike to photograph scenery and wildlife.
Boat, waterski, swim, or fish.
NO water–come prepared. Quiet 10pm-7am. 14-day limit.
2800 ft (840 m)

## LIMBERLOST
Willamette NF (503) 822-3381
State map: 5D
From MCKENZIE BRIDGE, travel 4.25 miles (6.8 k) E on OR 126 then .5 mile (800 m) E on OR 242 which has 35-ft limit–no large trailers or RVs.
FREE but choose a chore.
Open May–Oct.
12 close, screened sites.
Pit toilets, tables, fire rings.
On Lost Creek.
Enjoy seclusion. Fish for trout. Hike and photograph scenery.
NO water/trash facilities. 14-day limit.
1600 ft (480 m)

▲ ▲ ▲ ▲ ▲ ▲ ▲ ▲ ▲ ▲ ▲ ▲ ▲ ▲ ▲ ▲ ▲ ▲ ▲ ▲ ▲ ▲ ▲ ▲ ▲ ▲

## LITTLE APPLEGATE

BLM (503) 770-2200
State map: 9C
From OR 238 at RUCH (SW of MEDFORD), take Applegate River Rd S 1 mile (1.6 k). Turn onto Little Applegate River Rd and travel 16 miles (25.6 k). Park and walk 300-ft (90 m).
FREE but choose a chore.
Open May 15 – Nov 1; dry camping off-season.
10 scattered, open tent sites. Hand water pump, pit toilets, tables, grills.
On river bank in forest.
Hike on Sterling Mine Ditch Trail.
Crowded holidays. 14-day limit.
2500 ft (750 m)

## LITTLE BADGER

Mt Hood NF (503) 467-2291
State map: 3E
From TYGH VALLEY, take CR/FR 27 approximately 8 miles (12.8 k) W (past fairground and along Happy Ridge). Turn Left on FR 2710 for additional mile.
FREE but choose a chore.
Open Memorial Day – Labor Day; camping allowed off-season.
15 sites. Pit toilets.
On Little Badger Creek.
Fish, hike, or ride horses.
NO water. 16-ft limit.
2150 ft (645 m)

## LITTLE CULTUS LAKE

Deschutes NF (503) 388-5664
State map: 6D
From BEND, take FR 46 SW (Cascade Lakes Hwy) for 43 miles (68.8 k). Continue 1.5 miles (2.4 k) SW on FR 4635; 2 miles (3.2 k) on FR 4630; then 1 mile (1.6 k) W on FR 600.
FREE but choose a chore.
Open late May – late Sep.
10 sites. Hand water pump, pit toilets, tables, fire rings, boat ramp.
Boat, waterski, swim, and fish on lake.
Hike on forest trails to other lakes.
No trash pickup. 14-day/22-ft limits.
4800 ft (1440 m)

## LITTLE FAWN

Deschutes NF (503) 388-5664
State map: 5D
From BEND, take CR/FR 46 (Cascade Lakes Hwy) to Elk Lake – about 30 miles (48 k). Turn Left on FR 4625 then Left again on next road. (Also see South Elk Lake.)
$5/vehicle, $3/extra vehicle.
Open Jun – Sep.
Undesignated, individual sites on front loop plus group area on back loop.
Pit toilets, tables, fire rings, boat ramp.
With beach on Elk Lake.
Swim, boat, or fish.
NO water/trash facilities.
4900 ft (1470 m)

## LITTLE LAVA LAKE

Deschutes NF (503) 388-5664
State map: 5D
From BEND, take FR 46 (Cascade Lakes Hwy) about 34 miles (54.4 k) SW to Lava Lakes. Turn Left on FR 500 for additional mile.
FREE but choose a chore.
Open Jun – Sep.
14 sites. Hand water pump, pit toilets, tables, fire rings.
Near lake creating headwaters of Deschutes River.
Boat, fish, swim, or hike.
14-day/22-ft limits.
4800 ft (1440 m)

## LOBSTER CREEK

Siskiyou NF (503) 247-6651
State map: 8A
From GOLD BEACH, head NE on CR 595/FR 33 and go 8.5 miles (13.6 k). For more developed, fee-charged option, go another 2.8 miles (4.5 k) to **Quosatana** (42 sites).
FREE but choose a chore.
Open May 30 – Sep 10; camping allowed off-season.
5 tent sites.
Pit toilets, tables, fire rings, boat ramp.
On Rogue River.
Swim, boat, or fish.
NO water. 14-day limit.

▲ ▲ ▲ ▲ ▲ ▲ ▲ ▲ ▲ ▲ ▲ ▲ ▲ ▲ ▲ ▲ ▲ ▲ ▲ ▲ ▲ ▲ ▲ ▲ ▲ ▲ ▲ ▲ ▲ ▲ ▲ ▲

## LOFTON RESERVOIR

Fremont NF (503) 353-2427
State map: 8F
From BLY, take OR 140 SE for
13 miles (20.8 k). Turn Right (S) at
Quartz Mountain on FR 3715 and drive
7 miles (11.2 k) S. Turn Left (E) on
FR 013 for 1 mile NE–steep grades.
FREE but choose a chore.
Open May–Oct; dry camping off-season.
26 scattered, open sites.
Hand water pump, pit toilets, tables, fire
rings, boat ramp.
At edge of Great Basin.
Boating (no motors) and fishing.
No trash facilities. 14-day/22-ft limits.
6100 ft (1830 m)

## LONE PINE

BLM (503) 447-4115
State map: 4G
From KIMBERLY, travel N
1.5 miles (2.4 k) on paved road 402.
FREE but choose a chore.
Open All Year.
5 close, open sites.
Pit toilets, tables, fire rings.
In cottonwood grove providing shade in
high desert along North Fork of John
Day River.
Boat, swim, and fish in river. View and
photograph scenery and nature. Hike
and attend NPS ranger programs at
nearby John Day Fossil Beds NM.
NO water/trash facilities. 14-day limit.
Rattlesnakes. Hunting in season.
1200 ft (360 m)

## LOOKOUT

Willamette NF (503) 822-3317
State map: 5D
About 3 miles (4.8 k) N of
BLUE RIDGE via OR 126 then FR 15.
FREE but choose a chore.
Open All Year.
Undesignated sites. Pit toilet, boat
ramp–plans underway to add another
toilet, tables, grills, fire rings, and fee.
On grassy flat by Blue River Reservoir.
Hike, view and photograph nature. In
warm months, boat, swim, and fish in
reservoir. In snowy, cross-country ski.

14-day limit. Crowded holidays and
weekends. Hunting in season. FR 15 not
maintained in winter.
1200 ft (360 m)

## LOWER & UPPER OLALLIE

Willamette NF (503) 822-3381
State map: 5D
From MCKENZIE BRIDGE,
drive 11 miles (17.6 k) NE on OR 126.
(Also see Trail Bridge.)
$5. Open Apr–Oct (weather decides).
17 sites in two loops. Hand water pump,
pit toilets, tables, fire rings.
On McKenzie River at Olallie Creek in
stand of Douglas fir and cedar.
Raft and fish. Hike and take photos.
14-day/22-ft limits.
2000 ft (600 m)

## LOWER CANYON CREEK

Deschutes NF (503) 549-2111
State map: 4D
From SISTERS, drive NW
13 miles (20.8 k) on US 20/OR 126. Turn
on FR 12 and drive approximately
7 miles (11.2 k). Make hard Right (SE)
then bear Left on FR 400. Go .5 mile
(800 m).
FREE but choose a chore.
Open Apr 15–Oct 15.
5 sites.
Chemical toilets, tables, fire rings.
Fish or hike.
NO water/trash facilities (pack it out).
14-day/16-ft limits.
2900 ft (870 m)

## LOWER CROSSING

Mt Hood NF (503) 467-2291
State map: 2E
From DUFUR, travel 12 miles
(19.2 k) SW on CR 1; 4 miles (6.4 k) W
on FR 44; then 1 mile (1.6 k) N on
FR 167. (Also see Eightmile Crossing.)
FREE but choose a chore.
Open Jul 1–Sep 10.
3 sites. Pit toilets, tables, grills.
Fish on Eightmile Creek.
NO water. 10-day/16-ft limits. Hunting
in season.
3800 ft (1140 m)

▲ ▲ ▲ ▲ ▲ ▲ ▲ ▲ ▲ ▲ ▲ ▲ ▲ ▲ ▲ ▲ ▲ ▲ ▲ ▲ ▲ ▲ ▲ ▲ ▲ ▲ ▲ ▲

## MACKS CANYON

BLM (503) 447-4115
State map: 3E
Drive through town of
MAUPIN but do not cross bridge past
city park. Turn Left onto paved "Lower
Access Rd" and drive 9 miles (14.4 k).
Turn Right at stop sign then Left onto
gravel "Lower Access Rd." Signs read
"Deschutes River Recreation Lands" and
"Macks Canyon, Dead End, 17 miles."
Pass options: **Oakbrook** (3 sites), **Twin
Springs** (6 sites), **Jones Canyon** (7 sites),
**Gert Canyon** (4 sites), **Beavertail**
(18 sites), and **Rattlesnake** (8 sites). (Also
see Oasis Flat.)
$3/vehicle, $1/extra vehicle.
Open All Year.
16 scattered, open sites. Central water
faucet, pit toilets, tables, boat launch.
In high-desert environment within steep,
rugged Deschutes River canyon.
Boat (drift or raft), swim, and fish. View
and photograph geology, plants, and
animals.
14-day/30-ft limits. Quiet 10pm-7am.
Crowded summer weekends. Hot
summers. Limited shade. No fires from
Jun 1-Oct 15. Hunting in season.
500 ft (150 m)

## MAGONE LAKE

Malheur NF (503) 575-2110
State map: 4H
From MOUNT VERNON,
head N on US 395 for 9.5 miles (15.2 k).
Turn Right (E) on FR 36 and go 7 miles
(11.2 k). Bear Left (N) on FR 3618 and go
2 miles (3.2 k).
FREE but choose a chore.
Open May 30-Oct 15.
16 (3 tent-only) sites. ﾴ
Water, pit toilets, tables, fire rings, boat
launch.
On lake formed by landslide in 1800s.
Swim, boat, or fish. Hike trail around
lake beneath twisted trees.
No trash arrangements (pack it out).
5000 ft (1500 m)

## MALLARD MARSH

Deschutes NF (503) 388-5664
State map: 5D
From BEND, drive 31 miles
(49.6 k) W on FR 46 (Cascade Lakes
Hwy) then 2.75 miles (4.4 k) SW on
FR 4625.
FREE but choose a chore.
Open Jun 1-Sep 15.
15 sites. Pit toilets, tables, fire rings.
On Hosmer Lake.
Canoe or fly fish.
NO water/trash facilities. 14-day/22-ft
limits.
4900 ft (1470 m)

## MARSTER SPRINGS

Fremont NF (503) 943-3114
State map: 8F
From PAISLEY and OR 31,
head W on CR 28 (Mill Creek Rd) which
turns into FR 33. Drive 7 miles (11.2 k).
FREE but choose a chore.
Open Apr-Oct; dry camping off-season.
10 close, open sites.
Hand water pump, pit toilets, tables, fire
rings, and handicapped fishing access
(but not camping facilities).
On Chewaucan River.
Walk nature trail and view wildlife.
Swim, fish, or simply relax to soothing
sounds of river.
14-day/22-ft limits.
4845 ft (1452 m)

## MARY'S PEAK

Siuslaw NF (503) 487-5811
State map: 4B
From ALSEA, head NE on
OR 34 for 7 miles (11.2 k). Turn Left
(NW) on FR 30 for 4 miles (6.4 k). Bear
Right on FR 3010 for 3 miles (4.8 k).
$3. Open May 22-Oct 1.
6 sites. ﾴ
Water, pit toilets, tables, fire rings.
Sightsee and hike on mountain top.
No trash facilities. Small vehicles only.
4900 ft (1470 m)

▲ ▲ ▲ ▲ ▲ ▲ ▲ ▲ ▲ ▲ ▲ ▲ ▲ ▲ ▲ ▲ ▲ ▲ ▲ ▲ ▲ ▲ ▲ ▲

## MCBRIDE

Wallowa-Whitman NF
(503) 742-7511
State map: 3J
From CARSON (NW of HALFWAY), go
W on FR 7710 (Carson Grade) for
2.5 miles (4 k).
FREE but choose a chore.
Open Jun 1–Oct 31.
5 sites. Pit toilets, tables, fire rings.
Hike or fish along Brooks Ditch.
NO water. 10-day limit.
4800 ft (1440 m)

## MCCUBBINS GULCH

Mt Hood NF (503) 328-6211
State map: 3E
From MAUPIN, travel
24.5 miles (39.2 k) SW on
OR 216–almost to fee-charged Bear
Springs (21 sites). Turn Right (NE) for
1 mile (1.6 k) on FR 2110. Turn Right.
FREE but choose a chore.
Open May–Oct.
5 sites. Pit toilets, tables, grills.
Near Warm Springs Reservation.
Fish!
NO water. 14-day limit. Not
recommended for trailers or RVs.
3100 ft (930 m)

## MCCULLY FORKS

Wallowa-Whitman NF
(503) 523-6391
State map: 4I
From SUMPTER, head W on CR 520
(Elkhorn Dr) for 2.5 miles (4 k).
FREE but choose a chore.
Open May 1–Nov 15.
6 sites. Pit toilets, tables, fire rings.
Fish or hike along Powder River.
NO water. 10-day limit.
4600 ft (1380 m)

## MCKAY CROSSING

Deschutes NF (503) 388-5664
State map: 6E
From BEND, travel S on US 97
for 22 miles (35.2 k). Turn Left (SE) on
CR 21 and go 3 miles (4.8 k). Turn Left
(E) on FR 2120 and go 2 miles
(3.2 k)–beyond Ogden Group.

FREE but choose a chore.
Open Jun 1–Oct 31.
10 sites. Pit toilets, tables, fire rings.
On Paulina Creek near waterfalls.
Hike, bike, or ride horseback. Fish.
NO water/trash arrangements.
14-day/22-ft limits.
4400 ft (1320 m)

## MCKENZIE BRIDGE

Willamette NF (503) 822-3381
State map: 5D
From MCKENZIE BRIDGE,
travel 1 mile (1.6 k) W on OR 126.
$5/vehicle, $2.50/extra vehicle;
reservations accepted at (800) 283-2267
for additional $6.
Open May–Oct (weather decides).
20 close, screened sites. Hand water
pump, pit toilets, tables, grills, fire rings.
In forest beside McKenzie River.
Kayak and fish river. Hike to view and
photograph nature. Mountain bike too.
14-day/22-ft limits.
1400 ft (420 m)

## MCNEIL

Mt Hood NF (503) 622-3191
State map: 3D
From ZIGZAG, head N on
CR 18 for 4.75 miles (7.6 k). Bear Right
onto FR 1825 when entering NF. Nearby
options include Riley Horse Camp
within .5 mile (800 m) SE and Lost
Creek at end of FR 1825.
$4. Open Memorial Day–Labor Day.
34 sites. Water, pit toilets, tables.
On Clear Fork of Sandy River.
Fish. Bicycle. Walk nature trail. Hike into
Mt Hood Wilderness.
14-day/22-ft limits.
2000 ft (600 m)

## MEDITATION POINT
## WALK-IN/BOAT-IN

Mt Hood NF (503) 328-6211
State map: 3D
From GOVERNMENT CAMP,
drive US 26 SE for 15 miles (24 k) SE.
Turn Left (S) on FR 42 for 8 miles
(12.8 k). Turn Right (W) on FR 57 and go
5 miles (8 k). Park at Pine Point. Hike or

boat 1 mile (1.6 k). All vehicle-accessible sites at Timothy Lake charge fees—**Gone Creek, Hoodview, Oak Fork,** and **Pine Point.**
FREE but choose a chore.
Open May 15–Sep 30.
4 tent sites. Pit toilets, tables, fire rings.
On north shore of Timothy Lake.
Enjoy seclusion. Swim, fish, or boat.
NO water. 14-day limit.
3200 ft (960 m)

## MIDDLE FORK

Malheur NF (503) 575-2110
State map: 4H
From AUSTIN, head NW on CR 20 for 9 miles (14.4 k).
FREE but choose a chore.
Open May 30–Oct 15.
5 (2 tent-only) sites.
Water, pit toilets, tables, fire rings.
On Middle Fork of John Day River.
Fish. Explore. Enjoy getaway.
NO water/trash arrangements.
4100 ft (1230 m)

## MILE WALK-IN

Deschutes NF (503) 388-5664
State map: 5D
From BEND, travel 40 miles (64 k) SW on FR 46 (Cascades Lakes Hwy) to Lava Lakes. Hike short distance.
FREE but choose a chore.
Open May 15–Sep 15.
8 tent sites. Pit toilets, tables, fire rings.
On Upper Deschutes River.
Fish lakes or hike trails.
NO water/trash facilities. 14-day limit.
4700 ft (1410 m)

## MILL CREEK

Rogue River NF
(503) 560-3623
State map: 8C
2 miles (3.2 k) N of PROSPECT ranger station on OR 62, turn Right on FR 030 and drive 1 mile (1.6 k).
FREE but choose a chore.
Open Mar 15–Oct 31.
8 scattered, screened sites.
Pit toilets, tables, fire rings.
Birdwatch and fish along creek.

NO water. 14-day limit. Crowded holidays.
2800 ft (840 m)

## MINERAL

Umpqua NF (503) 942-5591
State map: 6C
From CULP CREEK, head SE on CR 2460 (Sharps Creek) for 12 miles (19.2 k).
FREE but choose a chore.
Open May 25–Sep 30; camping allowed off-season.
2 tent sites. Pit toilet, tables, fire rings.
Along Sharp Creek at base of historic Hardscrabble Grade.
Hike up Fairview Creek. Explore.
NO water. 14-day limit.
1800 ft (540 m)

## MONTY

Deschutes NF (503) 549-2111
State map: 4E
From CULVER, drive NE to Cove Palisades SP. Turn Left on CR 63 across Crooked River and Deschutes River. Go 10 miles (16 k) W on CR 64 to end of gravel road. Alternative is fee-charged **Perry South.**
FREE but choose a chore.
Open Apr 15–Oct 15.
20 sites.
Chemical toilets, tables, fire rings.
On Metolius River arm of Lake Billy Chinook.
Boat, swim, waterski, and fish. Hike too.
NO water/trash facilities (at fee-charged Perry South). 14-day/22-ft limits.
2000 ft (600 m)

## MOSS CREEK SPRINGS

Wallowa-Whitman NF
(503) 963-7186
State map: 3I
From COVE, head E on FR 6220 for 10 miles (16 k).
FREE but choose a chore.
Open Jun 1–Oct 31.
6 sites. Pit toilets, tables, fire rings.
At edge of Eagle Cap Wilderness.
Hike to Whiskey Flat or along Little Minam River. Enjoy solitude.

NO water. 10-day limit.
5400 ft (1620 m)

## MOTTET

Umatilla NF (509) 843-1891
State map: 2I
From WESTON, head E on
WA 204 for 18 miles (28.8 k). Turn Left
(NE) on FR 64 and go 12 miles (19.2 k).
Fee-charged **Jubilee Lake** (51 sites) is to
Right. Turn Left (N) on FR 6401/6403
and go 2.5 miles (4 k).
**FREE** but choose a chore.
Open Jun 1–Oct 31.
7 sites.
Water, pit toilets, tables, fire rings.
Near S edge of Wenaha-Tucannon
Wilderness.
Hike trail down to river.
10-day limit. Hunting in season.
5200 ft (1560 m)

## MT ASHLAND

Klamath NF (916) 465-2241
State map: 9C
Find camp .5 mile (800 m)
from Mt Ashland Ski Resort. From
ASHLAND, travel 12 miles (19.2 k) S on
I-5 to SISKIYOU/Mt Ashland Exit. Drive
1 mile (1.6 k) W on CR 993 then 9 miles
(14.4 k) on CR/FR 20 W.
**FREE** but choose a chore.
Open May–Oct; camping allowed
off-season.
9 scattered, open sites.
Pit toilets, tables, grills.
With good mountain views.
Along Pacific Coast Trail, hike in
summer and cross-country ski in winter.
Enjoy photography year-round.
NO water/trash arrangements.
14-day/24-ft limits. Hunting in season.
Snow closes road in winter.
6600 ft (1980 m)

## MT HEBO

Siuslaw NF (503) 392-3161
State map: 3B
From HEBO, take FR 14 E for
8 miles (9.6 k) to end. Pass fee-charged
**Hebo Lake**.
**FREE** but choose a chore.

Open May 15–Oct 31.
3 tent sites. Pit toilets, tables, fire rings.
At trailhead to Pioneer-Indian Trail.
Hike, explore, or relax.
NO water. 10-day limit.
3100 ft (930 m)

## MUD CREEK

BLM (503) 473-3144
State map: 2J
From TROY, go S for 6 miles
(9.6 k) of gravel road along Mud Creek.
**FREE** but choose a chore.
Open All Year.
Undesignated, close, open sites.
Pit toilets, tables, boat ramp.
With beach and spectacular views of
Grande Ronde corridor.
Boat, swim, or fish nearby. Take photos
of scenery and wildlife.
NO water/trash facilities. 14-day limit.
Quiet 10pm-7am. Hunting in season.

## MUD CREEK

Fremont NF (503) 947-3334
State map: 8F
From LAKEVIEW, drive
5 miles (8 k) N on US 395; 9 miles
(14.4 k) E on OR 140; then 7 miles
(11.2 k) N on FR 3615.
**FREE** but choose a chore.
Open May 15–Oct 31; dry camping
off-season.
7 scattered sites in choice of open or
screened settings. Central water spigot
(at spring), pit toilets, tables, fire rings.
In seclusion not far from Drake Peak.
Hike, fish, and birdwatch.
No trash arrangements (pack it out).
14-day/16-ft limits. Mosquitos.
6600 ft (1980 m)

## MULE SHOE

BLM (503) 447-4115
State map: 4G
Take OR 19 E from FOSSIL on
OR 19 W from SPRAY. Find sign to
campground 2 miles (3.2 k) E of Service
Creek Trading Post.
**FREE** but choose a chore.
Open All Year.
9 (4 tent-only) sites. &

▲ ▲ ▲ ▲ ▲ ▲ ▲ ▲ ▲ ▲ ▲ ▲ ▲ ▲ ▲ ▲ ▲ ▲ ▲ ▲ ▲ ▲ ▲

Pit toilets, tables, grills, fire rings, boat ramp.

Among juniper, sagebrush, and grass along John Day River.

Hike and attend ranger programs at nearby John Day Fossil Beds NM. Boat, swim, and fish in river. View and photograph nature.

NO water/trash facilities. 14-day limit. Hot summers. Little shade. Rattlesnakes. Hunting in season.

600 ft (180 m)

## MYRTLE GROVE

Siskiyou NF (503) 439-3011
State map: 8A
From POWERS, head SE on CR 219/FR 33 for 7.4 miles (11.8 k). (Also see Rock Creek.)

FREE but choose a chore.

Open May 30–Sep 10; camping allowed off-season.

5 tent sites. Pit toilets, tables, fire rings.

On South Fork of Coquille River.

Swim or fish. Visit nearby Elk Creek Falls and Port Orford Cedar Research Natural Area.

NO water. 14-day limit.

## NATURAL BRIDGE

Rogue River NF
(503) 560-3623
State map: 7C

From PROSPECT, drive 9.5 miles (15.2 k) N on Hwy 62 then 1 mile (1.6 k) W on FR 300.

FREE but choose a chore.

Open Memorial Day–Oct 31.

17 scattered, screened sites.

Pit toilets, tables, fire rings.

In Douglas fir near rocky, whitewater stretch of Rogue River.

Hike along Upper Rogue River Trail. Check out Mammoth Pines Nature Trail 4 miles (6.4 k) S. Study and photograph nature and geology (river disappears into volcanic hole). Fish. Attend ranger programs.

NO water. 14-day/22-ft limits. Crowded holidays. Hunting in season.

3200 ft (960 m)

## NENA CREEK

BLM (503) 447-4115
State map: 3E
Driving N on US 197 as you enter town of MAUPIN, take first Left onto gravel "Upper Access Rd," a rutted, former railroad grade, and drive about 6 miles (9.6 k). Pass **Wapinitia** (5 sites), **Long Bend** (8 sites), and **Devils Canyon** (5 sites). (Also see Oasis Flat.)

$3/vehicle, $1/extra vehicle.

Open All Year.

3 scattered, open sites.

Pit toilets, some tables, boat launch.

In high-desert environment within steep, rugged Deschutes River canyon.

Boat (drift or raft), swim, and fish. View and photograph geology, plants, and animals.

NO water. 14-day limit. Crowded summer weekends. Quiet 10pm-7am. Hot summers. Limited shade. No fires from Jun 1-Oct 15. Hunting in season.

980 ft (294 m)

## NESIKA PARK

Coos County Parks
(503) 396-3121
State map: 6A

On East Fork of Millicoma River, about 5 miles (8 k) E of ALLEGHENY. Gold and Silver Fall SP is about 5 miles (8 k) E. (Also see Rooke-Higgins.)

$3. Closed in winter.

20 sites. Natural spring beside road, chemical toilets, tables in day-use area.

Fishing, swimming, hiking, and sightseeing.

Call (503) 396-3121 ext 355 about opening and closing dates, vehicle lengths, and limit of stay.

## NORTH FORK

Rogue River NF
(503) 482-3333
State map: 8C

From MEDFORD, proceed 35 miles (56 k) E on OR 140 then .5 mile (800 m) S on FR 37.

$3 donation requested.

Open Apr 28–Nov 15.

9 (5 tent-only) scattered sites in open and

▲ ▲ ▲ ▲ ▲ ▲ ▲ ▲ ▲ ▲ ▲ ▲ ▲ ▲ ▲ ▲ ▲ ▲ ▲ ▲ ▲ ▲ ▲ ▲

screened settings. Hand water pump, pit toilets, tables, grills, fire rings.
Along lava flows and North Fork of Little Butte Creek near Fish Lake.
Hike. Observe and photograph nature. Boat, swim, fish. Attend ranger programs.
Crowded. 14-day limit.
4600 ft (1380 m)

## NORTH FORK ANTHONY CREEK

Wallowa-Whitman NF (503) 523-6391
State map: 3I
From NORTH POWDER, head SW on CR 102/FR 7312 (Pilcher Creek) for 12 miles (19.2 k).
FREE but choose a chore.
Open May 1–Nov 15.
4 sites. Pit toilets, tables, fire rings.
On creek near Elkhorn Wildlife Area.
Fish. Hike. Enjoy solitude.
NO water. 10-day limit.
4000 ft (1200 m)

## NORTH FORK CATHERINE

Wallowa-Whitman NF (503) 963-7186
State map: 3I
From UNION, head SE on OR 203 for 11 miles (17.6 k). Turn Left (E) on FR 7785 and go 5 miles (8 k).
FREE but choose a chore.
Open Jun 1–Oct 31.
6 sites. Pit toilets, tables, fire rings.
Fish on creek. Drive 2 miles (3.2 k) to end of road and access three good trails into Eagle Cap Wilderness.
NO water. 10-day limit.
4400 ft (1320 m)

## NORTH FORK JOHN DAY

Umatilla NF (503) 427-3231
State map: 3H
From GRANITE, head N on FR 73 for 8 miles (12.8 k).
FREE but choose a chore.
Open Jun 1–Nov 1; camping allowed off-season.
5 sites. Pit toilets, tables, fire rings.
On river next to wilderness.
Hike or fish. Enjoy solitude.

NO water. 14-day limit. Hunting in season.
5200 ft (1560 m)

## NORTH FORK MALHEUR

Malheur NF (503) 820-3311
State map: 5H
On S side of PRAIRIE CITY, head SE on CR 62 for 8 miles (12.8 k). Turn Left (E) on FR 13 and go about 16 miles (25.6 k). Bear Right (S) on FR 16 and go 2 miles (3.2 k)–just past Elk Creek (5 sites). Turn Right (SE) on FR 1675 and go 2 miles (3.2 k). For option, retrace route and continue S on FR 16 another 5 miles (8 k) to Little Crane (5 sites).
FREE but choose a chore.
Open May 30–Oct 15.
5 sites. Pit toilets, tables, fire rings.
On wild and scenic river.
Hike and fish. Enjoy solitude.
NO water (purify stream) or trash arrangements (pack it out).
4700 ft (1410 m)

## NORTH TWIN LAKE

Deschutes NF (503) 388-5664
State map: 6D
From BEND, take FR 46 (Cascade Lakes Hwy) about 62 miles (99.2 k) SW. Turn Left (E) on FR 42 and go 4 miles (6.4 k). Turn Right on FR 4260 Alternatives on 4260 charge fees: West South Twin and Gull Point. (Also see Sheep Bridge.)
FREE but choose a chore.
Open May 1–Sep 30.
13 sites. Pit toilets, tables, fire rings.
Boat and fish on lake.
NO water/trash facilities. 14-day/22-ft limits. Crowded weekends.
4300 ft (1290 m)

## OASIS FLAT

BLM (503) 447-4115
State map: 3E
Drive N on US 197 through MAUPIN but do not cross bridge past city park. Turn Left onto paved "Lower Access Rd," an old railroad grade that parallels Lower Deschutes River. Pass

▲ ▲ ▲ ▲ ▲ ▲ ▲ ▲ ▲ ▲ ▲ ▲ ▲ ▲ ▲ ▲ ▲ ▲ ▲ ▲ ▲ ▲ ▲ ▲

**Blue Hole** (5 sites), **Grey Eagle** (5 sites), and **Oak Springs** (9 sites). Access can also be obtained from OR 216, between Grass Valley and Tygh Valley. (Also see Macks Canyon and Nena Creek.)
$3/vehicle, $1/extra vehicle.
Open All Year.
15 scattered, open sites. Blue Hole: &
Pit toilets, some tables.
In high-desert environment within steep, rugged Deschutes River canyon.
Boat (drift or raft), swim, and fish. View and photograph geology, plants, and animals.
NO water. 14-day limit. Crowded summer weekends. Quiet 10pm-7am. Hot summers. Limited shade. No fires Jun 1-Oct 15. Hunting in season.
800 ft (240 m)

**OCHOCO**
Ochoco NF (503) 447-9645
State map: 4F
Drive about 15 miles (24 k) E of PRINEVILLE on US 26. Bear Right on CR 123 and go 8 miles (12.8 k).
$5/vehicle. Open Apr 30-Sep 30; dry camping off-season.
7 sites. &
Central water faucet, pit toilets, tables, grills, fire rings, picnic shelter.
Beside ranger station and Ochoco Creek in old-growth, mixed-conifer forest.
Hike trail to Lookout Mountain. Observe and photograph nature. Fish.
14-day limit.
4200 ft (1260 m)

**ODELL CREEK**
Deschutes NF (503) 433-2234
State map: 6D
From CRESCENT LAKE, take US 97 S for 10 miles (16 k). Turn Right (NW) on OR 58 and go about 17 miles (27.2 k) to Odell Lake. At eastern end of lake, turn Left on FR 2317 for .25 mile (400 m) SW.
$5/vehicle, $3/extra vehicle.
Open May 15-Sep 30.
22 sites. Hand water pump, pit toilets, tables, fire rings, boat ramp.
On southern end of Odell Lake.

Boat and fish lake. Hike into Diamond Peak Wilderness.
14-day/22-ft limits.
4800 ft (1440 m)

**ODESSA**
Winema NF (503) 883-6824
State map: 8D
From KLAMATH FALLS, take OR 140 about 22 miles (35.2 k) NW. Turn Right on FR 3639 for 1.5 miles (2.4 k) N. Another campground beside wildlife refuge is **Malone Springs** (2 sites) about 10 miles (16 k) up Westside Rd, but on FR 3459.
FREE but choose a chore.
Open May 15-Sep 30.
5 sites. Pit toilets, tables, fire rings.
On Odessa Creek near Upper Klamath Lake and its wildlife refuge.
Boat and fish. Observe waterfowl.
No water. 14-day limit.
4100 ft (1230 m)

**OLALLIE MEADOWS**
Mt Hood NF (503) 630-4256
State map: 4D
From ESTACADA, drive SE on OR 224 for 27 miles (43.2 k). Turn Right (S) on FR 46 for 22 miles (35.2 k); then SE on FR 4690 for 8 miles (12.8 k); then S on FR 4220 for another 1.5 miles (2.4 k). (Also see Camp Ten.)
FREE but choose a chore.
Open Jun 15-Sep 20.
5 sites. Pit toilets, tables, grills.
In great meadow.
Enjoy serenity. Hike along Pacific Crest Trail among others. Pick berries as ripen. Enjoy water activities at Olallie Lake (3 miles away).
NO water. 14-day/16-ft limits. Horses permitted at specific sites.
4500 ft (1350 m)

**OLIVE LAKE**
Umatilla NF (503) 427-3231
State map: 4H
From DALE, head SE on FR 10 about 26 miles (41.6 k).
FREE but choose a chore.
Open Jun 1-Nov 1; camping allowed

▲ ▲ ▲ ▲ ▲ ▲ ▲ ▲ ▲ ▲ ▲ ▲ ▲ ▲ ▲ ▲ ▲ ▲ ▲ ▲ ▲ ▲ ▲ ▲ ▲

off-season.

5 sites. Pit toilets, tables, fire rings.

On remote, glacier-formed lake in Blue Mountains near wilderness.

Hike, boat, or fish. Find old man-made lake (now meadow).

NO water. 14-day limit. Hunting in season.

6000 ft (1800 m)

## ONION

Siskiyou NF (503) 592-2166
State map: 9B
From CAVE JUNCTION, head N on US 199 for 4.5 miles (7.2 k). Turn Left (W) on FR 4201 and go 17 miles (27.2 k).

FREE but choose a chore.

Open May 30–Sep 10; camping allowed off-season.

3 tent sites. Pit toilets, tables, fire rings.

Near Kalmiopsis Wilderness and Babyfoot Lake Botanical Area amidst prolific wild onions.

Hike to Babyfoot Lake with rare Brewer's weeping spruce. Hike N toward Whetstone Butte with red cliffs. Explore, observe.

NO water. 14-day limit.

## OPAL LAKE WALK-IN

Willamette NF (503) 782-2283
State map: 6D
From OAKRIDGE, take OR 58 E. Turn Right (S) onto CR 360 (Kitson Springs Rd) and drive .5 mile (800 m). Turn Right onto FR 21 and proceed 32.5 miles (52 k). Turn Left on FR 2154 and follow signs to Timpanogas for 11 miles (17.6 k). Pass turnoff to Summit Lake. Turn Left on FR 399 then Left again onto FR 398. Opal Lake trailhead is .5 mile (800 m) on left. Walk in .2 mile (320 m). (Also see Timpanogas.)

FREE but choose a chore.

Open Jul–Oct; camping allowed off-season.

1 site. Pit toilet, fire ring.

In forest of Pacific silver, grand, and noble fir on small lake.

Enjoy solitude, photography, canoeing, fishing for brook trout, or hiking.

Check road conditions before traveling. NO water/trash arrangements. 16-day limit. Hunting in season.

5400 ft (1620 m)

## PAGE SPRINGS

BLM (503) 573-5241
State map: 7H
Find 4 miles (6.4 k) SE of FRENCHGLEN on Steens Mountain Loop Rd – check weather and road conditions.

$3/vehicle. Open May–Oct; dry camping off-season.

30 sites. 5 water faucets, pit toilets, tables, grills, fire rings.

On Blitzen River, bordering Malheur Wildlife Refuge.

Photograph wildlife (especially birds). Fish and hike.

14-day/24-ft limits.

4100 ft (1230 m)

## PARISH CABIN

Malheur NF (503) 575-2110
State map: 5H
From SENECA, head E on FR 16 for 11 miles (17.6 k). (Also see Canyon Meadows.)

FREE but choose a chore.

Open May 30–Oct 15.

20 sites.

Water, pit toilets, tables, fire rings.

Fish on Bear Creek. Explore nearby Strawberry Wilderness.

No trash arrangements (pack it out).

4900 ft (1470 m)

## PARK CREEK

BLM (503) 756-0100
State map: 7A
From COQUILLE, turn Left on Coquille–Fairview Rd and go 15 miles (24 k) S to FAIRVIEW. Turn Right on Coos Bay Wagon Rd and follow it 4 miles (6.4 k). Then turn Left onto Middle Creek Access Rd and go 15 miles (24 k). Turn on Park Creek access road.

FREE but choose a chore.

Open All Year.

Undesignated sites.

Pit toilets, tables, grills, fire rings.

▲ ▲ ▲ ▲ ▲ ▲ ▲ ▲ ▲ ▲ ▲ ▲ ▲ ▲ ▲ ▲ ▲ ▲ ▲ ▲ ▲ ▲ ▲ ▲ ▲ ▲

Among mature myrtlewood and maple along creek. Hike trails to observe and photograph wildlife.

NO water. 14-day limit. Camp with care—woods showing impact. Hunting in season.

500 ft (150 m)

## PARKER MEADOWS

Rogue River NF
(503) 865-3581
State map: 8C

From BUTTE FALLS, take CR 821/FR 30 for 9 miles (14.4 k). Turn Left (NE) on FR 3065/FR 37 and go 10.5 miles (16.8 k). (Also see Snowshoe.)

$3/vehicle, $1.50/extra vehicle.

Open May–Oct; dry camping off-season.

8 (3 tent-only) sites. Hand water pump, pit toilets, tables, grills, fire rings.

Along Parker Creek in cool, moist area full of wildlife.

Observe and photograph animals. Hike, fish, and pick berries when ripe.

14-day limit. Crowded hunting season.

5000 ft (1500 m)

## PENLAND LAKE

Umatilla NF (503) 676-9187
State map: 3G

From HEPPNER, head SE on CR 53 (Willow Creek) about 20 miles (32 k). Turn Right (S) on FR 21 and go 2.5 miles (4 k). Turn Left (E) on FR 2103 and go 2 miles (3.2 k). (Also see Cutsforth.)

FREE but choose a chore.

Open Jun 1–Nov 1; camping allowed off-season.

5 tent sites. Pit toilets, tables, fire rings.

Swim, boat (electric motors only), or fish on remote lake. Hike.

NO water. 14-day limit. Hunting in season.

4950 ft (1485 m)

## PINE MOUNTAIN

Deschutes NF (503) 388-5664
State map: 6E

From BEND, drive E on US 20 about 20 miles (32 k) to MILLICAN. Turn Right (S) on FR 2017. Go 6.5 miles

(10.4 k). Turn Right on 500.

FREE but choose a chore.

Open May 15–Oct 31.

3 tent sites. Pit toilets, tables, fire rings.

Near Pine Mountain Observatory.

Picnic and relax.

NO water/trash arrangements.

14-day/22-ft limits.

6200 ft (1860 m)

## POST CAMP

Mt Hood NF (503) 467-2291
State map: 3E

From WAMIC, travel 6 miles (9.6 k) W CR 226; 11 miles (17.6 k) SW on FR 48; 2 miles (3.2 k) NW on FR 339; then .75 mile (1.2 k) W on FR 468. (Also see Forest Creek.)

FREE but choose a chore.

Open Jul 10–Sep 10.

4 sites. Pit toilets, tables, fire rings.

Fishing good here.

NO water. 14-day/16-ft limits.

4000 ft (1200 m)

## PRINEVILLE RESERVOIR

BOR (503) 447-7957
State map: 5E

Drive 15 miles (24 k) SE of PRINEVILLE via OR 27, Juniper Canyon Rd, and Combs Flat Rd (Paulina Hwy).

FREE but choose a chore.

Open All Year.

Undesignated sites. Facilities vary from camp to camp. There are year-round restrooms at Jasper Point, Roberts Bay East, and Owl Creek. Open from Memorial Day to Labor Day, are restrooms at Juniper Bass, Cattleguard, Owl Field, Juniper Point, and Roberts Bay West.

Along 3030-acre reservoir offering 43 miles of shoreline.

Fish, boat, waterski, swim, view wildlife, and take photographs.

BOR personnel express concern over resource degradation (for example, travel across wetlands), litter, and basic sanitation. 14-day limit. Hunting in season. North Side Primitive Rd closes Dec 1–Mar 31.

3235 ft (969 m)

▲ ▲ ▲ ▲ ▲ ▲ ▲ ▲ ▲ ▲ ▲ ▲ ▲ ▲ ▲ ▲ ▲ ▲ ▲ ▲ ▲ ▲ ▲ ▲ ▲ ▲

## PRINGLE FALLS

Deschutes NF (503) 388-5664
State map: 6D
From LA PINE, head N on US 97 for 2 miles (3.2 k). Turn Left (W) on CR 43 and go 7 miles (11.2 k). Turn Right (N) on FR 4360 and go .5 mile (800 m). (Also see Bull Bend and Wyeth.)
FREE but choose a chore.
Open May–Sep.
10 sites. Pit toilets, tables, fire rings.
On Deschutes River at turbulent falls.
Enjoy scenery and fish.
NO water/trash facilities. 22-ft limit.
4300 ft (1290 m)

## RAAB

Mt Hood NF (503) 630-4256
State map: 3D
From ESTACADA, travel 27 miles (43.2 k) SE on OR 224; 4 miles (6.4 k) S on FR 46; then 1 mile (3.2 k) SE on FR 63.
FREE but choose a chore.
Open May 20–Sep 30.
27 (2 tent-only) sites. &
Pit toilets, tables, grills.
On Collawash River.
Fish here or create base to enjoy other forest recreation.
NO water (at Two Rivers Picnic Area 1 mile away). 14-day/22-ft limits.

## RAINBOW

Mt Hood NF (503) 630-4256
State map: 3D
From ESTACADA, 27 miles (43.2 k) SE on OR 224; then .1 mile (160 m) S on FR 46. Pass fee-charged **Ripplebrook** (14 sites). (Also see Riverford.)
$5. Open Apr 15–Oct 1.
17 sites. &
Water, tables, grills.
On Oak Grove Fork of Clackamas River.
Swim, fish, or hike.
14-day/16-ft limits.
1400 ft (420 m)

## RAINY LAKE

Mt Hood NF (503) 352-6002
State map: 2D
From PARKDALE, go 6 miles (9.6 k) N on CR 281 then 10 miles (16 k) W on FR 205.
FREE but choose a chore.
Open Jun 15–Sep 15.
4 sites. Pit toilets, tables, fire rings.
Near off-the-beaten path lake.
Canoe, swim, or fish. Hike and pick ripe berries.
NO water. 14-day/16-ft limits.
4100 ft (1230 m)

## RESERVOIR

Deschutes NF (503) 388-5664
State map: 6D
From BEND, drive 57 miles (91.2 k) W on FR 46 (Cascade Lake Hwy). Turn Left and drive 1.75 miles (2.8 k) E on FR 44.
FREE but choose a chore.
Open May–Sep.
28 sites. Pit toilets, tables, fire rings.
On logged, southern shore of Wickiup Reservoir.
Boating and fishing "good."
NO water/trash facilities (pack it out). 14-day/22-ft limits.
4400 ft (1320 m)

## RIVER

Wallowa-Whitman NF (503) 963-7186
State map: 3H
From LA GRANDE, head SW on OR 244 for 13 miles (20.8 k). Turn Left (S) on FR 51 (Grande Ronde River Rd) and go 10.5 miles (16.8 k). Pass **Bikini Beach** (5 sites), **Utopia** (2 sites), and **Time and a Half** (5 sites). For other options, continue 2 miles (3.2 k) then bear Left (SE) on FR 5125 for 4 miles (6.4 k) to **Woodley** (7 sites). River and Woodley have water.
FREE but choose a chore.
Open Jun 1–Oct 31.
6 sites.
Water, pit toilets, tables, fire rings.
On Grande Ronde River.
Fish. Hike. Pick berries in season.

NO water. 10-day limit.
3800 ft (1140 m)

**RIVER BRIDGE**
Rogue River NF
(503) 560-3623
State map: 8C
Go 4 miles (6.4 k) N of PROSPECT on
OR 62 then 1.5 miles (2.4 k) W on
FR 6210 (Kiter Rd).
**FREE** but choose a chore.
Open Mar 15–Oct 31.
6 scattered, screened sites.
Pit toilets, tables, fire rings.
On wide, quiet bend of Rogue River
among sugar pine trees.
Hike on Upper Rogue River Trail.
Observe and photograph nature. Fish.
NO water/trash facilities (pack it out).
14-day limit. Crowded holidays. Hunting
in season.
2800 ft (840 m)

**RIVERFORD**
Mt Hood NF (503) 630-4256
State map: 3D
From ESTACADA, drive
27 miles (43.2 k) SE on OR 224 then
3.5 miles (5.6 k) S on FR 46. Pass fee-
charged **Riverside** (16 sites). (Also see
Rainbow.)
**FREE** but choose a chore.
Open Apr 23–Sep 30.
10 sites. Pit toilets, tables, grills.
On Clackamas and Collawash rivers.
Swim with care due to river currents.
Fish. Hike and rockhound.
NO water (at nearby Two Rivers Picnic
Area). 14-day limit. Not recommended
for trailers or RVs.

**RIVERSIDE WALK-IN**
Deschutes NF (503) 549-2111
State map: 4E
From SISTERS, travel NW on
US 20 about 7 miles (11.2 k). Turn Right
(N) on CR/FR 14 and proceed 4 miles
(6.4 k)–first campground past Metolius
Spring. If you continue N, choose from
8 fee-charged camps or free **Candle
Creek**.
**FREE** but choose a chore.

Open Apr 15–Oct 15.
16 tent sites. Hand water pump,
chemical toilets, tables, fire rings.
Fish on Metolius River at Black Butte.
14-day limit.
3000 ft (900 m)

**ROBINHOOD**
Mt Hood NF (503) 352-6002
State map: 2E
From PARKDALE, travel
15 miles (24 k) S on OR 35.
$5. Open Memorial Day–Labor Day.
24 close, open sites. ♿
Central water faucet, pit toilets, tables,
grills, and fire rings.
In dense forest on East Fork of Hood
River at base of Mt Hood.
Hike, fish, or take pictures.
18-ft limit.
3600 ft (1080 m)

**ROCK CREEK**
Siskiyou NF (503) 439-3011
State map: 8A
From POWERS, head SE on
CR 219/FR 33 about 13 miles (20.8 k).
Bear Right (SW) on FR 3347 and go
1 mile (1.6 k). (Also see Myrtle Grove
and Squaw Lake.)
**FREE** but choose a chore.
Open May 30–Sep 10; camping allowed
off-season.
7 (3 tent-only) sites.
Pit toilets, tables, fire rings.
Fish on creek. Hike to Azalea Lake.
NO water. 14-day limit.

**ROCK SPRINGS**
Malheur NF (503) 575-1731
State map: 5H
From SILVIES, head S on
US 395 for 1.5 miles (2.4 k). Turn Left (E)
on CR 73 and go 4 miles (6.4 k). Bear
Right for .5 mile (800 m).
**FREE** but choose a chore.
Open May 15–Sep 30.
8 sites. Pit toilets, tables, fire rings.
Enjoy solitude at springs.
NO water.

▲ ▲ ▲ ▲ ▲ ▲ ▲ ▲ ▲ ▲ ▲ ▲ ▲ ▲ ▲ ▲ ▲ ▲ ▲ ▲ ▲ ▲ ▲ ▲

## ROOKE-HIGGINS PARK

Coos County Parks
(503) 396-3121
State map: 6A

Located on Millicoma River, 10 miles
(16 k) from COOS BAY and 5 miles (8 k)
from ALLEGHENY. (Also see Nesika.)

$3. Closed winters.

18 sites. Pit toilets, boat ramp.

Boat, fish, hike, and rockhound.

NO water. Call (503) 396-3121 ext 355 for
opening/closing dates, vehicle lengths,
and limit of stay.

## ROUND LAKE WALK-IN

Mt Hood NF (503) 630-4256
State map: 4D
From ESTACADA, drive
27 miles (43.2 k) SE on OR 224. Turn
Right (S) on FR 46 and go 3.5 miles
(5.6 k). Continue straight (S) on FR 63 for
12.5 miles (20 k). Bear Left (SE) on
FR 6370 for 6.75 miles (10.8 k) to parking
area. Walk .5 mile (800 m).

FREE but choose a chore.

Open Jun 15–Sep 15.

6 sites. Pit toilets, tables, grills.

At beautiful lake near Sugar Pine
Botanical Area.

Relax, swim or fish.

NO water. 14-day limit.

## ROUTSON

Hood River County Parks
(503) 386-6323
State map: 2E

Drive 22 miles (35.2 k) S of HOOD
RIVER on OR 35. (Also see Sherwood.)

$5. Open Apr–Oct.

Undesignated, scattered, screened sites.

Several water faucets, flush toilets,
tables, fire rings.

With woods and beach on Hood River.

Boat, waterski, swim, and fish. Hike and
birdwatch.

Hunting in season.

2600 ft (780 m)

## SACANDAGA

Willamette NF (503) 782-2283
State map: 6D
From OAKRIDGE, drive

2.25 miles (3.6 k) SE on OR 58. Turn
Right on CR 360 (Kitson Springs Rd) and
go .5 mile (800 m). Turn Right again on
FR 21 and proceed 23 miles (36.8 k).
(Also see Campers Flat and Indigo
Springs.)

FREE but choose a chore.

Open Apr 15–Nov 30.

15 scattered, screened sites.

Pit toilets, tables, fire rings.

On quiet Middle Fork of Willamette
River near historic Rigdon Meadows and
old military road.

Hike on Middle Fork Trail. Photograph
scenery and wildlife. Fish.

NO water/trash facilities. 16-day/22-ft
limits. Hunting in season.

2400 ft (720 m)

## SAND HILL CROSSING

Fremont NF (503) 943-3114
State map: 8F
From PAISLEY, drive 1 mile
(1.6 k) W on CR 28. Turn Right on
FR 3315 and go 22.5 miles (36 k). Turn
Left on FR 28 and go 1 mile (1.6 k) S.
Turn Right on FR 3411 for additional
7 miles (11.2 k). (Also see Lee Thomas.)

FREE but choose a chore.

Open Apr–Oct; dry camping off-season.

5 close, open sites. Hand water pump,
pit toilets, tables, grills.

Next to Sprague River.

Swim or fish. Hike into Gearhart
Wilderness.

No trash arrangements. 14-day/16-ft
limits. Snow pack controls opening.

6100 ft (1830 m)

## SAND PRAIRIE

Willamette NF (503) 782-2283
State map: 6C
From OAKRIDGE, drive
OR 58 SE for 2.25 miles (3.6 k). Turn
Right on CR 360 (Kitson Springs Rd) for
.5 mile (800 m). Turn Right again on
FR 21 for 12 miles (19.2 k) SE.

$5–7/vehicle.

Open Apr 15–Sep 30; dry camping
off-season.

20 scattered, screened sites. ♿

Central water faucet, flush/pit toilets,

tables, grills, fire rings.

In mixed stand of Douglas fir, western hemlock, cedar, and dogwood where Oregon Central Military Wagon Rd emerges from Middle Fork of Willamette River at Hills Creek Reservoir.

Hike Middle Fork Trail which begins here. Fish, of course, and enjoy photography.

14-day/22-ft limits. Hunting in season.

1600 ft (480 m)

## SAND SPRINGS

Deschutes NF (503) 388-5664
State map: 6E
From BEND, drive 20 miles (32 k) E on US 20. Turn Right (S) on FR 23 and go 18.5 miles (29.6 k) past Pine Mountain. Turn Left on FR 2312.

FREE but choose a chore.

Open May 15–Oct 31.

Undesignated sites.

Pit toilets, tables, fire rings.

Relax and enjoy seclusion.

NO water/trash facilities. 22-ft limit.

5100 ft (1530 m)

## SCAPONIA

Columbia County Parks
(503) 397-2353
State map: 2C
Find campground on Scappoose-Veronia Rd, 13 miles (20.8 k) W of SCAPPOOSE. **Big Eddy**, a fee-based county park, is nearby.

FREE but choose a chore.

Open All Year.

10 sites. Central water faucet, pit toilets, tables, fire rings.

Beside road in nature park with large conifers and deciduous trees, trails and footbridges.

Walk trails, take photographs, and birdwatch.

Crowded summer weekends. Quiet 10pm-7am. 7-day limit. Hunting in season.

680 ft (204 m)

## SCARED MAN

BLM (503) 672-4491
State map: 6C
From GLIDE, travel 21 miles (33.6 k) E on OR 138 to STEAMBOAT. Drive 3 miles (4.8 k) N on Canton Creek Rd.

FREE but choose a chore.

Open May 1–Oct 1.

10 sites. Pit toilets, tables, grills.

Swim in Canton Creek.

NO water. 14-day/21-ft limits.

## SCOTT LAKE WALK-IN

Willamette NF (503) 822-3381
State map: 5D
From MCKENZIE BRIDGE, drive 3.5 miles (5.6 k) E on OR 126; 14.5 miles (23.2 k) NE on narrow, steep OR 242 to milepost 71—not for trailers or RVs. Turn Left (SW) on gravel FR 260 1 mile (1.6 k).

FREE but choose a chore.

Open Jun–Oct; snow decides; camping allowed off-season.

Undesignated tent sites scattered in screened settings. Pit toilets, tables.

On small, pretty, no-motor lake with great views of Three Sisters Mountains. Canoe, swim, and fish. Hike into Mt Washington Wilderness. Practice photography.

NO water/trash facilities. 14-day limit.

4800 ft (1440 m)

## SECRET

Willamette NF (503) 782-2283
State map: 6C
From OAKRIDGE, take OR 58 SE for 2.25 miles (3.6 k). Turn Right on CR 360 (Kitson Springs Rd) and go .5 mile (800 m). Turn Right again on FR 21 and travel about 17 miles (27.2 k). (Also see Campers Flat and Sand Prairie.)

FREE but choose a chore.

Open Apr 15–Sep 30; camping allowed off-season.

6 scattered, open sites.

Pit toilets, tables, fire rings.

On Middle Fork of Willamette River among Douglas fir and maple trees,

▲ ▲ ▲ ▲ ▲ ▲ ▲ ▲ ▲ ▲ ▲ ▲ ▲ ▲ ▲ ▲ ▲ ▲ ▲ ▲ ▲ ▲ ▲ ▲ ▲ ▲

offering pretty fall color.
Fish, hike, and take photos.
NO water/trash arrangements.
14-day/15-ft limits.
2000 ft (600 m)

## SECRET CREEK

Siskiyou NF (503) 476-3830
State map: 8B
From MERLIN, head NW on
Merlin–Galice Access Rd for 12 miles
(19.2 k). Turn Left (S) on FR 25 and go
16 miles (25.6 k). Pass fee-charged **Big
Pine** (13 sites) at mile 12 and **Sam
Brown** (42 sites) at mile 13. (Also see Tin
Cup.)
FREE but choose a chore.
Open May 30–Oct 10; dry camping
off-season.
3 (2 tent-only) sites.
Water, pit toilets, tables, fire rings.
On creek (guess which one).
Hike, fish, and explore.
14-day limit.

## SHADY

Hells Canyon NRA
(503) 426-4978
State map: 3J
From LOSTINE, head S on FR 8210 for
16 miles (25.6 k). Pass **Williamson**
(10 sites), **Lillyville** (2 sites), and **French
Camp** (4 sites). In 1 mile (1.6 k), find
**Two Pan** (6 sites).
FREE but choose a chore.
Open Jun 15–Nov 1.
14 sites. Pit toilets, tables, fire rings.
On Lostine River surrounded by Eagle
Cap Wilderness.
Hike trail from camp to Maxwell Lake or
trail from Two Pan to Lost Lake. Fish.
NO water. 10-day/16-ft limits.
5400 ft (1620 m)

## SHADY COVE

Willamette NF (503) 854-3366
State map: 4D
From MEHAMA, drive
19 miles (30.4 k) NE on Little North
Santiam Rd.
FREE but choose a chore.
Open Apr–Oct; camping allowed

off-season.
10 tent sites scattered in open setting.
Pit toilets, tables, fire rings.
In old-growth forest at confluence of
Battle and Cedar creeks, creating Little
North Santiam Wild and Scenic River.
Swim or fish. Hike and take photos of
scenery and wildlife.
Treat river water to drink. Pack out
trash. Quiet 10pm-7am. 14-day limit.
1600 ft (480 m)

## SHARPS CREEK

BLM (503) 683-6600
State map: 6C
Go 1.5 miles (2.4 k) S of CULP
CREEK on Sharps Creek Rd (2-lane,
paved).
$5. Open May 15–Nov 30.
10 tent sites in scattered, screened
setting. Hand water pump, chemical
toilets, tables, and grills.
Within dense stand of second-growth
Douglas fir beside Sharps Creek.
Swim or fish. Take photos of wildlife.
14-day/25-ft limit.
2700 ft (810 m)

## SHEEP BRIDGE

Deschutes NF (503) 388-5664
State map: 6D
From BEND, take FR 46
(Cascade Lakes Hwy) about 62 miles
(99.2 k) SW. Turn Left (E) on FR 42 and
go 4 miles (6.4 k). Turn Right on FR 4260
and go .5 mile (800 m). Continue straight
(W) toward river. (Also see North Twin.)
FREE but choose a chore.
Open May 1–Sep 30.
17 open sites. Hand water pump, pit
toilets, tables, fire rings.
On Deschutes River channel of Wickiup
Reservoir.
Boat, waterski, swim, and fish.
14-day/22-ft limits.
4400 ft (1320 m)

## SHELLROCK CREEK

Mt Hood NF (503) 630-4256
State map: 3D
From ESTACADA, travel
27 miles (43.2 k) SE on OR 224. Continue

▲ ▲ ▲ ▲ ▲ ▲ ▲ ▲ ▲ ▲ ▲ ▲ ▲ ▲ ▲ ▲ ▲ ▲ ▲ ▲ ▲ ▲ ▲ ▲ ▲

7.5 miles (12 k) E on FR 57; then .5 mile (800 m) N on FR 58.
**FREE** but choose a chore.
Open Jun 15–Sep 10.
5 sites. Pit toilets, tables, grills.
At quiet place on Shellrock Creek.
Fish in creek or rockhound in area.
NO water. 16-ft limit.
2300 ft (690 m)

## SHERWOOD

Mt Hood NF (503) 352-6002
State map: 2E
From PARKDALE, travel
11 miles (17.6 k) S on OR 35. (Also see Robinhood and Routson.)
**$5.** Open Memorial Day–Labor Day; dry camping off-season.
14 sites. ♿
Central water faucet, pit toilets, tables, grills, and fire rings.
In open forest area on flat terrain near East Fork River.
Trout fish. Hike on Tamanawas Falls and East Fork trails. Take photographs.
14-day/16-ft limits.
3000 ft (900 m)

## SILVER CREEK

Fremont NF (503) 947-2107
State map: 7E
From SILVER LAKE, take
OR 31 W for 1 mile (1.6 k) then S on CR/FR 27 for 10 miles (16 k).
**FREE** but choose a chore.
Open May 1–Nov 14; dry camping off-season.
7 close, open sites.
Hand water pump, pit toilets, tables, grills, fire rings, buck and pole fence.
By Silver Creek, its marsh, and Thompson Reservoir.
Fish!
No trash arrangements. 14-day limit.
5000 ft (1500 m)

## SIXES RIVER

BLM (503) 756-0100
State map: 7A
From SIXES, drive E on
CR 184 (Sixes River Rd) for 11 miles (17.6 k)–watch for logging trucks. Turn

Right at sign.
**FREE** but choose a chore.
Open All Year.
20 scattered, open sites. Drinking water needs treating, pit toilets, tables, grills.
In wooded hills.
Swim and fish river. Try hand at mining.
Birdwatch and take photographs.
24-ft limit. Noise from mine dredges.
Crowded summers. 14-day limit.
1278 ft (381 m)

## SKOOKUM CREEK

Willamette NF (503) 782-2291
State map: 5D
From WESTFIR, drive
34.5 miles (55.2 k) NE on FR 19 (Aufderheide Scenic Byway) to Box Canyon. Turn Right (S) on FR 1957. Go 3.75 miles (6 k).
**FREE** but choose a chore.
Open May 30–Oct 15.
9 close, open sites.
Hand water pump, pit toilets, tables, fire rings, horse facilities.
At edge of Three Sisters Wilderness (need permit).
Hiking and horseback riding on forest trails. Enjoy fishing, birdwatching, and taking photographs.
No trash arrangements (pack it out).
14-day limit. Crowded summers.
Mosquitos. Hunting in season.
4500 ft (1350 m)

## SLIDE CREEK

Willamette NF (503) 822-3317
State map: 5D
From BLUE RIVER, drive
3.5 miles (5.6 k) E on US 126; Turn Right (S) on FR 19 (Aufderheide Scenic Byway) and go about 7 miles (11.2 k) to tip of Cougar Reservoir. Turn Left (N) on FR 500 (Eastside Rd) and go 2 miles (3.2 k). (Also see French Pete.)
**$5**/single site, **$10**/multiple site.
Open All Year.
16 close, open or screened sites.
Hand water pump, pit toilets, tables, grills, fire rings, bath house, boat ramp, horseshoe pit.
With swimming beach on east side of

▲ ▲ ▲ ▲ ▲ ▲ ▲ ▲ ▲ ▲ ▲ ▲ ▲ ▲ ▲ ▲ ▲ ▲ ▲ ▲ ▲ ▲ ▲ ▲ ▲

Cougar Reservoir at base of Three Sisters Wilderness.

Enjoy hiking, wildlife viewing, photography, boating, waterskiing, swimming, and fishing in summer. In winter, go cross-country skiing.

FR 19 not maintained for ice and snow. 14-day limit. Hunting in season.

1700 ft (510 m)

## SLOUGH

Deschutes NF (503) 388-5664
State map: 5E
From BEND, go 6.5 miles (10.4 k) SW on FR 46 (Cascades Lakes Hwy). Turn Left (S) on FR 41 and go 2 miles (3.2 k). Turn Left (SE) on FR 4120 then Right (S) on FR 100 and go 2 miles (3.2 k).

**FREE** but choose a chore.

Open Apr 15–Sep 30.

5 tent sites. Pit toilets, tables, fire rings.

Near Deschutes River.

Fish in river. Hike to observe and photograph nature.

NO water/trash facilities. 14-day limit. Crowded summers–bugs too.

4000 ft (1200 m)

## SMITH RIVER

BLM (503) 756-0100
State map: 6B
From REEDSPORT, drive N on US 101 and cross Umpqua River. Turn Right (E) on CR 48 (Smith River Rd) and continue about 20 miles (32 k).

**FREE** but choose a chore.

Open All Year.

Undesignated, scattered, open sites.

Pit toilets, tables, fire rings.

Along Smith River near falls.

Fishing good. Swimming and photography also.

NO water. 14-day limit. Crowded Jul–Aug. Hunting in season.

## SNIVELY HOT SPRINGS

BLM (503) 473-3144
State map: 6J
Find on Lake Owyhee Rd, 20 miles (32 k) S of NYSSA (route signed). From VALE, travel S on Lytle Blvd (Oregon Trail Route) 16 miles (25.6 k) to Cow Hollow Rd. Follow signs 10 miles (16 k) to lake. (Also see Twin Springs.)

**FREE** but choose a chore.

Open All Year.

Undesignated sites. Pit toilets.

Near popular hot spring (150 degrees) located on Owyhee River in shady Lower Owyhee Canyon.

Soak in hot spring. Watch and take photos of wildlife. Hike in surrounding open country. Boat, waterski, swim, and fish in Owyhee reservoir 10 miles away.

NO water. No large RVs. Crowded during day. Quiet 10pm-7am. Hunting in season.

2270 ft (681 m)

## SNOWSHOE

Rogue River NF
(503) 865-3581
State map: 8C
From BUTTE FALLS, take CR 821/FR 30 for 9 miles (14.4 k). Turn Left (NE) on FR 3065 and drive 5 miles (8 k). (Also see Fourbit and Parker Meadows.)

**FREE** but choose a chore.

Open May–Oct; camping allowed off-season.

5 scattered, open sites.

Pit toilets, tables, grills, fire rings.

In scenic area with lots of wildlife near Snowshoe Butte.

View and take photos of animals. Hike. NO water. 14-day limit. Hunting in season.

4000 ft (1200 m)

## SODA CREEK

Deschutes NF (503) 388-5664
State map: 5D
From BEND, take CR/FR 46 (Cascade Lakes Hwy) SW for 24 miles (38.4 k) to Sparks Lake. (Also see Devils Lake and Todd Lake.)

**FREE** but choose a chore.

Open Jul 1–Sep 30.

12 sites. Pit toilets, tables, fire rings.

Hike trails or fish Sparks Lake.

NO water/trash arrangements.

▲ ▲ ▲ ▲ ▲ ▲ ▲ ▲ ▲ ▲ ▲ ▲ ▲ ▲ ▲ ▲ ▲ ▲ ▲ ▲ ▲ ▲ ▲ ▲ ▲ ▲ ▲ ▲ ▲ ▲ ▲

## SOUTH ELK LAKE

Deschutes NF (503) 388-5664
State map: 5D
From BEND, take CR/FR 46 (Cascade Lakes Hwy) beyond North Elk Lake–about 30 miles (48 k). Turn Left (N) on loop FR 4625 and go 1 mile (1.6 k). (Also see Little Fawn.)
FREE but choose a chore.
Open Jun 1–Sep 15.
23 sites.
Chemical toilets, tables, fire rings.
Boat and fish on small lake.
NO water/trash facilities.
4900 ft (1470 m)

## SOUTH FORK

Rogue River NF
(503) 865-3581
State map: 8C
From BUTTE FALLS, go E for .5 mile (800 m). Turn Left (NE) on CR/FR 34. Go 13 miles (20.8 k). (Also see Big Ben.)
$3/vehicle, $1.50/extra vehicle.
Open May–Oct; dry camping off-season.
6 (2 tent-only) sites scattered in open setting. Hand water pump, pit toilets, tables, grills, fire rings.
On South Fork of Rogue River.
Hike into Sky Lakes Wilderness (trailhead 3 miles E on 3780). Observe and photograph nature. Fish.
14-day/16-ft limits. Crowded hunting season.
4000 ft (1200 m)

## SOUTH FORK

Wallowa-Whitman NF
(503) 446-3351
State map: 5I
From UNITY, head W on CR 610/FR 6005 for 7 miles (11.2 k). **Stevens Camp** and **Elk Creek** are couple of miles farther.
FREE but choose a chore.
Open May 1–Nov 15.
12 (2 tent-only) sites.
Water, pit toilets, tables, fire rings.
On South Fork Burnt River.
Fishing and hiking along river.
10-day limit.
4400 ft (1320 m)

## SOUTH JUNCTION

BLM (503) 447-4115
State map: 4E
From MADRAS, drive N on US 97 about 29 miles (46.4 k). At Shaniko junction of US 97 and US 197, turn Left on gravel road with small, brown sign indicating "BLM Recreation Site." (Also see Trout Creek.)
$3/vehicle, $1/additional vehicle.
Open All Year.
11 scattered, open sites.
Pit toilets, some tables, boat launch.
In high-desert environment surrounded by steep, rugged Deschutes River canyon walls.
Boat (drift and raft), swim, and fish. Photograph nature.
NO water. 14-day limit. Crowded summer weekends. Quiet 10pm-7am. Hot summers. Little shade. No fires Jun 1-Oct 15. Hunting in season.
1280 ft (384 m)

## SOUTHWEST SHORE

Wallowa-Whitman NF
(503) 523-6391
State map: 4I
From SUMPTER, head SE on CR 410/OR 7 for 6 miles (9.6 k). Turn Right (S) on FR 2226 and continue 2 miles (3.2 k). For alternative, check out **Millers Lane** (6 sites) in .5 mile (800 m) or, on N side of lake, fee-charged **Union Creek** (58 sites). (Also see Deer Creek.)
FREE but choose a chore.
Open May 1–Nov 15.
20 sites. Pit toilets, tables, fire rings.
On Phillips Lake.
Swim, boat, or fish. Hike in area.
NO water. 10-day limit.
4120 ft (1236 m)

## SPALDING POND

Siskiyou NF (503) 476-3830
State map: 8B
From GRANTS PASS, head SW on US 199 for 15 miles (24 k) to top of Hayes Hill. Turn Right (NW) on FR 25 and go 7 miles (11.2 k). Turn Left (W) on FR 2524 and go 5 miles (8 k).
FREE but choose a chore.

▲ ▲ ▲ ▲ ▲ ▲ ▲ ▲ ▲ ▲ ▲ ▲ ▲ ▲ ▲ ▲ ▲ ▲ ▲ ▲ ▲ ▲ ▲ ▲ ▲ ▲

Open May 30–Oct 10; dry camping
off-season.
4 tent sites. &
Water, pit toilets, tables, fire rings.
Fish in stocked pond. Explore region.
14-day limit.

## SPARKS LAKE
Deschutes NF (503) 388-5664
State map: 5D
From BEND, drive 24 miles
(38.4 k) on CR/FR 46 (Cascade Lakes
Hwy). Turn Left (S) and go 1 mile (1.6 k)
on FR 400. (Also see Soda Creek.)
FREE but choose a chore.
Open Memorial Day–Oct 15.
4 (2 tent-only) sites. Pit toilets, tables, fire
rings, boat launch.
On scenic lake at base of Mt Bachelor.
Boat (no motors), swim, and fly fish.
Ride ski lift in summer for view. Hike.
NO water/trash facilities.
5400 ft (1620 m)

## SPRING
BLM (503) 473-3144
State map: 5J
Drive 5 miles (8 k) E of
HUNTINGTON on mostly asphalt road
(short stretch of gravel) toward Brownlee
Reservoir.
FREE but choose a chore.
Open All Year.
Undesignated, close, open sites.
Water, pit toilets, tables, grills, fire rings,
boat ramp.
At remote beach on Snake River.
Fish, swim, or boat. Take photographs.
14-day/30-ft limits. Crowded holiday
weekends. Noisy around boat launch.
Quiet 10pm–6am. Hunting in season.
2500 ft (750 m)

## SQUAW LAKE
Siskiyou NF (503) 439-3011
State map: 8A
From POWERS, head SE on
CR 219/FR 33 about 12.5 miles (20 k).
Turn Left (E) on FR 3348 and go 3 miles
(4.8 k). Turn Right on FR 3348.080. If you
continue on 3348, there are several
additional primitive camp spots. (Also

see Rock Creek.)
FREE but choose a chore.
Open May 30–Sep 10; camping allowed
off-season.
7 sites. Pit toilets, tables, fire rings.
Hike or fish along lakeshore.
NO water. 14-day limit.
2900 ft (870 m)

## SQUAW LAKES WALK-IN
Rogue River NF
(503) 889-1812
State map: 9C
From JACKSONVILLE, drive 8 miles
(12.8 k) SW on OR 238; 14 miles (22.4 k)
SW on CR/FR 10; then 8 miles (12.8 k)
SE on FR 1075. Hike-in .5 mile (800 m).
$3; call (503) 899-1812 for reservations.
Open All Year.
Undesignated tent sites. Central water
faucet, pit toilets, tables, fire rings.
On Little Squaw Lake.
Hike to observe nature. Swim, boat (no
motors), and fish.
14-day limit.
3000 ft (900 m)

## STARR
Malheur NF (503) 575-2110
State map: 5H
From JOHN DAY, head S on
US 395 for 16 miles (25.6 k).
FREE but choose a chore.
Open May 30–Oct 15.
8 sites.
Water, pit toilets, tables, fire rings.
At Starr Bowl Winter Sports Area.
Explore then relax.
No trash arrangements (pack it out).
5100 ft (1530 m)

## STEAMBOAT FALLS
Umpqua NF (503) 496-3532
State map: 6C
From IDLEYLD PARK, head E
on OR 138 for 18 miles (28.8 k). Continue
NE on FR 38 for 6 miles (9.6 k). Pass fee-
charged Canton Creek (5 sites). Turn
Right (E) on FR 3810 for 1 mile (1.6 k).
(Also see Island.)
FREE but choose a chore.
Open All Year.

10 (3 tent-only) sites.
Pit toilets, tables, fire rings.
At confluence of Deep and Steamboat creeks with excellent scenery.
Swim. Hike. Watch steelhead trout jump falls during spawning runs.
NO water. 14-day/24-ft limits. No fishing.
1400 ft (420 m)

## STORE GULCH

Siskiyou NF (503) 592-2166
State map: 8B
From SELMA, head W on CR 5070/FR 4103 for 10 miles (16 k)–difficult when wet.
FREE but choose a chore.
Open May 30–Sep 10; camping allowed off-season.
3 tent sites. Pit toilets, tables, fire rings.
Swim and fish in Illinois River.
NO water. 14-day limit.

## STRAWBERRY

Malheur NF (503) 820-3311
State map: 5H
From PRAIRIE CITY, drive S on CR 60/FR 6001 for 11 miles (17.6 k).
Pass **McNaughton Spring** (4 sites) as well as **Slide Creek** (1 site).
FREE but choose a chore.
Open May 30–Oct 15.
11 sites.
Water, pit toilets, tables, fire rings.
On creek surrounded by Strawberry Wilderness.
Hike in scenic area. Fish.
No trash arrangements (pack it out).
5700 ft (1710 m)

## SUGAR CREEK

Ochoco NF (503) 477-3713
State map: 5G
From PAULINA, take CR 380 E 3.5 miles (5.6 k); CR 113 N for 6.5 miles (10.4 k); then FR 158 E for 1.75 miles (2.8 k).
$3. Open May 15–Oct 15; dry camping off-season.
15 (4 tent-only) sites. Central water faucet, pit toilets, tables, fire rings.
Among second-growth ponderosa pine

trees with eagle roost next to creek.
Watch birds. Bicycle, swim, or fish.
14-day/22-ft limits. Crowded hunting season.
4500 ft (1350 m)

## SUMMIT LAKE

Mt Hood NF (503) 328-6211
State map: 3D
From GOVERNMENT CAMP, drive 15 miles (24 k) SE on OR 26. Turn Right (S) on FR 42 and go 13 miles (20.8 k). Turn Right (W) on FR 141 for .5 mile (800 m).
FREE but choose a chore.
Open May 30–Oct 1.
4 tent sites.
Pit toilets, tables, grills, fire rings.
At mountain lake on western slopes of Cascades.
Enjoy scenery. Canoe (no motors on lake) and swim.
NO water. 14-day limit. No trailers or RVs.
4000 ft (1200 m)

## SUMMIT LAKE

Deschutes NF (503) 433-2234
State map: 6D
From CRESCENT, take US 97 S for 9 miles (14.4 k). Turn Right onto OR 58 and continue 7 miles (11.2 k). Turn Left on FR 6020 and go 9 miles (14.4 k) around S side of Crescent Lake. Just before **Tranquil Cove**, turn Left (W) on FR 6010 and continue 4 rough miles (6.4 k). (Also see Contorta Point and Opal Lake.)
FREE but choose a chore.
Open Jul 1–Sep 30.
3 sites. Pit toilets, tables, fire rings.
On northern shore of lake surrounded by Diamond Peak Wilderness.
Boat and fish. Hike Pacific Crest Trail.
NO water/trash arrangements.
14-day/22-ft limits.
5600 ft (1680 m)

▲ ▲ ▲ ▲ ▲ ▲ ▲ ▲ ▲ ▲ ▲ ▲ ▲ ▲ ▲ ▲ ▲ ▲ ▲ ▲ ▲ ▲ ▲ ▲ ▲

## SURVEYOR

BLM (503) 947-2177
State map: 8D
From KLAMATH FALLS,
travel 3 miles (4.8 k) S on US 97 to
WA 66. Follow WA 66 W for 15 miles
(24 k). Turn on Keno Access Rd and go
14 miles (22.4 k) NW to entrance.
FREE but choose a chore.
Open May 25–Oct 30 (weather decides);
camping allowed off-season.
5 close, screened sites. &
Spring water, "clean smelling" pit toilets,
tables, fire rings.
In ancient forest of large Douglas fir.
Find solitude. Study and photograph
nature. Mountain bike roads or relax.
Crowded in hunting season.
5200 ft (1560 m)

## SUTTLE LAKE

Deschutes NF (503) 549-2111
State map: 4D
From SISTERS, drive US 20
NW 13 miles (20.8 k) to Suttle Lake sign.
Turn Left.
FREE but choose a chore.
Open Apr 15–Oct 15.
8 sites. Hand water pump, pit toilets,
tables, fire ring, boat ramp.
On eastern end of lake.
Picnic. Boat, waterski, swim, or fish lake.
Hike trails.
No trash arrangements (pack it out).
3400 ft (1020 m)

## SWEDES LANDING

BLM (503) 473-3144
State map: 4J
Travel 12 miles (19.2 k) S of
RICHLAND via Snake River Rd (gravel
after short stretch of asphalt) toward
Brownlee Reservoir.
FREE but choose a chore.
Open All Year.
Undesignated, open sites. Pit toilets.
On Snake River bank with beach and
spectacular views of rugged mountains,
including Lookout Mountain.
Boating and fishing.
NO water/trash arrangements. 14-day
limit. Quiet 10pm-6am.

## TAMARACK

Wallowa-Whitman NF
(503) 742-7511
State map: 3J
From MEDICAL SPRINGS, head E on
FR 67 (Eagle Creek Rd) for 12 miles
(16 k). Turn Left (NE) on FR 77. For
alternative, continue 1 mile (1.6 k) to
Two Color (14 sites).
FREE but choose a chore.
Open Jun 1–Oct 31.
12 (10 tent-only) sites.
Water, pit toilets, tables, fire rings.
Fish or hike along creek.
10-day/22-ft limits.
4600 ft (1380 m)

## TENMILE CREEK

Siuslaw NF (503) 563-3211
State map: 5B
From YACHATS, head S on
US 101 for 12.5 miles (20 k). Turn Left
(E) on FR 56 and go 5.6 miles (9 k).
FREE but choose a chore.
Open All Year.
6 sites. Pit toilets, tables, fire rings.
Fish, hike, or relax along creek.
NO water. 22-ft limit.

## THOMPSON RESERVOIR

Fremont NF (503) 947-2107
State map: 7E
From SILVER LAKE, take
OR 31 W for approximately 1 mile
(1.6 k). Turn Left (S) on CR 27 for
13.5 miles (21.6 k). Take another Left on
FR 021 and go E 1 mile (1.6 k).
FREE but choose a chore.
Open May 1–Nov 15; dry camping
off-season.
19 close, open sites. Hand water pump,
pit toilets, tables, grills, fire rings.
Under ponderosa pine, close to reservoir
dam.
Boat and fish. Walk nature trail.
No trash facilities. 14-day/22-ft limits. In
drought, little water. Hunting in season.
5000 ft (1500 m)

▲▲▲▲▲▲▲▲▲▲▲▲▲▲▲▲ ▲▲▲▲▲▲▲▲▲▲▲▲▲▲▲▲

## THREE CREEK LAKE

Deschutes NF (503) 549-2111
State map: 5D
From SISTERS, travel 18 miles
(28.8 k) S to end of FR 16. (Also see
Driftwood.)
FREE but choose a chore.
Open Jun 15–Oct 15.
10 sites.
Chemical toilets, tables, fire rings.
In woods on southeastern shore.
Boat (no motors), swim, fish. Hike too.
NO water/trash arrangements.
14-day/16-ft limits.
6400 ft (1920 m)

## THREE FORKS

BLM (503) 473-3144
State map: 8J
Drive S on US 95 about
13 miles (20.8 k) from JORDAN
VALLEY. Turn Left (S) and drive
26 miles (41.6 k) on Three Forks Rd–dirt
road with steep grade requiring 4WD
when wet.
FREE but choose a chore.
Open All Year.
8 scattered, open layout sites.
1 chemical toilet, 4 fire rings.
In rye grass and sagebrush at confluence
of North Fork and Main Owyhee rivers.
Use game and livestock trails to hike,
ride horses, and mountain bike. Enjoy
boating (kayaks), swimming, and fishing.
Snap photos.
NO water/trash facilities. 14-day limit.
Quiet 10pm-6am. Fires only in rings.
Leash pets. Cows. Unpredictable spring
weather, rattlesnakes in summer, and
hunting in fall.
4000 ft (1200 m)

## THREEHORN

Umpqua NF (503) 825-3201
State map: 7C
From TILLER, take scenic
CR 1 (OR 227) S for 13 miles (20.8 k).
FREE but choose a chore.
Open All Year.
5 sites.
Pit toilets, tables, grills, fire rings.
In open stand of large pine and fir.

Hike or enjoy getaway.
NO water (pump broken) or trash
arrangements. 14-day limit.
1400 ft (420 m)

## TILLY JANE WALK-IN

Mt Hood NF (503) 352-6002
State map: 3E
Head S from PARKDALE on
OR 35 about 7 miles (11.2 k). Turn Right
(W) at Cooper Spur Rd junction. Turn
Left on FR 3512 and travel 11 miles
(17.6 k) on FR 3512, narrow but heavily
traveled road to Tilly Jane turnoff.
Continue another mile to **Cloud Cap
Saddle** (4 tent sites).
FREE but choose a chore.
Open Jun 20–Sep 15; camping allowed
off-season.
14 close, open tent sites.
Pit toilets, tables, grills, fire rings.
In alpine Cloud Cap/Tilly Jane
Historical Area.
Take trip back in time where settlers
crossed over Mt Hood to Willamette
Valley. Photograph remaining historic
structures. Hike trails. View site of
Pollalie Flood. Go mountain climbing
summers or snow skiing winters.
NO water. 14-day limit.
5900 ft (1770 m)

## TIMPANOGAS LAKE

Willamette NF (503) 782-2283
State map: 6D
From OAKRIDGE, take OR 58
E. Turn Right (S) onto CR 360 (Kitson
Springs Rd) and drive .5 mile (800 m).
Turn Right onto FR 21 and proceed
32.5 miles (52 k). Turn Left on FR 2154
and follow signs to Timpanogas for
11 miles (17.6 k). Turn Left on FR 399
then Right into campground. Access
point for **Indigo Lake Walk-In**. (Also see
Opal Lake Walk-In.)
**$4**. Open Jun–Sep; dry camping
off-season.
11 sites. Hand water pump, pit toilets,
tables, fireplaces, and boat ramp.
On lake, headwaters of Middle Fork of
Willamette River with views of Diamond
Peak, Sawtooth and Cow Horn

▲ ▲ ▲ ▲ ▲ ▲ ▲ ▲ ▲ ▲ ▲ ▲ ▲ ▲ ▲ ▲ ▲ ▲ ▲ ▲ ▲ ▲ ▲ ▲

mountains.
Boat (no motors), swim, and fish. Hike
to view and photograph nature.
16-day/22-ft limits. Hunting in season.
5200 ft (1560 m)

## TIN CUP

Siskiyou NF (503) 476 3830
State map: 8B
From MERLIN, head NW on
Merlin–Galice Access Rd for 12 miles
(19.2 k). Turn Left (S) on FR 25 and go
4 miles (6.4 k). (Also see Secret Creek.)
FREE but choose a chore.
Open May 30–Sep 10; camping allowed
off-season.
4 tent sites. Pit toilets, tables, fire rings.
On Taylor Creek.
Hike, explore, and observe nature.
NO water. 14-day limit.

## TODD LAKE WALK-IN

Deschutes NF (503) 388-5664
State map: 5D
From BEND, drive 25 miles
(40 k) W on CR/FR 46 (Cascade Lakes
Hwy) to Todd Lake sign. Turn Right and
drive .5 mile (800 m). Make .25 mile
(400 m) walk to lake. (Also see Soda
Creek.)
FREE but choose a chore.
Open Jul 1–Sep 15.
7 tent sites. Pit toilets, tables, fire rings.
On lake in scenic, alpine environment.
Canoe or fish. Hike or bike.
NO water/trash facilities.
6200 ft (1860 m)

## TOKETEE LAKE

Umpqua NF (503) 498-2531
State map: 7C
From IDLEYLD PARK, head E
on OR 138 for 37 miles (59.2 k). Turn
Left (N) on FR 34 and go 1.5 miles
(2.4 k). For alternative, continue 3 miles
(4.8 k) N to Lemolo (3 sites). (Also see
Boulder Flat and Clearwater Falls.)
FREE but choose a chore.
Open All Year.
33 sites. Pit toilets, tables, fire rings, boat
launch.
On NE side of 80-acre lake.

Boat, fish, or hike.
NO water. 14-day limit.
2500 ft (750 m)

## TOPSY

BLM (503) 947-2177
State map: 9D
From KLAMATH FALLS,
travel 3 miles (4.8 k) S on US 97. Turn
Right (W) on OR 66 and go 14.5 miles
(23.2 k) to Klamath River. Turn Left on
dirt Topsy Rd. Go 1 mile (1.6 k) SW.
$4. Open Apr–Sep; dry camping
off-season.
15 close, open sites. ₠
Central water faucets, "clean smelling"
pit toilets, gray-water dump, tables, fire
rings, boat ramp and dock.
In pine forest on Upper Klamath River at
John C Boyles Reservoir.
Boat (whitewater and powerboat),
waterski, swim, and fish. Hike to view
and photograph wildlife.
Hunting in season.
4200 ft (1260 m)

## TRAIL BRIDGE

Willamette NF (503) 822-3381
State map: 5D
From MCKENZIE BRIDGE,
take OR 126 NE for approximately
11 miles (17.6 k) then .25 mile (400 m)
SW on FR 732 (Trail Bridge Reservoir
Rd) to cross dam. (Also see Ice Cap
Creek and Olallie.)
$5/vehicle, $2.50/extra vehicle.
Open Apr 20–Oct 31 (weather decides);
dry camping off-season.
28 scattered, screened sites (plus RV
parking on "Flats" near reservoir).
Central water faucet, flush/pit toilets,
tables, fire rings, boat ramp.
In fir trees by Trail Bridge Reservoir.
Boat and fish for trout. Hike too.
10-day limit. Crowded opening day
fishing season. 5 mph speed limit
around reservoir.
2000 ft (600 m)

▲ ▲ ▲ ▲ ▲ ▲ ▲ ▲ ▲ ▲ ▲ ▲ ▲ ▲ ▲ ▲ ▲ ▲ ▲ ▲ ▲ ▲ ▲ ▲

## TROUT CREEK

BLM (503) 447-4115
State map: 4E
From MADRAS, drive N on US 97 approximately 3 miles (4.8 k) to Cora Dr. Follow this road to Gateway. Turn Right toward Deschutes River at Clemens Dr-steep, gravel road that's slippery when wet. (Also see South Junction.)
$3/vehicle, $1/additional vehicle.
Open All Year.
20 scattered, open sites.
Pit toilets, some tables, boat launch.
In high-desert environment surrounded by steep, rugged canyon walls.
Mountain bike from Trout Creek to Mecca Flat. Hike, view nature, and take photographs. Boat (drift or raft), swim, and fish on Deschutes River.
NO water. 14-day/30-ft limits. Crowded summer weekends. Quiet 10pm-7am. Hot summers. Little shade. No fires Jun 1-Oct 15. Hunting.
1300 ft (390 m)

## TROUT FARM

Malheur NF (503) 820-3311
State map: 5H
On S side of PRAIRIE CITY, head SE on CR 62/FR 14 for 15 miles (24 k). For alternative, go S additional 2 miles (3.2 k) to Crescent (4 sites).
FREE but choose a chore.
Open May 30-Oct 15.
9 (5 tent-only) sites.
Water, pit toilets, tables, fire rings.
On pond and creek.
Picnic and relax. Fish.
No trash arrangements (pack it out).
4700 ft (1410 m)

## TUCKER FLAT

BLM (503) 770-2200
State map: 8B
From I-5, take Exit 61 at MERLIN. Travel 20 miles (32 k) W on Galice Rd to Grave Creek Bridge. Turn Left onto Grave Creek-Marial National Backcountry Byway and travel another 33 miles (52.8 k) to site.
FREE but choose a chore.

Open May 15-Nov 1.
10 scattered, open tent sites. Central water faucet, pit toilets, tables, grills.
Within Rogue National Wild and Scenic River managed area.
Hike Rogue River Trail. Visit Rogue River Ranch NHS. Fish. Take photos.
14-day/20-ft limits.
1000 ft (300 m)

## TUMALO FALLS WALK-IN

Deschutes NF (503) 388-5664
State map: 5E
From BEND, take Franklin Ave to Drake Park. Turn Right on Galveston and continue to end of road. Make short walk to falls.
FREE but choose a chore.
Open May-Sep.
4 tent sites. Pit toilets, tables, fire rings.
On Tumalo Creek near 100-ft waterfall.
Picnic or camp. Hike or fish.
NO water/trash facilities.
5000 ft (1500 m)

## TWIN SPRINGS

BLM (503) 473-3144
State map: 6J
From VALE, travel S on Lytle Blvd (Oregon Trail Route) 16 miles (25.6 k). Turn on rough Cow Hollow Rd and go to Twin Springs Rd to camp-about 14 miles (22.4 k). High clearance recommended on vehicles-inaccessible in wet weather. (Also see Snively Hot Springs.)
FREE but choose a chore.
Open All Year.
Undesignated, open sites.
Spring water, pit toilets.
In sagebrush country, featuring grove of aspen and natural artesian well.
Create base for backcountry exploring. Photograph scenery and animals. Fish, rockhound, or mountain bike.
No trash arrangements. 14-day/20-ft limits. Quiet 10pm-6am. Bike on existing trails and roads only. Hunting in season.
3240 ft (972 m)

▲ ▲ ▲ ▲ ▲ ▲ ▲ ▲ ▲ ▲ ▲ ▲ ▲ ▲ ▲ ▲ ▲ ▲ ▲ ▲ ▲ ▲ ▲ ▲ ▲ ▲

## TWIN SPRINGS

Willamette NF (503) 822-3317
State map: 5D
From BLUE RIVER, take
US 126 E 3.5 miles (5.6 k); then FR 19 S
(Aufderheide Scenic Byway) for about
25 miles (40 k). (Pass French Pete and
Homestead but not Frissell Crossing.)
**FREE** but choose a chore.
Open All Year.
5 sites.
Pit toilets, tables, grills, fire rings.
Along South Fork of McKenzie River.
Hike to photograph nature. Boat, swim,
or fish in nearby Cougar Reservoir.
NO water/trash arrangements. Facilities
need repairs. 14-day limit. Road not
maintained during winter.
2400 ft (720 m)

## UMATILLA FORKS

Umatilla NF (509) 843-1891
State map: 2I
From GIBBON, head E on
CR/FR 32 about 10 miles (16 k).
**FREE** but choose a chore.
Open Apr 1–Nov 30.
15 (7 tent-only) sites.
Water, pit toilets, tables, fire rings.
On Umatilla River at edge of North Fork
Umatilla Wilderness.
Hike Buck Creek or Ninemile Ridge
trails. Fish river.
10-day limit.
2400 ft (720 m)

## UNION CREEK

Rogue River NF (503) 560-3623
State map: 7C
From PROSPECT, drive
10.75 miles (17.2 k) N on OR 62.
**$5**/vehicle, $2.50/extra vehicle.
Open Memorial Day–Oct 31.
78 scattered, open or screened sites.
Water near every site, pit toilets,
community kitchen, tables, fire rings.
With CCC-built structures in deep
woods along creek.
Hike to view and photograph nature.
Fish. Attend ranger programs.
14-day/22-ft limits. Crowded holidays.
3300 ft (990 m)

## UPPER ARM

Willamette NF (503) 854-3366
State map: 4D
From DETROIT, travel NE on
FR 46 (Breitenbush Rd) for 1 mile (1.6 k).
**FREE** but choose a chore.
Open Apr–Oct; camping off-season.
5 (2 tent only) scattered, open sites
Pit toilets, tables, fire rings.
On Detroit Lake where beautiful
Breitenbush River flows into lake.
Boat, sail, swim, and fish.
NO water. In off-season, pack out trash.
14-day/16-ft limits. Quiet 10pm-7am.
1600 ft (480 m)

## VIGNE

Hells Canyon NRA
(503) 426-4978
State map: 2J
From ENTERPRISE, go N on OR 3 for
15 miles (24 k). Turn Right (NE) on
FR 46 and go 12 miles (19.2 k) to Crow
Creek. Turn Right (SE) on FR 4625
(Chesnimnus Rd) and go 9 miles (14.4 k).
(Also see Coyote.)
**FREE** but choose a chore.
Open Apr 15–Nov 30; dry camping
off-season.
12 sites.
Water, pit toilets, tables, fire rings.
In remote setting next to spring.
Hike and explore.
10-day/22-ft-vehicle limits.
3500 ft (1050 m)

## WARM SPRINGS WALK-IN

Deschutes NF (503) 388-5664
State map: 6E
From BEND, drive S on US 97
about 20 miles (32 k). Turn Left on
CR 21 and go about 13 miles (20.8 k) to
Paulina Lake. Turn Left to fee-charged
**Little Crater**. Park and walk .5 mile
(800 m) to Warm Springs.
**FREE** but choose a chore.
Open May 15–Oct 31.
5 tent sites. Pit toilets, tables, fire rings.
On scenic Paulina Lake.
Boat and fish. Hike too.
NO water/trash facilities.
6300 ft (1890 m)

▲ ▲ ▲ ▲ ▲ ▲ ▲ ▲ ▲ ▲ ▲ ▲ ▲ ▲ ▲ ▲ ▲ ▲ ▲ ▲ ▲ ▲ ▲ ▲ ▲ ▲ ▲

## WETMORE

Wallowa-Whitman NF
(503) 446-3351
State map: 4I

From UNITY, head NW on US 26 for
10 miles (16 k). For alternatives, find
**Yellow Pine** (21 sites) in 1 mile (1.6 k)
and **Oregon** (8 sites) in 3 miles (4.8 k).
**FREE** but choose a chore.
Open May 1–Nov 15.
12 (4 tent-only) sites. ♿
Water, pit toilets, tables, fire rings.
On stream near Middle Fork Burnt
River.
Fish and hike.
10-day limit.
4320 ft (1296 m)

## WHISKEY SPRINGS

Rogue River NF
(503) 865-3581
State map: 8C

From BUTTE FALLS, take CR 821/FR 30
for 9 miles (14.4 k). Turn Left (NE) on
FR 3065 and go .25 mile (400 m). (Also
see Fourbit.)
**$5**/vehicle, $2.50/extra vehicle.
Open May–Oct.
36 (17 tent-only) sites in scattered, open
setting. ♿
Central water faucets, pit toilets, tables,
grills, fire rings.
Near Fourbit Creek.
Boat, swim, and fish. Stroll handi-
capped-accessible trail to observe and
photograph nature.
14-day/16-ft limits. Quiet 10pm-7am.
Crowded holidays. Hunting in season.
3200 ft (960 m)

## WHITE RIVER STATION

Mt Hood NF (503) 328-6211
State map: 3E

From GOVERNMENT CAMP,
drive 2 miles (3.2 k) E on US 26;
4.5 miles (7.2 k) N on OR 35; then
7 miles (11.2 k) NE on FR 30. (Also see
Barlow Crossing and Forest Creek.)
**FREE** but choose a chore.
Open May 15–Oct 1.
5 sites. Pit toilets, tables, grills.
On pioneer wagon trail (Old Barlow)

next to White River.
Fish. Explore wagon trail and other
hiking trails in forest.
NO water. 14-day limit. Not advised for
trailers or RVs.

## WHITTAKER CREEK

BLM (503) 683-6600
State map: 5B

From MAPLETON, drive
15 miles (24 k) E on OR 126 then S on
paved Siuslaw River Rd.
**$5**. Open May 15–Nov 30.
31 scattered, screened sites.
Hand water pump, chemical toilets,
tables, grills, fire rings, boat ramp.
Along both sides of Whittaker Creek
with beach near Siuslaw River.
Fish, swim, or boat (no motors). Hike.
Take photos of scenery and wildlife.
14-day limit. Hunting in season.
1300 ft (390 m)

## WICKIUP BUTTE

Deschutes NF (503) 388-5664
State map: 6D

From LA PINE, travel N on
US 97 for 2 miles (3.2 k). Turn Left (W)
on FR 43 and go 7 miles (11.2 k). Turn
Left (SW) on FR 44 and go about 7 miles
(11.2 k). Turn Right (W) on 4260 and go
1.5 miles (2.4 k).
**FREE** but choose a chore.
Open May–Sep.
5 sites.
Pit toilets, tables, fire rings, boat ramp.
On southeastern shore of Wickiup
Reservoir near dam.
Boat, waterski, swim, and fish.
NO water/trash arrangements.
14-day/22-ft limits.

## WILDCAT

Ochoco NF (503) 447-9641
State map: 4F

From PRINEVILLE, drive
9.25 miles (14.8 k) E on US 26; 4 miles
(6.4 k) N on CR 122; 7 miles (11.2 k) NE
on FR 33 (Mill Creek Rd).
**$4**. Open May 15–Oct 15.
17 sites. Hand water pump, pit toilets,
tables, fire rings.

In mixed conifers on East Fork of Mill Creek.
Hike into Mill Creek Wilderness via scenic Twin Pillars and Belknap Trails.
Observe and photograph nature.
14-day/32-ft limits.
3700 ft (1110 m)

## WILDHORSE
Siskiyou NF (503) 247-6651
State map: 8A
From GOLD BEACH, head S bearing Left at Buena Vista SP on CR 635/FR 3860-3318 and go about 20 twisting miles (32 k), always bearing Right. Another remote option is to turn Right at mile 10 on FR 1503 and go 2 miles (3.2 k) to Elko (3 sites).
FREE but choose a chore.
Open May 30-Sep 10; camping allowed off-season.
3 tent sites. Pit toilets, tables, fire rings.
In Wildhorse Prairie.
Hike, explore, picnic, and relax.
NO water. 14-day limit.
3500 ft (1050 m)

## WILDWOOD
Ochoco NF (503) 447-9645
State map: 4F
From PRINEVILLE, take US 26 E for 20 miles (32 k). Continue E on FR 22/2210 for 8 miles (12.8 k) – frequently closed by snow in winter.
FREE but choose a chore.
Open May 30-Sep 30; dry camping off-season.
7 (2 tent-only) sites. Central water faucet, pit toilets, tables, fire rings.
In mixed conifers.
Hike. Birdwatch. Enjoy solitude.
No trash arrangements. 14-day limit.
Hunting in season.
4800 ft (1440 m)

## WILEY FLAT
Ochoco NF (503) 447-9641
State map: 5F
From PRINEVILLE, travel 34 miles (54.4 k) SE on CR 380. Turn Right (S) at Wildcat Creek on FR 16 and go 10 miles (16 k). Turn Right (W) on

FR 400 for 1 mile (1.6 k).
FREE but choose a chore.
Open May 15-Oct 15 (weather decides).
5 sites. Pit toilets, tables, fire rings.
In mixed conifers along Wiley Creek.
Relax here.
NO water/trash arrangements.
14-day/32-ft limits. Hunting in season.
5000 ft (1500 m)

## WILLAMETTE PARK
City of Corvallis Parks
(503) 754-3748
State map: 4B
Drive S through CORVALLIS on 4th St (OR 99). Turn Left on Goodnight Ave. Campground on left at sign.
$5. Open Apr-Nov; dry camping off-season.
Undesignated sites.
Central water faucet, flush toilets, kitchen shelter, tables, grills, fire rings, ball fields, playground.
Next to day-use area of park in natural setting on Willamette River.
Make base to tour local art galleries, wineries, covered bridges, and historic buildings. Play golf among other recreational opportunities. On site, walk trails, watch birds, and fish.
14-day limit. Quiet 10pm-7am.

## WILLOW CREEK
Fremont NF (503) 947-3334
State map: 9F
From LAKEVIEW, drive 6 miles (9.6 k) N on US 395. Turn Right and go 8 miles (12.8 k) E on OR 140. Turn Right and go 9 miles (14.4 k) SE on FR 3915; then Right again for 1 mile S on FR 4011. (Also see Deep Creek.)
FREE but choose a chore.
Open Jun-Oct; camping allowed off-season.
8 sites.
Pit toilets, tables, grills, fire rings.
Beside shallow, meandering Willow Creek.
Play in water, fish, or hike.
NO water/trash arrangements.
14-day/22-ft limits.
5800 ft (1740 m)

▲ ▲ ▲ ▲ ▲ ▲ ▲ ▲ ▲ ▲ ▲ ▲ ▲ ▲ ▲ ▲ ▲ ▲ ▲ ▲ ▲ ▲ ▲ ▲ ▲ ▲ ▲

## WOLF CREEK

Ochoco NF (503) 477-3713
State map: 5G
From PAULINA, drive
3.5 miles (5.6 k) E on CR 380; 6.5 miles
(10.4 k) N on CR 113; then 1.5 miles
(2.4 k) N on FR 42.
$3. Open May 15–Oct 15.
15 (3 tent-only) sites. Central water
faucet, pit toilets, tables, fire rings.
Under ponderosa pine and other conifers
on small stream.
Enjoy peace and quiet. Observe and
photograph nature.
14-day limit.
4700 ft (1410 m)

## WOODLAND

Umatilla NF (509) 843-1891
State map: 2I
From WESTON, head E on
OR 204 for 23 miles (36.8 k). Pass fee-
charged **Woodward** (18 sites).
**FREE** but choose a chore.
Open Jun 1–Oct 31.
7 sites. Pit toilets, tables, fire rings.
On edge of North Fork Umatilla
Wilderness.
Explore!
NO water. 10-day limit. Hunting in
season.
5200 ft (1560 m)

## WRANGLE

Rogue River NF
(503) 889-1812
State map: 9C
Drive 11 miles (17.6 k) SE of ASHLAND
on I-5; 15 miles (24 k) W on CR/FR 20
(past Mt Ashland and Red Mountain);
then .5 mile (800 m) NW on FR 2030.
**FREE** but choose a chore.
Open All Year.
4 scattered, open tent sites.
Central water faucet, pit toilets,
community kitchen, tables, fire rings.
At headwaters of Wrangle Creek with
views of Siskiyou Mountains.
Hike on Pacific Coast Trail.
14-day/16-ft limits. Hunting in season.
6400 ft (1920 m)

## WYETH

Deschutes NF (503) 388-5664
State map: 6D
From LA PINE, head N on
US 97 for 2 miles (3.2 k). Turn Left (W)
on CR 43 and go 8 miles (12.8 k). Turn
Left (S) on FR 4370. (Also see Bull Bend
and Pringle Falls.)
**FREE** but choose a chore.
Open Apr 15–Sep 30.
7 sites.
Pit toilets, tables, fire rings, boat ramp.
Boat and fish on Deschutes River.
NO water/trash arrangements.
14-day/22-ft limits.
4300 ft (1290 m)

## YELLOW JACKET

Malheur NF (503) 573-7292
State map: 6G
From BURNS, head S on
US 395 for 3 miles (4.8 k). Turn Right
(NW) on CR 127/FR 47 and go 38 miles
(60.8 k). Turn Right (E) on FR 37 and go
2 miles (3.2 k). Bear Right (SE) on
FR 3745 and go 1 mile (1.6 k).
**FREE** but choose a chore.
Open May 30–Oct 15.
20 sites.
Water, pit toilets, tables, fire rings.
On lake.
Boat or fish. Enjoy remote spot.
No trash arrangements (pack it out).
4800 ft (1440 m)

## YELLOWBOTTOM

BLM (503) 375-5610
State map: 4D
From SWEET HOME, take
CR 11 NE along N side of Foster
Reservoir about 25 miles (40 k). Pass
**Whitcomb Creek County Park**.
$5. Open May 15–Oct 1.
22 close, screened sites. Hand water
pump, pit toilets, tables, fire rings.
On Quartzville Creek above Green Peter
Reservoir in foothills of Cascade Range.
Play in water–pan for gold as well as
swim or fish. Photograph activities,
animals, and scenery.
16-day limit.
1500 ft (450 m)

# Utah

Grid conforms to official state map. For your copy, write:
Utah Travel Council, Council Hall, Capitol Hill, Salt Lake City, UT 84114.

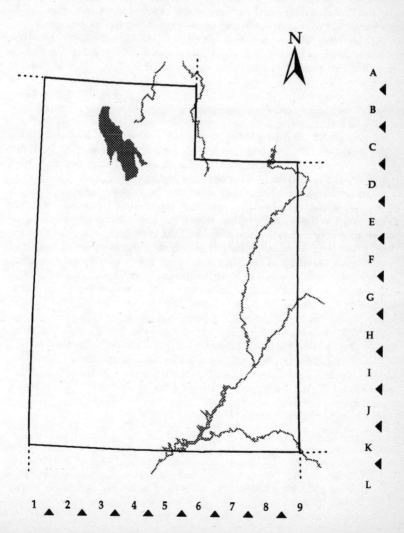

▲ ▲ ▲ ▲ ▲ ▲ ▲ ▲ ▲ ▲ ▲ ▲ ▲ ▲ ▲ ▲ ▲ ▲ ▲ ▲ ▲ ▲ ▲ ▲ ▲ ▲ ▲

Almost 80 percent of Utah is public land, making camping the perfect way to get close to natural beauty. The vast majority of the acreage is administered by the Bureau of Land Management (BLM), US Forest Service, National Park Service (NPS), and State of Utah.

The **BLM's** vast holdings include remote and unspoiled canyons in the east and southeast; almost-virgin mountain wilderness in the southcentral; colorful sand, cliffs, and rocks in the southwest; the Great Basin territory in the northwest; dinosaur remains, petroglyphs, and eroded rocks in the northeast.

One of the nation's most heavily visited forests, **Wasatch-Cache NF** offers canyons and peaks within a short distance of Utah's major cities. The Mount Naomi Wilderness in the north and the Mount Olympus and Twin Peaks wilderness areas near Salt Lake City provide many trails leading away from crowds. The crowning jewel remains scenic byway 150 (from Kamas, UT to Evanston, WY) with glimpses of and access to the High Uintas Wilderness.

**Ashley NF** also provides access to High Uintas and the only East–West mountain range in the US. While over half is above the timberline, below is an incredible variety of flora and fauna–especially birds. The Ashley also claims geologic wonders such as Sheep Creek Canyon and Flaming Gorge.

Moving south, **Uinta NF** features the Nebo Loop Scenic Byway. Mount Nebo, Mount Timponogas, and Peak wilderness areas provide scenic alternatives to developed sections.

Huge **Dixie NF** offers Pine Valley Wilderness in the west, colorful vistas in the Cedar Breaks–Strawberry Point–Navajo Lake central region, and Hell's Backbone plus Box-Death Hollow Wilderness in the eastern section. Dixie's remote corners, primitive roads, and trails provide seclusion and beauty.

**Fishlake NF** has three large sections but only two camps that qualify for this book. Take advantage of remote, primitive opportunities, especially near the Skyline Trail in the western Tushar Mountains. Enjoy Partridge Mountain, an undisturbed botanical showplace. Near Fish Lake itself, discover teaming streams such as River and Gooseberry Creek, or go north to a region known as The Rocks.

Segmented **Manti-LaSal NF** claims spectacular scenes of red sandstone spires and blue mountain lakes east of Moab, the remote Dark Canyon Wilderness west of Monticello, and gentle hills of central Utah. The more you explore, the more fascinating the discoveries: Arch Canyon, Cliffdwellers Pasture, Scad Canyon. Search for the rare Abert squirrel or alpine meadow rue.

The **NPS** administers some of the best rock gardens in the world. Don't miss any of them: Arches NP (backcountry), Bryce Canyon NP (backcountry), Canyonlands NP, Capitol Reef NP, Cedar Breaks National Monument (NM), Glen Canyon National Recreation Area (NRA), Natural Bridges NM, and Zion NP.

**Utah State Parks** (SPs) generally charge $9 for developed sites; eight listings feature more "primitive" camping.

Discover the natural beauty of Utah.

▲ ▲ ▲ ▲ ▲ ▲ ▲ ▲ ▲ ▲ ▲ ▲ ▲ ▲ ▲ ▲ ▲ ▲ ▲ ▲ ▲ ▲ ▲ ▲ ▲ ▲

**ARCHES NP-Backcountry**
(801) 259-8161
State map: H8
From MOAB, go 5 miles (8 k) N on US 191.
**FREE** but $3 entrance fee (or pass).

(**Devils Garden** Campground costs $7 from mid-Mar to mid-Oct. It's **free** during winter). Any time of year, obtain **free** backcountry permits at Visitor Center. Open All Year.

See nature's beautiful and powerful

▲ ▲ ▲ ▲ ▲ ▲ ▲ ▲ ▲ ▲ ▲ ▲ ▲ ▲ ▲ ▲ ▲ ▲ ▲ ▲ ▲ ▲ ▲ ▲

erosive forces at work–colorful sandstone fins, spires, pinnacles, balanced rocks, and arches. Hike, photograph, absorb, and reflect.

No established backcountry sites or trails. Hot in summer; below freezing in winter. No wood fires.
4500 ft (1350 m)

## BAKER DAM

BLM (801) 673-4654
State map: J2
From ST GEORGE, go 25 miles (40 k) N on UT 18.
FREE but choose a chore.
Open All Year.
10 scattered, screened sites.
Pit toilets, tables, grills.
On pinyon-juniper mesa overlooking Baker Reservoir and Santa Clara River. Excellent afternoon views of Pine Valley Mountains. Quiet, little-used retreat until scheduled reconstruction.
Fish in reservoir. Enjoy solitude while escaping valley's hotter temperatures.
NO water. 14-day limit.
5000 ft (1500 m)

## BALD MOUNTAIN

Wasatch-Cache NF
(801) 524-5030
State map: D6
From KAMAS, go E on UT 150 about 31 miles (49.6 k)–only free camp on this part of scenic byway.
FREE but choose a chore.
Open Jun 1–Sep 20.
5 close, open sites.
Pit toilets, tables, fire rings.
High camp with spectacular overlooks. Sightsee, hike, and relax. Listen to Moussorgsky's "Night on Bald Mountain." Imagine.
NO water. 14-day/20-ft limits.
10700 ft (3210 m)

## BEAVER VIEW

Wasatch-Cache NF
(801) 524-5030
State map: D6
From KAMAS, go E on UT 150 about 50 miles (80 k). One of several

camps along scenic byway near Wyoming line: **Sulphur** (26 sites), **Hayden's Fork** (9 sites), **Stillwater** (36 sites), **Bear River** (9 sites), **East Fork** (12 sites), and **Christmas Meadow** (16 sites) on FR 057.
FREE but choose a chore. If water's on, fees are charged.
Open May 15–Oct 15.
24 close, open sites.
Pit toilets, tables, fire rings.
On creek with trees.
Hike picturesque mountains and canyons. Find beaver dams and ponds.
NO water. 14-day limit.
8900 ft (2670 m)

## BIG BEND

BLM (801) 259-6111
State map: H8
From MOAB, go N on US 191 for 2 miles (3.2 k). Turn Right (E) on UT 128 and go 6 miles (9.6 k). For alternative, check out area at spur to Fisher Towers a few miles farther.
FREE but choose a chore.
Open All Year.
Undesignated scattered sites.
Pit toilets, tables, grills.
On banks of Colorado River among spectacular rock formations.
Fantastic sightseeing (location of many car commercials) plus some world-class mountain biking.
NO water. 14-day limit.
5100 ft (1530 m)

## BIRCH CREEK

BLM (801) 977-4300
State map: C5
From WOODRUFF, go 9 miles (14.4 k) W on UT 39. Turn on dirt road. Continue 1 mile (1.6 k).
FREE but choose a chore.
Open All Year.
4 scattered, open tent sites. (RVs may use parking lot).
Pit toilets, tables, grills, fire rings.
Grassy meadow at foot of reservoir.
Swim, boat, or fish.
NO water. 14-day limit. Gets crowded with people on weekends and mosquitos

when warm. Hunting in season.
7500 ft (2250 m)

## BLUE SPRUCE

Dixie NF (801) 826-4221
State map: I5
Take FR 154 NE from
ESCALANTE for 10 miles
(16 k). Turn on FR 153 and continue
5 miles (8 k). (Also see Posey Lake.)
$5. Open Jun 1–Sep 15; dry camping
off-season.
6 scattered, screened sites.
Water, pit toilets, tables, fire rings.
Under majestic spruce next to clear Pine
Creek. Fish or explore fantastic Box-
Death Hollow Wilderness.
14-day limit. No vehicles over 40 ft.
7800 ft (2340 m)

## BOUNTIFUL PEAK

Wasatch-Cache NF
(801) 524-5030
State map: D5
From FARMINGTON, go E on
steep FR 007 for 9 miles (14.4 k). (Also
see Sunset.)
FREE but choose a chore.
Open Jun 1–Sep 7.
79 close, open sites.
Water, pit toilets, tables, fire rings.
In woods along scenic drive.
Hike and picnic. Enjoy overlooks.
7-day limit.
7500 ft (2250 m)

## BRIDGE

Ashley NF (801) 789-1181
State map: D7
From ALTONAH, go NW on
Rd 10119 about 15 miles (24 k).
Developed (fee-charged) camps are
nearby Riverview, Swift Creek, and
Yellowstone. (Also see Reservoir.)
FREE but choose a chore.
Open Jun–Sep.
5 close, open sites &
Water, pit toilets, tables, fire rings.
On stream. Fish and relax.
14-day limit.
7700 ft (2310 m)

## BRIDGE HOLLOW

BLM (801) 789-1362
State map: D9
Go N from DUTCH JOHN on
US 191 to UT-WY line. Turn
Right (E) on dirt road (tough when wet),
follow signs to Brown's Park. (Also see
Indian Crossing.)
$3. Open May 1–Sep 30; dry camping
off-season.
13 (1 tent-only) scattered, open sites with
some screening.
Water, chemical toilets, tables, grills, fire
rings, pay phone, raft ramp.
Under cottonwood on banks of Green
River in Brown's Park.
Raft the Green. Fishing and birdwatching opportunities plus occasional
ranger programs.
14-day limit.
4200 ft (1260 m)

## BROWNE LAKE

Ashley NF (801) 789-1181
State map: D8
From MANILA, go S on UT 44
for 14 miles (22.4 k). Turn
Right (W) on second turnoff for FR 10218
and drive 3 miles (4.8 k). Go W for
.5 mile (800 m) on FR 10364 then turn
onto FR 10221 and go 3 miles (4.8 k).
(Also see Deep Creek.)
FREE but choose a chore.
Open Jun–Sep.
8 close, open tent sites. &
Water, pit toilets, tables, fire rings.
Next to small lake. If sites are wet, camp
in surrounding meadow and get
fantastic views of Uintas.
Explore remote area. Fish and relax.
14-day limit.
8200 ft (2460 m)

## BRYCE CANYON NP-Backcountry

(801) 834-5322
State map: J4
Enter from UT 63 off scenic
UT 12 at BRYCE CANYON.
FREE but $5 entrance fee (or pass). (Both
North and Sunset Campgrounds cost $6).
Obtain free backcountry permit (and
loan of snowshoes, if needed) at Sunrise

Nature Center or Visitor Center.
Open All Year.
Breathe clean air. Marvel at colors and ever-changing lighting nuances in geologic masterpieces. Enjoy overlooks before taking trails into canyon among sculpted rocks.
Crowded in summer; snowy in winter.
8100 ft (2430 m)

## CANYONLANDS NP-Willow Flat
(801) 259-7164
State map: H8
From MOAB, head N on US 191 for 10 miles (16 k). Turn Left (W) on UT 313 and drive 26 miles (41.6 k) to Island In The Sky section of park. (If you must have water and electricity, check out **Dead Horse Point SP**-fee charged).
**FREE** but $3 entrance fee (or pass). Also, **free** backcountry permits available for all sections of park (Island in the Sky, Maze, or Needles) at any ranger station.
Open All Year.
12 close, screened sites for small vehicles. Pit toilets, tables, grills.
Among pinyon-juniper on red sandstone mesa with incredible overlooks into both Green and Colorado river canyons.
Explore and hike. Attend ranger programs.
NO water. 14-day limit.

## CAPITOL REEF NP
(801) 425-3791
State map: H5
**FREE** but $3 entrance fee (or pass). Also, **free** backcountry permits are available at Visitor Center.
Open All Year.
Spectacular rock formations, colorful panoramas, and rugged landscape create superb hiking and photo opportunities.
▲ **Cathedral Valley**
Take UT 24 E from TORREY for 17 miles (27.2 k). Turn Left (N) on Hartnet dirt road and drive 25 miles (40 k). Road can often be impassable, except for high-clearance 4WD vehicles.
5 sites. Pit toilets, tables, grills.
Among pinyon-juniper in northern part

of park.
NO water. 14-day limit.
6000 ft (1800 m)
▲ **Cedar Mesa**
Take UT 24 E from TORREY for 21 miles (33.6 k) to park's eastern boundary. Turn Right (S) on Notom–Bullfrog dirt road and drive 35 miles (56 k). Road can often be impassable except for high-clearance 4WD vehicles. (Also see McMillan Spring.)
5 sites. Pit toilets, tables, grills.
In southern part of park.
Again, hike and take photos. Enjoy Waterpocket Fold.
NO water. 14-day limit.
6000 ft (1800 m)

## CARMEL
Ashley NF (801) 789-1181
State map: D8
From MANILA, go S on UT 44 for 5 miles (8 k). Turn Right (W) on FR 10218 for 1 mile (1.6 k). Turn Right (N) on FR 10193, go .5 mile (800 m). (Also see Deep Creek.)
**FREE** but choose a chore.
Open May 25–Sep 5.
10 close, open sites ♿
Water, pit toilets, tables, fire rings.
Entrance to Sheep Canyon–a most rewarding geological drive.
Explore and photograph canyon as light changes. Of course, there's also picnicking and fishing.
14-day limit.
6500 ft (1950 m)

## CEDAR CANYON
Dixie NF (801) 865-3200
State map: J3
Take Scenic Byway 14 E from CEDAR CITY 15 miles (24 k).
$5; reservations accepted.
Open May 15–Sep 30.
17 scattered, screened sites.
Water, flush toilets, tables, fire rings.
Cool location among spruce, fir, and aspen in narrow canyon.
Good area to relax.
14-day limit. Quiet hours.
8100 ft (2430 m)

## CHINA MEADOWS

Wasatch-Cache NF
(801) 524-5030
State map: D7
From MOUNTAIN VIEW, WY,
go S on WY 410 for 7 miles (11.2 k).
Continue S on unpaved FR 072 (pass
UT border) about 18 miles (28.8 k).
Another .5 mile (800 m) is **Trailhead
Camp** (4 sites)–great access to back-
country and Uinta Wilderness. (Also see
Marsh Lake.)
**FREE** but choose a chore.
Open Jun–Oct.
13 close, open sites.
Pit toilets, tables, fire rings.
Streamside setting near China Lake and
other small lakes.
Explore remote area. Hike, fish, picnic.
NO water. 14-day limit.
9500 ft (2850 m)

## CHINA ROW

Wasatch-Cache NF
(801) 524-5030
State map: B5
From LOGAN, take scenic
US 89 NE about 12 miles (19.2 k). Find
**Wood Camp** (6 sites) .5 mile (800 m) N
on FR 015.
**FREE** but choose a chore.
Open May 15–Oct 31; camp off-season.
4 sites. Pit toilets, tables, fire rings.
Beautiful area especially with fall color.
Discover Jardine Juniper, Logan Cave,
Hidden, and Ricks springs.
NO water. 7-day/20-ft limits.
5600 ft (1680 m)

## CLEAR CREEK

Sawtooth NF (208) 737-3200
State map: B2
From CLEAR CREEK, take
FR 001 SW.
**FREE** but choose a chore.
Open Jun–Oct.
7 close, open sites.
Water, pit toilets, tables, grills.
On stream near Idaho border.
Fish or relax. Hike up canyons.
14-day limit.
5300 ft (1590 m)

## DEEP CREEK

Ashley NF (801) 789-1181
State map: D8
From MANILA, go S on UT 44
for 14 miles (22.4 k). Turn
Right (W) on second turnoff for
FR 10210. Drive 3 miles (4.8 k). Turn
Right (N) on FR 10539. Go about 5 miles
(8 k). (See Browne Lake and Carmel.)
**FREE** but choose a chore.
Open Jun–Sep.
17 close, open sites. &
Water, pit toilets, tables, fire rings.
Among dark woods in steep canyon.
Terrific place in hot weather. Be sure to
drive through Sheep Creek Canyon.
Hike and fish.
14-day limit.
7800 ft (2340 m)

## DEWITT

Wasatch-Cache NF
(801) 524-5030
State map: B5
From LOGAN, take scenic
US 89 NE about 7 miles (11.2 k). Several
fee-charged choices such as **Spring
Hollow** and **Guinavah-Malibu** are a
few miles in either direction.
**FREE** but choose a chore.
Open May 15–Oct 15; camping allowed
off-season.
5 sites. Pit toilets, tables, fire rings.
In scenic area.
Hike 1-mile (1.6 k) trail to Wind Cave.
NO water. 7-day limit.
5200 ft (1560 m)

## DIAMOND

Uinta NF (801) 342-5260
State map: E5
From SPANISH FORK, go
10 miles (16 k) SE on US 89/6
to Diamond Fork Rd. Turn Left (NE) and
go 6 miles (9.6 k). (Also see Palmyra.)
**$5.** Open May–Oct.
35 sites.
Water, flush toilets, tables, fire rings.
Located on river where hiking, swimming, and relaxing are popular.
No trash arrangements. 14-day limit.
4200 ft (1260 m)

▲ ▲ ▲ ▲ ▲ ▲ ▲ ▲ ▲ ▲ ▲ ▲ ▲ ▲ ▲ ▲ ▲ ▲ ▲ ▲ ▲ ▲ ▲ ▲ ▲ ▲ ▲

## DRY FORK CANYON

BLM (801) 789-1362
State map: D8
From VERNAL, go W on
UT 121 for 3 miles (4.8 k). Turn
Right (N) on Red Cloud Loop and drive
12 miles (19.2 k).
FREE but choose a chore.
Open Apr 1–Oct 31; camping allowed
off-season.
6 scattered, screened tent sites.
Tables, grills, fire rings.
Under cottonwood, boxelder, and pine,
adjacent to ephemeral stream.
Hiking and birdwatching here.
NO water or toilets (come prepared).
14-day limit.
6500 ft (1950 m)

## EAST CANYON SP

(801) 829-6866
State map: D5
From SALT LAKE CITY, take
I-80 E to East Canyon Exit N.
From OGDEN, take I-84 E to Morgan
Exit S. Near junction of UT 65 and
66–about 30 miles (48 k) from either
city.
$5 primitive, $9 developed; reservations
accepted at (800) 322-3770 for an
additional $5.
Open All Year.
31 scattered, open sites.
Water, flush/pit toilets, dump station,
showers, tables, grills, fire rings, pay
phone, boat ramp, beach, nearby store
with ice and rentals.
In grassy area (few trees) next to
860-acre reservoir.
Hike, swim, fish, and boat. Birdwatch. In
cold weather, snowski.
14-day limit. Quiet hours.
5700 ft (1710 m)

## ELKHORN

Fishlake NF (801) 896-4491
State map: H5
From LOA, drive NE on UT 72
for 12 miles (19.2 k). Turn
Right (E) on FR 2062. Go 7 miles (11.2 k).
FREE but choose a chore.
Open Jun–Oct.

7 close, open sites.
Water, pit toilets, tables, fire rings.
In wooded setting on Thousand Lake
Mountain with views of Capitol Reef.
Hike trails (Great Western Trail nearby).
14-day limit.
9300 ft (2790 m)

## FISH CREEK

Manti-LaSal NF (801) 637-2817
State map: F6
From SCOFIELD, drive 4 miles
(6.4 k) NW on FR 008. Turn
Left (W) on FR 123. Go 1.5 miles (2.4 k).
FREE but choose a chore.
Open May–Oct.
5 close, open tent sites. Water, pit toilets,
tables, grills, fire rings, corral.
On creek used by horseback expeditions.
Hike Fish Creek National Recreation
Trail.
14-day limit.
8000 ft (2400 m)

## FREMONT INDIAN SP-Castle Rock

(801) 527-4631
State map: H4
From RICHFIELD, go 21 miles
(33.6 k) W on I-70 to Exit 17.
$5 primitive, $7 developed; reservations
accepted at (800) 332-2770 for an
additional $5.
Open Easter–Nov 1; dry camping
off-season.
31 close, screened sites.
Water, flush and chemical toilets, tables,
grills, fire rings, pay phone.
In canyon reminiscent of Bryce Canyon.
Rock formations plus many examples of
prehistoric Fremont Indian culture. Treat
all features (considered sacred by Paiute)
with great respect.
Learn more about past culture and
geology at Visitor Center. Ranger
programs available. Hike and fish.
14-day limit. Crowded around holidays.
5900 ft (1770 m)

# UTAH

338

▲ ▲ ▲ ▲ ▲ ▲ ▲ ▲ ▲ ▲ ▲ ▲ ▲ ▲ ▲ ▲ ▲ ▲ ▲ ▲ ▲ ▲ ▲

## GLEN CANYON NRA-Hite

(801) 684-2243
State map: J7
Go about 50 miles (80 k) SE of
HANKSVILLE on UT 95.
FREE but choose a chore.
Open All Year.
Undesignated sites; area mainly for tents.
Minimal facilities. Nearby private marina
with services.
At Hite Crossing (many consider this
most scenic part of lake).
Swim and boat immense Lake Powell.
Photograph fantastic scenery.
NO water or other amenities (come
prepared). 14-day limit.

## GOOSEBERRY

Fishlake NF (801) 896-4491
State map: H5
From SALINA, go SE on UT 70
for 7 miles (11.2 k). Turn Right
(S) on FR 540 and drive about 9 miles
(14.4 k).
FREE but choose a chore.
Open May-Nov.
6 close, open sites.
Water, pit toilets, tables, fire rings.
In scenic, wooded area by stream.
Explore, relax, fish.
14-day limit.
7800 ft (2340 m)

## GOOSENECKS SP

(801) 678-2238
State map: K8
From MEXICAN HAT, head N
for 4 miles (6.4 k) on US 183.
Turn Left (W) on UT 263 and then Left
(SW) again on UT 316 and drive about
3 miles (4.8 k).
FREE but choose a chore.
Open All Year.
4 close, open sites.
Pit toilets, tables, grills.
Panoramic views of 1000-ft chasm
created by meandering San Juan River.
Relax, photograph, and sightsee.
NO water.
4500 ft (1350 m)

## GUNLOCK SP

Snow Canyon SP
(801) 628-2255
State map: K1
Travel 16 miles (25.6 k) W of
ST GEORGE.
FREE but choose a chore.
Open All Year.
Undesignated sites.
Pit toilets, 4 tables, boat ramp.
On small reservoir with beach in
beautiful red-rock setting.
Use lake to swim, fish, and boat.
NO water.

## HATCH POINT

BLM (801) 259-6111
State map: H8
From MONTICELLO, go N on
US 191 for 22.5 miles (36 k).
Turn Left (W) on BLM road and follow
signs 22.5 more miles (36 k)-last
10 miles (16 k) are unpaved. Snow closes
road in winter. (Also see Wind Whistle.)
$5. Open Apr 1-Oct 30; dry camping
off-season.
10 scattered, screened sites. Water, pit
toilets, tables, grills, fire rings.
Quiet, isolated, lightly-used camp with
good sightseeing.
Hike region. Anticline and Needles overlooks make superb photo opportunities.
14-day limit.
5900 ft (1770 m)

## HENRY'S FORK TRAILHEAD

Wasatch-Cache NF
(801) 524-5030
State map: D7
From LONETREE, WY, go S a
couple of blocks then turn Right (W) on
CR. Go 1 mile (1.6 k), turn Left (S) on
CR/FR 077-swinging SW after first
2 miles (3.2 k). Drive 15 miles (24 k) to
end of road. Can also access from
MOUNTAIN VIEW, WY (see Marsh
Lake) by taking FR 017 when it forks off
FR 072.
FREE but choose a chore.
Open Jun-Oct.
8 close, open sites.
Pit toilets, tables, fire rings.

On creek with access to backcountry.
Explore remote area by foot or horseback. Hike, fish, picnic.
NO water. 14-day limit.
9600 ft (2880 m)

## HIGH CREEK

Wasatch-Cache NF
(801) 524-5030
State map: B5
From RICHMOND, go 2 miles
(3.2 k) N on US 91. Turn Right (E) on
CR to Richmond Knoll and go 4.5 miles
(7.2 k).
FREE but choose a chore.
Open Jun 15–Sep 15; camping allowed
off-season.
4 sites. Water (must be treated), pit
toilets, tables, fire rings.
On stream next to Mt Naomi Wilderness.
Fishing and hiking rate excellent.
7-day/20-ft limits.
5000 ft (1500 m)

## HOBBLE

Wasatch-Cache NF
(801) 524-5030
State map: C5
From HUNTSVILLE, take
scenic byway UT 39 E about 6 miles
(9.6 k). Second in series of seven camps
along UT 39 but only free one.
FREE but choose a chore.
Open May 15–Oct 31; camping allowed
off-season.
9 sites. Pit toilets, tables, fire rings.
On Ogden River.
Swim, fish, picnic, sightsee, or hike.
NO water. 7-day/20-ft limits.
5200 ft (1560 m)

## HONEYCOMB ROCKS

Dixie NF (801) 673-3431
State map: J1
From ENTERPRISE, go 5 miles
(8 k) W on UT 120 to FR. Turn
Left (SW) and continue 5 miles (8 k).
$5. Open May 15–Oct 31; dry camping
off-season.
22 sites. Water, flush toilets, tables, grills,
fire rings, boat ramp.
Unusual limestone formations around

reservoir. Fishing and waterskiing are
possible when reservoir is high (until
early summer). Explore rocks.
14-day limit.
5700 ft (1710 m)

## HOPE

Uinta NF (801) 342-5240
State map: E5
Take US 189 NE from PROVO
for 6 miles (9.6 k) Turn Right
on FR 27 and go 5 miles (8 k).
$5; for additional $6, reservations
accepted at (800) 283-2267.
Open Jun–Oct.
24 close, screened sites. Water, pit toilets,
tables, grills, fire rings.
Hiking possibilities.
14-day limit.
6000 ft (1800 m)

## HOVENWEEP NM-Square Tower

(303) 529-4461
State map: J9
From BLUFF, take US 191 N
for 11 miles (17.6 k). Turn
Right (E) on UT 262. Go 25 miles (40 k)–
first on paved then gravel surface. (Also
access from CORTEZ, CO.) Dirt access
roads become treacherous when wet.
$5 plus $5 entrance fee (or pass).
Open All Year.
31 scattered, open sites. Water, flush
toilets, tables, grills, sun shelters.
Mesa-top sites among sage and juniper
with fantastic panoramas including
Sleeping Ute Mountain. Excellent access
to prehistoric remains (fragile–be
extremely careful).
From short walks to lengthy canyon
treks, examine wide variety of Anasazi
buildings and rock art. Occasional ranger
programs help interpret culture.
May–Jun pesty gnats. Generator rules.
5240 ft (1572 m)

## INDIAN CROSSING

BLM (801) 789-1362
State map: D9
Go N from DUTCH JOHN on
US 191 to UT-WY line. Turn
Right (E) on dirt road (tough when wet)

▲ ▲ ▲ ▲ ▲ ▲ ▲ ▲ ▲ ▲ ▲ ▲ ▲ ▲ ▲ ▲ ▲ ▲ ▲ ▲ ▲ ▲

and follow signs to Brown's Park. (Also see Bridge Hollow.)
**FREE** but choose a chore.
Open May 1 – Sep 30; dry camping off-season.
10 (6 tent-only) scattered, open sites. Water, chemical toilets, tables, grills, fire rings, raft ramp.
On banks of Green River in Brown's Park (popular for rafting). There are fishing and birdwatching opportunities plus occasional ranger programs.
No trash arrangements. 14-day limit.
4200 ft (1260 m)

### JERICHO

BLM (801) 896-8221
State map: F4
Take US 6 S from EUREKA for 19 miles (30.4 k). Turn Right (W) on BLM road. Follow signs. (See Oasis, Sand Mountain, or White Sands.)
**$5**. Open All Year.
41 close, open sites. Water, flush toilets, tables, grills, shelters.
In large parking lot.
ATVs allowed on over two thirds of 60000 acres in Little Sahara RA. Sagebrush flats and freely shifting sand dunes provide interesting scenery for sightseer and photographer.
14-day limit. Crowded in spring and fall. ATVs create noise.
5100 ft (1530 m)

### LITTLE LYMAN LAKE

Wasatch-Cache NF
(801) 524-5030
State map: D6
From MOUNTAIN VIEW, WY, go S on WY 410, following as it turns W through Robertson–about 14 miles (22.4 k). As pavement ends, turn Left (S) on CR/FR 073 and drive into Utah around **Meeks Reservoir** (with developed camp) to fork, about 19 miles (30.4 k). Bear Right at fork on FR 058 and go 2 miles (3.2 k). Turn Right (N) on FR 635 and go .25 mile (400 m). If you go Left at fork on FR 065 and drive to end in 6 miles (9.6 k), find a backcountry access camp, **East Fork Black Fork**.

**FREE** but choose a chore.
Open Jun – Oct.
12 close, open sites.
Pit toilets, tables, fire rings.
In close proximity to several lakes and streams, so fish and relax at camp or take extended treks in scenic wild area.
NO water. 14-day limit.
9200 ft (2760 m)

### LITTLE VALLEY

Uinta NF (801) 342-5260
State map: E4
Go past EUREKA to Benmore. Take Rd 005 to site.
**FREE** but choose a chore.
Open May – Oct.
6 tent sites. Pit toilets, tables.
Among aspen in sage and grass.
Most campers come to fish or hike.
NO water/trash arrangements.
6000 ft (1800 m)

### LONESOME BEAVER

BLM (801) 896-8221
State map: I6
From HANKSVILLE, take rough, unpaved access road for 21.7 miles (34.7 k)–unsuitable for low clearance or large vehicles.
**$4**. Open May – Oct; dry camping off-season.
5 scattered, screened sites. Water, pit toilets, tables, grills, fire rings.
Under spruce, fir, and aspen in Sawmill Basin of Henry Mountains. Trail ascends Mt Ellen–1506 ft (3507 m)–for terrific hiking plus good photography.
No trash arrangements (pack it out). 14-day limit. Hunting in season.
8000 ft (2400 m)

### LOST CREEK SP

(801) 829-6866
State map: C5
From OGDEN, take I-84 E for 17 miles (27.2 k) to CRODEN Exit. Go NE on first paved then gravel access road.
**FREE** but choose a chore.
Open Apr – Nov (weather closes area); camping allowed off-season.

▲ ▲ ▲ ▲ ▲ ▲ ▲ ▲ ▲ ▲ ▲ ▲ ▲ ▲ ▲ ▲ ▲ ▲ ▲ ▲ ▲ ▲ ▲ ▲

Undesignated sites.
Pit toilets, boat ramp.
In forest next to mountain reservoir.
Swim, boat, and fish.
NO water. Quiet hours.
5900 ft (1770 m)

## LOWER PROVO

Wasatch-Cache NF
(801) 524-5030
State map: D6
From KAMAS, go E on UT 150
for 12 miles (19.2 k). Turn Right (S) on
FR 053 and go .5 mile (800 m).
FREE but choose a chore.
Open Jun 8–Sep 15.
10 close, open sites.
Water, pit toilets, tables, fire rings.
Fish, hike, or picnic along creek.
14-day/20-ft limits.
7700 ft (2310 m)

## MAPLE CANYON

Manti-LaSal NF (801) 283-4151
State map: F5
From FREEDOM, take dirt
Maple Canyon Rd W for
3.75 miles (6 k).
FREE but choose a chore.
Open May–Oct.
9 close, open sites.
Pit toilets, tables, grills.
In canyon with numerous hiking trails.
Walk Trail 158 to beautiful natural arch.
NO water. 14-day limit.
6700 ft (2010 m)

## MARSH LAKE

Wasatch-Cache NF
(801) 524-5030
State map: D7
From MOUNTAIN VIEW, WY,
go S on WY 410 for 7 miles (11.2 k).
Continue S on unpaved FR 072 (pass
UT border) about 16 miles (25.6 k). For
alternative, retrace N on 072 for 1 mile
(1.6 k), turn Right (SE) on FR 126 and go
1 mile (1.6 k) to check out **Bridger Lake**
(25 sites). Too, find primitive camping at
**Stateline Reservoir**. (Also see China
Meadows.)
FREE but choose a chore.

Open Jun–Oct.
38 close, open sites.
Pit toilets, tables, fire rings, boat ramp.
In woods on lake.
Explore remote area. Hike, boat (no
motors), fish, picnic.
NO water. 14-day limit.
9400 ft (2820 m)

## MCMILLAN SPRING

BLM (801) 896-8221
State map: I6
Take UT 24 W from
HANKSVILLE for 28.5 miles
(45.6 k). Turn Left (S) on rugged,
unpaved Notom–Bullfrog Rd. Go
31.6 miles (50.6 k). Access road is unsuitable for low-clearance or large vehicles.
(See Capitol Reef NP-Cedar Mesa.)
FREE but choose a chore.
Open May–Nov; dry camping
off-season.
10 scattered, screened sites.
Water, pit toilets, tables, grills.
Among ponderosa pine. Excellent views
of Waterpocket Fold and wildlife (bison).
Appreciate last-explored mountain
region in Lower 48.
14-day limit. Hunting in season.
8400 ft (2520 m)

## NATURAL BRIDGES NM

(801) 259-5174
State map: J8
From BLANDING, go 2 miles
(3.2 k) S on US 191. Turn Right
(W) on UT 95 and drive 38 miles (60.8 k)
to Spur 275. Turn Right (N) on Spur to
enter monument.
FREE but $3 entrance fee (or pass).
Open All Year.
13 (3 tent-only) scattered, screened sites.
Water at Visitor Center–.5 mile (800 m)
away, pit toilets, tables, grills.
Along small loop among pinyon-juniper
at start of scenic drive.
Enjoy three excellent examples of natural
rock bridges plus wonderful canyon
hiking and prehistoric artifact viewing
(take great care in this fragile environment). Nature study and ranger
programs round out stay.

▲ ▲ ▲ ▲ ▲ ▲ ▲ ▲ ▲ ▲ ▲ ▲ ▲ ▲ ▲ ▲ ▲ ▲ ▲ ▲ ▲ ▲

Crowded May–Sep. 7-day/21-ft limits.
Nearest supplies over 40 miles (64 k)
away.
6500 ft (1950 m)

## NEWSPAPER ROCK SP

(801) 678-2238
State map: I8
From MONTICELLO, go
15 miles (24 k) N on US 191.
Turn Left (W) on NV 211. Go 12 miles
(19.2 k).
FREE but choose a chore.
Open All Year.
8 scattered, screened sites.
Pit toilets, tables, grills, fire rings.
Next to small stream in riparian setting
on scenic road to Canyonlands NP.
Across road is incredible display of rock
art. Other excellent examples in area (do
not deface these national treasures).
NO water. 14-day/25-ft limits. Crowded
in spring and Oct. Gnats in late spring.

## OAK GROVE

Dixie NF (801) 586-2421
State map: K2
From ST GEORGE, go NE on
I-15 for 16 miles (25.6 k). Go
NW on FR 032 for 8 miles (12.8 k).
FREE but choose a chore.
Open Jun–Oct.
6 close, open sites.
Water, pit toilets, tables, fire rings.
In woods next to Pine Valley Mountain
Wilderness–ideal for short walks or
extended treks in natural setting.
14-day limit.
6800 ft (2040 m)

## OASIS

BLM (801) 896-8221
State map: F4
Take US 6 S from EUREKA for
19 miles (30.4 k). Turn Right
(W) on BLM road. Follow signs. (See
Jericho, Sand Mountain, or White Sands.)
$5. Open All Year.
84 scattered, screened sites.
Water, flush toilets, tables, grills, fire
rings, dump station.
Four loops among juniper adjacent to

20000 acres of active dunes–part of Little
Sahara RA.
ATVs allowed on over two thirds of
60000 acres. Sagebrush flats and freely
shifting sand dunes provide interesting
scenery for sightseer and photographer.
14-day limit. Crowded in spring and fall.
ATVs create noise.
5100 ft (1530 m)

## OOWAH LAKE

Manti-LaSal NF (801) 259-7155
State map: H9
About 8 miles (12.8 k) S of
MOAB on US 191, bear Left
(SE) on Mountain Loop Rd. Go 13 miles
(20.8 k), bearing Left on FR 062 to Mill
Creek Canyon Overlook. Continue
straight (E) on FR 076 (Oowah Access).
FREE but choose a chore.
Open Jun–Oct.
6 close, open sites.
Pit toilets, tables, fire rings.
On lakeshore, so enjoy water activities.
Enjoy trails too.
NO water. 14-day limit.
8800 ft (2640 m)

## PALMYRA

Uinta NF (801) 342-5260
State map: E5
From SPANISH FORK, go SE
on US 89/6 for 10 miles (16 k).
Turn Left (NE) on Diamond Fork Rd and
go 5 miles (8 k). (Also see Diamond.)
$5. Open May–Oct.
11 sites.
Water, pit toilets, tables, fire rings.
At bottom of Diamond Fork Canyon
next to river, warmer and drier than
surrounding region. Fifth Water and
Cottonwood Canyon trails.
Fish river and hike countryside.
14-day limit.
5200 ft (1560 m)

## PANGUITCH LAKE SOUTH

Dixie NF (801) 865-3200
State map: J3
From PANGUITCH, drive
19 miles (30.4 k) SW on
UT 143.

$5. Open May 23–Sep 15.
19 sites.
Water, flush toilets, tables, boat ramp.
Swim, waterski, boat, and fish on lake.
Enjoy nature and bike trails.
14-day limit.

## PARADISE PARK

Ashley NF (801) 789-1181
State map: E8
From LAPOINT, take CR 121
NW for 16.5 miles (26.4 k).
Continue NW on rough FR 104 for
8.75 miles (14 k).
FREE but choose a chore.
Open May 25–Sep 5.
15 close, open sites. &
Pit toilets, tables, fire rings.
Remote camp near stream.
Explore High Uintas Wilderness.
NO water. 14-day limit.
10000 ft (3000 m)

## PARIA MOVIE SET

BLM (801) 644-2672
State map: K4
From KANAB, go 34 miles
(54.4 k) E on US 89. Turn Left
(N) on unpaved spur road (impassable
when wet) and drive 5 miles (8 k).
FREE but choose a chore.
Open May 1–Oct 30; camping allowed
off-season.
3 tent sites.
Pit toilets, tables, grills, fire rings.
In deep valley along Paria River with
colorful rock walls of purples, yellows,
and reds.
Beautiful, relaxing place with good
photo possibilities.
NO water. Use trash receptacles (keep it
clean). 19-ft limit. Crowded in spring
and fall. Gnats can be pesty.
4265 ft (1278 m)

## PELICAN LAKE

BLM (801) 789-1362
State map: E8
Take US 40 W from VERNAL
for 15 miles (24 k). Turn Left
(S) on UT 88 and go 8 miles (12.8 k).
Camp is on south end of lake–access

around west side (unpaved).
FREE but choose a chore.
Open Apr 1–Oct 31; camping off-season.
14 scattered, open sites.
Chemical toilets, tables, grills, fire rings,
boat ramp, boat dock.
Along lake or under cottonwood.
Boating and fishing are mainstays.
NO water. 14-day limit.
4800 ft (1440 m)

## PINE PARK

Dixie NF (801) 673-3431
State map: J1
From ENTERPRISE, go
17 miles (27.2 k) on UT 120.
Turn Left (S) on FR 001. Go 5 miles (8 k).
FREE but choose a chore.
Open May–Nov; camping off-season.
11 tent sites. Pit toilets, tables.
Near interesting geologic formations.
Good hiking area.
NO water/trash arrangements.
6200 ft (1860 m)

## PIUTE SP

Otter Creek SP
(801) 624-3268
State map: I4
From JUNCTION, go N on
UT 89. Turn Right (E) and go 1.5 miles
(2.4 k).
FREE but choose a chore.
Open All Year.
7 scattered, open sites. Pit toilets, tables,
boat launch, boat dock.
Sagebrush with pinyon-juniper at north
end of Piute Reservoir.
Access to full range of water activities.
NO water. 14-day limit. Crowded in late
May and June. Flies, mosquitos, and
winds can spoil picnic.
6400 ft (1920 m)

## POLE CREEK LAKE

Ashley NF (801) 789-1181
State map: D7
From WHITEROCKS, head
NW 8 miles (12.8 k) on CR. Go
13.5 miles (21.6 k) NW on FR 10117.
FREE but choose a chore.
Open Jun–Sep.

▲ ▲ ▲ ▲ ▲ ▲ ▲ ▲ ▲ ▲ ▲ ▲ ▲ ▲ ▲ ▲ ▲ ▲ ▲ ▲ ▲ ▲ ▲ ▲ ▲

18 close, open sites. &
Pit toilets, tables, fire rings.
High-altitude camp near small lake.
Explore Uintas area.
NO water. 14-day limit.
8200 ft (2460 m)

## PONDEROSA

BLM (801) 644-2672
State map: K3
Take US 89 N from KANAB
for 7.5 miles (12 k). Turn Left
(W) on gravel road to **Coral Pink Sand Dunes SP**. Camp is 7 miles (11.2 k).
FREE but choose a chore.
Open Apr 15–Oct 31.
11 close, open sites.
Pit toilets, tables, grills, fire rings.
At northern edge of Coral Pink Sand Dunes SP among large ponderosa pines.
Nice sightseeing.
NO water. 14-day/22-ft limits. Use trash containers–keep it clean. Gets crowded and noisy on holidays due to ATVs.
Hunting in season.
6368 ft (1908 m)

## POSEY LAKE

Dixie NF (801) 826-4221
State map: I5
From ESCALANTE, take
FR 154 NE for 11 miles (17.6 k).
(Also see Blue Spruce.)
$5; for additional $6, reservations accepted at (800) 283-2267.
Open Jun 1–Sep 15; dry camping off-season.
30 scattered, screened sites.
Water, pit toilets, tables, fire rings.
In mixed vegetation on mountain lake.
Box-Death Hollow Wilderness only 5 miles (8 k) away.
Fish, canoe, or hike.
14-day limit. Quiet hours.
8200 ft (2460 m)

## PRICE CANYON

BLM (801) 259-6111
State map: F6
Go N on US 6 from PRICE for
15 miles (24 k). Turn Left (W)
on steep BLM road and continue 3 additional miles (4.8 k).
$5. Open Jun 1–Oct 15, snow determines.
18 scattered, screened sites. Water, pit toilets, tables, grills, fire rings.
Cool, high-elevation setting under ponderosa pines.
Photographic possibilities. Walk Bristlecone nature/hiking trails.
14-day limit.
8000 ft (2400 m)

## RED CLIFFS

BLM (801) 673-4654
State map: K2
Take LEEDS Exit off I-15
(about 14 miles N of ST
GEORGE). Follow signs.
$4. Open All Year.
10 close, open sites, some screening.
Water, chemical/pit toilets, tables, grills.
Spectacular, narrow, red-rock canyon with Pine Mountains as backdrop.
Wadeable stream. Green strip of vegetation. Near Zion NP and Quail Creek SP. Changes to alleviate overcrowding in planning stages.
Hike and relish scenery. Cool off in water or go to Quail Creek Reservoir for more serious swimming and boating.
Enjoy archeological display.
Springtime brings many day-users into joint camping/picnic area. Summers hot but less crowded. 14-day limit.
3600 ft (1080 m)

## RESERVOIR

Ashley NF (801) 789-1181
State map: D7
From ALTONAH, go NW on
Rd 10119 about 18 miles
(28.8 k). For more developed (fee-charged) camps, check out nearby **Riverview, Swift Creek, and Yellowstone**. (Also see Bridge.)
FREE but choose a chore.
Open Jun–Sep.
4 close, open sites. &
Water, pit toilets, tables, fire rings.
Streamside spot for fishing and relaxing.
14-day limit.
7900 ft (2370 m)

▲ ▲ ▲ ▲ ▲ ▲ ▲ ▲ ▲ ▲ ▲ ▲ ▲ ▲ ▲ ▲ ▲ ▲ ▲ ▲ ▲ ▲ ▲ ▲ ▲

## ROCKPORT SP (9 Areas)
(801) 336-2241
State map: D5
Go 36 miles (57.6 k) E on I-80
from SALT LAKE CITY. Take
WANSIP Exit to park.
**$5** primitive, $9 developed; reservations
accepted at (800) 322-3770 for an
additional $5. Open All Year.
300 scattered, open sites.
Water, flush and pit toilets, showers,
tables, grills, fire rings, pay phone, dump
station, boat ramp.
On east side of reservoir with beach
among pinyon, juniper, and cottonwood
in mountain setting.
Water draws most visitors with boating,
swimming, and fishing. Also
opportunities for birdwatching, hiking,
and cross-country skiing in winter.
14-day limit. Often crowded during
summer. Quiet hours.
6100 ft (1830 m)

## SAND ISLAND
BLM (801) 259-6111
State map: K8
From BLUFF, go 3 miles (4.8 k)
W on US 163.
**FREE** but choose a chore.
Open All Year.
6 scattered, open sites (small RVs ok).
Pit toilets, tables, grills, boat ramp.
Shaded spot next to San Juan River.
Spectacular prehistoric rock art panel
(please leave undisturbed).
Appreciate geologic and man-carved
wonders. Raft or boat San Juan River.
NO water. 14-day limit.
4300 ft (1290 m)

## SAND MOUNTAIN
BLM (801) 896-8221
State map: F4
Take US 6 S from EUREKA for
19 miles (30.4 k). Turn Right
(W) on BLM road. Follow signs. (Also
see Jericho, Oasis, and White Sands.)
**$5**. Open All Year.
300 close, open sites. Water, pit toilets.
Large parking area beside sand-covered
mountain and 20000 acres of active

dunes. In Little Sahara RA.
ATVs allowed on over two thirds of
60000 acres. Sagebrush flats and freely
shifting sand dunes provide interesting
scenery for sightseer and photographer.
14-day limit. Crowded in spring and fall.
ATVs create noise.
5100 ft (1530 m)

## SMITHFIELD CANYON
Wasatch-Cache NF
(801) 524-5030
State map: B5
From SMITHFIELD, go 4 miles
(4.8 k) NE on CR 049 toward White
Horse Village along Smithfield Summit
Creek.
**FREE** but choose a chore.
Open Jun 15–Sep 15; camping allowed
off-season.
7 (1 tent-only) sites.
Pit toilets, tables, fire rings.
On stream next to Mt Naomi Wilderness.
Fishing and hiking opportunities.
NO water. 7-day/20-ft limits.
5200 ft (1560 m)

## SOUTH FORK
Ashley NF (801) 789-1181
State map: D6
From HANNA, take FR 10134
NE for 16 miles (25.6 k). If full,
check out **Miners Gulch** a few miles
farther or, if you require water, there's
fee-charged **Yellowpine**.
**FREE** but choose a chore.
Open Jun–Sep.
4 close, open sites. &
Pit toilets, tables, fire rings.
Relax or fish in this streamside getaway.
NO water. 14-day limit.
7900 ft (2370 m)

## SOUTH WILLOW CANYON CAMPS
Wasatch-Cache NF
(801) 524-5030
State map: D3
From GRANTSVILLE, take
CR 138 (toward St John) S for 5 miles
(8 k). Turn Right (SW) on FR 171
(Willow Canyon) and go 4 miles (6.4 k).
Series of six camps–**Cottonwood, Intake,**

▲ ▲ ▲ ▲ ▲ ▲ ▲ ▲ ▲ ▲ ▲ ▲ ▲ ▲ ▲ ▲ ▲ ▲ ▲ ▲ ▲ ▲ ▲ ▲ ▲

**Boy Scout, Lower Narrows, Upper Narrows**, and **Loop**–along road next 3 miles (4.8 k).
**FREE** but choose a chore.
Open May 15–Oct 31; camping allowed off-season.
50 sites (tent-only except 4 sites at Cottonwood and 5 sites at Boy Scout).
Pit toilets, tables, fire rings.
Borders Desert Peak Wilderness.
Hike numerous trails.
NO water. 7-day/20-ft limits.
7000 ft (2100 m)

## SPRING

Wasatch-Cache NF
(801) 524-5030
State map: B5
From HYRUM, take UT 242 E about 8 miles (12.8 k). Turn Left (N) on FR 055 and drive 3.5 miles (5.6 k).
Companion camp **Friendship** (6 sites) is .75 mile (1.2 k) farther.
**FREE** but choose a chore.
Open May 15–Oct 31; camping allowed off-season.
3 sites. Pit toilets, tables, fire rings.
In Blacksmith Fork Canyon.
Access hiking trails across road or fish.
NO water. 7-day/20-ft limits.
6000 ft (1800 m)

## SPRING CITY

Manti-LaSal NF (801) 283-4151
State map: F5
From SPRING CITY, take rough, dirt FR 036 E for 4 miles (6.4 k).
**FREE** but choose a chore.
Open Jun–Oct.
5 close, open sites.
Water, pit toilets, tables, grills.
In canyon with numerous hiking trails.
Meadow Fork Trail scenic though strenuous with lots of hills.
Walk, explore, picnic, and relax.
14-day limit.
6500 ft (1950 m)

## STARR SPRING

BLM (801) 896-8221
State map: J6
From HANKSVILLE, take UT 95 S for 26.7 miles (42.7 k) to UT 276. Bear Right (S) on 276. Drive 17.3 miles (27.7 k) to Starr Spring Turnoff. Turn Right (W) on dirt road. Go 3.9 miles (6.2 k).
**$4**. Open Apr–Oct; dry camping off-season.
12 scattered, screened sites. Water, pit toilets, tables, grills, fire rings.
In patch of oak on Mt Hillers.
Seclusion and scenery make ideal spot for relaxing or taking short walks for spectacular views.
No trash arrangements. 14-day limit. No large vehicles. Mosquitos can get thick.
Hunting in season.
6300 ft (1890 m)

## SUNSET

Wasatch-Cache NF
(801) 524-5030
State map: D5
From FARMINGTON, go E on steep FR 007 for 4 miles (6.4 k). (Also see Bountiful Peak.)
**FREE** but choose a chore.
Open May 1–Oct 15.
32 close, open sites.
Pit toilets, tables, fire rings.
Wooded canyon along scenic drive.
Hike and picnic.
7-day limit.
6200 ft (1860 m)

## THE MAPLES

Wasatch-Cache NF
(801) 524-5030
State map: C5
From HUNTSVILLE, take UT 39 SW for 2.5 miles (4 k). Turn Left (S) on UT 226. Go 10 miles (16 k). Turn Right (W) on FR 122 for 2 miles (3.2 k).
**FREE** but choose a chore.
Open Jun 1–Oct 31; camping allowed off-season.
26 (16 tent-only) sites.
Pit toilets, tables, fire rings.
Relax in remote, quiet, scenic area near

▲ ▲ ▲ ▲ ▲ ▲ ▲ ▲ ▲ ▲ ▲ ▲ ▲ ▲ ▲ ▲ ▲ ▲ ▲ ▲ ▲ ▲ ▲ ▲ ▲ ▲ ▲ ▲ ▲ ▲ ▲ ▲

Snow Basin Ski Area.
NO water. 7-day/16-ft limits.
6200 ft (1860 m)

## UPPER PROVO

Wasatch-Cache NF
(801) 524-5030
State map: D6
From KAMAS, go E on UT 150
for 21 miles (33.6 k)–only free camp on
this section of scenic byway.
FREE but choose a chore.
Open Jun 1–Sep 20.
5 close, open sites.
Pit toilets, tables, fire rings.
On river near Provo Falls Overlook.
Hike and sightsee.
NO water. 14-day/20-ft limits.
9200 ft (2760 m)

## VERMILLION CASTLE

Dixie NF (801) 865-3200
State map: J3
From PAROWAN, go S on
UT 143 for 3 miles (4.8 k) to
FR. Turn Left (W) and go 1 mile (1.6 k).
$5. Open May 23–Sep 15; dry camping
off-season.
16 scattered, screened sites.
Water, pit toilets, tables, fire rings.
Narrow canyon with flaming red cliffs
and blue stream. Mountain bike trails.
Explore canyon by foot or bike.
14-day limit. Quiet hours.
7000 ft (2100 m)

## WANDIN

Ashley NF (801) 789-1181
State map: E7
From NEOLA, go N on
CR along Uinta River about
3 miles (4.8 k) beyond forest entrance.
Other fee-charged camps are within
1 mile (1.6 k).
FREE but choose a chore.
Open May 15–Sep 15.
7 (3 tent-only) close, open sites.
Pit toilets, tables, fire rings.
On river near Uintas Wilderness.
Hike strenuous trails to unspoiled lakes.
NO water. 14-day limit.
7700 ft (2310 m)

## WHITE HOUSE

BLM (801) 644-2672
State map: K4
Take US 89 E from KANAB for
40 miles (64 k). Turn Right (S)
on gravel road (prone to flash floods)
and proceed 2 miles (3.2 k).
FREE but choose a chore.
Open All Year.
5 close, open tent sites.
Pit toilets, tables, grills, fire rings.
Among junipers on banks of Paria River
at base of white sandstone cliffs. Good
access to Paria Wilderness creates hiking
opportunities.
NO water. 14-day/23-ft limits. Often
crowded during spring and fall. Gnats
and flies can get pesty.
4593 ft (1377 m)

## WHITE SANDS

BLM (801) 896-8221
State map: F4
Take US 6 S from EUREKA for
19 miles (30.4 k). Turn Right
(W) on BLM road. Follow signs. (See
Jericho, Oasis, or Sand Mountain.)
$5. Open All Year.
99 close, screened sites.
Water, flush toilets, tables, grills.
Three loops among juniper (part of Little
Sahara RA).
ATVs allowed on over two thirds of
60000 acres. Sagebrush flats and freely
shifting sand dunes provide interesting
scenery for sightseer and photographer.
14-day limit. Crowded in spring and fall.
ATVs create noise.
5100 ft (1530 m)

## WILLARD BASIN

Wasatch-Cache NF
(801) 524-5030
State map: C4
From BRIGHAM CITY, head E
on US 89/91 about 3 miles (4.8 k) to
Mantua Reservoir Exit. Go SE then bear
Right (S) on FR 084 and drive about
12 miles (19.2 k).
FREE but choose a chore.
Open May 15–Oct 31; dry camping
off-season.

▲ ▲ ▲ ▲ ▲ ▲ ▲ ▲ ▲ ▲ ▲ ▲ ▲ ▲ ▲ ▲ ▲ ▲ ▲ ▲ ▲ ▲ ▲ ▲ ▲ ▲ ▲ ▲ ▲

4 tent sites.
Water, pit toilets, tables, fire rings.
High camp with lookouts and trails.
Walk part of Skyline Trail or visit Inspiration Point.
7-day/20-ft limits.
9000 ft (2700 m)

## WIND WHISTLE

BLM (801) 259-6111
State map: H8
From MONTICELLO, go N on US 191 for 22.5 miles (36 k).
Turn Left (W) on BLM road (closed in winter) and drive 5 miles (8 k). (Also see Hatch Point.)
**$5.** Open Apr 1–Oct 30; dry camping off-season.
19 scattered, screened sites. Water, pit toilets, tables, grills, fire rings.
Surrounded by pinyon-juniper, scenic sandstone cliffs, and open north view.
Hike. Enjoy Anticline and Needles overlooks. Good photographic opportunities.
14-day limit.
6000 ft (1800 m)

## YELLOW PINE

Wasatch-Cache NF
(801) 524-5030
State map: D6
From KAMAS, go E on UT 150 for 6.8 miles (10.9 k). Nearby are three more camps (**Beaver** and **Shingle Creeks** with fees, **Taylors Forks** for ATVs).
**FREE** but choose a chore.
Open May 29–Sep 20.
33 close, open sites.
Pit toilets, tables, fire rings.
Fish, hike, and picnic along creek.
NO water. 14-day/16-ft limits.
7200 ft (2160 m)

## ZION NP-Lava Point

(801) 772-3256
State map: J2
From VIRGIN, take winding, hilly Kolob Terrace Rd (difficult when wet) N for 24 miles (38.4 k). Turn at Lava Point sign.
**FREE** but $5 entrance fee (or pass). Also, **free** backcountry permits available at Visitor Center.
Open when snow permits; camping allowed off-season.
6 close, screened sites.
Pit toilets, tables, fire rings.
In aspen grove.
Create base for short walks or extended exploration of fantastic park with 2000-ft deep gorge and colorful, eroded sandstone cliffs.
NO water. 14-day/22-ft limits. Crowded holidays and weekends.
7800 ft (2340 m)

# Washington

Grid conforms to official state map. For your copy, call (800) 554-1800 or write
Tourism Development Commission, 101 Gen Admin Bldg, Olympia, WA 98504.

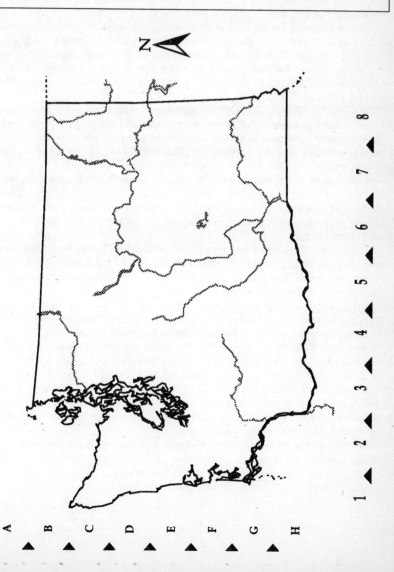

▲ ▲ ▲ ▲ ▲ ▲ ▲ ▲ ▲ ▲ ▲ ▲ ▲ ▲ ▲ ▲ ▲ ▲ ▲ ▲ ▲ ▲ ▲ ▲ ▲ ▲ ▲ ▲

Washington offers camping in coastal rainforests, among snowtopped mountains, beside mighty rivers and babbling streams, or on semiarid sagebrush plains.

The **National Park Service** (NPS) provides unusual opportunities. True rainforest experiences await in Olympic NP. In Mount Rainier NP, you'll find two qualifying campgrounds plus a challenging backcountry. In Northern Cascades NP Complex, there are a few drive-tos, including one accessible through Canada, plus a group reached by ferry then bus. Coulee Dam National Recreation Area (NRA) provides options for lake lovers (see Roosevelt Lake in Index). And, for volcano aficionados, there's Mount St Helens National Monument (NM) administered in conjunction with the Forest Service.

**Colville National Forest** (NF) dominates the northeastern part of the state. Gentle slopes, clear streams, and small lakes create a peaceful, serene atmosphere.

Moving west, the **Okanogan NF**, continues this pastoral feeling though it abuts the rugged Cascade Mountain Range. Its scenic byway WA 20 rates spectacular. In addition, the Pasayten Wilderness along the Canadian border provides ample room for seclusion.

The center of the state claims three large forests with huge wilderness areas. **Mount Baker-Snoqualmie NF** boasts more active glaciers in the Glacier Peak Wilderness then anywhere in the US, save Alaska. Add the beauty of the Alpine Lakes Wilderness, myriad waterfalls, wildflower meadows, wildly plunging streams, and lots of snow for winter sports activities.

Moving south to the **Wenatchee NF**, discover more campgrounds than any other national forest in the country. In addition, since it shares the Glacier Peak and Alpine Lakes wilderness areas and adds the Clearwater, Norse Peak, William O Douglas, and Goat Rocks Wilderness areas, there are wonderful remote, backcountry chances.

The **Gifford Pinchot NF** has two major mountains: Mount St Helens and Mount Adams. One has become a monument, the other a wilderness. If that's not enough, investigate Big Lava Bed, the Lewis River, seven more wilderness areas, and the Sawtooth Huckleberry fields.

On the peninsula, **Olympic NF** surrounds the national park, but only a single camp qualifies in cost. Among the many fee-based camps, however, find wonderful do-it-yourself spots for enjoying the rainforest environment.

**Washington State Parks** (SPs) are too expensive in general. Only one provides low-cost options. Remember, if you are on an extensive cycling or backpacking trek, many of the parks set aside spots for $4 per night. The **Washington Department of Natural Resources** (WA DNR) steps into the park vacuum by maintaining what's known as Multiple-Use Areas. Often surrounding lands have been severely logged but among the nearly seventy free camps, discover an escape from crowds and, perhaps, the perfect spot.

Rounding out the list, the **US Army Corps of Engineers** (COE), **Bureau of Land Management** (BLM), **Umatilla NF** (in the southeast corner but primarily in Oregon), and local communities offer additional options.

Explore the variety of natural beauty that is Washington.

## ADAMS FORK

Gifford Pinchot NF
(206) 497-7565
State map: G4

From RANDLE, head SE on FR 23 for 10 miles (16 k) to **North Fork** (33 sites). Turn Right on FR 21 and go 10 miles (16 k). Turn Right on FR 6401.
$3. Open May 15–Oct 30.
24 sites. Water, pit toilets, tables, grills, fire rings.
On Cispus River.
Swim or fish. Hike to Mouse Lake. Trek into nearby Mt Adams Wilderness.
14-day/24-ft limits.
2600 ft (780 m)

## AHTANUM

WA DNR (206) 753-2400
State map: F4

From TAMPICO, take A-2000 (Middle Fork Rd) W for 9.5 miles (15.2 k). (Also see Clover Flats, Snow Cabin, and Tree Phones.)
FREE but choose a chore.
Open All Year.
11 close, open sites.
Water, pit toilets, tables, grills.
Along wooded creek.
In summer–relax, fish, and picnic; in winter–snowmobile.
14-day limit.

## ALDER LAKE

WA DNR (206) 753-2400
State map: F3

From ELBE, go S on WA 7 for 2.1 miles (3.4 k). Turn Right (W) on Pleasant Valley Rd. Go 3.5 miles (5.6 k) staying Left during last .1 mile (160 m).
FREE but choose a chore.
Open All Year.
25 close, open sites. Water, pit toilets, tables, grills, boat launch.
On wooded lakeshore.
Float and fish lake. Relax and picnic.
14-day limit.

## ALDER THICKET

Umatilla NF (509) 843-1891
State map: G8

From POMEROY, head S on WA 128 for 10 miles (16 k). At fork, bear Right on CR/FR 40 for 7 miles (11.2 k). (Also see Teal.)
FREE but choose a chore.
Open May 15–Nov 15.
6 tent sites. Pit toilets, tables, fire rings.
At spring near Wenaha-Tucannon Wilderness.
Hike, pick berries, relax.
NO water. 14-day limit.
5100 ft (1530 m)

## ALDRICH LAKE

WA DNR (206) 753-2400
State map: E2

From TAHUYA, drive N on Belfair–Tahuya Rd for 4.1 miles (6.6 k). Turn Left (W) on Dewatto Rd and go 2.1 miles (3.4 k). Turn Left (S) on Robbins Lake Rd and drive .6 mile (1 k). Bear Right (left will go to Robbins Lake) and continue .7 mile (1.1 k). Make a final Right and go .1 mile (160 m).
FREE but choose a chore.
Open All Year.
4 close, open sites. Water, pit toilets, tables, grills, boat launch.
Quiet fishing and canoeing spot on lake.
14-day limit.

## ALPINE MEADOWS

Wenatchee NF (509) 763-3103
State map: D5

From COLES CORNER, take WA 207 N for 5 miles (8 k). Bear Right at state park toward Midway. Turn Left on FR 6100 toward Fish Lake and go 4 miles (6.4 k). At intersection with FR 6200 (Chiwawa River) turn Left (NW). Go 20 miles (32 k). (See Atkinson Flats, Finner, Nineteen Mile, Phelps Creek, Rock Creek, or Schaefer Creek.)
FREE but choose a chore.
Open May 1–Nov 1.
4 close, open sites.
Pit toilets, tables, fire rings.
With access to Chiwawa River.
Hike, fish, or picnic.
NO water/trash facilities. 14-day limit.
2700 ft (810 m)

▲ ▲ ▲ ▲ ▲ ▲ ▲ ▲ ▲ ▲ ▲ ▲ ▲     ▲ ▲ ▲ ▲ ▲ ▲ ▲ ▲ ▲ ▲ ▲

## ATKINSON FLATS

Wenatchee NF (509) 763-3103
State map: D5
From COLES CORNER, take
WA 207 N for 5 miles (8 k). Bear Right
at state park toward Midway. Turn Left
on FR 6100 toward Fish Lake and go
4 miles (6.4 k). At intersection with
FR 6200 (Chiwawa River) turn Left (NW)
and go 15 miles (24 k). (Also see Alpine
Meadows, Finner, Nineteen Mile, Phelps
Creek, Rock Creek, and Schaefer Creek.)
**FREE** but choose a chore.
Open May 1–Nov 1.
6 close, open sites.
Pit toilets, tables, fire rings.
Along Chiwawa River.
Hike, fish, or relax.
NO water/trash facilities. 14-day limit.
2550 ft (765 m)

## BALLARD

Okanogan NF (509) 996-2266
State map: B5
From MAZAMA, cross
Methow River to CR 1163. Turn Left
(NW) and go 7 miles (11.2 k) to gravel
FR 5400. Continue NW for 2 miles
(3.2 k). (Also see River Bend.)
**FREE** but choose a chore.
Open Jul 1–Sep 30; camping allowed
off-season.
6 (5 tent-only) close, open sites. &
Pit toilets, tables, fire rings.
Near river with access to Robinson
Creek, West Fork Meadow, and Lost
River/Monument trails. Hike!
NO water/trash facilities. 14-day limit.
2521 ft (756 m)

## BATTLE GROUND LAKE SP
## WALK-IN

(206) 687-4621
State map: H3
Follow signs from BATTLE
GROUND. Park is about 2.5 miles (4 k)
NE of town.
**$4** walk-in, **$5** horse, **$8** developed, **$10**
group, **$12** group building.
Open All Year.
50 (15 walk-in) close, screened sites.
Water, flush and pit toilets, showers,

tables, grills, fire rings, pay phone, dump
station, boat ramp, beach.
With wooded walk-in sites 100 yards
(91 m) to .25 mile (400 m) from parking.
Also, horse camp on far side of park
plus large group camp. Around lake
formed by collapsed caldera.
Swim, boat, and fish. Also, study nature,
hike, and ride horses.
10-day limit in summer. Crowded weekends. No amplified sound (including
radio). No fires in dry seasons.
Mosquitos.
50 ft (15 m)

## BEAR CREEK

WA DNR (206) 753-2400
State map: C1
Find just South of SAPPHO
at milepost 206 of US 101–S of road.
**FREE** but choose a chore.
Open All Year.
10 close, open sites.
Water, pit toilets, tables, grills.
On banks of Soleduck River.
Relax and fish. Make base to explore
part of Olympic Peninsula.
14-day limit.

## BEAVER LAKE

Okanogan NF (509) 486-2186
State map: B7
From WAUCONDA, go W
on WA 20 for 3 miles (4.8 k). Turn Right
(N) on CR 4953 and drive 5 miles (8 k).
Bear Right on FR 32 and continue about
6 miles (9.6 k). Turn Left (NW) on
CR 9480. (Also see adjacent Beth Lake
and Lost Lake.)
**$5**. Open May 15–Sep 30; dry camping
off-season.
12 close, open sites. Water, pit toilets,
tables, fire rings, boat ramp.
On shores of lake.
Swim, boat, fish, and hike.
14-day/22-ft limits.
3000 ft (900 m)

## BEDAL

Mt Baker-Snoqualmie NF
(206) 436-1155
State map: C4

From GRANITE FALLS, head NE on CR FH7 (Mountain Loop) for 30 miles (48 k). Go NE on FR 20 for 6.5 miles (10.4 k). For alternative, continue upriver on FR 49 to trailhead camp **Sloan Creek.**
FREE but choose a chore.
Open May–Sep.
19 close, open sites.
Pit toilets, tables, fire rings.
Next to Sauk River in old growth forest. Enjoy river sounds. Relax or mountain bike, hike, and fish.
NO water/trash arrangements (pack it out). 14-day/22-ft limits.
1250 ft (375 m)

### BETH LAKE

Okanogan NF (509) 486-2186
State map: B7
From WAUCONDA, go W on WA 20 for 3 miles (4.8 k). Turn Right (N) on CR 4953 and drive 5 miles (8 k). Bear Right on FR 32 and continue about 6 miles (9.6 k). Turn Left (NW) on CR 9480 for 1 mile (1.6 k). (Also see adjacent Beaver Lake and Lost Lake.)
$5. Open May 15–Sep 30; dry camping off-season.
15 close, open sites. Water, pit toilets, tables, fire rings, boat ramp.
On shores of lake.
Swim, boat, fish, or hike.
14-day/22-ft limits.
2900 ft (870 m)

### BEVERLY

Wenatchee NF (509) 674-4411
State map: E5
From CLE ELUM, head E on WA 970 for 8 miles (12.8 k). Turn Left (N) on CR 107 and drive 13 miles (20.8 k). Continue N on FR 9737 for 4 miles (6.4 k). For primitive trailhead camps, continue N 4 miles (6.4 k) to **De Roux** or another mile to **Esmeralda.**
FREE but choose a chore.
Open May 25–Sep 30.
16 (13 tent-only) close, open sites.
Pit toilets, tables, grills.
On North Fork of Teanaway River.
Hike to nearby wilderness. Fish at camp.
NO water. 14-day/22-ft limits. Crowded.

Motorcycles.
3200 ft (960 m)

### BIG MEADOWS LAKE

Colville NF (509) 684-4557
State map: B8
From IONE, go W on CR 2714 for 8 miles (12.8 k). Turn on CR 2695 (Meadow Creek) and go 1 mile (1.6 k).
FREE but choose a chore.
Open Apr 15–Sep 15.
15 close, open sites.
Pit toilets, tables, fire rings.
On lake.
Fish and picnic. Walk nature trail.
NO water. 14-day limit.
5400 ft (1620 m)

### BIRD CREEK

WA DNR (206) 753-2400
State map: G4
From GLENWOOD post office, go W .3 mile (480 m). Turn Right (N) on Bird Creek Rd for .9 mile (1.4 k). Turn Left, then Right on dirt road and continue .9 mile (1.4 k). Bear Left on K-3000 and go .3 mile (480 m). Cross gravel road then stay Right for 2 miles (3.2 k). (Also see Island Camp.)
FREE but choose a chore.
Open All Year.
8 close, open sites.
Pit toilets, tables, grills.
In secluded forest setting on stream.
Enjoy getaway with hiking in area.
NO water. 14-day limit.

### BLACK PINE LAKE

Okanogan NF (509) 997-2131
State map: C5
From TWISP, take FR 44 (Twisp River Rd) NW for 11 miles (17.6 k) to Buttermilk Creek. Turn Left across bridge. Go SE on FR 43 for 8 miles (12.8 k)–last 4 miles are gravel.
$5. Open Memorial Day–first freeze; dry camping off-season.
23 (3 tent-only) close, screened sites.
Water, pit toilets, tables, fire rings, boat ramp.
In mountainous area beneath mixed

conifers near lake.
Swim (cool), boat (no gas motors), and
fish. Explore pretty area.
14-day limit. Crowded holidays. Yellow
jackets and mosquitos.
4200 ft (1260 m)

## BLUE LAKE CREEK

Gifford Pinchot NF
(206) 497-7565
State map: G4

From RANDLE, head SE on FR 23 for
10 miles (16 k) to **North Fork** (33 sites).
Turn Right on FR 21 and go 4 miles
(6.4 k). (Also see Adams Fork.)
$3. Open May 15–Oct 30.
12 sites. Water, pit toilets, tables grills,
fire rings.
On creek near Cispus River.
Swim or fish. Hike to Blue Lakes.
14-day/24-ft limits.
1900 ft (570 m)

## BOARDMAN CREEK

Mt Baker-Snoqualmie NF
(206) 436-1155
State map: C4

From GRANITE FALLS, head NE on
CR FH7 (Mountain Loop) for 16.5 miles
(26.4 k). (Also see Red Bridge.)
FREE but choose a chore.
Open May–Sep.
10 (8 tent-only) close, open sites.
Pit toilets, tables, fire rings.
In low, riverside vegetation of alder and
vine maple. Close to road, but secluded.
Enjoy pleasant spot with easy access to
many backroads. Relax. Do a little
exploring, hiking, and fishing.
NO water/trash arrangements (pack it
out). 14-day/22-ft limits.
1350 ft (405 m)

## BONANZA

Wenatchee NF (509) 782-1413
State map: E5
From LEAVENWORTH,
head S on US 97 for 20 miles (32 k).
FREE but choose a chore.
Open May 25–Sep 30.
5 close, open sites.
Water, pit toilets, tables, fire rings.

On creek.
Hike, picnic, and relax.
No trash arrangements (pack it out).
14-day/16-ft limits.
3000 ft (900 m)

## BOULDER CREEK

Mt Baker-Snoqualmie NF
(206) 856-5700
State map: B4

From CONCRETE, head N on CR 25 for
9.5 miles (15.2 k). Continue N on CR 11
for 5.5 miles (8.8 k). (Also see Park Creek
and Shannon Creek.)
FREE but choose a chore.
Open May–Sep.
10 scattered, screened sites.
Pit toilets, tables, fire rings.
On banks of creek (but close to road)
with nice views of Mt Baker.
Pick berries in summer. Enjoy water
activities at nearby Baker Lake.
NO water/trash arrangements (pack it
out). 10-day/16-ft limits.
800 ft (240 m)

## BRADBURY BEACH

Coulee Dam NRA
(509) 633-9441
State map: B7

From KETTLE FALLS, take US 395 W
then immediately turn S on WA 25 and
drive 7 miles (11.2 k).
FREE but choose a chore.
Open All Year.
5 close, open tent sites. Water, pit toilets,
tables, fire rings, boat ramp.
On Roosevelt Lake.
Fishing and boating.
14-day limit.
1280 ft (384 m)

## BUCK LAKE

Okanogan NF (509) 996-2266
State map: C5
From WINTHROP, take
CR 1213 N for almost 7 miles (11.2 k) to
FR 51. Continue N for 2.8 miles (4.5 k) to
FR 5130. Bear Left (NW) and go .6 mile
(1 k). Turn on FR 100 and go 2.2 miles
(3.5 k). (Also see Flat, Honeymoon, Nice,
and Ruffled Grouse.)

▲ ▲ ▲ ▲ ▲ ▲ ▲ ▲ ▲ ▲ ▲ ▲ ▲ ▲ ▲ ▲ ▲ ▲ ▲ ▲ ▲ ▲ ▲ ▲ ▲ ▲ ▲ ▲

**FREE** but choose a chore.
Open May 15–Oct 15; camping allowed off-season.
9 close, open sites.
Pit toilets, tables, fire rings.
On shores of stocked lake.
Fish in early part of year. Boat (small allowed). Mountain bike. Explore.
NO water/trash arrangements (pack it out). 14-day limit.
3200 ft (960 m)

## BUCK MEADOWS

Wenatchee NF (509) 674-4411
State map: E5
From SW side of ELLENSBURG, head W on CR/FR 31 (along Manastash Creek) for 24 miles (38.4 k). (Also see Quartz Mountain or Tamarack Spring.)
**FREE** but choose a chore.
Open May 25–Sep 30.
5 close, open sites.
Pit toilets, tables, fire rings.
Along creek.
Hike to Keenan Meadows. Fish.
NO water. 14-day/22-ft limits.

## BUMPING CROSSING

Wenatchee NF (509) 653-2205
State map: F4
From NACHES, take US 12 W for 4 miles (6.4 k). Go NW on WA 410 for 28.5 miles (45.6 k). Turn Left on FR 18 and go 10 miles (16 k)–near GOOSE PRAIRIE. Also on FR 18, find six other choices. All charge fees–**Bumping Dam, Bumping Lake, Cedar Springs, Cougar Flat, Indian Flat,** and **Soda Springs.** For trailhead camp with great wilderness access, go S on FR 18 another 10 miles (16 k) to end and **Deep Creek.**
**FREE** but choose a chore.
Open May 25–Nov 15.
12 close, open sites.
Pit toilets, tables, fire rings.
On Bumping River.
Take hiking trails into Douglas Wilderness. Fish, picnic, and relax.
NO water/trash arrangements (pack it out). 14-day/16-ft limits.
3200 ft (960 m)

## CAMP 4

Okanogan NF (509) 996-2266
State map: C5
From WINTHROP, take CR 1213 N for almost 7 miles (11.2 k) to FR 51. Continue N another 11 miles (17.6 k). (Also see Chewuch and Falls Creek.)
**FREE** but choose a chore.
Open May 15–Oct 30; camping allowed off-season.
5 close, open sites.
Pit toilets, tables, fire rings.
Off paved road on Chewuch River.
Fish river. Hike and drive scenic area.
NO water/trash arrangements (pack it out). 14-day limit.
2384 ft (714 m)

## CAMP SPILLMAN

WA DNR (206) 753-2400
State map: E3
Take WA 300 SE out of BELFAIR for 3.5 miles (5.6 k). Turn Right on Belfair–Tahuya Rd and go .6 mile (1 k). Turn Right on Elfendahl Pass Rd and go 2.6 miles (4.2 k). Turn Left on Twin Lakes Rd and go .7 mile (1.1 k). (Also see Howell Lake, Twin Lakes, and Toonerville.)
**FREE** but choose a chore.
Open All Year.
6 close, open sites.
Water, pit toilets, tables, fire rings.
In forest along river.
Make base for hiking and exploring Tahuya State Forest.
14-day limit.

## CAMPBELL TREE GROVE

Olympic NF (206) 753-9534
State map: E2
From HUMPTULIPS, head NE beginning on US 101. Watch for FR 2200 on Right (West Fork of Humptulips) and follow signs for 23 miles (36.8 k). About halfway, turn Right then Left on FR 2204.
**FREE** but choose a chore.
Open May 15–Dec 1.
14 (8 tent-only) sites.
Water, pit toilets, tables, fire rings.

▲ ▲ ▲ ▲ ▲ ▲ ▲ ▲ ▲ ▲ ▲ ▲ ▲ ▲ ▲ ▲ ▲ ▲ ▲ ▲ ▲ ▲ ▲ ▲ ▲ ▲

On river near Colonel Bob Wilderness.
Enjoy surroundings. Make base for great
hiking. Pick berries in season.
14-day/16-ft limits.
1100 ft (330 m)

## CANYON CREEK

Colville NF (509) 738-6111
State map: B7
From KETTLE FALLS, take
US 395 NW for 3.5 miles (5.6 k). Turn W
on WA 20. Drive 11 miles (17.6 k). Turn
Left (S) on FR 136. Go .25 mile (400 m).
FREE but choose a chore.
Open May 25–Oct 30.
12 close, open sites.
Water, pit toilets, tables, fire rings.
On stream.
Explore interpretive center and nature
trail. Drive Bangs Mountain Auto Tour.
14-day limit.
2200 ft (660 m)

## CASCADE ISLANDS

WA DNR (206) 753-2400
State map: B4
In MARBLEMOUNT, take
Old Cascade Rd E for .7 mile (1.1 k).
Turn Right on Rockport Cascade Rd for
only .1 mile (160 m) then Left on South
Cascade Rd and continue 1.2 miles
(1.9 k). (Also see Marble Creek.)
FREE but choose a chore.
Open All Year.
15 close, open sites.
Water, pit toilets, tables, grills.
In woods along river.
Fish and picnic.
14-day limit.

## CAT CREEK

Gifford Pinchot NF
(206) 497-7565
State map: G4
From RANDLE, head SE on FR 23 for
10 miles (16 k) to North Fork (33 sites).
Turn Right on FR 21 and go 11.5 miles
(18.4 k). (Also see Adams Fork.)
FREE but choose a chore.
Open May 15–Sep 30.
6 sites. Pit toilets, tables, fire rings.
At confluence of creek and Cispus River

near Mt Adams Wilderness.
Swim or fish. Trek into wilderness.
NO water. 14-day/16-ft limits.
3000 ft (900 m)

## CHAIN OF LAKES

Gifford Pinchot NF
(206) 497-7565
State map: G4
From RANDLE, head SE on FR 23 for
10 miles (16 k) to North Fork (33 sites).
Turn Right on FR 21 and go 10 miles
(16 k). Turn Right on FR 6401 and drive
5.5 miles (8.8 k). Turn Left on
FR 022/2329 and continue 2 miles (3.2 k)
bearing Left at fork. Bearing Right leads
to Takhlakh Lake (54 sites; fee charged).
(Also see Olallie Lake.)
FREE but choose a chore.
Open Jun 15–Oct 30.
3 sites. Pit toilets, tables, fire rings.
On remote lake.
Fish. Hike to Horseshoe Lake. Trek into
Mt Adams Wilderness.
14-day/22-ft limits.
4300 ft (1290 m)

## CHEWELAH CITY PARK

State map: C8
Find just .25 mile (400 m) N
of CHEWELAH on US 395.
FREE but choose a chore.
Open All Year.
50 (25 tent-only) sites.
Water, flush toilets, tables, electric hook-
ups, playground.
On creek.
Swim, use bike paths, play tennis or golf.
3-day limit.

## CHEWUCH

Okanogan NF (509) 996-2266
State map: C5
From WINTHROP, take
CR 1213 N almost 7 miles (11.2 k) to
FR 51. Continue N for 8 miles (12.8 k).
(Also see Camp 4 and Falls Creek.)
FREE but choose a chore.
Open May 15–Oct 30; camping allowed
off-season.
4 close, open sites.
Pit toilets, tables, fire rings.

▲ ▲ ▲ ▲ ▲ ▲ ▲ ▲ ▲ ▲ ▲ ▲ ▲ ▲ ▲ ▲ ▲ ▲ ▲ ▲ ▲ ▲ ▲ ▲

In remote locale along Chewuch River. Fish. Bike, hike, and drive scenic area. NO water/trash arrangements (pack it out). 14-day/16-ft limits.
2278 ft (681 m)

## CHOPAKA LAKE

WA DNR (206) 753-2400
State map: B6
From LOOMIS, go N for 2.1 miles (3.4 k). Turn Right (E) onto steep 1-lane road. Go 3.4 miles (5.4 k). Bear Left and continue 1.7 miles (2.7 k). Turn Right and go 2 miles (3.2 k).
FREE but choose a chore.
Open All Year.
15 close, open sites.
Water, pit toilets, tables, boat launch.
Fish and boat on lake. View wildlife.
14-day limit.

## CLEAR CREEK

Mt Baker-Snoqualmie NF (206) 436-1155
State map: C4
From DARRINGTON, go S on CR FH7 (Mountain Loop) about 3 miles (4.8 k).
FREE but choose a chore.
Open May–Sep.
10 close, open sites.
Pit toilets, tables, fire rings.
On banks of Sauk River beneath old fir. At uncrowded spot for mountain biking, hiking, and fishing. Walk Frog Lake Nature Trail too.
NO water/trash arrangements (pack it out). 14-day limit.
600 ft (180 m)

## CLEAR LAKE SOUTH

Wenatchee NF (509) 653-2205
State map: F4
From NACHES, take US 12 W for 35.5 miles (56.8 k) past Rimrock Lake. Turn Left on FR 12 and go about 2 miles (3.2 k) to south side of lake. Go toward north side of Rimrock Lake for **Indian Creek** (fee charged).
FREE but choose a chore.
Open Apr 15–Nov 15.
23 close, open sites.
Pit toilets, tables, fire rings, boat ramp.

At lake with two locations–one with fee, one without.
Boating and fishing.
NO water. 14-day/22-ft limits.
3100 ft (930 m)

## CLOVER FLATS

WA DNR (206) 753-2400
State map: F4
From TAMPICO, take A-2000 (Middle Fork Rd) W for 18.7 miles (29.9 k)–last 6 miles are very steep–not recommended for large vehicles or trailers. (Also see Ahtanum, Snow Cabin, and Tree Phones.)
FREE but choose a chore.
Open All Year.
11 close, open sites.
Water, pit toilets, tables, grills.
At end-of-road in subalpine setting. Enjoy hiking to Eagle Nest Vista .3 mile (480 m) away and Goat Rock Wilderness a few miles W.
14-day limit.

## CLOVERLEAF

Coulee Dam NRA (509) 633-9441
State map: C7
From HUNTERS, go N on WA 25 for 15 miles (24 k).
FREE but choose a chore.
Open All Year.
7 close, open sites. Water, pit toilets, tables, fire rings, boat dock.
On Roosevelt Lake.
Swimming, fishing, and boating.
14-day limit.
1265 ft (378 m)

## COLD CREEK

WA DNR (206) 753-2400
State map: H3
From MEADOWGLADE, go E to WA 503 and drive S for 1.5 miles (2.4 k). Turn Left on NE 159th St and go 3 miles (4.8 k). Turn Right (S) on 182nd Ave and go 1 mile (1.6 k). Turn Left (E) on NE 139th (L-1400). Drive 8 miles (12.8 k). Turn Left on L-1000 and go 3.2 miles (5.1 k). Left again and go .8 mile (1.3 k). (See Rock Creek-Yacolt.)

▲ ▲ ▲ ▲ ▲ ▲ ▲ ▲ ▲ ▲ ▲ ▲ ▲ ▲ ▲ ▲ ▲ ▲ ▲ ▲ ▲ ▲ ▲ ▲

**FREE** but choose a chore.
Open All Year.
6 close, open sites. Water, pit toilets, tables, grills, group shelter.
Along stream in wooded locale.
Try good hiking and equestrian trails.
Enjoy quiet, pleasant setting.
14-day limit.

## COLD SPRINGS

WA DNR (206) 753-2400
State map: B6
From LOOMIS (grocery), go N for 2.1 miles (3.4 k). Turn Left (W) onto Toats Coulee Rd and drive 5.5 miles (8.8 k) to Toats Coulee Camp. Take OM-T-1000 for 2.1 miles (3.4 k). Turn Right on Cold Creek Rd. Drive .4 mile (600 m). Bear Right and go 1.8 miles (2.9 k); bear Left and go 2.7 miles (4.3 k). Pass picnic area.
**FREE** but choose a chore.
Open All Year.
9 scattered, open sites. Water, pit toilets, tables, grills, horse stalls.
In forest beside stream.
Take hiking/riding trails from camp.
Enjoy good wildlife viewing in region.
14-day limit.

## COLD SPRINGS INDIAN CAMP

Gifford Pinchot NF
(509) 395-2501
State map: G4
From TROUT LAKE, head W on WA 141 for 4 miles (6.4 k) to Ice Cave. Continue W on FR 24 for 15 miles (24 k). Pass fee-charged **Cultus Creek** (51 sites) and free **Meadow Creek Indian Camp**. Turn Right (NW) and go .5 mile (800 m). (Also see Little Goose and Surprise Lakes.)
**FREE** but choose a chore.
Open Jun 1–Sep 30.
8 sites. Pit toilets, tables, fire rings.
Near Indian Heaven Wilderness.
Enjoy seclusion. Hike.
NO water. 14-day/16-ft limits.
4000 ft (1200 m)

## COPPERMINE BOTTOM

WA DNR (206) 753-2400
State map: D1
From milepost 147 of US 101, drive N on Hoh–Clearwater Mainline for 12.6 miles (20.2 k)–through town of CLEARWATER. Turn Right on gravel C-1010 and drive 1.5 miles (2.4 k). (Also see Upper Clearwater and Yahoo Lake.)
**FREE** but choose a chore.
Open All Year.
9 close, open sites.
Pit toilets, tables, grills, boat launch.
In secluded spot on Clearwater River.
Float and canoe. Fish river.
NO water. 14-day limit.

## CORRAL PASS

Mt Baker-Snoqualmie NF
(206) 825-6585
State map: E4
From ENUMCLAW, take US 410 SE for 31 miles (49.6 k). Turn Left (E) on FR 7174 and drive 6 miles (9.6 k).
**FREE** but choose a chore.
Open Jun–Sep.
20 tent sites. Pit toilets, tables, fire rings.
In high, rustic setting next to Norse Peak Wilderness.
Hike to Hidden and Echo lakes. Pick berries in late summer.
NO water/trash arrangements. 14-day limit. No trailers (steep road).
5600 ft (1680 m)

## COTTONWOOD

WA DNR (206) 753-2400
State map: D1
About 15 miles (24 k) South of FORKS between mileposts 177-178 of US 101, go W on Oil City Rd for 2.3 miles (3.7 k). Turn Left on gravel H-4060 and go .9 mile (1.4 k).
**FREE** but choose a chore.
Open All Year.
6 close, open sites. Water, pit toilets, tables, grills, boat launch.
On Hoh River.
Float or canoe. Fish overlooked spot.
14-day limit.

## COTTONWOOD

Okanogan NF (509) 486-2186
State map: B6
From CONCONULLY, go 2.1 miles (3.4 k) NW on FR 38 (road begins as CR 2361). (Also see Kerr and Oriole.)
**$5.** Open May 15–Sep 30; camping allowed off-season.
4 close, open sites. Spring water, pit toilets, tables, fire rings.
Along Salmon Creek.
Fish creek. Picnic and relax.
14-day/22-ft limits.
2700 ft (810 m)

## COUNCIL LAKE

Gifford Pinchot NF
(206) 497-7565
State map: G4
From RANDLE, head SE on FR 23 for 10 miles (16 k) to **North Fork** (33 sites). Turn Right on FR 21 and drive 10 miles (16 k). Turn Right on FR 6401 and go 8 miles (9.6 k). Bear Right on FR 2334 for 1.5 miles (2.4 k). (Also see Chain of Lakes, Olallie, and Twin Falls.)
**FREE** but choose a chore.
Open Jun 15–Oct 30.
11 sites. Pit toilets, tables, fire rings.
On alpine lake with views of Mt Adams. Boat (no motors) and fish. Hike along Council Bluff. Trek into wilderness.
14-day/22-ft limits.
3700 ft (1110 m)

## CRAWFISH

Okanogan NF (509) 486-2186
State map: B6
From RIVERSIDE, go E on CR 9320 for 17.7 miles (28.3 k). Turn Right on FR 30 for 1.5 miles (2.4 k).
**FREE** but choose a chore.
Open May 15–Sep 30; camping allowed off-season.
19 close, open sites.
Pit toilets, tables, fire rings, boat ramp.
On shores of lake.
Enjoy swimming, boating, and fishing–catch a mess of crawfish.
NO water (water from Balanced Rock Spring not tested) or trash facilities.

14-day limit.
4500 ft (1350 m)

## CROW CREEK

Wenatchee NF (509) 653-2205
State map: F4
From NACHES, take US 12 W for 4 miles (6.4 k). Go NW on WA 410 for 24.5 miles (39.2 k). Continue straight (NW) on FR 1900 for 10.5 miles (16.8 k). Turn Left on FR 1902 and go .5 mile (800 m). On 1900, check out **Kaner Flat** (fee charged).
**FREE** but choose a chore.
Open Apr 15–Nov 15.
15 close, open sites.
Pit toilets, tables, fire rings.
On creek near Little Naches River.
Hike good trails in area. Fish, picnic, and relax at camp.
NO water/trash arrangements. 14-day limit. Crowded. Motorcycles.
2900 ft (870 m)

## DAVIS LAKE

Colville NF (509) 738-6111
State map: B7
From BOYDS, take US 395 S for .5 mile (800 m). Turn Right (W) on CR 460 and drive 3 miles (4.8 k). Turn Right (N) on CR 465 and twist 4 miles (6.4 k). Turn Left on CR 480/FR 80 and go W then N for 5 miles (8 k).
**FREE** but choose a chore.
Open May 25–Sep 30.
4 close, open sites. Pit toilets, tables, fire rings, boat launch.
In secluded lakeside location.
Picnic and do nothing. Canoe and fish.
NO water/trash arrangements (pack it out). 14-day limit.
3900 ft (1170 m)

## DEEP CREEK

Wenatchee NF (509) 763-3103
State map: D5
From COLES CORNER, take WA 207 N for 5 miles (8 k). Bear Right at state park toward Midway. Turn Left on FR 6100 toward Fish Lake and go 4 miles (6.4 k). At intersection with FR 6200 turn Right (SE) and go about

2 miles (3.2 k). For more developed (fee charged) option, check out **Goose Creek**. (Also see Deer Camp below.)
FREE but choose a chore.
Open May 1–Nov 1.
3 close, open sites.
Pit toilets, tables, fire rings.
Hike, fish, and picnic along creek.
NO water/trash arrangements (pack it out). 14-day limit.
2400 ft (720 m)

## DEER CAMP

Wenatchee NF (509) 763-3103
State map: D5
From COLES CORNER, take WA 207 N for 5 miles (8 k). Bear Right at state park toward Midway. Turn Left on FR 6100 toward Fish Lake and go 4 miles (6.4 k). At intersection with FR 6200 turn Right (SE) and go about 2 miles (3.2 k). Turn Left on FR 2722 and go 2 miles (3.2 k). (Also see Deep Creek above.)
FREE but choose a chore.
Open May 1–Nov 1.
3 close, open sites.
Pit toilets, tables, fire rings.
In quiet, isolated spot.
Hike, fish, and picnic.
NO water/trash arrangements (pack it out). 14-day limit.
3000 ft (900 m)

## DOG LAKE

Wenatchee NF (509) 653-2205
State map: F4
From PACKWOOD, take US 12 E for 22 miles (35.2 k). (Also see White Pass Lake.)
FREE but choose a chore.
Open May 25–Nov 15.
11 close, open sites.
Pit toilets, tables, fire rings, boat ramp.
Canoe and fish on lake. Take hiking trails into Douglas Wilderness.
NO water/trash arrangements (pack it out). 14-day/20-ft limits. No horses.
3400 ft (1020 m)

## DOUGAN CREEK

WA DNR (206) 753-2400
State map: H3
From WASHOUGAL, take WA 14 E for 9.5 miles (15.2 k). Turn Left (N) on WA 140 and go about 5 miles (8 k). Turn Right on Washougal River Rd and drive 7 miles (11.2 k).
FREE but choose a chore.
Open All Year.
7 close, open sites.
Water, pit toilets, tables, grills.
In secluded wooded setting at confluence of creek and river.
Picnic, relax, and, maybe, fish.
14-day limit.

## DOUGLAS FALLS

WA DNR (206) 753-2400
State map: B8
On E side of COLVILLE on WA 20, turn N on Aladdin Rd. Go 1.9 miles (3 k) and then continue N another 5 miles (8 k).
FREE but choose a chore.
Open All Year.
10 close, open sites. Water, pit toilets, tables, fire rings, baseball field.
On Mill Creek with short walk to falls.
Relax, do a little walking, and picnic.
14-day limit.

## DRAGOON CREEK

WA DNR (206) 753-2400
State map: D8
Starting at US 2/395 intersection in SPOKANE, head N on US 395 for exactly 10.2 miles (16.3 k). Turn Left (W) on Dragoon Creek Rd. Go .4 mile (640 m).
FREE but choose a chore.
Open All Year.
22 close, open sites.
Water, pit toilets, tables, grills.
In forest on creekbank.
Enjoy pleasant spot for relaxing.
14-day limit.

## EARLY WINTERS

Okanogan NF (509) 996-2266
State map: B5
Locate in town of MAZAMA

on WA 20. (Also see Klipchuck.)
$5. Open May 15–Oct 15; dry camping
off-season.
13 (7 tent-only) close, screened sites. &
Water, pit toilets, tables, fire rings.
On banks of Early Winters Creek with
great views of Goat Wall.
Stop at Visitor Center to locate hiking
trails and fishing spots.
14-day/16-ft limits.
2160 ft (648 m)

## EDGEWATER

Colville NF (509) 446-7500
State map: B8
From IONE, take WA 31 S
for 1 mile (1.6 k). Turn Left (E) on
CR 9345 and go just .3 mile (500 m) then
Left (N) on CR 3669 and drive 2 miles
(3.2 k). Turn Left (W) on FR 33101 and
go 1.75 miles (2.8 k).
FREE but choose a chore.
Open Apr 25–Sep 5.
23 close, open sites. Water, pit toilets,
tables, grills, boat ramp.
Along Pend Oreille River.
Fish, boat, or waterski. Enjoy easy-to-
reach but pastoral getaway.
14-day/22-ft limits.
2200 ft (660 m)

## ELBE HILLS

WA DNR (206) 753-2400
State map: F3
From ASHFORD, drive E on
WA 706 for 1.2 miles (1.9 k). Turn Right
(N) and go 3.1 miles (5 k). Bear Right for
another .6 mile (1 k). Turn Left and
continue .1 mile (160 m).
FREE but choose a chore.
Open All Year.
3 close, open sites. Pit toilets, tables, fire
rings, group shelter.
In forest at trailhead. Hike!
14-day limit. Noisy. 4X4s.

## ELWELL

WA DNR (206) 753-2400
State map: D4
From Stillwater (S of
MONROE on WA 203), take Kelley Rd N
for 3.2 miles (5.1 k). Turn Right on

Stossel Creek Rd. Drive 4.7 miles (7.5 k).
Bear Left and continue 1.4 miles (2.2 k).
FREE but choose a chore.
Open All-year.
18 close, open sites.
Water, pit toilets, tables, fire rings.
Along stream.
Enjoy nice, little-known getaway.
14-day limit.

## FALL CREEK

WA DNR (206) 753-2400
State map: F3
From OLYMPIA, go W on
US 101 for 4 miles (6.4 k) to Mud Bay
Exit. Drive S on Delphi Rd for 5.8 miles
(9.3 k). Go straight on Waddell Creek Rd
for 3 miles (4.8 k). Turn Right and go
1.4 miles (2.2 k) to fork. Take Left
(C-Line) for 1.9 miles (3 k). Turn Left on
C-4000 and go 2.5 miles (4 k). Turn Right
and go .2 mile (400 m). (Also see Mt
Molly and Sherman Valley.)
FREE but choose a chore.
Open All Year.
8 close, open sites. Water, pit toilets,
tables, grills, horse loading ramp.
In forest setting on streambank.
Try good hiking and equestrian trails.
14-day limit.

## FALLS CREEK

Okanogan NF (509) 996-2266
State map: C5
From WINTHROP, take
CR 1213 N for almost 7 miles (11.2 k) to
FR 51. Continue N another 4 miles
(6.4 k). (Also see Camp 4 and Chewuch.)
FREE but choose a chore.
Open May 15–Oct 30; camping allowed
off-season.
7 close, open sites. &
Pit toilets, tables, fire rings.
At confluence of Falls Creek and
Chewuch River.
Take short walk up creek to falls. Swim
and fish. Relax and picnic.
NO water/trash arrangements (pack it
out). 14-day limit.
2300 ft (690 m)

## FINNER

Wenatchee NF (509) 763-3103
State map: D5
From COLES CORNER, take
WA 207 N for 5 miles (8 k). Bear Right
at state park toward Midway. Turn Left
on FR 6100 toward Fish Lake and go
4 miles (6.4 k). At intersection with
FR 6200 (Chiwawa River) turn Left (NW)
and go 11 miles (17.6 k). (Also see
Atkinson Flats, Alpine Meadows, Finner,
Nineteen Mile, Phelps Creek, Rock
Creek, and Schaefer Creek.)
FREE but choose a chore.
Open May 1–Nov 1.
3 close, open sites.
Water, pit toilets, tables, fire rings.
Along Chiwawa River next to Rock
Creek Guard Station (only camp with
piped water).
Hike, fish, and picnic.
No trash arrangements. 14-day limit.
2500 ft (750 m)

## FISH LAKE

Wenatchee NF (509) 674-4411
State map: E4
From CLE ELUM, head N on
WA 903 for 22 miles (35.2 k). Turn Right
(NE) on unpaved, rough FR 43301 and
drive 11 miles (17.6 k). (Also see Owhi.)
FREE but choose a chore.
Open Jul 1–Oct 1.
15 close, open sites.
Pit toilets, tables, grills.
In scenic spot next to Tucquala Lake.
Canoe, swim, or fish. Enjoy excellent
hiking trails in Alpine Lake Wilderness.
NO water. 14-day/16-ft limits.
3400 ft (1020 m)

## FISH POND

Wenatchee NF (509) 763-3103
State map: D5
From COLES CORNER, take
WA 207 N for 1.25 miles (2 k).
FREE but choose a chore.
Open May 1–Nov 1.
3 close, open sites.
Pit toilets, tables, fire rings.
On Nason Creek.
Hike, fish, and picnic.

NO water/trash arrangements (pack it
out). 14-day/16-ft limits.
1800 ft (540 m)

## FLAT

Okanogan NF (509) 996-2266
State map: C5
From WINTHROP, take
CR 1213 N almost 7 miles (11.2 k) to
FR 51. Continue N for 2.8 miles (4.5 k) to
FR 5130. Bear Left (NW) and go 2 miles
(3.2 k)–easiest to reach camp in area for
trailers. (See Buck Lake, Honeymoon,
Nice, and Ruffled Grouse).
FREE but choose a chore.
Open May 15–Oct 15; camping allowed
off-season.
12 (9 tent-only) close, open sites. ૬
Pit toilets, tables, fire rings.
Along Eightmile Creek.
Mountain bike. Walk and explore. Fish.
NO water/trash facilities. 14-day limit.
2858 ft (855 m)

## FLODELLE CREEK

WA DNR (206) 753-2400
State map: B8
From US 395/WA 20
intersection in COLVILLE, head E on
WA 20 for 19.5 miles (31.2 k). Turn Right
(S) on gravel road. Drive .3 mile (480 m).
Turn Left and go .1 mile (160 m).
FREE but choose a chore.
Open All Year.
8 close, open sites.
Water, pit toilets, tables, fire rings.
In woods along creek.
Relax or do a little walking. Drive up to
Timber Mountain Lookout.
14-day limit. Dirt bikes.

## FOGGY DEW

Okanogan NF (509) 997-2131
State map: C5
Take WA 153 S from
CARLTON for 4 miles (6.4 k) to Gold
Creek Rd. Turn Right (W) and drive
5 miles (8 k).
FREE but choose a chore.
Open May 1–Oct 30; camping allowed
off-season.
13 close, screened sites.

Pit toilets, tables, fire rings.
On creek bank under mixed conifer canopy in mountainous area.
Enjoy multiple mountain bike opportunities plus hiking trails. Fish.
NO water/trash arrangements. 14-day limit. Mosquitos and yellow jackets.
Hunting in season.
2400 ft (720 m)

## FOX CREEK

Wenatchee NF (509) 784-1511
State map: D5
From ENTIAT, take US 97 S about 1.5 miles (2.4 k). Turn Right (NW) on CR 371 and drive 25 miles (40 k). Continue NW on FR 51 for 2 miles (3.2 k). For alternatives, **Lake Creek**, is another mile or more developed **Silver Falls** is 3 miles (4.8 k).
$4. Open May 1–Nov 1.
16 close, open sites.
Water, pit toilets, tables, fire rings.
On Entiat River at Fox Creek.
Relax, hike, or fish.
14-day/16-ft limits.
2300 ft (690 m)

## GODMAN

Umatilla NF (509) 843-1891
State map: G8
From DAYTON, head SE on CR 118 for 14 miles (22.4 k). Turn Right on FR 46 and go 11 miles (17.6 k). (Also see Tucannon.)
FREE but choose a chore.
Open Jun 15–Oct 30.
7 tent sites. Pit toilets, tables, fire rings.
Next to Wenaha-Tucannon Wilderness.
Hike trail into wilderness. Explore.
NO water. 14-day limit.
5100 ft (1530 m)

## GOOSE LAKE

Gifford Pinchot NF
(509) 395-2501
State map: H4
From TROUT LAKE, head W on WA 141 for 4 miles (6.4 k) to Ice Cave. Continue W on FR 24 for 2.5 miles (4 k) to fee-charged **Peterson Prairie** (30 sites). Continue W on FR 60 for 5.5 miles

(8.8 k). For alternative, go N on FR 6040 for 3 miles (4.8 k) to **Forlorn Lakes**.
FREE but choose a chore.
Open Jun 15–Sep 30.
25 sites. Pit toilets, tables, fire rings.
Near cluster of small lakes at northern boundary of Big Lava Bed.
Enjoy seclusion. Hike or fish.
NO water. 14-day/16-ft limits.
3200 ft (960 m)

## GRASSHOPPER MEADOWS

Wenatchee NF (509) 763-3103
State map: D5
From COLES CORNER, take WA 207 N for 9 miles (8 k) to ranger station, curving Left around state park. Continue NW on FR 6400 (White River) for 10 miles (16 k). (Also see Napeequa and White River Falls.)
FREE but choose a chore.
Open May 1–Nov 1.
3 close, open sites.
Pit toilets, tables, fire rings.
Along White River.
Hike, fish, or picnic.
NO water/trash arrangements (pack it out). 14-day limit.
2050 ft (615 m)

## GREEN MOUNTAIN CAMP

WA DNR (206) 753-2400
State map: E3
On WA 3 S of SILVERDALE, take Newberry Hill Rd W for 3.1 miles (5 k). Turn Left (S) on Seabeck Hwy for 2 miles (3.2 k). Turn Right (W) on Holly Rd and go 4 miles (6.4 k). Turn Left on Tahuya Lake Rd and go .9 mile (1.4 k). Turn Left on gravel Green Mountain Rd. Go 3.6 miles (5.8 k)–bear Left at junction.
FREE but choose a chore.
Open All Year.
9 close, open sites.
Water, pit toilets, tables, grills.
In quiet forest.
Enjoy trails and nice spot for relaxing.
14-day limit.

▲ ▲ ▲ ▲ ▲ ▲ ▲ ▲ ▲ ▲ ▲ ▲ ▲ ▲ ▲ ▲ ▲ ▲ ▲ ▲ ▲ ▲ ▲ ▲

## GREEN RIVER GORGE

WA DNR (206) 753-2400
State map: E3
From ENUMCLAW, go N on
WA 169 for 4.5 miles (7.2 k).
FREE but choose a chore.
Open All Year.
9 close, open sites.
Water, pit toilets, tables, grills.
In forest near Green River.
Raft or kayak. Explore or do nothing.
14-day limit.

## HAAG COVE

Coulee Dam NRA
(509) 633-9441
State map: B7
From KETTLE FALLS, take US 395 NW
for 3.5 miles (5.6 k). Turn SW on WA 20
and drive 4 miles (6.4 k). Turn Left (S)
on paved CR 3. Go 3 miles (4.8 k). Turn
Left (E). (Also see Northeast Lake Ellen.)
FREE but choose a chore.
Open All Year.
16 close, open sites. Water, pit toilets,
tables, grills, boat dock.
On Roosevelt Lake below Sherman
Creek.
Fishing and boating plus good photo
taking of wildlife around creek.
14-day/26-ft limits.
1265 ft (378 m)

## HALFWAY FLAT

Wenatchee NF (509) 653-2205
State map: F4
From NACHES, take US 12
W for 4 miles (6.4 k). Go NW on WA 410
for 21 miles (33.6 k). Turn Left on
FR 1704 and go 3 miles (4.8 k). More
developed sites along 410 include
**Cottonwood, Little Naches,** and **Sawmill
Flat** (all charge fees).
FREE but choose a chore.
Open Apr 1–Nov 15.
12 close, open sites.
Pit toilets, tables, fire rings.
On Naches River.
Hike trails in area. Fish and relax.
NO water/trash arrangements. 14-day
limit. Crowded. Motorcycles.
2050 ft (615 m)

## HART'S PASS

Okanogan NF (509) 996-2266
State map: B5
From MAZAMA, cross
Methow River to CR 1163. Turn Left
(NW) and go 7 miles (11.2 k) to gravel
FR 5400. Continue NW for 12.5 miles
(20 k). (Also see Meadows.)
FREE but choose a chore.
Open Jul 1–Sep 30; camping allowed
off-season.
5 close, open tent sites.
Pit toilets, tables, fire rings.
In alpine meadow at Hart's Pass near
Pacific Crest Trail and others leading
into Pasayten Wilderness.
Make high base-camp for exploring
beautiful, mountainous region.
NO water/trash arrangements. 14-day
limit. No trailers on steep, narrow access
road. Watch out for trucks.
6198 ft (1857 m)

## HAWK CREEK

Coulee Dam NRA
(509) 633-9441
State map: D7
From CRESTON, take Miles–Creston Rd
N for 10 miles (16 k). Look for sign.
FREE but choose a chore.
Open All Year.
28 close, open sites. Water, pit toilets,
tables, grills, boat ramp.
On Hawk Creek where it empties into
Roosevelt Lake.
Enjoy good spot for fishing, canoeing,
and power boating.
14-day/16-ft limits.
1277 ft (381 m)

## HELLER'S BAR

BLM (503) 473-3144
State map: G9
From ASOTIN, take Snake
River Rd SE for 28 miles (44.8 k).
FREE but choose a chore.
Open All Year.
Undesignated, open sites. Pit toilets, pay
phone, boat ramp, store.
On level, gravel parking area with river
access, beach, and spectacular view of
Snake River Canyon.

▲ ▲ ▲ ▲ ▲ ▲ ▲ ▲ ▲ ▲ ▲ ▲ ▲ ▲ ▲ ▲ ▲ ▲ ▲ ▲ ▲ ▲ ▲ ▲

Swimming, boating, skiing, and fishing. Good birdwatching too.
NO water/trash arrangements (pack it out). 14-day limit. Crowded holiday weekends. Noisy. Jet skis.

## HOH OXBOW

WA DNR (206) 753-2400
State map: D1
About 14 miles (24 k) S of FORKS, find on E side of US 101 next to river between mileposts 176-177.
FREE but choose a chore.
Open All Year.
5 close, open sites.
Pit toilets, tables, grills, boat launch.
On banks of Hoh River.
Float or canoe. Fish.
NO water. 14-day limit.

## HONEYMOON

Okanogan NF (509) 996-2266
State map: C5
From WINTHROP, take CR 1213 N almost 7 miles (11.2 k) to FR 51. Continue N for 2.8 miles (4.5 k) to FR 5130. Bear Left (NW) and go about 9 miles (14.4 k). (Also see Buck Lake, Flat, Nice, and Ruffled Grouse.)
FREE but choose a chore.
Open May 15–Oct 15; camping allowed off-season.
6 close, open sites.
Pit toilets, tables, fire rings.
On Eightmile Creek wedding night spot of ranger and his bride.
Create getaway. Enjoy access to Pasayten Wilderness just up road. Fish.
NO water/trash arrangements (pack it out). 14-day limit.
3280 ft (984 m)

## HORSESHOE LAKE

Gifford Pinchot NF
(206) 497-7565
State map: G4
From RANDLE, head SE on FR 23 for 10 miles (16 k) to **North Fork** (33 sites). Turn Right on FR 21 and go 10 miles (16 k). Turn Right on FR 6401 and drive 5.5 miles (8.8 k). Turn Left on FR 2329 and go 7 miles (11.2 k). Turn Left on

FR 078 and continue 1.3 miles (2.1 k). In another mile along 2329 find **Spring Creek** (3 sites) and **Keenes Horse Camp** (15 sites). (Also see Killen Creek and Olallie Lake.)
FREE but choose a chore.
Open Jun 15–Oct 30.
10 sites.
Pit toilets, tables, fire rings, boat ramp.
At lake near Mt Adams Wilderness.
Swim or fish. Trek into wilderness.
14-day/16-ft limits.
4200 ft (1260 m)

## HOWELL LAKE

WA DNR (206) 753-2400
State map: E3
Take WA 300 SE out of BELFAIR for 3.5 miles (5.6 k). Turn Right on Belfair–Tahuya Rd and go 4.5 miles (7.2 k). (Also see Camp Spillman, Twin Lakes, and Toonerville.)
FREE but choose a chore.
Open All Year.
6 close, open sites. Water, pit toilets, tables, fire rings, boat launch.
In quiet, lakeside location.
Hike and explore Tahuya State Forest.
14-day limit.

## HUTCHINSON CREEK

WA DNR (206) 753-2400
State map: B3
From ACME, on WA 9 go just N of Nooksack River Bridge and turn E on Mosquito Lake Rd. Drive 2.4 miles (3.8 k). Turn Right on gravel 1-lane road and go .4 mile (640 m).
FREE but choose a chore.
Open All Year.
11 close, open sites.
Pit toilets, tables, grills.
In pretty forest setting on creek.
Get away to fish and hike.
NO water. 14-day limit.

## ICEWATER CREEK

Wenatchee NF (509) 674-4411
State map: E5
From CLE ELUM, head SE on I-90 about 12 miles (19.2 k) to Thorp Exit. Go S .75 mile (1.2 k). Turn hard

▲ ▲ ▲ ▲ ▲ ▲ ▲ ▲ ▲ ▲ ▲ ▲ ▲ ▲ ▲ ▲ ▲ ▲ ▲ ▲ ▲ ▲ ▲ ▲ ▲ ▲

Right (NW) on CR/FR 33 (Taneum) and go 12 miles (19.2 k). Pass fee-charged **Taneum** (14 sites). (Also see Buck Meadows and Tamarack Spring.)
FREE but choose a chore.
Open May 15–Nov 15.
17 (9 tent-only) close, open sites.
Water, pit toilets, tables, grills.
Along creek.
Hike, picnic, fish, relax.
NO water. 14-day limit. Crowded.
Motorcycles.

## INDIAN CAMP

WA DNR (206) 753-2400
State map: E5
From CLE ELUM, take WA 970 E for 6.9 miles (11 k). Turn Left (N) on Teanaway Rd and drive 7.3 miles (11.7 k). Turn Left on West Fork Teanaway Rd and go 16 miles (25.6 k). Turn Right on Middle Fork Teanaway Rd and go 3.9 miles (6.2 k).
FREE but choose a chore.
Open All Year.
9 close, open sites.
Pit toilets, tables, grills.
On banks of Middle Fork of Teanaway.
Find quiet spot for fishing, picnicking, or just being alone.
NO water. 14-day limit.

## ISLAND CAMP

WA DNR (206) 753-2400
State map: G4
From GLENWOOD post office, go W .3 mile (480 m). Turn Right (N) on Bird Creek Rd for .9 mile (1.4 k). Turn Left, then Right on dirt road and continue .9 mile (1.4 k). Bear Left on K-3000 and go .3 mile (480 m). Cross gravel road then stay Right for 3.4 miles (5.4 k). (Also see Bird Creek.)
FREE but choose a chore.
Open All Year.
6 close, open sites.
Pit toilets, tables, grills, group shelter.
In remote forest on stream.
Explore nearby lava tubes and blow-holes. Hike. In winter, use snowmobile trails.
NO water. 14-day limit.

## JONES BAY

Coulee Dam NRA
(509) 633-9441
State map: D7
From WILBUR, head N on WA 21 for 12 miles (19.2 k). Turn Right (E) on rough road. Go 10 miles (16 k)–4WD advisable.
FREE but choose a chore.
Open All Year.
6 close, open tent sites. Water, pit toilets, tables, grills, boat dock.
In remote pine forest on Roosevelt Lake. Enjoy all types of boating plus fishing, mountain biking, or just doing nothing.
No trash arrangements (pack it out).
14-day/20-ft limits.
1282 ft (384 m)

## JONES CREEK

WA DNR (206) 753-2400
State map: H3
From CAMAS, take WA 500 N for 3.8 miles (6.1 k). Turn Right on 19th St and go .8 mile (1.3 k). Turn Left on 292 Ave and go 1.9 miles (3 k). Turn Right on Ireland for only .2 mile (400 m). Turn Left on Lessard and go 2 miles (3.2 k). Continue straight on Winters for 1.6 miles (2.6 k).
FREE but choose a chore.
Open All Year.
9 close, open sites.
Water, pit toilets, tables, grills.
With motorbike trail in forest.
14-day limit. Crowded weekends.

## JR

Okanogan NF (509) 997-2131
State map: C6
Take WA 20 E from TWISP about 11.5 miles (18.4 k) near Loup Loup Summit turnoff. (Also see Loup Loup.)
$4. Open Memorial Day–Sep 30; dry camping off-season.
6 close, screened sites.
Water, pit toilets, tables, fire rings.
On Frazer Creek under mixed conifers near popular ski area.
Find mountain biking and hiking opportunities. Fish in summer. Ski and snowmobile in winter.

14-day limit. Crowded holidays.
Mosquitos and yellow jackets. Hunting
in season.
3900 ft (1170 m)

## JUNIOR POINT

Wenatchee NF (509) 662-4355
State map: D5
From CHELAN, head W on
US 97 for 3 miles (4.8 k). Continue W on
CR along lake for 16 miles (25.6 k).
Continue SW on FR 5900 about 12 miles
(19.2 k). Pass **Ramona** and **Grouse
Mountain**. For alternatives, continue to
three trailhead camps–**Crescent Hill** in
1.5 miles (2.4 k), **Shady Pass** in 5 miles
(8 k), or **Halfway Spring** in another
3 miles (4.8 k).
FREE but choose a chore.
Open Jun 15–Sep 30.
5 sites. Pit toilets, tables, fire rings.
Overlooking Chelan Lake.
Explore or relax.
NO water. 14-day limit.
6700 ft (2010 m)

## KAMLOOPS

Coulee Dam NRA
(509) 633-9441
State map: B7
From KETTLE FALLS, take US 395 W
and N for 7 miles (11.2 k).
FREE but choose a chore.
Open All Year.
17 close, open tent sites. Water, pit
toilets, tables, fire rings, boat dock.
At spot where Kettle River flows into
Roosevelt Lake.
Fish and boat. Enjoy scenic and historical
diversions.
14-day limit.
1265 ft (378 m)

## KERR

Okanogan NF (509) 486-2186
State map: B6
From CONCONULLY, go
3.5 miles (5.6 k) NW on FR 38 (road
begins as CR 2361). (Also see
Cottonwood, Oriole and Salmon
Meadows.)
FREE but choose a chore.

Open May 15–Sep 30; camping allowed
off-season.
13 close, open sites.
Pit toilets, tables, fire rings.
Along Salmon Creek.
Fish creek. Picnic and relax.
NO water/trash arrangements (pack it
out). 14-day/22-ft limits.
3100 ft (930 m)

## KETTLE RANGE

Colville NF (509) 738-6111
State map: B7
From KETTLE FALLS, take
US 395 NW for 3.5 miles (5.6 k). Turn W
on scenic byway WA 20 and drive
19 miles (30.4 k).
FREE but choose a chore.
Open May 25–Sep 30.
9 close, open tent sites.
Water, pit toilets, tables, fire rings.
In woods at Sherman Pass.
Walk short trail. In .5 mile (800 m), it
hooks with two other longer trails. Enjoy
beautiful scenery. Relax.
14-day limit.
5300 ft (1590 m)

## KETTLE RIVER

Coulee Dam NRA
(509) 633-9441
State map: B7
From KETTLE FALLS, take US 395 NW
for 10 miles (16 k). (Also see Kamloops.)
FREE but choose a chore.
Open All Year.
12 close, open sites. Water, pit toilets,
tables, fire rings, boat dock.
In pine forest on Kettle River, a
few miles from Roosevelt Lake.
Fish and boat. Daydream.
14-day/20-ft limits.
1265 ft (378 m)

## KILLEN CREEK

Gifford Pinchot NF
(206) 497-7565
State map: G4
From RANDLE, head SE on FR 23 for
10 miles (16 k) to **North Fork** (33 sites).
Turn Right on FR 21 and go 10 miles
(16 k). Turn Right on FR 6401 and go

5.5 miles (8.8 k). Turn Left on FR 2329
and go 6 miles (9.6 k). Pass fee-charged
**Takhlakh** (54 sites). (Also see Horseshoe
Lake and Olallie Lake.)
**FREE** but choose a chore.
Open Jun 15–Oct 30.
10 sites. Pit toilets, tables, fire rings.
On creek across from Mt Adams Trail.
Make base for extended hikes.
14-day/16-ft limits.
4400 ft (1320 m)

## KLIPCHUCK

Okanogan NF (509) 996-2266
State map: B5
From MAZAMA, head W on
WA 20 for 1 mile (1.6 k). Turn Right (N)
on FR 300 and go 1 mile (1.6 k). (Also
see Early Winters.)
**$5.** Open May 15–Oct 15; dry camping
off-season.
46 (6 tent-only) close, screened sites. &
Water, flush and pit toilets, tables, fire
rings.
Set among majestic trees on banks of
Early Winters Creek.
Sample wonderful hiking trails leading
to meadows, waterfalls (Cedar), and
lake. See Early Winters Visitors Center.
14-day/32-ft limits. Rattlesnakes.
2920 ft (876 m)

## LAKE CREEK-WENATCHEE

Wenatchee NF (509) 763-3103
State map: D5
From COLES CORNER, take
WA 207 N for 9 miles (8 k) to ranger
station, curving Left around state park.
Continue NW about 1.5 miles (2.4 k) to
FR 6500 (Little Wenatchee). Turn Left
and drive 10 miles (16 k). (Also see Little
Wenatchee Ford, Soda Springs, and
Theseus Creek.)
**FREE** but choose a chore.
Open May 1–Nov 1.
8 close, open sites.
Pit toilets, tables, fire rings.
Along Little Wenatchee.
Hike, fish, or picnic.
NO water/trash facilities. 14-day limit.
2300 ft (690 m)

## LAKE MERRILL

WA DNR (206) 753-2400
State map: G3
From COUGAR, go .5 mile
(800 m) S on WA 503. Turn Right (NW)
on CR 8100 and go 5 miles (8 k).
**FREE** but choose a chore.
Open All Year.
11 sites. Water, pit toilets, tables, fire
rings, boat launch.
In forest on lake near Mt St Helens.
Boat and fish. Visit Ape Cave and Trail
of Two Forests.
14-day limit.
1550 ft (465 m)

## LEADER LAKE

WA DNR (206) 753-2400
State map: C6
From OKANOGAN, head W
on WA 20 for 8.4 miles (13.4 k). Turn
Right (N) on 1-lane Leader Lake Rd and
drive .4 mile (640 m).
**FREE** but choose a chore.
Open All Year.
16 close, open sites.
Pit toilets, tables, grills, boat launch.
On uncrowded lake.
Fish and boat.
NO water. 14-day limit.

## LEWIS RIVER

Gifford Pinchot NF
(509) 395-2501
State map: G4
Use forest map. Head W from TROUT
LAKE on WA 141 for 1 mile (1.6 k).
Turn Right (NW) on FR 88. Go about
18 miles (28.8 k). Continue W on FR 32
for 7 miles (11.2 k). Turn Right (N) on
FR 3241. Drive to end–5 miles (8 k). For
another remote alternative, turn Left off
FR 88 at mile 14 onto FR 8871/8854 for
**Steamboat Lake** (2 sites).
**FREE** but choose a chore.
Open Jun 15–Sep 30.
4 sites. Pit toilets, tables, fire rings.
On river across from Mt St Helens-
Lower Falls Campground.
Explore lots of secluded waterfalls. Fish.
NO water. 14-day/16-ft limits.
1500 ft (450 m)

▲ ▲ ▲ ▲ ▲ ▲ ▲ ▲ ▲ ▲ ▲ ▲ ▲ ▲ ▲ ▲ ▲ ▲ ▲ ▲ ▲ ▲ ▲ ▲ ▲ ▲ ▲ ▲ ▲

## LIBERTY LAKE

Spokane County Parks
(509) 456-4730
State map: D8

From SPOKANE, take I-90 E about
18 miles (28.8 k) to Exit 296. Go S on
Liberty Lake Rd for 4 miles (6.4 k).
$3.50 plus $1.50/person entry fee.
Open Memorial Day-Labor Day.
76 (50 tent-only) scattered, open sites.
Water, flush toilets, showers, tables,
grills, fire rings, electric hook-ups.
In a meadow on southeast shore of lake
with beach and mountain views.
Swim, fish, and boat. Hike on trails.
View deer, elk, bear, and owl.
4-night limit. Crowded July 4. Bear
country–store food carefully.
2100 ft (630 m)

## LILLIWAUP

WA DNR (206) 753-2400
State map: D2
About 11 miles (17.6 k) N of
HOODSPORT on US 101, turn Left (W)
on gravel FR 24 (Jorsted Creek Rd). Go
6.6 miles (10.6 k). (Also see Melbourne.)
FREE but choose a chore.
Open All Year.
13 close, open sites.
Water, pit toilets, tables, grills.
Along quiet, forest stream.
Get away from hectic life.
14-day limit.

## LION ROCK SPRING

Wenatchee NF (509) 674-4411
State map: E5
From NW side of
ELLENSBURG, take CR/FR 35 N for
20 miles (32 k)–bear Left during
last mile.
FREE but choose a chore.
Open All Year.
4 sites.
Water, pit toilets, tables, fire rings.
At base of Table Mountain.
Enjoy good hiking and seclusion.
No trash arrangements (pack it out).
14-day limit.
6300 ft (1890 m)

## LITTLE GOOSE

Gifford Pinchot NF
(509) 395-2501
State map: G4

From TROUT LAKE, head W on WA 141
for 4 miles (6.4 k) to Ice Cave. Continue
W on FR 24 for 9 miles (14.4 k). Pass
**Smokey Creek** (3 sites). Horse camp is
nearby. (See Cold Springs Indian Camp.)
FREE but choose a chore.
Open Jun 1–Sep 30.
24 sites. Water, pit toilets, tables, grills,
fire rings.
On creek near lake and Indian Heaven
Wilderness.
Fish. Hike into wilderness.
14-day/16-ft limits.
4000 ft (1200 m)

## LITTLE TWIN LAKES

Colville NF (509) 684-4557
State map: B8
From COLVILLE, go E on
WA 20 for 12.5 miles (20 k). Turn Left
(N) on CR 4939 and go 4.5 miles (7.2 k).
Take FR 150 N for 1.5 miles (2.4 k).
FREE but choose a chore.
Open May 25–Sep 15.
20 close, open sites. Water, pit toilets,
tables, fire rings, boat ramp.
Boat and fish lake. Walk nature trail.
14-day limit.
3900 ft (1170 m)

## LITTLE WENATCHEE FORD

Wenatchee NF (509) 763-3103
State map: D4
From COLES CORNER, take
WA 207 N for 9 miles (8 k) to ranger
station, curving Left around state park.
Continue NW about 1.5 miles (2.4 k) to
FR 6500 (Little Wenatchee). Turn Left
and drive 15 miles (24 k)–last several
are dirt. (Also see Lake Creek, Soda
Springs, and Theseus Creek.)
FREE but choose a chore.
Open May 1–Nov 1.
3 close, open sites.
Pit toilets, tables, fire rings.
Along Little Wenatchee at trailhead.
Makes great hiking base or getaway.
NO water/trash arrangements. 14-day

limit. Small vehicles only.
2900 ft (870 m)

## LONE FIR

Okanogan NF (509) 996-2266
State map: B5
From MAZAMA, go W on
WA 20 about 11 miles (17.6 k). (Also see
Klipchuck.)
**$5.** Open Jun 1–Oct 15; dry camping
off-season.
27 (21 tent-only) close, screened sites. &
Water, pit toilets, tables, fire rings.
Along Early Winters Creek (last camp
heading W for many miles).
Hike to Silver Star Glacier. Take short
trails at nearby Washington and Rainy
passes for views. Fish creek.
14-day/22-ft limits.
3640 ft (1092 m)

## LONG LAKE CAMP/PICNIC AREA

WA DNR (206) 753-2400
State map: D8
From REARDON, go N on
WA 231 for 14.2 miles (22.7 k). Turn
Right (E) on Long Lake Dam Rd. Drive
4.7 miles (7.5 k). Camp is on Right.
**FREE** but choose a chore.
Open All Year.
7 close, open sites.
Water, pit toilets, tables, grills.
Alongside Spokane River.
Walk across road to observe and learn
about Native American pictographs.
14-day limit.

## LONG SWAMP

Okanogan NF (509) 486-2186
State map: B6
Find approximately 20 miles
(32 k) NW of LOOMIS via FR 39.
**FREE** but choose a chore.
Open May 15–Sep 30; camping allowed
off-season.
2 close, open sites.
Pit toilets, tables, fire rings.
On stream (adopted and maintained by
Backcountry Horsemen).
Make base for extensive hiking and
horseback riding exploration.
NO water/trash arrangements (pack it

out). 14-day/22-ft limits.
5476 ft (1641 m)

## LOST LAKE

Okanogan NF (509) 486-2186
State map: B7
From WAUCONDA, go W
on WA 20 for 3 miles (4.8 k). Turn Right
(N) on CR 4953 and drive 5 miles (8 k).
Bear Right on FR 32 and continue about
2 miles (3.2 k). Turn Left (NW) on FR 33
and go 3.5 miles (5.6 k). Turn Left (S) on
FR 50 for .5 mile (800 m). (Also see
Beaver Lake and Beth Lake.)
**$5.** Open May 15–Sep 30; dry camping
off-season.
18 close, open sites. &
Water, pit toilets, tables, fire rings, boat
ramp.
On shore near Big Tree Botanical Area.
Swim, boat, and fish on lake. Hike trails.
Enjoy fall color.
14-day/22-ft limits.
3800 ft (1140 m)

## LOUP LOUP

Okanogan NF (509) 997-2131
State map: C6
Take WA 20 E from TWISP
about 11.5 miles (18.4 k) to Loup Loup
Summit turnoff. Turn Right (S) and go
about 1 mile (1.6 k). (Also see JR.)
**$4.** Open Memorial Day–Sep 30; dry
camping off-season.
25 close, screened sites.
Water, pit toilets, tables, fire rings.
Under mixed conifers close to highway
and popular ski area.
Good mountain biking and hiking.
Skiing and snowmobiling in winter.
14-day limit. Crowded holidays.
Mosquitos and yellow jackets. Hunting
in season.
4200 ft (1260 m)

## LYMAN LAKE

Okanogan NF (509) 486-2186
State map: B6
From TONASKET, go E on
WA 20 for 12.5 miles (4.8 k). Turn Right
(SE) on CR 9455 and drive 13 miles (8 k).
Turn Right (S) on CR 3785 and continue

▲ ▲ ▲ ▲ ▲ ▲ ▲ ▲ ▲ ▲ ▲ ▲ ▲ ▲ ▲ ▲ ▲ ▲ ▲ ▲ ▲ ▲ ▲ ▲ ▲ ▲

about 2.5 miles (9.6 k).
**FREE** but choose a chore.
Open May 15–Sep 30; camping allowed
off-season.
4 close, open sites.
Pit toilets, tables, fire rings.
On lakeshore.
Swimming and fishing here.
NO water/trash facilities. 14-day limit.
2900 ft (870 m)

## LYRE RIVER
WA DNR (206) 753-2400
State map: C2
From PORT ANGELES, head
W on WA 112 (off US 101) until just
past milepost 46. Turn Right (N) and
drive .4 mile (640 m). Camp is on Left.
**FREE** but choose a chore.
Open All Year.
11 sites. Water, pit toilets, tables, grills,
group shelter.
On riverbank, find good spot to picnic
(with a shelter when it rains). Fish.
14-day limit.

## MADAME DORION
COE (503) 922-3211
State map: G7
From WALLULA, head S on
US 12 for 1 mile (1.6 k).
**FREE** but choose a chore.
Open All Year.
30 close, open sites.
Water, pit toilets, tables, grills.
Boat, swim, or fish on lake.
14-day limit.
350 ft (105 m)

## MARBLE CREEK
Mt Baker-Snoqualmie NF
(206) 856-5700
State map: B4
From MARBLEMOUNT, head E on
CR 3528 for 8 miles (12.8 k). Turn Right
(S) on FR 1530 for 1 mile (1.6 k). (Also
see Cascade Islands and Mineral Park.)
**FREE** but choose a chore.
Open May–Sep.
23 scattered, open, spacious sites.
Pit toilets, tables, fire rings.
With stately old fir trees along river

bank in peaceful setting up old Cascade
River Rd.
Terrific location for relaxing or doing a
little mountain biking on roads, hiking
on trails, and fishing creek or river.
NO water/trash arrangements (pack it
out). 10-day/32-ft limits.
1000 ft (300 m)

## MARGARET MCKENNY
WA DNR (206) 753-2400
State map: F2
Go W from LITTLEROCK for
1 mile (1.6 k). Turn Right (N) on
Waddell Creek Rd and go 2.3 miles
(3.7 k). Turn Left and go .2 mile (400 m).
(Also see Middle Waddell.)
**FREE** but choose a chore.
Open All Year.
12 close, open sites.
Water, pit toilets, tables, grills.
Along forest stream.
Take hiking and horse trails scattered
through area. See Mima Mounds about
1.6 miles down Waddell Creek Rd.
14-day limit.

## MEADOW CREEK
Wenatchee NF (509) 763-3103
State map: D5
From COLES CORNER, take
WA 207 N for 5 miles (8 k). Bear Right
at state park toward Midway. Turn Left
on FR 6100 toward Fish Lake and go
3 miles (4.8 k). At intersection with
FR 6300 (Meadow Creek) turn Left (NW)
and go 2.5 miles (4 k).
**FREE** but choose a chore.
Open May 1–Nov 1.
4 close, open sites.
Pit toilets, tables, fire rings.
On creek next to Chiwawa River.
Hike, fish, or picnic.
NO water/trash facilities. 14-day limit.
2400 ft (720 m)

## MEADOWS
Okanogan NF (509) 996-2266
State map: B5
From MAZAMA, cross
Methow River to CR 1163. Turn Left
(NW) and go 7 miles (11.2 k) to gravel

▲ ▲ ▲ ▲ ▲ ▲ ▲ ▲ ▲ ▲ ▲ ▲ ▲ ▲ ▲ ▲ ▲ ▲ ▲ ▲ ▲ ▲ ▲ ▲ ▲ ▲ ▲ ▲ ▲

FR 5400. Continue NW for 12.5 miles (20 k). Turn Left (S) on FR 500 and go 1 mile (1.6 k). No trailers on steep, narrow access road–watch out for trucks. (Also see Hart's Pass.)
FREE but choose a chore.
Open Jul 1–Sep 30; camping allowed off-season.
14 close, open tent sites.
Pit toilets, tables, fire rings.
In alpine meadow near Hart's Pass, Pacific Crest Trail, and Pasayten Wilderness.
Create high base-camp for exploring gorgeous, mountainous region.
NO water/trash arrangements (pack it out). 14-day limit.
6200 ft (1860 m)

## MELBOURNE

WA DNR (206) 753-2400
State map: D2
About 11 miles (17.6 k) N of HOODSPORT on US 101, turn Left (W) on gravel FR 24 (Jorsted Creek Rd) and drive 5.5 miles (8.8 k). Turn Left and go 1.8 miles (2.9 k). Bear Left and continue .7 mile (1.1 k). (Also see Lilliwaup.)
FREE but choose a chore.
Open All Year.
5 close, open sites.
Pit toilets, tables, grills.
In secluded location on Melbourne Lake.
Savor quiet to canoe, fish, or relax.
NO water. 14-day limit.

## MIDDLE WADDELL

WA DNR (206) 753-2400
State map: F2
Go W from LITTLEROCK for 1 mile (1.6 k). Turn Right (N) on Waddell Creek Rd and go 3.1 miles (5 k). Turn Left and go .1 mile (200 m). (Also see Margaret McKenny and Yew Tree.)
FREE but choose a chore.
Open All Year.
3 close, open sites.
Pit toilets, tables, grills.
Along stream in forest.
NO water. 14-day limit. Crowded and noisy weekends. Dirt bikes.

## MIMA FALLS TRAILHEAD

WA DNR (206) 753-2400
State map: F2
Go W from LITTLEROCK for 1 mile (1.6 k). Turn Left (S) on Mima Rd and drive 1.3 miles (2.1 k). Turn Right on Bordeaux Rd and go .7 mile (1.1 k). Turn Right on Marksman Rd. Go .8 mile (1.3 k). Turn Left and go .2 mile (400 m).
FREE but choose a chore.
Open All Year.
5 close, open sites.
Water, pit toilets, tables, grills.
In quiet, forest location.
Enjoy delightful walk to falls. Relax.
14-day limit.

## MINE CREEK

WA DNR (206) 753-2400
State map: E4
Take Exit 34 off I-90 (E of NORTH BEND). Head N on 468 Ave SE for .5 mile (800 m). Turn Right (E) on SE Middle Fork Rd. Drive 4 miles (6.4 k).
FREE but choose a chore.
Open All Year.
13 close, open sites.
Pit toilets, tables, grills.
In quiet, forest on banks of Middle Fork of Snoqualmie.
Fish a bunch. Savor surroundings.
NO water. 14-day limit.

## MINERAL PARK

Mt Baker-Snoqualmie NF
(206) 856-5700
State map: B4
From MARBLEMOUNT, head E on CR 3528 for 15 miles (24 k). (Also see Marble Creek.)
FREE but choose a chore.
Open May–Sep.
6 (5 tent-only) scattered, open sites.
Pit toilets, tables, fire rings.
Up old Cascade River Rd on riverbank.
Take a hike into Glacier Peak Wilderness (Middle Fork Trail). Fish.
NO water/trash arrangements (pack it out). 10-day/16-ft limits.
1000 ft (300 m)

▲ ▲ ▲ ▲ ▲ ▲ ▲ ▲ ▲ ▲ ▲ ▲ ▲ ▲ ▲ ▲ ▲ ▲ ▲ ▲ ▲ ▲ ▲ ▲ ▲ ▲ ▲

## MINNIE PETERSON

WA DNR (206) 753-2400
State map: D1
About 15 miles (24 k) S of
FORKS between mileposts 178-179 of
US 101, go E on Hoh Rain Forest Rd for
3.5 miles (5.6 k). Camp on Right. (Also
see Willoughby Creek.)
**FREE** but choose a chore.
Open All Year.
3 close, open sites.
Pit toilets, tables, grills.
Fish on Hoh River.
NO water. 14-day limit.

## MORRISON CREEK

Gifford Pinchot NF
(509) 395-2501
State map: G4
From TROUT LAKE, head N on CR 17
for 1.5 miles (2.4 k). Continue N on
FR 80/8040 for 9 miles (14.4 k). For
alternative, continue NE on FR 500 for
2 miles to **Cold Springs**.
**FREE** but choose a chore.
Open Jun 15–Sep 15.
12 tent sites.
Pit toilets, tables, fire rings.
On creek near Mt Adams Wilderness.
Fish. Trek into wilderness.
NO water. 14-day/16-ft limits.
4600 ft (1380 m)

## MT RAINIER NP

(206) 569-2211
State map: F4
$5 entrance fee (or pass).
Also, **free** backcountry permits available
at Visitor Center or ranger stations.
Grandeur of ancient, but not extinct,
14410-ft (423-m) volcano lures sightseers,
campers, mountaineers, photographers,
and artists.
Explore forests, subalpine meadows
where flowers blossom Jul–Aug, as well
as glaciers.
▲ **Cougar Rock**
From ASHFORD, go 7 miles (11.2 k) E
on WA 706 to Nisqually entrance.
Continue 8 miles (12.8 k).
**$5**. Open May 25–Oct 25.
200 scattered, screened sites. &

Water, flush toilets, tables, grills, fire
rings, pay phone, dump station.
Along Nisqually River.
Hike along Wonderland Trail. Attend
ranger programs.
14-day limit. Crowded.
3300 ft (990 m)
▲ **Sunshine Point**
From ASHFORD, go 7 miles (11.2 k) E
on WA 706 (just inside Nisqually
entrance).
**$5**. Open All Year.
18 scattered, screened sites. Water,
chemical toilets, tables, grills, fire rings.
Along glacier-fed Nisqually River next to
main road.
Explore park (only all-year camp).
14-day/25-ft limits. Crowded.
2050 ft (615 m)

## MT ST HELENS NM-Lower Falls

(206) 247-5473
State map: G3
Take WOODLAND Exit 21
off I-5 and head NE on WA 503 for
30 miles (48 k). Turn on FR 90 and
continue E another 30 miles (48 k).
**FREE**. May add small fee.
Open Memorial Day–Labor Day; dry
camping off-season.
Undesignated sites with some screening.
Water, compost toilets, tables, grills, fire
rings.
On Lewis River in Gifford Pinchot NF
near southeast side of area's largest
volcanic eruption in recent years.
With ample choices for hiking, biking,
and exploring, view lava flow, learn
about nature's restorative process, as
well as see beautiful waterfalls.
14-day limit. Crowded holidays. Quiet
hours.
1500 ft (450 m)

## MT MOLLY

WA DNR (206) 753-2400
State map: F3
From OLYMPIA, go W on
US 101 for 4 miles (6.4 k) to Mud Bay
Exit. Drive S on Delphi Rd for 5.8 miles
(9.3 k). Go straight on Waddell Creek Rd
for 3 miles (4.8 k). Turn Right and go

▲ ▲ ▲ ▲ ▲ ▲ ▲ ▲ ▲ ▲ ▲ ▲ ▲ ▲ ▲ ▲ ▲ ▲ ▲ ▲ ▲ ▲ ▲

1.4 miles (2.2 k) to fork. Bear Left for .9 mile (1.4 k). (Also see Fall Creek.)
**FREE** but choose a chore.
Open All Year.
10 close, open sites.
Pit toilets, tables, grills.
In forest.
NO water. Crowded and noisy weekends. Dirt bikes.

## MYSTERY

Okanogan NF (509) 997-2131
State map: C5
From TWISP, take FR 44 (Twisp River Rd) NW about 18 miles (28.8 k). (Also see Poplar Flat and War Creek.)
**FREE** but choose a chore.
Open Memorial Day–Sep 30; camping allowed off-season.
4 close, screened sites.
Pit toilets, tables, fire rings.
Near Twisp River in mountainous, mixed-conifer setting.
Besides fishing, try hiking. Obtain map to trek along Reynolds Creek into adjacent North Cascades NP.
NO water/trash arrangements. 14-day limit. Crowded holidays. Mosquitos and yellow jackets. Hunting in season.
2800 ft (840 m)

## NAPEEQUA

Wenatchee NF (509) 763-3103
State map: D5
From COLES CORNER, take WA 207 N for 9 miles (8 k) to ranger station, curving Left around state park. Drive NW on FR 6400 (White River) for 7 miles (11.2 k). (Also see Grasshopper Meadows and White River Falls.)
**FREE** but choose a chore.
Open May 1–Nov 1.
5 close, open sites.
Pit toilets, tables, fire rings.
Along White River.
Hike to Twin Lakes. Fish and relax.
NO water/trash arrangements (pack it out). 14-day limit.
2000 ft (600 m)

## NICE

Okanogan NF (509) 996-2266
State map: C5
From WINTHROP, take CR 1213 N almost 7 miles (11.2 k) to FR 51. Continue N for 2.8 miles (4.5 k) to FR 5130. Bear Left (NW) and go about 4 miles (6.4 k). (Also see Buck Lake, Flat, Honeymoon, and Ruffled Grouse.)
**FREE** but choose a chore.
Open May 15–Oct 15; camping allowed off-season.
3 close, open sites.
Pit toilets, tables, fire rings.
Near beaver pond on Eightmile Creek.
Enjoy peaceful creek. Fish. Mountain bike. Walk and explore.
NO water/trash arrangements (pack it out). 14-day limit.
2728 ft (816 m)

## NINETEEN MILE

Wenatchee NF (509) 763-3103
State map: D5
From COLES CORNER, take WA 207 N for 5 miles (8 k). Bear Right at state park toward Midway. Turn Left on FR 6100 toward Fish Lake. Go 4 miles (6.4 k). At intersection with FR 6200 (Chiwawa River) turn Left (NW). Go 18 miles (28.8 k). (Also see Atkinson Flats, Alpine Meadows, Finner, Phelps Creek, Rock Creek, and Schaefer Creek.)
**FREE** but choose a chore.
Open May 1–Nov 1.
4 close, open sites.
Pit toilets, tables, fire rings.
With access to Chiwawa River.
Hike, fish, and picnic.
NO water/trash facilities. 14-day limit.
2600 ft (780 m)

## NORTH CASCADES NPS COMPLEX

North Cascades NP
(206) 873-4590
State map: B4
Complex encompasses North Cascades NP plus Lake Chelan and Ross Lake NRAs near Canadian border.
No entrance fee. Also, **free** backcountry permits available at any park office or ranger station. Open All Year though

▲ ▲ ▲ ▲ ▲ ▲ ▲ ▲ ▲ ▲ ▲ ▲ ▲ ▲ ▲ ▲ ▲ ▲ ▲ ▲ ▲ ▲ ▲ ▲ ▲

accessibility varies.

Among lofty, snowcapped peaks of Cascade Range.

▲ **Goodell Creek**

From NEWHALEM, go .5 mile (800 m) W on WA 20.

$5. Open All Year.

21 close, screened sites. Water, pit toilets, tables, grills, fire rings.

On Skagit River.

Make base to explore scenic region, take raft trip, mountain bike, or fish.

14-day limit. Crowded summer weekends.

500 ft (150 m)

▲ **Gorge Lake**

From NEWHALEM, go W on WA 20 for 7 miles (11.2 k).

FREE. Open All Year.

6 scattered, open sites.

Water (needs treating), pit toilets, tables, grills, fire rings, boat ramp.

On lakeshore.

Fish and boat. Hit trails for nature walks, extended treks, or cycling trips.

14-day limit. Crowded summer holidays and weekends.

700 ft (210 m)

**Ross Lake NRA**

(206)873-4590

State map: B4

▲ **Hozomeen**

From HOPE, BRITISH COLUMBIA, take Trans-Canada SE about 17 miles (27.2 k) to Silver Skagit Rd. Turn Right (S) on rough, gravel road and drive 23 miles (36.8 k), reentering US.

FREE. Open May 15–Oct 31.

122 close, open sites.

Water, pit toilets, tables, grills, fire rings, dump station, boat ramp.

At only drive-to spot on Ross Lake.

Fish and boat. Access more remote areas by foot or boat.

14-day/22-ft limits.

**Lake Chelan NRA**

(509) 682-2576

State map: C5

From CHELAN, take boat 55 miles (88 k) to STEHEKIN. Four-hour

boat trip from Chelan is $14 one-way ($21 round-trip). Leaves 8:30am. Shuttle bus is $3. Reserve space up to 30-days by writing North Cascades NPS Complex, Stehekin Ranger District, Box 7, Stehekin, WA 98284.

FREE. Open All Year.

▲ **Bridge Creek Bus/Walk-In**

7 scattered, screened tent sites.

Water (needs treating), pit toilets, tables, grills, fire rings, food storage.

In forest by creek near road.

Hike to observe nature. Fish stream. Bike in summer; ski in winter.

14-day limit. Rough bus ride. Crowded Jul–Aug (bus reservations a must).

2200 ft (660 m)

▲ **Cottonwood Bus/Walk-In**

5 scattered, screened tent sites.

Water (needs treating), pit toilets, tables, grills, fire rings, food storage.

At end-of-road in forested, shrubby area with mountain and cliff views.

Take off for mountains and serious hiking/climbing. Roam to enjoy natural beauty. Bike in summer; ski in winter.

14-day limit. Rough ride on bus. Biting flies in Aug.

2800 ft (840 m)

▲ **Dolly Varden Bus/Walk-In**

1 open tent site.

Water (needs treating), pit toilets, tables, grills, fire rings.

Next to road on Stehekin River.

Enjoy spot for relaxing as well as fishing. Bike in summer; ski in winter.

14-day limit. Rough bus ride. Crowded Jul–Aug (bus reservations a must).

2800 ft (840 m)

▲ **Flat Creek Bus/Walk-In**

2 open tent sites. Water (needs treating), pit toilets, tables, fire rings.

In private, shady sites across river from road (near its end).

Savor nature lover's spot with wonderful hiking and photo taking possibilities.

14-day limit. Rough bus ride. Crowded Jul–Aug (bus reservations a must).

2300 ft (690 m)

▲ **Harlequin Bus/Walk-In**

7 scattered, screened tent sites.

Water (needs treating), pit toilets, tables,

▲ ▲ ▲ ▲ ▲ ▲ ▲ ▲ ▲ ▲ ▲ ▲ ▲ ▲ ▲ ▲ ▲ ▲ ▲ ▲ ▲ ▲ ▲ ▲ ▲

grills, fire rings, food storage.
On forest flat by Stehekin River–fairly private setting.
Find good hiking and wildlife viewing.
Fish or canoe/kayak river. Bike in summer; ski in winter.
14-day limit. Vehicle noise. Crowded Jul–Aug (bus reservations a must).
1200 ft (360 m)

▲ **High Bridge Bus/Walk-In**
2 scattered, open tent sites.
Water (needs treating), pit toilets, tables, grills, fire rings, food storage.
On flat terrace overlooking river below– usually private.
Hike, fish, bike, or ski (in winter). Take photographs too.
14-day limit. Crowded Jul–Aug (bus reservations a must).
1700 ft (510 m)

▲ **Park Creek Bus/Walk-In**
2 scattered, open tent sites.
Water (needs treating), pit toilets, tables, grills, fire rings.
In forest near river and trails.
Hiking or fishing. Mountain biking in summer; skiing in winter.
No trash arrangements (pack it out).
14-day limit. Crowded Jul–Aug (bus reservations a must).
2300 ft (690 m)

▲ **Purple Point Walk-In**
7 scattered, screened tent sites.
Water (needs treating), pit toilets, tables, grills, fire rings, food storage.
Convenient location (a bit busy) with fairly flat sites in forest on hillside.
Nice walking on nature trail plus more extensive hiking possibilities. Fishing, boating, and swimming. Attending ranger programs. Biking in summer; skiing in winter.
14-day limit. Crowded Jul–Aug. Rattlesnakes.
1200 ft (360 m)

▲ **Shady Bus/Walk-In**
1 screened tent site. Water (needs treating), pit toilet, table, grill, fire ring.
In heavily-shaded, private location.
Relax and absorb natural surroundings.
Fish, bike, or cross-country ski.
14-day limit. Rough ride on bus.

Crowded Jul–Aug. Insects too.
2000 ft (600 m)

▲ **Tumwater Bus/Walk-In**
2 scattered, screened tent sites.
Water (needs treating), pit toilets, tables, grills, fire rings.
In forest next to roaring Stehekin River.
Become a nature aficionado-observe and photograph. Fish and bike in summer; ski in winter.
14-day limit. Crowded Jul–Aug (bus reservations a must).
1800 ft (540 m)

▲ **Weaver Point Boat/Walk-In**
30 scattered, screened tent sites.
Water, pit toilets, tables, grills, fire rings, summer boat ramp, beach.
On shore of forest lake.
Start more extensive trips from here.
Enjoy lake to swim, boat, and fish.
14-day limit.
1200 ft (360 m)

## NORTH CREEK

WA DNR (206) 753-2400
State map: F2
From OAKVILLE, head W on WA 12 for 2.7 miles (4.3 k). Turn Right (E) on D-Line Rd and drive 1.8 miles (2.9 k). Take Right fork and go 3.1 miles (5 k). Camp's on right.
FREE but choose a chore.
Open All Year.
5 close, open sites.
Water, pit toilets, tables, grills.
In quiet, streamside forest locale.
Find several good hiking trails as well as nice getaway spot.
14-day limit.

## NORTH FORK

Wenatchee NF (509) 784-1511
State map: D5
From ENTIAT, take US 97 S about 1.5 miles (2.4 k). Turn Right (NW) on CR 371 and drive 25 miles (40 k). Go NW on FR 51 for 8 miles (12.8 k). (Also see Fox Creek and Spruce Grove.)
$3. Open May 1–Nov 1.
8 close, open sites.
Water, pit toilets, tables, fire rings.
Along Entiat River.

Enjoy nearby Entiat Falls. Walk North Fork Trail.
14-day/16-ft limits.
2400 ft (720 m)

## NORTH FORK NINE MILE

WA DNR (206) 753-2400
State map: B6
From LOOMIS (grocery), go N for 2.1 miles (3.4 k). Turn Left (W) onto Toats Coulee Rd and drive 5.5 miles (8.8 k) to Toats Coulee camp. Take OM-T-1000 for 2.5 miles (4 k). (Also see Cold Springs.)
FREE but choose a chore.
Open All Year.
11 scattered, open sites.
Water, pit toilets, tables, grills.
Along forest stream.
View wildlife. Relax.
14-day limit.

## NORTH GORGE

Coulee Dam NRA
(509) 633-9441
State map: B7
From KETTLE FALLS, take US 25 N for 20 miles (32 k).
FREE but choose a chore.
Open All Year.
12 close, open tent sites. Water, pit toilets, tables, grills, boat ramp.
On shores of Roosevelt Lake.
Fish, swim, waterski, and boat.
14-day/16-ft limits.
1282 ft (384 m)

## NORTHEAST LAKE ELLEN

Colville NF (509) 738-6111
State map: B7
From KETTLE FALLS, take US 395 NW for 3.5 miles (5.6 k). Turn SW on WA 20 and drive 4 miles (6.4 k). Turn Left (S) on CR 3 and go 4.5 miles (7.2 k). Turn Right (SW) on CR 412/FR 2014 for 5.5 miles (8.8 k). (Also see Haag Cove.)
FREE but choose a chore.
Open May 25–Oct 30.
11 close, open sites. Water, pit toilets, tables, fire rings, boat ramp.
Swim, boat, and fish on lake. Hike.

14-day limit.
2300 ft (690 m)

## OBSTRUCTION PASS
## WALK/BOAT-IN

WA DNR (206) 753-2400
State map: B3
Go E out of OLGA on ORCAS ISLAND taking Doe Bay Rd for .6 mile (1 k). Turn Right on Obstruction Pass Rd and drive .7 mile (1.1 k). Bear Right for another .3 mile (480 m) then straight for .8 mile (1.3 k). Park and walk .5 mile (800 m) to camp.
FREE but choose a chore.
Open All Year.
9 close, open sites.
Pit toilets, tables, grills, 2 boat buoys.
In secluded forest on saltwater.
Enjoy excellent hiking good scenery, and favorite water activities.
NO water. 14-day limit.

## OKLAHOMA

Gifford Pinchot NF
(509) 395-2501
State map: H4
From WILLARD, head N on CR 86 for 7.5 miles (12 k). Turn Left on FR 181. On way, pass **Moss Creek** (18 sites) and **Big Cedar County Park**.
FREE but choose a chore.
Open May 15–Oct 15.
21 (12 tent-only) sites. &
Water, pit toilets, tables, fire rings.
On Little White Salmon River.
Swim, fish, or hike.
14-day/22-ft limits.
1700 ft (510 m)

## OLALLIE LAKE

Gifford Pinchot NF
(206) 497-7565
State map: G4
From RANDLE, head SE on FR 23 for 10 miles (16 k) to **North Fork** (33 sites). Turn Right on FR 21 and go 10 miles (16 k). Turn Right on FR 6401 and go 5 miles (8 k). (Also see Chain of Lakes and Council Lake.)
FREE but choose a chore.
Open Jun 15–Oct 30.

▲ ▲ ▲ ▲ ▲ ▲ ▲ ▲ ▲ ▲ ▲ ▲ ▲ ▲ ▲ ▲ ▲ ▲ ▲ ▲ ▲ ▲ ▲ ▲ ▲ ▲

6 sites. Pit toilets, tables, fire rings.
On shores of alpine lake with views of
Mt Adams.
Boat (no motors) and fish. Hike Canyon
Ridge Trail or into wilderness.
14-day/22-ft limits.
3700 ft (1110 m)

## OLYMPIC NP

(206) 452-4501
State map: D2
$3/vehicle or $2/person
entrance fee (or pass) at Elwha, Heart O'
the Hills/Hurricane Ridge, Hoh, and
Soleduck entrances from Memorial
Day–Labor Day. Also, free backcountry
permits available at all ranger stations.
Too, there's one primitive campground
(parking lot with toilets but no potable
water) at South Beach about 2.5 miles S
of Klaloch Ranger Station on US 101.
On the Olympic Peninsula, diverse
landscapes change from glacier-covered
peaks in Olympic Range to hot springs
to lush, temperate rainforests to rocky
ocean shores. Wildlife changes with
ecology–from marmot and Roosevelt elk
to harbor seal and migrating gray whale.

▲ **Deer Park**
From PORT ANGELES, go E on US 101
for 6 miles (9.6 k). Turn Right (S) on dirt
Blue Mountain Rd and drive 18 miles
(28.8 k) to road's end–trailers not
recommended.
FREE. Open May 30–Sep 30.
18 close, open tent sites.
Water, pit toilets, tables, grills.
In high country on Blue Mountain.
Make base to hike trails leading into
backcountry.
14-day limit.
5400 ft (1620 m)

▲ **Dosewallips**
Take US 101 S from QUILCENE for
13 miles (20.8 k). Turn Right (W) on dirt
FR 2610 and go 15 miles (24 k). Pass
Elkhorn–trailers not recommended.
FREE. Open All Year.
33 close, open tent sites. &
Water, pit toilets, tables, grills.
Along Dosewallips River.
Hike trails leading into heart of park.

Enjoy spot to fish and relax too.
14-day limit.
1540 ft (462 m)

▲ **Erickson's Bay Boat/Walk-In**
From OZETTE, go .5 mile (800 m) S to
lake. Must walk or boat to site. (For
vehicle camp, see Ozette on next page.)
FREE. Backcountry permit required for
camping beside lake.
Open All Year.
15 close, open tent sites.
Pit toilets, tables, grills.
Swim, boat, fish, and walk a few miles
to Pacific Ocean.
NO water/trash facilities. 14-day limit.
90 ft (27 m)

▲ **Graves Creek**
From QUINAULT, head NE on dirt
Quinault River Rd for 15 miles (24 k).
FREE. Open All Year.
30 close, open sites. &
Water, flush toilets, tables, grills.
At road's end in Quinault River Valley.
Hike trails leading into park's interior,
accessing several lakes. Fish and relax.
14-day/21-ft limits.
540 ft (162 m)

▲ **July Creek Walk-In**
From AMANDA PARK, go N for 2 miles
(3.2 k) on US 101. Turn Right (E) on
North Shore Rd. Drive 4 miles (6.4 k).
FREE. Open All Year.
29 close, open tent sites. &
Water, flush toilets, tables, grills.
On undeveloped side of Lake Quinault.
Swim or fish lake (check Quinault tribal
regulations).
14-day limit.
200 ft (60 m)

▲ **North Fork Quinault**
From AMANDA PARK, go N for 2 miles
(3.2 k) on US 101. Turn Right (E) on
North Shore Rd. Drive 18 miles (28.8 k).
FREE. Open All Year.
7 close, open tent sites.
Water, flush toilets, tables, grills.
In remote location close to rain forest.
Try fishing (check Quinault tribal
regulations). Explore trails.
14-day limit. No trailers.
520 ft (156 m)

▲ ▲ ▲ ▲ ▲ ▲ ▲ ▲ ▲ ▲ ▲ ▲ ▲ ▲ ▲ ▲ ▲ ▲ ▲ ▲ ▲ ▲ ▲ ▲ ▲ ▲

**▲ Ozette**

Find in LAKE OZETTE at end of gravel road. (Also see Erickson's Bay.)

**FREE. Open All Year.**

14 close, open sites. ઇ

Water, flush toilets, tables, grills.

At sea level near lake and ocean.

Find lots of fishing and hiking possibilities.

14-day/21-ft limits.

0 ft (0 m)

**▲ Queets**

From QUEETS, go about 5 miles (8 k) SE on US 101 to gravel Queets River Rd. Turn Left (E) and drive almost 14 miles (22.4 k) to end.

**FREE. Open All Year.**

20 close, open tent sites. ઇ

Pit toilets, tables, grills.

In remote, riverbank setting.

Hike into heart of park (check at ranger station). Enjoy excellent wildflower and wildlife observation. Fish and mountain bike too.

NO water (treat river water). 14-day limit. Small RVs possible.

290 ft (87 m)

**ORIOLE**

Okanogan NF (509) 486-2186
State map: B6
From CONCONULLY, go 2.6 miles (4.2 k) NW on FR 38 (road begins as CR 2361). Camp on Left. (Also see Cottonwood and Kerr.)

**$5.** Open May 15–Sep 30; dry camping off-season.

10 close, open sites.

Water, pit toilets, tables, fire rings.

Fish, picnic, and relax along Salmon Creek.

14-day/22-ft limits.

2900 ft (870 m)

**OWHI**

Wenatchee NF (509) 674-4411
State map: E4
From CLE ELUM, head N on WA 903 for 21 miles (33.6 k). Go NW on FR 228 for 5 miles (8 k). Turn Right (N) on FR 235 and go .25 mile (400 m). (Also see Fish Lake and Red Mountain.)

**FREE** but choose a chore.

Open May 25–Sep 30.

23 close, open tent sites.

Pit toilets, tables, grills, boat ramp.

Beside lake on wilderness boundary.

Canoe, swim, or fish. Take advantage of hiking possibilities.

NO water. 14-day limit.

2800 ft (840 m)

**PALMER LAKE**

WA DNR (206) 753-2400
State map: B6
From LOOMIS (grocery), go N (keeping Right) for 8.5 miles (13.6 k).

**FREE** but choose a chore.

Open All Year.

6 scattered, open sites.

Pit toilets, tables, grills.

On lakeshore.

View wildlife. Fish and boat.

NO water. 14-day limit.

**PANTHER CREEK**

Gifford Pinchot NF
(509) 427-5645
State map: H4
From COLSON, head NW on CR 30 for 8 miles (12.8 k). Turn Right (E) on FR 6517 and go 2 miles (3.2 k). For alternatives, retrace route to CR 30 and continue N for 3 miles (4.8 k) to **Beaver** (24 sites) or 7 more miles (11.2 k) to **Paradise Creek** (42 sites).

**$4.** Open Jun 15–Sep 15.

33 (2 tent-only) sites. ઇ

Water, pit toilets, tables, fire rings.

Hike or fish along creek.

14-day/22-ft limits.

1000 ft (300 m)

**PARK CREEK**

Mt Baker-Snoqualmie NF
(206) 856-5700
State map: B4
From CONCRETE, take CR 25 N for 9.5 miles (15.2 k). Continue N on FR 11 for 7.5 miles (12 k). Go NW of FR 1144 just a few hundred yards. (Also see Boulder Creek and Shannon Creek.)

**FREE** but choose a chore.

Open May–Sep.

12 close, open sites.
Pit toilets, tables, grills.
Near Baker Lake Resort on classic mountain stream that occasionally clouds with glacial silt. Open fir forest with bushy groundcover.
Pick berries in summer. Relax and fish anytime. Enjoy nearby Baker Lake.
NO water/trash arrangements (pack it out). 10-day/16-ft limits.
800 ft (240 m)

## PARTRIDGE POINT
WA DNR (206) 753-2400
State map: C3
On WA 20 halfway between milemarkers 25 and 26, go W on paved road 1.7 miles (2.7 k). Turn Left at park entrance. Go .8 mile (1.3 k).
FREE but choose a chore.
Open All Year.
8 close, open sites.
Pit toilets, tables, grills.
Hike trails. Savor saltwater location.
NO water. 14-day limit.

## PENINSULA
Wenatchee NF (509) 653-2205
State map: F4
From NACHES, take US 12 W for 22.5 miles (36 k). Turn Left on CR 2006/FR 12. Go 3 miles (4.8 k) Turn on FR 711. Go 1 mile (1.6 k). Nearby is smaller, tent-only Lonesome Cove.
FREE but choose a chore.
Open Apr 15–Nov 15.
19 close, open sites.
Pit toilets, tables, fire rings, boat ramp.
On Rimrock Lake.
Find full range of water activities–boat, waterski, swim, and fish.
NO water/trash arrangements (pack it out). 14-day/20-ft limits.
3000 ft (900 m)

## PHELPS CREEK
Wenatchee NF (509) 763-3103
State map: D5
From COLES CORNER, take WA 207 N for 5 miles (8 k). Bear Right at state park toward Midway. Turn Left on FR 6100 toward Fish Lake and go

4 miles (6.4 k). At intersection with FR 6200 (Chiwawa River), turn Left (NW) and go 21 miles (33.6 k). (Also see Atkinson Flats, Alpine Meadows, Finner, Nineteen Mile, and Schaefer Creek.)
FREE but choose a chore.
Open May 1–Nov 1.
7 close, open sites.
Pit toilets, tables, fire rings.
Hike, fish, picnic along Chiwawa River.
NO water/trash facilities. 14-day limit.
2800 ft (840 m)

## PIERRE LAKE
Colville NF (509) 738-6111
State map: B7
From ORIENT, take US 395 N for 3 miles (4.8 k). Turn Right (E) on CR/FR 4013. Go 5 miles (8 k) turning Right (S) after 3 miles (4.8 k). For remote setting, turn Left (N), go 3 miles (4.8 k) on FR 180 to Summit Lake (no water).
FREE but choose a chore.
Open May 25–Oct 30.
15 close, open sites.
Water, pit toilets, tables, fire rings.
On southwestern end of lake.
Hike 1-mile trail to north end. Enjoy canoeing and fishing.
14-day limit.
2100 ft (630 m)

## PINE FLAT
Wenatchee NF (509) 784-1511
State map: D5
From ENTIAT, head S on US 97 for 1.25 miles (2 k). Turn Left (W) on CR 371 and go 10 miles (16 k). Bear Left (W) on FR 1500. Go 3.5 miles (5.6 k).
FREE but choose a chore.
Open Apr 15–Nov 10.
9 sites. Pit toilets, tables, fire rings.
Hike trails along Mad River or Hornet Ridge. Fish too.
NO water. 14-day limit.

## PINE NEEDLE
Wenatchee NF (509) 653-2205
State map: F4
From NACHES, head W for 4.5 miles (7.2 k) on US 12. Bear Right (NW) on WA 410 and go 30.5 miles

▲ ▲ ▲ ▲ ▲ ▲ ▲ ▲ ▲ ▲ ▲ ▲ ▲ ▲ ▲ ▲ ▲ ▲ ▲ ▲ ▲ ▲ ▲ ▲

(48.8 k). Pass **Indian Flat** and on FR 1050
**American Forks** and **Cedar Springs** (all
with fees). In another 2 miles (3.2 k) is
**Hells Crossing** (fee charged).
FREE but choose a chore.
Open May 15–Sep 15.
6 sites. Pit toilets, tables, fire rings.
On American River.
Fish. Hike into William O Douglas
Wilderness.
NO water. 14-day limit.

## POLE PATCH

Gifford Pinchot NF
(206) 497-7565
State map: G4
From RANDLE, head S on FR 25 for
11 miles (17.6 k) to fee-charged **Iron
Creek** (98 sites). Turn Left (E) on FR 76
and go 4 miles (6.4 k). If you continue
straight, there's fee-charged **Tower Rock**
(22 sites) in 4 more miles (6.4 k). Turn
Right (S) on FR 77 and drive
17 twisting miles (27.2 k).
FREE but choose a chore.
Open Jun 15–Sep 30.
12 tent sites. Pit toilets, tables, fire rings.
Near Veta Creek and Greenhorn Buttes.
Enjoy seclusion. Explore.
14-day/22-ft limits.
4400 ft (1320 m)

## POPLAR FLAT

Okanogan NF (509) 997-2131
State map: C5
From TWISP, take Twisp
River Rd NW approximately 21 miles
(33.6 k)–last 3 are gravel. (Also see
Mystery, Roads End, and South Creek.)
$4. Open Memorial Day–Sep 15;
camping allowed off-season.
16 close, screened sites.
Water, pit toilets, tables, fire rings.
On Twisp River in mountainous, mixed-
conifer setting.
Fish and hike. Obtain map to trek into
adjacent North Cascades NP. Cross-
country ski in winter.
14-day limit. Crowded holidays.
Mosquitos and yellow jackets. Hunting
in season.
2900 ft (870 m)

## PORTER CREEK

WA DNR (206) 753-2400
State map: F2
From PORTER, take Porter
Creek Rd NE for 3 miles (4.8 k).
Continue straight for .5 mile (800 m).
FREE but choose a chore.
Open All Year.
14 close, open sites. Water, pit toilets,
tables, grills, horse ramp.
Along stream.
Hike or ride horses on trails.
14-day limit. Noisy. Motorbikes.

## QUARTZ MOUNTAIN

Wenatchee NF (509) 674-4411
State map: E5
From SW side of
ELLENSBURG, head W on CR/FR 31
(along Manastash Creek) for 33 miles
(52.8 k)–near end of FR 3100. (Also see
Buck Meadows.)
FREE but choose a chore.
Open May 25–Sep 30.
3 close, open sites.
Pit toilets, tables, fire rings.
In remote, scenic area.
Hike, mountain bike, and relax.
NO water. 14-day/22-ft limits.
6000 ft (1800 m)

## R F KENNEDY

WA DNR (206) 753-2400
State map: E3
From bridge in HOME, head
S on Longbranch Rd for 1.3 miles (2.1 k).
Turn Right (W) on Whiteman Rd and
drive 2.3 miles (3.7 k). Turn Right on Bay
Rd and go 1 mile (1.6 k).
FREE but choose a chore.
Open All Year.
8 close, open sites. Water, pit toilets,
tables, grills, boat launch, floating dock.
On saltwater.
Boat sound or picnic and relax on land.
14-day limit.

## RED BRIDGE

Mt Baker-Snoqualmie NF
(206) 436-1155
State map: C4
From GRANITE FALLS, head E on

CR FH7 (Mountain Loop) for 18 miles (28.8 k). (Also see Boardman Creek.)
FREE but choose a chore.
Open May–Sep.
14 close, screened sites.
Pit toilets, tables, fire rings.
Among shrubs and trees along riverbank with sand bar playground.
Relax. explore, hike, and fish.
NO water/trash arrangements (pack it out). 10-day/32 limits. Help rangers discourage noisy groups.
1300 ft (390 m)

## RED MOUNTAIN

Wenatchee NF (509) 674-4411
State map: E4
From CLE ELUM, head N on WA 903 for 19.5 miles (31.2 k). Nearby Cle Elum offers lakeside sites for a fee. (Also see Fish Lake and Owhi.)
FREE but choose a chore.
Open May 25–Sep 30.
12 (2 tent-only) close, open sites.
Pit toilets, tables, grills.
On river, not far from Cle Elum Lake.
Swim, boat, fish, or hike.
NO water. 14-day/16-ft limits.

## RED TOP

Wenatchee NF (509) 674-4411
State map: E5
From CLE ELUM, head E on WA 970 for 10 miles (16 k). Go N on US 97 for 8 miles (9.6 k). Turn Left (NW) on FR 9702. Travel to end of road–about 8 miles (12.8 k).
FREE but choose a chore.
Open May 15–Oct 15.
3 close, open sites.
Pit toilets, tables, grills, fire lookout.
With impressive overlooks.
Walk trails and snap a few pictures.
Rockhound too.
NO water. 14-day/22-ft limits.

## RHODODENDRON

WA DNR (206) 753-2400
State map: C3
Start from COUPEVILLE WA 20 intersection. Go S for 1.6 miles (2.6 k). Watch for entrance on Right.

FREE but choose a chore.
Open All Year.
6 close, open sites.
Water, pit toilets, tables, grills.
In quiet forest on Whidbey Island.
Create base for exploring. Enjoy getaway.
14-day limit.

## RIVER BEND

Okanogan NF (509) 996-2266
State map: B5
From MAZAMA, cross Methow River to CR 1163. Turn Left (NW) and go 7 miles (11.2 k) to gravel FR 5400. Continue NW for 2 miles (3.2 k). Just beyond Ballard Camp turn Left on FR 60 and go .5 mile (800 m). (Also see Ballard.)
FREE but choose a chore.
Open Jul 1–Sep 30; camping allowed off-season.
5 close, open sites. &
Pit toilets, tables, fire rings.
On Methow River with access to Robinson Creek, West Fork Meadow, and Lost River/Monument Trails.
Enjoy hiking and fishing opportunities.
NO water/trash arrangements (pack it out). 14-day/22-ft limits.
2600 ft (780 m)

## ROADS END

Okanogan NF (509) 997-2131
State map: C5
From TWISP, take Twisp River Rd NW approximately 25 miles (40 k)–last 7 are gravel. (Also see Mystery, Poplar Flat, and South Creek.)
FREE but choose a chore.
Open Memorial Day–Sep 15; camping allowed off-season.
7 close, screened sites.
Pit toilets, tables, fire rings.
At end of road near Twisp River in mountainous, mixed-conifer setting.
Enjoy hiking (obtain map to trek to Twisp Pass and into adjacent North Cascades NP). Observe nature. Fish.
NO water/trash arrangements (pack it out). 14-day/16-ft limits. Crowded holidays. Mosquitos and yellow jackets.

▲ ▲ ▲ ▲ ▲ ▲ ▲ ▲ ▲ ▲ ▲ ▲ ▲ ▲ ▲ ▲ ▲ ▲ ▲ ▲ ▲ ▲ ▲ ▲ ▲ ▲ ▲ ▲ ▲

Hunting in season.
3600 ft (1080 m)

## ROCK CREEK

Wenatchee NF (509) 763-3103
State map: D5
From COLES CORNER, take
WA 207 N for 5 miles (8 k). Bear Right
at state park toward Midway. Turn Left
on FR 6100 toward Fish Lake and go
4 miles (6.4 k). At intersection with
FR 6200 (Chiwawa River) turn Left (NW)
and go 13 miles (20.8 k). Next door is
new **Chiwawa Horse Camp** (10 sites)
and closeby is **Riverbend** (6 sites). (Also
see Atkinson Flats, Alpine Meadows,
Finner, Nineteen Mile, Phelps Creek, and
Schaefer Creek.)
**FREE** but choose a chore.
Open May 1–Nov 1.
4 close, open sites.
Pit toilets, tables, fire rings.
Hike and fish along Chiwawa River.
NO water/trash arrangements (pack it
out). 14-day limit.
2500 ft (750 m)

## ROCK CREEK-OKANOGAN

WA DNR (206) 753-2400
State map: C6
From OKANOGAN, head W
on WA 20 for 9.8 miles (15.7 k). Turn
Right (N) on dirt Loup Loup Canyon Rd
and drive 3.9 miles (6.2 k). (Also see
Rock Lakes.)
**FREE** but choose a chore.
Open All Year.
6 close, open sites. Water, pit toilets,
tables, grills, group shelter.
Along quiet, forest stream.
Picnicking and relaxing.
14-day limit.

## ROCK CREEK-YACOLT

WA DNR (206) 753-2400
State map: H3
From MEADOWGLADE, go
E to WA 503 and head S for 1.5 miles
(2.4 k). Turn Left on NE 159th St and go
3 miles (4.8 k). Turn Right (S) on 182nd
Ave and go 1 mile (1.6 k). Turn Left (E)
on NE 139th (L-1400) and drive about

8 miles (12.8 k). Turn Left on L-1000 and
go 3.7 miles (5.9 k). Turn Left again on
L-1200 and find camp in .2 mile (400 m).
(Also see Cold Creek-Yacolt.)
**FREE** but choose a chore.
Open All Year.
19 close, open sites. Water, pit toilets,
tables, grills, group shelter.
Along stream in wooded location.
Find good hiking and equestrian
possibilities in pleasant setting.
14-day limit.

## ROCK LAKES

WA DNR (206) 753-2400
State map: C6
From OKANOGAN, head W
on WA 20 for 9.8 miles (15.7 k). Turn
Right (N) on dirt Loup Loup Canyon Rd
and drive 4.8 miles (7.7 k). Pass Rock
Creek Camp. Turn Left (W) on Rock
Lakes Rd. Go 5.8 miles (9.3 k). Bear Left
and continue another .3 mile (480 m).
**FREE** but choose a chore.
Open All Year.
8 close, open sites.
Pit toilets, tables, grills.
On uncrowded lakeshore.
Hike area trails. Fish and boat.
NO water. 14-day limit.

## ROCKY LAKE

WA DNR (206) 753-2400
State map: B8
From US 395/WA 20 inter-
section in COLVILLE, head E on WA 20
for 6 miles (9.6 k). Turn Right (S) on
CR 3893 and drive 3.2 miles (5.1 k). Turn
Right (W) on 1-lane gravel road and go
.1 mile (160 m). Bear Left and continue
1.2 miles (1.9 k).
**FREE** but choose a chore.
Open All Year.
7 close, open sites.
Water, pit toilets, tables, fire rings.
On shore of shallow, rocky (aptly-
named) lake.
Enjoy picnicking and relaxing. Canoe on
lake. Take trip to nearby Little Pend
Oreille Wildlife Area for more extensive
nature opportunities.
14-day limit.

▲ ▲ ▲ ▲ ▲ ▲ ▲ ▲ ▲ ▲ ▲ ▲ ▲ ▲ ▲ ▲ ▲ ▲ ▲ ▲ ▲ ▲ ▲ ▲

## RUFFLED GROUSE

Okanogan NF (509) 996-2266
State map: C5
From WINTHROP, take
CR 1213 N almost 7 miles (11.2 k) to
FR 51. Continue N for 2.8 miles (4.5 k) to
FR 5130. Bear Left (NW) and go about
8 miles (9.6 k). (Also see Buck Lake, Flat,
Honeymoon, and Nice.)
FREE but choose a chore.
Open May 15–Oct 15; camping allowed
off-season.
4 close, open tent sites.
Pit toilets, tables, fire rings.
Fish Eightmile Creek. Hike into Pasayten
Wilderness. Bike roads.
NO water/trash arrangements (pack it
out). 14-day limit.
3120 ft (936 m)

## SALMON MEADOWS

Okanogan NF (509) 486-2186
State map: B6
From CONCONULLY, go
8.5 miles (13.6 k) NW on FR 38 (road
begins as CR 2361). (Also see Kerr.)
$5. Open May 15–Sep 30; dry camping
off-season.
7 close, open sites.
Water, pit toilets, tables, fire rings,
outdoor kitchen, corral.
In meadow with nearby stream.
Make base for extensive hiking or
horseback exploring. Observe wildlife.
14-day/22-ft limits.
4500 ft (1350 m)

## SAN JUAN

Mt Baker-Snoqualmie NF
(206) 677-2414
State map: D4
From INDEX, head E on FR 63
(Northfork Rd) for 15 miles (24 k). (Also
see Troublesome Creek.)
FREE but choose a chore.
Open May–Sep.
14 (12 tent-only) close, open sites.
Pit toilets, tables, fire rings.
In open forest setting on North Fork of
Skykomish.
Relax or fish. Access Henry M Jackson
Wilderness 6 miles (9.6 k) up FR 63.

NO water/trash arrangements (pack it
out). 14-day/22-ft limits.
1400 ft (420 m)

## SCHAEFER CREEK

Wenatchee NF (509) 763-3103
State map: D5
From COLES CORNER, take
WA 207 N for 5 miles (8 k). Bear Right
at state park toward Midway. Turn Left
on FR 6100 toward Fish Lake and go
4 miles (6.4 k). At intersection with
FR 6200 (Chiwawa River) turn Left (NW)
and go 14 miles (22.4 k). (Also see
Atkinson Flats, Alpine Meadows, Finner,
Nineteen Mile, and Phelps Creek.)
FREE but choose a chore.
Open May 1–Nov 1.
3 close, open sites.
Pit toilets, tables, fire rings.
Hike, fish, picnic along Chiwawa River.
NO water/trash facilities. 14-day limit.
2500 ft (750 m)

## SHANNON CREEK

Mt Baker-Snoqualmie NF
(206) 856-5700
State map: B4
From CONCRETE, take CR 25 N for
9.5 miles (15.2 k). Continue N on FR 11
for 12 miles (19.2 k). (Also see Boulder
Creek and Park Creek.)
FREE but choose a chore.
Open May–Sep.
18 close, open sites.
Pit toilets, tables, grills, boat ramp.
On north shore of Baker Lake in old-
growth forest.
Swim, boat, waterski, and fish. With
boat, head for Noisy Creek area.
NO water/trash arrangements (pack it
out). 10-day/22-ft limits.
800 ft (240 m)

## SHEEP CREEK

WA DNR (206) 753-2400
State map: B8
From NORTHPORT, go NE
on WA 25 for .8 mile (1.3 k). Turn Left
(W) on Sheep Creek Rd and drive
4.3 miles (6.9 k).
FREE but choose a chore.

▲ ▲ ▲ ▲ ▲ ▲ ▲ ▲ ▲ ▲ ▲ ▲ ▲ ▲ ▲ ▲ ▲ ▲ ▲ ▲ ▲ ▲ ▲ ▲

Open All Year.
11 close, open sites. Water, pit toilets, tables, grills, group shelter.
Along forest creek a few miles from Columbia River.
Fishing, hiking, or picnicking.
14-day limit.

## SHERMAN VALLEY

WA DNR (206) 753-2400
State map: F3
From OLYMPIA, go W on US 101 for 4 miles (6.4 k) to Mud Bay Exit. Drive S on Delphi Rd for 5.8 miles (9.3 k). Go straight on Waddell Creek Rd for 3 miles (4.8 k). Turn Right and go 1.4 miles (2.2 k) to fork. Take Left (C-Line) for 1.9 miles (3 k). Turn Left on C-4000. Go 6.1 miles (9.8 k). (Also see Fall Creek.)
FREE but choose a chore.
Open All Year.
7 close, open sites.
Pit toilets, tables, grills.
In forest setting on Porter Creek.
Good hiking trails.
NO water. 14-day limit.

## SKOOKUM CREEK

WA DNR (206) 753-2400
State map: C8
From USK, drive E across river–.9 mile (1.4 k). Turn Right (SE) on Leclerc Rd and go 2.2 miles (3.5 k). Turn Left on 1-lane gravel road and go .1 mile (160 m), then bear Left for .3 mile (500 m).
FREE but choose a chore.
Open All Year.
10 close, open sites.
Water, pit toilets, tables, grills.
Along quiet, forest creek (close to Pend-Oreille River).
Picnic, hike, fish, or boat (raft, canoe, kayak) nearby river.
14-day limit.

## SNAG COVE

Coulee Dam NRA
(509) 633-9441
State map: B7
From KETTLE FALLS, take US 395 W

and N for 15 miles (24 k). Turn Right (E) on CR and go 7 miles (11.2 k).
FREE but choose a chore.
Open All Year.
6 close, open sites. Water, pit toilets, tables, grills, boat dock.
In private spot on Roosevelt Lake.
Fish, swim, waterski, and boat.
14-day/20-ft limits.
1265 ft (378 m)

## SNOW CABIN

WA DNR (206) 753-2400
State map: F4
From TAMPICO, take A-2000 (Middle Fork Rd) W for 9.5 miles (15.2 k). Turn onto A-3000 (North Fork Ahtanum Rd) and go 4.5 miles (7.2 k). Keep Left and continue 2.6 miles (4.2 k). (Also see Ahtanum, Clover Flats, and Tree Phones.)
FREE but choose a chore.
Open All Year.
8 close, open sites.
Pit toilets, tables, grills.
Along remote, wooded stream.
Relaxing, picnic, fish, or hike. Retrace on A-3000 for 1.5 miles to find Gray Rock trailhead with motorbike trails.
NO water. 14-day limit.

## SODA LAKE

Columbia NWR
(509) 488-2668
State map: E6
From MOSES LAKE, go S on WA 17 about 10 miles (16 k). Turn Right (W) on Sullivan's Dam Rd. Drive until reaching Potholes Reservoir. Turn Left (S) at Columbia NWR sign.
FREE but choose a chore.
Open All Year.
Undesignated sites with 9 tables.
Chemical toilets, tables, boat ramp.
In bumper-to-bumper, elbow-to-elbow spot for desperate fishermen.
Fish and boat. Hike too.
NO water/trash arrangements (pack it out). Crowded.

▲ ▲ ▲ ▲ ▲ ▲ ▲ ▲ ▲ ▲ ▲ ▲ ▲ ▲ ▲ ▲ ▲ ▲ ▲ ▲ ▲ ▲ ▲ ▲

## SODA SPRINGS

Gifford Pinchot NF
(206) 494-5515
State map: F4

From PACKWOOD, head NE on US 12 for 8 miles (9.6 k). Pass fee-charged **La Wis Wis** (120 sites). Turn Left (N) on FR 4510 and go 6 miles (9.6 k). Pass free **Summit Creek** (7 sites).

FREE but choose a chore.

Open May 15–Sep 30.

8 tent sites.

Pit toilets, tables, fire rings.

On creek at border of William O Douglas Wilderness.

Hike to Jug or Frying Pan lakes. Take extended trek into wilderness. Visit Summit Creek Falls.

NO water. 14-day/16-ft limits.

3200 ft (960 m)

## SODA SPRINGS-WENATCHEE RIVER

Wenatchee NF (509) 763-3103
State map: D5

From COLES CORNER, take WA 207 N for 9 miles (8 k) to ranger station, curving Left around state park. Continue NW about 1.5 miles (2.4 k) to FR 6500 (Little Wenatchee). Turn Left. Drive 7.5 miles (12 k). Pass **Riverside** (7 sites). (Also see Lake Creek, Little Wenatchee Ford, and Theseus Creek.)

FREE but choose a chore.

Open May 1–Nov 1.

5 close, open sites.

Pit toilets, tables, fire rings.

Along Little Wenatchee plus own spring.

Hike, fish, or picnic.

NO water/trash arrangements (pack it out). 14-day limit. No trailers.

2000 ft (600 m)

## SOUTH CREEK

Okanogan NF (509) 997-2131
State map: C5

From TWISP, take Twisp River Rd NW approximately 22 miles (35.2 k)–last 4 are gravel. (Also see Mystery, Poplar Flat, and Roads End.)

FREE but choose a chore.

Open Memorial Day–Sep 15; camping allowed off-season.

4 close, screened sites.

Pit toilets, tables, fire rings.

In mountainous, mixed-conifer setting at confluence of South Creek and Twisp River.

Fish, hike, or relax. Take South Creek Trail into adjacent North Cascades NP. Cross-country ski in winter.

NO water/trash arrangements (pack it out). 14-day/16-ft limits. Crowded holidays. Mosquitos and yellow jackets. Hunting in season.

3100 ft (930 m)

## SOUTH FORK

Wenatchee NF (509) 653-2205
State map: F4

From NACHES, take US 12 W for 22.5 miles (36 k). Turn Left on CR 2006/FR 12 and go 4 miles (6.4 k). Go S on FR 1000 for .5 mile (800 m).

FREE but choose a chore.

Open May 25–Nov 15.

15 close, open sites.

Pit toilets, tables, fire rings.

On South Fork of Tieton River.

Swim and fish. Hike too.

NO water/trash arrangements (pack it out). 14-day/20-ft limits.

3000 ft (900 m)

## SOUTH FORK HOH

WA DNR (206) 753-2400
State map: D1

About 14 miles (22.4 k) South of FORKS at milepost 176 of US 101, go E on Hoh Mainline Rd for 6.6 miles (10.6 k). Turn Left on gravel H-1000 and go 7.4 miles (11.8 k).

FREE but choose a chore.

Open All Year.

3 close, open sites.

Pit toilets, tables, grills.

In private spot on river.

Enjoy place to relax and, perhaps, fish.

NO water. 14-day limit.

## SPRUCE GROVE

Wenatchee NF (509) 784-1511
State map: D5

From ENTIAT, take US 97 S about 1.5 miles (2.4 k). Turn Right (NW)

on CR 371 and drive 25 miles (40 k).
Continue NW on FR 51 for 10 miles
(16 k). In another mile, find **Three Creek**
(3 sites). For more developed, fee site,
drive 3 more miles to **Cottonwood**. (Also
see North Fork.)
**FREE** but choose a chore.
Open May 1–Nov 1.
3 close, open sites.
Pit toilets, tables, fire rings.
Along Entiat River.
Relax, picnic, and fish. Hike trails such
as Duncan Ridge or Middle Tommy.
NO water/trash arrangements (pack it
out). 14-day/16-ft limits.
2800 ft (840 m)

## SUGARLOAF

Okanogan NF (509) 486-2186
State map: B6
From CONCONULLY, take
CR 4015 NE for 4.5 miles (7.2 k).
**FREE** but choose a chore.
Open May 15–Sep 30; camping allowed
off-season.
4 close, open sites.
Pit toilets, tables, fire rings.
On northern shore of Lake Conconully.
Enjoy swimming, boating, and fishing.
NO water/trash arrangements (pack it
out). 14-day limit.
2400 ft (720 m)

## SURPRISE LAKES

Gifford Pinchot NF
(509) 395-2501
State map: G4
From TROUT LAKE, head W on WA 141
for 4 miles (6.4 k) to Ice Cave. Continue
W on FR 24 for 16 miles (25.6 k). (Also
see Cold Springs and Little Goose.)
**FREE** but choose a chore.
Open Jun 1–Sep 30.
9 sites. Pit toilets, tables, fire rings.
Near cluster of small lakes on Pacific
Crest Trail.
Enjoy seclusion. Hike or fish. Pick
huckleberries (best fields 1 mile W).
NO water. 14-day/16-ft limits.
4300 ft (1290 m)

## SWAUK

Wenatchee NF (509) 674-4411
State map: E5
From CLE ELUM, head E on
WA 970 for 10 miles (16 k). Go N on
US 97 for 17 miles (27.2 k). It's free
alternative to nearby **Mineral Springs**.
**FREE** but choose a chore.
Open May 25–Sep 30.
23 close, open sites.
Pit toilets, tables, grills, fire rings,
community kitchen, playing fields.
On scenic creek.
Walk nature trail or hike farther. Fish.
Ski and snowmobile in winter.
NO water. 14-day/22-ft limits.
3200 ft (960 m)

## TAMARACK SPRING

Wenatchee NF (509) 674-4411
State map: E5
From CLE ELUM, head SE
on I-90 about 12 miles (19.2 k) to Thorp
Exit. Go S .75 mile (1.2 k). Turn hard
Right (NW) on CR/FR 33 (Taneum) and
go 12.5 miles (20 k). Pass fee-charged
**Taneum** (14 sites). Turn Left (S) on
FR 3330 and go about 5 twisting miles
(8 k). Turn Left (E) on 3120 and go
1.5 miles (2.4 k). (Also see Buck
Meadows and Icewater Spring.)
**FREE** but choose a chore.
Open May 15–Nov 15.
4 close, open sites.
Water, pit toilets, tables, grills.
Hike, picnic, or relax in Willow Gulch.
14-day limit.

## TEAL SPRING

Umatilla NF (509) 843-1891
State map: G8
From POMEROY, head S on
WA 128 for 10 miles (16 k). At fork, bear
Right on CR/FR 40 for 12 miles
(19.2 k)–just past Clearwater Guard
Station. For alternatives, check out **Big
Springs** (6 sites and water) 3 miles
(4.8 k) NE of guard station on FR 42. Or
continue down FR 40 for 2.5 miles (4 k).
Bear Left on FR 44 to find **Wickiup**
(3 sites). (Also see Alder Thicket.)
**FREE** but choose a chore.

▲ ▲ ▲ ▲ ▲ ▲ ▲ ▲ ▲ ▲ ▲ ▲ ▲ ▲ ▲ ▲ ▲ ▲ ▲ ▲ ▲ ▲ ▲ ▲ ▲ ▲

Open May 15–Nov 15.
7 (5 tent-only) sites.
Pit toilets, tables, fire rings.
At spring near Wenaha-Tucannon
Wilderness.
Hike, pick berries, and relax.
NO water. 14-day limit.
5600 ft (1680 m)

## TEN MILE

Colville NF (509) 775-3305
State map: B7
From REPUBLIC, head S on
WA 21 for 10 miles (16 k). For another
alternative, continue 3 miles (4.8 k) to
Thirteen Mile.
FREE but choose a chore.
Open May 15–Oct 15.
13 sites. Pit toilets, tables, fire rings.
On Sanpoil River.
Hike or fish. Explore nearby lakes.
NO water. 14-day limit.
2170 ft (651 m)

## THESEUS CREEK

Wenatchee NF (509) 763-3103
State map: D5
From COLES CORNER, take
WA 207 N for 9 miles (8 k) to ranger
station, curving Left around state park.
Continue NW about 1.5 miles (2.4 k) to
FR 6500 (Little Wenatchee). Turn Left
and drive about 6 miles (9.6 k). Turn Left
(at Riverside) to cross river. Turn Right
on dirt FR 6701. Drive another 5 miles
(8 k) up river. (Also see Lake Creek,
Little Wenatchee Ford, or Soda Springs.)
FREE but choose a chore.
Open May 1–Nov 1.
3 close, open sites.
Pit toilets, tables, fire rings.
In isolated spot on Little Wenatchee.
Enjoy solitude. Hike, fish, or picnic.
NO water/trash facilities. 14-day limit.
2200 ft (660 m)

## TIFFANY SPRINGS

Okanogan NF (509) 486-2186
State map: B6
From CONCONULLY, go
total of 30.5 miles (48.8 k) NW on FR 38
(road begins as CR 2361), turning Left on

FR 39 a few miles after Salmon
Meadows Camp.
FREE but choose a chore.
Open May 15–Sep 30; camping allowed
off-season.
6 close, open sites.
Pit toilets, tables, fire rings.
Near Tiffany Mountain.
Hike about 1 mile (1.6 k) to Tiffany Lake.
Explore more distant options.
NO water/trash arrangements (pack it
out). 14-day/22-ft limits.
6800 ft (2040 m)

## TILLICUM

Gifford Pinchot NF
(509) 395-2501
State map: G4
From TROUT LAKE, head W on WA 141
for 4 miles (6.4 k) to Ice Cave. Drive W
on FR 24 for 19 miles (30.4 k)–circling W
around Twin Butte. On FR 2480 which
circles E, find South (9 sites) and Saddle
(12 sites). (Also see Surprise Lakes.)
FREE but choose a chore.
Open Jun 15–Oct 15.
49 (12 tent-only) sites.
Water, pit toilets, tables, fire rings.
On creek.
Hike or bike–E for Mosquito Lakes or W
for Meadow Lake and Squaw Butte.
14-day/16-ft limits.
4300 ft (1290 m)

## TOATS COULEE

WA DNR (206) 753-2400
State map: B6
From LOOMIS (grocery), go
N for 2.1 miles (3.4 k). Turn Left (W)
onto Toats Coulee Rd and drive
5.5 miles (8.8 k) to lower camp. Upper
camp is another .1 mile (160 m) at
junction of OM-T-1000 and OM-T-2000.
(Also see Cold Springs and North Fork
Nine Mile.)
FREE but choose a chore.
Open All Year.
9 scattered, open sites.
Pit toilets, tables, grills.
On forest stream.
Enjoy good wildlife viewing.
NO water. 14-day limit.

▲ ▲ ▲ ▲ ▲ ▲ ▲ ▲ ▲ ▲ ▲ ▲ ▲ ▲ ▲ ▲ ▲ ▲ ▲ ▲ ▲ ▲ ▲ ▲

## TOONERVILLE

WA DNR (206) 753-2400
State map: E3
Take WA 300 SE out of
BELFAIR for 3.5 miles (5.6 k). Turn Right
on Belfair–Tahuya Rd and go .6 mile
(1 k). Turn Right on Elfendahl Pass Rd
and go 3.6 miles (5.8 k) through
intersection with Goat Ranch Rd. Camp's
on left. (Also see Camp Spillman,
Howell Lake, and Twin Lakes.)
FREE but choose a chore.
Open All Year.
4 close, open sites.
Pit toilets, tables, fire rings.
Hike and explore Tahuya State Forest.
NO water. 14-day limit.

## TREE PHONES

WA DNR (206) 753-2400
State map: F4
From TAMPICO, take A-2000
(Middle Fork Rd) W for 15.3 miles
(24.5 k)–just before road begins steep
climb. (Also see Ahtanum, Clover Flats,
and Snow Cabin.)
FREE but choose a chore.
Open All Year.
14 close, open sites.
Pit toilets, tables, grills, group shelter.
On forest creek.
In summer, picnic, fish, or motorbike. In
winter, snowmobile.
NO water. 14-day limit. Noisy.

## TROUBLESOME CREEK

Mt Baker-Snoqualmie NF
(206) 677-2414
State map: D4
From INDEX, head E on CR 63 for
12 miles (19.2 k). (Also see San Juan.)
FREE but choose a chore.
Open May–Sep.
22 close, open sites.
Pit toilets, tables, fire rings.
In deep forest setting on creek.
Fish, splash, wade, and relax. Walk up to
Bear Falls.
NO water (can treat) or trash arrange-
ments. 14-day/22-ft limits.
1300 ft (390 m)

## TROUT LAKE

Colville NF (509) 738-6111
State map: B7
From KETTLE FALLS, take
US 395 NW for 3.5 miles (5.6 k). Turn W
on WA 20. Drive 5.5 miles (8.8 k). Turn
Right (N) on FR 020 and go 5 miles (8 k).
FREE but choose a chore.
Open May 25–Oct 30.
4 close, open sites.
Water, pit toilets, tables, fire rings.
Boat, swim, and fish on lake.
14-day limit.
3000 ft (900 m)

## TUCANNON

Umatilla NF (509) 843-1891
State map: G8
From DAYTON, head SE on
CR 118 for 14 miles (22.4 k). Turn Left
on FR 4620. Go 2 miles (3.2 k). Turn Left
(E) along Tucannon River. Go 3 miles
(4.8 k)–just beyond Camp Wooten. Turn
Right into camp. (Also see Godman.)
FREE but choose a chore.
Open All Year.
18 (10 tent-only) sites.
Water, pit toilets, tables, fire rings.
On river, near Wenaha-Tucannon
Wilderness.
Fish. Hike into wilderness. Explore.
14-day limit.
2600 ft (780 m)

## TWIN FALLS

Gifford Pinchot NF
(509) 395-2501
State map: G4
From TROUT LAKE, head N on CR 80
for 1 mile (1.6 k). Continue N on FR 23
for 16 miles (16 k). Turn Left (NW) on
FR 90 and go 4.5 miles (7.2 k). (Also see
Council Lake.)
FREE but choose a chore.
Open May 15–Sep 30.
5 sites. Pit toilets, tables, fire rings.
At confluence of creek and Lewis River
near Mt Adams Wilderness.
Enjoy scenery. Fish. Trek into
wilderness.
NO water. 14-day/16-ft limits.
2700 ft (810 m)

▲ ▲ ▲ ▲ ▲ ▲ ▲ ▲ ▲ ▲ ▲ ▲ ▲ ▲ ▲ ▲ ▲ ▲ ▲ ▲ ▲

## TWIN LAKES

WA DNR (206) 753-2400
State map: E3
Take WA 300 SE out of
BELFAIR for 3.5 miles (5.6 k). Turn Right
on Belfair–Tahuya Rd and go .6 mile
(1 k). Turn Right on Elfendahl Pass Rd
and go 2.6 miles (4.2 k). Turn Left on
Twin Lakes Rd and go 1.8 miles (2.9 k).
Turn Right and go .5 mile (800 m). (Also
see Camp Spillman, Howell Lake, and
Toonerville.)
FREE but choose a chore.
Open All Year.
6 close, open sites. Pit toilets, tables, fire
rings, boat launch.
In woods next to lake.
Create private base for hiking and
exploring Tahuya State Forest, floating
and fishing lakes, or doing nothing.
NO water. 14-day limit.

## UPPER CLEARWATER

WA DNR (206) 753-2400
State map: D1
From milepost 147 of US 101,
drive N on Hoh–Clearwater Mainline
for 12.9 miles (20.6 k)–through town of
CLEARWATER. Turn Right on gravel
C-3000. Drive 3.2 miles (5.1 k). (Also see
Coppermine Bottom and Yahoo Lake.)
FREE but choose a chore.
Open All Year.
6 close, open sites. Water, pit toilets,
tables, grills, boat launch.
On Clearwater River.
Float and canoe or fish.
14-day limit.

## WAR CREEK

Okanogan NF (509) 997-2131
State map: C5
From TWISP, take Twisp
River Rd NW about 14.4 miles (23 k).
(Also see Mystery and Poplar Flat.)
$4. Open Memorial Day–Sep 30; dry
camping off-season.
12 close, screened sites.
Water, pit toilets, tables, fire rings.
Near Twisp River in mountainous,
mixed-conifer setting.
Fish and hike (obtain map to trek into

adjacent North Cascades NP). Cross-
country ski in winter.
14-day limit. Crowded holidays.
Mosquitos and yellow jackets. Hunting
in season.
2400 ft (720 m)

## WESTERN LAKES

WA DNR (206) 753-2400
State map: G2
Near NASELLE at milepost 3
of WA 4, go N on gravel C-Line Rd up
hill for .9 mile (1.4 k). Turn Right on
C-4000 and go 1.4 miles (2.2 k). Turn
Left on 1-lane C-2600 and go .9 mile
(1.4 k). Turn Right on WA-WT-8520 for
just .3 mile (480 m).
FREE but choose a chore.
Open All Year.
3 close, open sites.
Pit toilets, tables, grills.
On isolated, wooded lakeshore.
Enjoy solitude and hiking trails.
NO water. 14-day limit.

## WHITE CHUCK

Mt Baker-Snoqualmie NF
(206) 436-1155
State map: C4
From DARRINGTON, head N about
1.2 miles (1.9 k) then turn Right (SE) on
FR 22. Go 10 miles (16 k). For trailhead
camp, continue SE on FR 23 for 10 miles
(16 k) to end.
FREE but choose a chore.
Open May–Sep.
7 (5 tent-only) close, open sites.
Pit toilets, tables, grills.
At confluence of White Chuck and Sauk
Rivers in old-growth forest with sparse
undergrowth.
Hike along White Chuck Bench to
Beaver Lake. Also, bike, fish or relax.
NO water/trash arrangements (pack it
out). 10-day/16-ft limits.
1000 ft (300 m)

## WHITE PASS LAKE

Wenatchee NF (509) 653-2205
State map: F4
From PACKWOOD, take
US 12 E for 20 miles (32 k). Turn Left

▲ ▲ ▲ ▲ ▲ ▲ ▲ ▲ ▲ ▲ ▲ ▲ ▲ ▲ ▲ ▲ ▲ ▲ ▲ ▲ ▲ ▲ ▲ ▲

(N) on FR 498 and go .3 mile (500 m). (Also see Dog Lake.)
FREE but choose a chore.
Open Jun 1–Nov 15.
16 close, open sites. Pit toilets, tables, fire rings, boat launch.
On lake with nearby horse camp.
Swim, boat (no motors), or fly fish. Hike couple of good trails.
NO water/trash arrangements (pack it out). 14-day/20-ft limits.
4500 ft (1350 m)

## WHITE PINE

Wenatchee NF (509) 763-3103
State map: D5
From COLES CORNER, take US 2 W about 9 miles (14.4 k)–just beyond Rayrock Store. Turn Left on FR 266 and go .5 mile (800 m).
FREE but choose a chore.
Open May 1–Nov 1.
5 close, open sites.
Pit toilets, tables, fire rings.
Close to highway.
Picnic or hike to explore area.
NO water/trash facilities. 14-day limit.
1900 ft (570 m)

## WHITE RIVER FALLS

Wenatchee NF (509) 763-3103
State map: D5
From COLES CORNER, take WA 207 N for 9 miles (8 k) to ranger station, curving Left around state park. Continue NW on FR 6400 (White River) for 11 miles (17.6 k). (Also see Grasshopper Meadows and Napeequa.)
FREE but choose a chore.
Open May 1–Nov 1.
5 close, open sites.
Pit toilets, tables, fire rings.
On White River near impressive falls.
Hike, fish, or picnic and relax.
NO water/trash facilities. 14-day limit.
Be careful of footing around waterfalls.
2100 ft (630 m)

## WILD ROSE

Wenatchee NF (509) 653-2205
State map: F4
From NACHES, take US 12

W for 20.5 miles (32.8 k). Other nearby choices are more developed camps (with fees): **Hause Creek, River Bend, Willows,** and **Windy Point.**
FREE but choose a chore.
Open Apr 15–Nov 15.
8 close, open sites.
Pit toilets, tables, fire rings.
On Tieton River.
Swim and fish. Hike area trails.
NO water/trash facilities (pack it out). 14-day/22-ft limits.
2400 ft (720 m)

## WILLIAM C DEARINGER

WA DNR (206) 753-2400
State map: C4
From DARRINGTON, go .3 mile (480 m) N on WA 530. Turn Right (E) on Mountain Loop Rd for .5 mile (800 m). Keep straight for another 4.9 miles (7.8 k). Turn Left on E Sauk Prairie Rd and drive .8 mile (1.3 k). Bear Right on SW-D-5000 for 2.7 miles (4.3 k). Stay Left another .8 mile (1.3 k) then turn Left on SW-D-5400 and go .2 mile (320 m).
FREE but choose a chore.
Open All Year.
12 close, open sites.
Pit toilets, tables, grills.
In secluded forest on Sauk River.
Enjoy peace and quiet.
NO water. 14-day limit.

## WILLIAMS LAKE

WA DNR (206) 753-2400
State map: B8
From COLVILLE, head W on US 395 for 1.5 miles (2.4 k). Turn Right (N) on Williams Lake Rd and drive 15.2 miles (24.3 k). Make 2 Lefts into camp.
FREE but choose a chore.
Open All Year.
8 sites. Water, pit toilets, tables, grills.
In woods on lakeshore.
Fish, canoe, and relax.
14-day limit.

▲ ▲ ▲ ▲ ▲ ▲ ▲ ▲ ▲ ▲ ▲ ▲ ▲ ▲ ▲ ▲ ▲ ▲ ▲ ▲ ▲ ▲ ▲ ▲

## WILLOUGHBY CREEK

WA DNR (206) 753-2400
State map: D1
About 15 miles (24 k) South
of FORKS between mileposts 178-179 of
US 101, go E on Hoh Rain Forest Rd for
3.5 miles (5.6 k). Camp on Right. (Also
see Minnie Peterson.)
FREE but choose a chore.
Open All Year.
3 close, open sites.
Pit toilets, tables, grills.
Fish on Hoh River.
NO water. 14-day limit.

## WINDUST PARK

COE (509) 399-2387
State map: F7
From KAHLOTUS, head S on
WA 263 for 9 miles (14.4 k).
FREE but choose a chore.
Open All Year.
20 (10 tent-only) scattered, open sites. &
Water, flush toilets, tables, grills,
playground.
On Lake Sacajawea below Monumental
Dam–swim, boat, or fish.
14-day limit.
400 ft (120 m)

## WINSTON CREEK

WA DNR (206) 753-2400
State map: F3
From MAYFIELD, go E on
US 12 for 2 miles (3.2 k). Turn Right (S)
on Winston Creek Rd and go 3.6 miles
(5.8 k). Turn Left (E) on Longbell Rd and
go 1 mile (1.6 k).
FREE but choose a chore.
Open All Year.
11 close, open sites.
Water, pit toilets, tables, grills.
In quiet streamside forest setting.
Fish and relax. Picnic.
14-day limit.
1050 ft (315 m)

## WOODLAND

WA DNR (206) 753-2400
State map: H3
From WOODLAND at Exit
21 off I-5, take WA 503 E for .1 mile

(200 m). Turn Right to East CC St. Go
just S of bridge. Turn Right on CR 38
and go 2.5 miles (4 k).
FREE but choose a chore.
Open All Year.
10 close, open sites. &
Water, pit toilets, tables, grills,
playground.
In forest near several towns.
Make handy layover or getaway.
14-day limit.

## YAHOO LAKE WALK-IN

WA DNR (206) 753-2400
State map: D1
From milepost 147 of US 101,
drive N on Hoh–Clearwater Mainline
for 12.9 miles (20.6 k)–through town of
CLEARWATER. Turn Right on gravel
C-3000 and drive 4 miles (6.4 k). Turn
Right on C-3100 and go 5.5 miles (8.8 k).
Bear Left and continue .6 mile (1 k).
Walk in. (Also see Coppermine Bottom
and Upper Clearwater.)
FREE but choose a chore.
Open All Year.
6 close, open tent sites. Pit toilets, tables,
grills, group shelter, boat dock.
On secluded, forest lake.
Hike. Canoe or fish.
NO water. 14-day limit.
1900 ft (570 m)

## YEW TREE

WA DNR (206) 753-2400
State map: F2
Go W from LITTLEROCK for
1 mile (1.6 k). Turn Right (N) on
Waddell Creek Rd and go 3.7 miles
(5.9 k). Turn Left and go .1 mile (200 m).
(Also see Middle Waddell.)
FREE but choose a chore.
Open All Year.
3 close, open sites.
Pit toilets, tables, grills.
On forest stream.
NO water. 14-day limit. Motorcycles.
Noisy.

# Wyoming

Grid conforms to official state map. For your copy, call (800) 225-5996
or write Division of Tourism, I-25 at College Dr, Cheyenne, WY 82002.

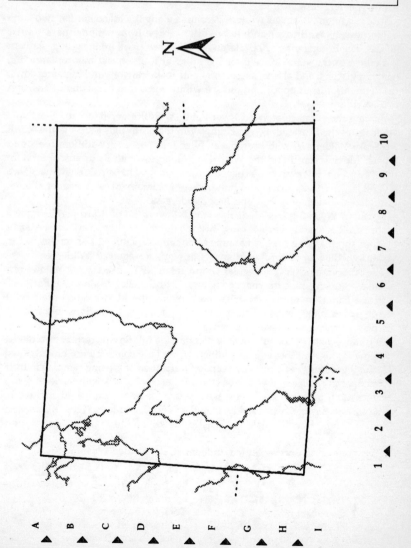

Wyoming's topography creates camping diversity. Switching from desert floor to rugged, snowcapped mountain takes only a short move. Fortunately, inexpensive choices abound due to state and local efforts as well as the US Forest Service, Bureau of Land Management (BLM), and National Park Service (NPS).

Sacred to the Plains Indians is land administered by **Bighorn National Forest** (NF) and it's easy to sense why. Arising suddenly from flatlands, this forested range has been a great source of game. Seek out special spots, such as Cloud Peak Primitive Area, Tensleep and Shell canyons, Bighorn Medicine Wheel, Fallen City, even the road east from Lovell.

**Black Hills NF** dominates the northeastern part of the state with the especially scenic Warren Peaks area.

**Bridger-Teton NF** covers western Wyoming along the Idaho border. Two large wilderness areas, Bridger and Teton, offer escape from national park tourist hordes. The Bridger offers 20 peaks above 12000 feet (3658 m) including Gannett, the tallest in the state. More than 500 miles of trails reveal moose, large elk, hanging glaciers, and alpine lakes. Among its rocky canyons and high meadows, the Teton affords an opportunity to see wildflowers, rare trumpeter swans, and breccia cliffs.

Sharing the spectacular Wind River Range with Bridger-Teton, the **Shoshone NF** features the Beartooth Scenic Highway in the north plus access to the North Absaroka Wilderness with bear, bison, lynx, and bobcat in addition to elk and moose. Moving south find the Washakie Wilderness with its extensive array of petrified wood. For even more rugged terrain, try the Fitzpatrick Wilderness with several large, active glaciers and hundreds of mountain lakes. A smaller, though formidable, challenge is the Popo Agie Wilderness.

Southern Wyoming has **Medicine Bow NF** with the postcard-perfect Snowy Mountain Range and Sierra Madres' historic mining territory. Farther east, sight bighorn sheep among rugged Laramie Mountains, fanciful rock shapes etched in Vedauwoo Glen, or colorful wildflowers in virgin Savage Run Wilderness.

The **NPS** administers spectacular Grand Teton NP (backcountry), Yellowstone NP (backcountry), plus the connecting John D Rockefeller, Jr Memorial Parkway.

In the flatter, more arid foothills and canyons, the **BLM** offers a number of scenic drives plus campsites near intriguing geologic formations, old mining districts, pioneer trails, lakes, and streams.

**Wyoming State Parks** (SPs) qualify and provide full service, recreation-centered camping throughout the state. In addition, many local communities through town or county governments continue a wonderful tradition of offering camping in their parks. Several are listed. If you need an overnight spot, check with the local police station. You'll probably discover a nearby free (or minimum-fee) alternative in these towns: Basin, Casper, Cody, Douglas, Fort Laramie, Kaycee, Kemmerer, Lander, Lewis, Lovell, Lusk, Newcastle, Rawlins, Sheridan, Sundance, and Torrington.

Find yourself in uncomplicated, unfettered, uncrowded Wyoming.

▲ ▲ ▲ ▲ ▲ ▲ ▲ ▲ ▲ ▲ ▲ ▲ ▲ ▲ ▲ ▲ ▲ ▲ ▲ ▲ ▲ ▲ ▲

## ALPINE

Targhee NF (208) 523-1412
State map: D1
From ALPINE, take US 26 W
for 3 miles (4.8 k).

$5; for additional $6, reservations accepted at (800) 283-2267.
Open Jun 1–Sep 15.
26 close, open sites. Water, pit toilets, tables, grills, fire rings.

▲ ▲ ▲ ▲ ▲ ▲ ▲ ▲ ▲ ▲ ▲ ▲ ▲ ▲ ▲ ▲ ▲ ▲ ▲ ▲ ▲ ▲

On stream.
Hike, fish, or ride horses.
14-day/26-ft limits.

## ATLANTIC CITY

BLM (307) 324-7171
State map: F4
From LANDER, take WY 28 S
about 17 miles (27.2 k) to Atlantic City
turnoff. Turn Left (E) and go about
.5 mile (800 m) on gravel road. For
companion camp, **Big Atlantic Gulch**
($4, 10 sites), turn Left on BLM 2324. Go
.25 mile (400 m).
**$5.** Open Jun 1–Nov 1; dry camping
off-season.
22 scattered, open sites. Water, pit toilets,
tables, grills, fire rings.
Among lodgepole pine and quaking
aspen near old Camp Stambaugh and
South Pass Historical District.
Good for mountain biking, touring old
mines, fishing, and relaxing. Skiing in
winter.
14-day limit. Crowded around Sep–Oct.
8100 ft (2430 m)

## BATTLE CREEK

Medicine Bow NF
(307) 327-5481
State map: H6
From ENCAMPMENT, take FH 11 W for
28 miles (44.8 k). Turn Left (S) on
FR 807. Go 2 miles (3.2 k).
**FREE** but choose a chore.
Open May 25–Oct 31; camping allowed
off-season.
4 close, open sites.
Pit toilets, tables, grills, fire rings.
Creek setting with nearby trails.
Good hiking. Also fishing, photography,
and birdwatching.
14-day/16-ft limits.
7800 ft (2340 m)

## BEARLODGE

Black Hills NF (307) 283-1361
State map: B10
Drive about 7 miles (11.2 k)
SE of ALVA on WY 24.
**FREE** but choose a chore.
Open May 22–Sep 8; camping off-season.

8 scattered, screened sites.
Pit toilets, tables, fire rings.
In quiet location among pines –
birdwatch and relax. Visit nearby Devils
Tower NM.
NO water/trash facilities (pack it out).
14-day/22-ft limits. Hunting in season.
4000 ft (1200 m)

## BEARTOOTH LAKE

Shoshone NF (307) 754-7207
State map: A3
From COOKE CITY, MT, take
one of country's most beautiful drives
US 212 (Beartooth Scenic Byway) E for
24.5 miles (39.2 k). Alternative **Island
Lake** is 3 miles (4.8 k) farther. (Also see
Fox Creek.)
**$5.** Open Jul 1–Sep 7; dry camping
off-season.
21 scattered, screened sites. Water, pit
toilets, tables, grills, fire rings.
On alpine lake next to picturesque
Absaroka Beartooth Wilderness.
Explore region with excellent hiking
possibilities. Fish and boat (no motors).
14-day/32-ft limits.
9000 ft (2700 m)

## BENNETT PEAK

BLM (307) 324-7171
State map: H7
From RIVERSIDE, take
WY 230 E for 4 miles (6.4 k). Turn Left
(N) on CR 660 and go 8 miles (12.8 k).
Turn Left on BLM 3404 and drive
6 miles (9.6 k). (Also see Corral Creek.)
**$3.** Open Jun 1–Nov 1; dry camping
off-season.
12 scattered, open sites. Water, pit toilets,
tables, fire rings, boat ramp.
Along North Platte River.
Pleasant spot for canoeing or floating
river. Fish and swim a bit; relax a lot.
14-day limit. Crowded around Aug–Sep.
7380 ft (2214 m)

## BIG SANDY

Bridger-Teton NF
(307) 733-2752
State map: F3
From BOULDER, take WY 353 SE for

15 miles (24 k). Continue SE on CR 23118 for 21 miles (33.6 k). Turn Left (NE) on FR 135. Go 6 miles (9.6 k).
FREE but choose a chore.
Open Jun 20–Sep 10.
12 scattered, open sites.
Pit toilets, tables, fire rings.
On Big Sandy River next to Bridger Wilderness.
Take a trek into scenic Wind River Range or stay around camp and swim, boat, or fish.
NO water/trash arrangements (pack it out). 14-day limit.
9100 ft (2730 m)

## BIG SANDY SRA

(307) 332-3684
State map: F3
From FARSON, take WY 191 N for 9 miles (14.4 k). Turn Right (E) (dirt road difficult when wet).
FREE but choose a chore.
Open Jun 1–Oct 1.
12 scattered, open sites. Water, pit toilets, tables, grills, fire rings, boat ramp.
Next to high-altitude desert reservoir with Wind River Mountain backdrop.
Water activities predominate: swimming, fishing, and boating.
Be prepared to clean up area as well as pack out trash. 14-day limit.
6580 ft (1974 m)

## BIGHORN CANYON NRA
### Barry's Landing

(406) 689-3155
State map: A5
From LOVELL, take US 14A E for 2 miles (3.2 k). Turn Left (N) on WY 37. Go 24 miles (38.4 k) into MT. Pass 126-site **Horseshoe Bend** (fee charged) at mile 11.
FREE but $3 entrance fee (or pass). Also, free backcountry permits available at Visitor Center.
Open All Year.
20 (5 tent-only) scattered, open sites.
Walk-in sites with some privacy.
Pit toilets, tables, fire rings, boat ramp.
In arid setting with creek and cottonwood trees.

Wander over to old Hillsboro townsite. Enjoy panorama of lake. Of course, most come to boat, waterski, swim, or fish.
NO water. 14-day/16-ft limits.
3700 ft (1110 m)

## BOBBIE THOMPSON

Medicine Bow NF
(307) 745-8971
State map: H7
From FOXPARK (a few miles N of MOUNTAIN HOME), go 11.2 miles (17.9 k) NW on FR 512–alternative to more popular, fee-charged **Rob Roy**.
$5. Open Jun 1–Oct 15; dry camping off-season.
10 close, open sites.
Water, tables, grills, fire rings.
On nice creek.
Fishing and hiking.
14-day/32-ft limits.
8800 ft (2640 m)

## BOSWELL CREEK

Medicine Bow NF
(307) 745-8971
State map: H8
From LARAMIE, go 38 miles (61 k) SW on WY 230. Turn Right (E) on unpaved FR 526 and continue 3 miles (4.8 k).
FREE but choose a chore.
Open Jun 1–Oct 15; camping allowed off-season.
9 close, open sites.
Pit toilets, tables, grills, fire rings.
On small creek near CO border, reduced maintenance schedule campground.
Fish in creek or take extended walks through surrounding mountains.
14-day/16-ft limits.
8900 ft (2670 m)

## BOTTLE CREEK

Medicine Bow NF
(307) 327-5481
State map: H7
From ENCAMPMENT, take FH 11 W for 7.1 miles (11.4 k).
$5. Open May 25–Oct 31; dry camping off-season.
12 close, open sites. Water, pit toilets, tables, grills, fire rings.

▲ ▲ ▲ ▲ ▲ ▲ ▲ ▲ ▲ ▲ ▲ ▲ ▲ ▲ ▲ ▲ ▲ ▲ ▲ ▲ ▲ ▲

On creek in beautiful region. Hike or kick back and relax. Fishing readily available.
14-day/16-ft limits.
8800 ft (2640 m)

## BOULDER LAKE

Bridger-Teton NF
(307) 733-2752
State map: E3

From BOULDER, take WY 353 E for 11 miles (17.6 k). Turn Left (N) on CR 114 and go 9 miles (14.4 k)–bearing Right when road becomes FR 114. On north side of lake, BLM maintains 5-unit site. For more primitive spot, try nearby **Burnt Lake**. (Also see Scab Creek.)
**FREE** but choose a chore.
Open Jun 1–Oct 15.
25 close, open sites.
Pit toilets, tables, fire rings.
On lake with access to scenic Bridger Wilderness.
Hike into Wind River Range or stay around camp and swim, boat, or fish.
NO water/trash facilities. 10-day limit.
7300 ft (2190 m)

## BOW RIVER

Medicine Bow NF
(307) 326-5258
State map: H7

From ELK MOUNTAIN, go S on unpaved CR 101 for 14 miles (22.4 k). Jog Left (SE) on FR 1013A for 1.3 miles (2.1 k) then Right (W) on FR 101 for .2 mile (300 m).
**$5**. Open Jun 15–Sep 15; dry camping off-season.
13 close, open sites. Water, pit toilets, tables, grills, fire rings.
Near several lakes.
Good wildlife viewing opportunities including birdwatching. Bring camera and/or fishing gear.
14-day/32-ft limits.
8600 ft (2580 m)

## BOYSEN SP-Lake Campgrounds

(307) 876-2796
State map: D5
Facilities start just N of

SHOSHONI off US 20.
**$4**. Open All Year.
180 scattered, open sites (some undesignated). Water, pit toilets, tables, grills, group shelters, pay phone, dump station, boat ramp, store with rentals.
In several spots, both above and below dam, around 19000-acre reservoir.
Fishing, swimming, and boating plus fishing derbies and volleyball tournaments. When cold, ski or participate in winter carnival.
14-day limit. Prepare to pack out trash.
4820 ft (1446 m)

## BOYSEN SP

### Upper & Lower Wind River

(307) 876-2796
State map: D5
Find 15 miles (24 k) N of

SHOSHONI off US 20.
**$4**. Open All Year.
45 scattered, open sites. Water, pit toilets, tables, grills, group shelters, pay phone, dump station.
Amidst cottonwood along Wind River.
Wonderful area for exploring, including some historic curiosities (old railroad and mining ventures). Fish river.
14-day limit. Pack out trash.
5000 ft (1500 m)

## BROWN MOUNTAIN

Shoshone NF (307)868-2379
State map: C3
From MEETEETSE, head W

on WY 29 past famous cattle ranches. Fork Left onto CR/FR 200 for total of 28 miles (44.8 k). (Also see Wood River.)
**FREE**, donations requested.
Open May 31–Nov 15; dry camping off-season.
6 scattered, screened sites. Water, pit toilets, tables, grills, fire rings.
In woods on streambank.
Besides fishing, take advantage of excellent hiking opportunities.
14-day/16-ft limits.
7600 ft (2280 m)

▲ ▲ ▲ ▲ ▲ ▲ ▲ ▲ ▲ ▲ ▲ ▲ ▲ ▲ ▲ ▲ ▲ ▲ ▲ ▲ ▲ ▲ ▲ ▲

## BUFFALO BILL SP

(307) 587-9227
State map: B3
From CODY, go 6 miles
(9.6 k) W on US 14/16/20.
$4. Open May 1–Oct 31.
71 (6 tent-only) scattered, open sites.
Water, pit toilets, tables, grills, fire rings,
dump station, boat ramp.
As Bureau of Reclamation expands reservoir, camping areas shift. Plans
keep sites open during reconstruction.
Excellent for boating, waterskiing,
swimming, and fishing.
14-day limit.
5300 ft (1590 m)

## BULL CREEK

Bighorn NF (307) 347-8291
State map: C6
From TEN SLEEP, head NE
on WY 16 for 25 miles (40 k). Turn Left
(N) on FR 432 and go .5 mile (800 m).
(Also see Lakeview.)
FREE but choose a chore.
Open Jun 1–Oct 31; camping allowed
off-season.
10 close, open sites.
Pit toilets, tables, fire rings, boat ramp.
On Meadowlark Lake.
Fishing and boating.
NO water. 14-day/16-ft limits.
8400 ft (2520 m)

## CABIN CREEK

Bighorn NF (307) 765-4435
State map: B5
From SHELL, go NE on US 14
for 15.7 miles (25 k).
$5. Open Jun 1–Oct 31; dry camping
off-season.
4 close, open sites.
Water, pit toilets, tables, fire rings.
On creek near trailer park, fishing is IT!
14-day limit.
7400 ft (2220 m)

## CAMPBELL CREEK

Medicine Bow NF
(307) 358-4690
State map: F8
From DOUGLAS, take WY 91 S for

20 miles (32 k) then go 13 more miles
(20.8 k) on CR 24.
FREE but choose a chore.
Open Jun 1–Oct 31; camping allowed
off-season. 9 close, open sites.
Pit toilets, tables, grills, fire rings.
Near couple of creeks plus rugged
hiking trails.
Hiking and fishing.
NO water. 14-day/22-ft limits.
8200 ft (2460 m)

## CANYON CAMPGROUND

Bighorn NF (307) 684-7891
State map: C6
From BUFFALO, head W on
WY 16 for 25.5 miles (40.8 k). Turn Left
(E) on FR 33 and go 2 miles (3.2 k).
FREE but choose a chore.
Open Jun 1–Sep 30; dry camping
off-season.
4 close, open sites.
Pit toilets, tables, fire rings.
In usually quiet locale on creek.
Nice getaway with a bit of fishing.
NO water. 14-day/16-ft limits.
7400 ft (2220 m)

## CASTLE GARDENS

BLM (307) 347-9871
State map: C6
From TEN SLEEP, go 1 mile
(1.6 k) W on US 16 to Castle Gardens
Scenic Area (dirt road). Follow signs
5 miles (8 k).
FREE but choose a chore.
Open May–Nov; camping allowed
off-season.
2 close, open sites.
Pit toilet, tables, grills, fire rings.
With outstanding desert scenery.
Explore area by walking nature trail or
hiking further afield. Good opportunities
for birdwatching and photography.
NO water/trash arrangements. 14-day
limit. Hunting in season.
4500 ft (1350 m)

## COFFEEN PARK

Bighorn NF (307) 672-0751
State map: B6
Take WY 335 SW from BIG

▲ ▲ ▲ ▲ ▲ ▲ ▲ ▲ ▲ ▲ ▲ ▲ ▲ ▲ ▲ ▲ ▲ ▲ ▲ ▲ ▲ ▲ ▲ ▲

HORN for 9.3 miles (14.9 k). Turn SW on FR 25 and go 8 miles (12.8 k). Head SW for 8 more miles (12.8 k) on very rough FR 293–may need 4WD near end. (Also see Cross Creek and Little Goose.)

**FREE** but choose a chore.

Open Jun 1–Oct 31; dry camping off-season.

5 close, open tent sites.

Pit toilets, tables, fire rings.

On creek next to beautiful Cloud Peak Wilderness.

Great base for extensive exploring.

NO water. 14-day/16-ft limits.

8500 ft (2550 m)

## COLD SPRINGS

Bighorn NF (307) 765-4435
State map: B6
From SHELL, take US 14 NE for 7.2 miles (11.5 k). Head NE on FR 344 for 11.3 miles (18.1 k).

**FREE** but choose a chore.

Open May 30–Oct 31; camping allowed off-season.

8 close, open sites.

Pit toilets, tables, fire rings.

In quiet spot near Paint Rock Creek.

Getaway with fishing possibilities.

NO water. 14-day/16-ft limits.

8600 ft (2580 m)

## CONNOR BATTLEFIELD SP

(307) 674-4589
State map: A6
Locate in RANCHESTER, about 2 blocks off US 14.

**FREE** but choose a chore.

Open May 1–Oct 15.

12 scattered, open sites. Water, pit toilets, tables, grills, fire rings.

In lush green park on Tongue River.

Learn about one of many episodes in white man vs red man battles which took place in 1800s.

14-day limit. Be prepared to pack out trash and keep this site clean.

3745 ft (1122 m)

## CORRAL CREEK

BLM (307) 324-7171
State map: H7
From RIVERSIDE, take WY 230 E for 4 miles (6.4 k). Turn Left (N) on CR 660 and go 8 miles (12.8 k). Turn Left on BLM 3404 and drive 5 miles (8 k). (Also see Bennett Peak).

**$3.** Open Jun 1–Nov 1; dry camping off-season.

12 close, open sites. Water, pit toilets, tables, fire rings, boat ramp.

In nice position near North Platte River for canoeing or floating. Fish, swim, relax a lot.

14-day limit. Crowded Aug–Sep.

7380 ft (2214 m)

## COTTONWOOD

BLM (307) 324-7171
State map: F5
From JEFFREY CITY, take US 287 E for 8 miles (12.8 k). Turn Right (S) on Green Mountain Rd. Go 8 miles (12.8 k)–follow signs.

**$4.** Open Jun 1–Nov 1; dry camping off-season.

21 scattered, screened sites. Water, pit toilets, tables, grills, fire rings.

Nestled among evergreens along Cottonwood Creek on Green Mountain.

Escape for mountain biking, wildlife viewing, fishing, and relaxing. Take a few pictures.

14-day limit. Crowds possible Sep–Oct.

7700 ft (2310 m)

## COTTONWOOD LAKE

Bridger-Teton NF
(307) 733-2752
State map: F1
From SMOOT, take WY 89 S for 1 mile (1.6 k). Turn Left (E) on CR/FR 10208 and go 7.5 miles (12 k).

**FREE** but choose a chore.

Open Jun 15–Sep 10.

7 close, open sites.

Pit toilets, tables, fire rings.

Canoe, swim, and fish from lakeside sites. Hike in nearby mountains.

NO water/trash arrangements (pack it out). 10-day/16-ft limits.

## CROSS CREEK

Bighorn NF (307) 672-0751
State map: B6
Take WY 335 SW from BIG
HORN for 9.3 miles (14.9 k). Turn SW on
FR 25 and go 8 miles (12.8 k). Head SW
for 6 miles (9.6 k) on very rough
FR 293–may need 4WD near end. (Also
see Coffeen Park and Little Goose.)
FREE but choose a chore.
Open Jun 1 – Oct 31; dry camping
off-season.
3 close, open tent sites.
Pit toilets, tables, fire rings.
In remote spot on creek.
Possible base for extensive exploring of
beautiful territory or getaway spot.
NO water. 14-day/16-ft limits.
8400 ft (2520 m)

## CURT GOWDY SP

(307) 632-7946
State map: H9
From CHEYENNE, take
Missile Dr (WY 210) Exit off I-25. Head
W on WY 210 for 23.5 miles (37.6 k) to
Happy Jack Rd.
$4. Open All Year.
280 scattered, open sites. Water, pit
toilets, tables, grills, fire rings, pay
phone, dump station, boat ramp, beach.
Amidst massive granite formations
framing timbered park with two
reservoirs: Crystal and Granite. Find
sites near water or among pines.
Natural area for hiking, lodge for group
activities, and, of course, two lakes with
boating, waterskiing, and fishing (sorry,
no swimming). Nature study and
photography also popular.
14-day limit. Quiet hours.
7200 ft (2160 m)

## CURTIS GULCH

Medicine Bow NF
(307) 358-4690
State map: F8
From DOUGLAS, take WY 91 S for
20 miles (32 k) then 14 more miles
(22.4 k) on CR 16 until reaching unpaved
FR 658. Turn Left (NE) and drive 4 miles
(6.4 k).

FREE but choose a chore.
Open Jun 1 – Oct 31; camping allowed
off-season.
6 close, open sites.
Pit toilets, tables, grills, fire rings.
Nice creekside location deep in forest.
Good hiking and fishing possibilities.
NO water. 14-day/22-ft limits.
6600 ft (1980 m)

## DEAD INDIAN

Shoshone NF (307) 754-7207
State map: A3
From CODY, take WY 120 N
for 17 miles (27.2 k). Turn Left (NW) on
MT 296 (Chief Joseph Scenic Byway) and
drive 25 miles (40 k). Another 17 miles
(27.2 k) NW on 296 is Hunter Peak (fee
charged); 4 more miles (6.4 k) is Lake
Creek (fee charged).
FREE but choose a chore.
Open May 1 – Nov 30; camping allowed
off-season.
12 scattered, screened sites.
Pit toilets, tables, grills, fire rings.
On creek near wilderness trailhead
means scenic area to explore. Fish too.
NO water. 14-day/32-ft limits.
6000 ft (1800 m)

## DEEP CREEK

Medicine Bow NF
(307) 326-5258
State map: H7
From ARLINGTON, take unpaved
FR 111 S for 11 miles (17.6 k). Turn S on
FR 101, drive 2 miles (3.2 k).
$5. Open Jul 1 – Sep 15; camping allowed
off-season.
12 close, open sites.
Pit toilets, tables, grills, fire rings.
Near excellent hiking trail.
Photographic opportunities complement
usual hiking and fishing activities.
NO water. 14-day/22-ft limits.
10100 ft (3030 m)

## DEER CREEK

Shoshone NF (307) 527-6921
State map: C3
From CODY, take WY 291 SW
(South Fork Dr) then continue on FR 479

for a total of 47 miles (75.2 k).
**FREE** but choose a chore.
Open All Year.
7 scattered, screened sites.
Pit toilets, tables, grills, fire rings.
On creekbank in beautiful region.
Exceptional access to Washakie Wilderness and southern part of Absaroka Mountains. Hike or fish.
NO water/trash arrangements (pack it out). 14-day/16-ft limits.
6400 ft (1920 m)

## DICKINSON CREEK

Shoshone NF (307) 332-5460
State map: E3
From LANDER, take US 26/287 NW for 15 miles (24 k). Turn Left at Hines Store on CR and go 5 miles (8 k). Continue on FR 167 for 14 miles (22.4 k) then 3 miles (4.8 k) on FR 303.
**FREE** but choose a chore.
Open Jul 1 – Sep 15; dry camping off-season.
15 scattered, screened sites. Water, pit toilets, tables, grills, fire rings.
In remote, creekside spot.
Fish. Explore Popo Agie Wilderness.
Enjoy peace and quiet.
14-day/20-ft limits.
9400 ft (2820 m)

## DOYLE

Bighorn NF (307) 684-7891
State map: C6
Take US 16 W from BUFFALO for 27 miles (43.2 k). Head SW on FR 484 and go 5.5 miles (8.8 k). Turn Left (SE) on FR 514 and go .3 mile (480 m).
**FREE** but choose a chore.
Open May 15 – Sep 15; camping allowed off-season.
18 close, open sites.
Pit toilets, tables, fire rings.
Getaway on creek with a little fishing thrown in.
NO water. 14-day/22-ft limits.
8100 ft (2430 m)

## EAGLE CREEK

Shoshone NF (307) 527-6921
State map: B2
From CODY, head W for 44.7 miles (71.5 k) on US 14/16/20. In next 5 miles (8 k), find series of three more camps with similar facilities and fees: **Sleeping Giant** (6 sites), **Three Mile** (33 sites), **Pahaska** (24 sites). (Also see Wapiti).
**$5**. Open Jun 1 – Sep 30; dry camping off-season.
20 scattered, screened sites. Water, pit toilets, tables, grills, fire rings.
Wooded streamside sites on road to Yellowstone NP.
Fish or relax around one of these camps. Access trails into Washakie Wilderness within .5 mile (800 m).
14-day/22-ft limits.
6500 ft (1950 m)

## EAST FORK

Bighorn NF (307) 672-0751
State map: B6
From BIG HORN, take WY 335 S for 9.3 miles (14.9 k). Head SW on FR 26 for 8 miles (12.8 k). Turn Left (S) on FR 293. Go .5 mile (800 m). (Also see Ranger Creek).
**$4**. Open Jun 1 – Oct 31; dry camping off-season.
12 close, open tent sites.
Water, pit toilets, tables, fire rings
Create creekside base for hiking and exploring secluded area. Fishing opportunities too.
14-day/22-ft limits. No trailers.
7600 ft (2280 m)

## ENCAMPMENT

BLM (307) 324-7171
State map: H7
From ENCAMPMENT, take FH 70 W for 1 mile (1.6 k). Turn Left (S) on CR 353 and go 1 mile (1.6 k). Turn Left (E) on BLM 3407 and go 1 mile (1.6 k).
**FREE** but choose a chore.
Open All Year.
7 close, open sites.
Pit toilets, tables, fire rings.

▲ ▲ ▲ ▲ ▲ ▲ ▲ ▲ ▲ ▲ ▲ ▲ ▲ ▲ ▲ ▲ ▲ ▲ ▲ ▲ ▲ ▲

On banks of Encampment River.
Offers river access for swimmers, kayakers, and fishermen. Encampment River Canyon Trailhead leads to BLM Wilderness Study Area and USFS Wilderness. NO water/trash arrangements (pack it out). 14-day limit. Hunting in season.
7380 ft (2214 m)

## ESTERBROOK

Medicine Bow NF
(307) 358-4690
State map: F9
From DOUGLAS, take WY 94 S for 17 miles (27.2 k) then 11 more miles (17.6 k) on CR 5 to unpaved FR 633. Turn Left (E). Go 3 miles (4.8 k).
**FREE** but choose a chore.
Open Jun 1 – Oct 15; dry camping off-season.
12 close, open sites. Water, pit toilets, tables, grills, fire rings.
With Laramie Peak backdrop, pretty choice camp.
Good hiking opportunities.
14-day/22-ft limits.
6500 ft (1950 m)

## FIDDLERS LAKE

Shoshone NF (307) 332-5460
State map: F4
Find on Loop Rd. Either take WY 131 S out of LANDER or drive from other end (near SOUTH PASS CITY off WY 28). Fiddler is 23.4 miles (37.4 k) from LANDER. (Also see Louis Lake, Popo Agie, and Worthen Meadows.)
**$5.** Open Jul 1 – Sep 15; dry camping off-season.
12 (5 tent-only) sites. &
Water, pit toilets, tables, grills, fire rings, boat ramp.
In pines near lake with access to Popo Agie Wilderness.
Great wildlife area. Wilderness at your doorstep – take a hike. Fish and swim (if brave). In winter, snowmobile or cross-country ski.
Road closed in winter.
9400 ft (2820 m)

## FONTENELLE CREEK RA

BLM (307) 382-5350
State map: F2
From LA BARGE, take US 189 S about 10 miles (16 k). (Also see Weeping Rock.)
**$5.** Open Jun 1 – Oct 5; dry camping off-season.
72 scattered, open sites.
Water, flush and pit toilets, tables, fire rings, boat ramps.
In four spots plus numerous access points to reservoir and Green River.
Water attractions include rafting, swimming, and fishing. Land-based opportunities for rockhounds, mountain bikers, wildlife viewers, historical trail buffs.
14-day limit.

## FOX CREEK

Shoshone NF (307) 754-7207
State map: A3
From COOKE CITY, MT, take US 212 (Beartooth Scenic Byway) E for 7.5 miles (12 k). For alternatives, continue E for **Crazy Creek** – 5 more miles (8 k) – and **Lake Creek** – 5.5 miles (8.8 k) then Right on WY 296 for 1 mile (1.6 k). (Also see Beartooth Lake in WY and Chief Joseph in MT.)
**$5.** Open Jun 1 – Sep 30; dry camping off-season.
27 scattered, screened sites. Water, pit toilets, tables, grills, fire rings.
On wooded creekbank near Clark Fork plus trailhead to exceptional wilderness. Hike and fish.
14-day/32-ft limits. Crowded in summer.
7100 ft (2130 m)

## FRENCH CREEK

Medicine Bow NF
(307) 326-5258
State map: H7
From SARATOGA, take WY 130 for 24 miles (38.4 k) E to FR 206 (South Brush Creek Rd). Turn Right (S) and continue 15 miles (24 k).
**$5.** Open Jun 1 – Oct 1; dry camping off-season.
11 close, open sites. Water, pit toilets, tables, grills, fire rings.

On creek in "Snowy Range" country with both fishing and hiking.

Like most Medicine Bow NF sites, find countless nearby secluded lakes, streams, and pastoral spots.

14-day/32-ft limits.

8000 ft (2400 m)

## FRIEND PARK

Medicine Bow NF
(307) 358-4690
State map: F9

From DOUGLAS, take WY 94 S for 17 miles (27.2 k) then 11 miles (17.6 k) on CR 5. Turn Left (SW) on FR 653. Drive 15 miles (24 k). Turn Left (SE) on FR 677. Go 3.5 miles (5.6 k).

FREE but choose a chore.

Open Jun 1–Oct 31; camping allowed off-season.

6 close, open sites.

Pit toilets, tables, grills, fire rings.

Walking and viewing opportunities abound with Laramie Peak Trail (moderately difficult due to elevation gain).

NO water. 14-day/22-ft limits.

7400 ft (2220 m)

## GLENDO SP

(307) 735-4433
State map: F9
Find just off I-25 outside GLENDO.

$4. Open All Year.

165 scattered, open sites.

Water, pit toilets, tables, grills, fire rings, pay phone, dump station, boat ramp, nearby store with ice and rentals.

On mammoth lake bordered by sandy beaches and forests.

Swim, boat, ski or fish. Sailboat regattas and fishing contests punctuate water sports. There's hiking and relaxing for land-based. Check out "Spanish Diggings" N of lake.

14-day limit.

4718 ft (1413 m)

## GRAND TETON NP-Backcountry

(307) 733-2880
State map: C1
Locate Visitor Center in MOOSE.

FREE but $10 entrance fee (or pass). (All campgrounds in park cost $8.) Obtain **free** backcountry permits at Visitor Center or at Jenny Lake Ranger Station (summer only).

Open All Year.

From rugged mountains to sagebrush flats, filled with rushing steams, alpine lakes, and varied wildlife.

Escape crowds by hiking into one of most spectacular, photogenic mountain ranges on earth.

Winter is long and blizzards, common. Weather can be extreme any time of year–come prepared.

6800 ft (2040 m)

## GRAVE SPRINGS

BLM (307) 261-7600
State map: E6
From ARMINTO, head N on rough WY 109 for 8 miles (12.8 k). Also, find single campsite at **Buffalo Creek**, a couple of miles back on 109.

FREE but choose a chore.

Open All Year.

3 scattered, open tent sites.

Pit toilets, tables, fire rings.

Along South Big Horn/Red Wall Scenic Byway.

Observe elk, mule deer, and antelope. You're near hideout of Butch Cassidy and "Hole-in-the-Wall" gang.

NO water. 14-day/16-ft limits.

## GUERNSEY SP

(307) 836-2334
State map: F9
Take WY 26 W from GUERNSEY for .5 mile (800 m). Turn Right (N) on WY 317 and drive 2 miles (3.2 k).

$4. Open May 1–Sep 30; dry camping off-season.

142 scattered, open sites. Water, pit toilets, tables, grills, fire rings, pay phone, dump station, boat ramp, beach. Protected by high bluffs, on warm water reservoir for boating enthusiasts with canyons as well as sandy beaches. Scattered 60-year-old CCC buildings.

Boat, ski, swim, and fish. Visit history

▲ ▲ ▲ ▲ ▲ ▲ ▲ ▲ ▲ ▲ ▲ ▲ ▲ ▲ ▲ ▲ ▲ ▲ ▲ ▲ ▲ ▲ ▲ ▲ ▲ ▲ ▲

museum and see Oregon Trail ruts. Reservoir drained for irrigation use during July (after 4th). Crowded on holidays. 14-day limit.
4354 ft (1305 m)

## HASKINS CREEK

Medicine Bow NF
(307) 327-5481
State map: H6
From ENCAMPMENT, take FH 11 W for 15.3 miles (24.5 k).
$5. Open Jun 15–Oct 31; dry camping off-season.
10 close, open sites. Water, pit toilets, tables, grills, fire rings.
In nice high-altitude setting along creek just off Battle Hwy.
Fishing plus exploring neighborhood. Check out Edison Monument at nearby Battle Lake and abandoned area mines.
14-day limit.
9000 ft (2700 m)

## HAWK SPRINGS SRA

(307) 836-2334
State map: G10
From HAWK SPRINGS, go 4 miles (6.4 k) S on US 85. Turn Left.
$4. Open All Year.
24 scattered, open sites. Water, pit toilets, tables, grills, fire rings, boat ramp.
On lake with a bit of shade.
Swim, fish, and ski reservoir or just enjoy the birds.
14-day limit. Weather can present bad road conditions.
4400 ft (1320 m)

## JACK CREEK

Shoshone NF (307) 868-2379
State map: C3
From MEETEETSE, head W on WY 290, forking Right onto CR/FR 208 for total of 20 miles (32 k).
FREE, donations requested.
Open All Year.
7 scattered, screened sites.
Pit toilets, tables, grills, fire rings.
In woods on creek.
Hike Greybull River Trail along river bottom in narrow canyon with views of

surrounding peaks. Fish and relax.
14-day/22-ft limits.
7600 ft (2280 m)

## JACK CREEK

Medicine Bow NF
(307) 327-5481
State map: H6
Take CR 500 W from ENCAMPMENT for 19.1 miles (30.6 k). Turn Left (S) on unpaved FR 405 and go 8.1 miles (13 k).
$5. Open Jun 5–Oct 31; dry camping off-season.
16 close, open sites. Water, pit toilets, tables, grills, fire rings.
On creekbank.
Besides fishing, take time to hike. Good photography and wildlife viewing.
No trash facilities. 14-day/22-ft limits.
8500 ft (2550 m)

## JOHN D ROCKEFELLER, JR
## MEMORIAL PARKWAY-Scattered

Grand Teton NP
(307) 733-2880
State map: C1
From MORAN JUNCTION, head NW on US 287 for 25 miles (40 k)–2 miles (3.2 k) before Yellowstone. Turn Left (W) at Flagg Village and take gravel Grassy Lake Rd (becomes FR 261) along Glade Creek. Eventually, road leads into Idaho S of Winegar Hole Wilderness.
FREE but $10 entrance fee (or pass). Also, free backcountry permits available at parkway or Grand Teton ranger stations. Open All Year.
Portable toilets, tables.
In clearings along creek in woods and near meadows.
Fish and hike. Enjoy several hot springs within walking distance.
NO water. Crowded in summer.
6800 ft (2040 m)

## KEYHOLE SP

(307) 756-3596
State map: B9
About 12 miles (19.2 k) E of MOORCROFT on I-90, take Exit 165 N to park.
$4. Open All Year.

▲ ▲ ▲ ▲ ▲ ▲ ▲ ▲ ▲ ▲ ▲ ▲ ▲ ▲ ▲ ▲ ▲ ▲ ▲ ▲ ▲ ▲ ▲ ▲ ▲

140 scattered, open sites.

Water, pit toilets, tables, grills, fire rings, pay phone, dump station, boat ramp, nearby store with ice.

Near water known for fishing and migrating bird flocks. View of Devils Tower in distance.

Reportedly excellent fishing for many varieties. Wildlife and birdwatching also superb. Swim and hike for exercise. Use as base to visit Devils Tower NM (camping over $5).

14-day limit.

4100 ft (1230 m)

## LAKEVIEW

Bighorn NF (307) 347-8291
State map: C6
From TEN SLEEP, take US 16 NE for 24 miles (38.4 k). (Also see Bull Creek.)

FREE but choose a chore.

Open Jun 1–Oct 31; camping allowed off-season.

11 close, open sites.

Pit toilets, tables, fire rings, boat ramp.

On shores of Meadowlark Lake.

Fishing and boating spot.

NO water. 14-day/22-ft limits.

8300 ft (2490 m)

## LIBBY CREEK RA
**Aspen, Pine, Spruce, & Willow Units**

Medicine Bow NF
(307) 745-8971
State map: H7

Go NW of CENTENNIAL on WY 130 for 2 miles (3.2 k) to series of four camps. Aspen and Pine Units are W on FR 351.

$5; for additional $6, reservations accepted at (800) 283-2267.

Open May 26–Sep 30; dry camping off-season.

38 close, open sites. Water, pit toilets, tables, grills, fire rings.

Next to Snowy Range Scenic Byway.

Fish creeks and lakes. Explore area and, perhaps, find a lost gold mine or two.

14-day/22-ft limits. Sometimes full on weekends.

8600 ft (2580 m)

## LINCOLN PARK

Medicine Bow NF
(307) 326-5258
State map: H7

Take scenic WY 130 SE from SARATOGA for 20.2 miles (32.3 k). Turn Left (NE) on FR 101. Go 2.6 miles (4.2 k). (Also see South Brush Creek.)

$5. Open May 15–Oct 1; dry camping off-season.

8 close, open sites.

Water, tables, grills, fire rings.

On Lincoln Creek with a bit more privacy than camps closer to WY 130. Enjoy creek or hike into mountains.

14-day limit. No vehicles over 32 ft.

7800 ft (2340 m)

## LITTLE GOOSE

Bighorn NF (307) 672-0751
State map: B6
From BIG HORN, take WY 335 SW for 9.3 miles (14.9 k). Turn S on FR 314 and proceed 2.5 miles (4 k)–may need 4WD near end. (Also see Coffeen Park and Cross Creek).

FREE but choose a chore.

Open Jun 1–Oct 31; camping allowed off-season.

3 close, open tent sites.

Pit toilets, tables, fire rings.

In remote creekside setting.

Possible base camp for extended treks.

NO water. 14-day/16-ft limits.

7000 ft (2100 m)

## LITTLE SANDSTONE

Medicine Bow NF
(307) 358-4690
State map: H6

From SAVERY, take FH 11 E for 23.6 miles (37.8 k). Turn of FR 801 and continue 2 miles (3.2 k).

FREE but choose a chore.

Open May 25–Oct 31; dry camping off-season.

9 close, open sites.

Pit toilets, tables, grills, fire rings.

Along creek.

Hike and view wildlife.

NO water. 14-day limit.

8400 ft (2520 m)

## LITTLE SUNLIGHT

Shoshone NF (307) 754-7207
State map: A3
From CODY, take WY 120 N
for 17 miles (27.2 k). Turn Left on MT
296 (Chief Joseph Scenic Byway) and
drive 23 miles (36.8 k). Turn on FR 101
and go 13 miles (20.8 k).
FREE but choose a chore.
Open May 1–Nov 30; dry camping
off-season.
4 scattered, screened sites.
Pit toilets, tables, grills, fire rings.
On creek near trailhead.
Remote region to explore. Hike and fish.
NO water. 14-day/32-ft limits.
6900 ft (2070 m)

## LOST CREEK

Medicine Bow NF
(307) 327-5481
State map: H6
Take FH 11 SW from ENCAMPMENT
for 17.3 miles (27.7 k).
$5. Open Jun 15–Oct 31; dry camping
off-season.
13 close, open sites. Water, pit toilets,
tables, grills, fire rings.
On Lost Creek (not hard to find).
Fish creek and explore mine-dotted
landscape. Hike and rockhound.
14-day/22-ft limits.
8800 ft (2640 m)

## LOUIS LAKE

Shoshone NF (307) 332-5460
State map: F4
Either take WY 131 S out of
LANDER or drive from other end (near
SOUTH PASS CITY off WY 28). Louis
Lake is about 28 miles (44.8 k) from
LANDER. (Also see Fiddlers Lake, Popo
Agie, and Worthen Meadows.)
$5. Open Jul 1–Sep 15; dry camping
off-season.
28 scattered, screened sites. Water, pit
toilets, tables, grills, fire rings.
In pines near lake with access to Popo
Agie Wilderness.
Great wildlife area with wilderness at
your doorstep–take a hike. Fish and
swim (if brave). In winter, snowmobile

or cross-country ski.
Road closed in winter.
8600 ft (2580 m)

## LYNX CREEK

Bridger-Teton NF
(307) 733-2752
State map: E1
From ALPINE, take US 89 S for .75 mile
(1.2 k). Continue straight on CR 1001
about .5 mile (800 m). Turn Left (SE) on
FR 10138. Drive 11.5 miles (18.4 k). More
developed, fee-charged sites at Murphy
Creek are 2 miles up FR 10138. (Also see
Moose Flat.)
FREE but choose a chore.
Open Jun 15–Sep 10.
14 close, open sites.
Pit toilets, tables, fire rings.
On Greys River.
Hike trails in area. Fish and relax.
NO water/trash arrangements (pack it
out). 10-day/16-ft limits.
6200 ft (1860 m)

## MEDICINE LODGE

Medicine Lodge Archaeo-
logical Site (307) 469-2234
State map: B5
From HYATTVILLE, take paved Cold
Springs Rd for 5 miles (8 k). Look for
gravel road on Left with Medicine Lodge
Habitat Area sign.
FREE but choose a chore.
Open All Year.
25 scattered, open sites. Water, pit toilets,
tables, grills, fire rings.
In cottonwood respite from sagebrush
grassland. On Medicine Lodge Creek at
canyon mouth with major native
American artifacts. Fragile pictographs
and petroglyphs. Visitor Center exhibits.
Excellent hiking and wildlife observation. Fishing and rockhounding too.
14-day limit. Summer weekends and
holidays get crowded. Be aware of
rattlesnakes and hunters in season.
4800 ft (1440 m)

▲ ▲ ▲ ▲ ▲ ▲ ▲ ▲ ▲ ▲ ▲ ▲ ▲ ▲ ▲ ▲ ▲ ▲ ▲ ▲ ▲ ▲ ▲ ▲

## MEDICINE LODGE LAKE

Bighorn NF (307) 765-4435
State map: B6
From SHELL, take US 14 NE
for 15.7 miles (25.1 k). Turn Right (SE)
on rough, dirt FR 17. Go 25 miles (40 k).
$5. Open May 30–Oct 31; dry camping
off-season.
8 close, open tent sites.
Water, pit toilets, tables, fire rings.
In idyllic location–high, remote area of
Bighorn Mountains near several lakes.
Great starting spot for hikes, including
Cloud Peak Wilderness. Relax and do
nothing or fish a favorite lake.
14-day limit. Not recommended for
trailers.
9300 ft (2790 m)

## MIDDLE FORK

BLM (307) 347-9871
State map: D6
From TEN SLEEP, go 20 miles
(32 k) S on WY 434 to BIG TRAILS. Turn
Left (E) on Stock Driveway Rd and
travel 13 miles (20.8 k) to Hazleton Rd.
Turn Right (S) and go another 17 miles
(27.2 k).
FREE but choose a chore.
Open Jun–Oct; camping off-season.
7 close, open sites.
Pit toilets, tables, grills, fire rings.
Next to high country stream in pine and
shrub environment.
Hike and enjoy photography, wildlife, or
fishing possibilities.
NO water/trash arrangements (pack it
out). 14-day limit. Road closed in winter.
Hunting nearby during season.
7500 ft (2250 m)

## MIDDLE PINEY LAKE

Bridger-Teton NF
(307) 733-2752
State map: F1
From BIG PINEY, take WY 350 W for
20 miles (32 k). Turn Right (N) on
FR 10046 and go 7 miles (11.2 k). For
more developed site, check out
**Sacajawea** (fee charged).
FREE but choose a chore.
Open Jul 1–Sep 30.

6 close, open sites. Pit toilets, tables, fire
rings, boat launch.
On lake.
Good spot for observing wildlife. Canoe,
swim, and fish or take a hike into
surrounding mountains.
NO water/trash arrangements (pack it
out). 10-day/16-ft limits.
8500 ft (2550 m)

## MILLER LAKE

Medicine Bow NF
(307) 745-8971
State map: H7
From FOXPARK (a few miles N of
MOUNTAIN HOME), go 1 mile (1.6 k) S
on FR 512.
$5. Open Jun 1–Oct 15; dry camping
off-season.
7 close, open sites. Water, pit toilets,
tables, grills, fire rings.
Next to high-altitude lake.
Swim (if you're tough), boat, and fish.
Walk surrounding countryside.
14-day/22-ft limits. Crowded weekends.
9100 ft (2730 m)

## MOOSE FLAT

Bridger-Teton NF
(307) 733-2752
State map: E1
From ALPINE, take US 89 S for .75 mile
(1.2 k). Continue straight on CR 1001
about .5 mile (800 m). Turn Left (SE) on
FR 10138. Drive 22.5 miles (36 k). For
more developed site, find **Forest Park**
13 more miles up FR 10138 (fee charged).
(Also see Lynx Creek.)
FREE but choose a chore.
Open Jun 15–Sep 10.
10 close, open sites.
Pit toilets, tables, fire rings.
Secluded spot on Greys River.
Good trails for hiking. Fish and relax.
NO water/trash arrangements (pack it
out). 10-day/16-ft limits.
6400 ft (1920 m)

## MORTON LAKE

BOR (307) 856-6138
State map: D4
From KINNEAR, go 1 mile
(1.6 k) N on good dirt road.
FREE but choose a chore.
Open All Year.
12 close, open sites. Water, pit toilets,
tables, grills, fire rings, shelters.
Swim, boat, waterski, or fish on lake.
5000 ft (1500 m)

## MUDDY MOUNTAIN-Lodgepole

BLM (307) 261-7600
State map: E7
From CASPER, head S on
WY 251 (Casper Mountain Rd) for
15 miles (24 k). Another option is
companion **Rim** camp with an open
feeling but no water (still charges $3), or,
about halfway from town, opt for **Casper
Mountain** or **Beartrap Meadow** county
parks (both have fees).
$3. Open All Year.
15 scattered, open sites. Water, pit toilets,
tables, grills, fire rings.
Beneath lodgepole pine.
Observe wildlife. Hike or mountain bike
East Overlook and Beaver trails.
14-day limit. Hunting in season.
8200 ft (2460 m)

## NATURAL BRIDGE PARK

Converse County Parks
(307) 358-3532
State map: E8
From DOUGLAS, go 12 miles (19.2 k) W
on I-5. Park is 5 miles (8 k) S on paved
road.
FREE but choose a chore.
Open Apr 1–Oct 31.
32 (20 tent-only, 12 RV-only) sites.
Water, pit toilets, tables, grills.
In horseshoe canyon with extra-large
picnic area for big gatherings.
Fishing and birdwatching are relaxing.
Admire geologic formations.
3-day/30-ft limits. Crowded weekends.
No generators after 9pm.
5200 ft (1560 m)

## NEW FORK

BLM (307) 382-5350
State map: F2
From MARBLETON, take
US 189 N for .75 mile (1.2 k). Turn Right
(E) on WY 351 and drive about 10 miles
(16 k) to New Fork River.
FREE but choose a chore.
Open All Year.
5 close, open sites.
Water, pit toilets, tables, fire rings.
Riverside sites provide good put-in/take
out spot for float trips. Fish.
14-day limit.

## NEW FORK LAKE

Bridger-Teton NF
(307) 733-2752
State map: E2
From CORA, head N on WY 352 for
11 miles (17.6 k). Turn Right on CR 107
(watch for sign) and drive 4.5 miles
(7.2 k). Continue on FR for 3 miles
(4.8 k). For more developed sites (with
postcard views), check out companion
**Narrows** camp (fee charged).
FREE but choose a chore.
Open Jun 1–Sep 10.
14 close, open sites. Pit toilets, tables, fire
rings, nearby boat ramp.
On lake in beautiful mountain setting.
Ski, swim, boat, and fish. Hike into
incredible Bridger Wilderness.
NO water/trash arrangements (pack it
out). 10-day/22-ft limits.
7800 ft (2340 m)

## NORTH FORK

Medicine Bow NF
(307) 745-8971
State map: H7
Take WY 130 W from CENTENNIAL for
3.5 miles (5.6 k). Turn on FR 101 and
continue 1.7 miles (2.7 k).
$5; for additional $6, reservations
accepted at (800) 283-2267.
Open Jun 15–Sep 30; dry camping
off-season.
60 sites. Water, pit toilets, tables, grills,
fire rings.
On three loops near Snowy Range Scenic
Byway on North Fork of Laramie River.

▲ ▲ ▲ ▲ ▲ ▲ ▲ ▲ ▲ ▲ ▲ ▲ ▲ ▲ ▲ ▲ ▲ ▲ ▲ ▲ ▲ ▲ ▲ ▲ ▲

Excellent fishing and hiking.
14–day/22-ft limits. Crowded weekends.
8600 ft (2580 m)

## OCEAN LAKE-Long Point

State Game and Fish
(307) 856-9005
State map: D4

From RIVERTON, go W on US 26 for
15 miles (24 k).
FREE but choose a chore.
Open All Year.
10 scattered, open sites.
Water, tables, grills, fire rings, shelters.
Along lake suitable for waterskiing,
swimming, boating, and fishing (ice-
fishing too).
5000 ft (1500 m)

## OUTLAW CAVE

BLM (307) 261-7600
State map: C6
From KAYCEE, head W on
WY 191 for 1 mile (1.6 k). Turn Left on
WY 190 (Barnum Rd) and drive
17.2 miles (27.5 k). Turn Left toward Bar
C Ranch. Drive 8.6 miles (13.8 k) past
Hole-in-the-Wall overlook.
FREE but choose a chore.
Open All Year.
4 scattered, open tent sites.
Pit toilets, tables, fire rings.
On gorgeous ledge above Middle Fork of
Powder River.
Hike down 660 ft into canyon and
explore caves. Walk West from camp
and admire Rock Art Cave (Do not
deface this heritage).
NO water. 14-day limit.

## PELTON CREEK

Medicine Bow NF
(307) 745-8971
State map: H7

From LARAMIE, go SW on WY 230 for
40 miles (64 k). Turn Right (NW) on
unpaved FR 898 and continue 9 miles
(14.4 k).
$5. Open Jun 15–Oct 15; dry camping
off-season.
15 close, open sites. Water, pit toilets,
tables, grills, fire rings.

On banks of Pelton and Douglas creeks,
next to Platte River Wilderness.
Fishing, hiking, wildlife observation
superb. Find black bear, bobcat,
mountain lion, lots of deer, many bird
species, and, of course, trout.
14–day/16-ft limits. Crowded weekends.
8100 ft (2430 m)

## PICKAROON & PIKE POLE

Medicine Bow NF
(307) 745-8971
State map: H7

From FOXPARK (a few miles N of
MOUNTAIN HOME), go 23 miles
(36.8 k) W on unpaved FR 512. Pike Pole
(6 sites) is another .5 mile (800 m).
FREE but choose a chore.
Open Jun 15–Oct 15; camping allowed
off-season.
8 close, open sites.
Pit toilets, tables, grills, fire rings.
On North Platte River and Douglas
Creek next to Savage Run Wilderness.
Excellent base for rewarding hikes. Fish
or splash in water. Birdwatching and
photography also popular.
NO piped water. 14-day limit. Trailers
over 16 ft not recommended.
7800 ft (2340 m)

## POPO AGIE

Shoshone NF (307) 332-5460
State map: E4
From LANDER, take WY 131
S for 6 miles (9.6 k). Continue on FR 200
(Loop Rd) for 20.3 miles (32.5 k). (Also
see Fiddlers Lake, Louis Lake, and
Worthen Meadows.)
FREE but choose a chore.
Open Jul 1–Sep 15; camping allowed
off-season.
4 scattered, screened sites.
Pit toilets, tables, grills, fire rings.
On Little Popo Agie (PO-PO-SHA) River
in Wind River Mountains.
Fishing is popular. Hiking is superb.
Arm yourself with map before venturing
into wilderness.
NO water. 14-day/16-ft limits.
8800 ft (2640 m)

▲ ▲ ▲ ▲ ▲ ▲ ▲ ▲ ▲ ▲ ▲ ▲ ▲ ▲ ▲ ▲ ▲ ▲ ▲ ▲ ▲ ▲ ▲

## PRYOR FLAT

BLM (307) 324-7171
State map: F5
From SINCLAIR, head N on
CR 351 past Miracle Mile section of
North Platte River. Turn Right on
CR 291. Go 1 mile (1.6 k). Turn Left on
CR 102. Go 12 miles (19.2 k).
FREE but choose a chore.
Open May – Nov; camping allowed
off-season.
5 close, screened sites.
Pit toilets, tables, fire rings.
Secluded getaway in stand of aspen.
NO water. 14-day limit. Hunting in
season.
7000 ft (2100 m)

## RANGER CREEK

Bighorn NF (307) 672-0751
State map: B6
From BIG HORN, take
WY 335 S for 9.3 miles (14.9 k). Head SW
on FR 26 for 10 miles (16 k). (Also see
East Fork and Little Goose)
$4. Open Jun 1 – Oct 31; dry camping
off-season.
11 close, open tent sites.
Water, pit toilets, tables, fire rings.
Creek base for hiking secluded area as
well as for fishing.
14-day/22-ft limits. NO trailers.
7800 ft (2340 m)

## REUNION FLAT

Targhee NF (208) 354-2312
State map: C1
From DRIGGS, ID, take Teton
Canyon Rd E for 6.2 miles (9.9 k). Turn
on FR 2009. Continue E for 2.8 miles
(4.5 k).
FREE but choose a chore.
Open Jun 1 – Sep 30; dry camping
off-season.
2 close, open sites. Water, pit toilets,
tables, grills, fire rings.
On stream at base of Grand Tetons close
to Jebediah Smith Wilderness.
Quiet location for relaxing, picnicking,
and fishing or as base camp for exploring fantastic wilderness.
No trash arrangements. 16-day limit.

## RIVERSIDE PARK

City of Douglas
(307) 358-9750
State map: E8
Locate on North Platte River in
DOUGLAS.
FREE but choose a chore.
Open All Year.
Undesignated sites. Water, flush toilets,
dump station, showers, tables, grills, pay
phone, boat ramp.
In grassy areas for overnight stops only.
Hiking and fishing possible.
1-day limit. Crowded summer and fall.
5000 ft (1500 m)

## RYAN PARK

Medicine Bow NF
(307) 326-5258
State map: H7
Take WY 230 E from SARATOGA for
23.3 miles (37.3 k).
$5; for additional $6, reservations
accepted at (800) 283-2267.
Open May 15 – Oct 15; dry camping
off-season.
34 close, open sites. Water, pit toilets,
tables, grills, fire rings.
Site for World War II prisoner of war
camp (self-guided tour). Popular spot for
investigating history and more remote
areas of forest.
14-day/32-ft limits.
8000 ft (2400 m)

## SCAB CREEK

BLM (307) 367-4358
State map: E3
From BOULDER, take
WY 353 E about 11 miles (17.6 k). Watch
for sign to Left. (Also see Boulder Lake.)
FREE but choose a chore.
Open All Year.
Undesignated scattered sites.
Pit toilets, tables, fire rings, corral.
At trailhead (managed as proposed
wilderness area) with access to Monroe
Lake and Bridger Wilderness.
Hike, backpack, fish, rock climb.
NO water/trash arrangements (pack it
out). 14-day limit.
7500 ft (2250 m)

▲ ▲ ▲ ▲ ▲ ▲ ▲ ▲ ▲ ▲ ▲ ▲ ▲ ▲ ▲ ▲ ▲ ▲ ▲ ▲ ▲ ▲

## SEMINOE SP

(307) 328-0115
State map: G6
From SINCLAIR, go N on oiled CR 351 for 34 miles (54.4 k)–tricky when wet.
$4. Open Apr 15–Oct 30; dry camping off-season.
94 scattered, open sites.
Water, pit toilets, tables, grills, fire rings, dump station, boat ramp, playground.
Two camping areas (North and South Red Hills) in high desert park. Mountains grace northern horizon, but little shade near huge reservoir.
Swimming, boating, and fishing. Nature trails and other opportunities abound. Watch for bighorn sheep, deer, antelope, and prairie dogs.
14-day limit. Crowded long weekends in summer.
6357 ft (1905 m)

## SINKS CANYON SP

(307) 332-3077
State map: E4
From LANDER, take WY 131 S for 6 miles (9.6 k). Only 2.7 miles (4.3 k) farther, **Sinks Canyon** NF camp has slightly higher fee.
$4. Open May 15–Oct 30.
30 close and scattered, screened sites.
Water, pit toilets, tables, grills, fire rings, pay phone.
In beautiful locale along Popo Agie River. River completely disappears into cavern (the Sinks) to emerge a few hundred yards downstream (the Rise).
Enjoy geologic oddity, two nature trails, and varied flora. Visitor Center has exhibits and information.
14-day limit. Quiet hours.
6000 ft (1800 m)

## SIX MILE GAP

Medicine Bow NF
(307) 327-5481
State map: H7
From ENCAMPMENT, take WY 230 SE for 24.6 miles (39.4 k). Turn Left (SE) on FR 492 and go 2 miles (3.2 k).
FREE but choose a chore.

Open May 15–Oct 31; dry camping off-season.
7 close, open sites.
Pit toilet, tables, grills, fire rings.
Near North Platte River in scenic area. Fish the Platte or hike banks. Relax.
NO water. 14-day/32-ft limits.
8000 ft (2400 m)

## SOUTH BRUSH CREEK

Medicine Bow NF
(307) 326-5258
State map: H7
Take scenic WY 130 SE from SARATOGA for 20.2 miles (32.3 k) to FR 101. Turn Left (NE) and proceed .2 mile (300 m). (Also see Lincoln Park).
$5. Open May 15–Oct 1; dry camping off-season.
20 close, open sites. Water, pit toilets, tables, grills, fire rings.
Excellent hiking possibilities into remote region plus good fishing spots.
14-day/32-ft limits.
7900 ft (2370 m)

## TETON RESERVOIR

BLM (307) 324-7171
State map: G6
From RAWLINS, head S on WY 71 for 12 miles (19.2 k). Turn Left on BLM 3418 and follow to west side of reservoir.
FREE but choose a chore.
Open All Year.
5 close, open sites.
Pit toilets, tables, fire rings, boat ramp.
On lakeshore.
Boating and fishing.
NO water/trash arrangements (pack it out). 14-day limit. Hunting in season.
7000 ft (2100 m)

## THE DUGWAY

BLM (307) 324-7171
State map: F5
From SINCLAIR, head N on CR 351 about 8 miles (12.8 k).
FREE but choose a chore.
Open All Year.
7 close, screened sites.
Pit toilets, tables, fire rings.

Adjacent to North Platte River.
Swim, canoe, kayak, boat, fish, and relax.
NO water. 14-day limit. Hunting in season.
6560 ft (1968 m)

## TIE CITY

Medicine Bow NF
(307) 745-8971
State map: H8
From LARAMIE, travel SE on I-80 for 12.3 miles (19.6 k). Take FR 722 E for 1.1 miles (16 k). (Also see Yellow Pine.)
**$5.** Open May 25–Oct 31; dry camping off-season.
18 close, open sites. Water (if it passes test), pit toilets, tables, grills, fire rings.
Near an Interstate and Summit Visitor Center. Several hiking trails in area.
14-day/32-ft limits.
8600 ft (2580 m)

## TRAIL LAKE

▲
Shoshone NF (307) 455-2466
State map: D3
Go 4 miles (6.4 k) SE of DUBOIS on US 26. Turn Right (S) on rough dirt road. Proceed 6 miles (9.6 k).
**FREE** but choose a chore.
Open May 1–Nov 1; camping allowed off-season.
Undesignated open meadow sites.
Pit toilets.
Swim, boat, and fish on lake. Trails plus photo opportunities.
NO water.
5600 ft (1680 m)

## UPPER GREEN RIVER

▲
BLM (307) 367-4358
State map: E2
From PINEDALE, take US 192 NW for 23 miles (36.8 k) to Green River.
Turn Right on gravel access road and drive N for 10 miles (16 k). (Also see Warren Bridge.)
**FREE** but choose a chore.
Open All Year.
12 close, open sites.
Pit toilets, tables, fire rings.
From the bridge N, find 12 access points along Green River with scattered

facilities (toilets, tables, dumpster at base of road).
Put-in spots for floating or fishing river.
NO water. 14-day limit.

## VEDAUWOO

Medicine Bow NF
(307) 745-8971
State map: H9
Take I-80 SE out of LARAMIE for 19.1 miles (30.5 k). Travel E on FR 700 for 1.7 miles (2.7 k) to FR 720. Another .5 mile (800 m) to camp.
**$5.** Open May 1–Oct 31; dry camping off-season.
11 close, open sites. Water, pit toilets, tables, grills, fire rings.
Rocks! Wild formations perhaps thrown up by mischievous Earth according to Cheyenne (Vedauwoo roughly means "born of the earth.") Scramble over rocks while taking lots of photographs.
14-day/32-ft limits. Often full weekends.
8200 ft (2460 m)

## WAPITI

▲
Shoshone NF (307) 527-6921
State map: B3
From CODY, head W for 29 miles (46.4 k) on US 14/16/20. Within next 8 miles (9.6 k) a series of six camps with similar facilities and fees: **Big Game** (16 sites), **Elk Fork** (13 sites), **Clearwater** (32 sites), **Rex Hale** (8 sites), **Newton Creek** (31 sites). (Also see Eagle Creek.)
**$5.** Open Jun 1–Sep 30; dry camping off-season.
41 scattered, screened sites. Water, pit toilets, tables, grills, fire rings.
On wooded stream in Wapiti Valley on road to Yellowstone NP.
Fish or relax around one of these camps.
Access trails into Washakie Wilderness.
Clearwater Camp has trail to volcanic outcrops.
14-day/22-ft limits (Big Game and Clearwater can handle larger rigs).
6000 ft (1800 m)

▲ ▲ ▲ ▲ ▲ ▲ ▲ ▲ ▲ ▲ ▲ ▲ ▲ ▲ ▲ ▲ ▲ ▲ ▲ ▲ ▲ ▲ ▲ ▲ ▲

## WARREN BRIDGE
BLM (307) 367-4358
State map: E2
From PINEDALE, take US 192
NW for 23 miles (36.8 k) to Green River.
(Also see Upper Green River.)
$5. Open Jun 1–Sep 30; dry camping
off-season.
17 close, open sites.
Water, pit toilets, tables, fire rings.
Riverside sites for floating or fishing.
14-day limit

## WEEPING ROCK
BLM (307) 382-5350
State map: G2
From LA BARGE, take US 189
S for 24 miles (38.4 k). Turn Left (E) on
WY 372 and go 5 miles (8 k) to just
below Fontenelle Reservoir Dam. Other
spots within 1 mile (1.6 k) are **Tailrace**
and **Slate Creek**. (Also see Fontenelle
RA.)
FREE but choose a chore.
Open All Year.
4 close, open sites.
Pit toilets, tables, fire rings.
In riverside location a few miles N of
Seedskadee NWR.
Good put-in spot for river floating (Slate
Creek is 1 mile downstream). Fishing
and wildlife observation possibilities.
NO water. 14-day limit.

## WILLOW LAKE
Bridger-Teton NF
(307) 733-2752
State map: E2
Just out of PINEDALE, go N on Soda
Lake Rd 12 miles (19.2 k).
FREE but choose a chore.
Open Jun 1–Oct 1.
8 close, open sites. Pit toilets, tables, fire
rings, nearby boat ramp.
On beautiful mountain lake.
Hike away from civilization or canoe
and fish from camp.
NO water/trash arrangements (pack it
out). 10-day/22-ft limits.
7800 ft (2340 m)

## WOOD RIVER
Shoshone NF (307) 868-2379
State map: C3
From MEETEETSE, head W
on WY 290, forking Left onto CR/FR 200
for total of 25 miles (40 k). (Also see
Brown Mountain.)
FREE, donations requested.
Open May 31–Nov 15; dry camping
off-season.
5 scattered, screened sites. Water, pit
toilets, tables, grills, fire rings.
In woods on stream.
Fish near camp. Hike Middle Fork or
South Fork Trails; either gives wonderful
views of high peaks.
14-day/16-ft limits.
7300 ft (2190 m)

## WORTHEN MEADOWS
Shoshone NF (307)332-5460
State map: F4
Either take WY 131 S out of
LANDER or drive from other end (near
SOUTH PASS CITY off WY 28). Camp is
approximately 18 miles (28.8 k) from
LANDER. (Also see Fiddlers Lake, Louis
Lake, and Popo Agie.)
$5. Open Jul 1–Sep 15; dry camping
off-season.
28 close, open sites. Water, pit toilets,
tables, grills, fire rings, boat ramp.
In pines near lake with two trailheads
into Popo Agie Wilderness.
Great wildlife observation area with
fishing and hiking. Winter access by
snowmobile or cross-country ski.
Road closed in winter.
8500 ft (2550 m)

## YELLOW PINE
Medicine Bow NF
(307) 745-8971
State map: H9
Take I-80 SE from LARAMIE for
12.3 miles (19.6 k). Go E on FR 722 for
3.1 miles (5 k). (Also see Tie City.)
$5. Open May 25–Sep 30; dry camping
off-season.
19 close, open sites. Water, pit toilets,
tables, grills, fire rings.
In pines couple of miles farther from

highway than Tie City.
Hike surrounding mountains or indulge
in a little birdwatching.
14-day/32-ft limits. Crowded weekends.
8400 ft (2520 m)

## YELLOWSTONE NP-Backcountry

(307) 344-7381
State map: B1
Enter park from S (US 191), E
(US 14/20), NE (US 212), N (US 89), or
W (US 20).
**FREE** but $10 entrance fee (or pass).
(Campgrounds in park cost $6–$10.)
Obtain free backcountry permits at any
ranger station or Visitor Center.
Open All Year.
In volcanic-formed landscape filled with
spectacular geysers and hot springs,
fantastic canyons and waterfalls,
beautiful meadows and alpine lakes as
well as rugged mountains–several parks
and ecologies in one.
By hiking away from roads and camp-
grounds, find a natural wonderland
without crowds.
Designated backcountry sites with stays
limited to 1–3 days each. Bear country.
Pack out all trash.
6800 ft (2040 m)

# Index

Index includes towns used in directions (ALL CAPS), bonus camps mentioned as alternatives in listings (**bolded**), plus major rivers and lakes.

NEAREST TOWNS          Bodies of Water          **Bonus Camps**

▲ ▲ ▲ ▲ ▲ ▲ ▲ ▲ ▲ ▲ ▲ ▲ ▲ ▲ ▲ ▲ ▲ ▲ ▲ ▲ ▲ ▲ ▲ ▲ ▲ ▲ ▲

▲ ▲ ▲ ▲ ▲ ▲ ▲ ▲ ▲ ▲ ▲ ▲ ▲ ▲ ▲ ▲ ▲ ▲ ▲ ▲ ▲ ▲ ▲ ▲ ▲ ▲

NEAREST TOWNS        Bodies of Water        **Bonus Camps**

▲ ▲ ▲ ▲ ▲ ▲ ▲ ▲ ▲ ▲ ▲ ▲ ▲ ▲ ▲ ▲ ▲ ▲ ▲ ▲ ▲ ▲ ▲ ▲ ▲ ▲

▲ ▲ ▲ ▲ ▲ ▲ ▲ ▲ ▲ ▲ ▲ ▲ ▲ ▲ ▲ ▲ ▲ ▲ ▲ ▲ ▲ ▲ ▲ ▲ ▲

**NEAREST TOWNS**          Bodies of Water          **Bonus Camps**

▲ ▲ ▲ ▲ ▲ ▲ ▲ ▲ ▲ ▲ ▲ ▲ ▲ ▲ ▲ ▲ ▲ ▲ ▲ ▲ ▲ ▲ ▲ ▲

▲ ▲ ▲ ▲ ▲ ▲ ▲ ▲ ▲ ▲ ▲ ▲ ▲ ▲ ▲ ▲ ▲ ▲ ▲ ▲ ▲ ▲ ▲ ▲

NEAREST TOWNS        Bodies of Water        **Bonus Camps**

▲ ▲ ▲ ▲ ▲ ▲ ▲ ▲ ▲ ▲ ▲ ▲ ▲ ▲ ▲ ▲ ▲ ▲ ▲ ▲ ▲ ▲ ▲ ▲ ▲ ▲ ▲ ▲

▲ ▲ ▲ ▲ ▲ ▲ ▲ ▲ ▲ ▲ ▲ ▲ ▲ ▲ ▲ ▲ ▲ ▲ ▲ ▲ ▲ ▲ ▲ ▲ ▲ ▲ ▲ ▲

NEAREST TOWNS          Bodies of Water          **Bonus Camps**

▲ ▲ ▲ ▲ ▲ ▲ ▲ ▲ ▲ ▲ ▲ ▲ ▲ ▲ ▲ ▲    ▲ ▲ ▲ ▲ ▲ ▲ ▲ ▲ ▲ ▲ ▲ ▲ ▲ ▲

▲ ▲ ▲ ▲ ▲ ▲ ▲ ▲ ▲ ▲ ▲ ▲ ▲ ▲ ▲ ▲ ▲ ▲ ▲ ▲ ▲ ▲ ▲ ▲ ▲ ▲ ▲ ▲

NEAREST TOWNS      Bodies of Water      **Bonus Camps**

▲ ▲ ▲ ▲ ▲ ▲ ▲ ▲ ▲ ▲ ▲ ▲ ▲ ▲ ▲ ▲ ▲ ▲ ▲ ▲ ▲ ▲ ▲ ▲ ▲ ▲ ▲

▲ ▲ ▲ ▲ ▲ ▲ ▲ ▲ ▲ ▲ ▲ ▲ ▲ ▲ ▲ ▲ ▲ ▲ ▲ ▲ ▲ ▲ ▲ ▲ ▲

**NEAREST TOWNS**　　　　Bodies of Water　　　　**Bonus Camps**

NEAREST TOWNS      Bodies of Water      **Bonus Camps**

▲ ▲ ▲ ▲ ▲ ▲ ▲ ▲ ▲ ▲ ▲ ▲ ▲ ▲ ▲ ▲ ▲ ▲ ▲ ▲ ▲ ▲ ▲ ▲ ▲ ▲

▲ ▲ ▲ ▲ ▲ ▲ ▲ ▲ ▲ ▲ ▲ ▲ ▲ ▲ ▲ ▲ ▲ ▲ ▲ ▲ ▲ ▲ ▲ ▲ ▲

NEAREST TOWNS        Bodies of Water        **Bonus Camps**

▲ ▲ ▲ ▲ ▲ ▲ ▲ ▲ ▲ ▲ ▲ ▲ ▲ ▲ ▲ ▲ ▲ ▲ ▲ ▲ ▲ ▲ ▲ ▲ ▲ ▲

▲ ▲ ▲ ▲ ▲ ▲ ▲ ▲ ▲ ▲ ▲ ▲ ▲ ▲ ▲ ▲ ▲ ▲ ▲ ▲ ▲ ▲ ▲ ▲ ▲ ▲

**NEAREST TOWNS**          Bodies of Water          **Bonus Camps**

▲ ▲ ▲ ▲ ▲ ▲ ▲ ▲ ▲ ▲ ▲ ▲ ▲ ▲ ▲ ▲ ▲ ▲ ▲ ▲ ▲ ▲ ▲ ▲ ▲ ▲ ▲

▲ ▲ ▲ ▲ ▲ ▲ ▲ ▲ ▲ ▲ ▲ ▲ ▲ ▲ ▲ ▲ ▲ ▲ ▲ ▲ ▲ ▲ ▲ ▲ ▲ ▲ ▲

NEAREST TOWNS          Bodies of Water          **Bonus Camps**

▲ ▲ ▲ ▲ ▲ ▲ ▲ ▲ ▲ ▲ ▲ ▲ ▲ ▲ ▲ ▲ ▲ ▲ ▲ ▲ ▲ ▲ ▲ ▲

▲ ▲ ▲ ▲ ▲ ▲ ▲ ▲ ▲ ▲ ▲ ▲ ▲ ▲ ▲ ▲ ▲ ▲ ▲ ▲ ▲ ▲ ▲ ▲

NEAREST TOWNS          Bodies of Water          **Bonus Camps**

NEAREST TOWNS        Bodies of Water        **Bonus Camps**